The Justices of the Peace
in Wales and Monmouthshire
1541 to 1689

The Justices of the Peace
in Wales and Monmouthshire
1541 to 1689

LISTS COMPILED AND EDITED

by

J. R. S. PHILLIPS

Lecturer in Medieval History, University College, Dublin

PUBLISHED ON BEHALF OF THE BOARD OF CELTIC STUDIES

CARDIFF
UNIVERSITY OF WALES PRESS
1975

ISBN 0 7083 0563 6

QUALITEX PRINTING LIMITED CARDIFF

Preface

The material in this volume was largely compiled and edited between 1966 and 1968 while I was a researcher for the History and Law Committee of the Board of Celtic Studies. Many people have offered me assistance during the course of my work but in particular I should like to thank Sir Goronwy Edwards, Sir David Evans, Professor Glanmor Williams, Professor J. Gwynn Williams, Dr. Penry Williams, Dr. R. Brinley Jones and Mr. W. R. B. Robinson for their help and advice at various times. My fellow researcher, Mr. G. R. Thomas, put me on the track of important documents among the collections of the National Library of Wales. I am also indebted to the staff of many archives and libraries, especially to those of the British Museum and Public Record Office and, most of all, to the members of the department of manuscripts at the National Library of Wales who had to put up with my repeated requests for large quantities of bulky and often extremely dusty Great Sessions records.

University College, Dublin   J. R. S. Phillips
September 1974]

Contents

Introduction

To adapt a famous saying, there are lies, damned lies and commissions of the peace. This exaggerates the difficulties involved in establishing accurate lists of the holders of the office of justice of the peace[1], but it is essential to begin by warning potential users of these lists that there is no single easily consulted source which provides full and reliable information on the dates of issue of commissions of the peace and on the detailed changes in their composition. Instead it is necessary to make use of a variety of sources all of which present problems to the researcher, either because of their inherent shortcomings or because only a small proportion of the original records remains extant or for a combination of both causes[2]. The lists of justices of the peace in this volume are therefore only as complete and as accurate as the sources will allow and the main purpose of this introduction is to explain the nature of the materials used and their individual strengths and weaknesses.

The origins and functions of the office of justice of the peace[3] and the historical background to its introduction into Wales have already been

---

[1] A few lists of justices of the peace are already available for individual Welsh counties: e.g., for Caernarvon between 1541 and 1558 in the *Calendar of the Caernarvonshire Quarter Sessions Records,* vol. 1, *1541–1558,* ed. W. O. Williams (Caernarvon, 1956); for Merioneth between 1733 and 1765 in the *Calendar of the Merioneth Quarter Sessions Rolls,* vol. 1, *1733–1765,* ed. K. Williams-Jones (Aberystwyth, 1965); for Flint between 1540 (*sic*) and 1889 in the *Guide to the Flintshire Record Office: Flintshire Quarter Sessions and Other Records,* ed. M. Bevan-Evans (Flintshire Record Office, 1955). The Flintshire list in fact starts in 1543 and not in 1540 and also does not make use of the information from the plentiful Great Sessions records available for that county.

[2] With the exception of the county of Caernarvon, there are, for example, no extant quarter sessions records for the Welsh counties during the period covered in this volume. The fate of some of the Welsh records is graphically illustrated in a frequently quoted passage from W. H. Black's report in 1840: 'But I have discovered by diligent enquiry, that a great quantity of ancient records had been deposited in a kind of cellar in the basement of the building (the office of the protonotary of North Wales in Caernarvon) and suffered to go to decay; which were cleared out by order of the magistrates about twenty or thirty years ago, and partly sold together with old Acts of Parliament and other waste paper, by the hundred weight, and partly thrown upon dungheaps and wheeled into the Menai, as rotten and worthless. Some of these records were bought or otherwise obtained by Mr. David Williams, of Turkey Shore, Caernarvon; who for many years past has supplied tailors and others with parchment for various purposes, out of the materials': *Report of the Deputy Keeper of the Public Records, First Report, 1840: Report on Welsh Records by W. H. Black,* pp. 90–1.

[3] On the origins of the justice of the peace see especially Bertha H. Putnam, 'The Transformation of the Keepers of the Peace into the Justices of the Peace', *Transactions of the Royal Historical Society,* 4th series, vol. 12 (1929), and Bertha H. Putnam, 'Keepers of the Peace and Justices of the Peace', in *The English Government at Work, 1327–1336,* vol. 3, ed. J. F. Willard, W. A. Morris, W. H. Dunham, Medieval Academy of America Publication 56 (Cambridge, Mass., 1950). For studies of the justices of the peace in the sixteenth and seventeenth centuries and their relation to the politics of the period see, for example, J. H. Gleason, *The Justice of the Peace in England, 1558–1640* (Oxford, 1969), and T. G. Barnes, *Somerset 1625–1640, A County's Government during the 'Personal Rule'* (Harvard, 1961). A good example of how the Welsh commissions of the peace were affected by one period of political crisis is to be found in A. H. Dodd, '"Tuning" the Welsh Bench, 1680', *National Library of Wales Journal,* vol. 6 (1950).

dealt with fully elsewhere[4] so that there is no need to discuss these questions in any detail. The only point that needs to be clarified is the date at which justices of the peace can first positively be proved to have been acting in the counties of Wales and Monmouthshire. Contrary to widely held opinion, justices of the peace did not make their appearance in Wales either in 1536, the year of the Act, 27 Henry VIII, c.5, which first authorised their appointment, or in the years immediately following 1536[5]. The first definite pieces of evidence that justices of the peace were acting in Wales are provided by the examination of a prisoner before Thomas Stradling, a justice in Glamorgan, on 2 October 1541 and by the holding of a Quarter Session at Caernarvon on 6 October 1541[6]. This implies that justices of the peace had been appointed for at least these two counties by October 1541, but there

---

[4] Among older views of the administrative changes introduced in Wales after 1536 are T. H. Lewis, 'The Justice of the Peace in Wales', *Transactions of the Honourable Society of Cymmrodorion,* 1943–44; A. H. Dodd, 'Wales's Parliamentary Apprenticeship (1536–1625)', *Transactions of the Honourable Society of Cymmrodorion,* 1942; W. Rees, 'The Union of England and Wales', *Transactions of the Honourable Society of Cymmrodorion,* 1937; J. F. Rees, 'Tudor Policy in Wales', *Studies in Welsh History* (Cardiff, 1947); W. O. Williams, op. cit., Introduction. For the most recent views, which have substantially modified earlier work, see J. G. Edwards, 'The Principality of Wales, 1267–1967', *Caernarvonshire Historical Society* (Caernarvon, 1969); P. R. Roberts, *The 'Acts of Union' and the Tudor Settlement of Wales,* Ph.D. (Cambridge, 1966); P. S. Edwards, *The Parliamentary Representation of Wales and Monmouthshire, 1542–1558,* Ph.D. (Cambridge, 1970).

[5] For the view that justices of the peace did appear quickly after the 1536 Act see, for example, A. H. Dodd, 'Wales's Parliamentary Apprenticeship (1536–1625)', p. 8; T. H. Lewis, op. cit., p. 121; K. Williams-Jones, op. cit., p. XV. There are several pieces of evidence which appear to suggest that justices of the peace were soon introduced but none of them stands up to close examination. T. H. Lewis, op. cit., p. 121, quoted a writ of 20 December, 28 Henry VIII (1536), summoning the justices of the peace to attend quarter sessions at Caernarvon on the Monday after Epiphany 1537. Study of this document (Caernarvonshire Record Office, Q.S.2/1, item 5) shows that its actual date is 20 December, 38 Henry VIII (1546), which presents no problems of interpretation. The writ has been published under its correct date, together with a facsimile, in W. O. Williams, op. cit., p. 33. Another piece of apparently very early evidence is the document of 24 February 1536 which is printed as a commission of the peace and of oyer and terminer in *Letters & Papers of the Reign of Henry VIII,* vol. 10, no. 392(48). Reference to the original Patent Roll from which the commission is taken (P.R.O., C.66/667/m.26d.) shows that it is not a commission of the peace but a commission appointing justices in eyre. This point was first noticed by W. R. B. Robinson in 'Early Tudor Policy towards Wales', part 3, *Bulletin of Board of Celtic Studies,* vol. 21 (1965–66), p. 343, n. 4. It has also been suggested that as early as 1538 John ap Robert was acting as clerk of the peace in Caernarvon: W. O. Williams, op. cit., p. CX, quoting E. A. Lewis, *Early Chancery Proceedings concerning Wales,* Board of Celtic Studies, University of Wales, *History & Law Series,* no. 3 (Cardiff, 1937), p. 17. This item occurs in a file of Early Chancery Proceedings which covers the years 1538 to 1544 but whose individual contents bear no precise date: P.R.O., C.1/971/3. John ap Robert may be the John Gruffydd alias Vaughan who was appointed as clerk of the peace in Caernarvon in July 1541 (*Letters & Papers of the Reign of Henry VIII,* vol. 16, no. 1056) but, even if this identification is wrong, there is no reason to suppose that John ap Robert held the office as early as 1538.

[6] N.L.W., Wales 4/591/item 5; W. O. Williams, op. cit., p. 251.

is no reason to believe that their appointment was other than recent[7]. The earliest surviving records of the new courts of Great Sessions provide lists of justices active in Cardigan and Radnor in 1542[8], while the names of the justices acting in Monmouthshire in the early part of the same year are supplied in the sheriff's account enrolled on the Pipe Roll of 33 Henry VIII[9]. The first complete details of all the Welsh commissions of the peace are contained in a *liber pacis* which records a set of commissions issued for Wales and Monmouth on 12 March 1543[10]. By the Act of 34 and 35 Henry VIII, c.26, the borough of Haverfordwest was separated from the county of Pembroke to become an additional county in its own right[11]. This made it necessary to issue a special commission of the peace for Haverfordwest but the earliest surviving details of this commission date only from 1555.

[7] Justices of the peace were also active in Denbigh and Flint at the time of the session of the Parliament which met between 16 January and 1 April 1542, since an Act of Parliament of that session transferring some territory from Denbigh to Flint interrupted proceedings before the justices of the peace of those counties: P. R. Roberts, op. cit., pp. 255–6. The dates on which the clerks of the peace were first appointed provide another important indication of when the quarter sessions of justices of the peace began to function. The first recorded appointment is for Glamorgan in July 1539, followed by Monmouth in July 1540, Denbigh in December 1540, Caernarvon in July 1541, Radnor, Brecon, Montgomery, Pembroke, Cardigan and Carmarthen in December 1541, and Merioneth and Anglesey in February 1542: P. R. Roberts, op. cit., p. 256, citing *Letters & Papers of the Reign of Henry VIII*. It is likely that the clerks of the peace were appointed some time before the justices of the peace because of the need to set up the organisation of the new quarter sessions, but the length of the intervening period is difficult to estimate and probably in any case varied from county to county.

[8] Cardigan: 18 September 1542 (N.L.W., Wales 4/883/1); Radnor: 13 March 1542 (N.L.W., Wales 4/461/1). There is also a list for Glamorgan on 27 March 1542 (N.L.W., Wales 4/591/1). This evidence comes from the Gaol Files drawn up for the sessions of the Great Sessions of the above dates. There can be little doubt that all the other counties of Wales also had justices of the peace in 1542.

[9] P.R.O., E.372/387/m.27.

[10] P.R.O., C.193/12/1. The date can be established by the description of the book on the cover as 'Liber pacis de tricesimo quarto Regis Henrici octavi' and the words, 'Commiss. T.R. apud Westm' XII die Marcii', which follow a list on folio 48v of the members of the Council in the Marches of Wales. The book contains many names which were added later as corrections but the presence in all the commissions in an uncorrected form of the name of John Russell, the Keeper of the Privy Seal, who was appointed to his office on 3 December 1542, suggests that the book belongs to very late 1542 or early 1543. The name of the President of the Council in the Marches of Wales is given only as R., Bishop of Coventry and Lichfield. This could refer either to Rowland Lee, Bishop of Coventry and Lichfield, who held the office of Lord President until his death on 24 January 1543, or to Richard Sampson, who succeeded Lee in both offices, being confirmed as Bishop on 9 March 1543 and appointed as Lord President at about the same time. However, the name of the President of the Council in the Marches appears as a part of the basic list of justices in each commission of the peace and not as a later correction, which would be the case if the commissions had been issued before the death of Lee. The most likely explanation is that the Welsh commissions were all renewed on 12 March 1543 in order to record Richard Sampson's appointment as Lord President.

[11] Clause LXI of the Act of 34 & 35 Henry VIII, c.26, printed in *Statutes of the Realm*, vol. 3, *1509–1547* (London, 1817), p. 936. In the lists of *nomina ministrorum* attached to the Gaol Files for the county of Carmarthen information is included on justices of the peace who sat especially for the borough of Carmarthen. Their names differ in some respects from those included in the commission for the county but there is no evidence that a separate commission was ever issued for the borough.

The reasons for the long delay between the enabling legislation of 1536 and the first recorded appearance of justices of the peace in 1541 have been explained by Dr. P. R. Roberts in his important study of the administrative changes introduced into Wales by the 'Acts of Union'.[12]. One reason was the time taken to perform the essential preliminary task of fixing the boundaries of the new Welsh shires, but the major cause was the suspension of the operation of the 1536 'Act of Union', 27 Henry VIII, c.26, by a royal proclamation on 20 February 1537.[13] In consequence there were extended delays in the appointment not only of the first justices of the peace,[14] the sheriffs of the Welsh shires and the justices of the courts of Great Sessions[15] but also in the election of the first Welsh members of Parliament.[16]

SOURCE MATERIALS ON THE JUSTICES OF THE PEACE IN WALES AND MONMOUTHSHIRE, 1541 to 1689.

The sources available for compiling lists of justices of the peace have already been described and critically assessed in a valuable article by T. G. Barnes and A. Hassell Smith[17]. The details and comments that follow therefore draw considerably on their work to which the reader may refer for further information. Their survey of sources starts however with the year 1558 so that it has been necessary to search for material prior to that date. It has also been possible to add a few items from within their period of study, together with some miscellaneous evidence which relates solely to Wales and therefore lies outside their terms of reference. A full guide to all the sources actually used in compiling the present volume is to be found in the Bibliography.

[12] P. R. Roberts, *The 'Acts of Union' and the Tudor Settlement of Wales,* Ph.D. (Cambridge, 1966).

[13] *Tudor Royal Proclamations,* vol. 1, *The Early Tudors (1485–1553),* eds. P. L. Hughes & J. F. Larkin (New Haven & London, 1964), no. 172, p. 254. The Act, 28 Henry VIII, c.3, which was passed in the Parliament which began on 8 June 1536, gave the King powers to alter or suspend the Act, 27 Henry VIII, c.26, for three years after the end of that Parliament: P. R. Roberts, op. cit., p. 180. The question of the suspension of the 1536 Act is discussed at length in P. R. Roberts, op. cit., chapter four, 'Delay and Deferment, 1536–1541'.

[14] Justices of the peace had been authorised for Wales by the Act, 27 Henry VIII, c.5, and not by the Act, 27 Henry VIII, c.26, but the suspension of the latter Act made it impossible for its predecessor to come into operation.

[15] The beginning of the functions of the courts of Great Sessions is particularly important for the history of the justices of the peace because of the information on the commissions of the peace which is contained in the Gaol Files of the courts.

[16] Despite the absence of any surviving returns of members attending the Parliaments of 1536 and 1539, it has usually been assumed that Welsh members were present. In fact Welsh members were not summoned to either Parliament and first attended Parliament in January 1542. For further information on this question see P. R. Roberts, op. cit., p. 223, and P. S. Edwards, *The Parliamentary Representation of Wales and Monmouthshire, 1542–1558* Ph.D. (Cambridge, 1970), pp. 1–2.

[17] 'Justices of the Peace from 1558 to 1688—a Revised List of Sources', *Bulletin of the Institute of Historical Research,* vol. 32 (1959). This superseded the earlier list by Bertha H. Putnam in ibid., vol. 4 (1926–7).

There are six basic types of source which provide evidence on the commissions of the peace:—

1. Original Commissions of the Peace

These are naturally the ideal source of information since they are the original letters patent which recorded the commission of the peace and gave the justices of the peace their legal authority. The commission itself can be divided into two distinct sections: the *ex officio* members comprising the great officers of state and in Wales the members of the Council in the Marches and the justices of Great Sessions; and the smaller active portion of the commission made up of justices who were closely linked with the county in which they exercised jurisdiction. Selected justices who supposedly had special legal knowledge were also appointed to the quorum one of whom was always required to take part in certain of the functions of the justices of the peace. By the early seventeenth century the quorum had been extended to cover practically all the members of the commission so that the original distinction ceased to have much meaning.

By their very nature as original documents the commissions of the peace, once engrossed and sealed, passed out of the custody of the Crown Office where they were produced, so that the historian wishing to use them is dependent on the preservation of the commissions in the localities to which they were sent. In the case of the English county of Somerset there are 105 surviving original commissions for dates between 1600 and 1691, while 127 commissions between 1598 and 1700 are preserved for Lancashire. But this abundance of material is exceptional and for Wales, in particular, original commissions are very rare. The only ones used in this volume are three commissions for Merioneth dated between 1627 and 1643 (N.L.W., Pennal Towers Mss. (unscheduled) and U.C.N.W., Nannau Mss. 320 and 346), and a series of fourteen commissions for Denbigh between 1649 and 1686 which exist among the papers of the Myddelton family of Chirk.[18]

The scarcity of surviving commissions is largely explained by the frequency with which they were issued, since 'whenever a justice was appointed, dismissed or repositioned in the commission because of a change in status, a whole new commission for the county had to be issued, a fact not to be obscured by the chancery parlance, that the commission was "renewed"'[19] In the year 1630 no less than 133 commissions were issued

---

[18] A member of the Myddelton family was *custos rotulorum* for the county during nearly the whole of this period so that the presence of the commissions among their family papers is not surprising.

[19] Barnes and Hassell Smith, op. cit., p. 224. It was also normal for all the English and Welsh commissions to be renewed at the same time at the start of a new reign or to add the name of a newly appointed officer of state, such as the Chancellor or Treasurer, even though such renewals did not necessarily have any effect upon the active portion of the commission. For Wales the appointment of a President of the Council in the Marches of Wales was also the occasion of a general renewal of the commissions. General renewals of the commissions were also common at times of national disturbance, such as the years following the Civil War, during the Exclusion Crisis and during the reign of James II, when major alterations might be made in the commissions for political reasons.

for England and Wales.[20] On occasions commissions might succeed one another within a very short period. On 12 June 1630 a new commission was issued for Pembrokeshire in order to incorporate the newly succeeded Earl of Pembroke, Philip Herbert, as *custos rotulorum*; only a week later, on 19 June, another new commission was produced to record the appointment of Owen Edwards as a justice of the peace.[21] The frequency of new commissions and the low fee which was paid to the Crown Office for their production have drawn the comment that these documents 'were among the meanest instruments that passed the great seal'.[22] Under these circumstances it is not surprising that as each commission was superseded and ceased to have any legal value it became merely a piece of waste parchment to be put to whatever use seemed appropriate.

The removal of a justice from the commission by administrative action invariably required a new commission. But this was not the case if death were the cause of removal, partly one assumes because the deceased justice was in the nature of things unlikely to pay the necessary fee for producing a new commission. If there were a long interval between commissions, as sometimes occurred, and if several justices died in the meantime, it was therefore possible for the commission that was still legally in force to bear little resemblence to reality.[23] Even when first issued, the commission was not immune from error, such was the haste and carelessness with which it was drawn up. It was possible for an existing member of the commission to be omitted accidentally when the commission was renewed to add the name of a newly appointed justice. This may explain why it was necessary to issue a new commission for Denbigh on behalf of Peter Salisbury on 19 August 1595, only four days after the previous commission for the county.[24] One of the rare surviving original commissions reveals that although the Denbigh commission was renewed on 4 September 1660 to insert the name of Robert Milward as a justice of Great Sessions, the commission as actually issued contained the name of Arthur Trevor in place of Milward. This particular commission also shows that there could be a discrepancy between the date borne by a commission and the date on which it was actually engrossed or sealed, since the commission includes the name of the Treasurer, the Earl of Southampton, who was not appointed to his office until 8 September 1660, four days after the nominal date of the commission.[25] This last point is however largely a technical one and for the ordinary purposes of research the date carried by an original commission can be treated as its actual date.[26]

[20] Barnes and Hassell Smith, op. cit., p. 225.

[21] P.R.O., Index 4212/pp. 33, 35.

[22] Barnes and Hassell Smith, op. cit., p. 224.

[23] No new commission was issued for Pembrokeshire between 18 July 1666 and 11 March 1670: P.R.O., Index 4214/pp. 289, 363.

[24] Ibid., 4208/f.4v.

[25] N.L.W., Chirk Castle Ms. F.9926. The nominal date is that given in the docquet book: P.R.O., Index 4214/p. 35.

[26] This problem is discussed in Barnes and Hassell Smith, op. cit., pp. 225-6.

2. Enrolled Commissions of the Peace (P.R.O., C.66)

In quantity the enrolments of commissions of the peace on the patent rolls (P.R.O., C.66) are a plentiful source but in quality they are far from satisfactory. As Barnes and Hassell Smith have pointed out, 'the enrolment of commissions of the peace, if it took place at all, was in grudging obedience to the lord chancellor's order, which was in effect no more than an obeisance to time-honoured though by then archaic chancery practice'.[27] Of the counties covered in this volume, Monmouth is the only one for which there are any enrolments before 1558, being represented by commissions for 1543, 1544 and 1547. There are then enrolments for Monmouth and the twelve Welsh counties for 1562 and 1564 after which there are no further enrolments until 1594. This gap of thirty years was caused by dereliction of duty on the part of the officials of the Crown Office, notably by Thomas Powle who was Clerk of the Crown and also one of the Six Clerks. Sir Thomas Egerton, Master of the Rolls, was largely responsible for the resumption of the practice of enrolment which continued until the outbreak of the Civil War. The enrolments were briefly restarted after 1660 but were finally abandoned altogether by 1670.[28]

The mid-sixteenth century enrolments usually bear an individual date which can probably be regarded as accurate, but those produced after 1594 are in a different category. The commissions for each regnal year were entered on the patent roll in alphabetical order, beginning with the commission for Bedfordshire which was dated. The remaining commissions were then entered with their dates being given merely as *ut supra*. This practice is extremely misleading. The date of the Bedfordshire commission may be correct for that one county but bore little or no relation to the dates of the other commissions. Nor is there any guarantee that the commission enrolled even belonged to the same regnal year as the patent roll on which it was entered. Many of the commissions on the patent roll of 10 Charles I (P.R.O., C.66/2654) are in fact commissions of 7 Charles I. It was also common for the same commission to be entered on the rolls of two successive years, regardless of any changes in the real state of the commission in the meantime.[29]

The enrolment of commissions of the peace was therefore made in a very casual fashion. Since the original commission would have been sent to its destination long before it was enrolled, the information for the enrolment was probably taken instead from the copy of the commission in the Crown Office entry book.[30] The entry book was systematically corrected to keep

---

[27] Ibid., p. 230.

[28] Ibid., pp. 230–1. The patent rolls, P.R.O., C.66/2858 and 2859, ostensibly containing the enrolled commissions of 15 Charles I, were not made up and finally delivered to the petty bag office until 1655 and 1667 respectively. See R. B. Pugh, 'The Patent Rolls of the Interregnum', *Bulletin of the Institute of Historical Research*, vol. 23 (1950), and Barnes and Hassell Smith, op. cit., p. 231, n. 4.

[29] The Carmarthen commission of 13 December 1630 was entered on the rolls of both 6 and 7 Charles I: P.R.O., C.66/2536 and 2577.

[30] See sections five and six of this introduction for a discussion of the entry books.

up with official additions and omissions from the commissions. But it also noted the deaths of justices as these were reported to the Chancellor so that the information contained in the entry book would not necessarily corre- pond with the commission as originally issued. Errors of this kind naturally made their way into the enrolments. A good example is the omission from the enrolment of the Montgomery commission of 17 December 1600 of the Earls of Pembroke and Essex, both of whom died early in 1601 before the commission had been enrolled.[31] Many other errors arose from carelessness in the making of the enrolment. Justices whose names appear in the enrolment as members of the quorum are often left out of the list of the full commission or their names might be omitted altogether. James Bowen, who was appointed to the Pembrokeshire commission on 19 February 1621, remained a member of the commission when it was again renewed only a week later on 26 February but was omitted when the commission was enrolled.[32] The patent roll entries might also provide justices with post- humous careers. Two members of the Flintshire commission, John Conway and William Griffith, who died in 1614 were still to be found in an enrolment of 1616.[33] Another source of confusion to the researcher was created when a member of the commission of the peace was appointed as sheriff for the same county. In such a situation the sheriff was removed from his place on the commission during his year of office and afterwards restored as a justice of the peace. If the commission were not enrolled until after the justice concerned had finished acting as sheriff and had returned to the commission, the enrolment would naturally not reveal that there had been any break in his service as justice of the peace. This was probably the case with the enrolment of the Glamorgan commission of 28 June 1594 which includes the name of Sir Thomas Mansel even though he was sheriff of the county in 1593 to 1594.[34]

If the patent roll entries were used in isolation it would therefore be impossible to provide anything like accurate lists of justices of the peace. Fortunately, however, when the enrolled commissions are used in con- junction with other sources it is possible to overcome or at least to detect many of their deficiencies.[35] The accurate information contained in the Crown Office docket books on the dates of issue of commissions of the

---

[31] P.R.O., C.66/1549/m.31d. The commission is dated by the docket book entry in P.R.O., Index 4208/f.100.

[32] P.R.O., Index 4211/ff.119v., 120; P.R.O., C.66/2234/m.43d. Bowen was however included in another copy of the 26 February commission in B.M., Harleian Ms. 1933/f.26.

[33] P.R.O., C.66/2076/m.24d. The Gaol File list of the justices acting on 9 May 1614 has both men marked as dead, which implies that they were either already dead or that they died soon afterwards and that the list was corrected accordingly: N.L.W., Wales 4/976/7.

[34] P.R.O., C.66/1421/m.15d. Mansel was correctly omitted from the Gaol File list of justices acting on 22 July 1594: N.L.W., Wales 4/592/5. Discrepancies of this kind have been noted in the text.

[35] The unreliability of the patent rolls is correctly emphasised in Barnes and Hassell Smith, op. cit., pp. 230-3, but they perhaps slightly underestimate the extent to which information can be salvaged from this source when used in conjunction with other types of records.

peace and on the names of those justices who were added or removed often makes it possible to assign dates to the enrolled copies of the commissions. Frequently a commission which is enrolled on the patent roll can also be found in a *liber pacis* or Crown Office entry book, so providing a further check on the accuracy of the enrolment.[36] A careful watch on the dates of appointment, dismissal or death of the major office holders among the *ex officio* portion of the commission will also show if names contained in the original commission have been left out at the time of enrolment. Similarly, reference to the lists of sheriffs for each county will indicate occasions when the name of a justice who also served as sheriff should have been omitted from the enrolment. Many other occasions of proved or probable error can also be identified and noted. Nevertheless, the patent roll enrolments of commissions can never be wholly satisfactory, however much care is taken over their use as evidence, and for counties where other superior sources exist the enrolments can be discarded altogether.

3. CROWN OFFICE DOCQUET BOOKS (P.R.O., Indexes 4208, 4210–4215. These items have now been reclassified as C.231/1-8).

The docquet books were the Crown Office's record of the dates of issue of commissions of the peace and other instruments under the Great Seal. In the case of commissions of the peace, the docquet books also give the names of those who were added or removed from the commissions each time they were renewed, sometimes also giving a reason. The docquet books used in this volume are those covering the periods 1595 to 1603 and 1615 to 1699. The books from before 1595 and for over half the reign of James I are not extant. The precision of the information contained in the docquet books makes them of obvious value since, even in the absence of other sources, they provide at least a summary of the dates of new commissions and of the changes in the commissions. The docquet books also have the most important additional value of enabling the researcher to establish the dates of undated copies of the commissions of the peace when these are found enrolled on the patent rolls or written into entry books or *libri pacis*.

The docquet books however provide their own problems. The purpose of the docquets was to state simply the names of justices who were added or removed from the commission of the peace by administrative action. They do not state what other corrections were made to the commissions to allow for the deaths of individual justices. This means that if other sources are not available, it is not possible to supply full details of the commissions. This explains, for example, the very inadequate lists compiled for Anglesey between 1666 and 1680. The dates given in the docquet books for the issue of commissions of the peace can also cause some difficulties, since it does not invariably follow that the date of the docquet was the same as the date on the commission as actually issued. The original Denbigh commission of 9 March 1669 is dated four days after the docquet which records its issue.[37]

---

[36] See section three of this introduction for information on the docquet books and sections five and six for the entry books and *libri pacis*.

[37] N.L.W., Chirk Castle Ms. F.12910; P.R.O., Index 4214/p. 342.

However for most purposes the date of the docquet can be regarded as the date of the commission itself, unless by some rare chance the original commission has survived to contradict this evidence.[38]

Apart from these technical limitations, the docquet books are prone to several types of error, many of which can fortunately be detected. On some occasions the docquet books do not contain any entries to correspond with commissions which are known to have been issued or which were probably issued. There are no docquet book entries of the same date or approximately the same date as the two original Denbigh commissions of 23 June 1665 and 22 November 1677. In another instance a docquet book entry of 26 July 1616 records the issue of a new commission for Anglesey to include Francis Eure, a newly appointed justice of Great Sessions for the North Wales circuit. Eure's appointment would normally have required new commissions for Caernarvon and Merioneth, the other two counties in the circuit, but there is no record of such commissions in the docquet book and it is reasonable to conclude that the omission was an error.[39] Other docquet book errors which have been traced include the entry for Montgomery on 19 December 1676 which refers to Edward instead of Richard Herbert of Kerry and the reference to John in place of Roger Puleston in the entry of 1 July 1684 for Flint;[40] the entry for Caernarvon on 25 June 1656 runs together the names of Richard Griffith of Llanfair and Maurice Griffith of Methlan as Richard Griffith of Methlan; an incomplete entry for Pembrokeshire on 9 July 1616 records that the Bishop of St. Davids was added to the commission but fails to mention Sir Thomas Chamberlain, the new Justice of Chester, who was almost certainly added at the same time.[41]

4. Gaol Files Lists of Nomina Ministrorum (N.L.W., Wales 4; P.R.O., Assize 5)

Twice a year before the sessions of the courts of Great Sessions the clerk of the peace drew up a list of *nomina ministrorum* containing the names of the justices of the peace and other officials in his county. The names of the justices of the peace were obtained from the most recent commission to have reached the clerk of the peace. The completed list was then handed to the clerk of the justices of Great Sessions who made a mark against the name of each justice of the peace to show whether or not he was present at the Great Session or whether he was dead. The information gathered in this way enabled the justices of Great Sessions to tell the Chancellor what changes were required in the commission of the peace. The lists of *nomina ministrorum* remained in the possession of the justices of Great Sessions and were preserved as the outer parchment wrapping of the Gaol File of the

---

[38] See section one of this introduction for the dating problems posed by original commissions.

[39] N.L.W., Chirk Castle Mss. F.12899 and F.1119; P.R.O., Index 4211/f.24v.

[40] P.R.O., Index 4214/p.519 and Index 4215/p. 104.

[41] P.R.O., Index 4213/p. 337 and Index 4211/f.23v.

Great Session for which they had been produced.[42] Each Gaol File list of *nomina* can readily be dated by means of the attached writ summoning the Great Session to which the file belonged. Another advantage that the *nomina* have over other sources is that the regularity with which they were copied out makes them a very sensitive guide to changes in the commission of the peace. This sensitivity is shown when a member of the commission was appointed as sheriff for the same county, which meant that he temporarily ceased to act as a justice of the peace. Owen Brereton, who was sheriff of Denbigh in 1587 to 1588, was correctly left out of the lists of *nomina ministrorum* for the Great Sessions of 29 April and 19 August 1588 and was then correctly restored to the lists in 1589.[43]

The Gaol Files can therefore be a very valuable and regular source of information on the composition of the commissions of the peace and very extensive use has been made of them in compiling the lists in this volume. Unfortunately their state of preservation varies very widely from county to county. For the counties of the North Wales circuit of the courts of Great Sessions, Anglesey, Caernarvon and Merioneth, virtually no Gaol Files survive at all, while on the other hand they are very plentiful for the counties of the Chester circuit, Denbigh, Flint and Montgomery. The state of the files for the Carmarthen and Brecon circuits lies between these two extremes. In the case of Monmouth, which belonged to the English Assize system, there are only three usable files left in existence.[44]

One of the shortcomings of the *nomina* is the absence of any record of which justices were also members of the quorum and of the name of the *custos rotulorum*. This information can however sometimes be supplied by collating the *nomina* with other copies of the commission from about the same date taken from the patent rolls, entry books or *libri pacis*. Another problem arises from the fact that the *nomina ministrorum* were based on the most recent commission of the peace to have arrived in the county. Since there was often a considerable delay in the arrival of a new commission at its destination, it was possible for the *nomina* to represent an out of date commission. Where the contemporary docquet books survive and give a record of the dates on which new commissions were issued it is possible to discover without difficulty whether the *nomina* were out of step. This was the case with the *nomina* for Denbigh of 19 April 1630 which were a copy of the commission issued for the county on 8 July 1629 and not of the latest commission of 7 April 1630 which had not yet arrived.[45] This instance is a

---

[42] See also Barnes and Hassell Smith, op. cit., pp. 227–8. The same procedure was followed at the Assizes in England.

[43] N.L.W., Wales 4/7/4 and 5; ibid./8/1.

[44] For fuller information on the state of these records see Barnes and Hassell Smith, op. cit., pp. 236–7, and also the full lists printed in *Public Record Office List and Index*, no. XL, *List of Records of the Palatinates of Chester, Durham and Lancaster, the Honour of Peveril and the Principality of Wales* (London, 1914). It should be noted that quite frequently the Gaol File for a particular session has survived while the *nomina ministrorum* which formed the outer wrapper of the file has been destroyed or is too badly damaged for use, even under ultra-violet light.

[45] N.L.W., Wales 4/19/3; P.R.O., Index 4212/pp. 14, 29.

reminder that the date of a list of *nomina ministrorum* is one on which the justices of the peace were acting and not the date of their appointment.

The *nomina ministrorum* present the most intractable problems at times when there was a long interval between the issue of new commissions. It was normal for the clerk of the justices of Great Sessions to mark the *nomina* to show which justices of the peace had died and some attempt was certainly made to omit the names of dead justices from succeeding lists. But this was a rather haphazard process. Frequently the name of a deceased justice was omitted from the *nomina* drawn up for the Great Session which followed his death. However when the clerk of the peace copied out the *nomina* for the next session, possibly six months later, he would simply follow the information in the most recent commission in his possession. If a new commission had not been received in the meantime, the deceased justice would therefore reappear in the *nomina* as if he had been restored to the commission. A good example of the kind of situation that might arise is to be found in Pembrokeshire for which no new commission was issued between 18 July 1666 and 11 March 1670. Four of the justices of the peace for the county, Hugh Butler, Walter Vaughan, George Hayward and Thomas Wogan, were included in the *nomina ministrorum* for the sessions of 7 and 25 August 1668 but in both cases they were marked as dead. They were duly omitted from the *nomina* for the session of 12 April 1669 but they then reappeared on 30 August 1669 and were not finally omitted until 11 April 1670, by which time the new commission of 11 March 1670 had reached Pembrokeshire and brought the commission up to date.[46] This is an extreme example of justices being credited with posthumous careers but the problem has always to be borne in mind. For this reason it would be unwise for a researcher seeking biographical information to treat the date at which a justice finally disappears from the *nomina ministrorum* as more than a very general indication of the point at which he ceased to be a justice or of the date of his death.[47] Many other variations which occur between one set of *nomina* and another are not so readily explicable as the example just given and may be the result simply of carelessness on the part of the clerk of the peace or of some good but unrecorded reason. In such cases it is possible only to draw attention to the variation without offering an explanation.[48]

[46] N.L.W., Wales 4/793/4, 5, 6 and 7; ibid., 794/1; P.R.O., Index 4214/pp. 289, 363. They may still have been alive when the *nomina* were produced in August 1668 and have died shortly afterwards.

[47] Another case of a posthumous career is that of Sir John Salisbury who died in 1684 but was not finally omitted from the Flintshire commission as recorded in the *nomina* until after 3 October 1687: N.L.W., Wales 4/992/6. To confuse the issue still further there were two other men named John Salisbury in the Flintshire commission at this time. No systematic attempt has been made to discover the date of death of each of the hundreds of individuals who served as justices of the peace in Wales between 1541 and 1689 and so to decide at what date they should have been omitted from records of the commissions of the peace.

[48] Thomas Wynn ap Richard and William Myddelton were both left out of the *nomina* for Denbigh on 7 July 1600 but reappeared in later lists: N.L.W., Wales 4/11/4. There is no obvious reason for these changes.

5. Crown Office Entry Books: Borough Commissions (P.R.O., C.181)

These volumes contain the Crown Office's official record of commissions of the peace issued for boroughs. The entry books are a particularly accurate and valuable source since each commission was copied out in full complete with its date and details of the quorum. They also provide a useful check on the dates given in the corresponding docquet book entries. The only Welsh borough for which a separate commission was issued was Haverfordwest so that the entry books make only a small contribution to the lists in this volume.[49]

6. Crown Office Entry Books and Libri Pacis: County Commissions

Strictly speaking, the entry books and *libri pacis* were two distinct types of record with different purposes. In practice however they present closely related problems to the researcher and it is in any case rarely possible to be certain to which class any given book originally belonged.

The entry books were a series of working records kept by the Crown Office to provide the Chancellor with up to date information on the state of the commissions of the peace. Each entry book was therefore steadily amended to show new appointments to the commissions and to cross out the names of justices who had died or had been removed for other reasons. Barnes and Hassell Smith have identified two books preserved in the Public Record Office which in their opinion are definitely entry books (P.R.O., C.193/13/4 (1652) and ibid., 5 (1657)) and suggest that six others may be of the same type (P.R.O., C.193/12/1 (1543); ibid., 3 (1662); ibid., 4 (1680); C.193/13/1 (1621); ibid., 2 (1634); ibid., 6 (1656)).[50]

The *libri pacis* were also produced by the Crown Office. They were not however formal records in the same sense as the entry books since their function was to provide information on the justices of the peace for other government agencies such as the Privy Council or Treasury. The *libri pacis* were annotated in the same way as the entry books, although less systematically, and were discarded when their useful life had ended. Some of them are still to be found among various classes of material in the Public Record Office (e.g., C.193, C.220, E.163, and State Papers), but many *libri pacis* remained in the possession of the officials for whom they had been produced and for this reason are preserved among private manuscript collections now in the British Museum (e.g., Lansdowne, Harleian, Egerton, Stowe, Royal Mss.) and in other miscellaneous locations (e.g., Hatfield House, Cambridge University Library, Kent County Record Office).

The entry books and *libri pacis* have the practical research advantage of providing evidence on the state of the commissions of the peace at periods when other sources may be scarce, particularly in the sixteenth century. Without these two sources it would be virtually impossible to give details of the commissions for Anglesey, Caernarvon and Merioneth

---

[49] For further information see Barnes and Hassell Smith, op. cit., pp. 228–9, 232–3.

[50] Ibid., pp. 228–30, 237–40. One reason why the enrolments on the patent rolls were so carelessly made was that they had become merely a formal record and had been replaced by the entry books as the real working source of reference for administrative purposes.

for any date much before 1600. It is also common to find copies of the same commission recorded in more than one entry book or *liber pacis*, so providing a useful cross-check. The Glamorgan commission of 24 February 1651 is to be found in three different places, P.R.O., C.193/13/4/f.120v., Cambridge University Ms. Dd.VIII.1/f.127, and B.M., Stowe Ms. 577/f.64. On many occasions the entry books and *libri pacis* contain details of commissions which are also enrolled on the patent rolls and can therefore be used to test the accuracy of the enrolments.[51]

The entry books and *libri pacis* present certain technical difficulties which fortunately are not often insuperable. The books usually contain some statement of the year in which they were produced but the individual commissions which they record are not dated.[52] This means that in the case of sixteenth-century books it is possible only to say that the justices of a particular county were acting in a given year. However the surviving docquet books for the years 1595 to 1603 and 1615 to 1699 make it feasible to assign an exact date to the commissions contained in the entry books or *libri pacis* during those periods. Another practical problem which can largely be overcome with care arises from the large number of corrections in the entry books and *libri pacis*.[53] Any justice of the peace whose name has been crossed through can be assumed to have been a member of the commission as originally entered. The names of justices who were added to the commission at a later date can usually be distinguished by differences in the hand in which they were entered or by their insertion in the blank spaces left between names when the commission was first copied out. The docquet books can again help by identifying the justices who were appointed subsequent to the original commission.

When the commissions were recorded in the entry books they were always entered in full with details of both the *ex officio* and active members of the commission. In the case of the *libri pacis*, on the other hand, two books of the same year will sometimes differ, one giving the complete commission and the other only the active portion. The commissions of 1558 to 1559, for example, are listed in full in B.M., Lansdowne Ms. 1218 and in part in P.R.O., S.P.12/2/17.

7. MISCELLANEOUS UNPRINTED SOURCES

In addition to the six main sources just discussed, information on commissions of the peace can sometimes be found in other miscellaneous sources. Material of this kind which has been used in this volume includes the register of the Council in the Marches of Wales between 1569 and

---

[51] The Anglesey commission of 26 February 1621 is recorded in both P.R.O. C.66/2234/m 41d. and in B.M., Harleian Ms. 1974/f.22. The name of Francis Eure, a Justice of Great Sessions for Anglesey, is correctly included in the Harleian Ms. copy but is omitted from the enrolment in C.66/2234, which suggests that the enrolment was made after the death of Eure on 1 May 1621.

[52] The entry books of county commissions therefore differ in this respect from the entry books of borough commissions (P.R.O., C.181) which are discussed in the preceding section of this introduction.

[53] The entry book of 1543 (P.R.O., C.193/12/1), for example, is very heavily corrected.

1591,[54] a few lists of justices for North Wales counties among the Wynn Papers in the National Library of Wales, and the details of the politically-inspired changes in the commissions in 1680 and 1686 which are recorded in the Privy Council registers of those years.

8. PRINTED SOURCES

These form another small miscellaneous category. They include such items as the lists of justices of the peace published by Thomas Walkley in 1650 and by N.S., Esq., in 1680, Rice Merrick's *Booke of Glamorganshire Antiquities* of 1578, and a published manuscript from the House of Lords containing details of the changes in the commissions in 1680.

EDITORIAL METHOD

The amount of available source material varies considerably from county to county. For counties where evidence is scarce and where there are frequent gaps in the sources it is desirable to present what material there is more or less in full. For other counties which are far better served by surviving original documents it would obviously be impracticable to quote every list of justices that exists without some condensation. The basic principle adopted has therefore been to try to achieve a working compromise between too much and too little information and so satisfy both the demands of scholarship and the need to economize on space. In general full details of each county commission are supplied for about one year in three. In this way it is possible to show regularly where newly appointed justices were fitted into the commission and so establish the justices' order of precedence, a point of very considerable social importance.[55] Where a rapid turnover in the membership of the commission makes it desirable, the full commission is given more frequently. The changes that took place in the intervening years are summarized to indicate only the names of those justices who were added or who disappeared from the commission.[56]

In order to assist users of the lists in tracing variations in the size of the commissions, the number of names in the commission is provided in brackets at the end of each full and of each summary entry. On some occasions the size of the commission for a particular county may appear to vary widely

---

[54] Bodleian library, Bodley Ms. 904. The original manuscript has been used in preference to the printed edition edited by R. Flenley (*Cymmrodorion Record Series,* no. 8 (London, 1916)) which is not always accurate.

[55] The order of precedence in the commission established the order in which the justices sat on the bench at quarter sessions and was also an indication of their social status. It was not unknown for a justice to attempt to have his name raised a few places when a new commission was issued. In the sixteenth century membership of the quorum of the commission was also connected with social prestige as well as with any presumed knowledge of the law. In the seventeenth century the great majority of justices were also members of the quorum. For further discussion of these questions see Barnes and Hassell Smith, op. cit., pp. 223–4.

[56] This information includes all the docquet book entries giving the dates of issue of new commissions and the names of the justices who were added or removed by administrative action.

from one year to the next. This sometimes occurs at times of political unrest such as the Civil War or the Exclusion Crisis but frequently it is merely the result of different methods of recording the commission rather than of real changes in its size. This latter reason explains, for example, why a list of the members of the Anglesey commission in 1579 contains forty-six names while another of 1581 has only ten.[57] Another important point to keep in mind when using the lists is that the dates attached to some copies of the commission represent the actual date on which the commission was issued, while other dates are merely those on which the members of the commission can be said to have been acting. This distinction in dating has been indicated clearly in the text and should present no serious difficulties.

A substantial part of any Welsh commission was composed of the great officers of state, the justices of Great Sessions and members of the Council in the Marches who were all appointed *ex officio* and were not intended to be active as justices of the peace. This portion of the commission has been retained since to omit it would give a misleading impression of the appearance of a commission. Such a procedure would also distort the order of precedence on the commission and would introduce errors since there is no precise dividing line between the *ex officio* and active portions of the commissions. However, in order to save space the amount of information given on the *ex officio* justices has been abbreviated wherever possible. In general full details of the name and rank of the major office holders are given only on their first appearance in the commission and are largely omitted in subsequent entries, except where necessary for clarity.

The period covered by the lists in this volume starts nominally in 1541 when the first evidence is to be found of justices of the peace acting in Wales, although, as explained earlier, such evidence is available for only two counties. The remaining lists start in practice in 1542 or 1543 as evidence first appears. The volume ends in approximately 1689, partly for the practical reasons that this provides a manageable period of roughly 150 years and that the survey of sources by Barnes and Hassell Smith ends in 1688, but also because this makes it possible to show the effect on the commissions of the Revolution of 1688. The order in which the lists are presented is not alphabetical but instead follows the pattern of the four circuits in which the Welsh counties were grouped for the courts of Great Sessions. Monmouthshire formed part of the English Assize system and is therefore placed on its own at the end of the volume.

For the sake of completeness it would also have been useful to have included lists of the clerks of the peace alongside those of the justices of the peace. The clerks of the peace are unfortunately not mentioned in the same material as the justices of the peace and there is no obvious source of information on the subject, so that it has not proved feasible to try to identify the clerks systematically. Such evidence as there is on the clerks of the peace

---

[57] P.R.O., S.P.12/145/f.57v.; Bodleian Library, Bodley Ms. 904/f.207. The 1581 list gives the names only of the active portion of the commission and not of its *ex officio* members. In theory there were supposed to be only eight active members of the commission, in addition to the *ex officio* justices, but this number was soon exceeded.

has however been collected by Sir L. E. Stephens in *The Clerks of the Counties, 1360–1960*.[58]

To achieve consistency and clarity the spelling of family names has been standardized, usually on the basis of the forms adopted in *The Dictionary of Welsh Biography*,[59] while Christian names have been abbreviated to save space. Where the records state the place of origin of a justice of the peace this information has been included but no attempt has been made to supply such details in other cases because the possibility of a wrong and misleading identification is often too great. As might be expected, the spellings of Welsh place names in record material are frequently garbled almost beyond recognition but in the great majority of cases it has been possible to discover the correct form.[60]

As has already been explained, the lists of justices of the peace in this volume are composed from a variety of sources each of which poses its own problems of interpretation. So far as possible the inconsistencies of this material have been traced and corrected or, when this is not feasible, they have been pointed out to the reader. But in the nature of things it cannot be claimed that the lists are either complete or free from errors. It is hoped that some users will find them a useful source of reference while others will use them as a basis for further research. Provided that due note is taken of the problems discussed in this introduction and of the comments incorporated in the text, the lists should be helpful.

[58] Published by the Society of Clerks of the Peace of Counties and of Clerks of County Councils (Newport, 1961). Similar material can also be found for the county of Glamorgan in G. Williams, *A List of the Names and Residences of the High Sheriffs of Glamorgan from 1541–1966* (Cheltenham, 1966).

[59] *The Dictionary of Welsh Biography down to 1940*, Honourable Society of Cymmrodorion (London, 1959). Where the dictionary does not include a particular family other miscellaneous reference books have been consulted, in particular the *Index to Archaeologia Cambrensis, 1846–1900*, Cambrian Archaeological Association (Cardiff, 1964).

[60] Especially useful for this purpose is the gazeteer in M. Richards, *Welsh Territorial and Administrative Units* (Cardiff, 1969). Other valuable sources of information on place-names include the *Gazeteer of Welsh Place-Names*, ed. E. Davies (Cardiff, 1967) and the Index to *Archaeologia Cambrensis, 1846–1900*. Where doubt remains about the correct form of a place-name this has been noted in the text.

Abbreviations

B.M.: British Museum.

H.M.C.: Historical Manuscripts Commission.

N.L.W.: National Library of Wales.

P.R.O.: Public Record Office.

U.C.N.W.: University College of North Wales.

p: In *libri pacis* the symbol p for *preses* is used to indicate the holder of the office of *custos rotulorum* and its use has been retained here.

*: This indicates membership of the quorum.

Bibliography

This is limited to the sources used in compiling the lists of justices of the peace for each county. The material cited in the Introduction is referred to in the footnotes.

Unprinted Sources

1. ORIGINAL COMMISSIONS OF THE PEACE

N.L.W., Pennal Towers Mss. (unscheduled): Merioneth commission of 15 March 1627.

N.L.W., Chirk Castle Mss. F.1115, F.9926, F.114, F.1120, F.4709, F.4721, F.12899, F.4719, F.184, F.12910, F.1119, F.1118, F.1116, F.1117: Denbigh commissions of 31 March 1649, 4 September 1660, 1 June 1661, 8 November 1661, 20 March 1662, 17 July 1662, 23 June 1665, 11 January 1667, 30 June 1668, 9 March 1669, 22 November 1677, 1 July 1684, 23 June 1685, 2 December 1686.

U.C.N.W., Nannau Ms. 320: Merioneth commission of 22 February 1632.

U.C.N.W., Nannau Ms. 346: Merioneth commission of 29 April 1643.

2. ENROLLED COMMISSIONS OF THE PEACE

P.R.O., C.66: Patent Rolls.

P.R.O., C.67: Supplementary Patent Rolls.

3. CROWN OFFICE DOCQUET BOOKS

P.R.O., Index 4208 (1595–1603), Index 4211 (1615–29), Index 4212 (1629–43), Index 4210 (1642–46), Index 4213 (1644–60), Index 4214 (1660–79), Index 4215 (1679–99). These items have now been reclassified as P.R.O., C.231/1–8.

4. GAOL FILES NOMINA MINISTRORUM

N.L.W., Wales 4: Gaol Files of the Courts of Great Sessions. These records were formerly deposited at the Public Record Office.

P.R.O., Assize 5: Gaol Files of Monmouthshire Assizes.

5. CROWN OFFICE ENTRY BOOKS (Borough Commissions)

P.R.O., C.181/1–7: Entry Books, 1601–1673.

6. LIBRI PACIS AND CROWN OFFICE ENTRY BOOKS (County Commissions)

In origin these were two distinct types of record but in practice it is often very difficult or impossible to say to which class any given item belonged. Fuller details of these sources can be obtained in T. G. Barnes & A. Hassell Smith, 'Justices of the Peace from 1558 to 1688', *Bulletin of the Institute of Historical Research,* 32, 1959, pp. 237–40. In most cases the dates of the records listed here follow those given by Barnes and Hassell Smith. Items which are not included in their list are marked by an asterisk.

*P.R.O., C.193/12/1: 1543
*P.R.O., S.P.11/5: 1555
 B.M., Lansdowne Ms. 1218: 1558–59
 P.R.O., S.P.12/2/no. 17: 1559
 B.M., Lansdowne Ms. 1218: 1561
 P.R.O., S.P.12/93/part 2: 1573–74
 B.M., Egerton Ms. 2345: 1573–74
 P.R.O., S.P.12/104: 1575
 P.R.O., S.P.12/106/part 2: 1575
 P.R.O., S.P.12/121: 1577
 Hatfield House Ms. 223.7: 1578
 P.R.O., S.P.12/145: 1579
 B.M., Lansdowne Ms. 35: 1582
 B.M., Royal Ms. 18.D.III: 1583
 P.R.O., E.163/14/8: 1584
 Hatfield House Ms. 278: 1591
 Kent Record Office Ms. U.350.03: 1593
 P.R.O., S.P.13/Case F/no. 11: 1596
*B.M., Harleian Ms. 1974: 1601
 B.M., Additional Ms. 38139: 1604
 P.R.O., S.P.14/33: 1608
*B.M., Harleian Ms. 1933: 1621
 P.R.O., C.193/13/1: 1621
 B.M., Harleian Ms. 1622: 1626
 P.R.O., C.193/12/2: 1626
 P.R.O., E.163/18/12: 1626
 P.R.O., S.P.16/212: 1632
 P.R.O., C.193/13/2: 1634
 P.R.O., S.P.16/405: 1636
 P.R.O., C.193/13/3: 1649
 B.M., Stowe Ms. 577: 1652
 P.R.O., C.193/13/4: 1652
 Cambridge University Ms. Dd.VIII.1: 1652
 P.R.O., C.193/13/6: 1656
 P.R.O., C.193/13/5: 1657
 P.R.O., C.220/9/4: 1660
*B.M., Egerton Ms. 2557: 1661
 P.R.O., C.193/12/3: 1662
 P.R.O., C.193/12/4: 1680
 P.R.O., C.193/12/5: 1685

7. MISCELLANEOUS

Bodleian Library, Bodley Ms. 904: Register of the Council in the Marches of Wales, 1569–1591.

Huntington Library, Ellesmere Ms. 2513: List of Monmouthshire justices of the peace in 1609.

N.L.W. Ms. 11020E: Letter of Duke of Beaufort, 26 June 1687, recommending certain men for appointment as justices of the peace in Anglesey, Brecon, Caernarvon, Denbigh, Monmouth.

N.L.W., Chirk Castle Ms. F.10172: *dedimus potestatem* of 15 July 1615 for administering to Thomas Myddelton, Esq., the oath of a justice of the peace in Denbigh.

N.L.W., Wynn Papers No. 2209: Lists of the justices of the peace in Anglesey, Caernarvon and Denbigh in 1659.

N.L.W., Wynn Papers No. 2836: Copies of the Caernarvon and Denbigh Commissions of 20 September 1683.

P.R.O., E.372/387: Pipe Roll of 33 Henry VIII.

P.R.O., P.C.2/68 and 71: Privy Council Registers of 1680 and 1686.

Printed Sources

Calendar of the Caernarvonshire Quarter Sessions Records, vol. 1, *1541–1558,* ed. W. O. Williams (Caernarvon, 1956).

Calendar of Letters and Papers of the Reign of Henry VIII, vols. 10, 18, 20.

Calendar of Patent Rolls, 1547–48.

Calendar of the Register of the Council in the Marches of Wales, 1569–1591, ed R. Flenley, Cymmrodorion Record Series, no. 8 (London, 1916).

Gleason, J. H., *The Justices of the Peace in England, 1558–1640* (Oxford, 1969).

Historical Manuscripts Commission, Eleventh Report, Appendix, Part 2 (London, 1887).

Merrick, Rice, Esq., *A Booke of Glamorganshire Antiquities, 1578,* ed. J. A. Corbett (London, 1887).

N. S., Esq., *A catalogue of the names of all . . . justices . . . according to the late alterations, to which is added the names of those formerly in commission now left out* (London, 1680).

Owen, George, *The Description of Pembrokeshire,* vol. 1, ed. H. Owen, Cymmrodorion Record Series, no. 1 (London, 1892).

Walkley, Thomas, *The names of the justices of the peace this Michaelmas term* (London, 1650).

1543: 12 March
*Th. Audley, kt., Chancellor; *D. of Norfolk, Treasurer; *D. of Suffolk, President of Council; *J. Russell, kt., Keeper of Privy Seal; *B. of Coventry & Lichfield, President of the Council in the Marches of Wales; Bishops of *St. Asaph, Bangor; Walter, Lord Ferrers; *Nich. Hare, Ed. Croft, Rice Mansel, *J. Vernon, kts.; *J. Pakington; *p Th. Holte; *David Brooke; J. ap Rice; *Rich. Hassall; *J. Arnold; J. Lewis; *J. ap Rice ap Llewelyn ap Hulkyn; *Roderick ap David; Rich. ap Rhydderch; David ap Rice ap Llewelyn ap Gruffydd; *Rich. Meyrick. *Later additions to list*: *Rich. Bulkeley, kt.; *Th. Bromley, serjeant at law; *Adam Mytton; Lewis ap Payn ap Llewelyn ap Owen; Roland Griffith; Th. Griffith: C.193/12/1/f.47. (24 names plus 6 corrections).

1555: (Acting)
Rich. Bulkeley, kt.; W. Lewis; Lewis Owen ap Meyrick; Roderick ap David; Th. Bulkeley, clerk; J. ap Rice ap Llewelyn ap Hulkyn; W. Roberts, clerk: S.P.11/5/f.59v.   (7)

1558–59: (Acting)
*Nich. Bacon, kt., Keeper of Great Seal; *Marquess of Winchester, Treasurer; *E. of Arundel, Steward; Bishops of *Bath & Wells, *St. Asaph, *Chester; *J. Throckmorton, Justice of Chester; *J. Vaughan, *Adam Mytton, *p Rich. Bulkeley, kts.; *J. Scudamore of Holm; *Chas. Fox; *J. Welsh; *Reg. Corbet; *W. Symonds; *W. Gerard; *Rich. Seaborne; Rees Thomas; *Roland Meredith; *W. Roberts, clerk; *Th. Powell; W. Lewis; *Rich. ap Rhydderch; W. Wood; David ap Richard ap David ap Gwilym; Roderick ap David; Owen ap Hugh: B.M., Lansdowne Ms.1218/f.41. (Except for the omission of the *ex officio* members of the commission, the same list also appears in S.P.12/2/17/p.65).   (27)

1561: (Acting)
*Bacon; *Winchester; *Arundel; *H. Sidney, kt., President of the Council in the Marches of Wales; *B. of Bangor; *Reg. Corbet, Justice of Great Sessions; *Nich. Bagnall, kt.; *Th. Powell; *Rees Thomas; *Lewis Owen ap Meyrick; Roland Meredith; *W. Wood; Rich. ap Rhydderch; *Owen Wood; Owen ap Hugh: B.M., Lansdowne Ms. 1218/f.88.   (15)

1562: 13 June
As in 1561: C.66/985/m.41d.   (15)

1564: (Acting)
*Bacon; *Winchester; *Arundel; *Sidney; Bishops of *Bangor, *St. Asaph; *Corbet; *J. Throckmorton, Justice of Chester; *p Rich. Bulkeley, *Nich. Bagnall, kts.; *W. Gerard; *Chas. Fox; *Rich. Wye; *Rich. Seaborne; *Ellis Price, Ll.D.; *Rich. Pates; *J. Price; *Rich. Smith; *Th. Powell; *W. Lewis; *Lewis Owen ap Meyrick; Roland Meredith; Maurice Griffith of Porthaml; *Hugh Morgan, Ll.B.; Rich. ap Rhydderch; *Owen Wood: C.66/998/m.11d.   (26)

I

1573–4: (Acting)
*Bacon; *W., Lord Burghley, Treasurer; *Sidney; *B. of Bangor; *Hugh
Cholmondeley, kt.; *Geo. Bromley, Justice of Great Sessions; *Throck-
morton; *Gerard; *Fox; *Seaborne; *Price; *Pates; *p Rich. Bulkeley;
*W. Lewis; *Rich. Owen Tudor; *Lewis ap Owen ap Meyrick; *Roland
Thomas, D.C.L.; *Edm. Meyrick, D.C.L.; *Maurice Griffith of Porthaml;
Owen Wood; *Roland Meredith; Owen ap Hugh: S.P.12/93/part 2/f.36
& B.M., Egerton Ms. 2345/f.46v. (22)

1575: (Acting)
As in 1573–4, except: *Roland Bulkeley of Porthaml, *added*. Hugh Cholmondeley, *omitted*: S.P.12/106/part 2/f.10v. (22)

1577: (Acting)
As in 1575, except: *Hugh Hughes, *added*. Roland Thomas; Edm. Meyrick,
omitted: S.P.12/121/f.41. (21)

1578: (Acting)
*Bacon; *Burghley; *Sidney, President of the Council in the Marches of
Wales; *B. of Worcester, Vice-President of the Council in the Marches of
Wales; Earls of *Worcester, *Pembroke; Bishops of *Hereford, *Bangor,
*St. Davids, *St. Asaph; *Jas. Croft, Household Controller; *Throck-
morton; *Andrew Corbet, *J. Perrot, *Nich. Arnold, *Hugh Cholmon-
deley, *J. Littleton, *J. Huband, *p Rich, Bulkeley, kts.; *Geo. Bromley,
Justice of Great Sessions; *David Lewis, Ll.D.; *W. Gerard; *W. Aubrey;
*Chas. Fox; *W. Glaseor; *Ellis Price, Ll.D.; *Ed. Leighton; *Rich. Pates;
*Ralph Barton; *Jerome Corbet; *J. Puckering; *Fabian Phillips; H.
Townshend; *W. Leighton; *W. Lewis; *Lewis ap Owen ap Meyrick;
Owen Wood; Rich. ap Owen Tudor; Roland Bulkeley of Porthaml;
*Maurice Griffith; Roland Meredith; Owen ap Hugh; *Hugh Hughes.
Later additions to list: *Th. Bromley, kt., Chancellor; *W. Herbert, kt.;
*J. Price; *J. Nuttall; *W. Thomas; J. Griffith of Trefarthen; Th. Glynn:
Hatfield House Ms. 223.7. (43 names plus 7 corrections).

1579: post 26 April
As in 1578, except: Bacon; Rich. ap Owen Tudor; Roland Bulkeley; Roland
Meredith, *omitted*: S.P.12/145/f.57v. (All corrections to 1578 list form part
of basic 1579 list. List dated by appointment of Bromley as Chancellor on
26 April.) (46)

1581: 20 November (Acting)
Rich. Bulkeley, kt.; W. Lewis; Lewis ap Owen Meyrick; Owen Wood;
Maurice Griffith of Porthaml; Th. Glynn; J. Griffith; Hugh Hughes; Rich.
Owen Tudor; Owen ap Hugh: Bodleian, Bodley Ms. 904/f.207. (10)

1582: (Acting)
J. Huband, Rich. Bulkeley, W. Herbert, kts.; W. Lewis; Rich. Owen Tudor;
Lewis ap Owen ap Meyrick; Maurice Griffith; Roland Meredith; J. Nuttall;
W. Thomas; Owen Wood; Hugh Hughes; Owen ap Hugh; Th. Glynn:
B.M., Lansdowne Ms. 35/f.139v. (14)

1584: (Acting)
*Bromley, Chancellor; *Burghley, Treasurer; *Sidney, President of the Council in the Marches of Wales; *p E. of Leicester; Earls of *Worcester, *Pembroke; Bishops of *Hereford, *Bangor, *St. Asaph; *Croft, Household Controller; *Geo. Bromley, kt., Justice of Chester; *W. Leighton & *Fabian Phillips, Justices of Great Sessions; *J. Perrot, *Hugh Cholmondeley, *J. Littleton, *Rich. Bulkeley, *W. Herbert, kts.; *J. Puckering; *W. Aubrey; *Chas. Fox; *Ellis Price; *Ed. Leighton; *H. Townshend; *Rich. Pates; *Ralph Barton; *Jerome Corbet; *W. Glaseor; *W. Lewis; *Owen Wood; *Lewis ap Owen ap Meyrick; *W. Griffith, Ll.D.; *Rich. Owen Tudor; *Maurice Griffith; *Roland Meredith; W. Thomas; W. Morris; *Hugh Hughes; *Rich. White; *J. Griffith; Owen ap Hugh; Th. Glynn. *Later additions to list*: *Christopher Hatton, Chancellor (1587); David Owen Tudor; Hugh Lewis: E.163/14/8/f.55v. (42 names plus 3 corrections).

1590–91: (Acting)
*Hatton, Chancellor; *Burghley; *E. of Pembroke, President of the Council in the Marches of Wales; *B. of St. Asaph; *J. Perrot, kt.; *W. Leighton & *Fabian Phillips, Justices of Great Sessions; *Hugh Cholmondeley, *p Rich. Bulkeley, *W. Herbert, kts.; *J. Puckering; *W. Aubrey; *Ellis Price, Ll.D.; *Ed. Leighton; *H. Townshend; *Jerome Corbet; *W. Lewis; *Owen Wood; *W. Griffith, Ll.D.; W. Morris; *Hugh Hughes; *Roland Meredith; *Owen Holland; Maurice Griffith; David Owen Tudor; *Rich. White; *J. Griffith; Owen ap Hugh; Th. Glynn; Hugh Lewis of Bodewryd: Hatfield House Ms. 278/f.62. (30)

1592–3: (Acting)
As in 1590–91, except: *Rich. Shuttleworth, kt., Justice of Chester; *Rich. Bulkeley, Esq.; Piers Lloyd; *W. Glynn, *added*. Hatton; J. Perrot; Owen Wood; W. Griffith; Roland Meredith, *omitted:* Kent Record Office Ms. U.350.03. (J. Puckering is now Keeper of Great Seal (28 May 1592)) (29)

1594: 15 July
*J. Puckering, kt., Keeper of Great Seal; *Burghley; *E. of Pembroke, President of the Council in the Marches of Wales; *B. of St. Asaph; *Rich. Shuttleworth, kt., Justice of Chester; *W. Leighton & *Rich. Broughton, Justices of Great Sessions; *Hugh Cholmondeley, *p Rich. Bulkeley, *W. Herbert, kts.; *W. Aubrey; *Ellis Price, Ll.D.; *H. Townshend; *Jerome Corbet; *Fabian Phillips; *W. Lewis; *W. Morris; *Hugh Hughes; *J. Griffith; *Rich. Bulkeley; *Owen Holland; Maurice Griffith; David Owen Tudor; Rich. White; Owen ap Hugh; Piers Lloyd; Th. Glynn; *W. Glynn; Hugh Lewis of Bodewryd: C.66/1421/m.16d. (29)

1595: 15 August
As in 1594, except: *W. Fowler; *Arthur Bulkeley; Hugh Wood; Hugh ap Rice Wynn, *added*. W. Aubrey; Ellis Price; W. Morris; J. Griffith; Maurice Griffith; Th. Glynn; W. Glynn, *omitted*: C.66/1435/m.21d. General renewal of Welsh commissions on 15 August: Index 4208/f.4v. (26)

1596: 12 March
Commission renewed to *restore* J. Griffith of Trefarthen; Piers Lloyd, late sheriff: Index 4208/f.13.

1596: 13 July
*Th. Egerton, kt., Keeper of Great Seal; *Burghley; *E. of Pembroke, President of the Council in the Marches of Wales; *E. of Worcester; *B. of St. Asaph; *W., Lord Chandos; *Shuttleworth, Justice of Chester; *Leighton & *Broughton, Justices of Great Sessions; *Hugh Cholmondeley, *p Rich. Bulkeley, *W. Herbert, *J. Harington, *H. Poole, kts.; *Geo. Kingsmill, serjeant at law; *H. Townshend; *Jerome Corbet; *Fabian Phillips; *Rich. Atkins; *Rich. Corbet of Morton; *Th. Cornwall; *W. Fowler; *W. Lewis; *Hugh Hughes, Queen's attorney; *J. Griffith of Trefarthen; *Rich. Bulkeley; *Owen Holland; David Owen Tudor; *Th. Glynn; *Rich. White; *Arthur Bulkeley; Owen ap Hugh; Piers Lloyd; Hugh Wood; Hugh Lewis of Bodewryd: C.66/1468/m.16d. & S.P.13/Case F, no. 11/f.42v. Commission renewed to *restore* Th. Glynn: Index 4208/f.18.   (35)

1597: 16 November
Commission renewed to *add* Rich. Meyrick: Index 4208/f.22v.

1597: 17 December
*Egerton; *Burghley; *Pembroke; *B. of St. Asaph; *Shuttleworth; *Leighton & *Broughton; *p Rich. Bulkeley, *W. Herbert, kts.; *H. Townshend; *Jerome Corbet; *Th. Mostyn; *W. Lewis; *Hugh Hughes, attorney; *J. Griffith of Trefarthen; *Rich. Bulkeley; *Owen Holland; David Owen Tudor; *Th. Glynn; *Rich. White; *Arthur Bulkeley; Owen ap Hugh; Piers Lloyd; Hugh Wood; *Rich. Meyrick; Hugh Lewis of Bodewryd: C.66/1468/m.31d. Commission renewed to *add* Th. Mostyn: Index 4208/f.43.   (26)

1598: 15 March
Commission renewed to *add* Owen ap Robert Owen: Index 4208/f.47.

1598: 31 May
Commission renewed to *add* Hugh ap Rice: Index 4208/f.50v.

1598: 3 July
Commission renewed to *add* W. Lewis of Whayne: Index 4208/f.51v.

1598: 1 December
As on 17 December 1597, except: *Hugh Owen; W. Lewis of Whayne; Owen ap Robert Owen; Hugh ap Rice Wynn, *added*. Burghley; Jerome Corbet, *omitted*: C.66/1482/m.18d. Commission renewed to *add* Hugh Owen: Index 4208/f.60.   (28)

1599: 12 July
As on 1 December 1598, except: *Th., Lord Buckhurst, Treasurer; *H., B. of Bangor, *added*: C.66/1493/m.28d. Commission renewed to *add* B. of Bangor: Index 4208/f.74.   (30)

1600: 16 July
Commission renewed to *add* W. Griffith of Trefarthen; Rich. Hampton, and *omit* W. Herbert: Index 4208/f.93.

1600: 23 October
*Egerton; *Buckhurst; *E. of Pembroke, President of the Council in the Marches of Wales; Bishops of *Bangor, *St. Asaph; *Rich. Lewkenor, kt., Justice of Chester; *Leighton & *Broughton; *p Rich. Bulkeley, kt.; *Th. Mostyn, kt.; *H. Townshend; *W. Lewis; *Hugh Hughes, attorney; *J. Griffith of Trefarthen; *Rich. Bulkeley; *Hugh Owen; *W. Lewis of Whayne; David Owen Tudor; *Th. Glynn; *Rich. White; Owen ap Robert Owen; Owen ap Hugh; Piers Lloyd; Hugh Wood; W. Griffith of Trefarthen; Rich. Hampton; *Rich. Meyrick; Hugh Lewis of Bodewryd; H. Lloyd of Bodwyn: C.66/1523/m.30d. Commission renewed to *add* H. Lloyd of Bodwyn: Index 4208/f.97. (29)

1600: 10 December
Commission renewed to *add* Owen Wynn: Index 4208/f.99v.

1601: 27 April
As on 23 October 1600, except: *Th. Holland; Owen Wynn, *added*. E. of Pembroke; B. of St. Asaph, *omitted*: C.66/1549/m.32d. & B.M., Harleian Ms. 1974/f.23. Commission renewed to *add* Th. Holland: Index 4208/f.109. (29)

1602: 7 July
Commission renewed to *add* Rich. Barker, Justice of Great Sessions: Index 4208/f.139v.

1602: 25 July
General renewal of Welsh commissions to *add* Ed., Lord Zouch, President of Council in the Marches of Wales: Index 4208/f.141.

1602: 1 October
As on 27 April 1601, except: *Ed., Lord Zouch; *Rich. Barker; Piers Lloyd junior, *added*. Rich. Broughton; Owen ap Hugh, *omitted*: C.66/1594/m.35d. Commission renewed to *add* Piers Lloyd junior: Index 4208/f.142v. (30)

1603: (Acting)
*Egerton; *Buckhurst; *Ed., Lord Zouch, President of the Council in the Marches of Wales; *B. of Bangor; *Rich. Lewkenor, kt., Justice of Chester; *W. Leighton & *Rich. Barker, Justices of Great Sessions; *p Rich Bulkeley, kt.; *Th. Mostyn, kt.; *H. Townshend; *W. Lewis; *Hugh Hughes, attorney; *J. Griffith of Trefarthen; *Rich. Bulkeley; *Hugh Owen; *W. Lewis of Whayne; David Owen Tudor; *Th. Glynn; *Rich. White; *Th. Holland; Owen ap Robert Owen; Piers Lloyd; Hugh Wood; Owen Wynn; W. Griffith of Trefarthen; Piers Lloyd junior; Rich. Hampton; *Rich. Meyrick; Hugh Lewis of Bodewryd; Hugh Lloyd of Bodwyn: C.66/1620/m.12d. (30)

1604: (Acting)
As in 1603, except: *Owen Wood, Dean of Armagh; *J. Lewis; Jasper Price; Roland Griffith, *added*. W. Lewis (Sheriff, 1603–4), *omitted*: C.66/1662/ m.20d. & B.M., Add. Ms. 38139/f.166. (33)

1605: (Acting)
As in 1604, except: Owen Hughes, *added*. Ed., Lord Zouch, *omitted*: C.66/ 1682/m.5d. (33)

1606: (Acting)
As in 1605: C.66/1698/m.27d. (33)

1607: post 12 September
*Th. Egerton, Lord Ellesmere, Chancellor; *Lord Buckhurst, E. of Dorset, Treasurer; *Ralph, Lord Eure, President of Council in the Marches of Wales (appointed on 12 September); *B. of Bangor; *Lewkenor, Justice of Chester; *Ed. Herne, kt. & *Rich. Barker, Justices of Great Sessions; *p Rich. Bulkeley; *Th. Mostyn, *H. Townshend, *Hugh Owen, *W. Glynn, kts.; *Owen Wood, Dean of Armagh; *Hugh Hughes, attorney; *J. Lewis; *Rich. Bulkeley; *Hugh Wood; *Owen Wynn; *W. Lewis of Whayne; David Owen Tudor; *Th. Holland; Owen ap Robert Owen; Piers Lloyd; W. Griffith of Trefarthen; Jasper Price; Piers Lloyd junior; Rich. Hampton; *Rich. Meyrick; Owen Hughes; H. Lloyd of Bodwyn; Roland Griffith: C.66/1748/m.28d. (31)

1608–9: (Acting)
As in 1607, except: *E. of Salisbury, Treasurer; *E. of Northampton, Keeper of Privy Seal; Sackville Trevor, kt.; Roland White; Owen Wood, Esq.; Hugh Lewis, *added*. E. of Dorset *omitted*: C.66/1786/m.28d. (36)

1610: (Acting)
As in 1608–9, except: *Lewis Prowde, Justice of Great Sessions; W. Owen, *added*. Ed. Herne; Owen Wood, Dean of Armagh; Hugh Hughes; Owen Wynn; Owen ap Robert Owen; Piers Lloyd senior, *omitted*: C.66/1822/m.24d. (32)

1610–11: (Acting)
As in 1610: C.66/1897/m.17d. (32)

1611–12: (Acting)
As in 1610–11: C.66/1898/m.25d. (32)
(The commission may not in fact have been as unaltered between 1610 and 1612 as appears here.)

1614: post 11 July
As in 1611–12, except: *E. of Suffolk, Treasurer (appointed on 11 July); J. Bodvel, *added*. E. of Salisbury; E. of Northampton, *omitted* (both dead): C.66/1988/m.25d. (32)

1614–15: (Acting)
As in 1614: C.66/2047/m.19d. (32)

1615: 8 July
Commission renewed to *add* Th. Chamberlain, Justice of Great Sessions;
Rich. Williams: Index 4211/f.7.

1616: 19 February
*Lord Ellesmere, Chancellor; *E. of Suffolk, Treasurer; *E. of Worcester,
Keeper of Privy Seal; *Ralph, Lord Eure, President of the Council in the
Marches of Wales; *B. of Bangor; *Rich. Lewkenor, kt., Justice of Chester;
*Th. Chamberlain, serjeant at law & *Lewis Prowde, Justices of Great
Sessions; *p Rich. Bulkeley, *Th. Mostyn, H. Townshend, Sackville
Trevor, *W. Glynn, kts.; *J. Lewis; J. Bodvel; W. Owen; *Rich. Bulkeley;
*W. Griffith of Trefarthen; *W. Lewis of Whayne; Roland White; Owen
Wood; *Th. Holland; Jasper Price; Piers Lloyd; *Rich. Meyrick; *Hugh
Lewis; H. Lloyd of Bodwyn; Rich. Williams; Roland Griffith; W. Jones;
Rich. Prydderch: C.66/2076/m.22d. Commission renewed to *add* W. Jones;
Rich. Prydderch: Index 4211/f.16. (31)

1616: 26 July
Commission renewed to *add* Francis Eure, Justice of Great Sessions:
Index 4211/f.24v.

1617: 30 January
Commission renewed to *add* Lewis, B. of Bangor: Index 4211/f.32d.

1617: 19 March
Commission renewed to *add* Francis Bacon, kt., Keeper of Great Seal; Th.,
Lord Gerard, President of Council in the Marches of Wales; Index 4211/f.38.

1617: 6 June
Commission renewed to *add* Rob. White, clerk: Index 4211/f.43.

1617: post 24 November
*Francis Bacon, kt., Keeper of Great Seal; *Suffolk; *Worcester; *D. of
Lennox, Steward; *W., Lord Compton, President of Council in the Marches
of Wales (appointed on 24 November); *B. of Bangor; *Th. Chamberlain,
kt., Justice of Chester; *Francis Eure, kt. & *J. Jeffreys, Justices of Great
Sessions; *p Rich. Bulkeley, *Th. Mostyn, *H. Townshend, Sackville
Trevor, *W. Glynn, *W. Jones, serjeant at law, kts.; *J. Lewis; *J. Bodvel;
W. Owen; *Rich. Bulkeley; *W. Griffith of Trefarthen; *W. Lewis of
Whayne; *Roland White; Owen Wood; *Th. Holland; Rich. Prydderch;
Jasper Price; *Rob. White, clerk; Piers Lloyd; *Rich. Meyrick; *Hugh
Lewis; H. Lloyd of Bodwyn; Rich. Williams; Roland Griffith: C.66/2147/
m.21d. (33)

1618: 1 April
Commission renewed to *omit* Th. Holland: Index 4211/f.61d.

1618: 20 June
Commission renewed to *restore* Th. Holland: Index 4211/f.65.

1618–19: (Acting)
As in 1617, except: E. of Suffolk, *omitted*: C.66/2174/m.17d.   (32)

1619: 29 May
Commission renewed to *add* Hugh Wynn: Index 4211/f.84v.

1619: 12 July
Commission renewed to *add* Griffith Hughes, D.D.: Index 4211/f.90v.

1619: 14 November
Commission renewed to *restore* Jasper Price: Index 4211/f.93.

1620: 4 November
General renewal of Welsh commissions to *add* Jas. Whitlock, kt., Justice of Chester: Index 4211/f.114.

1620: 2 December
Commission renewed to *add* W. Thomas: Index 4211/f.115.

1621: 26 February
*Francis Bacon, kt., Viscount St. Alban, Chancellor; *H., Viscount Mandeville, Treasurer; *Worcester; *Lennox; *E. of Northampton, President of the Council in the Marches of Wales; *B. of Bangor; *Jas. Whitlock, kt., serjeant at law, Justice of Chester; *Eure & *Jeffreys, Justices of Great Sessions; *p Rich. Bulkeley, *H. Townshend, *Sackville Trevor, *W. Glynn, *W. Jones, *J. Bodvel, kts.; *Rob. White, D.D.; *Griffith Hughes, Chancellor of Bangor; *J. Lewis; *W. Owen; *Rich. Bulkeley; *W. Griffith of Trefarthen; *W. Lewis of Whayne; *Roland White; *Owen Wood; *Th. Holland; Rich. Prydderch; Jasper Price; Piers Lloyd; Rich. Meyrick; H. Lloyd of Bodwyn; *Rich. Williams; Hugh Wynn; Roland Griffith; W. Thomas: B.M., Harleian Ms. 1974/f.22. General renewal of Welsh commissions to *add* Viscount Mandeville: Index 4211/f.120. (This commission is also entered upon the patent roll (C.66/2234/m.41d.) but there omits the name of Francis Eure and must therefore have been enrolled after his death on 1 May 1621).   (34)

1621: 29 June
Commission renewed to *add* Ed. Littleton, Justice of Great Sessions: Index 4211/f.126.

1621: 3 July
Commission renewed to appoint Roland White as *custos rotulorum*: Index 4211/f.126v.

1622: 28 February
As on 26 February 1621, except: *J., B. of Lincoln, Keeper of Great Seal; *Lionel Cranfield, Treasurer; *Ed. Littleton, Justice of Great Sessions,

added. Viscount St. Alban; B. of Bangor; Francis Eure; Rich. Bulkeley, kt.; H. Townshend, kt.; W. Glynn, kt., *omitted*: C.66/2259/m.24d. Commission renewed to *restore* Hugh Wynn, late Sheriff: Index 4211/f.136.   (31)

1622: 24 October
Commission renewed to *add* W. Owen of Brondegie: Index 4211/f.145.

1622: 25 November
As on 28 February 1622, except: *B. of Bangor; *Peter Mutton, Justice of Great Sessions; W. Owen, *added.* J. Jeffreys, *omitted*: C.66/2285/m.31. Commission renewed to *add* Peter Mutton: Index 4211/f.146.   (33)

1624: 25 June
Commission renewed to *add* Owen Wood; Rich. Owen Tudor; J. Lloyd, clerk: Index 4211/f.168v.

1625: 1 April
*B. of Lincoln, Keeper of Great Seal; *Jas., Lord Ley, Treasurer; *Viscount Mandeville; *E. of Worcester, Keeper of Privy Seal; *E. of Northampton, President of Council in the Marches of Wales; *B. of Bangor; *W. Jones, kt., Justice *ad placita*; *Th. Chamberlain, kt., Justice of Chester; *Peter Mutton, kt. & *Ed. Littleton, Justices of Great Sessions; Sackville Trevor, *J. Bodvel, *Th. Holland, kts.; *Rob. White, D.D.; *Griffith Hughes, Chancellor of Bangor; *Sampson Eure; *Rob. Brooke; *W. Owen of Bodeon; *Rich. Bulkeley of Porthaml; *W. Griffith of Trefarthen; *p Roland White; *Owen Wood; *W. Lewis of Whayne; Rich. Prydderch; Piers Lloyd; *Rich. Owen Tudor; Rich. Meyrick; Jasper Price; *Rich. Williams; *Hugh Wynn of Mossoglen; Roland Griffith; W. Thomas; W. Owen of Brondegie; J. Lloyd, clerk: C.66/2367/m.26d. General renewal of all Welsh commissions: Index 4211/f.180v.   (34)

1625: 22 December
As on 1 April 1625, except: *Th. Coventry, kt., Keeper of Great Seal, *added.* Th. Chamberlain, *omitted*: B.M., Harleian Ms. 1622/f.87. General renewal of Welsh commissions to *add* Th. Coventry: Index 4211/f.194v. (34)

1626: 20 March
As on 22 December 1625, except: J. Bridgeman, kt., Justice of Chester; Rich. Williams, kt.; Rich. Bulkeley, *added.* Griffith Hughes; W. Lewis of Whayne; Piers Lloyd; Jasper Price; Hugh Wynn; Roland Griffith; J. Lloyd, *omitted*: E.163/18/12/f.89 & C.193/12/2/f.65. Commission renewed to *add* J. Bridgeman; Rich. Bulkeley: Index 4211/f.199.   (30)

1627: 20 February
As on 20 March 1626, except: *Timothy Turneur; *Hugh Wynn of Mossoglen, *added.* E. of Worcester; Rich. Williams, kt.; Rob. Brooke, *omitted*: C.66/2449/m.33d. Commission renewed to *restore* Hugh Wynn: Index 4211/f.218v.   (29)

1628: post 14 December

As on 20 February 1627, except: *Rich., Lord Weston, Treasurer; *Ed. Viscount Conway, President of Council (appointed on 14 December); *E. of Pembroke, *added*. Jas., Lord Ley; W. Owen of Bodeon; Rich. Williams, Esq., *omitted*: C.66/2495/m.25d. (29)

1629–30: (Acting)

As in 1628: C.66/2527/m.27d. (29)

1631: 26 January

*Th., Lord Coventry, Keeper of Great Seal; *Rich., Lord Weston, Treasurer; *H., (Viscount Mandeville) E. of Manchester, Keeper of Privy Seal; Bishops of *Lincoln, *Bangor; *W. Jones, kt., Justice *ad placita*; *J. Bridgeman, kt., Justice of Chester; *Mutton & *Littleton, Justices of Great Sessions; Sackville Trevor, *J. Bodvel, *Th. Holland, kts.; *Rob. White, D.D.; *Rich. Bulkeley; *Sampson Eure; *Timothy Turneur; *Rich. Bulkeley; *W. Griffith of Trefarthen; *Roland White; *Owen Wood; Rich. Prydderch; W. Owen; *Rich. Owen Tudor; *Rich. Meyrick; *Hugh Wynn; W. Thomas; *Hugh ap William Pritchard: C.66/2536/m.19d. Commission renewed to *add* Hugh ap William Pritchard: Index 4212/p.47. (27)

1631: 20 July

As on 26 January 1631, except: *Marmaduke Lloyd, kt.; *W. Griffith, Ll.D., Chancellor of Bangor; *J. Bodychen, *added:* C.66/2577/m.12d & S.P.16/212/f.68v. Commission renewed to *add* W. Griffith, Chancellor of Bangor: Index 4212/p.64. (30)

1632: 3 May

Commission renewed to *add* David, B. of Bangor: Index 4212/p.80.

1632: 20 June

Commission renewed to *add* Rich. Weston, Justice of Great Sessions: Index 4212/p.83.

1632: 30 June

As on 20 July 1631, except: *E. of Bridgwater, President of Council in the Marches of Wales; *David, B. of Bangor; *Rich. Weston, Justice of Great Sessions, *added*. Lewis, B. of Bangor; Ed. Littleton; J. Bodvel; W. Owen, *omitted*: C.66/2598/m.19d. Commission renewed to record appointment of W. Griffith, Chancellor of Bangor, as a Master in Chancery: Index 4212/p.84. (29)

1633–4: (Acting)

As on 30 June 1632: C.66/2623/m.22d. (29)

1634: 6 June

Commission renewed to *add* W. Robinson: Index 4212/p.137.

1634: 2 July
Commission renewed to *add* Timothy Turneur, Justice of Great Sessions:
Index 4212/p.141.

1634: 8 July
As in 1633-4, except: *Edm., B. of Bangor; *W. Robinson, *added*. David, B.
of Bangor; Rich. Weston, *omitted*: C.193/13/2/f.74v. (Timothy Turneur,
Justice of Great Sessions, was already in commission before his promotion).
Commission renewed to *add* Edm., B. of Bangor: Index 4212/p.143.   (29)

1636: post 6 March
As on 8 July 1634, except: *W., B. of London, Treasurer (appointed on
6 March); W. Owen, *added*. Rich., Lord Weston, E. of Portland, *omitted*:
S.P.16/405/f.72v.   (30)

1637: 31 July
Commission renewed to *omit* Timothy Turneur, Justice of Great Sessions:
Index 4212/p.258.

1637: 1 December
Commission renewed to *add* Hugh Owen: Index 4212/p.270.

1638: 21 April
Commission renewed to *add* W., B. of Bangor: Index 4212/p.289.

1638: 26 May
*Coventry, Keeper of Great Seal; *London, Treasurer; *Manchester,
Keeper of Privy Seal; *Bridgewater, President of the Council in the Marches
of Wales; *B. of Bangor; *W. Jones, kt., Justice *ad placita*; *Th. Milward,
kt., Justice of Chester; *Adam Littleton & *Rob. Brerewood, Justices of
Great Sessions; *Marmaduke Lloyd, kt.; *Rich. Prydderch, second Justice
of Chester; *Th. Holland, kt.; *W. Griffith, Ll.D., Master in Chancery;
*Rob. White, D.D.; *Rich. Bulkeley; Th. Glynn; *Sampson Eure; Hugh
Owen; *W. Griffith of Trefarthen; *p Roland White; *W. Robinson;
*Owen Wood; W. Owen; *J. Bodychen; *Rich. Owen Tudor; Rich.
Meyrick; W. Thomas; *Hugh ap William Pritchard: C.66/2761/m.18d.
Commission renewed to *add* Th. Glynn: Index 4212/p.293.   (28)

1639: 4 February
Commission renewed to *add* Griffith Williams, D.D., Dean of Bangor:
Index 4212/p.322.

1639: 12 August (Acting)
As on 26 May 1638, except: Griffith Williams, D.D., *added*. Rich. Bulkeley
(Sheriff, 1638-9); W. Thomas, *omitted*: Wales 4/262/1.   (27)

1640: 15 February
*J. Finch, kt., Keeper of Great Seal; *London; *Manchester; *Bridgewater,
President of the Council in the Marches of Wales; *B. of Bangor; *W. Jones,

kt., Justice *ad placita*; *Milward, Justice of Chester; *Littleton & *Brere-wood, Justices of Great Sessions; *Marmaduke Lloyd, kt.; *p Arthur Tirringham, kt.; *Rich. Prydderch, second Justice of Chester; *Th. Holland, kt.; *Griffith Williams, Dean of Bangor; *W. Griffith, Ll.D., Master in Chancery; *Rob. White, D.D.; *Rich, Bulkeley; Th. Glynn; *Sampson Eure; *W. Morgan; Hugh Owen; *W. Griffith of Trefarthen; *W. Robinson; *Owen Wood; W. Owen; *J. Bodychen; *Rich. Owen Tudor; Rich. Meyrick; W. Thomas; Hugh ap William Pritchard: C.66/2858/m.22d Commission renewed to *add* Arthur Tirringham as *custos rotulorum*: Index 4212/p.367. (30)

1640: 25 July
Commission renewed to *add* Owen Griffith; Th. Bulkeley; H. White; W. Bould: Index 4212/p.399.

1641: 10 April
Commission renewed to *add* W. Williams, Bt.: Index 4212/p.441.

1642: 19 March
Commission renewed to *add* Hugh Owen, kt. & Bt., *custos rotulorum*: Index 4212/p.514.

1643: 30 May
Commission renewed to *restore* Hugh Owen, omitted by mistake: Index 4210/p.20.

1643: 26 August
Commission renewed to *add* J. Bodvel, *custos rotulorum*; Owen Holland; Roland Bulkeley, and to *omit* Hugh Owen, Bt.: Index 4210/p.32.

1644: 29 April
Commission renewed to *add* Timothy Littleton, serjeant at law, Justice of Great Sessions: Index 4210/p.107.

1646: 11 August
Commission renewed (no details): Index 4213/p.54.

1647: 22 March
Commission renewed to *add* Rich. Keble & W. Littleton, Justices of Great Sessions: Index 4213/p.85.

1649: 6 July
Commission renewed to *add* W. Bould; Th. Madryn; Owen Bromley; Th. Williams; Rich. Dryhurst: Index 4213/p.157.

1649: 18 July
*W. Lenthall, Speaker of House of Commons; *Th., Lord Fairfax; *J. Bradshaw, President of Council; *Bulstrode Whitelock, *Rich. Keble, *J. Lisle, Commissioners of Great Seal; Earls of *Kent, *Manchester; *H. Rolle, Chief Justice of Upper Bench; *W. Littleton & *Ed. Bulstrode,

Justices of Great Sessions; *Edm. Prideaux, Attorney-General; *W. Williams, Bt.; *Hugh Owen, kt. & Bt.; *Th. Cheadle, kt.; *J. Glynn, serjeant at law; *Th. Mytton; *W. Bould; *Th. Madryn; *W. Williams; Rich. Cheadle; Owen Bromley; Th. Williams; Rich. Dryhurst: C.193/13/3/ f.7ov. Commission renewed to add Th. Cheadle, kt.; W. Williams; Rich. Cheadle, and to omit Th., Viscount Bulkeley: Index 4213/p.162.   (24)

1650: 25 July
*Lenthall; *Oliver Cromwell, Lord General; *Bradshaw; *Whitelock, *Keble & *Lisle; *E. of Denbigh; *Rolle; *Oliver St. John, Chief Justice of Court of Common Pleas; *J. Wilde, Chief Baron of Exchequer; *Littleton & *Bulstrode, Justices of Great Sessions; *Prideaux; *p Hugh Owen, Bt.; *J. Jones; *Nich. Bagnall; *Th. Mytton; *Owen Wood; *Th. Madryn; *Rich. Meyrick; *W. Bould; *Rich. Owen; *Owen Holland; J. Wood; Rich. Dryhurst; Rob. Lewis; W. Lewis; W. Williams; Rich. Bolton senior: Lists published by Th. Walkley (1650), p.62. Commission renewed to add J. Jones; Nich. Bagnall; Owen Wood; Rich. Meyrick; Rich. Owen; Owen Holland; J. Wood; Rob. Lewis; Rich. Bolton, and omit W. Williams, Bt.; Th. Cheadle, kt.; and others (un-named): Index 4213/p.197.   (29)

1651: 3 July
Commission renewed to add Hugh Courtney, omit Owen Holland; Rob. Lewis; Rich. Dryhurst, and place Rich. Bolton on quorum: Index 4213/p.219.

1652: 12 February
*Lenthall; *Cromwell; *Whitelock, *Keble & *Lisle; *Denbigh; *Bradshaw; *Rolle, *St. John; *Wilde; *Littleton & *Bulstrode, Justices of Great Sessions; *Prideaux; *p Hugh Owen, Bt.; *J. Jones; Nich. Bagnall; *Th. Mytton; *Owen Wood; *Hugh Courtney; *Geo. Twistleton; *Piers Lloyd; *Owen Holland; *Edm. Glynn; Th. Madryn; Rich. Meyrick; *W. Bould; *Rich. Owen Tudor; *Rich. Bolton; *J. Wood; W. Williams; Rob. Lewis; Rich. Dryhurst; Owen Bromley: Cambridge Univ. Ms. Dd. VIII.1/f.117. Commission renewed to add Geo. Twistleton; Piers Lloyd; Rich. Owen Tudor; Owen Holland; Edm. Glynn; Rob. Lewis: Index 4213/p.231.   (33)

1653: 27 July
Commission renewed to add Th. Swift; J. Sydenham, to appoint Th. Madryn as custos rotulorum, and omit Hugh Owen and others (no details): Index 4213/p.264.

1654: 7 July
Commission renewed according to a general list: Index 4213/p.293.

1655: 12 December
Commission renewed to add Colonel James Berry: Index 4213/p.321.

1656: post 26 March
*Nathaniel Fiennes & *J. Lisle, Commissioners of Great Seal; *Bulstrode Whitelock, kt., *Th. Widdrington, kt., *Ed. Montagu & *W. Sydenham, Commissioners of Treasury; *J. Glynn, Chief Justice of Upper Bench;

*W. Lenthall, Master of Rolls; *Oliver St. John, Chief Justice of Common Bench; *Edm. Prideaux, Attorney-General; *Ed. Bulstrode & *Evan Seys, serjeant at law, Justices of Great Sessions (Seys was appointed on 26 March); *Hugh Owen, Bt.; *Colonel Jas. Berry; *J. Jones; *Th. Mytton; *Owen Wood; *J. Carter; *Hugh Courtney; *p Th. Madryn; *Geo. Twistleton; *Owen Holland; *Edm. Glynn; *Rich. Owen Tudor; *Rich. Bolton; *J. Wood; Th. Swift; J. Sydenham: C.193/13/6/f.98.   (28)

1658: 24 September
General renewal of Welsh commissions to *add* Richard Cromwell, Lord Protector: Index 4213/p.405.

1659: 8 July
Commission renewed according to a general list: Index 4213/p.438.

1659: 5 October
Commission renewed to *add* W. Shepherd & Rich. Vaughan, Justices of Great Sessions: Index 4213/p.443.

1659: (Acting)
J. Jones; p Th. Madryn; Rich. Owen Tudor; Th. Swift; J. Sydenham; Owen Hughes; Rich. Bolton; Rich. Jones of Beaumaris; J. Lloyd of Llanddona; Th. Williams of Bodley: N.L.W., Wynn Papers no. 2209. (This list of the justices in 1659 probably represents the commission of 8 July or of 5 October, with the omission of all the *ex officio* members). (10)

1660: 3 March
Commission renewed according to a general list: Index 4213/p.452.

1660: 10 March
Commission renewed to *add* W. Williams: Index 4213/p.453.

1660: 6 September
Commission renewed to *add* Robert, Viscount Bulkeley, as *custos rotulorum*; Timothy Littleton, serjeant at law, & J. Griffith, Justices of Great Sessions: Index 4214/p.36.

1660: post 8 September
*Ed Hyde, kt., Chancellor; *E. of Southampton, Treasurer (appointed on 8 September); *D. of Albemarle; *Marquess of Ormond, Steward; *E. of Lindsey, Great Chamberlain; *E. of Manchester, Household Chamberlain; *p Rob., Viscount Bulkeley; *Timothy Littleton & *J. Griffith, Justices of Great Sessions; *Th. Bulkeley; *Hugh Owen, Bt.; *J. Carter, kt.; J. Bodvel; *Nich. Bagnall; *Piers Lloyd senior; Th. Wood; *Piers Lloyd junior; *W. Bould; *Rich. Owen Tudor; *J. Robinson; Roland Bulkeley; Rich. Meyrick; *J. Griffith of Carreglwyd; J. Wynn of Bodewryd; *Roland White; H. Jones; W. Williams of Nantanog; J. Owen of Maethley; J. Owen of Penrhos; *Th. Williams of Glan-y-gor; Rich. Bolton: C.220/9/4/f.98 & B.M., Egerton Ms. 2557/f.97.   (31).

1661: 8 November
As in 1660, except *J., Lord Robartes, Keeper of Privy Seal; *E. of Carbery, President of Council in the Marches of Wales, *added*: C.193/12/3/f.112v. General renewal of Welsh commissions to *add* E. of Carbery, President of Council in the Marches of Wales: Index 4214/p.144.   (33)

1663: 27 July
As on 8 November 1661, except: *Job Charlton, kt., serjeant at law, Justice of Chester; *Th. Jones, Justice of Great Sessions; *Owen Griffith, King's attorney, *added*. J. Griffith; J. Bodvel, *omitted*: C.66/3022/m.32d. Commission renewed to *add* Th. Jones, Justice of Great Sessions: Index 4214/p.211.   (34)

1665–66: (Acting)
As on 27 July 1663: C.66/3074/m.33d.   (34)

1670: 1 July
Commission renewed to *add* Kenrick Eyton, Justice of Great Sessions; Hugh Owen; Rich. Meyrick; Th. Holland; Roland White; Coningsby Williams; J. Wynn; Ed. Price; J. Owen; Rich. Wynn; Owen Hughes: Index 4214/p.371.

1680: 1 April
*Prince Rupert; *Archbishop of Canterbury; *Lord Finch, Chancellor; *E. of Radnor, President of Privy Council; *E. of Anglesey, Keeper of Privy Seal; Dukes of *Monmouth, *Albemarle, *Newcastle, *Lauderdale, *Ormond; *Marquess of Winchester; *Marquess of Worcester, President of the Council in the Marches of Wales; Earls of *Lindsey, *Arlington, *Salisbury, *Bridgewater, *Sunderland, *Essex, *Bath, *Halifax, *Carbery; *Viscount Fauconberg; *p Rob., Viscount Bulkeley; *B. of London; *Laurence Hyde; *H. Coventry; *Francis North, kt., Chief Justice of Bench; *J. Ernley, kt., Chancellor of Exchequer; *Th. Chichley, kt., Chancellor of Duchy of Lancaster; *W. Temple, Bt.; *Ed. Seymour; *Daniel Finch; *Leoline Jenkins; *Sidney Godolphin; *Th. Bulkeley; *Kenrick Eyton & *Thomas Walcott, Justices of Great Sessions; *Ed. Jennings, King's attorney; *Lewis Meyrick, King's attorney in Wales; *Francis Manley; *Nich. Bagnall; *J. Robinson; *Th. Holland; *Coningsby Williams; *W. Williams of Nantanog; *J. Griffith of Carreglwyd; *Roland White of Friars; *Owen Hughes; H. Jones; J. Owen of Penrhos: C.193/12/4/f.134. Commission renewed to *remove* recusants and to *add* others: Index 4215/p.26. (The only recorded change in the Anglesey commission is the removal of the Duke of Buckingham by a warrant of 5 February: *H.M.C., Eleventh Report, Appendix*, Part 2, p. 172).   (50)

1682: 28 March
Commission renewed to *add* Rich. Hopton, Justice of Great Sessions: Index 4215/p.64.

1683: 8 March
Commission renewed to *add* J. Grosvenor: Index 4215/p.80.

1684: 27 March
Commission renewed to *add* H. Sparrow: Index 4215/p.100.

1685: 7 March
Commission renewed to *add* Rob., Viscount Bulkeley, as *custos rotulorum*: Index 4215/p.122.

1685: post 28 September
*Archbishop of Canterbury; *Geo., Lord Jeffreys, Chancellor (appointed on 28 September); *E. of Rochester, Treasurer; *Marquess of Halifax, President of Privy Council; *E. of Clarendon, Keeper of Privy Seal; Dukes of *Albemarle, *Newcastle, *Ormond; *Duke of Beaufort, President of Council in the Marches of Wales; Marquesses of *Winchester, *Worcester; Earls of *Lindsey, *Ailesbury, *Bridgewater, *Sunderland, *Bath, *Nottingham, *Carbery; *Viscount Fauconberg; *p Rob., Viscount Bulkeley; *B. of London; *Sidney, Lord Godolphin; *H. Coventry; *J. Ernley, kt., Chancellor of Exchequer; *Th. Chichley, Chancellor of Duchy of Lancaster; *Ed. Seymour; *Th. Bulkeley; *Rich. Hopton & *Th. Powell, Justices of Great Sessions; *J. Grosvenor; *Francis Manley; *Ed. Jennings, King's attorney; *J. Ellis, Professor of Theology; *Nich. Bagnall; *Th. Holland; *Coningsby Williams; *W. Williams of Nantanog; *J. Griffith of Carreglwyd; *Owen Hughes; *H. Sparrow; H. Jones; J. Owen of Penrhos: C.193/12/5/f.158.   (42)

1686: 17 December
Order by the Privy Council for the *removal* from the Anglesey commission of Th. Bulkeley; W. Williams; J. Owen, and the *addition* of Lord Dungannon; Th. Price: P.C.2/71/p.376.

1687: 26 June
D. of Beaufort recommends appointment of Robert Parry of Amlwch as a J.P.: N.L.W. Ms. 11020E.

1687: 29 August
General renewal of Welsh commissions to add the clause of dispensation: Index 4215/p.179.

1688: 14 April
Commission renewed (no details): Index 4215/p.191.

1688: 6 October
General renewal of Welsh commissions: Index 4215/p.200.

1688: 27 November
Commission renewed to *add* J. Griffith and others (no details): Index 4215/p.204.

Caernarvon

1541: 6 October (Acting)
Rich. Bulkeley, kt., & others not named: *Calendar of the Caernarvonshire Quarter Sessions Records,* vol. 1, *1541–1558,* ed. W. O. Williams (Caernarvon, 1956), p.251. (These details are taken from the table showing the attendance of justices of the peace at some meetings of the Quarter Sessions between 1541 and 1558. The entry above is the first date at which a justice of the peace is named for the county of Caernarvon and is antedated only by a reference to a justice of the peace acting in Glamorgan on 2 October 1541).

1542: 12 January (Acting)
Hugh Peick; Rhys Gruffydd; Gruffydd Davies: ibid.

1543: 12 March
*Th. Audley, kt., Chancellor; *D. of Norfolk, Treasurer; *D. of Suffolk, President of Council; *J. Russell, kt., Keeper of Privy Seal; *B. of Coventry & Lichfield, President of Council in the Marches of Wales; Bishops of *St. Asaph, *Bangor; Walter, Lord Ferrers; *Nich. Hare, Ed. Croft, Rice Mansel, *J. Vernon, kts.; *p Rich. Bulkeley, kt.; *J. Pakington; *Th. Holte; *David Brooke; *J. ap Rice; *Rich. Hassall; *Rob. Evans, clerk; Rees Griffith; *J. Arnold; J. Puleston; *J. Wynn ap Meredith; W. Glynn of Caernarvon, alias ap Robert; *Hugh Peke; *Th. ap William ap Robert; Griffith Davy. *Later additions to list*: *Th. Bromley, serjeant at law; *Adam Mytton; Ellis ap Maurice; Griffith Vaughan: C.193/12/1/f.46v. (Note that in reproducing this and later commissions the spelling of names has been standardised on the basis of the most commonly accepted form in each case. Entries from the *Calendar of Quarter Sessions Records* however follow the spellings found in the sources). (27 names plus 4 corrections).

1543: 15 October (Acting)
B. of Bangor and others not named: W. O. Williams, op. cit., p.251.

1544: 10 January (Acting)
Hugh Peick; Gruffydd Davies: ibid.

1544: 9 July (Acting)
Hugh Peick; Gruffydd Davies: ibid.

1544: 1 October (Acting)
B. of Bangor; Gruffydd Davies: op. cit., p.252.

1550: 16 April (Acting)
J. Puleston, kt.; J. Wyn ap Meredydd; Eliza ap Moris; Gruffydd ap Robert Fychan; Gruffydd Davies: ibid.

1551: 15 April (Acting)
J. Wyn ap Meredydd; Eliza ap Moris; Gruffydd ap Robert Fychan; W. Roberts, clerk; W. Glyn: ibid.

1552: 9 February (Acting)
W. Glyn; Eliza ap Moris; Gruffydd ap Robert Fychan; W. Glyn of Glynllifon; Gruffydd Davies; Robert Evans, clerk: ibid.

1552: 26 April (Acting)
(Rhys) Gruffydd, kt.; J. Wyn ap Meredydd; Rice Thomas; Gruffydd ap Robert Fychan: ibid.

1552: 18 July (Acting)
J. Wyn ap Meredydd; Rice Thomas; J. Wynn ap Hugh; Eliza Moris; Gruffydd ap Robert Fychan: ibid.

1552: 17 October (Acting)
J. Wyn ap Meredydd; Rice Thomas; J. Wyn ap Hugh: ibid.

1553: 24 January (Acting)
Rhys Gruffydd, kt.; J. Wyn ap Meredydd; Rice Thomas; Eliza ap Moris; Gruffydd ap Robert Fychan: ibid.

1555: 5 November (Acting)
J. Wyn ap Hugh; Eliza ap Moris; Gruffydd Davies; ibid.

1555: (Acting)
Rich. Bulkeley, kt.; Rees Griffith, kt.; J. Wynn ap Meredith; Maurice Wynn; J. Wynn ap Hugh; W. ap William; Ellis Morris; Griffith ap Robert Vaughan; Griffith Davies; Lewis Owen: S.P.11/5/f.59v.   (10)

1558: 24 October (Acting)
Eliza Moris; Maurice Wyn; J. Wynn ap Hugh; David Lloyd ap Thomas; Gruffydd Madryn; Robert Gruffydd: W. O. Williams, op. cit., p.252.

1558–59: (Acting)
*Nich. Bacon, kt., Keeper of Great Seal; *Marquess of Winchester, Treasurer; *E. of Arundel, Steward; Bishops of *Bath & Wells, *Chester, *St. Asaph; *J. Throckmorton, Justice of Chester; *J. Vaughan, kt.; *J. Scudamore of Holm; *Chas. Fox; *J. Welsh; *Reg. Corbet; *W. Symonds; *W. Gerard; *Rich. Seaborne; *p J. Wynn ap Meredith; *Ellis ap Maurice; J. Wynn ap Hugh; *Griffith Davies; Maurice Wynn; David Lloyd ap Thomas; Griffith Madryn; Rob. ap Hugh; *Th. Powell; Rob. Griffith; W. Griffith of Caernarvon: B.M., Lansdowne Ms. 1218/f.40v. (Except for the omission of the *ex officio* members of the commission, the same list also appears in S.P.12/2/17/p.69).   (26)

1561: (Acting)
*Bacon; *Winchester; *Arundel; *H. Sidney, kt., President of Council in the Marches of Wales; Bishops of *Bangor, *St. Asaph; *Reg. Corbet, Justice of Great Sessions; *Nich. Bagnall, kt.; *Ellis Price, Ll.D.; *p Maurice Wynn; *Th. Powell; *Rees Thomas; *Griffith Davies; *David Lloyd ap Thomas; Griffith Madryn; Ellis ap Morris; W. Griffith of Caernarvon: B.M., Lansdowne Ms. 1218/f.88.   (17)

1562: 13 June
As in 1561: C.66/985/m.41d.   (17)

1564: (Acting)
*Bacon; *Winchester; *Arundel; *Sidney; Bishops of *Bangor, *St. Asaph;
*Corbet, Justice of Great Sessions; *J. Throckmorton, Justice of Chester;
*Rich. Griffith, *Nich. Bagnall, kts.; *W. Gerard; *Chas. Fox; *Rich. Wye;
*Ellis Price, Ll.D.; *Rich. Seaborne; *Rich. Pates; *J. Price; *Rich.
Smith; *p Maurice Wynn; *Th. Powell; *Rees Thomas; *Griffith Davies;
David Lloyd ap Thomas; *Griffith Madryn; W. Glynn; Ellis ap Morris;
Hugh Puleston: C.66/998/m.11d.   (27)

1573–4: (Acting)
*Bacon; *W., Lord Burghley, Treasurer; *E. of Leicester; *Sidney; *B. of
St. Asaph; *B. of Bangor; *Hugh Cholmondeley, kt.; *Throckmorton,
Justice of Chester; *Geo. Bromley, Justice of Great Sessions; *Rich.
Griffith, kt.; *W. Gerard; *Chas. Fox; *Ellis Price, Ll.D.; *J. Gwynn,
Ll.D.; *Jas. Ellis, Ll.D.; *Rich. Seaborne; *Rich. Pates; *p Maurice
Wynn; *J. Wynn ap Hugh; *Roland Thomas, D.C.L.; *Edm. Meyrick,
D.C.L.; *Rich, Vaughan; *Rob. Gwynn; *J. Griffith of Llyn; Ed. Williams;
*Th. Madryn; Rich. Mostyn; *W. Glynn; Ed. Conway; Roland Puleston;
Hugh Gwynn; Rob. Owen of Botysllyn: S.P.12/93/part 2/f.35v. & B.M.,
Egerton Ms. 2345/f.45v.   (32)

1575: (Acting)
As in 1573–4, except: *Rees Thomas; *Griffith Davies; *W. Williams;
Roland ap Robert; *W. Thomas; W. Morris; W. Griffith, *added*. Hugh
Cholmondeley; J. Gwynn, *omitted*: S.P.12/106/part 2/f.9v.   (37)

1577: (Acting)
*Bacon; *Burghley; *Leicester; *Sidney; Bishops of *St. Asaph, *Bangor;
*Throckmorton, Justice of Chester; *Bromley, Justice of Great Sessions;
*Rich. Griffith, kt.; *W. Gerard; *Chas. Fox; *Ellis Price, Ll.D.; *Rich.
Seaborne; *Rich. Pates; *p Maurice Wynn; *Roland Thomas, D.C.L.;
*Rees Thomas; Roland Puleston; *Griffith Davies; *Rich. Mostyn; *Th.
Madryn; Rob. Owen of Botysllyn; Rich. Griffiths; *W. Thomas; Hugh
Gwynn; Ed. Conway: S.P.12/121/f.40v.   (26)

1578–79: (Acting)
*Bacon; *Burghley; *Sidney; *B. of Worcester, Vice-president of Council
in the Marches of Wales; Earls of *Leicester, *Worcester, Pembroke;
Bishops of *Hereford, *Bangor, *St. Davids, *St. Asaph; *Croft, Household
Controller; *Throckmorton, Justice of Chester; *Andrew Corbet, *J.
Perrot, *Nich. Arnold, *Hugh Cholmondeley, *J. Littleton, *J. Huband,
*Rich. Griffith, kts.; *Bromley, Justice of Great Sessions & Attorney of
Duchy of Lancaster; *David Lewis, Ll.D.; *W. Gerard; *W. Aubrey;
*Chas. Fox; *W. Glaseor; *Ellis Price, Ll.D.; *Ed. Leighton; *Rich. Pates;
*Ralph Barton; *Jerome Corbet; *J. Puckering; *Fabian Phillips; *H.
Townshend; *W. Leighton; *p Maurice Wynn; *Roland Thomas, D.C.L.;
*Rees Thomas; Roland Puleston; *Griffith Davies; *Rich. Mostyn; Rob.

Owen of Botysllyn; W. Morris; *Rich. Griffiths; *W. Thomas; Ed. Conway: Hatfield House Ms. 223.7 & B.M., Royal Ms. 18.D.III/f.112.   (46)

1579: post 26 April
As in 1578–9, except: *Th. Bromley, kt., Chancellor (appointed on 26 April); *J. Price; *J. Nuttall; *W. Griffith; *W. Glynn of Glynllifon; *Rich. Vaughan; *J. ap Hugh ap Richard, *added*. Bacon; Rees Thomas; Roland Puleston; Rich. Griffiths, *omitted*: S.P.12/145/f.56v.   (49)

1581: 20 November (Acting)
B. of Bangor; Roland Thomas; J. Wynn; W. Thomas; W. Morris; Roland Puleston; W. Griffith; Rob. Wynn; Rich. Mostyn; W. Glynn; Th. Madryn; Rich. Vaughan; Owen Wynn; J. ap Hugh ap Richard; Rob. Owen; Ed. Conway; Th. Mostyn: Bodleian, Bodley Ms. 904/f.207.   (17)

1582: (Acting)
Rich. Griffith, kt.; J. Price; Edm. Meyrick, D.C.L.; W. Thomas; J. Wynn; Roland Thomas, D.C.L.; Rob. Wynn; Ed. Williams; Owen Wynn; J. Nuttall; Th. Mostyn; Roland Puleston; Th. Madryn; W. Griffith; W. Morris; Maurice Griffith; W. Glynn; Griffith Davies; Ed. Conway; Rich. Mostyn; J. ap Hugh ap Richard; Rob. Owen: B.M., Lansdowne Ms. 35/f.139v.   (22)

1584: (Acting)
*Bromley, Chancellor; *Burghley, Treasurer; *Sidney, President of Council in the Marches of Wales; Earls of *p Leicester, *Worcester, *Pembroke; Bishops of *Hereford, *Bangor, *St. Asaph; *Croft, Household Controller; *Geo. Bromley; *W. Leighton & *Fabian Phillips, Justices of Great Sessions; *J. Perrot, *Hugh Cholmondeley, *J. Littleton, *Rich, Bulkeley, kts.; *J. Puckering; *W. Aubrey; *Chas. Fox; *Ellis Price, Ll.D.; *Ed. Leighton; *H. Townshend; *Rich. Pates; *Ralph Barton; *Jerome Corbet; *W. Glaseor; *Th. Mostyn; *W. Thomas; *Hugh Gwynn; *W. Morris; *W. Griffith, Ll.D.; *Roland Thomas, D.C.L.; *Rob. Wynn; *Ed. Williams; Roland Puleston; *Th. Madryn; *W. Griffith; Maurice Griffith; W. Glynn; *Griffith ap John Griffith; *Rich. Mostyn; J. ap Hugh ap Richard; Maurice Kyffin. *Later additions to list*: *Christopher Hatton, Chancellor; *Hugh, B. of Bangor; *J. Wynn; J. Griffith; Griffith Vaughan; Roland ap Robert: E.163/14/8/f.54v.   (44 names plus 6 corrections).

1590–91: (Acting)
*Hatton, Chancellor; *Burghley, Treasurer; *E. of Pembroke, President of Council in the Marches of Wales; *B. of Bangor; *B. of St. Asaph; *J. Perrot, kt.; *Rich. Shuttleworth, kt., Justice of Chester; *Leighton & *Phillips, Justices of Great Sessions; *p W. Russell, kt.; *Hugh Cholmondeley, *Rich. Bulkeley, kts.; *J. Puckering; *W. Aubrey; *Ellis Price, Ll.D.; *Ed. Leighton; *H. Townshend; *Jerome Corbet; *Th. Mostyn; *W. Morris, deputy *custos rotulorum*; *W. Griffith, Ll.D.; W. Williams; *Hugh Gwynn; *J. Wynn; *Hugh Hughes, Queen's attorney; *Rob. Wynn;

*Ed. Williams; *Roland Puleston; *J. Griffith; *Th. Madryn; Rich. Gwynn;
W. Glynn; Maurice Griffith; *Hugh Hookes; Griffith Vaughan; Th.
Vaughan; *Rich. Mostyn; Maurice Kyffin; *Roland ap Robert; Evan ap
Hugh: Hatfield House Ms. 278/f.60v.   (40)

1592–3: (Acting)
As in 1590–1, except: *Griffith ap John Griffith; *Rob. Brinker; Ed.
Holland; Rob. ap Richard, added. Hatton; J. Perrot; W. Russell; W. Griffith;
Th. Madryn; Rich. Mostyn; Roland ap Robert, omitted: Kent Record Office
Ms. U.350.03.   (37)

1594: 15 July
*J. Puckering, kt., Keeper of Great Seal; *Burghley; *Pembroke, President
of Council in the Marches of Wales; Bishops of *Bangor, *St. Asaph;
*Shuttleworth, Justice of Chester; *W. Leighton & *Rich. Broughton,
Justices of Great Sessions; *Hugh Cholmondeley, *Rich. Bulkeley, kts.;
*W. Aubrey; *Ellis Price, Ll.D.; *H. Townshend; *Jerome Corbet;
*Fabian Phillips; *p W. Morris; *Th. Mostyn; *J. Wynn; *Hugh Gwynn;
*W. Williams; *Hugh Hughes; *H. Roland Vaughan; *J. Griffith; *Rob.
Wynn; *Ed. Williams; *Roland Puleston; *Griffith ap John Griffith; *Rob.
Brinker; *Rich. Gwynn; W. Glynn; Maurice Griffith; *Hugh Hookes;
Griffith Vaughan; Th. Vaughan; *Hugh Gwynn of P.; *Rob. Madryn;
Maurice Kyffin; Ed. Holland; Rob. ap Richard; Evan ap Hugh: C.66/1421/
m.16d.   (40)

1595: 15 August
*Puckering; *Burghley; *Pembroke; *B. of St. Asaph; *Shuttleworth,
Justice of Chester; *Leighton & *Broughton, Justices of Great Sessions;
*Hugh Cholmondeley, *Rich. Bulkeley, kts.; *H. Townshend; *Jerome
Corbet; *Fabian Phillips; *W. Fowler; *p W. Morris; *Th. Mostyn;
*J. Wynn; W. Williams; *Hugh Hughes; *H. Rowland, Dean of Bangor;
*J. Griffith; *Roland Puleston; *Griffith ap John Griffith; *Rob. Brinker;
Th. Glynn; Maurice Griffith; Th. Vaughan; *Hugh Gwynn of Pennarth;
*Rob. Madryn; Maurice Kyffin; Ed. Holland; Evan ap Hugh: C.66/1435/
m.20d. General renewal of Welsh commissions on 15 August: Index
4208/f.4v.   (31)

1596: 2 July
Commission renewed to appoint Th. Mostyn as custos rotulorum: Index
4208/f.17.

1596: 7 July
Commission renewed to add Hugh Gwynn of Bodvel; W. Williams of
Faenol: Index 4208/f.17v.

1596: 8 July
As on 15 August 1595, except: *Th. Egerton, kt., Keeper of Great Seal;
*Hugh Gwynn of Bodvel; *W. Thomas; *W. Williams of Faenol, added.
J. Puckering, omitted: C.66/1468/m.16d. & S.P.13/Case F, no.11/f.42.
Commission renewed to add W. Thomas: Index 4208/f.18.   (34)

1597: 9 June
As on 8 July 1596, except: *Rob. Wynn; *Hugh Hookes, *added*. Hugh
Cholmondeley; Fabian Phillips; W. Morris (Sheriff, 1595–6), *omitted*:
C.66/1468/m.31d. Commission renewed to *restore* Rob. Wynn; Hugh
Hookes: Index 4208/f.34v. (33)

1598: 7 July
Commission renewed to *add* Rich. Gwynn: Index 4208/f.52.

1598: 21 July
As on 9 June 1597, except: *W. Morris; *Rich. Gwynn; Griffith Hughes,
added. Burghley; W. Fowler, *omitted*: C.66/1482/m.18d. Commission
renewed to *add* Griffith Hughes: Index 4208/f.54. (34)

1599: 11 July
*Egerton, Keeper of Great Seal; *Th., Lord Buckhurst, Treasurer;
*Pembroke, President of Council in the Marches of Wales; Bishops of
*Bangor, *St. Asaph; *Shuttleworth, Justice of Chester; *Leighton &
*Broughton, Justices of Great Sessions; *Rich. Bulkeley, *Th. Mostyn,
kts.; *H. Townshend; *W. Morris; *J. Wynn; *Hugh Gwynn of Bodvel;
W. Williams; *Hugh Hughes, Queen's attorney in Caernarvon; *J. Griffith;
*Rob. Wynn; *Roland Puleston: *Griffith ap John Griffith; *Rob. Brinker;
*Rich. Gwynn; Th. Glynn; Maurice Griffith; *Hugh Hookes; Th. Vaughan;
*W. Thomas; *Hugh Gwynn of Pennarth; *W. Williams of Faenol; *Rob.
Madryn; Maurice Kyffin; Ed. Holland; Evan ap Hugh; Griffith Hughes:
C.66/1493/m.28d. Commission renewed to *add* H., B. of Bangor: Index
4208/f.74. (34)

1600: 7 June
Commission renewed to *add* J. Griffith of Llyn: Index 4208/f.90.

1600: 20 June
As on 11 July 1599, except: *Rich. Lewkenor, kt., Justice of Chester;
J. Griffith of Llŷn; Rich. Wynn of Bangor: Hugh Bodwrda, *added*. Rich.
Shuttleworth; Griffith ap John Griffith; Rob. Wynn; Evan ap Hugh,
omitted: C.66/1523/m.30d. Commission renewed to *add* Rich. Wynn of Ban-
gor; Hugh Bodwrda: Index 4208/f.91v. (34)

1600: 10 December
Commission renewed to *add* W. Johns; W. Bould: Index 4208/f.99.

1601: 29 January
As on 20 June 1600, except: *W. Johns; W. Glynn; J. Hookes; W. Bould,
added. E. of Pembroke; B. of St. Asaph; Hugh Hookes, *omitted*: B.M.,
Harleian Ms. 1974/f.103. Commission renewed to *add* W. Glynn; J. Hookes:
Index 4208/f.101v. (The patent roll enrolment of this commission (C.66/
1549/m.32d.) also omits Th. Glynn, probably in error). (35)

1602: 2 January
Commission renewed to *add* Rich. Vaughan and *omit* Hugh Gwynn of Bodvel; W. Williams; W. Thomas: Index 4208/f.127.

1602: 25 February
Commission renewed to *add* W., B. of St. Asaph: Index 4208/f.130.

1602: 26 February
Commission renewed to *restore* W. Thomas: Index 4208/f.130v.

1602: 26 June
Commission renewed to *add* W. Glynn of Lleuar: Index 4208/f.138.

1602: 7 July
Commission renewed to *add* Rich. Barker, Justice of Great Sessions: Index 4208/f.139v.

1602: 25 July
*Egerton; *Buckhurst; *Ed., Lord Zouch, President of Council in the Marches of Wales; Bishops of *Bangor, *St. Asaph; *Rich. Lewkenor, kt., Justice of Chester; *W. Leighton & *Rich. Barker, Justices of Great Sessions; *Rich. Bulkeley, *p Th. Mostyn, kts.; *H. Townshend; *W. Morris; *J. Wynn; *Hugh Hughes, Queen's attorney; *J. Griffith; *Roland Puleston; *Rob. Brinker; *Rich. Gwynn; Th. Glynn; J. Griffith of Llyn; *W. Williams of Faenol; *W. Johns; W. Glynn; Maurice Griffith; *J. Hookes; Th. Vaughan; Rich. Vaughan; *W. Thomas; *Rich. Wynn of Bangor; *Hugh Gwynn of Pennarth; *Rob. Madryn; Maurice Kyffin; Griffith Hughes; Hugh Bodwrda; W. Glynn of Lleuar; W. Bould: C.66/1594/m.35d. General renewal of Welsh commissions to *add* Lord Zouch, President of Council in the Marches of Wales: Index 4208/f.141. (36)

1603: (Acting)
As on 25 July 1602, except: Rob. ap Richard, *added*. Roland Puleston; Maurice Kyffin, *omitted*: C.66/1620/m.13d. (35)

1604: (Acting)
As in 1603: C.66/1662/m.21d. & B.M., Add. Ms. 38139/f.169. (35)

1605: (Acting)
As in 1604, except: W. Vaughan; Humph. Meredith, *added*. Lord Zouch; Rich. Vaughan, *omitted*: C.66/1682/m.3d. (35)

1606: (Acting)
*Th. Egerton, Lord Ellesmere, Chancellor; *Th., Lord Buckhurst, E. of Dorset, Treasurer; Bishops of *Bangor, *St. Asaph; *Lewkenor, Justice of Chester; *Leighton & *Barker, Justices of Great Sessions; *Rich. Bulkeley, *p Th. Mostyn, *W. Morris, *W. Thomas, *H. Townshend, *Rich. Gwynn, *J. Wynn, W. Glynn, kts.; *Hugh Hughes, King's attorney; *J. Griffith; *Rob. Brinker; Th. Glynn; J. Griffith of Llŷn; *W. Williams of Faenol;

*W. Jones; Maurice Griffith; Th. Vaughan; W. Vaughan; *Rich. Wynn of Bangor; *Hugh Gwynn of Pennarth; *Rob. Madryn; Griffith Hughes; Hugh Bodwrda; W. Glynn of Lleuar; W. Bould; Humph. Meredith; Rob. ap Richard: C.66/1698/m.28d. (34)

1607: post 12 September
As in 1606, except: *Ralph, Lord Eure, President of Council in the Marches of Wales (appointed on 12 September); *Ed. Herne, kt., Justice of Great Sessions; W. Humfreys, *added*. W. Leighton; J. Griffith; Th. Glynn; W. Glynn of Lleuar, *omitted*: C.66/1748/m.29d. (33)

1608–9: (Acting)
As in 1607, except: *E. of Salisbury, Treasurer; *E. of Northampton, Keeper of Privy Seal, *added*. E. of Dorset, *omitted*: C.66/1786/m.29d. (34)

1609–10: (Acting)
As in 1608–9, except: *Lewis Prowde, Justice of Great Sessions; Th. Bodvel; Rob. Griffith; W. Griffith; J. Gwynn, *added*. Ed. Herne; Hugh Hughes; Maurice Griffith; W. Vaughan; Rob. Madryn; W. Bould; Rob. ap Richard, *omitted*: C.66/1822/m.25d. (32)

1610–11: (Acting)
As in 1609–10: C.66/1897/m.18d. (32)

1611–12: (Acting)
*Ellesmere; *Salisbury, Treasurer; *Northampton, Keeper of Privy Seal; *Eure, President of Council in the Marches of Wales; Bishops of *Bangor, *St. Asaph; *Lewkenor, Justice of Chester; *Rich. Barker & *Lewis Prowde, Justices of Great Sessions; *J. Wynn, kt. & Bt.; *Rich. Bulkeley, *p Th. Mostyn, *W. Morris, *W. Thomas, *H. Townshend, *Rich. Gwynn, W. Glynn, kts. *Rob. Brinker; J. Griffith of Llŷn; *W. Williams of Faenol; *W. Jones; Th. Bodvel; Rob. Griffith; W. Griffith; Th. Vaughan; *Rich. Wynn of Bangor; *Hugh Gwynn of Pennarth; W. Humfreys; Griffith Hughes; Hugh Bodwrda; Humph. Meredith; J. Gwynn: C.66/1898/m.26d. (32)

1614: post 11 July
As in 1611–12, except: *E. of Suffolk, Treasurer (appointed on 11 July); *Griffith Vaughan; Arthur Williams, clerk, *added*. Salisbury; Northampton; Rob. Griffith, *omitted*: C.66/1988/m.26d. (32)

1614–15: (Acting)
As in 1614: C.66/2047/m.20d. (32)

1615: 8 July
Commission renewed to *add* Th. Chamberlain, Justice of Great Sessions: Index 4211/f.7v.

1616: 19 February
*Ellesmere; *E. of Suffolk, Treasurer; *E. of Worcester, Keeper of Privy Seal; *Eure, President of Council in the Marches of Wales; Bishops of *Bangor, *St. Asaph; *Lewkenor, Justice of Chester; *Th. Chamberlain, serjeant at law & *Lewis Prowde, Justices of Great Sessions; *J. Wynn, kt. & Bt.; *Rich. Bulkeley, *p Th. Mostyn, *W. Morris, *W. Thomas, *H. Townshend, *Rich. Gwynn, W. Glynn, kts.; *Rob. Brinker; J. Griffith of Llŷn; *W. Williams of Faenol; *Griffith Vaughan; *W. Jones; W. Griffith; Th. Vaughan; *Rich. Wynn of Bangor; Arthur Williams, clerk; W. Humfreys; Griffith Hughes; Hugh Bodwrda; Humph. Meredith; J. Gwynn; J. Bodvel; W. Vaughan: C.66/2076/m.23d. Commission renewed to *add* J. Bodvel; W. Vaughan: Index 4211/f.16v.   (33)

1616: 26 July
Anglesey commission renewed to *add* Francis Eure, Justice of Great Sessions: Index 4211/f.24v. (The Caernarvon commission should also have been renewed, but there is no Docquet Book entry for this date.)

1617: 30 January
Commission renewed to *add* Lewis, B. of Bangor: Index 4211/f.32v.

1617: 19 March
Commission renewed to *add* Francis Bacon, kt., Keeper of Great Seal; Th., Lord Gerard, President of Council in Wales: Index 4211/f.38.

1617: post 24 November
*Francis Bacon, kt., Keeper of Great Seal; *Suffolk, Treasurer; *Worcester, Keeper of Privy Seal; *D. of Lennox, Steward; *W., Lord Compton, President of Council in the Marches of Wales (appointed on 24 November); Bishops of *St. Asaph, *Bangor; *Th. Chamberlain, kt., Justice of Chester; *Francis Eure, kt. & *J. Jeffreys, Justices of Great Sessions; *J. Wynn, kt. & Bt.; *Rich. Bulkeley, *p Th. Mostyn, *W. Morris, *W. Thomas, *H. Townshend, *Rich. Gwynn, *W. Glynn, *W. Jones, serjeant at law, kts.; *J. Griffith of Llŷn; *W. Williams of Faenol; W. Vaughan; W. Griffith; *Th. Vaughan; Arthur Williams, clerk; W. Humfreys; Griffith Hughes; Hugh Bodwrda; Humph. Meredith; J. Gwynn: C.66/2147/m.22d.   (30)

1618: 12 March
Commission renewed to *add* J. Wynn, kt. & Bt., as *custos rotulorum*; W. Holland of Conway: Index 4211/f.60v.

1618: (Acting)
As in 1617, except: *J. Bodvel, kt.; W. Holland of Conway, *added*. E. of Suffolk; Th. Mostyn; Rich. Gwynn; W. Griffith; Th. Vaughan, *omitted*: C.66/2174/m.19d.   (27)

1619: 14 May
Commission renewed to *add* Edm. Griffith, Dean of Bangor: Index 4211/f.84.

1619: 24 May
Commission renewed to *add* H. Bodvel: Index 4211/f.84.

1619: 12 July
Commission renewed to *add* Griffith Hughes, Chancellor of Bangor; Ellis Brinker: Index 4211/f.90.

1620: 4 November
General renewal of Welsh commissions to *add* Jas. Whitlock, kt., Justice of Chester: Index 4211/f.114.

1621: 26 February
*Francis Bacon, Viscount St. Alban, Chancellor; *H. ,Viscount Mandeville, Treasurer; *Worcester; *Lennox; *E. of Northampton, President of Council in the Marches of Wales; *B. of St. Asaph; *B. of Bangor; *Jas. Whitlock, kt., Justice of Chester; *Eure and *Jeffreys, Justices of Great Sessions; *p J. Wynn, kt. & Bt.; *Rich. Bulkeley, *W. Morris, *W. Thomas, *H. Townshend, *W. Glynn, *Roger Mostyn, *J. Bodvel, *W. Jones, serjeant at law, kts.; *Edm. Griffith, Dean of Bangor; *Griffith Hughes, Chancellor of Bangor; *J. Griffith of Llŷn; *W. Williams of Faenol; W. Vaughan; W. Griffith; *Th. Vaughan; *Th. Glynn; Ellis Brinker; Arthur Williams, clerk; W. Humfreys; Griffith Hughes; Hugh Bodwrda; H. Bodvel; Humph. Meredith; J. Gwynn; *W. Holland of Conway: B.M., Harleian Ms. 1974/f.106. Commission renewed to *add* Viscount Mandeville; Th. Glynn: Index 4211/f.120. (The patent roll entry of this commission (C.66/2234/m.42d.) omits the names of Francis Eure (who died on 1 May 1621) and Th. Vaughan, the commission evidently being enrolled after their deaths). (36)

1621: 29 June
Commission renewed to *add* Ed. Littleton, Justice of Great Sessions: Index 4211/f.126.

1622: 20 April
As on 26 February 1621, except: *B. of Lincoln, Keeper of Great Seal; *Lionel Cranfield, Treasurer; *Ed. Littleton, Justice of Great Sessions; Owen Wynn; Rich. Evans, *added*. Viscount St. Alban; B. of Bangor; Francis Eure; Rich. Bulkeley; H. Townshend; W. Glynn; Th. Vaughan, *omitted*: C.66/2259/m.24d. Commission renewed to *add* Owen Wynn; Rich. Evans: Index 4211/f.138. (34).

1622: 17 July
Commission renewed to *add* Rich. Williams and *omit* H. Bodvel: Index 4211/f.142.

1622: 24 October
Commission renewed to *add* Th. Williams: Index 4211/f.145.

1622: 25 November
As on 20 April 1622, except: *B. of Bangor; *Peter Mutton, kt., Justice of
Great Sessions; *W. Williams, Bt.; *Th. Williams; Rich. Williams, *added*.
J. Jeffreys; W. Morris; Arthur Williams; W. Humfreys; Hugh Bodwrda;
H. Bodvel, *omitted*: C.66/2285/m.32d. Commission renewed to *add* Peter
Mutton: Index 4211/f.146. (33)

1623: 5 August
Commission renewed to *restore* H. Bodvel: Index 4211/f.156v.

1623: 11 October
As on 25 November 1622, except: *H. Bodvel, *added*. D. of Lennox; B. of
St. Asaph; W. Williams of Faenol; Griffith Hughes; Rich. Evans, *omitted*:
C.66/2310/m.29d. Commission renewed to *omit* Rich. Evans: Index
4211/f.157v. (29)

1624: 10 July
Commission renewed to *add* J. Bodwrda: Index 4211/f.169.

1625: 1 April
*B. of Lincoln, Keeper of Great Seal; *Jas., Lord Ley, Treasurer; *Viscount
Mandeville; *Worcester, Keeper of Privy Seal; *Northampton, President
of Council in the Marches of Wales; *B. of Bangor; *W. Jones, kt., Justice
ad placita; *Th. Chamberlain, kt., Justice of Chester; *Peter Mutton, kt. &
*Ed. Littleton, Justices of Great Sessions; *p J. Wynn, kt. & Bt.; *W.
Williams, Bt.; *W. Thomas, *Roger Mostyn, *J. Bodvel, kts.; *Edm.
Griffith, Dean of Bangor; *Griffith Hughes, Chancellor of Bangor;
*Sampson Eure; *Rob. Brooke; *Th. Williams; Th. Glynn; *J. Griffith of
Llŷn; W. Vaughan; *W. Griffith; Owen Wynn; Ellis Brinker; *H. Bodvel;
Humph. Meredith; J. Gwynn; *W. Holland of Conway; Rich. Williams;
*J. Bodwrda: C.66/2367/m.28d. General renewal of Welsh commissions:
Index 4211/f.180v. (32)

1625: 30 May
Commission renewed to *add* W. Thomas: Index 4211/f.188v.

1625: 22 December
As on 1 April, 1625, except: *Th. Coventry, kt., Keeper of Great Seal;
*W. Thomas, *added*. Th. Chamberlain, *omitted*: B.M., Harleian Ms. 1622/f.92.
General renewal of Welsh commissions to *add* Th. Coventry: Index 4211/
f.194v. (33)

1626: 20 March
As on 22 December 1625, except: *J. Bridgeman, kt., Justice of Chester;
*Rich. Bulkeley, *added*. W. Williams; Griffith Hughes; Owen Wynn; W.
Holland; Rich. Williams; W. Thomas, *omitted*: E.163/18/12/f.93v. &
C.193/12/2/f.67v. Commission renewed to *add* J. Bridgeman; Rich. Bulkeley:
Index 4211/f.199. (29)

1627: 5 March
Commission renewed to *add* Rich. Wynn, kt. & Bt., as *custos rotulorum* in place of his father, J. Wynn, deceased: Index 4211/f.219v.

1627: 16 March
Commission renewed to *add* Owen Wynn: Index 4211/f.220v.

1627: 22 June
Commission renewed to *add* Rich. Vaughan: Index 4211/f.228v.

1627: 13 July
*Coventry, Keeper of Great Seal; *Jas. Ley, E. of Marlborough, Treasurer; *H., (Viscount Mandeville), E. of Manchester, Keeper of Privy Seal; *Northampton, President of Council in the Marches of Wales; Bishops of *Lincoln, *Bangor; *W. Jones, kt., Justice *ad placita*; *J. Bridgeman, kt., Justice of Chester; *Mutton & *Littleton, Justices of Great Sessions; *p Rich. Wynn, kt. & Bt.; *Th. Williams, Bt.; *W. Thomas, *Roger Mostyn, *J. Bodvel, kts.; *Edm. Griffith, Dean of Bangor; *Rich. Bulkeley; *Sampson Eure; *Timothy Turneur; Th. Glynn; *J. Griffith of Llŷn; W. Vaughan; *W. Griffith; *J. Wynn; *Owen Wynn; *J. Bodwrda; Ellis Brinker; *H. Bodvel; Humph. Meredith; Rich. Vaughan: C.66/2449/m.32d. Commission renewed to *add* J. Wynn: Index 4211/f.231v.   (30)

1627: 20 December
Commission renewed to *add* Th. Glynn of Nanley (probably Nanlle): Index 4211/f.237v.

1628: post 14 December
As on 13 July 1627, except: *Rich., Lord Weston, Treasurer; *Ed., Viscount Conway, President of Council (appointed on 14 December); *E. of Pembroke; Th. Glynn of Nanley (probably Nanlle), *added*. E. of Marlborough; Ellis Brinker; Humph. Meredith, *omitted*: C.66/2495/m.26d.   (31)

1629–30: (Acting)
As in 1628: C.66/2527/m.28d.   (31)

1630: 10 June
Commission renewed to *add* Griffith Jones; W. Thomas: Index 4212/p.33.

1632: 22 February
Commission renewed to *add* Humphrey Jones, King's Receiver in North Wales: Index 4212/p.76.

1632: 3 May
Commission renewed to *add* David, B. of Bangor: Index 4212/p.80.

1632: 20 June
*Coventry; *Rich. Weston, E. of Portland, Treasurer; *Manchester; *E. of Bridgewater, President of Council in the Marches of Wales; Bishops of *Lincoln, *Bangor; *W. Jones, kt., Justice *ad placita*; *Bridgeman, Justice

of Chester; *Peter Mutton, kt. & *Rich. Weston, Justices of Great Sessions;
*p Rich. Wynn, kt. & Bt.; *Th. Williams, Bt.; *W. Thomas, *Roger
Mostyn, *Marmaduke Lloyd, *J. Bodvel, kts.; *Edm. Griffith, Dean of
Bangor; *Rich. Bulkeley; *Sampson Eure; *Timothy Turneur; *Griffith
Jones; Th. Glynn; *J. Griffith of Llŷn; W. Vaughan; *W. Griffith; *Owen
Wynn; Humph. Jones, King's Receiver in North Wales; *J. Bodwrda;
Rich. Vaughan; Th. Glynn of Nanley (probably Nanlle); W. Thomas:
C.66/2598/m.21d. Commission renewed to *add* Rich. Weston, Justice of
Great Sessions: Index 4212/p.81.   (31)

1634: 2 July
As on 30 June 1632, except: *Edm., B. of Bangor; Owen Griffith, King's
attorney, *added*. David, B. of Bangor; Rich. Weston; J. Bodvel; Edm.
Griffith, *omitted*: C.66/2623/m.23d. Commission renewed to *add* Owen
Griffith and record appointment of Timothy Turneur as Justice of Great
Sessions (Turneur was on the commission before his promotion): Index
4212/p.141.   (29)

1635: 26 June
Commission renewed to *add* Griffith Thomas: Index 4212/p.173.

1636: post 6 March
As on 2 July 1634, except: *B. of London, Treasurer (appointed on 6 March);
Griffith Thomas, *added*. E. of Portland; Th. Williams, Bt.; W. Thomas, kt.,
omitted: S.P.16/405/f.76v.   (28)

1637: 9 May
Commission renewed to *add* Griffith Williams, D.D.: Index 4212/p.241.

1638: 15 February
*Coventry; *B. of London, Treasurer; *Manchester; *Bridgewater, President
of Council in the Marches of Wales; *W. Jones, kt., Justice *ad placita*;
*p Rich. Wynn, kt. & Bt.; *Roger Mostyn, *Marmaduke Lloyd, kts.;
*Rich. Prydderch, second Justice of Chester, *Griffith Williams, D.D.,
Dean of Bangor; *Rich. Bulkeley; *Sampson Eure; *Owen Griffith, King's
attorney; *Griffith Jones; Th. Glynn; *J. Griffith of Llŷn; *W. Griffith;
*Owen Wynn; *Humph. Jones, King's Receiver in North Wales; W.
Lloyd; *J. Bodwrda; Th. Glynn of Nanley (probably Nanlle); W. Thomas;
Griffith Thomas: C.66/2725/m.19d. Commission renewed to *add* W. Lloyd:
Index 4212/p.279.   (24)

1638: 21 April
As on 15 February 1638, except: *W., B. of Bangor; *Th. Milward, kt.,
Justice of Chester; *Adam Littleton & *Rob. Brerewood, Justices of Great
Sessions, *added*: C.66/2761/m.17d. Commission renewed to *add* W., B. of
Bangor: Index 4212/p.289.   (28)

1639: 3 April
Commission renewed to *add* Hugh Griffith: Index 4212/p.337.

1640: post 17 January

*J. Finch, kt., Keeper of Great Seal (appointed on 17 January); *London; *Manchester; *Bridgewater, President of Council in the Marches of Wales; *B. of Bangor; *W. Jones, kt., Justice *ad placita*; *Th. Milward, kt., Justice of Chester; *Adam Littleton & *Rob. Brerewood, Justices of Great Sessions; *p Rich. Wynn, kt. & Bt.; *Roger Mostyn, *Marmaduke Lloyd, kts.; *Rich. Prydderch, second Justice of Chester; *Griffith Williams, Dean of Bangor; *Rich. Bulkeley; *Sampson Eure; *W. Morgan; *Owen Griffith, King's attorney; *Griffith Jones; Th. Glynn; *J. Griffith of Llyn; *W. Griffith; *Owen Wynn; *Humph. Jones, King's Receiver in North Wales; *W. Lloyd; *J. Bodwrda; Th. Glynn of Nanley (probably Nanlle); W. Thomas; Griffith Thomas; Hugh Griffith: C.66/2858/m.21d.   (30)

1640: 25 July

Commission renewed to *add* Th. Bulkeley; J. Griffith of Llŷn; J. Owen; Th. Madryn; Arthur Williams; Hugh Wynn: Index 4212/p.399.

1641: 10 April

Commission renewed to *add* W. Williams, Bt.: Index 4212/p.441.

1641: 27 May

Commission renewed to *add* W. Hooke and place Th. Glynn on quorum: Index 4212/p.449.

1643: 4 December

Commission renewed to *add* W. Griffith, Ll.D.; Maurice Wynn; Ed. Williams; Roger Mostyn senior; Griffith Williams; Th. Pugh; Rob. Jones; Th. Wynn; W. Griffiths of Cefnamlwch: Index 4210/p.54.

1644: 29 April

Commission renewed to *add* Timothy Littleton, serjeant at law, Justice of Great Sessions, and others (no details): Index 4210/p.107.

1646: 4 July

Commission renewed (no details): Index 4213/p.49.

1647: 22 March

Commission renewed to *add* Rich. Keble & W. Littleton, Justices of Great Sessions: Index 4213/p.85.

1648: 7 July

Commission renewed (no details): Index 4213/p.119.

1649: 31 March

Commission renewed (no details): Index 4213/p.147.

1649: 6 July

*W. Lenthall, Speaker of House of Commons; *Th., Lord Fairfax; *J. Bradshaw, President of Council; *Bulstrode Whitelock, *Rich. Keble, *J. Lisle, Commissioners of Great Seal; Earls of *Pembroke, *Denbigh;

*H. Rolle, Chief Justice of Upper Bench; *Oliver St. John, Chief Justice of Common Pleas; *J. Wilde, Chief Baron of Exchequer; *W. Littleton & *Ed. Bulstrode, Justices of Great Sessions; *Edm. Prideaux, Attorney-General; *W. Williams, Bt.; *Griffith Jones; Th. Mytton; *Th. Mason; *Th. Williams; *Th. Madryn; *Ed. Williams; *J. Carter; Hugh Griffith of Madryn; *Edm. Glynn; *J. Wynn of Gwynfryn; J. Owen; *Rich. Anwyl; Griffith Williams of Conway; W. Stoddart; *Maurice Wynn; Rich. Coytmore: C.193/13/3/f.74. Commission renewed to *add* Ed. Bulstrode: Index 4213/p.157. (31)

1650: 25 July
*Lenthall; *Oliver Cromwell, Lord General; *Bradshaw; *Whitelock, *Keble & *Lisle; *Denbigh; *Rolle; *St. John; *Wilde; *Littleton & *Bulstrode; *Prideaux; *Owen Wynn, Bt.; *J. Jones; *J. Glynn, serjeant at law; *J. Carter; *Th. Mason; *Geo. Twistleton; *p Griffith Jones; *Th. Madryn; *Owen Griffith; *W. Foxwist; J. Owen; W. Williams; W. Lloyd: *Lists published by Th. Walkley* (1650), p.65. Commission renewed to *add* Owen Wynn, Bt.; J. Jones; Geo. Twistleton; Owen Griffith; W. Foxwist; W. Williams; W. Lloyd, and to *omit* Th. Williams; Ed. Williams; and others: Index 4213/p.198. (26)

1651: 1 May
Commission renewed to record appointment of J. Carter as *custos rotulorum*: Index 4213/p.214.

1651: 3 July
*Lenthall; *Cromwell; *Whitelock, *Keble, *Lisle; *Denbigh; *Bradshaw; *Rolle; *St. John; *Wilde; *Littleton & *Bulstrode; *Prideaux; *Owen Wynn, Bt.; *J. Jones; *J. Glynn, serjeant at law; *p J. Carter; *Griffith Williams; *Th. Mason; *Geo. Twistleton; *Griffith Jones; *Th. Madryn; *W. Foxwist; *Edm. Glynn; J. Owen; W. Williams; W. Lloyd; Hugh Griffith; W. Stoddart; J. Parry: Cambridge Univ. Ms. Dd. VIII.1/f.122v. & C.193/13/4/f.116. Commission renewed to *add* Griffith Williams; Hugh Griffith; W. Stoddart; J. Parry, and *omit* Owen Griffith: Index 4213/p.219. (30)

1653: 27 July
Commission renewed to *add* Rob. Williams, and *omit* Owen Wynn, Bt., and others (no details): Index 4213/p.264.

1654: 7 July
Commission renewed according to a general list: Index 4213/p.293.

1654: 15 September
Commission renewed to *add* W. Williams, Bt.; Th. Williams; J. Wynn of the Abbey; Rob. Wynn; J. Wynn of Gwynfryn: Index 4213/p.296.

1655: 12 December
Commission renewed to *add* Colonel James Berry: Index 4213/p.321.

1656: 25 June
Commission renewed to *add* Rich. Griffith of Methlan; Jeffrey Parry of Rhydolion; Rich. Edwards of Llanharon; Rob. Evans of Llanarmon, to appoint W. Lloyd of Bodfean as *custos rotulorum*, and to *omit* Griffith Williams; Griffith Jones; and others: Index 4213/p.337. (See note after next entry).

1656: 4 July
*Nathaniel Fiennes & *J. Lisle, Commissioners of Great Seal; *Bulstrode Whitelock, kt., *Th. Widdrington, kt., *Ed. Montagu & *W. Sydenham, Commissioners of Treasury; *J. Glynn, Chief Justice of Upper Bench; *W. Lenthall, Master of Rolls; *Oliver St. John, Chief Justice of Common Bench; *Ed. Bulstrode & *Evan Seys, serjeant at law, Justices of Great Sessions; *Edm. Prideaux, Attorney-General; *W. Williams, Bt.; *Major-Gen. James Berry; *J. Nicholas; *Rowland Dawkins; *J. Jones; *Hugh Price; *p J. Carter; *Griffith Williams; *Griffith Jones; *Rob. Williams; *Edm. Glynn; *Th. Mason; *Geo. Twistleton; *Th. Madryn; *W. Foxwist; *W. Lloyd of Bodfean; *Rich. Griffith of Llanfair; *Maurice Griffith of Methlan; J. Wynn of the Abbey; *Hugh Griffith; *Jeffrey Parry of Rhydolion; *Rich. Edwards of Llanharon; W. Stoddart; Rob. Evans of Llanarmon: C.193/13/6/f.102v. & C.193/13/5/f.123. Commission renewed to *add* Griffith Williams; Griffith Jones; Edm. Glynn, and to appoint J. Carter as *custos rotulorum*: Index 4213/p.339. (The Docquet Book entry of 25 June should probably begin: Rich. Griffith of Llanfair and Maurice Griffith of Methlan. The two names are apparently run together in the entry to appear as Rich. Griffith of Methlan). (36)

1658: 24 September
General renewal of Welsh commissions to *add* Rich. Cromwell, Lord Protector: Index 4213/p.405.

1659: 8 July
Commission renewed according to a general list: Index 4213/p.438.

1659: 5 October
Commission renewed to *add* W. Shepherd & Rich. Vaughan, Justices of Great Sessions: Index 4213/p.443.

1659: (Acting)
p J. Jones; Geo. Twistleton; Th. Madryn; Griffith Jones; W. Foxwist; W. Lloyd; Maurice Griffith; Rich. Edwards; Jeffrey Parry; Hugh Griffith; W. Stoddart; Rob. Evans: N.L.W., Wynn Papers no. 2209. (This list of the justices acting in 1659 is probably based on the commission of 8 July or of 5 October, with the omission of the *ex officio* members of the commission). (12)

1660: 3 March
Commission renewed according to a general list: Index 4213/p.453.

1660: 6 September
Commission renewed to appoint Rich. Wynn, Bt., as *custos rotulorum*, and *add* Timothy Littleton & J. Griffith, Justices of Great Sessions; and others (no details): Index 4214/p.36.

1660: post 8 September
*Ed. Hyde, kt., Chancellor; *E. of Southampton, Treasurer (appointed on 8 September); *D. of Albemarle; *Marquess of Ormond, Steward; *E. of Lindsey, Great Chamberlain; *E. of Manchester, Household Chamberlain; *Timothy Littleton, serjeant at law & *J. Griffith, Justices of Great Sessions; *p Rich. Wynn, Bt.; *Roger Mostyn, kt. & Bt.; *J. Owen, *Rich. Lloyd, kts.; *J. Glynn, serjeant at law *Griffith Jones; *J. Bodvel; *Griffith Williams; *W. Griffith; W. Vaughan; *Hugh Wynn; J. Bodwrda; *Maurice Wynn; Th. Wynn; Rob. Williams of Conway; *Edm. Glynn of Hendre; *Owen Griffith; Rich. Griffith; W. Wynn; J. Lloyd of Nantgwnnadl; Owen Wynn; *Griffith Bodwrda; Th. Vaughan; W. Hookes; Rich. Glynn: C.220/9/4/f.102v. & B.M., Egerton Ms. 2557/f.101v.   (33)

1661: 8 November
As in September 1660, except: *J., Lord Robartes, Keeper of Privy Seal; *E. of Carbery, President of Council in the Marches of Wales, *added*: C.193/12/3/f.117v. General renewal of Welsh commissions to *add* E. of Carbery, President of Wales: Index 4214/p.144.   (35)

1662: 17 July
Commission renewed to *add* Rob., Viscount Cashel; Th. Bulkeley; Rob. Wynn of Conway; Rob. Coytmore of Cwmowen; W. Wynn of Pengwern; W. Williams of Conway; Hugh Bodwrda of Aberdaron; Edm. Glynn of Bryn-y-Gwdion; W. Wynn of Llanwnda: Index 4214/p.179.

1663: 27 July
*E. of Clarendon, Chancellor; *Southampton; *J., Lord Robartes, Keeper of Privy Seal; *Albemarle; *Ormond; *Lindsey; *Manchester; *E. of Carbery, President of Council in the Marches of Wales; *Rob., Viscount Cashel; *Timothy Littleton & *Th. Jones, Justices of Great Sessions; *Th. Bulkeley; *p Rich. Wynn, Bt.; *Roger Mostyn, kt. & Bt.; *J. Glynn, serjeant at law, *J. Owen, *Rich. Lloyd, kts.; *Griffith Jones; *J. Bodvel; *Griffith Williams; *W. Griffith; W. Vaughan; *Hugh Wynn; J. Bodwrda; *Maurice Wynn; Rob. Williams of Conway; Rob. Wynn of Conway; Rob. Coytmore of Cwmowen; *Edm. Glynn of Hendre; W. Wynn of Pengwern; W. Williams of Conway; *Owen Griffith; Edm. Glynn of Bryn-y-Gwdion; W. Wynn of Llanwnda; Rich. Griffith; J. Williams of Meilionydd; W. Wynn; *Hugh Bodwrda of Aberdaron; J. Lloyd of Nantgwnnadl; *Owen Wynn; *Griffith Bodwrda; Th. Vaughan; W. Hookes; Rich. Glynn: C.66/2986/m.31d. Commission renewed to *add* Th. Jones, Justice of Great Sessions: Index 4214/p.211.   (44)

1665: 26 May
Commission renewed to *add* J. Wynn: Index 4214/p.260.

1670: 1 July
Commission renewed to *add* Kenrick Eyton, Justice of Great Sessions; J. Glynn; Th. Madryn; Owen Wynn; J. Hookes; Rich. Kyffin; J. Wynn; W. Thomas: Index 4214/p.371.

1672: 21 March
Commission renewed to *add* Th. Glynn of Plas Newydd: Index 4214/p.411.

1673: 18 March
Commission renewed to *add* Th. Mostyn: Index 4214/p.444.

1673: 16 September
Commission renewed to *omit* W. Wynn: Index 4214/p.461.

1674: 5 December
Commission renewed to *add* Roger Mostyn, Bt., *custos rotulorum*: Index 4214/p.486.

1677: 19 July
Commission renewed to *add* Humphrey, B. of Bangor: Index 4214/p.530.

1679: 3 May
Commission renewed to *add* Rich. Bulkeley, *custos rotulorum*: Index 4215/p.6.

1679: 2 June
Commission renewed to *add* Rob. Wynn; Rob. Hookes: Index 4215/p.8.

1680: 1 April
*Prince Rupert; *Archbishop of Canterbury; *Lord Finch, Chancellor; *E. of Radnor, President of Privy Council; *E. of Anglesey, Keeper of Privy Seal; Dukes of *Albemarle, *Monmouth, *Newcastle, *Lauderdale, *Ormond; Marquess of *Winchester; Marquess of *Worcester, President of Council in the Marches of Wales; Earls of *Lindsey, *Arlington, *Salisbury, *Bridgewater, *Sunderland, *Essex, *Bath, *Halifax, *Carbery; Viscounts *Fauconberg, *Bulkeley; Bishops of *London, *Bangor; *Laurence Hyde; *H. Coventry; *Francis North, kt., Chief Justice of Bench; *J. Ernley, kt., Chancellor of Exchequer; *Th. Chichley, kt., Chancellor of Duchy of Lancaster; *W. Temple, Bt.; *Ed. Seymour; *Daniel Finch; *Leoline Jenkins; *Sidney Godolphin; *Kenrick Eyton & *Th. Walcott, Justices of Great Sessions; *Th. Bulkeley; *p Rich. Bulkeley; *Roger Mostyn, kt. & Bt.; *Rob. Owen, Bt.; Rob. Williams, Bt.; *Ed. Jennings, King's attorney; *Lewis Meyrick, King's attorney in Wales; *Francis Manley; *W. Griffith; *J. Wynn; *J. Glynn; *Th. Madryn; *Owen Wynn of Ystumcegid; Rob. Coytmore of Cwmowen; W. Wynn of Llanwnda; *Rob. Wynn; *Rich. Griffith; *Rob. Hookes; *Hugh Bodwrda of Aberdaron; *J. Wynn; *W. Glynn; *Th. Vaughan; *Ed. Williams; *Randolph Wynn; *Rich. Kyffin: C.193/12/4/f.142. Commission renewed to *remove* recusants and to *add* others (no details): Index 4215/p.26. (In 1680 the *removal* from the commission of the Duke of Buckingham, Th. Mostyn and Griffith Bodwrda was ordered by a warrant of 5 February and the *addition*

of Rob. Owen, Bt., W. Glynn, and Randolph Wynn by a warrant of 18 February: *H.M.C Eleventh Report, Appendix*, Part 2, p.175. The lists published in 1680 by N.S., Esq., (p.25) record only the omissions). (62)

1682: 28 March
Commission renewed to *add* Rich. Hopton, Justice of Great Sessions: Index 4215/p.64.

1683: 20 September
*Archbishop of Canterbury; *Francis North, kt., Keeper of Great Seal; *E. of Radnor, President of Council; *Marquess of Halifax, Keeper of Privy Seal; Dukes of *Albemarle, *Newcastle, *Ormond; *D. of Beaufort, President of Council in the Marches of Wales; Marquesses of *Winchester, *Worcester; Earls of *Lindsey, *Arlington, *Bridgewater, *Sunderland, *Bath, *Nottingham, *Rochester, *Carbery; *Viscount Fauconberg; *Viscount Bulkeley; Bishops of *London, *Bangor; *H. Coventry; *J. Ernley, kt., Chancellor of Exchequer; *Th. Chichley, kt., Chancellor of Duchy of Lancaster; *Ed. Seymour; *Leoline Jenkins, kt.; *Sidney Godolphin; *Geo. Jeffreys, kt. & Bt., Justice of Chester; *Th. Walcott, kt. & *Rich. Hopton, Justices of Great Sessions; *Th. Bulkeley; *p Rich. Bulkeley; *Roger Mostyn, kt. & Bt.; *Rob. Owen, Bt.; Rob. Williams, Bt.; *Ed. Jennings, King's attorney in Caernarvon; *Lewis Meyrick, Attorney-General for Wales; *Francis Manley; *W. Griffith; *J. Wynn; *J. Glynn; *Th. Madryn; *Owen Wynn of Ystumcegid; Rob. Coytmore of Cwmowen; W. Wynn of Llanwnda; Rob. Wynn; *Rich. Griffith; *Rob. Hookes; *Hugh Bodwrda of Aberdaron; *J. Wynn; *W. Glynn; *Rich. Brooke; *Th. Vaughan; *Ed. Williams; *Randolph Wynn; *Rich. Kyffin: N.L.W., Wynn Papers no. 2836. (This is a dated copy of the Caernarvon commission of 20 September 1683). Commission renewed to *add* Rich. Brooke: Index 4215/p.89. (57).

1685: 7 March
Commission renewed to reappoint Rich. Bulkeley as *custos rotulorum* and to *add* Th. Powell, Justice of Great Sessions: Index 4215/p.122.

1685: post 28 September
*Archbishop of Canterbury; *Geo., Lord Jeffreys, Chancellor (appointed on 28 September); *E. of Rochester, Treasurer; *Marquess of Halifax, President of Council; *E. of Clarendon, Keeper of Privy Seal; Dukes of *Albemarle, *Newcastle, *Ormond; *D. of Beaufort, President of Council in the Marches of Wales; *Marquess of Winchester; *Marquess of Worcester; Earls of *Lindsey, *Ailesbury, *Bridgewater, *Sunderland, *Bath, *Nottingham, *Carbery; Viscounts *Fauconberg, *Bulkeley; Bishops of *London, *Bangor; *Sidney, Lord Godolphin; *H. Coventry; *J. Ernley, kt., Chancellor of Exchequer; *Th. Chichley, kt., Chancellor of Duchy of Lancaster; *Ed. Seymour; *Rich. Hopton & *Th. Powell, Justices of Great Sessions; *Th. Bulkeley; *p Rich. Bulkeley; *Roger Mostyn, kt. & Bt.; *Rob. Owen, Bt.; *Rob. Williams, Bt.; *Ed. Jennings, King's attorney in Caernarvon; *Lewis Meyrick, Attorney-General for Wales; *Francis Manley; *W. Griffith; *J. Wynn; *J. Glynn; *Th. Madryn; *Owen Wynn of

Ystumcegid; *Rob. Coytmore of Cwmowen; W. Wynn of Llanwnda; *Rob. Wynn; *Rich. Griffith; *Rob. Hookes; *Hugh Bodwrda of Aberdaron; *J. Wynn; *W. Glynn; *Rich. Brooke; *Th. Vaughan; *Ed. Williams; *Randolph Wynn: C.193/12/5/f.167. (54)

1686: 17 December
Order by Privy Council to *add* to the Caernarvon commission W. Pugh of Penrhyn; Maurice Wynn of Graianllyn; J. Rowlands; Th. Price; J. Griffith; Rob. Wynn of Bodysgallen; Geo. Twistleton, and to *omit* Th. Bulkeley; Th. Madryn; Robert (i.e. Richard) Brooke; Randolph Wynn; W. Griffith: P.C.2/71/p.377.

1687: 26 June
D. of Beaufort recommends appointment of Hugh Lewis as a J.P.: N.L.W. Ms. 11020 E.

1687: 29 August
General renewal of Welsh commissions to add the clause of dispensation: Index 4215/p.179.

1688: 14 April
Commission renewed: Index 4215/p.191.

1688: 6 October
General renewal of Welsh commissions: Index 4215/p.200.

1688: 27 November
Commission renewed to *add* Rawleigh Mansel and others (no details): Index 4215/p.204.

Merioneth

1543: 12 March
*Th. Audley, kt., Chancellor; *D. of Norfolk, Treasurer; *D. of Suffolk, President of Council; *J. Russell, kt., Keeper of Privy Seal; *B. of Coventry and Lichfield, President of Council in the Marches of Wales; Bishops of *St. Asaph, *Bangor; Walter, Lord Ferrers; *Nich. Hare, Ed. Croft, Rice Mansel, *J. Vernon, *Rich. Bulkeley, kts.; *J. Pakington; *Th. Holte; *David Brooke; *J. ap Rice; *Rich, Hassall; Ellis Price, clerk; *J. Arnold; *Rich. Mytton; *p J. Wynn ap Meredith; *Rob. Salisbury; *Ed. Stanley; *Lewis Owen; J. Powes; *J. Spysar. *Later additions to list*: *Th. Bromley, serjeant at law; *Adam Mytton; *Roland Meyrick, clerk; Hugh Lloyd, clerk: C.193/12/1/f.47v. (27 names plus 4 corrections).

1555: (Acting)
Rich. Mytton; J. Wynn ap Meredith; Ellis Price; Lewis Owen; Owen ap John ap Howel Vaughan; Maurice Wynn; Ed. Stanley; J. Powes; Roderick ap David ap Meredith; J. Vaughan: S.P.11/5/f.60. (10)

1558–59: (Acting)
*Nich. Bacon, kt., Keeper of Great Seal; *Marquess of Winchester, Treasurer; *E. of Arundel, Steward; Bishops of *Bath & Wells, *Chester; *J. Throckmorton, Justice of Chester; *Adam Mytton, *J. Vaughan, kts.; *J. Scudamore of Holm; *Chas. Fox; *J. Welsh; *Reg. Corbet; *W. Symonds; *W. Gerard; *Rich. Seaborne; *p Ellis Price, Ll.D.; *Ed. Herbert; *Rich. Mytton; *J. Wynn ap Meredith; *Th. Powell; *Owen ap John ap Howel Vaughan; J. Price of Derwen; *Rees Vaughan; Maurice Wynn; *J. ap Hugh; Ed. Stanley; Rees Hughes; J. Powes; *J. David Lloyd; Roderick ap David ap Meredith; J. Vaughan; Hugh Vaughan: B.M., Lansdowne Ms. 1218/f.42. (Except for the omission of the *ex officio* members of the commission, the same list appears in S.P.12/2/17/p.73). (32)

1561: (Acting)
*Bacon; *Winchester; *Arundel; *H. Sidney, kt., President of Council in the Marches of Wales; Bishops of *Bangor, *St. Asaph; *Reg. Corbet, Justice of Great Sessions; *Ellis Price, Ll.D.; *Th. Powell; *Maurice Wynn; *p Owen ap John ap Howel Vaughan; *Th. Mytton; *J. ap David Lloyd; Hugh Vaughan; *Rees Vaughan; J. Powes: B.M., Lansdowne Ms. 1218/f.88v. (16)

1562: 13 June
As in 1561: C.66/985/m.41d. (16)

1564: (Acting)
*Bacon; *Winchester; *Arundel; *Sidney; *Bangor; *St. Asaph; *Corbet, Justice of Great Sessions; *J. Throckmorton, Justice of Chester; *W. Gerard; *Chas. Fox; *Rich. Wye; *Rich. Seaborne; *p Ellis Price, Ll.D.; *Rich. Pates; *J. Price; *Rich. Smith; *Th. Powell; *Maurice Wynn; *Owen ap John ap Howel Vaughan; *Ed. Stanley; *Hugh Vaughan; *Rees Hughes; J. Powes; J. Lewis Owen; J. Lewis ap Evan ap David: C.66/998/m.11d. (25)

1573-4: (Acting)
*Bacon; *W., Lord Burghley, Treasurer; *Sidney; *St. Asaph; *Bangor; *Hugh Cholmondeley, kt.; *Throckmorton, Justice of Chester; *Geo. Bromley, Justice of Great Sessions; *W. Gerard; *Chas. Fox; *p Ellis Price, Ll.D.; *J. Gwynn, Ll.D.; *Jas. Ellis, Ll.D.; *Rich. Seaborne; *Rich. Pates; *Ed. Davies; *Maurice Wynn; *Edm. Meyrick, D.C.L.; *J. Price of Gogerddan; Rees Vaughan; *Rich. Vaughan; *J. Owen; *Rob. Wynn; *Owen Wynn; *Roland ap Hugh; J. Wynn ap Cadwalader; J. ap David Lloyd; Hugh Owen; J. Lewis ap Evan ap David; *Rees Hughes: S.P.12/93/part 2/f.36 & B.M., Egerton Ms. 2345/f.47.   (30)

1575: (Acting)
As in 1573-4, except: *J. Vaughan; Rob. Vaughan, *added*. Hugh Cholmondeley; J. Gwynn, Ll.D., *omitted*: S.P.12/106/part 2/f.11.   (30)

1577: (Acting)
As in 1575, except: *W. Lewis; *Lewis ap Owen ap Meyrick; Owen Wood; Rich. ap Owen Tudor; Roland Bulkeley of Porthaml; *Maurice Griffith; J. Salisbury of Rug, *added*. Jas. Ellis, Ll.D.; Ed. Davies; Maurice Wynn; J. Price of Gogerddan; Rees Vaughan; Rob. Wynn; Owen Wynn; Roland ap Hugh, *omitted*: S.P.12/121/f.41.   (29)

1578: (Acting)
*Bacon; *Burghley; *Sidney; *B. of Worcester; Earls of *Worcester, *Pembroke; Bishops of *Hereford, *Bangor, *St. Davids, *St. Asaph; *Throckmorton, Justice of Chester; *Andrew Corbet, *J. Perrot, *Nich. Arnold, *Hugh Cholmondeley, *J. Littleton, *J. Huband, kts.; *Geo. Bromley, Justice of Great Sessions; *David Lewis, Ll.D.; *W. Gerard; *W. Aubrey; *Chas. Fox; *W. Glaseor; *Ellis Price, Ll.D.; *Ed. Leighton; *Rich. Pates; *Ralph Barton; Jerome Corbet; *J. Puckering; *Fabian Phillips; *H. Townshend; *W. Leighton; *Edm. Meyrick, D.C.L.; *Rich. Vaughan; J. Owen; J. Salisbury of Rug; *J. Lewis ap Evan ap David; *J. Wynn ap Cadwalader; J. Lloyd ap David; Rees Hughes; J. Vaughan; Rob. Vaughan; Hatfield House Ms. 223.7.   (42)

1579: post 26 April
As in 1578, except: *Th. Bromley, kt., Chancellor (appointed on 26 April); *p E. of Leicester; *J. Price; *J. Nuttall; W. Thomas; Ednyfed Griffith; Morgan ap Robert, *added*. Bacon, *omitted*: S.P.12/145/f.58v.   (48)

1581: 20 November (Acting)
Rich. Vaughan; J. Lewis; J. Owen; Evan Lloyd ap David ap John; J. Wynn ap Cadwalader; Rob. Vaughan; Morgan ap Robert; Edm. Meyrick; J. Vaughan; Rees Hughes; Ednyfed Griffith: Bodleian, Bodley Ms. 904/f.207.   (11)

1582: (Acting)
W. Aubrey; Edm. Meyrick, D.C.L.; J. Nuttall; W. Thomas; Rich. Vaughan; J. Owen; J. Salisbury of Rug; J. ap Lewis ap Evan ap David; J. Wynn ap Cadwalader; J. Wynn; J. Lloyd ap David; Rob. Wynn; Owen Wynn; Rees

Hughes; J. Vaughan; Rob. Vaughan; Ednyfed Griffith; Morgan ap Robert:
B.M., Lansdowne Ms. 35/f.139v.   (18)

1584: (Acting)

*Bromley, Chancellor; *Burghley, Treasurer; *Sidney, President of Council
in the Marches of Wales; *p E. of Leicester; Earls of *Worcester, *Pem-
broke; Bishops of *Hereford, *Bangor, *St. Asaph; *Jas. Croft, Household
Controller; *Geo. Bromley, kt., Justice of Chester; *W. Leighton &
*Fabian Phillips, Justices of Great Sessions; *J. Perrot, *Hugh Cholmon-
deley, *J. Littleton, kts.; *J. Puckering; *W. Aubrey; *Chas. Fox; *Ellis
Price, Ll.D.; *Ed. Leighton; *H. Townshend; *Rich. Pates; *Ralph Barton;
*Jerome Corbet; *W. Glaseor; *Edm. Meyrick, D.C.L.; *W. Morris;
*Evan Lloyd of Yale; W. Thomas; *J. Owen; *J. Wynn ap Cadwalader;
*J. Wynn; *Rob. Wynn; Rees Hughes; *Rob. Vaughan; Hugh Owen:
E.163/14/8/f.56v.   (37)

1590–91: (Acting)

*Christopher Hatton, kt., Chancellor; *Burghley, Treasurer; *E. of
Pembroke, President of Council in the Marches of Wales; *B. of St. Asaph;
*J. Perrot, kt.; *Rich. Shuttleworth, kt., Justice of Chester; *Leighton &
*Phillips, Justices of Great Sessions; *Hugh Cholmondeley, kt.; *J.
Puckering; *W. Aubrey; *p Ellis Price, Ll.D.; *Ed. Leighton; *H.
Townshend; *Jerome Corbet; *Edm. Meyrick, D.C.L.; *Rob. Salisbury;
*J. Wynn; *W. Morris; *Hugh Hughes; *Owen Wynn; *J. Owen;
Cadwalader Wynn; *Griffith Vaughan; Th. Vaughan; *J. Lewis ap Evan
ap David; *Hugh Nanney; *Rob. Wynn; *Morgan ap Robert; Rees Hughes;
Hugh Owen; Piers Lloyd; *J. Vaughan; *Rob. Lloyd; Rich. ap Hugh;
J. Roberts: Hatfield House Ms. 278/f.62v.   (36)

1592–3: (Acting)

As in 1590–1, except: *Edm. Price, Archdeacon of Merioneth; Ednyfed
Griffith; Th. Price; Maurice Lewis; Roland ap Elissa, added. Hatton;
J. Perrot; J. Lewis ap Evan ap David, omitted: Kent Record Office U.350.03.
(Rob. Salisbury is now custos rotulorum).   (38)

1594: 28 June

*J. Puckering, kt., Keeper of Great Seal; *Burghley; *Pembroke, President
of Council in the Marches of Wales; *B. of St. Asaph; *Shuttleworth,
Justice of Chester; *W. Leighton & *Rich. Broughton, Justices of Great
Sessions; *Hugh Cholmondeley, kt.; *W. Aubrey; *Ellis Price, Ll.D.;
*H. Townshend; *Jerome Corbet; *Fabian Phillips; *p Rob. Salisbury of
Rug; *Edm. Meyrick, D.C.L.; *Edm. Price, Archdeacon of Merioneth;
*J. Wynn; *W. Morris; *Hugh Hughes; *Owen Wynn; *J. Owen;
*Cadwalader Wynn; *Griffith Vaughan; Th. Vaughan; Owen Vaughan;
*Hugh Nanney; *Rob. Wynn; *Morgan ap Robert; Ednyfed Griffith;
Th. Price; Rees Hughes; Hugh Owen; *Piers Lloyd; J. Roberts; *J.
Vaughan; *Rob. Lloyd: C.66/1421/m.16d.   (36)

1595: 15 August

General renewal of Welsh commissions: Index 4208/f.4v.

1595 : 28 November
As on 28 June 1594, except: *W. Fowler; Maurice Lewis; Humph. Hughes, *added*. W. Aubrey; Ellis Price; Owen Wynn; Owen Vaughan; Rob. Wynn; Morgan ap Robert; Th. Price; Rees Hughes; Piers Lloyd, *omitted*: C.66/1435/m.21d. Commission renewed to *restore* Maurice Lewis, late sheriff: Index 4208/f.11v. (30)

1596 : 7 July
As on 28 November 1595, except: *Th. Egerton, kt., Keeper of Great Seal; *Jas. Price, *added*. J. Puckering, *omitted*: S.P.13/Case F, no. 11/f.43v. Commission renewed to *add* Jas. Price: Index 4208/f.17v. (31)

1596 : 30 October
*Th. Egerton, kt., Keeper of Great Seal; *Burghley; *Pembroke, President of Council in the Marches of Wales; *B. of St. Asaph; *Shuttleworth, Justice of Chester; *Leighton & *Broughton, Justices of Great Sessions; *Hugh Cholmondeley, *p Rob. Salisbury, kts.; *H. Townshend; *Jerome Corbet; *Fabian Phillips; *W. Fowler; *Edm. Meyrick, D.C.L.; *Edm. Price, Archdeacon of Merioneth; *J. Wynn; *W. Morris; *Hugh Hughes, Queen's attorney in Merioneth; *J. Owen; *Cadwalader Wynn; *Griffith Vaughan; Th. Vaughan; *Hugh Nanney; *Jas. Price; Ednyfed Griffith; *Hugh Owen; *J. Vaughan; J. Roberts; *Rob. Lloyd; Math. Herbert; Maurice Lewis; Humph. Hughes: C.66/1468/m.17d. Commission renewed to *add* Math. Herbert: Index 4208/f.21v. (32)

1596 : 12 November
Commission renewed to *add* Cadwalader Pierce: Index 4208/f.22v.

1597 : 7 January
Commission renewed to *add* Piers Lloyd: Index 4208/f.25v.

1597 : 13 May
As on 30 October 1596, except: *Piers Lloyd; Rob. ap Evan ap Morgan; Cadwalader Pierce, *added*. Hugh Cholmondeley; Fabian Phillips, *omitted*: C.66/1468/m.32d. Commission renewed to *add* Rob. ap Evan ap Morgan: Index 4208/f.33. (33)

1598 : (Acting)
As on 13 May 1597, except: Burghley; W. Fowler, *omitted*: C.66/1482/m.18d. (31)

1599 : 12 July
Commission renewed to *add* H., B. of Bangor: Index 4208/f.74.

1599 : 24 July
As in 1598, except: *Th., Lord Buckhurst, Treasurer; *H., B. of Bangor; *p Th. Myddelton, *added*. Rob. Salisbury; Jerome Corbet, *omitted*: C.66/1493/m.28d. Commission renewed to *add* Th. Myddelton as *custos rotulorum*: Index 4208/f.75. (32)

1599: 7 December
Commission renewed to *omit* Cadwalader Wynn: Index 4208/f.79v.

1600: post 11 March
As on 24 July 1599, except: *Rich. Lewkenor, kt., Justice of Chester, *added*. Rich. Shuttleworth; Cadwalader Wynn, *omitted*: C.66/1523/m.31d. (Lewkenor was appointed on 11 March). (31)

1600: 19 December
Commission renewed to *add* H. ap Evan Lloyd: Index 4208/f.100.

1600: 22 December
Commission renewed to *add* Griffith Nanney: Index 4208/f.100v.

1601: 14 May
Commission renewed to *add* W. David Lloyd of Peniarth: Index 4208/f.110.

1601: 25 September
*Egerton; *Buckhurst, Treasurer; *B. of Bangor; *Rich. Lewkenor, kt., Justice of Chester; *Leighton & *Broughton, Justices of Great Sessions; *H. Townshend; *p Th. Myddelton; *Edm. Meyrick, D.C.L.; *Edm. Price, Archdeacon of Merioneth; *J. Wynn; *W. Morris; *Hugh Hughes, Queen's attorney; *J. Owen; *Griffith Vaughan; Th. Vaughan; *Hugh Nanney; *Jas. Price; Ednyfed Griffith; *Hugh Owen; *J. Vaughan; Rob. ap Evan ap Morgan; *Rob. Lloyd; Math. Herbert; Maurice Lewis; H. ap Evan Lloyd; Griffith Nanney; W. David Lloyd of Peniarth; Humph. Hughes; J. Vaughan of Caergai: C.66/1549/m.32d. Commission renewed to *add* J. Vaughan of Caergai, and *omit* Cadwalader Pierce: Index 4208/f.122v. (30)

1602: 25 February
Commission renewed to *add* W., B. of St. Asaph: Index 4208/f.130.

1602: 1 March
Commission renewed to *add* J. Lloyd: Index 4208/f.130v.

1602: 5 June
Commission renewed to *add* Roland ap Elissa: Index 4208/f.135v.

1602: 2 July
Commission renewed to *add* Rob. Lewis: Index 4208/f.138.

1602: 25 July
General renewal of Welsh commissions to *add* Ed., Lord Zouch, President of the Council in the Marches of Wales: Index 4208/f.141.

1602: 27 August
*Egerton; *Buckhurst; *Ed., Lord Zouch, President of Council in the Marches of Wales; Bishops of *Bangor, *St. Asaph; *Lewkenor, Justice of Chester; *W. Leighton & *Rich. Barker, Justices of Great Sessions; *H. Townshend; *p Th. Myddelton; *Edm. Meyrick, D.C.L.; *Edm. Price,

Archdeacon of Merioneth; *J. Wynn; *W. Morris; *Hugh Hughes, Queen's attorney; *J. Owen; *Griffith Vaughan; Th. Vaughan; *Hugh Nanney; *Jas. Price; *J. Lloyd; Ednyfed Griffith; *Hugh Owen; Rob. ap Evan ap Morgan; *Rob. Lloyd; Math. Herbert; Maurice Lewis; H. ap Evan Lloyd; Griffith Nanney; W. David Lloyd of Peniarth; Humph. Hughes; J. Vaughan of Caergai; Roland ap Elissa; Rob. Lewis; Humph. Hughes of Maesypandy: C.66/1594/m.36d. Commission renewed to *add* Humph. Hughes of Maesypandy: Index 4208/f.142.   (35)

1603: (Acting)
As on 27 August 1602, except: Th. Needham, *added*: C.66/1620/m.12d.   (36)

1604: (Acting)
As in 1603, except: Edm. Meyrick, D.C.L.; Hugh Owen, *omitted*: C.66/1662/m.22d.   (34)

1605: (Acting)
As in 1604, except: Ed., Lord Zouch; J. Owen, *omitted*: C.66/1682/m.2d. (32)

1606: (Acting)
As in 1605: C.66/1698/m.30d.   (32)

1607: post 12 September
*Th. Egerton, Lord Ellesmere, Chancellor; *Th., Lord Buckhurst, E. of Dorset, Treasurer; *Ralph, Lord Eure, President of Council in the Marches of Wales (appointed on 12 September); Bishops of *Bangor, *St. Asaph; *Lewkenor, Justice of Chester; *Ed. Herne, kt. & *Rich. Barker, Justices of Great Sessions; *W. Morris, *H. Townshend, *p Th. Myddelton, *J. Wynn, kts.; *Jas. Price; *Edm. Price, Archdeacon of Merioneth; *Hugh Hughes, King's attorney in Merioneth; J. Wynn; *Griffith Vaughan; J. Price; Th. Vaughan; *Hugh Nanney; *Th. Needham; *J. Lloyd; *Humph. Hughes; Ednyfed Griffith; Rob. ap Evan ap Morgan; *Rob. Lloyd; Math. Herbert; H. ap Evan Lloyd; Griffith Nanney; W. David Lloyd of Peniarth; J. Vaughan of Caergai; *Roland ap Elissa; Rob. Lewis; Humph. Hughes of Maesypandy: C.66/1748/m.31d.   (34)

1608-9: (Acting)
As in 1607, except: *E. of Salisbury, Treasurer; *E. of Northampton, Keeper of Privy Seal; W. Lewis Anwyl, *added*. E. of Dorset, *omitted*: C.66/1786/m.31d.   (36)

1610: (Acting)
As in 1608-9, except: *Lewis Prowde, Justice of Great Sessions; Simon Thelwall, *added*. Ed. Herne; Hugh Hughes; Griffith Nanney; Humph. Hughes of Maesypandy, *omitted*: C.66/1822/m.27d.   (34)

1611: (Acting)
As in 1610, except: Griffith Nanney; Humph. Hughes of Maesypandy, *added*: C.66/1897/m.19d. (These two justices may have been omitted in error from the 1610 enrolment of the commission).   (36)

1612: (Acting)

*Ellesmere; *E. of Salisbury, Treasurer; *E. of Northampton, Keeper of Privy Seal; *Eure, President of Council in the Marches of Wales; Bishops of *Bangor, *St. Asaph; *Lewkenor, Justice of Chester; *Rich. Barker & *Lewis Prowde, Justices of Great Sessions; *J. Wynn, kt. & Bt.; *W. Morris, *H. Townshend, *p Th. Myddelton, *Jas. Price, kts.; *Edm. Price, Archdeacon of Merioneth; J. Wynn; *Griffith Vaughan; J. Price; Th. Vaughan; *Hugh Nanney; *Th. Needham; Simon Thelwall; *J. Lloyd of Rhiwedog; *Humph. Hughes; W. Lewis Anwyl; Ednyfed Griffith; Rob. ap Evan ap Morgan; *Rob. Lloyd; Math. Herbert; H. ap Evan Lloyd; W. David Lloyd of Peniarth; J. Vaughan of Caergai; *Roland ap Elissa; Rob. Lewis: C.66/1898/m.28d. (35)

1614: post 11 July

As in 1612, except: *E. of Suffolk, Treasurer (appointed on 11 July); *W. Salisbury; *J. Lloyd of Faenol; *Piers Lloyd; J. Vaughan of Caethle, *added*. E. of Salisbury; E. of Northampton; J. Price; Th. Needham; Ednyfed Griffith; Math. Herbert; H. ap Evan Lloyd; J. Vaughan of Caergai (Sheriff, 1613–14); Roland ap Elissa, *omitted*: C.66/1988/m.28d. (31)

1615: (Acting)

As in 1614: C.66/2047/m.21d. (31)

1615: 8 July

Commission renewed to *add* Th. Chamberlain, Justice of Great Sessions: Index 4211/f.7v.

1616: 19 February

*Ellesmere; *E. of Suffolk, Treasurer; *E. of Worcester, Keeper of Privy Seal; *Eure, President of Council in the Marches of Wales; *B. of Bangor; *B. of St. Asaph; *Lewkenor, Justice of Chester; *Th. Chamberlain, serjeant at law & *Lewis Prowde, Justices of Great Sessions; *J. Wynn, kt. & Bt.; *W. Morris, *H. Townshend, *p Th. Myddelton, *Jas. Price, kts.; *Edm. Price, Archdeacon of Merioneth; J. Wynn; *W. Salisbury; *Griffith Vaughan; Th. Vaughan; *Hugh Nanney; *Piers Lloyd; Simon Thelwall; *J. Lloyd; J. Lloyd of Rhiwedog; *Humph. Hughes; W. Lewis Anwyl; Rob. ap Evan ap Morgan; *Rob. Lloyd; W. David Lloyd of Peniarth; J. Vaughan of Caethle; Rob. Lewis; Owen Vaughan; Lewis Gwynn: C.66/2076/m.24d. Commission renewed to *add* Owen Vaughan; Lewis Gwynn: Index 4211/f.16v. (33)

1616: 26 July

The commission was probably renewed on this date to *add* Francis Eure, Justice of Great Sessions. The Anglesey commission was renewed for this purpose on 26 July and a new commission would therefore be required for Merioneth too: Index 4211/f.24v.

1617: 30 January

Commission renewed to *add* Lewis, B. of Bangor: Index 4211/f.32v.

1617: 19 March
Commission renewed to *add* Francis Bacon, kt., Keeper of Great Seal; Th., Lord Gerard, President of Council in the Marches of Wales; W. Vaughan: Index 4211/ff.37v., 38.

1617: 16 June
Commission renewed to *restore* Piers Lloyd: Index 4211/f.43v.

1617: 30 June
Commission renewed to appoint W. Salisbury as *custos rotulorum*: Index 4211/f.43v.

1617: 14 July
Commission renewed to *add* Peter Meyrick: Index 4211/f.46.

1617: post 24 November
*Francis Bacon, kt., Keeper of Great Seal; *Suffolk; *Worcester; *D. of Lennox, Steward; *W., Lord Compton, President of Council in the Marches of Wales (appointed on 24 November); Bishops of *Bangor, *St. Asaph; *Th. Chamberlain, kt., Justice of Chester; *Francis Eure, kt. & *J. Jeffreys, Justices of Great Sessions; *J. Wynn, kt. & Bt.; *W. Morris, *H. Townshend, *Th. Myddelton, *Jas. Price, kts.; *Edm. Price, Archdeacon of Merioneth; *p W. Salisbury; W. Vaughan; Th. Vaughan; *Hugh Nanney; *Piers Lloyd; Simon Thelwall; *J. Lloyd; J. Lloyd of Rhiwedog; *Humph. Hughes; W. Lewis Anwyl; Rob. ap Evan ap Morgan; *Rob. Lloyd; W. David Lloyd of Peniarth; Lewis Gwynn; J. Vaughan of Caergai; J. Vaughan of Caethle; Rob. Lewis; Peter Meyrick: C.66/2147/m.23d.   (34)

1618: 18 February
As in 1617, except: *Rob. Vaughan *added*. E. of Suffolk; W. Vaughan; Th. Vaughan; Piers Lloyd, *omitted*: C.66/2174/m.19d. Commission renewed to *add* Rob. Vaughan: Index 4211/f.58. (31)

1620: 4 November
General renewal of Welsh commissions to *add* Jas. Whitlock, kt., Justice of Chester: Index 4211/f.114.

1621: 26 February
*Francis Bacon, kt., Viscount St. Alban, Chancellor; *H., Viscount Mandeville, Treasurer; *Worcester; *Lennox; *E. of Northampton, President of Council in the Marches of Wales; Bishops of *St. Asaph, *Bangor; *Jas. Whitlock, kt., Justice of Chester; *J. Jeffreys, Justice of Great Sessions; *J. Wynn, kt. & Bt.; *W. Morris, *H. Townshend, *Th. Myddelton, *Jas. Price, kts.; *Edm. Price, Archdeacon of Merioneth; *p W. Salisbury; *Rob. Vaughan; W. Vaughan; *Hugh Nanney; Simon Thelwall; *J. Lloyd; *J. Lloyd of Rhiwedog; W. Lewis Anwyl; *Rob. Lloyd; Lewis Gwynn; J. Vaughan of Caergai; J. Vaughan of Caethle; Rob. Lewis; Peter Meyrick: C.66/2234/m.43d. General renewal of Welsh commissions to *add* Viscount Mandeville: Index 4211/f.120. (Note that Francis Eure, kt., Justice of Great Sessions, was included in the commission

as originally issued on 26 February. Eure died on 1 May 1621 and was therefore omitted when the commission was enrolled. Compare with Anglesey and Merioneth commissions of 26 February 1621). (29)

1621: 29 June
Commission renewed to *add* Ed. Littleton, Justice of Great Sessions: Index 4211/f.126.

1621: post 29 September
As on 26 February 1621, except: *J., B. of Lincoln, Keeper of Great Seal; *Lionel Cranfield, Treasurer (appointed on 29 September); *Ed. Littleton, Justice of Great Sessions, *added*. Viscount St. Alban; B. of Bangor; H. Townshend, *omitted*: C.66/2259/m.25d. (The ex-Treasurer, Viscount Mandeville, remained on the commission). (29)

1622: 26 January
Commission renewed to *add* Francis Herbert: Index 4211/f.133v.

1622: 24 July
Commission renewed to *add* J. Price of Rhiwlas: Index 4211/f.142v.

1622: 25 November
*B. of Lincoln, Keeper of Great Seal; *Lionel Cranfield, E. of Middlesex, Treasurer; *Viscount Mandeville; *Worcester; *Lennox; *Northampton, President of Council in the Marches of Wales; Bishops of *St. Asaph, *Bangor; *Whitlock, Justice of Chester; *Peter Mutton, kt. & *Ed. Littleton, Justices of Great Sessions; *J. Wynn, kt. & Bt.; *Th. Myddelton, *Jas. Price, *Rob. Vaughan, kts.; *Edm. Price, Archdeacon of Merioneth; *p W. Salisbury; J. Price of Rhiwlas, W. Vaughan; *Hugh Nanney; Simon Thelwall; *J. Lloyd; *J. Lloyd of Rhiwedog; W. Lewis Anwyl; *Rob. Lloyd; Lewis Gwynn; J. Vaughan of Caergai; J. Vaughan of Caethle; Rob. Lewis; Peter Meyrick; Francis Herbert: C.66/2285/m.33d. Commission renewed to *add* Peter Mutton, Justice of Great Sessions: Index 4211/f.146. (31)

1623: 28 May
As on 25 November 1622, except: H. Price, *added*. D. of Lennox; B. of St. Asaph; Edm. Price; Hugh Nanney, *omitted*: C.66/2310/m.30d. Commission renewed to *add* H. Price: Index 4211/f.152v. (28)

1624: 12 April
Commission renewed to *add* J. Davies, D.D.: Index 4211/f.164.

1624: 25 June
Commission renewed to *add* Hugh Nanney: Index 4211/f.168v.

1625: 1 April
*Lincoln; *Jas., Lord Ley, Treasurer; *Mandeville; *Worcester; *Northampton, President of Council in the Marches of Wales; *B. of Bangor; *Th. Chamberlain, kt., Justice of Chester; *Mutton & *Littleton, Justices

of Great Sessions; *J. Wynn, kt. & Bt.; *Th. Myddelton, *Jas. Price, *J. Lloyd, serjeant at law, kts.; *J. Davies, D.D.; *Sampson Eure; *Rob. Brooke; *p W. Salisbury; *J. Price of Rhiwlas; *W. Vaughan; *Hugh Nanney; Simon Thelwall; *J. Lloyd of Rhiwedog; W. Lewis Anwyl; *Rob. Lloyd; Lewis Gwynn; J. Vaughan of Caergai; J. Vaughan of Caethle; Rob. Lewis; *Peter Meyrick; *Francis Herbert; H. Price: C.66/2367/m.29d. General renewal of Welsh commissions: Index 4211/f.180v. (31)

1625: 12 July
Commission renewed to *add* Owen Wynn: Index 4211/f.191.

1625: 22 December
As on 1 April 1625, except: *Th. Coventry, kt., Keeper of Great Seal; *Owen Wynn, *added*. B. of Lincoln; Th. Chamberlain, *omitted*: B.M., Harleian Ms. 1622/f.98v. General renewal of Welsh commissions to *add* Th. Coventry, Keeper of Great Seal: Index 4211/f.194v. (31)

1626: 20 March
As on 22 December 1626, except: *J. Bridgeman, kt., Justice of Chester, *added*. Jas. Price; Owen Wynn; Lewis Gwynn; J. Vaughan of Caergai; J. Vaughan of Caethle; Rob. Lewis; H. Price, *omitted*: E.163/18/12/f.99 & C.193/12/2/f.71v. Commission renewed to *add* J. Bridgeman, kt., Justice of Chester: Index 4211/f.199. (25)

1627: 15 March
*Th. Coventry, kt., Keeper of Great Seal; *Jas. Ley, E. of Marlborough, Treasurer; *E. of Manchester (Viscount Mandeville), President of Council; *E. of Worcester, Keeper of Privy Seal; *Northampton, President of Council in the Marches of Wales; *B. of Bangor; *J. Bridgeman, kt., Justice of Chester; *Mutton & *Littleton, Justices of Great Sessions; *J. Wynn, kt. & Bt.; *Th. Myddelton, *J. Lloyd, serjeant at law, kts.; *J. Davies, D.D.; *Sampson Eure; *Rob. Brooke; *p W. Salisbury; *J. Price of Rhiwlas; *W. Vaughan; *Hugh Nanney; Simon Thelwall; *J. Lloyd of Rhiwedog; W. Lewis Anwyl; *Rob. Lloyd; *Peter Meyrick; *Francis Herbert; *H. Price: N.L.W., Pennal Towers Mss. (unscheduled). Commission renewed to *restore* H. Price: Index 4211/f.220v. (26)

1627: 18 July
Commission renewed to *restore* Jas. Price, kt.: Index 4211/f.232.

1627: 14 December
Commission renewed to *restore* Lewis Gwynn: Index 4211/f.237.

1628: 1 March
Commission renewed to *add* Griffith Lloyd: Index 4211/f.240v.

1628: 8 July
As on 15 March 1627, except: *Jas. Price, kt.; *Timothy Turneur; Lewis Gwynn; *J. Vaughan of Caergai; *Griffith Lloyd, *added*. E. of Worcester; J. Wynn, kt. & Bt.; Rob. Brooke, *omitted*. C.66/2449/m.31d. Commission renewed to *add* J. Vaughan of Caergai: Index 4211/f.248v. (28)

1628: 1 August
Commission renewed to *add* Lewis Anwyl: Index 4211/f.253v.

1629: 12 February
As on 8 July 1628, except: *Rich., Lord Weston, Treasurer; *Ed., Viscount Conway, President of the Council; *E. of Pembroke; *Lewis Anwyl, *added*. E. of Marlborough; W. Salisbury, *omitted*: C.66/2495/m.27d. & C.66/2527/m.30d. Commission renewed to appoint Hugh Nanney as *custos rotulorum* and *omit* W. Salisbury: Index 4211/f.264. (30)

1630: 6 July
As on 12 February 1629, except: Edm. Meyrick *added*. Viscount Conway; E. of Pembroke; E. of Northampton; J. Price of Rhiwlas; J. Vaughan of Caergai; Peter Meyrick, *omitted*: C.66/2536/m.21d. Commission renewed to *add* Edm. Meyrick: Index 4212/p.38. (25)

1631: 20 July
*Coventry; *Rich., Lord Weston, Treasurer; *E. of Manchester, Keeper of Privy Seal; *B. of Bangor; *Bridgeman, Justice of Chester; *Mutton & *Littleton, Justices of Great Sessions; *Th. Myddelton, *Jas. Price, *Marmaduke Lloyd, *J. Lloyd, serjeant at law, kts.; *J. Davies, D.D.; *Sampson Eure; *Timothy Turneur; *W. Vaughan; *W. Lewis Anwyl; *p Hugh Nanney; Simon Thelwall; *Francis Herbert; *J. Lloyd of Rhiwlas; J. Lloyd of Rhiwedog; *Rob. Lloyd; *Lewis Anwyl; Lewis Gwynn; *H. Price; *Griffith Lloyd; Edm. Meyrick: C.66/2577/m.10d. & S.P.16/212/f.76. Commission renewed to *add* J. Lloyd of Rhiwlas: Index 4212/p.64. (27)

1632: 22 February
Commission renewed to *add* Humph. Jones, King's Receiver in North Wales: Index 4212/p.77. (The original of this commission survives in a damaged state as Nannau Ms. 320, U.C.N.W., Bangor).

1632: 20 June
Commission renewed to *add* Rich. Weston, Justice of Great Sessions: Index 4212/p.83.

1632: 2 December
Commission renewed to *add* J. Lewis: Index 4212/p.95.

1633: 16 March
As on 20 July 1631, except: *E. of Bridgewater, President of Council in the Marches of Wales; *Rich. Weston, Justice of Great Sessions; Humph. Jones, King's Receiver; J. Lewis; W. Wynn of Glynn, *added*. Lewis, B. of Bangor; Ed. Littleton; Th. Myddelton, kt.; J. Lloyd, kt.; Lewis Gwynn, *omitted*: C.66/2598/m.22d. & C.66/2623/m.24d. Commission renewed to *add* W. Wynn of Glynn: Index 4212/p.103. (27)

1634: 2 July
*Coventry; *Rich. Weston, E. of Portland, Treasurer; *Manchester; *E. of Bridgewater, President of Council in the Marches of Wales; *Bridgeman,

Justice of Chester; *Peter Mutton, kt. & *Timothy Turneur, Justices of Great Sessions; *Jas. Price, *Marmaduke Lloyd, kts.; *J. Davies, D.D.; *Sampson Eure; *W. Vaughan; *W. Lewis Anwyl; *p Hugh Nanney; Simon Thelwall; *Humph. Jones, King's Receiver in North Wales; *Francis Herbert; *J. Lloyd of Rhiwlas; *J. Lloyd of Rhiwedog; *Rob. Lloyd; *H. Price; *Lewis Anwyl; W. Wynn of Glynn; *J. Lewis; *Griffith Lloyd; Edm. Meyrick: C.193/13/2/f.83. Commission renewed to *add* Timothy Turneur, Justice of Great Sessions: Index 4212/p.141.   (26)

1636: 7 April
As on 2 July 1634, except: *B. of London, Treasurer, *added*. E. of Portland; W. Vaughan; Griffith Lloyd, *omitted*: S.P.16/405/f.81. Commission renewed to *omit* Griffith Lloyd: Index 4212/p.202.   (24)

1637: 30 March
Commission renewed to *restore* Griffith Lloyd: Index 4212/p.237.

1638: post 23 March
As on 7 April 1636, except: *Th. Milward, kt., Justice of Chester (appointed on 23 March); *Adam Littleton & *Rob. Brerewood, Justices of Great Sessions; *Griffith Lloyd, *added*. J. Bridgeman; Peter Mutton; Timothy Turneur, *omitted*: C.66/2761/m.16d.   (25)

1639: 26 November
Commission renewed to *add* Lewis Nanney: Index 4212/p.359.

1640: post 17 January
*J. Finch, kt., Keeper of Great Seal (appointed on 17 January); *B. of London, Treasurer; *Manchester; *Bridgewater, President of Council in the Marches of Wales; *Th. Milward, kt., Justice of Chester; *Adam Littleton & *Rob. Brerewood, Justices of Great Sessions; *Jas. Price, Marmaduke Lloyd, kts.; *J. Davies, D.D.; *Sampson Eure; *W. Morgan; *W. Lewis Anwyl; *Hugh Nanney; Simon Thelwall; *Humph. Jones, King's Receiver in North Wales; *Francis Herbert; *J. Lloyd of Rhiwlas; *J. Lloyd of Rhiwedol; *Rob. Lloyd; *H. Price; *Lewis Anwyl; *Lewis Nanney; *Griffith Lloyd; W. Wynn of Glynn; *J. Lewis; Edm. Meyrick: C.66/2858/m.20d.   (27)

1640: 25 July
Commission renewed to *add* Owen Griffith; Humph. Hughes: Index 4212/p.399.

1642: 10 February
Commission renewed to *add* W. Price: Index 4212/p.505.

1643: 22 February
Commission renewed to *add* Griffith Nanney; Rob. Wynn; J. Wynn; J. Morgan, and to *omit* Edm. Meyrick: Index 4210/p.4.

1643: 29 April
(Edward, Lord Littleton), Keeper of Great Seal; D. of Richmond & Lennox, Steward; E. of Arundel; E. of Bridgewater; Peter Wyche, kt., Household Controller; Ed. Nicholas, kt.; (Th. Milward, kt., Justice of Chester); Adam Littleton & Rob. Brerewood, Justices of Great Sessions; Sampson Eure; Jas. Price, Marmaduke Lloyd, Rich. Lloyd, kts.; Owen Griffith; W. ? ; J. Lloyd of Rhiwedog; Owen Salisbury; Rob. Anwyl; W. Wynn of Glynn; Edm. Meyrick; Griffith Lloyd; Humph. Hughes; J. Lewis;Rowland Vaughan; Griffith Nanney; J. Wynn; J. Morgan: Nannau Ms. 346, U.C.N.W., Bangor. Commission renewed to *add* Owen Salisbury; Rob. Anwyl; Edm. Meyrick; Rob. Wynn; J. Vaughan of Cefnbodig; Rowland Vaughan; J. Lloyd of Ceiswyn; Hugh Owen of Llanegryn: Index 4210/p.15. (Nannau Ms. 346 is an original commission of the peace. The document is however badly mutilated and some of the names of the justices are certainly missing. The names in brackets have been supplied by comparison with the list of justices acting in Denbigh in January 1644: Wales 4/24/3. It can be assumed that all eight men whom the Docquet Book entry gives as being added to the commission on 29 April were in fact present in the commission as issued). (27)

1643: 8 May
Commission renewed to *add* Rob. Corbet; Vincent Corbet: Index 4210/p.16.

1644: 29 April
Commission renewed to *add* Timothy Littleton, serjeant at law, Justice of Great Sessions: Index 4210/p.107.

1647: 11 March
Commission renewed (no details): Index 4213/p.79.

1647: 22 March
Commission renewed to *add* Rich. Keble & W. Littleton, Justices of Great Sessions: Index 4213/p.84.

1649: 30 March
Commission renewed (no details): Index 4213/p.147.

1649: 6 July
*W. Lenthall, Speaker of House of Commons; *Th., Lord Fairfax; *J. Bradshaw, President of Council; *Bulstrode Whitelock, *Rich. Keble, *J. Lisle, Commissioners of Great Seal; *E. of Pembroke and Montgomery; *E. of Denbigh; *H. Rolle, Chief Justice of Upper Bench; *Oliver St. John, Chief Justice of Court of Common Pleas; *J. Wilde, Chief Baron of Exchequer; *W. Littleton & *Ed. Bulstrode, Justices of Great Sessions; *Edm. Prideaux, Attorney-General; *Th. Myddelton, kt.; *Th. Mytton; *Owen Salisbury; *Rob. Anwyl; *J. Jones; *Ed. Meyrick; *Howel Vaughan; *Griffith Nanney; *J. Vaughan; *W. Wynn of Glynn; *Griffith Lloyd; *Lewis Lloyd; Rob. Wynn; *Lewis Owen; *Rob. Vaughan; J. Vaughan of Caergai; Lewis Gwynn of Bala; J. Lloyd of Carog; *Maurice Wynn; Maurice Lewis: C.193/13/3/f.78. Commission renewed to *add* Ed. Bulstrode, Justice of Great Sessions: Index 4213/p.162. (34)

1650: 25 July
*Lenthall; *Oliver Cromwell, Lord General; *Bradshaw; *Whitelock, *Keble & *Lisle; *Denbigh; *Rolle; *St. John; *Wilde; *Littleton & *Bulstrode, Justices of Great Sessions; *Prideaux; *Th. Myddelton, kt.; *Owen Wynn, Bt.; *Th. Mytton; *p Owen Salisbury; *Griffith Nanney; *J. Jones; *H. Wynn; *Rob. Anwyl; *Lewis Owen; *Rob. Vaughan; *W. Wynn; Lewis Lloyd; Howel Vaughan; *J. Lloyd; J. Vaughan; Griffith Lloyd: *Lists published by Th. Walkley* (1650), p.69. Commission renewed to *add* Owen Wynn, Bt.; H. Wynn; J. Lloyd of Maesypandy, and to *omit* Ed. Meyrick; Rob. Wynn; Lewis Gwynn of Bala; Maurice Wynn; Maurice Lewis: Index 4213/p.196. (29)

1653: 28 July
Commission renewed to *add* J. Lloyd of Maesypandy; J. Lloyd of Carog; J. Vaughan of Caergai; Rob. Owen of Dolserau; J. Price; Rob. Vaughan, and to *omit* E. of Denbigh; Th. Myddelton; Owen Wynn; H. Wynn; Lewis Owen of Maesypandy; J. Lloyd of Caergai: Index 4213/p.265.

1653: 13 October
Commission renewed according to a general list to *add* Ellis Hughes; Daniel Lloyd; Lewis Price; H. Williams, and to *omit* Rob. Anwyl and others (no details): Index 4213/p.271.

1654: 7 July
Commission renewed according to a general list: Index 4213/p.293. (The Merioneth commission is not actually recorded as being renewed on this date, but those for Anglesey and Caernarvonshire were renewed and it is likely that the same course was followed for Merioneth).

1656: 25 June
*Nathaniel Fiennes & *J. Lisle, Commissioners of the Great Seal; *Bulstrode Whitelock, kt., *Th. Widdrington. kt., *Ed. Montagu, *W. Sydenham, Commissioners of the Treasury; *J. Glynn, Chief Justice of Upper Bench; *W. Lenthall, Master of Rolls; *Oliver St. John, Chief Justice of Common Bench; *Ed. Bulstrode & *Evan Seys, serjeant at law, Justices of Great Sessions; *Edm. Prideaux, Attorney-General; *Major-General Jas. Berry; *J. Nicholas; *Rowland Dawkins; *p J. Jones; *Owen Salisbury; *Rob. Vaughan of Hengwrt; *Howel Vaughan of Gwengraig; *Lewis Owen of Peniarth; *Rob. Owen of Dolserau; *Maurice Wynn of Moelyglo; Owen Humphreys of Llwyngwril; Owen Lewis of Garthgynfor: C.193/13/5/f.129 & C.193/13/6/f.108. Commission renewed according to a general list: Index 4213/p.337. (24)

1658: 7 January
Commission renewed to *add* W. Vaughan of Corsygedol; J. Lloyd of Maesypandy; W. Vaughan of Caethle; Rich. Anwyl senior of Park; J. Vaughan of Cefnbodig; J. Wynn; Nathaniel Jones: Index 4213/p.382.

1658: 24 September
General renewal of Welsh commissions to *add* Rich. Cromwell, Lord Protector: Index 4213/p.405.

1659: 8 July
Commission renewed according to a general list: Index 4213/p.438.

1659: 5 October
Commission renewed to *add* W. Shepherd & Rich. Vaughan, Justices of Great Sessions: Index 4213/p.443.

1660: 3 March
Commission renewed according to a general list: Index 4213/p.453.

1660: 31 August
Commission renewed to *add* Th. Myddelton, kt., *custos rotulorum*: Index 4214/p.33.

1660: post 8 September
*Ed. Hyde, kt., Chancellor; *E. of Southampton, Treasurer (appointed on 8 September); *D. of Albemarle; *Marquess of Ormond, Steward; *E. of Lindsey, Great Chamberlain; *E. of Manchester, Household Chamberlain; *Ed., Lord Herbert; *Timothy Littleton, serjeant at law & *J. Griffith, Justices of Great Sessions; *Rich. Wynn, Bt.; *Th. Myddelton, Bt.; *p Th. Myddelton, kt.; *J. Carter, *J. Owen, kts.; *Rich. Wynn; *W. Price; *W. Vaughan; *W. Salisbury; *Maurice Wynn of Crogen; *Howel Vaughan; *J. Lloyd; *Edm. Meyrick; Lewis Owen; Lewis Lloyd; Rich. Anwyl; *Rob. Wynn of Glynn; Humph. Hughes; W. Vaughan of Caethle; J. Vaughan; Roland Vaughan; Griffith Lloyd; Maurice Williams; Ellis Edwards; J. Wynn; *Vincent Corbet; Howel Vaughan: C.220/9/4/f.109 & B.M., Egerton Ms. 2557/f.108.   (36)

1661: 9 April
Commission renewed to *add* J. Morgan: Index 4214/p.96.

1661: 8 November
As in 1660, except: *J., Lord Robartes, Keeper of Privy Seal; *E. of Carbery, President of Council in the Marches of Wales; J. Morgan, *added*: C.193/12/3/f.124. General renewal of Welsh commissions to *add* E. of Carbery, President of Council in the Marches of Wales: Index 4214/p.144.   (39)

1663: 22 July
*E. of Clarendon, Chancellor; *Southampton; *J., Lord Robartes, Keeper of Privy Seal; *Albemarle; *Ormond; *Lindsey; *Manchester; *E. of Carbery, President of Council in the Marches of Wales; *Ed., Lord Herbert; *Job Charlton, kt., serjeant at law, Justice of Chester; *Timothy Littleton, serjeant at law & *Th. Jones, Justices of Great Sessions; *Rich. Wynn, Bt.; *Th. Myddelton, *J. Owen, *J. Carter, kts.; *Rich. Wynn; *W. Price; *W. Vaughan; *W. Salisbury; *Maurice Wynn of Crogen; *Howel Griffith, King's attorney in Merioneth; *Howel Vaughan; *J. Lloyd; *Edm. Meyrick; Lewis Owen; Lewis Lloyd; Rich. Anwyl; *Rob. Wynn of Glynn; Humph. Hughes; W. Vaughan of Caethle; J. Vaughan; Roland Vaughan; Griffith Lloyd; Maurice Williams; Ellis Edwards; J. Wynn; *Vincent Corbet; J. Morgan; Howel Vaughan: C.66/3022/m.37d. Commission renewed to appoint J. Owen, kt., as *custos rotulorum*: Index 4213/p.210.   (40)

1670: 1 July
Commission renewed to *add* Kenrick Eyton, Justice of Great Sessions; J. Wynn, kt.; H. Wynn; Hugh Nanney; Roger Mostyn; Peter Meyrick: Index 4214/p.371.

1677: 24 November
Commission renewed to *add* Jenkin Vaughan: Index 4214/p.535.

1678: 25 March
Commission renewed to *add* J. Wynn, *custos rotulorum*; Ed. Vaughan; Rich. Mostyn; J. Lloyd of Aberllwyfein; Edm. Meyrick: Index 4214/p.542.

1678: 12 July
Commission renewed to *add* Roland Price: Index 4214/p.547.

1680: 1 April
*Prince Rupert; *Archbishop of Canterbury; *Lord Finch, Chancellor; *E. of Radnor, President of Privy Council; *E. of Anglesey, Keeper of Privy Seal; Dukes of *Albemarle, *Monmouth, *Newcastle, *Lauderdale, *Ormond; *Marquess of Winchester; *Marquess of Worcester, President of Council in the Marches of Wales; Earls of *Lindsey, *Arlington, *Salisbury, *Bridgewater, *Essex, *Sunderland, *Bath, *Halifax, *Carbery; *Viscount Fauconberg; *B. of London; *Laurence Hyde; *H. Coventry; *Francis North, kt., Chief Justice of Bench; *J. Ernley, kt., Chancellor of Exchequer; *Th. Chichley, kt., Chancellor of Duchy of Lancaster; *W. Temple, Bt.; *Leoline Jenkins; *Sidney Godolphin; *Kenrick Eyton & *Th. Walcott, Justices of Great Sessions; *p J. Wynn, kt. & Bt.; *Ed. Vaughan of Llwydiarth; *Ed. Jennings, King's attorney; *Lewis Meyrick, King's attorney in Wales; *Francis Manley; *W. Price; *Griffith Vaughan; *Owen Wynn of Glynn; *Rob. Wynn of Maes-y-neuadd; *J. Lloyd; *Nathaniel Jones; *Owen Anwyl; *Lewis Owen; *W. White; *Rich. Anwyl; *Humph. Hughes; *Jenkin Vaughan; *Rich. Mostyn; J. Wynn; J. Lloyd of Aberllwyfein; Edm. Meyrick; *Roland Price; W. Wynn: C.193/12/4/f.151. Commission renewed to *remove* recusants and to *add* others (no details): Index 4215/p.26. (In 1680 the *removal* of the Duke of Buckingham from the Merioneth commission was ordered by a warrant of 5 February and the *addition* of Griffith Vaughan, Owen Wynn of Glynn, Rob. Wynn of Maes-y-neuadd, Nathaniel Jones, Owen Anwyl and W. White was ordered by a warrant of 25 April: *H.M.C., Eleventh Report, Appendix*, Part 2, p.184. The names of all those added to the commission in 1680 are included in the commission identified above as that of 1 April 1680 and which is the only recorded commission to be issued for Merioneth in 1680. The explanation of this discrepancy may either be that there was a commission issued on or soon after 25 April of which no record has survived in the Docquet Book (Index 4215) or that the changes ordered on 25 April were incorporated in the commission of 1 April when it was inserted in the C.193 Entry Book. The order for the *addition* to the commission of Griffith Vaughan, Owen Wynn of Glynn, Rob. Wynn of Maes-y-neuadd, Nathaniel Jones and Owen Anwyl was given by the Privy Council on 17 April 1680, effect being given to the order by the warrant of 25 April: P.C.2/68/p.482). (56)

1682: 28 March
Commission renewed to *add* Rich. Hopton, Justice of Great Sessions:
Index 4215/p.64.

1682: 14 August
Commission renewed to *add* Rob. Owen, kt., and *omit* Roland Price:
Index 4215/p.69.

1684: 14 October
Commission renewed to *add* J. Edwards, Ll.D.: Index 4215/p.108.

1685: 3 April
Commission renewed to *add* J. Wynn, kt. & Bt., as *custos rotulorum*: Index
4215/p.125.

1685: 7 September (Acting)
Archbishop of Canterbury; Lord Guilford, Keeper of Great Seal; E. of
Rochester, Treasurer; Marquess of Halifax, President of Council; E. of
Clarendon, Keeper of Privy Seal; Dukes of Albemarle, Ormond; D. of
Beaufort, President of Council in the Marches of Wales; Marquesses of
Winchester, Worcester; Earls of Lindsey, Arlington, Bridgewater, Sunder-
land, Bath, Nottingham, Middleton, Carbery; Viscount Fauconberg;
B. of London; Sidney, Lord Godolphin; H. Coventry; J. Ernley, kt.,
Chancellor of Exchequer; Th. Chichley, kt., Chancellor of Duchy of
Lancaster; Ed. Seymour; Leoline Jenkins; Geo. Jeffreys, kt. & Bt., Chief
Justice of Pleas *coram Rege*; Rich. Hopton & Th. Powell, Justices of Great
Sessions; J. Wynn, kt. & Bt., *custos rotulorum*; Rob. Owen, kt.; Ed. Vaughan
of Llwydiarth; Ed. Jennings, King's attorney in Merioneth; Lewis Meyrick,
King's attorney in Wales; W. Price; Griffith Vaughan; Rob. Wynn of
Maes-y-Neuadd; J. Lloyd; Owen Anwyl; Lewis Owen; W. White; Jenkin
Vaughan; Rich. Mostyn; J. Lloyd of Aberllwyfein; Edm. Meyrick; Vincent
Corbet: Wales 4/310/3. (46)

1686: 17 December
Order by the Privy Council to *add* to the Merioneth commission Gabriel
Salisbury; Rob. Price; Owen Salisbury; Griffith Nanney; Oliver Thomas;
Rich. Owen; Ed. Owen; W. Pugh; J. Vaughan; Th. Price: P.C.2/71/p.378.

1687: 29 August
General renewal of Welsh commissions to add the clause of dispensation:
Index 4215/p.179.

1688: 14 April
Commission renewed to *add* Marquess of Powys as *custos rotulorum*: Index
4215/p.191.

1688: 6 October
General renewal of Welsh commissions: Index 4215/p.200.

Denbigh

1543: 12 March
*Th. Audley, kt., Chancellor; *D. of Norfolk, Treasurer; *D. of Suffolk, President of Council; *J. Russell, kt., Keeper of Privy Seal; *B. of Coventry & Lichfield, President of Council in the Marches of Wales; *B. of St. Asaph; Walter, Lord Ferrers; *Nich. Hare, Ed. Croft, Rice Mansel, *J. Vernon, *Roger Puleston, kts.; *J. Pakington; *Th. Holte; *David Brooke; *J. ap Rice; *Rich. Hassall; *p J. Salisbury senior; *J. Puleston senior; J. Puleston junior; *Walter Blount; Ellis Price, clerk; J. Edwards; *Ed. Almer; Griffith ap Evan; *W. Holcroft; *David ap Robert ap Rice; *J. ap Rice junior; Geoff. Bromfield. *Later additions to list*: *Th. Bromley, serjeant at law; *Adam Mytton; *J. Salisbury junior; Rob. Salisbury; Tudor ap Robert; J. Owen ap John; David Holland; Th. Williams; Cadwalader ap Morris; Hugh Dryhurst: C.193/12/1/f.44v. (29 names plus 10 corrections).

1553: 30 October (Acting)
B. of Winchester, Chancellor; Marquess of Winchester, Treasurer; E. of Bedford, Keeper of Privy Seal; E. of Arundel; E. of Pembroke, President of Council in the Marches of Wales; E. of Worcester; B. of St. Asaph; Lord Stafford; Rob. Townshend, kt.; David Brooke, Chief Baron of Exchequer; Th. Bromley, kt.; J. Pollard; J. Seyntlowe, Rice Mansel, Th. Jones, Walter Dennys, Ed. Carne, Roland Hill, J. Price, Adam Mytton, J. Salisbury, kts.; Griffith Leyson, Ll.D.; Reg. Corbet; J. Scudamore of Holm; Rich. Hassall; W. Sheldon; J. Throckmorton; Edm. Plowden; Rob. Puleston; J. Edwards; Tudor ap Robert; Fulk Lloyd; J. Owen; Cadwalader ap Morris; Ed. Almer; Geoff. Bromfield; J. Williams; J. Price: Wales 4/1/2. (38)

1555: (Acting)
J. Salisbury, Ed. Puleston, kts.; Ellis Price; Rob. Puleston; J. Edwards; Tudor ap Robert; Ed. Almer; Evan Lloyd of Yale; Geoff. Bromfield; J. Owen; Cadwalader ap Morris; J. Price; Th. Billot; Fulk Lloyd: S.P.11/5/f.59. (14)

1558–59: (Acting)
*Nich. Bacon, kt., Keeper of Great Seal; *Marquess of Winchester, Treasurer; *E. of Arundel, Steward; Bishops of *Bath & Wells, *St. Asaph, *Chester; *J. Throckmorton, Justice of Chester; *J. Vaughan, *Adam Mytton, *p J. Salisbury, *Ed. Puleston, kts.; *J. Scudamore of Holm; Chas. Fox; *J. Welsh; *Reg. Corbet; *W. Symonds; *W. Gerard; *Rich. Seaborne; *Ellis Price, Ll.D.; *Ed. Almer; *Tudor ap Robert; Evan Lloyd of Yale; *J. Price of Derwen; *Ralph Broughton; Fulk Lloyd; *J. Price of Eglwysegl: B.M., Lansdowne Ms. 1218/f.38v. (Except for the omission of the *ex officio* members of the commission, the same list appears in S.P.12/2/17/p.70). (26)

1559: 16 December (Acting)
Bacon; Winchester; Arundel; H. Sidney, kt., President of Council in the Marches of Wales; Bishops of Hereford, Bangor, Worcester, St. Davids, St. Asaph; Throckmorton, Justice of Chester; Nich. Arnold, Adam Mytton,

J. Salisbury, J. Vaughan, Ed. Puleston, kts.; Chas. Fox; J. Scudamore of Holm; Ellis Price, Ll.D.; Rich. Seaborne; Rich. Wye; W. Gerard; Geo. Bromley; Rich. Pates; —— Whitehead (the first name is destroyed); Ed. Almer; Tudor ap Robert; Rob. Puleston; Evan Lloyd of Yale; J. Price of Eglwysegl; J. Price of Derwen; J. Trevor of Trevalyn; Ralph Broughton; Fulk Lloyd; Th. Billot; Rob. Lloyd of Chirkland: Wales 4/1/3.   (35)

1561: 13 October (Acting)
*Bacon; *Winchester; *Arundel; *Sidney; Bishops of *Bangor, *St. Asaph; *Throckmorton, Justice of Chester; *p J. Salisbury, Ed. Puleston, kts.; *Ellis Price, Ll.D.; *Geo. Bromley; *Ed. Almer; Tudor ap Robert; Rob. Puleston; Evan Lloyd of Yale; *J. Price of Eglwysegl; *J. Price of Derwen; Ralph Broughton; Fulk Lloyd; Th. Billot; J. Trevor of Trevalyn: Wales 4/1/5. (Details of *quorum* supplied by B.M., Lansdowne Ms. 1218/f.86v. which contains a list of the justices in 1561 identical to the one above, except for the addition of *Ralph Leicester, kt., after Ed. Puleston).   (21)

1562: 13 June
*Bacon; *Winchester; *Arundel; *Sidney; Bishops of *Bangor, *St. Asaph; *Throckmorton, Justice of Chester; *p J. Salisbury, Ed. Puleston, *Ralph Leicester, kts.; *Ellis Price, Ll.D.; *Geo. Bromley; *Ed. Almer; Tudor ap Robert; Rob. Puleston; Evan Lloyd of Yale; *J. Price of Eglwysegl; *J. Price of Derwen; Ralph Broughton; Fulk Lloyd; *Th. Billot; J. Trevor of Trevalyn: C.66/985/m.41d.   (22)

1563: 2 August (Acting)
As on 13 June 1562, except: Reg. Corbet; W. Gerard; Chas. Fox; Rich. Wye; Rich. Seaborne; Rich. Smith; Hugh Evans, clerk; Rob. Lloyd of Chirkland, *added*. Ralph Leicester; Geo. Bromley, *omitted*: Wales 4/2/1. (28)

1564: (Acting)
As on 2 August 1563, except: *Rich. Pates, *added*: C.66/998/m.10d.   (29)

1565: 26 February (Acting)
As in 1564, except: Simon Thelwall, *added*: Wales 4/2/2.   (30)

1565: 10 September (Acting)
As on 26 February 1565, except: W. Glaseor; J. Salisbury of Rug; J. Edwards; Th. Morris; Hugh ap Hugh; Jas. Eyton, *added*. Tudor ap Robert, *omitted*: Wales 4/2/3.   (35)

1566: 20 May (Acting)
Bacon; Winchester; Arundel; Sidney, President of Council in the Marches of Wales; B. of St. Asaph; Throckmorton, Justice of Chester; Reg. Corbet, Justice *coram Regina*; J. Salisbury, Ed. Puleston, kts.; W. Symonds; Chas. Fox; Rich. Wye; Ellis Price, Ll.D.; Rich. Seaborne; Rich. Pates; W. Glaseor; J. Price of Eglwysegl; Rich. Smith; Hugh Evans, clerk; Ed. Almer; Rob. Puleston; Simon Thelwall; J. Salisbury of Rug; Evan Lloyd of Yale;

J. Edwards; J. Price of Derwen; Th. Morris; Fulk Lloyd; Th. Billot; J. Trevor of Trevalyn; Hugh ap Hugh; Rob. Lloyd of Chirk; Jas. Eyton: Wales 4/2/4. (33)

1567: 12 May (Acting)
As on 20 May 1566, except: B. of Bangor; W. Gerard; Maurice Wynn, *added*. Reg. Corbet; Ed. Puleston; W. Symonds; Fulk Lloyd, *omitted*: Wales 4/2/6. (32)

1568: 9 February (Acting)
As on 12 May 1567, except: E. of Pembroke, Steward; J. Gwynn, Ll.D.; Peter Owen; W. Holland, *added*. Evan Lloyd of Yale (Sheriff, 1567-8), *omitted*: Wales 4/2/7. (35)

1569: 28 March (Acting)
Bacon; Winchester; E. of Pembroke, Steward; Earls of Arundel, Leicester; Sidney, President of Council in the Marches of Wales; Bishops of St. Asaph, Bangor; Throckmorton, Justice of Chester; J. Salisbury, kt.; W. Gerard; Chas. Fox; Rich. Wye; J. Gwynn, Ll.D.; Rich. Seaborne; Rich. Pates; W. Glaseor; J. Price of Eglwysegl; Rich. Smith; Hugh Evans, clerk; Maurice Wynn; Ed. Almer; Rob. Puleston; Simon Thelwall; J. Salisbury of Rug; Evan Lloyd of Yale; J. Edwards; J. Price of Derwen; Th. Billot; J. Trevor of Trevalyn; Hugh ap Hugh; Rob. Lloyd of Chirk; Peter Owen; J. Rogers; Hugh Puleston; W. Holland; Jas. Eyton: Wales 4/3/1. (37)

1571: 7 May (Acting)
As on 28 March 1569, except: Hugh Cholmondeley, kt., Vice-President of Council in the Marches of Wales; Ellis Price, Ll.D.; Fulk Lloyd; Th. Morris; Owen Brereton, *added*. Rich. Seaborne; J. Salisbury of Rug, *omitted*: Wales 4/3/3. (40)

1571: 15 October (Acting)
As on 7 May 1571, except: E. of Pembroke; Rich. Wye; Rich. Smith, *omitted*: Wales 4/3/5. (37)

1572: 11 February (Acting)
*Bacon; *Winchester; *p E. of Leicester; *Sidney, President of Council in the Marches of Wales; Bishops of *St. Asaph, *Bangor; *Hugh Cholmondeley, kt., Vice-President of Council in the Marches of Wales; Throckmorton, Justice of Chester and of Great Sessions; *J. Salisbury, kt.; *W. Gerard; *Chas. Fox; *Ellis Price, Ll.D.; *J. Gwynn, Ll.D.; *Rich. Seaborne; *Rich. Pates; *W. Glaseor; *Ed. Davies; J. Salisbury of Rug; *Rob. Puleston; *Evan Lloyd; J. Edwards; *Fulk Lloyd; Hugh ap Hugh; Rob. Lloyd of Chirk; Th. Morris; Th. Lloyd; J. Matthew (these last two are described as Aldermen & Justices of the town of Denbigh): Wales 4/3/4. (Details of the quorum are taken from two lists of 1573-4: S.P.12/93/ part 2/f.34 & B.M., Egerton Ms. 2345/f.44). (27)

1572: 15 September (Acting)
As on 11 February 1572, except: W., Lord Burghley, Treasurer; Lord Howard of Effingham, Keeper of Privy Seal; Maurice Wynn; J. Trevor;

W. Almer; Owen Brereton, *added*. Marquess of Winchester; J. Salisbury of Rug; Th. Lloyd; J. Matthew; Rob. Lloyd of Chirk, *omitted*: Wales 4/3/6. (28)

1574: 22 March (Acting)
As on 15 September 1572, except: Hugh Evans, Dean of St. Asaph; J. Price of Derwen, *added*. Lord Howard, *omitted*: Wales 4/4/1. (29)

1574: 16 August (Acting)
As on 22 March 1574, except: J. Price of Eglwysegl; Simon Thelwall; Ed. Hughes; Peter Owen; W. Holland; Ed. Jones, *added*. J. Trevor, *omitted*: Wales 4/4/2. (34)

1575: 11 July (Acting)
As on 16 August 1574, except: J. Gwynn, Ll.D., *omitted*: Wales 4/4/3. (33)

1575: (Acting)
*Bacon; *Burghley; *p E. of Leicester; *Sidney, President of Council in the Marches of Wales: Bishops of *Bangor, *St. Asaph; (*Hugh Cholmondeley, kt., Vice-President of Council in the Marches of Wales: omitted from this list but included in Great Sessions lists (Wales 4) of the same year); *Throckmorton, Justice of Chester & Great Sessions; *J. Salisbury, kt.; *W. Gerard; *Chas. Fox; *Ellis Price, Ll.D.; *Rich. Seaborne; *Rich. Pates; *W. Glaseor; *J. Price of Eglwysegl; *Hugh Evans, Dean of St. Asaph; *Ed. Davies; *Maurice Wynn; *Rob. Puleston; *Simon Thelwall; *Evan Lloyd; *Fulk Lloyd; J. Edwards; *Ed. Hughes; *W. Almer; *Owen Brereton; *Peter Owen; J. Price of Derwen; *Th. Morris; W. Holland; Hugh ap Hugh; Ed. Jones: S.P.12/106/part 2/f.7. (32 names (33 names if Cholmondeley is included)).

1576: 13 August (Acting)
As on 11 July 1575, except: Ed. Jones (Sheriff, 1575–6), *omitted*: Wales 4/4/5. (32)

1576: 22 October (Acting)
As on 13 August 1576: Wales 4/4/6. (32)

1577: 5 August (Acting)
As on 22 October 1576, except: Lewis Lloyd, *added*: Wales 4/5/1. (33)

1579: 23 February (Acting)
*Bacon; *Burghley; *Sidney, President of Council in the Marches of Wales; *B. of Worcester, Vice-President of Council in the Marches of Wales; *p E. of Leicester; Earls of *Worcester, *Pembroke; Bishops of *Hereford, *Bangor, *St. Davids, *St. Asaph; *Jas. Croft, kt., Household Controller; *Throckmorton, Justice of Chester & of Great Sessions; *J. Perrot, *Nich. Arnold, *Hugh Cholmondeley, *J. Littleton, *J. Huband, kts.; *David Lewis, Ll.D., Judge of the Court of Admiralty; *Geo. Bromley, Attorney of Duchy of Lancaster; *W. Gerard; *W. Aubrey; *Chas. Fox; *W. Glaseor; *Ellis Price, Ll.D.; *Ed. Leighton; *Rich. Pates; *Ralph Barton;

*Jerome Corbet; *J. Puckering; *Fabian Phillips; *H. Townshend;
*W. Leighton; *J. Price of Eglwysegl; *Simon Thelwall; *Evan Lloyd of
Yale; *J. Edwards; *Rob. Puleston; J. Salisbury of Rug; *W. Almer;
Fulk Lloyd; Ed. Hughes; Owen Brereton; *Ed. Jones; Geoff. Holland:
Wales 4/5/3. (Details of the quorum are taken from two lists of 1578–79:
Hatfield House Ms. 223.7 & S.P.12/145/f.53v.).   (45)

1579: 14 September (Acting)
As on 23 February 1579, except: Th. Bromley, kt., Chancellor; J. Price;
Roger Puleston; Th. Powell; Peter Owen, *added*. Bacon; J. Edwards,
omitted: Wales 4/5/4.   (48)

1580: 16 May (Acting)
As on 14 September 1579, except: J. Price of Derwen; J. Edwards, *added*.
Ed. Leighton, *omitted*: Wales 4/5/5.   (49)

1581: 17 April (Acting)
As on 16 May 1580,: Wales 4/6/2.   (49)

1581: 2 October (Acting)
Th. Bromley, kt., Chancellor; Burghley; H. Sidney, kt., President of Council
in the Marches of Wales; B. of Worcester, Vice-President of Council in the
Marches of Wales; Earls of Leicester, Worcester, Pembroke; Bishops of
Hereford, Bangor, St. Davids, St. Asaph; Croft, Household Controller;
Geo. Bromley, kt. & H. Townshend, Justices of Chester & of Great
Sessions; J. Perrot, Hugh Cholmondeley, J. Littleton, J. Huband, W.
Gerard, kts.; J. Puckering, serjeant at law; David Lewis, Ll.D.; W. Aubrey,
Ll.D.; Chas. Fox; W. Glaseor, Ellis Price, Ll.D.; Rich. Pates; Ralph Barton;
Jerome Corbet; Fabian Phillips; W. Leighton; J. Price; J. Price of
Eglwysegl; J. Salisbury; Simon Thelwall; Evan Lloyd of Yale; J. Edwards;
Rob. Puleston; Th. Morris; Ed. Hughes; Peter Owen; Fulk Lloyd; W.
Wynn; Th. Powell; J. Price; Roger Puleston; W. Almer; Geoff. Holland:
Wales 4/6/1.   (47)

1581: 20 November (Acting)
Ellis Price, Ll.D.; Fulk Lloyd; W. Wynn; Peter Owen; Geoff. Holland;
Simon Thelwall; J. Price of Derwen; Th. Morris; Evan Lloyd of Yale;
J. Price of Eglwysegl; J. Edwards; Roger Puleston; Rob. Puleston; Owen
Brereton; W. Almer; Th. Powell; Ed. Hughes: Bodleian, Bodley Ms.
904/f.207. (This list omits all the *ex officio* members of the commission and
also gives the names in an order different from that in the Wales 4 lists).   (17)

1583: 8 July (Acting)
As on 2 October 1581, except: Owen Brereton; Ed. Thelwall; Rob.
Turbridge, *added*. B. of St. Davids; W. Gerard; J. Salisbury, *omitted*:
Wales 4/6/3.   (47)

1584: 18 May (Acting)
Bromley; Burghley; Sidney, President of Council in the Marches of Wales;
Earls of Leicester, Worcester, Pembroke; Bishops of Hereford, Bangor,

St. Asaph; Croft; Bromley & Townshend, Justices of Chester & of Great Sessions; J. Perrot, Hugh Cholmondeley, J. Littleton, kts.; David Lewis, Ll.D.; J. Puckering, serjeant at law; W. Aubrey, Ll.D.; Chas. Fox; W. Glaseor; Ellis Price, Ll.D.; Rich. Pates; Ralph Barton; Jerome Corbet; Fabian Phillips; W. Leighton; J. Price; Simon Thelwall; Roger Puleston; Owen Brereton; W. Almer; Evan Lloyd of Yale; Rob. Puleston; J. Price of Eglwysegl; Ed. Hughes; Fulk Lloyd; W. Wynn; Ed. Thelwall; Rob. Turbridge; Geoff. Holland: Wales 4/6/5. (40)

1586: 26 September (Acting)
*Bromley; *Burghley; *p E. of Leicester; Earls of *Worcester, *Pembroke; Bishops of *St. Asaph, *Hereford, *Bangor; *Croft, *Bromley & *Townshend, Justices of Chester & of Great Sessions; *J. Perrot, *Hugh Cholmondeley, *J. Littleton, kts.; *J. Puckering, serjeant at law; *W. Aubrey; *Chas. Fox; *Ellis Price, Ll.D.; *Rich. Pates; *Ralph Barton; *Jerome Corbet; *Fabian Phillips; *W. Leighton; *W. Glaseor; *Roger Puleston; *Owen Brereton; *W. Almer; *Evan Lloyd of Yale; *J. Price of Eglwysegl; *Ed. Hughes; *Peter Owen; Fulk Lloyd; Ed. Thelwall; Rob. Turbridge: Wales 4/7/1. (Details of the quorum are taken from a list of 1584: E.163/14/8/f.51v). (34)

1587: 8 May (Acting)
As on 26 September 1586, except: W. Wynn, added. Th. Bromley; Roger Puleston; W. Almer (Sheriff, 1586–7); Evan Lloyd, omitted: Wales 4/7/3. (31)

1588: 29 April (Acting)
As on 8 May 1587, except: Christopher Hatton, kt., Chancellor; Roger Puleston; David Powell, D.D.; W. Almer, added. B. of Hereford; B. of Bangor; Ralph Barton; W. Glaseor; W. Wynn; Owen Brereton (Sheriff, 1587–8); Peter Owen, omitted: Wales 4/7/4. (28)

1588: 19 August (Acting)
As on 29 April 1588, except: Evan Lloyd; J. Edwards, added: Wales 4/7/5. (30)

1589: 15 September (Acting)
As on 19 August 1588, except: E. of Warwick; J. Salisbury; Rob. Salisbury; Owen Brereton; J. Lloyd; Th. Powell; W. Wynn; Th. Salisbury; H. ap Evan Lloyd, added. E. of Leicester; E. of Worcester; Geo. Bromley; Evan Lloyd; Rich. Pates, omitted: Wales 4/8/1. (34)

1590: 19 October (Acting)
*Hatton, Chancellor; *Burghley, Treasurer; *E. of Pembroke, President of Council in the Marches of Wales; *B. of St. Asaph; *J. Perrot, kt.; *Rich. Shuttleworth, kt. & *H. Townshend, Justices of Chester & of Great Sessions; *Hugh Cholmondeley, *J. Littleton, kts.; *J. Puckering, serjeant at law; *p Th. Egerton, Solicitor-General; *W. Aubrey, Ll.D.; *Chas. Fox; *Ellis Price, Ll.D.; *Jerome Corbet; *Fabian Phillips; *W. Leighton; *J. Salisbury; *Roger Puleston; *Rob. Salisbury; *Owen Brereton; *David

Powell, D.D.; *J. Edwards; *W. Almer; J. Lloyd; *J. Price of Eglwysegl; Th. Powell; *Ed. Hughes; Fulk Lloyd; W. Wynn; *Th. Salisbury; Rob. Turbridge; H. ap Evan Lloyd: Wales 4/8/3. (Details of the quorum are taken from a list of 1590–91: Hatfield House Ms. 278/f.58). (33)

1591: 26 April (Acting)
As on 19 October 1590, except:Ed.Thelwall; Peter Salisbury; Th. Wynn ap Richard, *added*. J. Littleton; Th. Powell (Sheriff, 1590–1), *omitted*: Wales 4/8/4. (34)

1591: 18 October (Acting)
As on 26 April 1591: Wales 4/8/5. (34)

1592: 10 April (Acting)
As on 18 October 1591, except: Th. Powell; Hugh Beeston; Th. Price, *added*. Christopher Hatton; J. Perrot; Chas. Fox; Fulk Lloyd (Sheriff, 1591–2), *omitted*: Wales 4/9/1. (33)

1594: 15 July
*J. Puckering, kt., Keeper of Great Seal; *Burghley; *Pembroke, President of Council in the Marches of Wales; Bishops of *St. Asaph, Chester; *p Th. Egerton, kt.; *Shuttleworth & *Townshend, Justices of Chester & of Great Sessions; *Hugh Cholmondeley, *Rob. Salisbury, kts.; *W. Aubrey; *Ellis Price, Ll.D.; *Jerome Corbet; *Fabian Phillips; *W. Leighton; *Roger Puleston; *Owen Brereton; *David Powell, D.D.; *J. Edwards; *Ed. Thelwall; Th. Myddelton; *J. Lloyd; W. Wynn; *J. Price of Eglwysegl; *Th. Powell; Fulk Lloyd; *W. Wynn; *J. Lloyd of St. Asaph; Rich. Trevor; *Hugh Beeston; Rich. Leighton; Th. Price; Rob. Turbridge; H. ap Evan Lloyd; *Peter Salisbury; Th. Wynn ap Richard; Rich. Evans: C.66/1421/m.15d. (37)

1594: 14 October (Acting)
As on 15 July 1594, except: W. Wynn, *omitted*: Wales 4/9/4. (36)

1595: 21 July (Acting)
As on 14 October 1594, except: J. Salisbury; Th. Salisbury, *added*. B. of Chester; Ellis Price; Owen Brereton; Th. Wynn ap Richard (Sheriff, 1594–5), *omitted*: Wales 4/10/1. (34)

1595: 15 August
General renewal of Welsh commissions: Index 4208/f.4v.

1595: 19 August
Commission renewed to *add* Peter Salisbury: Index 4208/f.4v. (Peter Salisbury was a member of the commission on 21 July 1595. His name may have been omitted in error in the renewal of the commission on 15 August).

1596: 12 February
As on 21 July 1595, except: Th. Wynn ap Richard, *added*. W. Aubrey; J. Edwards; J. Price of Eglwysegl; J. Lloyd of St. Asaph; Rich. Evans, *omitted*: C.66/1435/m.20d. Commission renewed to *restore* Th. Wynn ap Richard, late Sheriff of Denbigh: Index 4208/f.11. (30)

1596: 3 May (Acting)
As on 12 February 1596: Wales 4/10/2.   (30)

1596: 27 June
Commission renewed to record appointment of Roger Puleston as *custos rotulorum*: Index 4208/f.16v.

1596: 27 August
Commission renewed to *add* W. Penrhyn: Index 4208/f.20.

1596: 24 September
*Th. Egerton, kt., Keeper of Great Seal; *Burghley; *Pembroke, President of Council in the Marches of Wales; *B. of St. Asaph; *Shuttleworth & *Townshend, Justices of Chester & of Great Sessions; *Hugh Cholmondeley, *Rob. Salisbury, kts.; *Jerome Corbet; *Fabian Phillips; *W. Leighton; *J. Salisbury; *p Roger Puleston; *David Powell, D.D.; *Ed. Thelwall; Th. Myddelton; *J. Lloyd; *Th. Powell; Fulk Lloyd; *W. Wynn; *Th. Salisbury; *J. Lloyd of Faenol; Rich. Trevor; *Hugh Beeston; Rich. Leighton; Th. Price; Rob. Turbridge; H. ap Evan Lloyd; *Peter Salisbury; *Th. Wynn ap Richard; *W. Penrhyn: C.66/1468/m.16d. Commission renewed to *add* J. Lloyd of Faenol: Index 4208/f.20v.   (31)

1597: 3 March
Commission renewed to *add* David Holland: Index 4208/f.29v.

1597: 17 March
As on 24 September 1596, except: *David Holland; *Ed. Brereton, *added*. Hugh Cholmondeley; Fabian Phillips; Th. Powell; Fulk Lloyd, *omitted*: C.66/1468/m.31d. Commission renewed to *add* Ed. Brereton: Index 4208/f.30v.   (29)

1597: 24 October (Acting)
As on 17 March 1597, except: Th. Powell; Fulk Lloyd, *added*. Rob. Salisbury, (Sheriff, 1596–7), *omitted*: Wales 4/10/5.   (30)

1598: 22 April
Commission renewed to *add* Th. Egerton junior, kt.: Index 4208/f.48.

1598: 14 October
As on 24 October 1597, except: *Rob. Salisbury, kt.; *Th. Egerton junior, kt.; *J. Wynn of Gwydir, *added*. W., Lord Burghley, *omitted*: C.66/1482/m.17d. Commission renewed to *add* J. Wynn of Gwydir: Index 4208/f.56v. (32)

1599: 19 March
Commission renewed to *add* Owen Vaughan: Index 4208/f.66v.

1599: 20 April
Commission renewed to *add* W. Myddelton: Index 4208/f.68.

1599: 11 July
*Egerton; *Th., Lord Buckhurst, Treasurer; *Pembroke, President of Council in the Marches of Wales; Bishops of *Chester, *St. Asaph; *Shuttleworth & *Townshend, Justices of Chester & of Great Sessions; *Rob. Salisbury, *Rich. Trevor, kts.; *Rich. Parry, Dean of Bangor; *W. Leighton; *J. Salisbury; *p Roger Puleston; *J. Wynn of Gwydir; *David Powell, D.D.; Owen Vaughan; *Ed. Thelwall; Th. Myddelton; *J. Lloyd; *Th. Powell; *W. Wynn; *Th. Salisbury; *David Holland; *J. Lloyd of Faenol; *Hugh Beeston; Rich. Leighton; Th. Price; Rob. Turbridge; H. ap Evan Lloyd; *Peter Salisbury; *Th. Wynn ap Richard; *W. Penrhyn; W. Myddelton: C.66/1493/m.27d. Commission renewed to *add* B. of Chester: Index 4208/f.74.   (33)

1599: 15 October (Acting)
As on 11 July 1599, except: Jerome Corbet, *added*. Lord Buckhurst; B. of Chester; Rich. Parry, Dean of Bangor (these first three omissions are probably errors); Rob. Salisbury; David Powell, *omitted*: Wales 4/11/3.   (29)

1600: 22 January
Commission renewed to *add* Ed. Lloyd of Llysfeisir: Index 4208/f.82.

1600: 18 March
Commission renewed to *add* Rich. Lewkenor, kt., Justice of Chester & of Great Sessions; Hugh Conway of Bryneurin: Index 4208/f.84.

1600: 3 June
Commission renewed to *add* David Yale, Ll.D.: Index 4208/f.89.

1600: 7 July (Acting)
As on 15 October 1599, except: Lord Buckhurst, Treasurer; B. of Chester; Rich. Lewkenor, kt., Justice of Chester; Rich. Parry, Dean of Bangor; David Yale, Ll.D.; Ed. Lloyd of Llysfeisir; Hugh Conway of Bryneurin, *added*. Rich. Shuttleworth; Jerome Corbet; J. Salisbury; Th. Wynn ap Richard; W. Myddelton, *omitted*: Wales 4/11/4.   (31)

1600: 19 August
As on 7 July 1600, except: *Th. Wynn ap Richard; W. Myddelton, *added* (these two were probably omitted in error from the 7 July list). Ed. Thelwall, *omitted*: C.66/1523/m.29d. Commission renewed to *omit* Ed. Thelwall: Index 4208/f.95v.   (32)

1601: 2 September
Commission renewed to *add* J. Salisbury, kt.; Th. Trafford: Index 4208/f.122.

1601: 11 September
As on 19 August 1600, except: *J. Salisbury, kt.; Th. Trafford of Esclusham; Roger Langford, *added*. E. of Pembroke; B. of St. Asaph, *omitted*: C.66/1549/m.30d. Commission renewed to *add* Roger Langford: Index 4208/f.122v.   (33)

1602: 25 February
Commission renewed to *add* B. of St. Asaph: Index 4208/f.130.

1602: 2 April
Commission renewed to *add* Rob. Sontley; Cadwalader Wynn, and to *omit* Th. Trafford: Index 4208/f.131v.

1602: 29 May
Commission renewed to *add* Peter Mutton; J. Jeffreys: Index 4208/f.135.

1602: 6 July
Commission renewed to *add* W. Wynn: Index 4208/f.139v.

1602: 25 July
*Egerton; *Buckhurst; *Ed., Lord Zouch, President of Council in the Marches of Wales; Bishops of Chester, *St. Asaph; *Rich. Lewkenor, kt. & *H. Townshend, Justices of Chester & of Great Sessions; *Rich. Trevor, *J. Lloyd, *J. Salisbury, kts.; *Rich. Parry, Dean of Bangor; David Yale, Ll.D., one of the Masters in Chancery; *W. Leighton; *p Roger Puleston; *J. Wynn of Gwydir; *Owen Vaughan; *Hugh Beeston; Th. Myddelton; *Th. Powell; *W. Wynn; *Th. Salisbury; *David Holland; *J. Lloyd of Faenol; Rich. Leighton; Th. Price; Rob. Turbridge; H. ap Evan Lloyd; *Peter Salisbury; *Th. Wynn ap Richard; *W. Penrhyn; W. Myddelton; Ed. Lloyd of Llysfeisir; *Peter Mutton; *J. Jeffreys; Ed. Price; Hugh Conway of Bryneurin; Roger Langford: C.66/1594/m.34d. Commission renewed to *add* Ed., Lord Zouch; Ed. Price: Index 4208/f.141.   (37)

1603: 20 June (Acting)
As on 25 July 1602, except: Rob. Sontley; Cadwalader Wynn, *added*. W. Wynn; Th. Salisbury, *omitted*: Wales 4/13/1.   (37)

1603: 17 October (Acting)
As on 20 June 1603, except: Th. Wynn ap Richard, *omitted*: Wales 4/13/2. (36)

1604: (Acting)
As on 17 October 1603, except: *J. Williams, D.D.; *W. Wynn, *added*. Hugh Conway, *omitted*: C.66/1662/m.21d.   (37)

1605: 9 September (Acting)
As in 1604, except: Th. Trafford, *added*. Rich. Parry; Cadwalader Wynn (Sheriff, 1604–5); Ed. Price, *omitted*: Wales 4/14/1.   (35)

1606: 13 October (Acting)
As on 9 September 1605, except: Cadwalader Wynn; Evan Meredith, *added*. Ed., Lord Zouch; B. of Chester; J. Lloyd, kt.; Roger Langford, *omitted*: Wales 4/14/3.   (33)

1607: post 12 September
As on 13 October 1606, except: *Ralph, Lord Eure, President of Council in the Marches of Wales, *added*. W. Leighton; Th. Price, *omitted*: C.66/ 1748/m.30d. (Eure was appointed on 12 September). (32)

1608: 10 October (Acting)
*Th. Egerton, Lord Ellesmere, Chancellor; *E. of Salisbury, Treasurer; *E. of Northampton, Keeper of Privy Seal; *Ralph, Lord Eure, President of Council in the Marches of Wales; *B. of St. Asaph; *Lewkenor & *Townshend, Justices of Chester & of Great Sessions; *Rich. Trevor, *J. Salisbury, *Hugh Beeston, Th. Myddelton, *J. Wynn, kts.; *J. Williams, D.D.; David Yale, Ll.D., Master in Chancery; *p Roger Puleston; *Owen Vaughan; *Th. Powell; *W. Wynn; *David Holland; *J. Lloyd of Faenol; *Th. Trafford; *Peter Mutton; *J. Jeffreys; Rich. Leighton; Rob. Turbridge; H. ap Evan Lloyd; *W. Penrhyn; Rob. Sontley; Cadwalader Wynn; W. Myddelton; Evan Meredith; Rich. Evans; W. Vaughan: Wales 4/15/1. (Details of quorum taken from undated patent roll enrolment of 1608: C.66/1786/m.29d.) (33)

1610: (Acting)
As on 10 October 1608, except: Th. Price, *added*. J. Salisbury, kt.; Rob. Sontley (Sheriff, 1610–11), *omitted*: C.66/1822/m.26d. (32)

1611: (Acting)
As in 1610, except: Rob. Sontley, *added*: C.66/1897/m.19d. (33)

1612: (Acting)
As in 1611, except: Evan Lloyd, *added*. Rob. Sontley, *omitted* (probably in error): C.66/1898/m.26d. (33)
(N.B., the apparent changes in the commissions, c.1610–12, should be approached with caution as there were probably errors in the enrolment of the commissions on the patent rolls).

1613: 5 July (Acting)
*Ellesmere; *Northampton; *Eure, President of Council in the Marches of Wales; *B. of St. Asaph; *Lewkenor & *Townshend, Justices of Chester & of Great Sessions; *J. Wynn, kt. & Bt.; *Rich. Trevor, Th. Myddelton, kts.; *J. Williams, D.D.; *David Yale, Ll.D., Master in Chancery; *Rich. Barker; *p Roger Puleston; *Owen Vaughan; *Th. Powell; *David Holland; *W. Wynn; Simon Thelwall; Evan Lloyd; *J. Lloyd of Faenol; *Th. Trafford; *Peter Mutton; *J. Jeffreys; Th. Lloyd; Rich. Leighton; Th. Price; Rob. Turbridge; H. ap Evan Lloyd; *W. Penrhyn; Rob. Sontley; Cadwalader Wynn; W. Myddelton; Evan Meredith; W. Vaughan; Geo. Bostock: Wales 4/16/1. (Details of quorum taken from undated patent roll enrolments of 1612 and 1614: C.66/1898/m.26d. & ibid./1988/m.27d.) (35)

1614: post 11 July
As on 5 July 1613, except: *E. of Suffolk, Treasurer (appointed on 11 July); W. Salisbury; *Th. Needham; Simon Parry; Hugh Morris, *added*. E. of Northampton; Th. Powell: Rich. Leighton; Cadwalader Wynn, *omitted*: C.66/1988/m.27d. (36).

1615: 15 July
Commission renewed to *add* Th. Myddelton, Esq.: Index 4211/f.6v. (The original *dedimus potestatem* of the same date directing Roger Puleston and Th. Lloyd to administer the oath of a justice of the peace to Th. Myddelton survives as N.L.W., Chirk Castle Ms. F.10172).

1615: 8 September
Commission renewed to *add* Th. Goodman: Index 4211/f.9v.

1615: 9 October (Acting)
As in 1614, except: Th. Myddelton; Th. Goodman, *added*. Rich. Barker; Rob. Turbridge; H. ap Evan Lloyd, *omitted*: Wales 4/16/3. (According to the writ attached to this Gaol File the present list of justices was made for a Great Session held at Ruthin on 17 July 1615. This date however cannot be reconciled with the addition to the commission of Th. Myddelton only two days before on 15 July nor with the addition of Th. Goodman on 8 September, two months after the apparent date of the session. Examination of the Gaol Kalendar attached to the File shows that in fact the session was held on 9 October 1615, a date which causes no problems of interpretation. The likely reason for the error is that the writ originally belonged to the lost File for the summer session of 1615 and accidentally became attached to the File for the autumn session). (35)

1616: 12 February
*Ellesmere; *Suffolk, Treasurer; *E. of Worcester, Keeper of Privy Seal; *Eure, President of Council in the Marches of Wales; *B. of St. Asaph; *Lewkenor & *Townshend, Justices of Chester & of Great Sessions; *J. Wynn, kt. & Bt.; *Rich. Trevor, *Th. Myddelton, kts.; *J. Williams, D.D.; *David Yale, Ll.D., Master in Chancery; *p Roger Puleston; *Owen Vaughan; *David Holland; Th. Myddelton; W. Salisbury; Evan Lloyd; *W. Wynn; *Simon Thelwall; Rich. Williams; *Th. Trafford; *Peter Mutton; *J. Jeffreys; *W. Vaughan; Th. Lloyd; *Th. Needham; *W. Penrhyn; Rob. Sontley; W. Myddelton; Evan Meredith; *Simon Parry; Geo. Bostock; Hugh Morris; Th. Goodman: C.66/2076/m.23d. Commission renewed to *add* Rich. Williams, and *omit* Th. Price: Index 4211/f.15v. (35)

1616: 21 May
Commission renewed to *add* Th. Chamberlain, kt., Justice of Chester & of Great Sessions: Index 4211/f.19v.

1616: 28 June
Commission renewed to place Evan Lloyd on quorum: Index 4211/f.22.

1617: 19 March
Commission renewed to *add* Francis Bacon, kt., Keeper of Great Seal; Th., Lord Gerard, President of Council in the Marches of Wales; J. Panton: Index 4211/ff.37v., 38.

1617: 12 May (Acting)
As on 12 February 1616, except: Francis Bacon, kt., Keeper of Great Seal;
Th., Lord Gerard, President of Council in the Marches of Wales; Th.
Chamberlain, kt., Justice of Chester; J. Panton, *added*. Ellesmere; Eure;
Lewkenor; Owen Vaughan; David Holland, *omitted*: Wales 4/16/4. (34)

1617: 5 July
Commission renewed to *add* Lewis, B. of Bangor; Hugh Meredith: Index
4211/f.44.

1617: 22 November
Commission renewed to *add* H. Salisbury: Index 4211/f.51v.

1617: post 24 November
As on 12 May 1617, except: *D. of Lennox, Steward; *W., Lord Compton,
President of Council in the Marches of Wales (appointed on 24 November);
*B. of Bangor; *H. Salisbury; Hugh Meredith, *added*. Lord Gerard, *omitted*:
C.66/2147/m.23d. (38)

1618: 7 February
Commission renewed to *add* Rob. Vaughan: Index 4211/f.56v.

1618: 26 February
Commission renewed to *add* Piers Holland: Index 4211/f.59.

1618: 16 May
Commission renewed to *add* Rob. Salisbury; Fulk Vaughan: Index 4211/
f.62v.

1618: 5 October (Acting)
As at end of 1617, except: Rob. Vaughan; Piers Holland; Rob. Salisbury;
Fulk Vaughan, *added*. Rich Williams, *omitted*: Wales 4/17/2. (41)

1618: 21 November
Commission renewed to *add* W. Robinson: Index 4211/f.74.

1618: 23 December
*Francis Bacon, kt., Chancellor; *E. of Worcester, Keeper of Privy Seal;
*D. of Lennox, Steward; *W. Compton, E. of Northampton, President
of Council in the Marches of Wales; Bishops of *St. Asaph, *Bangor; *Th.
Chamberlain & *H. Townshend, kts., Justices of Chester & of Great
Sessions; *J. Wynn, kt. & Bt.; *Rich. Trevor, *Th. Myddelton, Th.
Myddelton junior, kts.; *J. Williams, D.D.; *David Yale, Ll.D., Master in
Chancery; *J. Jeffreys; *H. Salisbury; *Rob. Vaughan; W. Salisbury;
*p Evan Lloyd; *W. Wynn; *Simon Thelwall; *Th. Trafford; Piers Holland;
*Peter Mutton; *W. Vaughan; Th. Lloyd; *Th. Needham; *W. Penrhyn;
Rob. Sontley; W. Myddelton; Evan Meredith; *Simon Parry; W. Robinson;
Geo. Bostock; Hugh Morris; Th. Goodman; Hugh Meredith; Rob.
Salisbury; Fulk Vaughan: C.66/2174/m.19d. Commission renewed to
record appointment of Evan Lloyd as *custos rotulorum*: Index 4211/f.76. (39)

1619: 14 May
Commission renewed to *add* Rob. Pritchard, clerk: Index 4211/f.84.

1619: 12 June
Commission renewed to *add* Francis Eure, kt.: Index 4211/f.86.

1620: 4 November
General renewal of Welsh commissions to *add* Jas. Whitlock, kt., serjeant at law, Justice of Chester & Justice of Great Sessions in Denbigh: Index 4211/f.114.

1621: 26 February
*Francis Bacon, kt., Viscount St. Alban, Chancellor; *H., Viscount Mandeville, Treasurer; *Worcester; *Lennox; *Northampton, President of Council in the Marches of Wales; Bishops of *St. Asaph, *Bangor; *Jas. Whitlock, serjeant at law & *H. Townshend, kts., Justices of Chester & of Great Sessions; *J. Wynn, kt. & Bt.; *H. Salisbury, Bt.; *Rich. Trevor, *Th. Myddelton, Th. Myddelton junior, *Rob. Vaughan, kts.; *J. Williams, D.D.; *David Yale, Ll.D., Master in Chancery; *J. Jeffreys; W. Salisbury; *p Evan Lloyd; *W. Wynn; *Simon Thelwall; *Th. Trafford; Piers Holland; *Peter Mutton; *Geo. Puleston; *W. Vaughan; Th. Lloyd; *Th. Needham; *W. Penrhyn; Rob. Sontley; W. Myddelton; Evan Meredith; *Simon Parry; W. Robinson; Geo. Bostock; Hugh Morris; *Th. Goodman; Hugh Meredith; Rob. Salisbury; Fulk Vaughan; Rob. Pritchard, clerk: C.66/2234/m.42d. General renewal of Welsh commissions to *add* Viscount Mandeville, Treasurer: Index 4211/f.120.   (42)

1621: post 29 September
As on 26 February 1621, except: *Lionel Cranfield, Treasurer (appointed on 29 September), *added.* Viscount St. Alban; B of Bangor; H. Townshend; Geo. Puleston, *omitted:* C. 66/2259/m.25d. (Viscount St. Alban was replaced as Keeper of Great Seal by J. Williams, D.D., now B. of Lincoln. The ex-Treasurer, Viscount Mandeville, remained on the commission).   (39)

1622: 29 April
Commission renewed to *add* Marmaduke Lloyd, kt., Second Justice of Chester & Justice of Great Sessions: Index 4211/f.138.

1622: 7 August
Commission renewed to *add* E. of Bridgewater; Geo. Puleston; J. Bayly, M.A., clerk: Index 4211/f.143v.

1622: 14 September
Commission renewed to *add* Rich. Lloyd, D.D.; Gerrard Eyton; Fulk Myddelton: Index 4211/f.144.

1623: 12 February
*B. of Lincoln, Keeper of Great Seal; *Lionel Cranfield, E. of Middlesex, Treasurer; *Viscount Mandeville, President of Privy Council; *Worcester; *Lennox; *Northampton, President of Council in the Marches of Wales;

*E. of Bridgewater (not included in enrolment but probably omitted in error); Bishops of *St. Asaph, *Bangor; *Jas. Whitlock & *Marmaduke Lloyd, kts., Justices of Chester & of Great Sessions; *J. Wynn, kt. & Bt.; *H. Salisbury, Bt.; *Rich. Trevor, *Th. Myddelton, Th. Myddelton junior, *Rob. Vaughan, *Peter Mutton, kts.; *Rich, Lloyd, D.D.; *David Yale, Ll.D., Master in Chancery; W. Salisbury; *p Evan Lloyd; *W. Wynn; *Simon Thelwall; *Th. Trafford; Piers Holland; *Geo. Puleston; *W. Vaughan; Th. Lloyd; *Th. Needham; *W. Penrhyn; W. Myddelton; Evan Meredith; *Simon Parry; W. Robinson; Geo. Bostock; *Th. Goodman; Hugh Meredith; Fulk Vaughan; Gerrard Eyton; Fulk Myddelton; Rob. Wynn; David Morris; Rob. Pritchard, clerk; J. Bayly, clerk: C.66/2285/m.32d. Commission renewed to *add* Rob. Wynn; David Morris: Index 4211/f.149. (45)

1623: 28 April (Acting)

As on 12 February 1623, except: W. Penrhyn, *omitted*: Wales 4/17/5. (The E. of Bridgewater is included in this list after E. of Northampton). (44)

1624: pre 25 April

As on 28 April 1623, except: D. of Lennox; B. of St. Asaph; Th. Goodman, *omitted*: C.66/2310/m.30d. (The E. of Middlesex was suspended from office on 25 April). (41)

1624: 25 June

Commission renewed to *add* Ed. Broughton: Index 4211/f.168v.

1624: 20 September (Acting)

As pre 25 April 1624, except: B. of St. Asaph; Ed. Broughton, *added*. E. of Middlesex; Rob. Vaughan, *omitted*: Wales 4/17/6. (41)

1624: 28 October

Commission renewed to *add* Th. Chamberlain, kt., First Justice of Chester & Justice of Great Sessions in Denbigh: Index 4211/f.171v.

1624: 25 November

Commission renewed to *add* J. Roberts: Index 4211/f.172v.

1625: 1 April

*Lincoln; *Jas., Lord Ley, Treasurer; *Mandeville; *Worcester; *Northampton, President of Council in the Marches of Wales; *E. of Bridgewater; *B. of Bangor; *Th. Chamberlain & *Marmaduke Lloyd, kts., Justices of Chester & of Great Sessions; *J. Wynn, kt. & Bt.; *H. Salisbury, Bt.; *Rich. Trevor, *Th. Myddelton, *Th. Myddelton junior, *Ed. Broughton, *Peter Mutton, kts.; *Rich. Lloyd, D.D.; *David Yale, Ll.D., Master in Chancery; *Sampson Eure; *Rob. Brooke; W. Salisbury; *p Evan Lloyd; *W. Wynn; *Simon Thelwall; Th. Trafford; Piers Holland; *Geo. Puleston; *W. Vaughan; Th. Lloyd; *Th. Needham; W. Myddelton; Evan Meredith; *Simon Parry; W. Robinson; Geo. Bostock; Hugh Meredith; Fulk Vaughan; *Gerrard Eyton; Fulk Myddelton; *Rob. Wynn; *David Morris; *J. Roberts; Rob. Pritchard, clerk; J. Bayly, clerk: C.66/2367/m.28d. General renewal of all Welsh commissions: Index 4211/f.180v. (44)

1625: 9 July
Commission renewed to *add* Rob. Wynn of Foelas: Index 4211/f.191. (Note that the commission now includes two men named Rob. Wynn).

1625: 22 December
As on 1 April 1625, except: *Th. Coventry, kt., Keeper of Great Seal; *Rob. Wynn of Foelas, *added*. B. of Lincoln; Th. Chamberlain, *omitted*: B.M., Harleian Ms. 1622/f.93v. General renewal of Welsh commissions to *add* Th. Coventry, Keeper of Great Seal: Index 4211/f.194d. (44)

1626: 9 March
Commission renewed to *add* J. Bridgeman, kt., First Justice of Chester & Justice of Great Sessions in Denbigh: Index 4211/f.198v.

1626: 3 April (Acting)
As on 22 December 1626, except: J. Bridgeman, kt., Justice of Chester, *added*. B. of St. Asaph; David Yale; Piers Holland; W. Vaughan; Evan Meredith; Hugh Meredith; Rob. Wynn (this is the Rob. Wynn added on 12 February 1623); David Morris; Rob. Pritchard, *omitted*: Wales 4/18/2. (36)

1626: 22 June
Commission renewed to record appointment of Th. Myddelton junior as *custos rotulorum*: Index 4211/f.204.

1626: 4 July
*Th. Coventry, kt., Keeper of Great Seal; *Jas. Ley, E. of Marlborough, Treasurer; *E. of Manchester (Viscount Mandeville), President of Privy Council; *Worcester; *Northampton, President of Council in the Marches of Wales; *Bridgewater; *B. of Bangor; *J. Bridgeman & *Marmaduke Lloyd, kts., Justices of Chester & of Great Sessions; *J. Wynn, kt. & Bt.; *H. Salisbury, Bt.; *Rich. Trevor, *Th. Myddelton, *p Th. Myddelton junior, *Ed. Broughton, *Peter Mutton, kts.; *Rich. Lloyd, D.D.; *Sampson Eure; *Rob. Brooke; W. Salisbury; *Evan Lloyd; *W. Wynn; *Simon Thelwell; *Th. Trafford; *Geo. Puleston; *Rob. Wynn of Foelas; Th. Lloyd; *Th. Needham; W. Myddelton; *Simon Parry; *W. Robinson; Geo. Bostock; *Fulk Vaughan; *Gerrard Eyton; Fulk Myddelton; *David Morris; J. Bayly, clerk: E.163/18/12/f.94d. Commission renewed to *add* David Morris: Index 4211/f.204v. (37)

1626: 16 November
As on 4 July 1626, except: Rob. Wynn; W. Dolben, *added*: C.193/12/2/f.68d. Commission renewed to *restore* Rob. Wynn and to *add* W. Dolben: Index 4211/f.217. (39)

1627: 16 March
As on 16 November 1626, except: *Timothy Turneur; *Owen Wynn, *added*. E. of Worcester; Rob. Brooke; H. Salisbury, *omitted*: C.66/2449/m.32d. Commission renewed to *add* Owen Wynn: Index 4211/f.220v. (38)

1627: 16 April (Acting)
Coventry; Marlborough; Manchester; Worcester; Northampton, President of Council in the Marches of Wales; Bridgewater; B. of Bangor; Bridgeman & Lloyd, Justices of Chester & of Great Sessions; H. Salisbury, Bt.; Rich. Trevor, Th. Myddelton, Th. Myddelton junior, Peter Mutton, Ed. Broughton, kts.; Rich. Lloyd, D.D.; Sampson Eure; Rob. Brooke; W. Salisbury; Evan Lloyd; W. Wynn; Simon Thelwall; Th. Trafford; Geo. Puleston; Th. Lloyd; Th. Needham; Rob. Wynn of Foelas; W. Myddelton; Simon Parry; W. Robinson; Fulk Vaughan; Gerrard Eyton; Fulk Myddelton; David Morris; Rob. Wynn; W. Dolben; J. Bayly, clerk: Wales 4/18/3. (37)

1627: 24 September (Acting)
As on 16 April 1627, except: Simon Parry, *omitted*: Wales 4/18/4. (36)

1628: 5 May (Acting)
As on 24 September 1627, except: E. of Worcester; H. Salisbury (Sheriff, 1627–8); Rob. Brooke, *omitted*: Wales 4/18/5. (33)

1628: 10 December
Commission renewed to *add* Ed. Trevor, kt.; J. Wynn; Ed. Thelwall: Index 4211/f.260.

1629: 15 April
Commission renewed to *add* Geo. Bostock: Index 4211/f.267.

1629: 27 April (Acting)
*Coventry; *Rich., Lord Weston, Treasurer; *E. of Marlborough, President of Privy Council; *Manchester; *E. of Pembroke; *Northampton, President of Council in the Marches of Wales; *Bridgewater; *B. of Bangor; *Th. Trevor, kt., Baron of Exchequer; *Bridgeman & *Lloyd, Justices of Chester & of Great Sessions; *H. Salisbury, Bt.; *Rich. Trevor, *J. Trevor, *Th. Myddelton, *p Th. Myddelton junior, *Ed. Trevor, *Ed. Broughton, *Peter Mutton, kts.; *Rich. Lloyd, D.D.; *Sampson Eure; *Timothy Turneur; W. Salisbury; *Evan Lloyd; *W. Wynn; *Simon Thelwall; *Th. Trafford; *Geo. Puleston; *Rob. Wynn of Foelas; Th. Lloyd; W. Myddelton; *W. Robinson; J. Wynn; *Owen Wynn; Ed. Thelwall; *Fulk Vaughan; *Gerrard Eyton; Fulk Myddelton; *Rob. Wynn; *David Morris; *W. Dolben; Geo. Bostock; J. Bayly, clerk: Wales 4/19/1. (Details of the quorum are taken from the enrolled commission of 8 July 1629: C.66/2495/m. 27d.) (43)

1629: 8 July
As on 27 April 1629, except: *Viscount Conway, President of Privy Council; *Ed. Meredith; *Peter Ellis; Gabriel Goodman, *added*. E. of Marlborough; W. Salisbury, *omitted*: C.66/2495/m.27d. Commission renewed to *add* Ed. Meredith; Peter Ellis; Gabriel Goodman: Index 4212/p.14. (45)

1630: 7 April
As on 8 July 1629, except: *B. of St. Asaph, *added*: C.66/2527/m.29d. Commission renewed to *add* J., B. of St. Asaph: Index 4212/p.29. (46)

1630: 19 April (Acting)
Coventry; Weston; Viscount Conway, President of Council; Manchester; Pembroke; Northampton, President of Council in the Marches of Wales; Bridgewater; B. of Bangor; Th. Trevor, kt., Baron of Exchequer; Bridgeman & Lloyd, Justices of Chester & of Great Sessions; H. Salisbury, Bt.; Rich. Trevor, J. Trevor, Th. Myddelton, Th. Myddelton junior, Ed. Trevor, Ed. Broughton, Peter Mutton, kts.; Rich. Lloyd, D.D.; Sampson Eure; Timothy Turneur; Evan Lloyd; W. Wynn; Simon Thelwall; Th. Trafford; Geo. Puleston; Rob. Wynn of Foelas; Ed. Meredith; Th. Lloyd; W. Myddelton; Owen Wynn; Ed. Thelwall; Fulk Vaughan; Gerrard Eyton; Fulk Myddelton; Rob. Wynn; Peter Ellis; Gabriel Goodman; David Morris; W. Dolben; Geo. Bostock; J. Bayly, clerk: Wales 4/19/3. (Note that the absence from the present list of the Bishop of St. Asaph indicates that it is based upon an earlier commission, presumably that of 8 July 1629). (43)

1630: 18 October (Acting)
As on 19 April 1630, except: E. of Northampton, *omitted*: Wales 4/19/4. (Note that the renewal of the commission on 7 April 1630 is still not reflected in the Gaol File list). (42)

1631: 2 May (Acting)
As on 18 October 1630, except: B. of St. Asaph; W. Robinson, *added*. Viscount Conway; J. Trevor, kt.; Rob. Wynn of Foelas (Sheriff, 1630–31), *omitted*: Wales 4/20/1. (41)

1631: post 11 July
*Coventry; *Weston; *Manchester; *E. of Bridgewater, President of Council in the Marches of Wales (appointed on 11 July); *B. of St. Asaph; *Th. Trevor, kt., Baron of Exchequer; *Bridgeman & *Lloyd, Justices of Chester & of Great Sessions; *H. Salisbury, Bt.; *Rich. Trevor, *p Th. Myddelton, *Ed. Trevor, *Ed. Broughton, *Peter Mutton, Master in Chancery, kts.; *Rich. Lloyd, D.D.; *Sampson Eure; *Timothy Turneur; *Evan Lloyd; *W. Wynn; *Simon Thelwall; *Th. Trafford; *Geo. Puleston; *Rob. Wynn of Foelas; *Ed. Meredith; Th. Lloyd; W. Myddelton; *W. Robinson; J. Wynn; *Owen Wynn; Ed. Thelwall; *Fulk Vaughan; *Gerrard Eyton; Fulk Myddelton; *Rob. Wynn; *Peter Ellis; Gabriel Goodman; *David Morris; *W. Dolben; Geo. Bostock; J. Bayly, clerk: S.P.16/212/f.72v. (40)

1633: 9 January
Commission renewed to *add* Roger Holland: Index 4212/p.96.

1633: 29 January
Commission renewed to *add* J. Lloyd: Index 4212/p.97.

1633: 20 February
Commission renewed to *add* W. Wynn of Llanfair: Index 4212/p.98.

1633: 16 March
As in 1631, except: *W. Wynn of Llanfair; *J. Lloyd (not actually listed in the enrolment, but probably omitted in error); Roger Holland; Edm. Vaughan, *added*. H. Salisbury, Bt.; Evan Lloyd; W. Wynn; J. Wynn; Fulk Vaughan; Fulk Myddelton, *omitted*: C.66/2598/m.21d. Commission renewed to *add* Edm. Vaughan: Index 4212/p.103. (38)

1633: 26 July
Commission renewed to *add* Th. Salisbury, Bt.: Index 4212/p.112.

1633: 20 December
Commission renewed to *add* J. Parry of Llanbedr: Index 4212/p.120.

1634: 28 April (Acting)
*Coventry; *Rich. Weston, E. of Portland, Treasurer; *Manchester; *Bridgewater, President of Council in the Marches of Wales; *B. of St. Asaph; *Th. Trevor, kt.; *Bridgeman & *Lloyd, Justices of Chester & of Great Sessions; *Th. Salisbury, Bt.; *Rich. Trevor, *p Th. Myddelton, *Ed. Trevor, *Ed. Broughton, *Peter Mutton, kts.; *Rich. Lloyd, D.D.; *Sampson Eure; *Timothy Turneur; *W. Wynn of Llanfair; *Simon Thelwall; *Th. Trafford; *Geo. Puleston; *J. Lloyd; *Rob. Wynn of Foelas; *Ed. Meredith; W. Myddelton; *W. Robinson; *Owen Wynn; *Ed. Thelwall; *Gerrard Eyton; *Rob. Wynn; *Peter Ellis; Gabriel Goodman; *W. Dolben; Geo. Bostock; Edm. Vaughan; J. Parry of Llanbedr: Wales 4/21/1. (Details of quorum based on list of 25 June 1634: C.193/13/2/f.79v). (36)

1634: 25 June
As on 28 April 1634, except: *Evan Lloyd; Roger Holland; *David Morris; J. Roydon, *added*. W. Robinson; Owen Wynn; Peter Ellis; Gabriel Goodman; Geo. Bostock; J. Parry, *omitted*: C.193/13/2/f.79v. Commission renewed to *add* J. Roydon, and to *omit* W. Robinson; Owen Wynn; Peter Ellis; Gabriel Goodman: Index 4212/p.140. (34)

1636: 13 June
*Coventry; *B. of London, Treasurer; *Manchester; *Bridgewater, President of Council in the Marches of Wales; *B. of St. Asaph; *Th. Trevor, kt., Baron of Exchequer; *J. Bridgeman, kt., Justice of Chester & of Great Sessions; *Th. Salisbury, Bt.; *Th. Powell, Bt.; *Rich. Trevor, *p Th. Myddelton, *Ed. Trevor, *Ed. Broughton, *Peter Mutton, Master in Chancery, kts.; *Rich Lloyd, D.D.; *Sampson Eure; *Timothy Turneur; *Evan Lloyd; *W. Wynn of Llanfair; *Simon Thelwall; *Th. Trafford; *Geo. Puleston; *J. Lloyd; *Rob. Wynn of Foelas; *Ed. Meredith; W. Myddelton; Ed. Thelwall; *Gerrard Eyton; *Rob. Wynn; J. Parry of Llanbedr; Roger Holland; J. Roydon; *W. Dolben: S.P.16/405/f.77v. Commission renewed to *add* Th. Powell, Bt.: Index 4212/p.210. (33)

1637: 15 June
Commission renewed to *add* Rich. Lloyd: Index 4212/p.247.

1638: 20 February
Commission renewed to *add* Gabriel Parry, B.D.: Index 4212/p.280.

1638: 3 April
*Coventry; *London; *Manchester; *Bridgewater, President of Council in
the Marches of Wales; *B. of St. Asaph; *Th. Trevor, kt., Baron of
Exchequer; *Th. Milward, serjeant at law & *Rich. Prydderch, Justices of
Chester & of Great Sessions; *Marmaduke Lloyd, kt.; *Th. Salisbury, Bt.;
*Th. Powell, Bt.; *Rich. Trevor, *p. Th. Myddelton, *Ed. Trevor, *Ed.
Broughton, kts.; *Rich. Lloyd, D.D.; *Sampson Eure; *W. Wynn of
Llanfair; *Simon Thelwall; *Th. Trafford; *J. Lloyd; *Rob. Wynn of
Foelas; *Ed. Meredith; Ed. Thelwall; *Gerrard Eyton; *Rich. Lloyd;
Roger Holland; J. Roydon; Gabriel Parry, B.D.; *W. Dolben: C.66/2725/
m.19d. Commission renewed to *add* Th. Milward, Justice of Chester:
Index 4212/p.287. (30)

1638: 21 April
Commission renewed to *add* B. of Bangor: Index 4212/p.289.

1638: 10 August
As on 3 April 1638, except: *B. of Bangor, *added*. W. Dolben, *omitted*:
C.66/2761/m.17d. Commission renewed to *omit* W. Dolben: Index 4212/
p.305. (30)

1639: 9 November
Commission renewed to *add* Rob. Davies: Index 4212/p.358.

1640: post 17 January
*J. Finch, kt., Keeper of Great Seal; *London; *Manchester; *Bridgewater,
President of Council in the Marches of Wales; Bishops of *St. Asaph,
*Bangor; *Th. Trevor, kt., Baron of Exchequer; *Milward & *Prydderch,
Justices of Chester & of Great Sessions; *Marmaduke Lloyd, kt.; *Th.
Salisbury, Bt.; *Th. Powell, Bt.; *p Th. Myddelton, *Ed. Trevor, *Ed.
Broughton, kts.; *Rich. Lloyd, D.D.; *Sampson Eure; *W. Morgan;
*J. Lloyd; *W. Wynn of Llanfair; *Rob. Davies; *Simon Thelwall; *Th.
Trafford; *Rob. Wynn of Foelas; *Ed. Meredith; *Ed. Thelwall; *Gerrard
Eyton; *Rich. Lloyd; Roger Holland; J. Roydon; Gabriel Parry, B.D.:
C.66/2858/m.21d. (J. Finch was appointed on 17 January 1640 and was
created Lord Finch on 7 April following). (31)

1640: 12 December
Commission renewed to *add* Geo. Bostock: Index 4212/p.418.

1641: 18 May
Commission renewed to *add* J. Wynn; H. Ashpoole: Index 4212/p.447.

1641: 27 May
Commission renewed to *add* Roger Kynaston: Index 4212/p.449.

1641: 4 October (Acting)

Edward, Lord Littleton, Keeper of Great Seal; London; Manchester; Bridgewater, President of Council in the Marches of Wales; Bishops of St. Asaph, Bangor; Th. Trevor, kt., Baron of Exchequer; Milward & Prydderch, Justices of Chester & of Great Sessions; Marmaduke Lloyd, kt.; Th. Salisbury, Bt.; Th. Powell, Bt.; Th. Myddelton, Ed. Trevor, Ed. Broughton, kts.; Rich. Lloyd, D.D.; Gabriel Parry, B.D.; Sampson Eure; Simon Thelwall; Th. Trafford; W. Wynn; J. Lloyd; W. Morgan; Rob. Wynn of Foelas; —————; Ed. Meredith; Ed. Thelwall; Gerrard Eyton; Rich. Lloyd; Roger Holland; J. Roydon; Geo. Bostock: Wales 4/23/5. (List damaged). (32)

1641: 17 December

Commission renewed to *add* Kenrick Eyton: Index 4212/p.495.

1642: 10 February

Commission renewed to *add* W. Price: Index 4212/p.505.

1642: 2 May (Acting)

Lord Littleton, Keeper of Great Seal; Manchester; Bridgewater, President of Council in the Marches of Wales; Milward & Prydderch, Justices of Chester & of Great Sessions; Marmaduke Lloyd, kt.; Th. Salisbury, Bt.; Th. Powell, Bt.; Sampson Eure; Th. Myddelton, Ed. Trevor, Ed. Broughton, kts.; Rich. Lloyd, D.D.; W. Morgan; W. Price; J. Lloyd; W. Wynn of Llanfair; Simon Thelwall; Th. Trafford; Rob. Wynn of Foelas; Ed. Meredith; Ed. Thelwall; Gerrard Eyton; Kenrick Eyton; Geo. Bostock; Roger Holland; J. Roydon: Wales 4/23/4. (27)

1642: 5 August

Commission renewed to *add* J. Trevor; Th. Yate, and to appoint Th. Salisbury, Bt., as *custos rotulorum*: Index 4212/p.534.

1642: 23 August

Commission renewed to *add* Geo. Bostock: Index 4212/p.541. (Bostock may have been omitted in error in the renewal of the commission on 5 August since he was already a member of the commission before that date).

1643: 22 February

Commission renewed to *add* Ellis Wynn of Plas Bella: Index 4212/p.546 & Index 4210/p.4.

1643: 15 March

Commission renewed to *add* Chas. Chambers: Index 4212/p.546 & Index 4210/p.9.

1643: 29 April

Commission renewed to *add* J. Edwards of Chirk; Ed. Goodman; Th. Ravenscroft; Rich. Myddelton of Cadwgan; J. Robinson; Rob. Wynn of Garthewin; Rob. Price of Geeler; Ed. Williams: Index 4210/p.14.

1643: 17 July
Commission renewed to appoint W. Wynn as *custos rotulorum*: Index 4210/p.27.

1643: 26 October
Commission renewed to appoint W. Price as *custos rotulorum*: Index 4210/p.46.

1644: 22 January (Acting)
Littleton; D. of Richmond & Lennox, Steward; E. of Arundel; Bridgewater, President of Council in the Marches of Wales; Th., Viscount Saville, Treasurer of Household; Geo., Lord Digby; Peter Wyche, kt., Household Controller; Ed. Nicholas, kt.; Milward & Prydderch, Justices of Chester & of Great Sessions; Marmaduke Lloyd, kt.; Th. Powell, Bt.; W. Meredith, kt. & Bt.; Sampson Eure, kt., serjeant at law; Ed. Broughton, Rich. Lloyd, Gerrard Eyton, kts.; W. Morgan; W. Price; Rob. Davies; Simon Thelwall; Th. Trafford; Rob. Wynn of Foelas; Ed. Thelwall; J. Wynn; Kenrick Eyton; J. Roydon; Roger Kynaston; Geo. Bostock; J. Trevor; J. Edwards of Chirk; Ed. Goodman; Rich. Myddelton of Cadwgan; Th. Ravenscroft; J. Robinson; Ellis Wynn of Plas Bella; Chas. Chambers: Wales 4/24/3.   (37)

1644: 20 April
Commission renewed to *add* W. Wynn of Garthgynan; Rich. Myddelton of Llansilin, and to *omit* J. Edwards of Chirk; Geo. Bostock of Holt; Rich. Myddelton of Cadwgan; Ellis Wynn of Plas Bella; Chas. Chambers: Index 4210/p.102.

1644: 27 April
Commission renewed to *restore* J. Edwards of Chirk; Geo. Bostock of Holt; Rich. Myddelton of Cadwgan; Ellis Wynn of Plas Bella; Chas. Chambers: Index 4210/p.105.

1646: 13 July
Commission renewed (no details): Index 4213/p.52.

1646: 1 September
Commission renewed to *add* Th. Myddelton, kt., *as custos rotulorum*: Index 4213/p.56.

1647: 22 March
Commission renewed to *add* J. Bradshaw & Peter Warburton, Justices of Chester & of Great Sessions: Index 4213/p.84.

1647: 1 October
Commission renewed (no details): Index 4213/p.98.

1648: 3 March
Commission renewed (no details): Index 4213/p.110.

1648: 9 October (Acting)
E. of Denbigh; E. of Manchester; W. Lenthall, Speaker of House of Commons; J. Bradshaw & Peter Warburton, Justices of Chester & of Great

Sessions; Rich. Wynn, kt. & Bt.; Th. Myddelton, J. Trevor, kts.; J. Puleston; Th. Myddelton; Simon Thelwall junior; Rob. Sontley; J. Edisbury; Th. Johns; Owen Salisbury; Ed.? Thelwall; Th. Ravenscroft; ——————; Fulk Myddelton; plus six other names: Wales 4/24/5. (The end of the list is too badly damaged for use). (25)

1648: 23 December
Commission renewed to *add* Simon Thelwall senior; Rob. Wynn of Foelas; W. Wynn of Llanfon; Ed. Thelwall; J. Carter; J. Langford; Rob. Lloyd of Isclawdd: Index 4213/p.130.

1649: 31 March
*W. Lenthall, Speaker of House of Commons; *Th., Lord Fairfax, General; *Bulstrode Whitelock, *Rich. Keble, *J. Lisle, Commissioners of the Great Seal; *E. of Pembroke & Montgomery; *E. of Denbigh; *H. Rolle, Chief Justice of Upper Bench; *Oliver St. John, Chief Justice of Common Bench; *J. Wilde, Chief Baron of Exchequer; *J. Bradshaw & *Peter Warburton, Justices of Chester & of Great Sessions; *p Th. Myddelton, *J. Trevor, kts.; *J. Puleston, serjeant at law; *Th. Mytton; *Simon Thelwall senior; *Rob. Wynn; *Rob. Sontley; *J. Jones; *J. Edisbury; *Geo. Twistleton; *Owen Salisbury; *Th. Ravenscroft; *Ed. Thelwall; *J. Carter; Fulk Myddelton; *Ed. Wynn of Llanfychan; *J. Peck; Owen Thelwall; J. Kynaston; Rich. Egerton; Leighton Owen; Th. Ball; Rich. Bassett; J. Langford; Rob. Lloyd of Isclawdd: N.L.W., Chirk Castle Ms. F.1115 (original commission of the peace). Renewal of commission: Index 4213/p.147. (37)

1649: post 10 August
As on 31 March 1649, except: *Th. Fell, Justice of Chester & of Great Sessions, *added.* Peter Warburton, *omitted*: C.193/13/3/f.75. (Th. Fell was appointed on 10 August 1649). (37)

1650: 25 July
*Lenthall; *Oliver Cromwell, Lord General; *J. Bradshaw, President of Council; *Whitelock, *Keble & *Lisle; *E. of Denbigh; *Rolle; *St. John; *Humph. Mackworth & *Th. Fell, Justices of Chester & of Great Sessions; *Edm. Prideaux, Attorney-General; *p Th. Myddelton, kt.; *J. Trevor, kt.; *J. Puleston, Justice of Common Pleas; *J. Bradshaw, attorney-general in Denbigh; *Simon Thelwall senior; *Rob. Sontley; *Th. Tirrell; *Ed. Thelwall of Glantanat; *Th. Ravenscroft; *J. Carter; *Geo. Twistleton; *Owen Thelwall; *Th. Ball; J. Peck; W. Wynn; Rich. Myddelton: *Lists published by Th. Walkley* (1650), p.66. Commission renewed to *add* Humph. Mackworth; J. Bradshaw, attorney-general in Denbigh; Th. Tirrell: Ed. Thelwall of Glantanat; W. Wynn; Rich. Myddelton, and to *omit* Th. Mytton; Rich. Wynn; J. Edisbury; and others (no details): Index 4213/p.198. (28)

1651: 13 October (Acting)
As on 25 July 1650, except: J. Wilde, Chief Baron of Exchequer, *added.* W. Wynn (Sheriff, 1650–51); Rich. Myddelton, *omitted*: Wales 4/24/6. (27)

1652: 29 July
As on 13 October 1651, except: *Rob. Duckenfield; *Simon Thelwall junior; *J. Edisbury; *Jas. Duckenfield; W. Wynn; Rich. Myddelton (the last two men may have been omitted in error in 1651); J. Kynaston; Ed. Wynn, *added*: Cambridge University Ms. Dd.VIII.1/f.124. Commission renewed to *add* J. Kynaston; Simon Thelwall junior; J. Edisbury; Ed. Wynn; Rob. & Jas. Duckenfield: Index 4213/p.243.   (35)

1653: 27 July
Commission renewed to *add* Andrew Ellis; Daniel Lloyd; Rob. Sontley; Hugh Pritchard, and to *omit* Th. Myddelton and others (no details): Index 4213/p.264.

1653: 13 October
Commission renewed to *add* J. Bradshaw, Chancellor of Duchy of Lancaster; J. Jones; W. Morris; Roger Sontley; to appoint J. Kynaston as *custos rotulorum*, and to *omit* others (no details): Index 4213/p.272.

1654: 23 March
Commission renewed according to a general list: Index 4213/p.286.

1655: 24 September (Acting)
W. Lenthall, Master of the Rolls; Whitelock, Keble & Lisle; J. Bradshaw, Chancellor of the Duchy of Lancaster; E. of Denbigh; J. Glynn, Chief Justice of Upper Bench; St. John; W. Steele, Chief Baron of the Exchequer; J. Puleston; Th. Fell; Edm. Prideaux, Attorney-General; Th. Myddelton, J. Trevor, kts.; J. Bradshaw; Simon Thelwall; Rob. Duckenfield; Th. Tirrell; Ed. Thelwall of Glantanat; Th. Ravenscroft of Pickhill; J. Carter; Geo. Twistleton; J. Edisbury; Jas. Duckenfield; Ed. Thelwall; Th. Ball; J. Peck; W. Wynn; Rich. Myddelton; J. Kynaston: Wales 4/24/7.   (30)

1655: 12 December
Commission renewed to *add* Colonel Jas. Berry: Index 4213/p.321.

1656: 24 March
Commission renewed to place J. Edisbury & J. Peck on the quorum: Index 4213/p.331.

1656: 25 June
*Nathaniel Fiennes & *J. Lisle, Commissioners of Great Seal; *Bulstrode Whitelock, kt., *Th. Widdrington, kt., *Ed. Montagu, *W. Sydenham, Commissioners of Treasury; *J. Glynn, Chief Justice of Upper Bench; *W. Lenthall, Master of Rolls; *Oliver St. John, Chief Justice of Common Bench; *J. Bradshaw & *Th. Fell, Justices of Chester & of Great Sessions; *Edm. Prideaux, Attorney-General; *p Th. Myddelton, *J. Trevor, kts.; *Major-General Jas. Berry; *J. Nicholas; *Rowland Dawkins; *J. Jones; *Simon Thelwall senior; *J. Robinson; *Rob. Sontley; *J. Carter; *Geo. Twistleton; *Andrew Ellis; *J. Peck; *Th. Ball; *J. Kynaston; *Th. Ravenscroft; *Owen Thelwall; W. Wynn of Ruthin; Roger Sontley; Hugh Pritchard; *J. Edisbury; Rob. Duckenfield; Andrew Ellis; Gerrard Barber;

Peter Moyle of Ruthin; Watkin Kyffin: C.193/13/6/f.104 & C.193/13/5/f.124v. Commission renewed to *add* J. Nicholas; Rowland Dawkins; J. Robinson; Gerrard Barber; Peter Moyle; Watkin Kyffin: Index 4213/p.337. (38)

1658: 24 March
Commission renewed to *add* Ed. Thelwall: Index 4213/p.389.

1658: 24 September
General renewal of Welsh commissions to *add* Richard Cromwell, Lord Protector: Index 4213/p.405.

1659: 8 July
Commission renewed according to a general list: Index 4213/p.438.

1659: (Acting)
p Th. Myddelton; Rob. Saltonstall, kt.; J. Jones; J. Trevor, kt.; Simon Thelwall; ———— Puleston (the first name is not given); Th. Myddelton; Andrew Ellis; Rob. Duckenfield; Th. Ball; Watkin Kyffin; W. Wynn; J. Manley; Roger Sontley; J. Edisbury; Ed. Trevor; Th. Cooper; Geo. Twistleton; Geo. Trevor; Hugh Courtney; Rob. Myddelton; J. Peck; Owen Thelwall; Peter Moyle; Fulk Myddelton; Hugh Pritchard: N.L.W., Wynn Papers no. 2209. (This list of justices acting in 1659 probably represents the commission of 8 July 1659 with the omission of the *ex officio* members of the commission). (26)

1659: 5 October
Commission renewed to *add* J. Kynaston, and to *omit* Th. Myddelton and others (no details): Index 4213/p.443.

1660: 3 March
Commission renewed according to a general list: Index 4213/p.453.

1660: 4 September
Commission renewed to *add* Rob. Milward, Justice of Chester & of Great Sessions: Index 4214/p.35 (See note after next entry).

1660: 4 September
*Ed. Hyde, kt., Chancellor; *E. of Southampton, Treasurer; *D. of Albermarle, General; *Marquess of Ormond, Steward; *E. of Lindsey, Great Chamberlain; *E. of Manchester, Household Chamberlain; *Timothy Turneur, Justice of Chester & of Great Sessions; *Arthur Trevor; *p Th. Myddelton, kt.; *Rich. Wynn, Bt.; *J. Salisbury, Bt.; *Th. Powell, Bt.; *Evan Lloyd, Bt.; *Th. Myddelton, Bt.; *Roger Mostyn, kt. & Bt.; *Rich. Lloyd, *J. Carter, *Rob. Agborough, Ed. Broughton, kts.; *W. Wynn of Garthgynan; Rich. Wynn; *Roger Grosvenor; Rich. Myddelton; *Simon Thelwall; J. Wynn of Melai; *Kenrick Eyton; *J. Robinson; J. Thelwall; J. Edisbury; J. Wynn of Wynnstay; Chas. Salisbury; *J. Dolben; W. Parry of Hendre; Rob. Price of Geeler; Owen Thelwall; Rob. Wynn; Bevis Lloyd; Chas. Goodman; Watkin Kyffin; Eubule Thelwall; J. Puleston; Francis

Manley; Fulk Myddelton; W. Price; *Hugh Wynn of Berth-ddu; J. Wynn; J. Thelwall; Th. Vaughan of Pantlas; W. Owen of Llunddun; Geo. Bostock: N.L.W., Chirk Castle Ms. F.9926 (original commission of the peace). (Through an error in the drawing up of the commission Arthur Trevor is named as a Justice of Chester & of Great Sessions in place of Robert Milward for whom the commission was in fact issued and who in consequence does not appear in the commission. Note also that, although the commission was issued under a docquet of 4 September, it was probably not drawn up on that date and it was therefore possible to incorporate in the commission the name of the Earl of Southampton who was appointed as Treasurer on 8 September 1660). (50)

1661: 18 March
Commission renewed to *add* J. Peck: Index 4214/p.91.

1661: 1 June
As on 4 September 1660, except: *J., Lord Robartes, Keeper of Privy Seal, *added*. Rich. Wynn; J. Wynn (this is the J. Wynn named after Hugh Wynn of Berth-ddu), *omitted*: N.L.W., Chirk Castle Ms. F.114. (original commission of the peace). Commission renewed to place several persons on the quorum: Index 4214/p.111. (The main reason for the renewal was probably to add Lord Robartes who was appointed Keeper of Privy Seal on 15 May 1661). (49)

1661: 26 August
Commission renewed to *add* Geoff. Palmer, kt. & Bt., Attorney-General & Justice of Chester: Index 4214/p.136.

1661: 8 November
*E. of Clarendon, Chancellor; *Southampton; *J., Lord Robartes, Keeper of Privy Seal; *Albemarle; *Ormond; *Lindsey; *Manchester, Household Chamberlain; *E. of Carbery, President of Council in the Marches of Wales; *Geoff. Palmer, kt. & Bt., Attorney-General & Justice of Chester and of Great Sessions; *Job Charlton, serjeant at law & *Rob. Milward, deputy Justices of Chester & of Great Sessions; *p Th. Myddelton, kt.; *Rich. Wynn, *J. Salisbury, *Th. Powell, *Evan Lloyd, *Th. Myddelton, Baronets; *Roger Mostyn, kt. & Bt.; *Rich. Lloyd, *J. Carter, *Rob. Agborough, Ed. Broughton, kts.; *Roger Grosvenor; Rich. Myddelton; *Simon Thelwall; W. Wynn; *J. Wynn of Wynnstay; *J. Wynn of Melai; *Kenrick Eyton; *J. Robinson; J. Thelwall; J. Edisbury; Chas. Salisbury; *J. Dolben; W. Parry of Hendre; *Rob. Price of Geeler; Owen Thelwall; *Rob. Wynn of Foelas; Bevis Lloyd; Chas. Goodman; Watkin Kyffin; Eubule Thelwall; J. Puleston; Francis Manley; Fulk Myddelton; W. Price; *Hugh Wynn of Berth-ddu; J. Thelwall; Th. Vaughan of Pantlas; W. Owen of Llunddun; Geo. Bostock; J. Peck: N.L.W., Chirk Castle Ms. F.1120 (original commission of the peace). General renewal of Welsh commissions to *add* E. of Carbery, President of Council in the Marches of Wales: Index 4214/p.144. (52)

1662: 20 March

As on 8 November 1661, except: Rich. Wynn; *David Morris, *added*. Geoff. Palmer, kt. & Bt., *omitted*: N.L.W., Chirk Castle Ms. F.4709 (original commission of the peace). Commission renewed to *add* Job Charlton, serjeant at law, Chief Justice of Chester; David Morris: Index 4214/p.163. (53)

1662: 17 July

As on 20 March 1662, except: *Th. Walcott, King's attorney, *added*. Roger Grosvenor; J. Peck, *omitted*: N.L.W., Chirk Castle Ms. F.4721 (original commission of the peace). Commission renewed to *add* Th. Walcott, King's attorney: Index 4214/p.180. (This commission is enrolled in C.66/2986/ m.31d). (52)

1663: 17 August (Acting)

As on 17 July 1662, except: Th. Myddelton, Bt.; Simon Thelwall; J. Dolben; Geo. Bostock, *omitted*: Wales 4/25/4. (48)

1663: 19 October (Acting)

As on 17 August 1661, except: Evan Lloyd, Bt., *omitted*: Wales 4/25/5. (47)

1664: 11 July (Acting)

As on 19 October 1663, except: J. Carter; J. Thelwall (this is the J. Thelwall listed after Hugh Wynn of Berth-ddu), *omitted*: Wales 4/26/1. (45)

1664: 26 September (Acting)

As on 11 July 1664, except: Job Charlton; Rob. Milward, *omitted*: Wales 4/26/2. (These two men were probably omitted in error as there is no apparent cause for their removal at this date). (43)

1665: 17 April (Acting)

As on 26 September 1664, except: W. Wynn, *omitted*: Wales 4/26/3. (42)

1665: 23 June

*Clarendon; *Southampton; *Robartes; *Albemarle; *Ormond; *Lindsey; *Manchester; *Carbery, President of Council in the Marches of Wales; *Job Charlton, kt., serjeant at law & *Rob. Milward, Justices of Chester & of Great Sessions; *J. Glynn, kt., serjeant at law; *p Th. Myddelton, kt.; *Rich. Wynn, *J. Salisbury, *Th. Powell, *Evan Lloyd, *Th. Myddelton, Baronets; *Roger Mostyn, kt. & Bt.; *Rich. Lloyd, *J. Carter, *Rob. Agborough, Ed. Broughton, *J. Wynn, kts.; *Kenrick Eyton; *Th. Walcott, King's attorney; Rich. Myddelton; *Simon Thelwall; *Rich. Wynn; *J. Wynn of Melai; *J. Robinson; J. Thelwall; J. Edisbury; Chas. Salisbury; *J. Dolben; W. Parry of Hendre; *Rob. Price of Geeler; Owen Thelwall; *Rob. Wynn of Foelas; Bevis Lloyd; Chas. Goodman; Watkin Kyffin; Eubule Thelwall; J. Puleston; *Francis Manley; Fulk Myddelton; W. Price; *Hugh Wynn of Berth-ddu; J. Thelwall; Th. Vaughan of Pantlas; *David Morris; W. Owen of Llunddun; Geo. Bostock: N.L.W., Chirk Castle Ms. F.12899 (original commission of the peace). (52)

1666: 24 December
Commission renewed to *add* Ed., Lord Herbert of Cherbury, as *custos rotulorum*: Index 4214/p.297.

1667: 11 January
*Clarendon; *Southampton; *Robartes; *Albemarle; *Ormond; *Lindsey; *Manchester; *Carbery, President of Council in the Marches of Wales; *p Ed., Lord Herbert of Cherbury; *Charlton & *Milward, Justices of Chester & of Great Sessions; *Rich. Wynn, *J. Salisbury, *Th. Powell, Baronets; *Roger Mostyn, kt. & Bt.; *Rich. Lloyd, *J. Carter, *Rob. Agborough, *J. Wynn, kts.; *Th. Walcott, King's attorney; *Kenrick Eyton; Chas. Myddelton; Timothy Myddelton; Rich. Myddelton; *Simon Thelwall; *Rich. Wynn; *J. Wynn of Melai *J. Robinson; *J. Edisbury; *Chas. Salisbury; *J. Dolben; *W. Parry of Hendre; *Rob. Price of Geeler; Owen Thelwall; *Rob. Wynn of Foelas; Bevis Lloyd; Chas. Goodman; *Watkin Kyffin; *Eubule Thelwall; J. Puleston; *Francis Manley; Fulk Myddelton; W. Price; *Hugh Wynn of Berth-ddu; J. Thelwall; Th. Vaughan of Pantlas; *David Morris; W. Owen of Llunddun; Geo. Bostock; Humph. Lloyd: N.L.W., Chirk Castle Ms. F.4719 (original commission of the peace). Commission renewed to *add* Chas. & Timothy Myddelton; Hugh Roberts; J. Mathews; Humph. Lloyd: Index 4214/p.298. (Although apparently added to the commission on this date, neither Hugh Roberts nor J. Mathews appears on this original commission or on any later one, their appointment as justices having presumably been cancelled for some unspecified reason). (50)

1668: 30 June
*Orlando Bridgeman, kt. & Bt., Keeper of Great Seal; *Robartes; *Albemarle; *Ormond; *Lindsey; *Manchester; *Carbery, President of Council in the Marches of Wales; *p Ed., Lord Herbert of Cherbury; *Charlton & *Milward, Justices of Chester & of Great Sessions; *Rich. Wynn, *J. Salisbury, *Th. Powell, Baronets; *Roger Mostyn, kt. & Bt.; *Rich. Lloyd, *J. Carter, *Rob. Agborough, *J. Wynn, kts.; *J. Trevor; *Th. Walcott, King's attorney in Denbigh; *Kenrick Eyton; Chas. Myddelton; Timothy Myddelton; Rich. Myddelton; *Simon Thelwall; *Rich. Wynn; *J. Wynn of Melai; *J. Robinson; J. Thelwall; *J. Edisbury; *W. Parry of Hendre; *Rob. Price of Geeler; Owen Thelwall; *Rob. Wynn of Foelas; Bevis Lloyd; Chas. Goodman; *Watkin Kyffin; Eubule Thelwall; J. Puleston; *Francis Manley; Fulk Myddelton; W. Price; *Hugh Wynn of Berth-ddu; J. Thelwall; Th. Vaughan of Pantlas; *Ed. Brereton; *David Morris; W. Owen of Llunddun; Humph. Lloyd: N.L.W., Chirk Castle Ms. F.184. (Original commission of the peace). Commission renewed to *add* J. Trevor: Index 4214/p.331. (49)

1669: 9 March
*Bridgeman; *Robartes; *D. of Buckingham, Master of the Horse; *Albemarle; *Ormond; *Lindsey; *Manchester; *Carbery, President of Council in the Marches of Wales; *p Ed., Lord Herbert of Cherbury; *Charlton & *Milward, Justices of Chester & of Great Sessions; *Rich. Wynn, *J. Salisbury, *Th. Powell, Baronets; *Roger Mostyn, kt. & Bt.; *Rich. Lloyd,

*J. Carter, *Rob. Agborough, *J. Wynn, kts.; *Th. Walcott, King's attorney in Denbigh; *Kenrick Eyton; *J. Trevor; W. Owen; Owen Holland; *Mutton Davies; Chas. Myddelton; Timothy Myddelton; Rich. Myddelton; *Simon Thelwall; *Rich. Wynn; *J. Wynn of Melai; *J. Robinson; J. Thelwall; *J. Edisbury; *W. Parry of Hendre; *Rob. Price of Geeler; Owen Thelwall; *Rob. Wynn of Foelas; Bevis Lloyd; Chas. Goodman; *Watkin Kyffin; *Eubule Thelwall; J. Puleston; *Francis Manley; Fulk Myddelton; W. Price; *Hugh Wynn of Berth-ddu; J. Thelwall; Th. Vaughan of Pantlas; *Ed. Brereton; *David Morris; Humph. Lloyd: N.L.W., Chirk Castle Ms. F.12910 (original commission of the peace). Commission renewed to *add* Mutton Davies: Index 4214/p.342. (Note that the date of this commission is given in the Docquet Book (Index 4214) as 5 March. The discrepancy in date may be an error but is probably the result of delay in the production of the commission after receipt of the order to do so). (52).

1669: 26 April (Acting)

As on 9 March 1669, except: Owen Holland, *omitted*: Wales 4/27/4. (51)

1669: 13 September (Acting)

Robartes; Albemarle; Lindsey; Ormond; Manchester; Carbery, President of Council in the Marches of Wales; Ed., Lord Herbert of Cherbury; Charlton & Milward, Justices of Chester & of Great Sessions; Rich. Wynn, J. Salisbury, Th. Powell, Baronets; Roger Mostyn, kt. & Bt.; Rich. Lloyd, J. Carter, Rob. Agborough, J. Wynn, kts.; Th. Walcott, King's attorney in Denbigh; Kenrick Eyton; Chas. Myddelton; Rich. Myddelton; Rich. Wynn; J. Wynn of Melai; J. Robinson; J. Thelwall; Ed. Brereton; J. Trevor; Rob. Price of Geeler; Owen Thelwall; Rob. Wynn of Foelas; Bevis Lloyd; Chas. Goodman; Watkin Kyffin; Eubule Thelwall; J. Puleston; Francis Manley; Hugh Wynn of Berth-ddu; Th. Vaughan; David Morris; W. Owen of Llunddun; Humph. Lloyd: Wales 4/27/5. (41).

1670: 25 April (Acting)

As on 13 September 1669, except: D. of Albermarle; Rob. Price, *omitted*: Wales 4/28/1. (39)

1670: 19 September (Acting)

As on 25 April 1670, except: W. Parry, *added*. Watkin Kyffin, *omitted*: Wales 4/28/2. (39)

1670: 15 November

Commission renewed to *add* W. Williams: Index 4214/p.381.

1671: 8 May (Acting)

As on 19 September 1670, except: Orlando Bridgeman, Keeper of Great Seal; D. of Buckingham; B. of Bangor; J. Edisbury; W. Williams; W. Price, *added*. Rich. Wynn, *omitted*: Wales 4/28/3. (44)

1672: 29 February
Commission renewed to *add* Ed. Thelwall; Ed. Vaughan of Llwydiarth; Jas. Thelwall; J. Lloyd of Llanynys: Index 4214/p.409.

1672: 9 September (Acting)
As on 8 May 1671, except: E. of St. Albans, Household Chamberlain; B. of St. Asaph; Rob. Powell, D.D., Chancellor of St. Asaph; Owen Wynn; Ed. Thelwall; Mutton Davies; Simon Thelwall; Rich. Wynn; Ed. Vaughan of Llwydiarth; Jas. Thelwall; J. Lloyd of Llanynys, *added*. E. of Manchester; Ed. Brereton, *omitted*: Wales 4/28/5. (53)

1673: 14 April (Acting)
Orlando Bridgeman, kt. & Bt., Keeper of Great Seal; D. of Buckingham, Master of the Horse; Ormond; Lindsey; E. of St. Albans, Household Chamberlain; Carbery, President of Council in the Marches of Wales; Bishops of Bangor, St. Asaph; Ed., Lord Herbert of Cherbury; Charlton & Milward, Justices of Chester & of Great Sessions; Rich. Wynn, J. Salisbury, Th. Powell, Baronets; Roger Mostyn, kt. & Bt.; Rich. Lloyd, J. Carter, Rob. Agborough, J. Wynn, J. Trevor, kts.; Rob. Powell, D.D., Chancellor of St. Asaph; Owen Wynn; Th. Walcott, King's attorney in Denbigh; Kenrick Eyton; Ed. Thelwall; W. Owen of Llunddun; Mutton Davies; Chas. Myddelton; Timothy Myddelton; Rich. Myddelton; Simon Thelwall; Rich. Wynn; J. Wynn of Melai; J. Robinson; J. Thelwall; J. Edisbury; W. Parry of Hendre; Owen Thelwall; Rob. Wynn of Foelas; Bevis Lloyd; Chas. Goodman; Eubule Thelwall; W. Williams; J. Puleston; Francis Manley; Fulk Myddelton; W. Price; Hugh Wynn of Berth-ddu; J. Thelwall; Th. Vaughan of Pantlas; Ed. Brereton; David Morris; Humph. Lloyd; Ed. Vaughan of Llwydiarth; Jas. Thelwall; J. Lloyd of Llanynys: Wales 4/29/1. (56)

1673: 7 July
Commission renewed to *add* Cadwalader Wynn: Index 4214/p.454.

1673: 22 September (Acting)
As on 14 April 1673, except: E. of Shaftesbury, Chancellor; Viscount Osborne, Treasurer; E. of Anglesey, Keeper of Privy Seal; Marquess of Worcester, President of Council in the Marches of Wales; Cadwalader Wynn, *added*. Orlando Bridgeman; E. of St. Albans; E. of Carbery, *omitted*: Wales 4/29/2. (58)

1673: 8 December
Commission renewed to *add* Th. Myddelton, kt., *custos rotulorum*: Index 4214/p.468.

1674: 30 May
Commission renewed to *add* Rich. Parry: Index 4214/p.477.

1674: 5 October (Acting)
Heneage Finch, kt. & Bt., Keeper of Great Seal; E. of Latimer, Treasurer; E. of Anglesey, Keeper of Privy Seal; Buckingham; Ormond; Marquess of

Worcester, President of Council in the Marches of Wales; Lindsey; St. Albans; E. of Carbery; Bishops of Bangor, St. Asaph; Job Charlton, kt. & Geo. Johnson, Justices of Chester & of Great Sessions; Th. Myddelton, Rich. Wynn, J. Salisbury, Th. Powell, Baronets; Roger Mostyn, kt. & Bt.; Rich. Lloyd, J. Carter, Rob. Agborough, J. Trevor, kts.; Rob. Powell, D.D.; Owen Wynn, King's attorney; Th. Walcott, King's attorney in Denbigh; Kenrick Eyton; Ed. Thelwall; W. Owen of Llunddun; Mutton Davies; Rich. Myddelton of Bodlith; J. Wynn of Melai; J. Robinson; J. Thelwall; J. Edisbury; W. Parry of Hendre; Owen Thelwall; Bevis Lloyd; Chas. Goodman; Eubule Thelwall; W. Williams; J. Puleston; Francis Manley; W. Price; Hugh Wynn of Berth-ddu; Th. Vaughan of Pantlas; Ed. Brereton; David Morris; Ed. Vaughan of Llwydiarth; Rich. Parry; Cadwalader Wynn; J. Lloyd of Llanynys: Wales 4/29/4. (51)

1675: 12 April (Acting)
As on 5 October 1674, except: D. of Monmouth; J. Wynn, kt.; Chas. Myddelton; J. Thelwall (after Hugh Wynn); Th. Lloyd, *added*: Wales 4/29/5. (56)

1675: 13 September (Acting)
As on 12 April 1675, except: Rich. Wynn, Bt.; J. Puleston; Hugh Wynn; Th. Lloyd; J. Thelwall (this is the J. Thelwall after Hugh Wynn), *omitted*: Wales 4/29/6. (51)

1676: 3 April (Acting)
As on 13 September 1675: Wales 4/30/1. (51)

1676: 9 June
Commission renewed to *add* Th. Carter: Index 4214/p.513.

1676: 18 September (Acting)
As on 3 April 1676, except: E. of Arlington, *added*: Wales 4/30/2. (52)

1677: 1 March
Commission renewed to *add* Th. Rossindale: Index 4214/p.524.

1677: 30 April (Acting)
Finch; E. of Danby (Viscount Osborne), Treasurer; E. of Arlington, Household Chamberlain; Anglesey; Buckingham; D. of Monmouth, Master of the Horse; Ormond; Worcester, President of Council in the Marches of Wales; Lindsey; Carbery; Bishops of St. Asaph, Bangor; Charlton & Johnson, Justices of Chester & of Great Sessions; Th. Myddelton, J. Salisbury, Th. Powell, Baronets; Roger Mostyn, kt. & Bt.; Rob. Agborough, kt.; J. Wynn, kt. & Bt.; J. Trevor, kt.; Kenrick Eyton, kt.; Rob. Powell, D.D.; Owen Wynn; Th. Walcott, King's attorney in Denbigh; Ed. Thelwall; W. Owen of Llunddun; Mutton Davies; Chas. Myddelton; Rich. Myddelton of Bodlith; J. Wynn of Melai; J. Robinson; J. Thelwall; W. Parry of Hendre; Owen Thelwall; Bevis Lloyd; Chas. Goodman; W. Price; Th. Vaughan of Pantlas; Ed. Brereton; David Morris; Rich. Parry; Ed. Vaughan; Cadwalader Wynn; J. Lloyd of Llanynys:

Wales 4/30/3. (This is probably based on an outdated commission since Th. Rossindale's addition to the commission on 1 March is not reflected). (45).

1677: 25 July
Commission renewed to *omit* Th. Rossindale: Index 4214/p.531.

1677: 1 October (Acting)
As on 30 April 1677, except: Lewis Meyrick, Attorney-General for Wales; Eubule Thelwall; W. Williams; Francis Manley; Th. Carter, *added*. B. of Bangor; Owen Wynn, *omitted*: Wales 4/30/4. (Thomas Rossindale was included in this list when it was first drawn up but his name was later erased). (48)

1677: 22 November
*Finch; *Danby; *Anglesey; *Buckingham; *Monmouth; *Ormond; *Worcester, President of Council in the Marches of Wales; *Lindsey; *Arlington; *Carbery; *B. of St. Asaph; *Charlton & *Johnson, Justices of Chester & of Great Sessions; *p Th. Myddelton, Bt.; *J. Wynn, kt. & Bt.; *J. Salisbury, *Th. Powell, Baronets; *Roger Mostyn, kt. & Bt.; *Rob. Agborough, *J. Trevor, *Kenrick Eyton, kts.; *Rob. Powell, D.D.; *Lewis Meyrick, Attorney-General for Wales; *Owen Wynn; *Th. Walcott, King's attorney in Denbigh; *Ed. Thelwall; W. Owen of Llunddun; *Mutton Davies; Chas. Myddelton; *Rich. Myddelton of Bodlith; *J. Wynn of Melai; *J. Robinson; J. Thelwall; *W. Parry of Hendre; Owen Thelwall; Bevis Lloyd; Chas. Goodman; *Eubule Thelwell; *W. Williams; *Francis Manley; *Th. Carter; W. Price; J. Thelwall; Th. Vaughan of Pantlas; *Ed. Brereton; *David Morris; *Rich. Parry; *Ed. Vaughan of Llwydiarth; *Cadwalader Wynn; J. Lloyd of Llanynys: N.L.W., Chirk Castle Ms. F.1119 (original commission of the peace). (50)

1678: 18 April
Commission renewed to *add* Sidney Godolphin: Index 4214/p.542.

1678: 30 September (Acting)
As on 22 November 1677, except: B. of Bangor, *added*. Owen Wynn; Ed. Thelwall; W. Owen; J. Thelwall (listed after W. Price); Ed. Brereton (Sheriff, 1677–8); David Morris; J. Lloyd of Llanynys, *omitted*: Wales 4/30/5. (Sidney Godolphin's addition is not yet reflected). (44)

1679: 6 February
Commission renewed to *add* J. Salisbury: Index 4215/p.1.

1679: 28 April (Acting)
As on 30 September 1678, except: Owen Wynn; Sidney Godolphin; J. Salisbury of Bachygraig; J. Wynn; Ed. Brereton, *added*. B. of Bangor; Rich. Myddelton, *omitted*: Wales 4/31/1. (47)

1679: 13 October (Acting)
As on 28 April 1679: Wales 4/31/2. (47)

1680: 1 April

*Prince Rupert; *Archbishop of Canterbury; *Heneage, Lord Finch, Chancellor; *E. of Radnor, President of Council; *E. of Anglesey, Keeper of Privy Seal; Dukes of *Albemarle, *Monmouth, *Newcastle, *Lauderdale, *Ormond; *Marquess of Winchester; *Marquess of Worcester, President of Council in the Marches of Wales; *E. of Lindsey, Great Chamberlain; *E. of Arlington, Household Chamberlain; Earls of *Salisbury, *Bridgewater, *Sunderland, *Essex, *Bath, *Halifax, *Carbery; *Viscount Fauconberg; *B. of London; *Laurence Hyde; *H. Coventry; *Francis North, kt., Chief Justice of the Bench; *J. Ernley, kt., Chancellor of Exchequer; *Th. Chichley, kt., Chancellor of Duchy of Lancaster; *W. Temple, Bt.; *Daniel Finch; *Ed. Seymour; *Leoline Jenkins; *Sidney Godolphin; *Geo. Johnson, Justice of Chester; *p Th. Myddelton, Bt.; *J. Wynn, kt. & Bt.; *J. Salisbury, Bt.; *Th. Powell, Bt.; Roger Mostyn, kt. & Bt.; *Rob. Agborough, *J. Trevor, *Kenrick Eyton, kts.; *Rob. Powell, Professor of Theology; *Owen Wynn; *Lewis Meyrick, Attorney-General for Wales; *Th. Walcott, King's attorney in Denbigh; *Ed. Thelwall; W. Owen of Llunddun; *Mutton Davies; Chas. Myddelton; *Rich. Myddelton of Bodlith; *J. Wynn of Melai; J. Thelwall; *W. Parry of Hendre; Owen Thelwall; Bevis Lloyd; Chas. Goodman; Eubule Thelwall; Rich. Myddelton of Plas Newydd; *Francis Manley; *J. Myddelton of Gwaenynog; *Th. Carter; *J. Salisbury of Bachygraig; W. Price, J. Thelwall; Th. Vaughan of Pantlas; *J. Wynn; *Ed. Brereton; *David Morris; *Rich. Parry; *Ed. Vaughan of Llwydiarth; *Cadwalader Wynn; J. Lloyd of Llanynys: C.193/12/4/f.144. Commission renewed to *remove* recusants and to *add* others (no details): Index 4215/p.26. (The commission given above also contains the following corrections which were made to it over a number of years: *D. of Beaufort (Marquess of Worcester), President of Council in the Marches of Wales; Earls of *Conway, *Nottingham (Heneage Finch), *Rochester (Laurence Hyde); *Chas., Lord Herbert; *J. Warren, Second Justice of Chester; *Evan Lloyd, Bt.; *Geoff. Shackerley, kt.; *Th. Powys, King's attorney in Denbigh; *Sidney Godolphin; *J. Lloyd of Gwrych; *Hugh Meredith; Hedd Lloyd; J. Dolben. In 1680 orders were given for the *removal* from the Denbigh commission of the Duke of Buckingham and W. Williams by a warrant of 5 February and for the *addition* of Rich. Myddelton and J. Myddelton of Gwaenynog by warrants of 5 and 18 February respectively: *H.M.C., Eleventh Report, Appendix,* Part 2, p.176). (73)

1680: 26 August (Acting)

As on 1 April 1680, except: B. of St. Asaph; Job Charlton, kt., Justice of Chester; Geo. Jeffreys, kt.; J. Robinson, *added*: Wales 4/31/4. (Note that Job Charlton's name should probably not be on this list since he was superseded as Chief Justice of Chester by Geo. Jeffreys who was appointed to the office on 27 April 1680: Index 4215/p.28). (77)

1681: 3 March

Commission renewed to *add* Th. Powys, King's attorney in Denbigh: Index 4215/p.44.

1681: 5 March
Commission renewed to *add* Evan Lloyd, Bt.; Geoff. Shackerley, kt.: Index 4215/p.44.

1681: 4 April (Acting)
As on 26 August 1680, except: B. of St. Asaph; Job Charlton; Rob. Powell; Ed. Thelwall; W. Owen; Rich. Myddelton of Bodlith; J. Robinson; W. Parry; J. Lloyd, *omitted*: Wales 4/31/3. (Note that the additions made in March are not reflected in the Gaol File list of active justices). (68)

1681: 18 August
Commission renewed to *add* Hedd Lloyd; J. Dolben: Index 4215/p.54.

1681: 5 September (Acting)
As on 4 April 1681: Wales 4/31/5. (68)

1681: 23 December
Commission renewed to *add* J. Lloyd of Gwrych; Hugh Meredith: Index 4215/p.58.

1682: 17 April (Acting)
As on 5 September 1681, except: Chas., Lord Herbert; J. Warren, second Justice of Chester; Evan Lloyd, Bt.; Geoff. Shackerley, kt.; Th. Powys, King's attorney in Denbigh; Sidney Godolphin, Esq. (There are two men of this name on the commission, father and son); J. Lloyd of Gwrych; Hugh Meredith; Hedd Lloyd; J. Dolben, *added*. D. of Monmouth; Earls of Salisbury, Sunderland, Essex; W. Temple, Bt.; Geo. Johnson; Kenrick Eyton, *omitted*: Wales 4/31/6. (71)

1682: 11 September (Acting)
As on 17 April 1682: Wales 4/31/7. (71)

1683: 2 April (Acting)
Rupert; Canterbury; E. of Nottingham (Heneage Finch), Chancellor; Radnor; Anglesey; Dukes of Albemarle, Newcastle, Lauderdale, Ormond; Marquess of Winchester; Marquess of Worcester, President of Council in the Marches of Wales; Lindsey; Arlington; Earls of Bridgewater, Bath, Halifax, Carbery; Chas., Lord Herbert; Viscounts Fauconberg, Hyde; B. of London; Daniel, Lord Finch; H. Coventry; Francis North, kt., Chief Justice of King's Bench; J. Ernley, kt., Chancellor of Exchequer; Th. Chichley, kt., Chancellor of Duchy of Lancaster; Ed. Seymour; Leoline Jenkins, kt.; Sidney Godolphin; Geo. Jeffreys, kt. & Bt. & J. Warren, Justices of Chester & of Great Sessions; Th. Myddelton, Bt.; J. Wynn, kt. & Bt.; J. Salisbury, Bt.; Th. Powell, Bt.; Roger Mostyn, kt. & Bt.; Evan Lloyd, Bt.; Geoff. Shackerley, Rob. Agborough, kts.; J. Trevor, kt., one of King's Council; Th. Walcott, kt., serjeant at law; Owen Wynn; Lewis Meyrick, Attorney-General for Wales; Th. Powys, King's attorney in Denbigh; Mutton Davies; Sidney Godolphin; Chas. Myddelton; J. Wynn of Melai; J. Thelwall; Owen Thelwall; Bevis Lloyd; Chas. Goodman; Eubule Thelwall; Rich. Myddelton; Francis Manley; J. Myddelton of

Gwaenynog; Th. Carter; J. Salisbury of Bachygraig; J. Lloyd of Gwrych; W. Price; Hugh Meredith; J. Thelwall; Th. Vaughan of Pantlas; J. Wynn; Ed. Brereton; David Morris; Rich. Parry; Ed. Vaughan of Llwydiarth; Cadwalader Wynn; Hedd Lloyd; J. Dolben: Wales 4/32/1. (71)

1683: 3 September (Acting)
As on 2 April 1683: Wales 4/32/2. (71)

1683: 20 September
*Archbishop of Canterbury; *Francis North, kt., Keeper of Great Seal; *E. of Radnor, President of Council; *Marquess of Halifax, Keeper of Privy Seal; Dukes of *Albemarle, *Newcastle, *Ormond; *D. of Beaufort, President of Council in the Marches of Wales; Marquesses of *Winchester, *Worcester; Earls of *Lindsey, *Arlington, *Bridgewater, *Sunderland, *Bath, *Nottingham, *Rochester, *Carbery; *Viscount Fauconberg; *B. of London; *H. Coventry; *J. Ernley, kt., Chancellor of Exchequer; *Th. Chichley, kt., Chancellor of Duchy of Lancaster; *Ed. Seymour; *Leoline Jenkins, kt.; *Sidney Godolphin; *Geo. Jeffreys, kt. & Bt. & *J. Warren, Justices of Chester; *p Th. Myddelton, Bt.; *J. Wynn, kt. & Bt.; *J. Salisbury, Bt.; *Th. Powell, Bt.; *Roger Mostyn, kt. & Bt.; *Evan Lloyd, Bt.; *Geoff. Shackerley, *Rob. Agborough, *J. Trevor, *Th. Walcott, kts.; *Owen Wynn; *Lewis Meyrick, Attorney-General for Wales; *Th. Powys, King's attorney in Denbigh; *Mutton Davies; *Sidney Godolphin; Chas. Myddelton; *W. Jones of Carreghofa; *J. Wynn of Melai; J. Thelwall; Owen Thelwall; *Bevis Lloyd; *Chas. Goodman; *Eubule Thelwall; *Rich. Myddelton of Plas Newydd; *Francis Manley; *J. Myddelton of Gwaenynog; *Th. Carter; *J. Salisbury of Bachygraig; *J. Lloyd of Gwrych; *W. Price; *Hugh Meredith; *J. Thelwall; *Th. Vaughan of Pantlas; *Rich. Brooke; *J. Wynn; *Ed. Brereton; *David Morris; *Rich. Parry; *Ed. Vaughan of Llwydiarth; *Cadwalader Wynn; J. Lloyd of Llanynys; Hedd Lloyd; J. Dolben: N.L.W., Wynn Papers no. 2836. (This is a dated copy of the Denbigh commission of 1683). Commission renewed to *add* Rich. Brooke: Index 4215/p.89. (71)

1684: 13 February
Commission renewed to *add* Rich. Myddelton, Bt., *as custos rotulorum*: Index 4215/p.97.

1684: 17 March (Acting)
As on 20 September 1683, except: Ed. Herbert, kt., Justice of Chester; Rich. Myddelton, Bt., *added*. Geo. Jeffreys; Th. Myddelton; Th. Walcott, *omitted*: Wales 4/32/3. (70)

1684: 1 July
*Canterbury; *Francis North, Lord Guildford, Keeper of Great Seal; *Radnor; *Halifax; Dukes of *Albemarle, *Newcastle, *Ormond; *D. of Beaufort, President of Council in the Marches of Wales; Marquesses of *Winchester, *Worcester; *Lindsey; *Arlington; Earls of *Bridgewater, *Sunderland, *Bath; *Earl of Nottingham (i.e. Daniel, Lord Finch); *E. of Rochester (i.e. Laurence, Viscount Hyde); *E. of Carbery; *Viscount

Fauconberg; *B. of London; *H. Coventry; *J. Ernley, kt., Chancellor of Exchequer; *Th. Chichley, kt., Chancellor of Duchy of Lancaster; *Ed. Seymour; *Leoline Jenkins, kt.; *Sidney Godolphin; *Ed. Herbert, kt. & *J. Warren, Justices of Chester & of Great Sessions; *p Rich. Myddelton, Bt.; *J. Wynn, kt. & Bt.; *J. Salisbury, Bt.; *Th. Powell, Bt.; *Roger Mostyn, kt. & Bt.; *Evan Lloyd, Bt.; *Geoff. Shackerley, *Rob. Agborough, *J. Trevor, *Roger Puleston, kts.; *Owen Wynn, serjeant at law; *Lewis Meyrick, Attorney-General for Wales; *Th. Powys, King's attorney in Denbigh; *Mutton Davies; *Sidney Godolphin; Chas. Myddelton; *W. Jones of Carreghofa; *J. Wynn of Melai; J. Thelwall; Owen Thelwall; Bevis Lloyd; Chas. Goodman; *Eubule Thelwall; *Francis Manley; *J. Myddelton of Gwaenynog; *Th. Carter, *J. Salisbury of Bachygraig; *J. Lloyd of Gwrych; W. Price; *Hugh Meredith; J. Thelwall; *Ed. Wynn; Th. Vaughan of Pantlas; *Rich, Brooke; *J. Wynn; *Ed. Brereton; *David Morris; *Rich. Parry; *Ed. Vaughan of Llwydiarth; *Cadwalader Wynn; J. Lloyd of Llanynys; *Hedd Lloyd; *J. Dolben: N.L.W., Chirk Castle Ms. F.1118 (original commission of the peace). Commission renewed to *add* J. Puleston, kt.; Index 4215/p.104. (This must be an error for Roger Puleston, kt.). (71)

1685: 16 April
Commission renewed to record appointment of Rich. Myddelton, Bt., as *custos rotulorum*: Index 4215/p.126.

1685: 23 June
As on 1 July 1684, except: *E. of Clarendon, Keeper of Privy Seal; *E. of Middleton; *Geo., Lord Jeffreys, Chief Justice *coram Rege*; *Rob. Davies, *added*. E. of Radnor; Mutton Davies; Francis Manley, *omitted*: N.L.W., Chirk Castle Ms. F.1116 (original commission of the peace). Commission renewed to *add* Rob. Davies: Index 4215/p.131. (72)

1685: 24 August (Acting)
As on 23 June 1685, except: J. Salisbury, Bt.; J. Lloyd of Llanynys, *omitted*: Wales 4/33/2. (Both names may be omitted in error). (70)

1686: 2 March
Commission renewed to *add* Peter Ellis: Index 4215/p.147.

1686: 2 September
*Archbishop of Canterbury; *Geo., Lord Jeffreys, Chancellor; *E. of Rochester, Treasurer; *E. of Sunderland, President of Council; *E. of Clarendon, Keeper of Privy Seal; Dukes of *Albemarle, *Newcastle, *Ormond; *D. of Beaufort, President of Council in the Marches of Wales; Marquesses of *Winchester, *Worcester; *Lindsey; *E. of Mulgrave, Household Chamberlain; Earls of *Bridgewater, *Bath, *Nottingham, *Middleton; *Viscount Fauconberg; *B. of London; *Sidney, Lord Godolphin; *H. Coventry; *J. Ernley, kt., Chancellor of Exchequer; *Th. Chichley, kt., Chancellor of Duchy of Lancaster; *Ed. Herbert, kt., Chief Justice *coram Rege*; *Ed. Seymour; *J. Trevor, kt., Master of Rolls of Chancery Court; *Job Charlton, kt. & Bt. & *J. Warren, Justices of

Chester & of Great Sessions; *p Rich. Myddelton, Bt.; *J. Wynn, kt. &
Bt.; *J. Salisbury, Bt.; *Th. Powell, Bt.; *Roger Mostyn, kt. & Bt.; *Evan
Lloyd, Bt.; *Geoff. Shackerley, *Rob. Agborough, *Roger Puleston, kts.;
*Owen Wynn, serjeant at law; *Lewis Meyrick, Attorney-General for
Wales; *Ed. Jennings, King's attorney in Denbigh; *Rob. Davies; *Sidney
Godolphin; Chas. Myddelton; *W. Jones of Carreghofa; *J. Wynn of Melai;
J. Thelwall; Owen Thelwall; Bevis Lloyd; Chas. Goodman; *Eubule
Thelwall; *Rob. Price; *J. Myddelton of Gwaenynog; *Th. Carter; *J.
Salisbury of Bachygraig; W. Price; *Hugh Meredith; J. Thelwall; *Ed.
Wynn; Th. Vaughan of Pantlas; *Rich. Brooke; *J. Wynn; *Ed. Brereton;
*David Morris; *Rich. Parry; Ed. Vaughan of Llwydiarth; *Cadwalader
Wynn; Peter Ellis; J. Lloyd of Llanynys; Sidney Binner; *Hedd Lloyd;
*J. Dolben: N.L.W., Chirk Castle Ms. F.1117 (original commission of the
peace). Commission renewed to *add* Job Charlton as Chief Justice of Chester:
Index 4215/p.160.   (71)

1686: 17 December
Order by the Privy Council to *add* Ellis Lloyd; J. Maesmore; J. Parry of
Tywysog; Maurice Wynn of Graianllyn; Owen Salisbury; W. Pugh to the
Denbigh commission, and to *omit* Rich. Brooke; J. Lloyd: P.C.2/71/p.377.

1687: 26 June
D. of Beaufort recommends appointment of John Parry of Coedmarchan
as a J.P.: N.L.W. Ms. 11020E.

1687: 29 August
General renewal of Welsh commissions to add the clause of dispensation:
Index 4215/p.179.

1687: 26 September (Acting)
Canterbury; Jeffreys; Sunderland; H., Lord Arundell, Keeper of Privy Seal;
Dukes of Ormond, Albemarle, Newcastle; D. of Beaufort, President of
Council in the Marches of Wales; Marquesses of Winchester, Powys,
Worcester; Lindsey; Mulgrave; Earls of Bath, Nottingham, Middleton;
Viscounts Fauconberg, Preston; B. of Durham; J., Lord Belasyse; Geo.,
Lord Dartmouth; Sidney, Lord Godolphin; H., Lord Dover; J. Ernley, kt.;
Ed. Herbert, kt., Chief Justice of the Bench; J. Trevor, kt., Master of
Chancery Rolls; Job Charlton, kt. & Bt. & J. Warren, Justices of Chester
& of Great Sessions; Rich. Myddelton, Bt.; J. Wynn, kt. & Bt.; Th. Powell,
Bt.; Roger Mostyn, kt. & Bt.; Evan Lloyd, Bt.; Geoff. Shackerley, Roger
Puleston, kts.; Owen Wynn, serjeant at law; Griffith Jeffreys, kt.; Lewis
Meyrick, Attorney-General for Wales; Ed. Jennings, King's attorney in
Denbigh; J. Maesmore; J. Parry of Tywysog; Maurice Wynn of Graianllyn;
Rob. Davies; Sidney Godolphin; Chas. Myddelton; W. Jones of Carreghofa;
Owen Salisbury; W. Pugh; J. Wynn of Melai; Ellis Lloyd; Owen Thelwall;
Bevis Lloyd; Chas. Goodman; Eubule Thelwall; Rob. Price; Th. Carter;
W. Price; Hugh Meredith; Ed. Wynn; Th. Vaughan of Pantlas; J. Wynn;
Ed. Brereton; David Morris; W. Wynn; Ed. Vaughan of Llwydiarth;
Cadwalader Wynn; Peter Ellis; Sidney Binner; Hedd Lloyd; J. Dolben:
Wales 4/33/6.   (70)

1688: 2 April (Acting)
As on 26 September 1687: Wales 4/33/7. (70)

1688: 14 April
Commission renewed (no details): Index 4215/p.191.

1688: 1 October (Acting)
As on 2 April 1688: Wales 4/33/8. (70)

1688: 6 October
General renewal of Welsh commissions: Index 4215/p.200.

1689: 15 June
Commission renewed to *add* Rob. Cotton, kt., *custos rotulorum*: Index 4215/p.228.

1689: 2 September (Acting)
Archbishop of Canterbury; J. Maynard, Anthony Keck, W. Rawlinson, kts., Commissioners of the Great Seal; Marquess of Carmarthen, President of the Council; Marquess of Halifax, Keeper of the Privy Seal; D. of Norfolk; D. of Bolton; E. of Lindsey, Great Chamberlain; E. of Devonshire, Steward; E. of Dorset & Middlesex, Household Chamberlain; E. of Oxford; E. of Shrewsbury; E. of Bedford; E. of Bath; E. of Macclesfield, President of Council in the Marches of Wales; E. of Nottingham; J. Trenchard, serjeant at law, Justice of Chester & of Great Sessions; J. Wynn, kt. & Bt.; Walter Bagot, Bt.; Th. Powell, Bt.; Evan Lloyd, Bt.; Rich. Myddelton, Bt.; Roger Mostyn, kt. & Bt.; W. Williams, kt. & Bt.; Rob. Cotton, kt.; Rob. Owen, kt.; W. Williams; Rob. Davies; Th. Carter; ———— Thelwall (first name not given); Ed. Brereton; Joshua Edisbury; Cadwalader Wynn; Owen Thelwall; Ellis Lloyd; Hedd Lloyd; J. Dolben; J. Parry; Roger Whitley; Th. Whitley; Ed. Williams: Wales 4/34/1. (42)

Flint

1543: 12 March

*Th. Audley, kt., Chancellor; *D. of Norfolk, Treasurer; *D. of Suffolk, President of Council; *J. Russell, kt., Keeper of Privy Seal; *B. of Coventry & Lichfield, President of Council in the Marches of Wales; *B. of St. Asaph; Walter, Lord Ferrers; *p Nich. Hare, Ed. Croft, Rice Mansel, *J. Vernon, *Th. Hanmer, kts.; *J. Pakington; *Th. Holte; *David Brooke; *J. ap Rice; *Rich. Hassall; *Th. ap Richard ap Hywel; J. Hanmer of Bettisfield; Humph. Dymock; *J. Davies; *Ranulph Lloyd. *Later additions to list*: *Th. Bromley, serjeant at law; *Adam Mytton; *Peter Mutton; Peter Mostyn; H. Conway fitz Peter Conway; Th. Mostyn; Peter ap Richard ap Hywel; J. Griffith: C.193/12/1/f.46. (22 names plus 8 corrections).

1544: September (Acting)

Th., Lord Wriothesley, Chancellor; Norfolk; Suffolk; Russell; B. of Coventry & Lichfield, President of Council in the Marches of Wales; B. of St. Asaph; Lord Ferrers; Nich. Hare, Ed. Croft, Rice Mansel, J. Vernon, Th. Hanmer, kts.; Th. Bromley, serjeant at law; J. Pakington; Th. Holte; ———— (rest of list missing): Wales 4/966/5. (15)

1551: 5 October (Acting)

Richard, Lord Rich., Chancellor; E. of Wiltshire, Treasurer; E. of Warwick, President of Council; E. of Bedford, Keeper of Privy Seal; Marquess of Northampton, Great Chamberlain; E. of Worcester; Walter Ferrers, Viscount Hereford; B. of St. Asaph; W. Herbert, kt., President of Council in the Marches of Wales; Rob. Townshend, Th. Bromley, Ed. Carne, J. Subey, Rich. Cotton, J. Bridges, Anth. Kingston, J. Seyntlowe, Geo. Herbert, Rice Mansel, Th. Jones, Walter Dennys, Walter Herbert, Th. Holcrofte, Roland Hill, Th. Hanmer, Roger Brereton, W. Brereton, Jas. Croft, Hugh Cholmondeley, J. Salisbury, Rob. Acton, J. Price, Adam Mytton, kts.; J. Pollard, serjeant at law; Griffith Leyson, Ll.D.; J. Scudamore; Nich. Arnold; Rich. Hassall; W. Sheldon; Th. Mostyn; Peter Mostyn; J. Edwards; Th. Salisbury; J. Griffith; Th. Ravenscroft; H. Conway of Rhuddlan; Ranulph Lloyd; Humph. Dymock: Wales 4/966/9. (48)

1554: 24 September (Acting)

B. of Winchester, Chancellor; Marquess of Winchester, Treasurer; E. of Bedford, Keeper of Privy Seal; E. of Arundel; B. of Worcester, President of Council in the Marches of Wales; Earls of Pembroke, Worcester; B. of St. Asaph; H., Lord Stafford; Rob. Townshend, Th. Bromley, kts.; J. Pollard; David Brooke, serjeant at law; J. Seyntlowe, Rice Mansel, Th. Jones, Walter Dennys, Ed. Carne, Roland Hill, J. Price, Adam Mytton, kts.; Griffith Leyson, Ll.D.; Reg. Corbet; J. Scudamore; Rich. Hassall; W. Sheldon; J. Throckmorton; Edm. Plowden; W. Symonds; Th. Mostyn; Peter Mostyn; Ed. Stanley; J. Davies; Rich. Grosvenor; Humph. Dymock; Rob. Massey; Th. Salisbury of Flint; J. ap Griffith ap Hugh; Brian Fowler: Wales 4/967/2. (39)

1555: 20 May (Acting)
B. of Winchester; Marquess of Winchester; Arundel; Bedford; B. of Worcester, President of Council in the Marches of Wales; Earls of Worcester, Pembroke; Viscount Hereford; Bishops of Hereford, St. Davids; J. Bridges, kt., Lord Chandos; Th. Bromley, Rich. Morgan, David Brooke, Rob. Townshend, Geo. Herbert, Rice Mansel, Andrew Corbet, Ed. Carne, Th. Jones, Th. Stradling, J. Vaughan, J. Wogan, J. Price, Adam Mytton, kts.; J. Pollard; Rich. Hassall; J. Welsh; W. Gerard; Griffith Leyson, Ll.D.; Hugh Curwen, Ll.D.; J. Scudamore; J. Oteley; W. Symonds; Reg. Corbet; Geo. Wood; Edm. Plowden; Rich. Seaborne; Th. Mostyn; Rob. Massey; Peter Mostyn; J. Conway; Th. Salisbury of Flint; Brian Fowler; J. Davies; H. Conway of Rhuddlan: Wales 4/967/3. (46)

1558: Spring (Acting)
Archbishop of York, Chancellor; Marquess of Winchester; Arundel; W., Lord Paget, Keeper of Privy Seal; E. of Pembroke, President of Council in the Marches of Wales; E. of Worcester; Viscount Hereford; Bishops of Worcester, Gloucester, St. Davids, St. Asaph, Chester, Bangor; Lord Stafford; David Brooke, Geo. Herbert, Rice Mansel, Ed. Carne, Th. Jones, Roger Vaughan, J. Salisbury, J. Vaughan, Adam Mytton, Th. Hanmer, kts.; J. Scudamore; William ———, Ll.D. (surname omitted); David Lewis, Ll.D.; W. Sheldon; W. Symonds; J. Welsh; Reg. Corbet; Geo. Wood; Gilbert Gerard; Edm. Plowden; W. Wightman; W. Gerard; Rich. Seaborne; Th. Mostyn; Peter Mostyn; J. Griffith; Ed. Stanley; J. Conway; Rich. Grosvenor; J. Davies; Fulk Lloyd; Th. Salisbury of Flint; H. Conway of Rhuddlan: Wales 4/967/6. (47)

1558–59: (Acting)
*Nich. Bacon, kt., Keeper of Great Seal; *Marquess of Winchester, Treasurer; *E. of Arundel, Steward; Bishops of *Bath & Wells, *St. Asaph, *Chester; *J. Throckmorton, Justice of Chester; *J. Vaughan, *Adam Mytton, *Th. Hanmer, kts.; *J. Scudamore of Holm; *Chas. Fox; *J. Welsh; *Reg. Corbet; *W. Symonds; *W. Gerard; *Rich. Seaborne; *Peter Mostyn; *p J. Griffith; *Ed. Stanley; Rich. Grosvenor; J. Davies; Fulk Lloyd; *H. Conway of Rhuddlan: B.M., Lansdowne Ms. 1218/f.40. (Except for the omission of the *ex officio* members of the commission, the same list also appears in S.P. 12/2/17/p.71). (24)

1561: (Acting)
*Bacon; *Winchester; *Arundel; *H. Sidney, kt., President of Council in the Marches of Wales; *B. of St. Asaph; *J. Throckmorton, Justice of Chester & of Great Sessions; *Th. Hanmer, kt.; *W. Gerard; *Geo. Bromley; Peter Mostyn; *p J. Griffith; Rich. Grosvenor; W. Hanmer of Fens; Humph. Hanmer; Roger Puleston: B.M., Lansdowne Ms. 1218/f.87v. (15)

1562: 13 June
As in 1561: C.66/985/m.41d. (15)

1562: 3 August (Acting)
As on 13 June 1562, except: Ralph Leicester, kt.; Hugh Jones; H. ap Harry, added: Wales 4/968/3. (18)

1564: (Acting)
*Bacon; *Winchester; *Arundel; *Sidney; *B. of St. Asaph; *Throckmorton, Justice of Chester & of Great Sessions; *Reg. Corbet; Ralph Leicester, *Th. Hanmer, kts.; *W. Gerard; *Chas. Fox; *Rich. Wye; *Rich. Seaborne; *Rich. Pates; *J. Price; *Rich. Smith; *Hugh Evans, clerk; *Peter Mostyn; *p J. Griffith; W. Hanmer of Fens; Humph. Hanmer; *Geo. Ravenscroft; H. ap Harry; Ed. Lloyd; Roger Puleston; *Brian Fowler; J. Conway: C.66/998/m.10d. (27)

1569: 10 October (Acting)
Bacon; Winchester; E. of Pembroke, Steward; Earls of Arundel, Leicester; H. Sidney, kt., President of Council in the Marches of Wales; Throckmorton, Justice of Chester & of Great Sessions; Th. Hanmer, Ralph Leicester, kts.; W. Gerard; Chas. Fox; Rich. Wye; Ellis Price, Ll.D.; Rich. Seaborne; Rich. Pates; J. Price; Rich. Smith; W. Mostyn; Hugh Evans, clerk; J. Conway; Peter Mostyn; J. Griffith; W. Hanmer; Griffith Jones, clerk; Geo. Ravenscroft; H. ap Harry; Simon Thelwall; J. Hanmer; Jas. Barker; Ed. Lloyd; J. Trevor; Brian Fowler; Roger Puleston; Roger Brereton: Wales 4/968/7. (34)

1571: 30 April (Acting)
Bacon; Winchester; E. of Leicester; Sidney, President of Council in the Marches of Wales; B. of St. Asaph; Throckmorton, Justice of Chester; Ralph Leicester, kt.; W. Gerard; Chas. Fox; J. Rastall; Ellis Price, Ll.D.; Rich. Seaborne; Rich. Pates; J. Price; Roger Puleston; Hugh Evans, clerk; J. Conway; Peter Mostyn; J. Griffith; Griffith Jones, clerk; Geo. Ravenscroft; H. ap Harry; Simon Thelwall; Jas. Barker; Ed. Lloyd; Brian Fowler; Roger Puleston; J. Hanmer; Roger Brereton: Wales 4/968/8. (29)

1571: 8 October (Acting)
As on 30 April 1571, except: Th. Hanmer, kt., added. Jas. Barker, omitted: Wales 4/968/9. (29)

1573: (Acting)
*Bacon; *W., Lord Burghley, Treasurer; *Leicester; *Sidney, President of Council in the Marches of Wales; *B. of St. Asaph; *Hugh Cholmondeley, kt.; *Throckmorton, Justice of Chester & of Great Sessions; *Th. Hanmer, kt.; *W. Gerard; *Chas. Fox; *Ellis Price, Ll.D.; *Rich. Seaborne; *Rich. Pates; *p J. Griffith; *W. Mostyn; *Roger Puleston; *J. Conway; W. Hanmer of Fens; H. ap Harry; *J. Trevor; *Geo. Ravenscroft; *J. Hanmer; *Roger Brereton; Ed. Lloyd: S.P.12/93/part 2/f.35 & B.M., Egerton Ms. 2345/f.45. (24)

1574: 22 February (Acting)
As in 1573, except: Peter Mostyn, added: Wales 4/968/12. (25)

1575: 26 September (Acting)
*Bacon; *Burghley; *Leicester; *Sidney; *B. of St. Asaph; *Throckmorton, Justice of Chester & of Great Sessions; *Th. Hanmer, kt.; *W. Gerard; *Chas. Fox; *Ellis Price, Ll.D.; *Rich. Seaborne; *Rich. Pates; *Hugh Evans, Dean of St. Asaph; *p J. Griffith; *W. Mostyn senior; *Roger Puleston; *J. Conway; W. Hanmer of Fens; H. ap Harry; *J. Trevor; *Geo. Ravenscroft; *J. Hanmer; *Roger Brereton; Peter Mostyn; Ed. Lloyd; W. Mostyn junior; *Ed. Morgan: Wales 4/969/2. (This list is identical to another of the same year among the State Papers (S.P.12/106/ part 2/f.9) from which details of the quorum are taken). (27)

1576: August (Acting)
As on 26 September 1575: Wales 4/969/3. (27)

1576: 8 October (Acting)
As in August 1576, except: W. Mostyn junior (Sheriff, 1575–6), *omitted*: Wales 4/969/4. (26)

1577: 12 April (Acting)
As on 8 October 1576, except: Th. Mostyn; W. Mostyn junior, *added*. W. Mostyn senior, *omitted*: Wales 4/969/5. (27)

1577: 22 July (Acting)
As on 12 April 1577, except: J. Trevor; J. Hanmer; W. Mostyn junior, *omitted*: Wales 4/969/6. (This list tallies exactly with an undated list of the same year in S.P.12/121/f.40). (24)

1578: 15 September (Acting)
*Bacon; *Burghley; *Sidney, President of Council in the Marches of Wales; *B. of Worcester, Vice-President of Council in the Marches of Wales; Earls of *Leicester, *Worcester, *Pembroke; Bishops of *Hereford, *Bangor, *St. Davids, *St. Asaph; *Jas. Croft, Household Controller; *J. Throckmorton, kt., Justice of Chester & of Great Sessions; *Andrew Corbet, *J. Perrot, *Nich. Arnold, *Hugh Cholmondeley, *J. Littleton, *J. Huband, *Th. Hanmer, kts.; *David Lewis, Ll.D., Justice of the Court of Admiralty; *Geo. Bromley, attorney of Duchy of Lancaster; *W. Gerard; *W. Aubrey; *Chas. Fox; *W. Glaseor; *Ellis Price, Ll.D.; *Ed. Leighton; *Rich. Pates; *Ralph Barton; *Jerome Corbet; *J. Puckering; *Fabian Phillips; *H. Townshend; *W. Leighton; *Hugh Evans, Dean of St. Asaph; *p J. Griffith; *Roger Puleston; J. Hanmer; J. Conway; W. Hanmer of Fens; H. ap Harry; Geo. Ravenscroft; Ed. Morgan; *Peter Mostyn junior; *W. Mostyn; *Roger Brereton; Ed. Lloyd: Wales 4/969/7. (Details of the quorum are taken from an undated list of the same year in Hatfield House Ms. 223.7). (48)

1579: 2 March (Acting)
As on 15 September 1578, except: Th. Mostyn, *added*. Geo. Ravenscroft (Sheriff, 1578–9), *omitted*: Wales 4/970/1. (48)

1579: 7 September (Acting)
As on 2 March 1579, except: Th. Bromley, kt., Chancellor; Evan Lloyd of Yale; Geo. Massey, *added*. Bacon; Andrew Corbet; J. Conway, *omitted*: Wales 4/970/2. (48)

1580: 9 May (Acting)
As on 7 September 1579, except: Geo. Ravenscroft; Peter Griffith, *added*. J. Griffith; H. ap Harry, *omitted*: Wales 4/970/3. (48)

1581: 10 April (Acting)
Th. Bromley, kt., Chancellor; Burghley; Sidney, President of Council in the Marches of Wales; B. of Worcester, Vice-President of Council in the Marches of Wales; Earls of Leicester, Worcester, Pembroke; Bishops of Hereford, Bangor, St. Davids, St. Asaph; Croft; Geo. Bromley, kt. & H. Townshend, Justices of Chester & of Great Sessions; J. Perrot, Hugh Cholmondeley, J. Littleton, J. Huband, Th. Hanmer, W. Gerard, kts.; J. Puckering, serjeant at law; David Lewis, Ll.D.; W. Aubrey, Ll.D.; Chas. Fox; W. Glaseor; Ellis Price, Ll.D.; Ed. Leighton; Rich. Pates; Ralph Barton; Jerome Corbet; Fabian Phillips; W. Leighton; J. Price; Hugh Evans, Dean of St. Asaph; Evan Lloyd of Yale; Th. Mostyn; Roger Puleston; J. Hanmer; W. Hanmer of Fens; J. Conway; H. ap Harry; Geo. Ravenscroft; Ed. Morgan; Peter Mostyn; W. Mostyn; Geo. Massey; Peter Griffiths; Ed. Lloyd: Wales 4/970/5. (48)

1581: 25 September (Acting)
As on 10 April 1581, except: E. of Derby, *added*. W. Gerard, *omitted*: Wales 4/970/6. (48)

1581: 20 November (Acting)
B. of St. Asaph; Th. Hanmer, kt.; Hugh Evans, clerk; Evan Lloyd of Yale; Th. Mostyn; Roger Puleston; J. Hanmer; W. Hanmer; J. Conway; H. ap Harry; Geo. Ravenscroft; Peter Mostyn; Ed. Morgan; W. Mostyn; Roger Brereton; Peter Griffith; Ed. Lloyd; Geo. Massey of Puddington, Cheshire: Bodleian, Bodley Ms. 904/f.207. (This is a list of justices active in Flint on the above date. All the men named also appear in the full commission listed in the Gaol Files of 1581 (Wales 4) with the exception of Roger Brereton who is not listed in a Gaol File until 24 September 1582). (18)

1582: 30 April (Acting)
As on 25 September 1581, except: Peter Griffith (Sheriff, 1581–2), *omitted*: Wales 4/970/7. (47)

1582: 24 September (Acting)
As on 30 April 1582, except: Roger Brereton, *added*: Wales 4/970/8. (48)

1583: 15 April (Acting)
As on 24 September 1582, except: Simon Thelwall; Peter Griffith, *added*. Hugh Cholmondeley (Sheriff, 1582–3), *omitted*: Wales 4/971/1. (49)

1584: (Acting)
*Bromley; *Burghley; *Sidney, President of Council in the Marches of Wales; *p E. of Leicester; Earls of *Worcester, *Pembroke; Bishops of *Hereford, *Bangor, *St. Asaph; *Croft; *Bromley & *Townshend, Justices of Chester & of Great Sessions; *J. Perrot, *Hugh Cholmondeley, *J. Littleton, kts.; *J. Puckering; *W. Aubrey; *Chas. Fox; *Ellis Price, Ll.D.; *Ed. Leighton; *W. Leighton; *Rich. Pates; *Ralph Barton; *Jerome Corbet; *Fabian Phillips; *W. Glaseor; *Roger Brereton; *Roger Puleston; *J. Hanmer; *Th. Mostyn; *Evan Lloyd of Yale; *W. Hanmer of Fens; *J. Conway; *Th. Sherer; H. ap Harry; *Geo. Ravenscroft; *Ed. Morgan; Peter Mostyn junior; *W. Mostyn; Peter Griffith: E.163/14/8/f.53v.   (40)

1585: 3 May (Acting)
As in 1584, except: E. of Derby; B. of Worcester; B. of St. Davids; Simon Thelwall; J. Price; Geo. Massey, *added*. J. Conway (Sheriff, 1584–5), *omitted*: Wales 4/971/5. (Too much notice should not be taken of these changes in the composition of the commission. All the men apparently added in 1585 are on earlier Gaol File lists).   (45)

1586: 25 April (Acting)
As on 3 May 1585, except: J. Conway, *added*. B. of Bangor, *omitted*: Wales 4/971/6.   (45)

1586: 11 October (Acting)
Bromley; Burghley; Earls of Derby, Leicester; B. of Worcester; Earls of Worcester, Pembroke; Bishops of Hereford, St. Asaph, St. Davids; Croft; Bromley & Townshend, Justices of Chester & of Great Sessions; J. Perrot, Hugh Cholmondeley, J. Littleton, kts.; J. Puckering; W. Aubrey; Chas. Fox; W. Glaseor; Ellis Price, Ll.D.; Ed. Leighton; Rich. Pates; Ralph Barton; Jerome Corbet; Fabian Phillips; W. Leighton; J. Price; Roger Brereton; Roger Puleston; J. Hanmer; Th. Mostyn; J. Conway; Geo. Ravenscroft; W. Hanmer of Fens; H. ap Harry; Peter Mostyn; Th. Egerton; Ed. Morgan; W. Mostyn; Peter Griffith; Geo. Massey: Wales 4/969/8. (This file is wrongly identified in the printed list of Great Sessions records as belonging to 20 Elizabeth).   (42)

1587: 18 September (Acting)
As on 11 October 1586, except: Christopher Hatton, kt., Chancellor; Th. Sherer, *added*. Th. Bromley; E. of Derby; B. of Worcester; B. of Hereford; B. of St. Davids; W. Glaseor; Ralph Barton; J. Price; Geo. Massey, *omitted*: Wales 4/971/8.   (35)

1588: 12 August (Acting)
As on 18 September 1587, except: J. Lloyd, *added*. W. Hanmer (Sheriff, 1587–8), *omitted*: Wales 4/971/9.   (35)

1589: 8 September (Acting)
Chris. Hatton, kt., Chancellor; Burghley; Derby; Pembroke, President of Council in the Marches of Wales; E. of Warwick; B. of St. Asaph; Croft; J. Perrot, kt.; Rich, Shuttleworth, kt. & H. Townshend, Justices of Chester

& of Great Sessions; Hugh Cholmondeley, J. Littleton, kts.; Th. Egerton, Solicitor-General; J. Puckering; W. Aubrey; Chas. Fox; Ellis Price, Ll.D.; Ed. Leighton; W. Leighton; Jerome Corbet; Fabian Phillips; J. Hanmer; Roger Brereton; Roger Puleston; Th. Mostyn; J. Lloyd; Geo. Ravenscroft; J. Conway; Th. Sherer; H. ap Harry; Ed. Morgan; Roger Mostyn; Rob. Davies; Th. Hanmer; Roger Salisbury; W. Mostyn; Peter Griffith: Wales 4/972/1. (37)

1590–91 (Acting)
As on 8 September 1589, except: *B. of Chester; *J. Lloyd of St. Asaph; J. Conway of Gwerneigron; W. Griffith of Pant-y-Llawndy, added. E. of Warwick; J. Littleton; Chas. Fox; H. ap Harry; omitted: Hatfield House Ms. 278/f.59v. (37).

1593: 30 April (Acting)
As in 1590–91, except: *J. Salisbury; *J. Hope; Rich. Trevor, added. Chris. Hatton; J. Perrot, omitted: Wales 4/972/6. (J. Puckering, the new Keeper of the Great Seal, was already on the commission before his promotion. This list tallies with a list of 1592–3 contained in Kent Record Office Ms. U.350.03 which also supplies details of the quorum). (38)

1594: 27 June
*J. Puckering, kt., Keeper of Great Seal; *Burghley; *Pembroke, President of Council in the Marches of Wales; Bishops of *St. Asaph, *Chester; *p Th. Egerton, kt.; *Shuttleworth & *Townshend, Justices of Chester & of Great Sessions; *Hugh Cholmondeley, kt.; *W. Aubrey; *Ellis Price, Ll.D.; *W. Leighton; *Jerome Corbet; *Fabian Phillips; *J. Hanmer; *J. Salisbury; *Roger Puleston; *Th. Mostyn; *Roger Brereton; J. Lloyd; *Th. Ravenscroft; W. Hanmer; *J. Conway; *Th. Sherer; *W. Griffith; Ed. Morgan; *J. Hope; Th. Hanmer; Roger Mostyn; *J. Lloyd of St. Asaph; *Rob. Davies; Rich. Trevor; *Peter Griffith; Peter Mostyn; Roger Salisbury; J. Conway of Gwerneigron; W. Mostyn: C.66/1421/m.16d. (37)

1595: 15 August
As on 27 June 1594, except: *W. Fowler; Th. Evans, added. B. of Chester; W. Aubrey; Ellis Price; Th. Hanmer; Roger Mostyn; Roger Salisbury; J. Conway of Gwerneigron; W. Mostyn; Th. Sherer, omitted:C.66/1435/m.2od. General renewal of Welsh commissions: Index 4208/f.4v. (30)

1595: 19 September
Commission renewed to add J. Salisbury: Index 4208/f.5v.

1596: 12 February
Commission renewed to restore Th. Ravenscroft, former Sheriff of Flint: Index 4208/f.11.

1596: 26 April (Acting)
As on 15 August 1595, except: Rob. Davies (Sheriff, 1595–6), omitted: Wales 4/972/11. (29)

1596: 28 June

As on 26 April 1596, except: *Rob. Davies, *added*. J. Puckering, *omitted* (Puckering's successor as Keeper of the Great Seal, Th. Egerton, was already on the commission before his promotion): C.66/1468/m.16d. & S.P.13/Case F, no. 11/f.41v. Commission renewed to record appointment of Th. Ravenscroft as *custos rotulorum*: Index 4208/f.16v. (29)

1596: 25 November

Commission renewed to *add* W. Dymock: Index 4208/f.23.

1597: 12 February

*Th. Egerton, kt., Keeper of Great Seal; *Burghley; *Pembroke, President of Council in the Marches of Wales; *B. of St. Asaph; *Shuttleworth & *Townshend, Justices of Chester & of Great Sessions; *Rich. Trevor, kt.; *W. Leighton; *Jerome Corbet; *W. Fowler; *J. Hanmer; *J. Salisbury; *Roger Puleston; *Th. Mostyn; *Roger Brereton; J. Lloyd; *p. Th. Ravenscroft; W. Hanmer; *J. Conway; *W. Griffith; Ed. Morgan; *J. Hope; *J. Lloyd of St. Asaph; *Rob. Davies; Th. Evans; W. Dymock; *Peter Griffith; Peter Mostyn; J. Conway of Gwerneigron: C.66/1468/ m.31d. Commission renewed to *add* J. Conway of Gwerneigron: Index 4208/f.27v. (29)

1598: 22 April

As on 12 February 1597, except: *Th. Egerton junior, kt., *added*. Burghley; W. Fowler; J. Salisbury, *omitted*: C.66/1482/m.18d. Commission renewed to *add* Th. Egerton junior: Index 4208/f.48. (27)

1599: 11 July

As on 22 April 1598, except: *Th., Lord Buckhurst, Treasurer; *B. of Chester; *J. Salisbury (possibly omitted in error in 1598), *added*. Th. Egerton junior; Jerome Corbet, *omitted*: C.66/1493/m.28d. Commission renewed to *add* B. of Chester: Index 4208/f.74. (28)

1600: 27 February

Commission renewed to *add* Roger Salisbury: Index 4208/f.84.

1600: 12 March

Commission renewed to *add* Rich. Lewkenor, kt., Justice of Chester & of Great Sessions: Index 4208/f.85.

1600: 16 June

*Egerton; *Th., Lord Buckhurst, Treasurer; *Pembroke, President of Council in the Marches of Wales; Bishops of *Chester, *St. Asaph; *Rich. Lewkenor, kt. & *H. Townshend, Justices of Chester & of Great Sessions; *Rich. Trevor, *Th. Mostyn, J. Lloyd, kts.; *W. Leighton; *J. Hanmer; *Roger Puleston; *Roger Brereton; *p Th. Ravenscroft; W. Hanmer; *J. Conway; *W. Griffith; Ed. Morgan; *J. Hope; *J. Lloyd of St. Asaph; *Rob. Davies; *Th. Evans; W. Dymock; *Peter Griffith; Peter Mostyn; Roger Salisbury; J. Conway of Gwerneigron; David Holland: C.66/1523/ m.30d. Commission renewed to *add* David Holland: Index 4208/f.91v. (29)

1601: 27 April (Acting)
As on 16 June 1600, except: B. of St. Asaph; W. Dymock (Sheriff, 1600–1), *omitted*: Wales 4/973/8. (27)

1601: 12 May
Commission renewed to *add* Roger Mostyn: Index 4208/f.110.

1601: 2 September
As on 27 April 1601, except: *J. Salisbury, kt.; *Roger Mostyn; W. Dymock, *added*. E. of Pembroke; W. Hanmer; J. Hope; Peter Griffith, *omitted*: C.66/1549/m.31d. Commission renewed to *add* J. Salisbury, kt., and to *omit* W. Hanmer: Index 4208/f.122. (26)

1602: 25 February
Commission renewed to *add* B. of St. Asaph; J. Conway junior: Index 4208/f.130.

1602: 9 May
Commission renewed to *add* Peter Mutton: Index 4208/f.135.

1602: 25 July
General renewal of Welsh commissions to *add* Ed., Lord Zouch, President of Council in the Marches of Wales: Index 4208/f.141.

1602: 27 November
*Egerton; *Buckhurst; *Ed., Lord Zouch, President of Council in the Marches of Wales; Bishops of *Chester, *St. Asaph; *Lewkenor & *Townshend, Justices of Chester & of Great Sessions; Rich. Trevor, *Th. Mostyn, J. Lloyd, *J. Salisbury, kts.; *W. Leighton; *J. Hanmer; *Roger Puleston; *H. Mostyn, Ll.D.; *Roger Brereton; *p Th. Ravenscroft; *Roger Mostyn; *J. Conway; *W. Griffith; Ed. Morgan; *J. Lloyd of St. Asaph; *Rob. Davies; *Th. Evans; W. Dymock; Peter Mostyn; Roger Salisbury; J. Conway of Gwerneigron; *Peter Mutton; David Holland; J. Conway junior: C.66/1594/m.34d. Commission renewed to *add* H. Mostyn, Ll.D.: Index 4208/f.146v. (31)

1603: 6 June (Acting)
Egerton; Buckhurst; Zouch, President of Council in the Marches of Wales; Bishops of Chester, St. Asaph; Lewkenor & Townshend, Justices of Chester & of Great Sessions; Rich. Trevor, Th. Mostyn, J. Salisbury, kts.; W. Leighton; J. Hanmer; Roger Puleston; H. Mostyn, Ll.D.; Roger Brereton; Th. Ravenscroft; Roger Mostyn; J. Conway; W. Griffith; Ed. Morgan; Th. Evans; W. Dymock; Peter Mostyn; Roger Salisbury; J. Conway of Gwerneigron; Peter Mutton; David Holland; J. Conway junior: Wales 4/974/1. (28).

1603: 10 October (Acting)
As on 6 June 1603, except: J. Lloyd, kt., *added*. (He appears to have been added to the list after it was drawn up): Wales 4/974/2. (29)

1605: 3 June (Acting)
As on 10 October 1603, except: J. Egerton senior, kt.; W. Hanmer, kt.; Th. Hanmer, kt.; J. Lloyd of St. Asaph; Geo. Hope; Rob. Davies, *added*. B. of Chester; B. of St. Asaph; J. Hanmer; Peter Mostyn; J. Conway junior, *omitted*: Wales 4/974/4. (30)

1605: 16 September (Acting)
As on 3 June 1605, except: B. of St. Asaph; J. Conway, kt., *added*: Wales 4/974/5. (Both names appear to have been added after the making of the list. J. Conway may be the former J. Conway junior). (32)

1606: 28 July (Acting)
As on 16 September 1605, except: B. of Chester, *added*. Th. Hanmer (Sheriff, 1606–7); Th. Evans, *omitted*: Wales 4/974/6. (31)

1607: 20 April (Acting)
*Th. Egerton, Lord Ellesmere, Chancellor; *E. of Dorset (Lord Buckhurst), Treasurer; *Zouch, President of Council in the Marches of Wales; Bishops of *Chester, *St. Asaph; *Lewkenor & *Townshend, Justices of Chester & of Great Sessions; Rich. Trevor, *J. Egerton senior, *Th. Mostyn, *J. Salisbury, *W. Hanmer, *Th. Hanmer, J. Conway, *Roger Mostyn, kts.; *W. Leighton; *Roger Puleston; *H. Mostyn, Ll.D.; *Roger Brereton; *David Holland; *W. Griffith; Ed. Morgan; *J. Lloyd of St. Asaph; W. Dymock; Roger Salisbury; J. Conway of Gwerneigron; *Geo. Hope; *Peter Mutton; Rob. Salisbury; Rob. Davies: Wales 4/974/7. (Details of the quorum are taken from C.66/1748/m.30d.) (30)

1607: 28 September (Acting)
As on 20 April 1607, except: Ralph, Lord Eure, President of Council in the Marches of Wales; Th. Ravenscroft, *added*. Lord Zouch, *omitted*: Wales 4/974/8. (Lord Zouch was included in the list as it was first drawn up but later his name was erased and that of Lord Eure inserted. Eure was appointed on 12 September. Th. Ravenscroft, who was Sheriff of Flint in 1606–7, was added when his term of office expired). (31)

1608: 11 July (Acting)
As on 28 September 1607, except: E. of Salisbury, Treasurer; E. of Northampton, Keeper of Privy Seal, *added*. E. of Dorset; W. Leighton; Rob. Davies (Sheriff, 1607–8), *omitted*: Wales 4/975/1. (30)

1608: 3 October (Acting)
As on 11 July 1608, except: B. of Chester, *omitted*: Wales 4/975/2. (29)

1610: 1 October (Acting)
As on 3 October 1608, except: Th. Evans; J. Eyton; Rob. Davies, *added*. J. Salisbury; W. Hanmer; Roger Salisbury; Rob. Salisbury, *omitted*: Wales 4/975/6. (28)

1611: 8 April (Acting)
*Ellesmere; *Salisbury; *E. of Northampton, Keeper of Privy Seal; *Ralph, Lord Eure, President of Council in the Marches of Wales; *B. of St. Asaph; *Lewkenor & *Townshend, Justices of Chester & of Great Sessions; Rich. Trevor, *J. Egerton senior, *Th. Mostyn, *W. Hanmer, *Th. Hanmer, J. Conway, *Roger Mostyn, kts.; *Roger Puleston; *H. Mostyn, Ll.D.; *Roger Brereton; *p Th. Ravenscroft; *David Holland; *W. Griffith; Ed. Morgan; *J. Lloyd of St. Asaph; *Th. Evans; W. Dymock; J. Conway of Gwerneigron; *Geo. Hope; *Peter Mutton; J. Eyton; Rob. Davies: Wales 4/976/1. (Details of quorum taken from C.66/1897/m.19d.)   (29)

1611: 7 October (Acting)
As on 8 April 1611: Wales 4/976/2.   (29)

1611–12: (Acting)
As on 7 October 1611, except: *J. Conway, Esq., *added*: C.66/1898/m.27d. (The apparent addition of J. Conway at this time is probably misleading since he appears consistently after David Holland in patent roll enrolments of commissions after 1607. For some reason however his name does not appear in Gaol File lists of the same period. To avoid confusion it should be noted that there are three men named J. Conway on the commission after 1607).   (30)

1612: 28 September (Acting)
As in 1611–12, except: E. of Salisbury; J. Conway, Esq. (see note under last entry); Ed. Morgan, *omitted*: Wales 4/976/4.   (27)

1613: 11 July (Acting)
As on 28 September 1612, except: W. Griffith; J. Eyton, *omitted*: Wales 4/976/5.   (25)

1613: 4 October (Acting)
As on 11 July 1613: Wales 4/976/6.   (25)

1614: 9 May (Acting)
As on 4 October 1613, except: J. Conway, Esq.; W. Griffith, *added*. Rich. Trevor (Sheriff, 1613–14); J. Egerton, *omitted*: Wales 4/976/7.   (25)

1614: 26 September (Acting)
As on 9 May 1614, except: E. of Northampton; J. Conway, Esq.; W. Griffith; J. Conway of Gwerneigron; Geo. Hope; Peter Mutton, *omitted*: Wales 4/976/8. (Of the six men omitted on this date, the last three all re-appear on the Gaol File list for 24 April 1615. J. Conway, Esq., and W. Griffith were both marked as dead on the Gaol File list of 9 May 1614 and are therefore correctly omitted from the present list. However both men continue to appear in the commissions as enrolled on the patent rolls and have a posthumous career until about 1616).   (19)

1615: 24 April (Acting)
*Ellesmere; *Eure, President of Council in the Marches of Wales; *B. of St. Asaph; *Lewkenor & *Townshend, Justices of Chester & of Great Sessions; Rich. Trevor, *Th. Mostyn, *W. Hanmer, *Th. Hanmer, J. Conway, *Roger Mostyn, kts.; *Roger Puleston; *H. Mostyn, Ll.D.; *Roger Brereton; *p Th. Ravenscroft; *David Holland; *J. Lloyd of St. Asaph; *Th. Evans; W. Dymock; J. Conway of Gwerneigron; *Geo. Hope; *Peter Mutton; Rob. Davies: Wales 4/976/9. (Quorum based on details in C.66/2047/m.20d. Note that the commission of c.1614–15 enrolled in C.66/2047/m.20d. contains 26 names, the additional names being those of *E. of Suffolk, Treasurer; *J. Conway, Esq.; *W. Griffith; J. Eyton. Rich. Trevor, kt., is omitted). (23)

1615: 2 October (Acting)
As on 24 April 1615: Wales 4/976/10. (23)

1615: 23 December
Commission renewed to *add* Th. Mostyn: Index 4211/f.12v.

1616: 21 May
Commission renewed to *add* Th. Chamberlain, kt., serjeant at law, Justice of Chester; David Crewe, kt., serjeant at law: Index 4211/f.19v.

1616: 8 July (Acting)
As on 2 October 1615, except: E. of Suffolk, Treasurer; Th. Chamberlain, Justice of Chester; Th. Mostyn, *added*. Rich. Lewkenor; J. Conway, kt.; J. Lloyd; W. Dymock, *omitted*: Wales 4/977/1. (22)

1616: 21 September
Commission renewed to *add* Th., B. of Chester: Index 4211/f.26v.

1617: 19 March
Commission renewed to *add* Francis Bacon, kt., Keeper of Great Seal; Th., Lord Gerard, President of Council in the Marches of Wales: Index 4211/f.38.

1617: 5 May (Acting)
As on 8 July 1616, except: Bacon, Keeper of Great Seal; E. of Worcester, Keeper of Privy Seal; Lord Gerard, President of Council in the Marches of Wales; B. of Chester, *added*. Lord Ellesmere; Lord Eure; Th. Hanmer (Sheriff, 1616–17); H. Mostyn; Roger Brereton; David Holland, *omitted*: Wales 4/977/3. (20)

1617: 8 September (Acting)
As on 5 May 1617, except: J. Conway of Gwerneigron, *omitted*: Wales 4/977/4. (Note that Conway appears on the enrolled commission of 16 January 1618, although he disappears thereafter). (19)

1617: 15 November
Commission renewed to *add* Th. Brereton, kt.: Index 4211/f.51.

1617: 22 November
Commission renewed to *add* H. Salisbury: Index 4211/f.51v.

1617: 27 November
Commission renewed to *add* J. Hanmer: Index 4211/f.52v.

1617: 22 December
Commission renewed to *add* J. Conway, kt.: Index 4211/f.54v.

1618: 16 January
*Francis Bacon, kt., Chancellor; *E. of Suffolk, Treasurer; *E. of Worcester, Keeper of Privy Seal; *D. of Lennox, Steward; *W., Lord Compton, President of Council in the Marches of Wales; Bishops of *St. Asaph, *Chester; *Th. Chamberlain, kt. & *H. Townshend, kt., Justices of Chester & of Great Sessions; *Rich. Trevor, *Th. Mostyn, *W. Hanmer, *Th. Hanmer, *J. Conway, *Roger Mostyn, *Roger Puleston, *Th. Brereton, kts.; *p Th. Ravenscroft; *H. Salisbury; J. Hanmer; *Th. Mostyn; *Th. Evans; J. Conway of Gwerneigron; *Geo. Hope; *Peter Mutton; Rob. Davies; J. Eyton: C.66/2147/m.23d. Commission renewed to *add* J. Eyton: Index 4211/f.55v. (27)

1618: 28 September (Acting)
As on 16 January 1618, except: Th. Mostyn, kt.; J. Conway of Gwerneigron, *omitted*: Wales 4/977/5. (25)

1619: 12 April (Acting)
As on 28 September 1618, except: Roger Puleston, *omitted*: Wales 4/977/6. (24)

1619: 12 June
Commission renewed to *add* Francis Eure, kt.: Index 4211/f.86v.

1619: 12 July
Commission renewed to *add* J. Williams, D.D.: Index 4211/f.90v.

1619: 27 September (Acting)
As on 12 April 1619, except: Francis Eure, kt.; J. Williams, D.D., *added*. E. of Suffolk; Th. Hanmer, *omitted*: Wales 4/977/7. (24)

1620: 24 July (Acting)
As on 27 September 1619: Wales 4/977/8. (24)

1620: 25 October (Acting)
As on 24 July 1620, except that H. Salisbury and J. Hanmer are now Baronets: Wales 4/977/9. (24)

1620: 4 November
General renewal of Welsh commissions to *add* Jas. Whitlock, kt., serjeant at law, Justice of Chester: Index 4211/f.114.

1621: 12 February
*Francis Bacon, kt., Viscount St. Alban, Chancellor; *H., Viscount Mandeville, Treasurer; *Worcester; *Lennox; *E. of Northampton, President of Council in the Marches of Wales; *B. of St. Asaph; *Jas. Whitlock, kt., serjeant at law & *H. Townshend, kt., Justices of Chester & of Great Sessions; *H. Salisbury, Bt.; *J. Hanmer, Bt.; *Rich. Trevor, *W. Hanmer, *J. Conway, *Roger Mostyn, *Th. Brereton, kts.; *J. Williams, D.D.; *p Th. Ravenscroft; *Th. Mostyn; *Th. Evans; *Geo. Hope; *Peter Mutton; *Humph. Dymock; Rob. Davies; J. Eyton: C.66/2234/m.42d. Commission renewed to *add* Humph. Dymock: Index 4211/f.119. (The commission was also almost certainly renewed in order to add Viscount Mandeville for whom the commissions in nine other counties in Wales were renewed on 26 February: Index 4211/f.120). (24)

1621: 16 April (Acting)
As on 12 February 1621, except: W. Hanmer, *omitted*: Wales 4/978/1. (23)

1621: 10 September (Acting)
As on 16 April 1621, except: J. Williams, D.D., *omitted*: Wales 4/978/2. (22)

1621: 10 November
As on 10 September 1621, except: *B. of Lincoln, Keeper of Great Seal; *Lionel Cranfield, Treasurer; J. Salisbury, *added*. Viscount St. Alban; H. Townshend, kt., *omitted*: C.66/2259/m.25d. Commission renewed to *add* J. Salisbury: Index 4211/f.130. (23)

1622: 20 February
Commission renewed to *add* Rob. Morgan: Index 4211/f.135.

1622: 29 April
Commission renewed to *add* Marmaduke Lloyd, kt., second Justice of Chester & of Great Sessions: Index 4211/f.138.

1622: 7 August
*B. of Lincoln, Keeper of Great Seal; *Lionel Cranfield, E. of Middlesex, Treasurer; *Viscount Mandeville, President of Council; *Worcester; *Lennox; *Northampton, President of Council in the Marches of Wales; *E. of Bridgewater; *B. of St. Asaph; *Jas. Whitlock, kt. & *Marmaduke Lloyd, kt., Justices of Chester & of Great Sessions; *H. Salisbury, Bt.; *J. Hanmer, Bt.; *Rich. Trevor, *J. Conway, *Roger Mostyn, *Th. Brereton, *Peter Mutton, kts.; *p. Th. Ravenscroft; *Th. Mostyn; *Geo. Puleston; *Th. Evans; *Geo. Hope; *Humph. Dymock; Rob. Davies; *J. Salisbury; J. Eyton; Rob. Morgan; Roger Ellis of Alltdref; Th. Jones of Halkyn: C.66/2285/m.33d. Commission renewed to *add* Geo. Puleston; Roger Ellis; Th. Jones: Index 4211/f.143v. (29)

1624: 10 February
As on 7 August 1622, except: *Th. Mostyn, kt., *added*. D. of Lennox; B. of St. Asaph; Th. Jones of Halkyn, *omitted*: C.66/2310/m.30d. Commission renewed to *add* Th. Mostyn, kt.: Index 4211/f.160. (27)

1624: 28 October
Commission renewed to *add* Th. Chamberlain, kt., Chief Justice of Chester & of Great Sessions: Index 4211/f.171v.

1625: 1 April
General renewal of Welsh commissions at start of new reign: Index 4211/f.180v.

1625: 13 April
*Lincoln; *Jas., Lord Ley, Treasurer; *Mandeville; *Worcester; *Northampton, President of Council in the Marches of Wales; *Bridgewater; *Th. Chamberlain & *Marmaduke Lloyd, kts., Justices of Chester & of Great Sessions; *H. Salisbury, Bt.; *Rich. Trevor, *J. Conway, *Roger Mostyn, *Th. Brereton, *Peter Mutton, *Th. Mostyn, kts.; *Sampson Eure; *Rob. Brooke; *p Th. Ravenscroft; *Th. Mostyn; *Geo. Puleston; *Th. Evans; *Geo. Hope; *Humph. Dymock; *Rob. Davies; *J. Salisbury; Rob. Ravenscroft; J. Eyton; *Rob. Morgan; Roger Ellis of Alltdref: C.66/2367/m.28d. Commission renewed to *add* Rob. Ravenscroft: Index 4211/f.183v. (29)

1625: 22 December
As on 13 April 1625, except: *Th. Coventry, kt., Keeper of Great Seal, *added*. B. of Lincoln; Th. Chamberlain, *omitted*: B.M., Harleian Ms. 1622/ f.95v. General renewal of Welsh commissions to *add* Th. Coventry, Keeper of Great Seal: Index 4211/f.194v. (28)

1626: 9 March
Commission renewed to *add* J. Bridgeman, kt., Chief Justice of Chester & of Great Sessions: Index 4211/f.198v.

1626: 18 August
As on 22 December 1625, except: *J. Bridgeman, kt., Justice of Chester, etc., *added*. Th. Evans; Roger Ellis, *omitted*: C.193/12/2/f.69v & E.163/ 18/12/f.96. Commission renewed to *restore* J. Conway, kt.: Index 4211/f.208v. (Conway had presumably been omitted from the commission of 9 March, though whether by accident or design is not clear). (27)

1627: 30 March
Commission renewed to *add* Jas., Lord Strange: Index 4211/f.221v.

1627: 26 April
Commission renewed to *restore* Th. Evans: Index 4211/f.223.

1628: 23 February
*Coventry, Keeper of Great Seal; *Jas., Lord Ley, E. of Marlborough, Treasurer; *E. of Manchester (Viscount Mandeville), Keeper of Privy Seal; *Northampton, President of Council in the Marches of Wales; *Bridgewater; *Jas., Lord Strange; *J. Bridgeman & *Marmaduke Lloyd, kts., Justices of Chester & of Great Sessions; *H. Salisbury, Bt.; *Rich. Trevor, *J. Conway, *Roger Mostyn, *Th. Brereton, *Peter Mutton, *Th. Mostyn, Philip

Oldfield, kts.; *Sampson Eure; *Timothy Turneur; *p Th. Ravenscroft;
*Th. Mostyn; *Geo. Puleston; *Th. Evans; *Geo. Hope; *Humph.
Dymock; Rob. Davies; *J. Salisbury; Rob. Ravenscroft; J. Eyton; *Rob.
Morgan: C.66/2449/m.32d. Commission renewed to *add* Philip Oldfield, kt.:
Index 4211/f.240. (29).

1628: 6 October (Acting)
As on 23 February 1628, except: E. of Marlborough; E. of Manchester;
Th. Mostyn, Esq. (Sheriff, 1627–8), *omitted*: Wales 4/979/7. (26)

1628: 17 November
Commission renewed to *add* W. Ravenscroft: Index 4211/f.258v.

1628: post 14 December
As on 6 October 1628, except: *Rich., Lord Weston, Treasurer; *Ed.,
Viscount Conway, President of Council; *E. of Manchester; *E. of Pembroke; *Th. Trevor, kt., Baron of Exchequer; *J. Trevor, kt.; *Th. Mostyn,
Esq., *added*: C.66/2495/m.27d. (Conway was appointed President of Council
on 14 December 1628. The commission by which he was added as a justice
of the peace was probably issued early in 1629). (33)

1630: 7 April
As at the end of 1628, except: *B. of St. Asaph, *added*: C.66/2527/m.29d.
Commission renewed to *add* J., B. of St. Asaph: Index 4212/p.29 (34)

1630: 11 October (Acting)
As on 7 April 1630, except: J. Lloyd, *added*. E. of Pembroke; E. of Northampton; J. Trevor, *omitted*: Wales 4/980/4. (Note that this list does not
reflect the addition of B. of St. Asaph in April). (31)

1631: post 3 January
As on 11 October 1630, except: B. of St. Asaph, *added*. Viscount Conway,
omitted: C.66/2536/m.21d. (The same commission is enrolled in C.66/2577/
m.10d. Viscount Conway died on 3 January 1631). (31)

1632: 10 January
*Coventry; *Lord Weston, Treasurer; *Manchester; *E. of Bridgewater,
President of Council in the Marches of Wales; *B. of St. Asaph; *Lord
Strange; *Th. Trevor, kt., Baron of Exchequer; *Bridgeman & *Lloyd,
Justices of Chester & of Great Sessions; *H. Salisbury, Bt.; *Rich. Trevor,
*Roger Mostyn, *Th. Brereton, *Peter Mutton, *Th. Mostyn, Philip
Oldfield, kts.; *W. Griffith, Ll.D., Chancellor of St. Asaph; *Sampson Eure;
*Timothy Turneur; *p Th. Ravenscroft; *Th. Mostyn; *Geo. Puleston;
*Th. Evans; *Geo. Hope; *Humph. Dymock; *Rob. Davies; *J. Salisbury;
*J. Lloyd; Rob. Ravenscroft; J. Eyton; *Rob. Morgan: S.P.16/212/f.74.
Commission renewed to *add* W. Griffith, Ll.D.: Index 4212/p.72. (31)

1632: 6 April (Acting)
As on 10 January 1632, except: J. Conway, kt., *added*. (This is probably an
error since Conway was omitted from all enrolled commissions from 1632

and from all Gaol File lists subsequent to this one). Philip Oldfield, kt.;
Th. Evans; Humph. Dymock, *omitted* (Dymock's omission appears to be
an error): Wales 4/980/7.   (29)

1632: 5 May
As on 6 April 1632, except: *Th. Hanmer, Bt.; *Humph. Dymock, *added*.
H. Salisbury; J. Conway; J. Lloyd, *omitted*: C.66/2598/m.21d. Commission
renewed to *add* Th. Hanmer, Bt.: Index 4212/p.81.   (28)

1634: 21 February
Commission renewed to *add* Th. Davies: Index 4212/p.124.

1634: 19 May
As on 5 May 1632, except: *Th. Davies; Peter Wynn of Bagillt, *added*.
Rob. Davies, *omitted*: C.66/2623/m.23d. Commission renewed to *add* Peter
Wynn of Bagillt: Index 4212/p.135.   (29)

1634: 10 December
*Coventry; *E. of Portland (Lord Weston), Treasurer; *Manchester;
*Bridgewater, President of Council in the Marches of Wales; *B. of St.
Asaph; *Lord Strange; *Th. Trevor, kt., Baron of Exchequer; *Bridgeman
& *Lloyd, Justices of Chester & of Great Sessions; *Th. Salisbury, Bt.;
*Th. Hanmer, Bt.; *Rich. Trevor, *Roger Mostyn, *Th. Brereton, *Peter
Mutton, *Th. Mostyn, kts.; *W. Griffith, Ll.D., Chancellor of St. Asaph;
*Sampson Eure; *Timothy Turneur; *p Th. Ravenscroft; *Th. Mostyn;
*Humph. Dymock; *J. Salisbury; Rob. Ravenscroft; J. Eyton; *Rob.
Morgan; W. Mostyn; *Th. Davies; Peter Wynn of Bagillt: C.66/2654/m.23d.
Commission renewed to *add* Th. Salisbury, Bt.; W. Mostyn: Index 4212/
p.151.   (29)

1635: 19 June
Commission renewed to *add* Rich Grosvenor: Index 4212/p.170.

1635: 19 October (Acting)
As on 10 December 1634, except: Rich. Grosvenor, *added*. E. of Portland,
omitted: Wales 4/981/6.   (29)

1636: post 6 March
As on 19 October 1635, except: *B. of London, Treasurer (appointed on
6 March), *added*: S.P.16/405/f.78v.   (30).

1637: 23 February
Commission renewed to *add* Rich. Grosvenor to the quorum, and to *omit*
Th. Salisbury, Bt.; Rich. Trevor, kt.; Th. Brereton, kt.; Th. Davies, because
they did not attend the Judges to be sworn and were not excused because of
infirmity or other cause: Index 4212/p.231.

1637: 22 September
Commission renewed to *add* Peter Evans: Index 4212/p.261.

1638: 3 April

*Coventry; *B. of London, Treasurer; *Manchester; *Bridgewater, President of Council in the Marches of Wales; *B. of St. Asaph; *Lord Strange; *Th. Trevor, kt., Baron of Exchequer; *Th. Milward, kt. & *Rich. Prydderch, Justices of Chester & of Great Sessions; *Marmaduke Lloyd, kt.; *Th. Salisbury, Bt.; *Th. Hanmer, Bt.; *Roger Mostyn, *Th. Brereton, *Th. Mostyn, kts.; *W. Griffith, Ll.D., Chancellor of St. Asaph; *Sampson Eure; *p Th. Ravenscroft; *Rich. Grosvenor; *Humph. Dymock; *J. Salisbury; Peter Evans; Rob. Ravenscroft; J. Eyton; *Rob. Morgan; *W. Mostyn; Peter Wynn of Bagillt: C.66/2725/m.19d. Commission renewed to *add* Th. Milward, Justice of Chester, etc.: Index 4212/p.287. (Note that of the four men omitted from the commission on 23 February 1637, Th. Salisbury and Th. Brereton had returned to the commission by 16 October 1637 (Wales 4/982/2), having presumably been restored when the commission was renewed on 22 September 1637. The other two omitted, Trevor and Davies, did not return to the commission and may both have died soon after their omission). (27).

1639: 29 April (Acting)

As on 3 April 1638, except: Timothy Turneur; Th. Mostyn, Esq., *added*. J. Eyton (Sheriff, 1638–9), *omitted*: Wales 4/982/5. (28)

1639: 26 September

Commission renewed to record appointment of Rob. Ravenscroft as *custos rotulorum*: Index 4212/p.355.

1639: 14 October (Acting)

As on 29 April 1639, except: Lord Strange; Marmaduke Lloyd; Th. Ravenscroft, *omitted*: Wales 4/982/6. (25)

1639: 9 November

Commission renewed to *add* Rob. Davies: Index 4212/p.358.

1640: 20 April (Acting)

As on 14 October 1639, except: J. Finch, kt., Keeper of Great Seal, *added*. Lord Coventry; Rob. Ravenscroft, *omitted*: Wales 4/982/8. (Note that this list does not record the addition of Rob. Davies). (24)

1640: 27 April

*J., Lord Finch, Keeper of Great Seal; *London; *Manchester; *Bridgewater, President of Council in the Marches of Wales; *B. of St. Asaph; *Lord Strange; *Th. Trevor, kt., Baron of Exchequer; *Milward & *Prydderch, Justices of Chester & of Great Sessions; *Marmaduke Lloyd, kt.; *Th. Salisbury, Bt.; *Th. Hanmer, Bt.; *Roger Mostyn, *Th. Brereton, *Th. Mostyn, kts.; *W. Griffith, Ll.D., Chancellor of St. Asaph; *Sampson Eure; *W. Morgan; *p Th. Ravenscroft; *Rich. Grosvenor; *Th. Mostyn; *Rob. Davies; *Humph. Dymock; *J. Salisbury; Peter Evans; J. Eyton; *Rob. Morgan; W. Mostyn: C.66/2858/m.20d. Commission renewed to *add* Th. Ravenscroft as *custos rotulorum*: Index 4212/p.382. (28)

1640: 21 September (Acting)
As on 27 April 1640: Wales 4/982/7.   (28)

1641: 10 May (Acting)
As on 21 September 1640, except: Lord Finch, *omitted*: Wales 4/983/1.
(Ed. Littleton, kt., was appointed as Keeper of Great Seal on 18 January
1641 but does not appear on this list which records the office as vacant).   (27)

1641: 17 August
Commission renewed to *add* Kenrick Eyton: Index 4212/p.475.

1641: 27 September (Acting)
As on 10 May 1641, except: Ed. Littleton, kt., Keeper of Great Seal, *added*:
Wales 4/983/2. (The list is damaged so that any further changes in its
composition and its full size are unknown).

1641: 13 November
Commission renewed to *add* Ralph Hughes: Index 4212/p.487.

1642: 14 March
Commission renewed to *add* Peter Griffith: Index 4212/p.512.

1642: 25 April (Acting)
As on 10 May 1641, except: Littleton, Keeper of Great Seal; Rich. Lloyd;
Peter Griffith; Kenrick Eyton; Ralph Hughes, *added*. B. of London; B. of
St. Asaph; Th. Trevor, kt.; Th. Mostyn, kt.; Rob. Morgan, *omitted*: Wales
4/983/3.   (27)

1642: 5 August
Commission renewed to *add* Ed. Kynaston; J. Jones, and to appoint Th.
Hanmer, Bt., as *custos rotulorum*: Index 4212/p.534.

1642: 17 October (Acting)
Ed., Lord Littleton, Keeper of Great Seal; E. of Manchester, Keeper of
Privy Seal; D. of Richmond & Lennox, Steward; E. of Arundel & Surrey;
Bridgewater, President of Council in the Marches of Wales; Viscount
Saville, Household Treasurer; Viscount Falkland, King's Secretary; Lord
Strange; Peter Wyche, kt., Household Controller; Ed. Nicholas, kt.,
King's Secretary; Th. Milward & Rich. Prydderch, kts., Justices of Chester
& of Great Sessions; Marmaduke Lloyd, kt.; Th. Salisbury, Bt.; Th.
Hanmer, Bt.; Sampson Eure, Th. Brereton, kts.; W. Griffith, Ll.D.,
Chancellor of St. Asaph; Rich. Lloyd; W. Morgan; Rich. Grosvenor; Ed.
Kynaston; Rob. Davies; Peter Griffith; J. Eyton; Kenrick Eyton; Ralph
Hughes; W. Mostyn; J. Jones: Wales 4/983/4.   (29)

1643: 27 February
Commission renewed to *add* Roger Mostyn: Index 4210/p.12.

1643: 29 April
Commission renewed to *add* W. Conway; Th. Ravenscroft; David Pennant;
Th. Whitley; Ed. Lloyd: Index 4210/p.31.

1643: 29 May (Acting)
As on 17 October 1642, except: E. of Derby; W. Conway; Th. Ravenscroft; Th. Whitley; David Pennant; Ed. Lloyd; Roger Mostyn, *added*. E. of Manchester; Lord Strange, *omitted*: Wales 4/983/5. (34)

1644: 29 January (Acting)
As on 29 May 1643: Wales 4/983/6. (34)

1647: 15 January
Commission renewed (no details): Index 4213/p.74.

1647: 22 March
Commission renewed to *add* J. Bradshaw & Peter Warburton, Justices of Chester & of Great Sessions: Index 4213/p.84.

1648: 27 March (Acting)
E. of Manchester; W. Lenthall, Speaker of House of Commons; J. Bradshaw & Peter Warburton, Justices of Chester & of Great Sessions; Th. Myddelton, J. Trevor, kts; J. Glynn, Recorder of City of London; Th. Myddelton; J. Trevor; Simon Thelwall junior; J. Puleston; Th. Ravenscroft; J. Salisbury senior; Peter Evans; J. Aldersey; Roger Ellis; Luke Lloyd: Wales 4/983/7. (17)

1648: 2 October (Acting)
As on 27 May 1648: Wales 4/983/8. (17)

1649: 29 March
Commission renewed (no details): Index 4213/p.147.

1649: 11 June
*W. Lenthall, Speaker of House of Commons; *Lord Fairfax, General; *J. Bradshaw, President of Council; *Bulstrode Whitelock, *Rich. Keble, *J. Lisle, Commissioners of Great Seal; *E. of Pembroke & Montgomery; *E. of Denbigh; *H. Rolle, Chief Justice of Upper Bench; *Oliver St. John, Chief Justice of Court of Common Pleas; *J. Wilde, Chief Baron of Exchequer; *Peter Warburton & *J. Puleston, Justices of Chester & of Great Sessions; *Edm. Prideaux, Attorney-General; *Th. Myddelton, *J. Trevor, kts.; *Th. Ravenscroft; *J. Jones; *J. Aldersey; J. Salisbury; *Humph. Dymock; *Humph. Mackworth; *Roger Hanmer; *Th. Holford; *Luke Lloyd; Peter Evans; Roger Ellis; Th. Lloyd of Halghton; Rich. Young; David Jones; H. Birkenhead; Peter Foulkes; Piers Conway: C.193/13/3/f.76. Commission renewed to *add* Humph. Mackworth; Roger Hanmer; Th. Holford: Index 4213/p.152. (33)

1649: 10 September (Acting)
As on 11 June 1649, except: Th. Ravenscroft (Sheriff, 1649), *omitted*: Wales 4/983/9. (32)

1650: 25 July
*Lenthall; *Oliver Cromwell, Lord General; *Bradshaw; *Whitelock, *Keble & *Lisle; *E. of Pembroke & Montgomery; *E. of Denbigh;

*Rolle; *St. John; *Wilde; *J. Puleston and *Peter Warburton, Justices of Common Pleas; *Th. Fell & *Humph. Mackworth, Justices of Chester & of Great Sessions; *Prideaux, Attorney-General; *J. Trevor, kt.; *J. Bradshaw, attorney in Flint; *p. Th. Ravenscroft; *J. Jones; *J. Aldersey; *J. Salisbury; *Humph. Dymock; *Roger Hanmer; Th. Holford; Peter Evans; Roger Ellis; Rich. Young; David Jones; H. Birkenhead; Peter Foulkes; Piers Conway; J. Conway; J. Peck: *Lists published by Th. Walkley* (1650), p.67. Commission renewed to *add* J. Bradshaw, attorney in Flint; J. Peck, and to *omit* Th. Myddelton, kt.; Luke Lloyd; Th. Lloyd of Halghton: Index 4213/p.196. (34)

1651: 13 August
As on 25 July 1650, except: *Th. Crichley, *added*. J. Conway, *omitted*: C.193/13/4/f.119. Commission renewed to *add* Th. Crichley: Index 4213/p.224. (34)

1652: 31 August
As on 13 August 1651, except: *Rob. Eyton, kt.; *Th. Dymock; *Ralph Hughes, *added*. Humph. Dymock, *omitted*: Cambridge University Ms. Dd.VIII.1/f.125v. Commission renewed to *add* Rob. Eyton, kt.; Th. Dymock; Ralph Hughes: Index 4213/p.246. (36)

1652: 27 September (Acting)
As on 31 August 1652: Wales 4/984/6. (36)

1653: 28 July
Commission renewed to *add* Andrew Ellis; Th. Ball; Geo. Twistleton, and to *omit* E. of Pembroke; E. of Denbigh; J. Trevor, kt.; Rob. Eyton, kt.; Th. Ravenscroft; J. Aldersey; J. Salisbury; Th. Dymock; Roger Hanmer; Th. Holford; Peter Evans; Roger Ellis; Peter Foulkes; Piers Conway; J. Peck: Index 4213/p.265.

1653: 13 October
Commission renewed to *add* J. Trevor, kt.; Luke Lloyd; Geo. Manley; Peter Foulkes, and to *omit* J. Bradshaw, attorney, and others (no details): Index 4213/p.271.

1654: 23 March
Commission renewed according to a general list: Index 4213/p.285. (This was probably the occasion for adding to the commission J. Bradshaw, who was appointed as Justice of Chester & of Great Sessions on 16 February: Ibid./p.279).

1654: 23 April (Acting)
Whitelock, Keble & Lisle; Rolle; W. Lenthall, Master of the Rolls; St. John; J. Bradshaw & Th. Fell, Justices of Chester & of Great Sessions; Edm. Prideaux, Attorney-General; J. Trevor, Rob. Eyton, kts.; J. Glynn, serjeant at law; J. Jones; Th. Ravenscroft; Luke Lloyd; Geo. Twistleton; Andrew Ellis; Rich. Young; H. Birkenhead; Th. Ball; Ralph Hughes; Th. Crichley; Th. Dymock; J. Peck: Wales 4/984/8. (24)

1654: 16 October (Acting)
As on 23 April 1654, except: Humph. Mackworth, member of Lord Protector's Council; Peter Foulkes, *added*. Oliver St. John, *omitted*: Wales 4/984/9. (25)

1655: 1 October (Acting)
As on 16 October 1654, except: Oliver St. John, *added*. Humph. Mackworth; Peter Foulkes (Sheriff, 1654–5), *omitted*: Wales 4/985/1. (24)

1655: 12 December
Commission renewed to *add* Colonel Jas. Berry: Index 4213/p.321.

1656: 24 March
*Nathanial Fiennes & *J. Lisle, Commissioners of Great Seal; *Bulstrode Whitelock, kt., *Th. Widdrington, kt., *Ed. Montagu & *W. Sydenham, Commissioners of Treasury; *J. Glynn, Chief Justice of Upper Bench; *Lenthall; *St. John; *Bradshaw & *Fell, Justices of Chester & of Great Sessions; *Edm. Prideaux, Attorney-General; *J. Trevor, *Rob. Eyton, kts.; *Major-General Jas. Berry; *Ralph Hughes; *J. Jones; *Th. Ravenscroft; *Luke Lloyd; *Geo. Twistleton; *p Andrew Ellis; *J. Peck; *Rich. Young; *David Jones; *H. Birkenhead; *Th. Ball; *Peter Foulkes; *Th. Crichley; Th. Dymock; Peter Foulkes: C.193/13/5/f.126 & ibid./6/f.105v. Commission renewed to place J. Peck on the quorum: Index 4213/p.331. (Note that the apparent presence of two men named Peter Foulkes may be caused by a later correction to the list to move Peter Foulkes higher up in the order of justices). (30)

1656: 7 April (Acting)
As on 24 March 1656, except: David Jones; Peter Foulkes; Th. Dymock (Sheriff, 1655–6); Peter Foulkes, *omitted*: Wales 4/985/2. (Comparison between this list and the commission of 24 March is in fact misleading since the present list is clearly based on a commission of before 24 March, the latter commission having presumably not yet reached Flint. But at the same time it is also apparent that the total number of justices listed in each Gaol File runs consistently a little below that of other sources). (26)

1656: 13 October (Acting)
As on 7 April 1656: Wales 4/985/3. (26)

1657: 13 April (Acting)
As on 13 October 1656, except: Rob. Eyton, kt., *omitted*: Wales 4/985/4. (25)

1657: 28 September (Acting)
As on 13 April 1657, except: Th. Dymock, *added*: Wales 4/985/5. (26)

1658: 12 April (Acting)
As on 28 September 1657, except: Rob. Eyton, kt., *added*. (Probably omitted in error in 1657). Ralph Hughes (Sheriff, 1657–8), *omitted*: Wales 4/985/6. (26)

1658: 24 September
General renewal of Welsh commissions to *add* Rich. Cromwell, Lord
Protector: Index 4213/p.405.

1658: 25 September (Acting)
As on 12 April 1658, except: Rob. Eyton, *omitted*: Wales 4/985/7.   (25)

1659: 18 April (Acting)
As on 25 September 1658: Wales 4/985/8. (Note that the name of Rich.
Cromwell is not included, presumably because of his fall from power early
in 1659).   (25)

1659: 8 July
Commission renewed according to a general list (no details): Index 4213/
p.438.

1659: 5 October
Commission renewed to *omit* J. Peck: Index 4213/p.443.

1660: 3 March
Commission renewed according to a general list: Index 4213/p.453.

1660: 16 August
Commission renewed to *add* Th. Hanmer, Bt., *custos rotulorum*, and others
(no details): Index 4214/p.28. (Kenrick Eyton, appointed King's attorney
in Flint on 3 August, (ibid./p.23), was probably added on this date).

1660: 4 September
Commission renewed to *add* Timothy Turneur & Rob. Milward, Justices of
Chester & of Great Sessions; W. Mostyn; Th. Crichley: Index 4214/p.35.

1660: 10 September (Acting)
*Ed. Hyde, kt., Chancellor; *E. of Southampton, Treasurer; *D. of
Albemarle, General; *Marquess of Ormond, Steward; *E. of Lindsey,
Great Chamberlain; *E. of Manchester, Household Chamberlain; *Timothy
Turneur & *Rob. Milward, Justices of Chester & of Great Sessions; *p
Th. Hanmer, Bt.; *Evan Lloyd, Bt.; *Roger Mostyn, Bt.; H. Conway, Bt.;
*Th. Myddelton, *J. Hanmer, *J. Carter, kts.; *Kenrick Eyton; *Rob.
Davies; *W. Price; *Th. Ravenscroft; *W. Mostyn; *Roger Puleston;
Rob. Whitley; *Roger Whitley; *W. Hanmer; Th. Lloyd; *J. Parry; *Th.
Crichley; Roger Grosvenor; J. Broughton; J. Salisbury: Wales 4/986/1.
(Details of the quorum are taken from two identical lists of about the same
date contained in C.220/9/4/f.106 & B.M., Egerton Ms. 2557/f.105).   (30)

1661: 7 March
Commission renewed to *add* Peter Griffith; Th. Mostyn; J. Peck; Chas.
Jones: Index 4214/p.88.

1661: 25 March (Acting)
As on 10 September 1660, except: Peter Griffith; Th. Mostyn; J. Peck;
Chas. Jones, *added*: Wales 4/986/2.   (34)

1661: 26 August
Commission renewed to *add* Geoff. Palmer, kt. & Bt., Justice of Chester & of Great Sessions: Index 4214/p.136.

1661: 8 November
General renewal of Welsh commissions to *add* E. of Carbery, President of Council in the Marches of Wales: Index 4214/p.144.

1662: 20 March
As on 25 March 1661, except: *Lord Robartes, Keeper of Privy Seal; *E. of Carbery, President of Council in the Marches of Wales; *Job Charlton, kt., Justice of Chester and of Great Sessions, *added* (Palmer's appointment as Justice of Chester did not last long enough to be reflected in any of the surviving lists of justices). Timothy Turneur; Th. Ravenscroft; J. Peck, *omitted*: C.66/2986/m.32d. & C.193/12/3/f.120v. Commission renewed to *add* Job Charlton, kt., serjeant at law, Justice of Chester, etc.: Index 4214/p.163. (34)

1662: 21 July (Acting)
As on 20 March 1662, except: Th. Ravenscroft, *added*. Roger Puleston; Roger Grosvenor, *omitted*: Wales 4/986/4. (33)

1662: 20 October (Acting)
As on 21 July 1662: Wales 4/986/5. (33)

1663: 24 August (Acting)
As on 20 October 1662, except: Roger Puleston, *added*: Wales 4/986/7. (34)

1663: 26 October (Acting)
As on 24 August 1663, except: Evan Lloyd, Bt., *omitted*: Wales 4/986/6. (33)

1664: 18 July (Acting)
*E. of Clarendon, Chancellor; *Southampton; *Lord Robartes, Keeper of Privy Seal; *Albemarle; *Ormond; *Lindsey; *Manchester; *E. of Carbery, President of Council in the Marches of Wales; *Job Charlton, kt., serjeant at law & *Rob. Milward, Justices of Chester & of Great Sessions; *Th. Hanmer, Bt.; *Roger Mostyn, kt. & Bt.; *H. Conway, Bt.; *Th. Myddelton, *J. Hanmer, *J. Carter, kts.; *Kenrick Eyton; *W. Price; *Th. Ravenscroft; *W. Mostyn; *Rob. Davies; *Roger Puleston; Rob. Whitley; *Roger Whitley; *W. Hanmer; *J. Parry; *Peter Griffith; *Th. Crichley; Th. Mostyn; Chas. Jones; J. Broughton; J. Salisbury: Wales 4/986/8. (The quorum is based mainly on an enrolled commission of about 1663: C.66/3022/m.36d.) (32)

1664: 3 October (Acting)
As on 18 July 1664: Wales 4/986/9. (32)

1665: 24 April (Acting)
As on 3 October 1664, except: Th. Lloyd, *added*. J. Salisbury, *omitted*: Wales 4/986/10. (32)

1665: 11 September (Acting)
As on 24 April 1665, except: Roger Grosvenor; J. Peck; J. Salisbury, *added*: Wales 4/986/11. (Some of the variations between 1662 and 1665 may be the effects of working from an outdated commission, since there appears to have been no renewal during this time. The Gaol File list of 11 September 1665, for example, contains the name of Evan Lloyd, Bt., although he had died in October 1663). (35)

1666: 7 March
Commission renewed to *add* W. Griffith: Index 4214/p.278.

1666: 26 March (Acting)
As on 11 September 1665, except: J. Glynn, serjeant at law; W. Griffith, *added*. Th. Ravenscroft; Roger Grosvenor; J. Peck, *omitted*: Wales 4/986/12. (34)

1666: 13 August (Acting)
As on 26 March 1666: Wales 4/986/13. (34)

1667: 22 April (Acting)
Clarendon; Southampton; Robartes; Albemarle; Ormond; Lindsey; Manchester; Carbery, President of Council in the Marches of Wales; Charlton & Milward, Justices of Chester & of Great Sessions; Th. Hanmer, Bt.; Roger Mostyn, kt. & Bt.; H. Conway, Bt.; J. Hanmer, J. Carter, kts.; Kenrick Eyton; W. Price; Th. Ravenscroft; W. Mostyn; W. Griffith; Roger Puleston; Rob. Whitley; Roger Whitley; W. Hanmer; Th. Lloyd; J. Parry; Peter Griffith; Th. Crichley; Chas. Jones; J. Broughton; J. Salisbury: Wales 4/987/1. (31)

1667: 16 September (Acting)
As on 22 April 1667, except: Clarendon; Southampton; Roger Puleston, *omitted*: Wales 4/987/2. (28)

1668: 29 June (Acting)
As on 16 September 1667: Wales 4/987/3. (28)

1668: 28 September (Acting)
As on 29 June 1668: Wales 4/987/4. (28)

1669: 5 March
Commission renewed to *add* Mutton Davies: Index 4214/p.342.

1669: 20 April
Commission renewed to *add* Ed. Pennant: Index 4214/p.343.

1669: 3 May (Acting)
As on 28 September 1668, except: Orlando Bridgeman, kt. & Bt., Keeper of Great Seal; D. of Buckingham; Mutton Davies, *added*. J. Broughton (Sheriff, 1668-9), *omitted*: Wales 4/987/5. (30)

1669: 27 September (Acting)
As on 3 May 1669, except: Ed. Pennant, *added.* H. Conway; W. Hanmer, *omitted*: Wales 4/987/6. (29)

1670: 22 April (Acting)
Orlando Bridgeman, kt. & Bt., Keeper of Great Seal; Robartes; D. of Buckingham; Ormond; Lindsey; Manchester; Carbery, President of Council in the Marches of Wales; Charlton & Milward, Justices of Chester & of Great Sessions; Th. Hanmer, Bt.; Evan Lloyd, Bt.; Roger Mostyn, kt. & Bt.; J. Hanmer, J. Carter, kts.; Kenrick Eyton, King's attorney in Flint; W. Price; Th. Ravenscroft; W. Griffith; Rob. Whitley; Roger Whitley; Th. Lloyd; J. Parry; Peter Griffith; Th. Crichley; Chas. Jones; Ed. Pennant; J. Broughton; J. Salisbury: Wales 4/988/1. (28)

1670: 22 September (Acting)
As on 22 April 1670, except: Evan Lloyd, Bt., *omitted* (probably in error): Wales 4/988/2. (27)

1671: 18 April
Commission renewed to *add* Kenrick Eyton senior: Index 4214/p.390.

1671: 12 May (Acting)
As on 22 September 1670, except: Evan Lloyd, Bt., *added*: Wales 4/988/3. (Eyton's addition was too recent to be reflected in this list). (28)

1671: 25 July
Commission renewed to *add* Rob. Powell, D.D.: Index 4214/p.399.

1672: 8 April (Acting)
As on 12 May 1671, except: E. of St. Albans, Household Chamberlain; B. of St. Asaph; Rich. Lloyd, kt.; Th. Myddelton, kt.; Kenrick Eyton senior; Mutton Davies; W. Mostyn, *added.* Lord Robartes; E. of Manchester, *omitted*: Wales 4/988/5. (33)

1672: 23 May
Commission renewed to *restore* Roger Mostyn, Bt., who had been omitted from the commission by accident: Index 4214/p.415. (Mostyn had probably been omitted from the commission issued on 25 July 1671 to add Rob. Powell. This commission had clearly not reached the county by 8 April 1672 since in the list of justices drawn up for the Great Session held on that date the name of Rob. Powell appears as a later addition in a different hand. Roger Mostyn is named in this list but his name is partly erased, presumably in response to the details given in the newly arrived commission).

1672: 20 June
Commission renewed to *add* J. Salisbury, Bt.: Index 4214/p.416.

1672: 16 September (Acting)
As on 8 April 1672, except: J. Salisbury, Bt.; Rob. Powell, D.D., Chancellor of St. Asaph; Owen Wynn; Th. Mostyn, *added.* W. Mostyn, *omitted*: Wales 4/988/6. (36)

1673: 25 April (Acting)
As on 16 September 1672: Wales 4/988/7.   (36)

1673: 2 July
Commission renewed to *add* Th. Hanmer: Index 4214/p.453.

1673: 29 September (Acting)
E. of Shaftesbury, Chancellor; Viscount Osborne, Treasurer; E. of Anglesey, Keeper of Privy Seal; Buckingham; Ormond; Marquess of Worcester, President of Council in the Marches of Wales; Earls of Lindsey, St. Albans, Carbery; B. of St. Asaph; Charlton & Milward, Justices of Chester & of Great Sessions; Th. Hanmer, J. Salisbury, Evan Lloyd, Baronets; Roger Mostyn, kt. & Bt.; Rich. Lloyd, Th. Myddelton, J. Hanmer, J. Carter, kts.; Rob. Powell, D.D., Chancellor of St. Asaph; Kenrick Eyton senior; Owen Wynn; Kenrick Eyton junior, King's attorney in Flint; W. Price; Th. Ravenscroft; Mutton Davies; Th. Hanmer; W. Mostyn; W. Griffith; Rob. Whitley; Roger Whitley; W. Hanmer; Th. Lloyd; J. Parry; Peter Griffith; Th. Crichley; Th. Mostyn; Chas. Jones; Ed. Pennant; J. Broughton; J. Salisbury: Wales 4/988/8.   (42)

1674: 4 May (Acting)
As on 29 September 1674, except: Geo. Johnson, second Justice of Chester, etc.; Roger Puleston, *added*. E. of Shaftesbury; Rob. Milward; W. Hanmer, *omitted*: Wales 4/988/9.   (41)

1674: 28 September (Acting)
As on 4 May 1674, except: Th. Mostyn, *omitted*: Wales 4/988/10. (The omission of both W. Hanmer and Th. Mostyn in the course of 1674 may be an error since both reappear on the Gaol File of 19 April 1675).   (40)

1675: 19 April (Acting)
As on 28 September 1674, except: Lord Finch, Keeper of Great Seal; D. of Monmouth; W. Hanmer; Th. Mostyn, *added*. Roger Puleston, *omitted*: Wales 4/989/1.   (43)

1675: 6 September (Acting)
As on 19 April 1675, except: Peter Griffith, *omitted*: Wales 4/989/2.   (42)

1676: 8 August
Commission renewed to *add* Ed. Ravenscroft; Th. Evans; Ralph Whitley: Index 4214/p.517.

1676: 11 September (Acting)
As on 6 September 1675, except: E. of Arlington; Lewis Meyrick; Ed. Ravenscroft; Th. Evans; Ralph Whitley, *added*. E. of St. Albans; Rich. Lloyd; Evan Lloyd; Owen Wynn; W. Hanmer; Ed. Pennant, *omitted*: Wales 4/989/4.   (41)

1677: 7 May (Acting)
(Lord Finch, Chancellor); E. of Danby, Treasurer; Anglesey; Dukes of Buckingham, Monmouth, Ormond; Marquess of Worcester, President of Council in the Marches of Wales; Earls of Lindsey, Arlington, Carbery; B. of St. Asaph; Job Charlton, kt. & Geo. Johnson, Justices of Chester & of Great Sessions; Th. Hanmer, Bt.; J. Salisbury, Bt.; Roger Mostyn, kt. & Bt.; Th. Myddelton, J. Hanmer, Kenrick Eyton, kts.; Rob. Powell, D.D., Chancellor of St. Asaph; Lewis Meyrick, King's attorney in Wales; Kenrick Eyton junior, King's attorney in Flint; W. Price; Th. Ravenscroft; Mutton Davies; Th. Hanmer of Fens; Ed. Ravenscroft; W. Mostyn; W. Griffith; Rob Whitley; Roger Whitley; Th. Lloyd; J. Parry; Th. Evans; Th. Crichley; Th. Mostyn; Ralph Whitley; Chas. Jones; J. Broughton; J. Salisbury: Wales 4/989/5. (The name of the Chancellor is omitted from the actual list). (40)

1677: 25 July
Commission renewed to *add* Th. Griffith of Caerwys; Th. Eyton of Leeswood; Th. Edwards of Rhual: Index 4214/p.531.

1677: 8 October (Acting)
As on 7 May 1677, except: Th. Griffith of Caerwys; Th. Eyton of Leeswood; Th. Edwards of Rhual, *added*: Wales 4/989/6. (43)

1678: 15 April (Acting)
As on 8 October 1677: Wales 4/989/7. (43)

1678: 23 July
Commission renewed to *add* J. Trevor, kt.; Owen Barton: Index 4214/p.547.

1678: 19 November
Commission renewed to *add* Roger Mostyn, Bt., as *custos rotulorum*: Index 4214/p.551.

1679: 6 February
Commission renewed to *add* J. Salisbury: Index 4215/p.1.

1679: 5 April
Commission renewed to *add* Th. Hanmer, kt.; W. Hanmer: Index 4215/p.4.

1679: 5 May (Acting)
As on 15 April 1678, except: J. Trevor, kt.; Th. Hanmer, kt.; J. Salisbury of Bachygraig; Owen Barton, J. Wynn, *added*. E. of Danby; Th. Hanmer, Bt.; Th. & Ed. Ravenscroft; J. Parry, *omitted*: Wales 4/990/1. (43)

1679: 20 June
Commission renewed to *add* Rich. Parry; W. Rutter: Index 4215/p.9.

1679: 6 October (Acting)
As on 5 May 1679, except: W. Hanmer, *added*. (Hanmer should have been included in the previous Gaol File list). W. Mostyn, *omitted*: Wales 4/990/2. (43)

1680: 20 April
Commission renewed to *remove* recusants and to *add* others (no details):
Index 4215/p.27. (The removal from the Flint commission of the Duke of
Buckingham; Th. Ravenscroft; Th. Mostyn; and Ralph Whitley was
ordered by a warrant of 5 February 1680: *H.M.C., Eleventh Report,
Appendix*, Part 2, p.179).

1680: 11 June
*Prince Rupert; *Archbishop of Canterbury; *Lord Finch, Chancellor;
*E. of Radnor, President of Privy Council; *E. of Anglesey, Keeper of
Privy Seal; Dukes of *Albemarle, *Monmouth, *Newcastle, *Ormond,
*Lauderdale; *Marquess of Winchester; *Marquess of Worcester, President
of Council in the Marches of Wales; Earls of *Lindsey, *Arlington, *Salis-
bury, *Bridgewater, *Sunderland, *Essex, *Bath, *Halifax, *Carbery;
*Viscount Fauconberg; *B. of London; *Laurence Hyde; *H. Coventry;
*Francis North, kt., Chief Justice of Bench; *J. Ernley, kt., Chancellor of
Exchequer; *Th. Chichley, kt., Chancellor of Duchy of Lancaster; *W.
Temple, Bt.; *Ed. Seymour; *Daniel Finch; *Leoline Jenkins; *Sidney
Godolphin; *Geo. Jeffreys, kt. & Bt. & *Geo. Johnson, Justices of Chester
& of Great Sessions; *J. Salisbury, Bt.; *p Roger Mostyn, Bt.; *Th.
Myddelton, kt.; *Th. Hanmer, kt.; *J. Trevor, kt.; *Kenrick Eyton, kt.;
*Robert Powell, D.D.; *Lewis Meyrick, King's attorney in Wales; *Kenrick
Eyton junior, King's attorney in Flint; *W. Price; *Mutton Davies; *Th.
Hanmer of Fens; *Ed. Ravenscroft; *W. Mostyn; *W. Griffith; Rob.
Whitley; *Roger Whitley; *J. Salisbury of Bachygraig; Th. Lloyd; *W.
Hanmer; *Rich. Parry; *Th. Evans; *Th. Crichley; *W. Rutter; *Owen
Barton; *Th. Griffith of Caerwys; *Chas. Jones; *Th. Eyton of Leeswood;
*J. Wynn; *Ed. Pennant; Th. Edwards of Rhual; J. Broughton; J. Salisbury:
C.193/12/4/f.146v. Commission renewed to *add* Chas. Jones: Index 4215/
p.32. (68)

1680: 20 August (Acting)
As on 11 June 1680, except: E. of Ossory; J. Hanmer, kt., *added*. Ed.
Ravenscroft; W. Mostyn; Ed. Pennant; J. Salisbury, *omitted*: Wales 4/990/3.
(Some of these omissions may not be real). (66)

1681: 28 March (Acting)
As on 20 August 1680, except: J. Salisbury, *added*. Th. Evans (Sheriff,
1680–81), *omitted*: Wales 4/990/4. (66)

1681: 12 September (Acting)
As on 28 March 1681, except: Geo. Johnson; J. Salisbury, *omitted*: Wales
4/990/5. (64)

1682: 10 April (Acting)
As on 12 September 1681, except: J. Salisbury; Th. Evans, *added*. Kenrick
Eyton senior; Rob. Powell; Chas. Jones; Th. Edwards of Rhual (Sheriff,
1681–2), *omitted*: Wales 4/991/1. (62)

1682: 18 September (Acting)
As on 10 April 1682, except: D. of Lauderdale; J. Salisbury; Lewis Meyrick, *omitted*: Wales 4/991/2. (59)

1683: 9 April (Acting)
As on 18 September 1682, except: D. of Lauderdale; Geo. Johnson; Kenrick Eyton senior; Rob. Powell, D.D.; Lewis Meyrick; Ed. Ravenscroft; W. Mostyn; Chas. Jones; Ed. Pennant; Th. Edwards of Rhual; J. Salisbury, *added*: Wales 4/991/3. (These additions are all of men who had apparently been left out of the commission since 11 June 1680. It is unlikely that any of these omissions was genuine). (70)

1683: 10 September (Acting)
As on 9 April 1683, except: D. of Monmouth; E. of Essex; Geo. Johnson; Chas. Jones; Ed. Pennant; J. Salisbury, *omitted*: Wales 4/991/4. (64)

1684: 24 March (Acting)
As on 10 September 1683, except: Monmouth; Essex; Geo. Johnson; Chas. Jones; Ed. Pennant; J. Salisbury, *added*. Th. Crichley; Th. Eyton (Sheriff, 1683–4), *omitted*: Wales 4/991/5. (68)

1684: 25 March
Commission renewed to *add* Th. Jones of Halkyn: Index 4215/p.100.

1684: 1 July
Commission renewed to *add* Roger Puleston, kt.: Index 4215/p.104. (The original entry gives the name incorrectly as John Puleston).

1684: 4 August (Acting)
Canterbury; Lord Guildford, Keeper of Great Seal; Radnor; Marquess of Halifax, Keeper of Privy Seal; Dukes of Albemarle, Newcastle, Ormond; D. of Beaufort, President of Council in the Marches of Wales; Marquesses of Winchester, Worcester; Earls of Lindsey, Arlington, Bridgewater, Sunderland, Bath, Nottingham, Rochester, Carbery; Viscount Fauconberg; B. of London; H. Coventry; J. Ernley, kt., Chancellor of Exchequer; Th. Chichley, kt., Chancellor of Duchy of Lancaster; Ed. Seymour; Leoline Jenkins, kt.; Sidney Godolphin; Ed. Herbert, kt. & J. Warren, Justices of Chester & of Great Sessions; Roger Mostyn, Bt.; J. Hanmer, kt. & Bt.; J. Trevor, Roger Puleston, Th. Hanmer, kts.; Lewis Meyrick, King's attorney in Wales; Kenrick Eyton, King's attorney in Flint; W. Price; Mutton Davies; Th. Hanmer of Fens; Ed. Ravenscroft; W. Griffith; Rob. Whitley; Roger Whitley; J. Salisbury of Bachygraig; Th. Lloyd; W. Hanmer; Rich. Parry; Th. Evans; Th. Crichley; W. Rutter; J. Wynn; Th. Edwards of Rhual; Th. Jones of Halkyn; J. Broughton: Wales 4/991/6. (53)

1685: 30 March (Acting)
As on 4 August 1684, except: Th. Eyton, *added*. Mutton Davies; Ed. Ravenscroft; Th. Crichley; J. Wynn, *omitted*: Wales 4/992/1. (Some at least of these omissions are probably erroneous). (50)

1685: 16 June
Commission renewed to record appointment of Roger Mostyn, Bt., as *custos rotulorum*. (This is in fact a reappointment): Index 4215/p.131.

1685: 7 August (Acting)
As on 30 March 1685, except: E. of Clarendon, Keeper of Privy Seal; E. of Middleton; Lord Jeffreys, Chief Justice of Pleas *coram Rege*; J. Salisbury, Bt.; Rob. Davies; W. Mostyn; Ed. Ravenscroft; Th. Crichley; Owen Barton; Th. Griffith; J. Wynn, *added*. E. of Radnor, *omitted*: Wales 4/992/2. (60)

1686: 2 March (Acting)
As on 7 August 1685, except: Ed. Lutwich, kt., Chief Justice of Chester & of Great Sessions, *added*. Lord Guilford; J. Salisbury, Bt.; W. Mostyn; Ed. Ravenscroft; J. Salisbury of Bachygraig; Th. Eyton; Th. Crichley; Th. Griffith, *omitted*: Wales 4/992/3. (Note that J. Salisbury, Bt., died in 1684 and is therefore being provided with a posthumous career). (53)

1686: 2 September
Commission renewed to *add* Job Charlton, kt., Chief Justice of Chester & of Great Sessions: Index 4215/p.160.

1686: 4 October (Acting)
*Canterbury; *Lord Jeffreys, Chancellor; *E. of Rochester, Treasurer; *E. of Sunderland, President of Council; *E. of Clarendon, Keeper of Privy Seal; Dukes of *Albemarle, *Newcastle, *Ormond; *D. of Beaufort, President of Council in the Marches of Wales; Marquesses of *Winchester, *Worcester; Earls of *Lindsey, *Mulgrave, *Bridgewater, *Bath, *Nottingham, *Middleton, *Carbery; *Viscount Fauconberg; *B. of London; *Sidney, Lord Godolphin; *H. Coventry; *J. Ernley, kt., Chancellor of Exchequer; *Th. Chichley, kt., Chancellor of Duchy of Lancaster; *Ed. Herbert, kt., Lord Chief Justice; *Ed. Seymour; *J. Trevor, kt., Master of Rolls of Chancery; *Job Charlton, kt. & *J. Warren, Justices of Chester & of Great Sessions; *p Roger Mostyn, kt. & Bt.; *J. Hanmer, kt. & Bt.; *Roger Puleston, *Th. Hanmer, kts.; *Lewis Meyrick, King's attorney in Wales; *Kenrick Eyton junior, King's attorney in Flint; *W. Price; *Rob. Davies; *Th. Hanmer of Fens; *W. Griffith; Rob. Whitley; *Roger Whitley; Th. Lloyd; *W. Hanmer; *Rich. Parry; *Th. Evans; *W. Rutter; *Owen Barton; *Th. Eyton; *J. Wynn; Th. Edwards of Rhual; *Th. Jones of Halkyn; J. Broughton: Wales 4/992/4. (Quorum based on undated list of about 1685: C.193/12/5/f.172v.). (52)

1686: 17 December
Order by Privy Council to *omit* from the Flint commission Roger Whitley and to *add* Ed. Mostyn, kt.; Geo. Pennant; Piers Mostyn; Ed. Pennant; Ed. Petre; W. Fitzherbert; Th. Mostyn of Brimford: P.C.2/71/p.377. (Note that these changes are not reflected in the Gaol File lists until 3 October 1687, following the renewal of all the Welsh commissions on 29 August 1687).

1687: 28 March (Acting)
As on 4 October 1686, except: J. Salisbury, Bt. (see note under 2 March 1686); Ed. Ravenscroft; W. Mostyn; J. Salisbury of Bachygraig; Th. Crichley (probably an error as he was noted as dead in the list of 7 August 1685); Th. Griffith of Caerwys, *added.* E. of Carbery, *omitted*: Wales 4/992/5. (57)

1687: 29 August
General renewal of Welsh commissions to add the clause of dispensation: Index 4215/p.179.

1687: 3 October (Acting)
Canterbury; Jeffreys; Sunderland; Lord Arundell of Wardour, Keeper of Privy Seal; Dukes of Ormond, Albemarle, Newcastle; D. of Beaufort, President of Council in the Marches of Wales; Marquesses of Winchester, Powys, Worcester; Earls of Lindsey, Mulgrave, Bath, Nottingham, Middleton; Viscounts Fauconberg, Preston; J., Lord Belasyse; Geo., Lord Dartmouth; Sidney, Lord Godolphin; J. Ernley, kt., Chancellor of Exchequer; Ed. Herbert, kt., Chief Justice of the Bench; J. Trevor, kt., Master of the Rolls; Charlton & Warren, Justices of Chester & of Great Sessions; J. Salisbury, Bt. (see note under 2 March 1686); Roger Mostyn, Bt.; J. Hanmer, kt. & Bt.; Roger Puleston, Ed. Mostyn, Th. Hanmer, kts.; Lewis Meyrick, Attorney-General for Wales; Kenrick Eyton junior, King's attorney in Flint; Geo. Pennant; Piers Mostyn; W. Price; Ed. Pennant; Ed. Petre; Rob. Davies; Th. Hanmer of Fens; W. Fitzherbert; Th. Mostyn of Brimford; W. Griffith; Rob. Whitley; Th. Lloyd; W. Hanmer; Rich. Parry; Th. Evans; Th. Crichley; W. Rutter; Owen Barton; Ed. Lloyd; J. Wynn; Th. Edwards; Th. Jones; J. Broughton: Wales 4/992/6. (57)

1688: 9 April (Acting)
As on 3 October 1687: Wales 4/992/7. (57)

1688: 14 April
Commission renewed (no details): Index 4215/p.191.

1688: 6 October
General renewal of Welsh commissions: Index 4215/p.200.

1688: 8 October (Acting)
Canterbury; Jeffreys; Sunderland; Arundell of Wardour; Dukes of Norfolk, Ormond, Albemarle, Newcastle; D. of Beaufort, President of Council in the Marches of Wales; Marquesses of Winchester, Powys, Worcester; Earls of Lindsey, Mulgrave, Bath, Nottingham, Middleton, Castlemaine; Viscounts Montgomery, Fauconberg, Preston; B. of Durham; Lords Belasyse, Dartmouth, Godolphin, Dover; J. Ernley, kt., Chancellor of Exchequer; Ed. Herbert, kt., Chief Justice of the Bench; J. Trevor, kt., Master of the Rolls; Job Charlton, kt. & Bt. & J. Warren, Justices of Chester & of Great Sessions; J. Hanmer, kt. & Bt.; Ed. Mostyn, kt.; Rich. Parry; Ed. Pennant; J.——nor; Th. Lloyd of Bangor; Kenrick Eyton junior; Geo. Pennant; Piers Mostyn; Ed. Petre; W. Fitzherbert; J. Wynn; Th. Edwards

of Rhual; H. Mostyn; Th. Mostyn of Kelston; Philip Henry, clerk; Rob. Roberts; Geo. Da——; Th. Price of Bryn-y-Pys: Wales 4/992/8. (This list is probably based on the commission of 14 April 1688 rather than of 6 October 1688 which could not have reached the county by 8 October. Parts of the list are no longer legible). (50).

1691: 19 September (Acting)
Archbishop of Canterbury; Marquess of Carmarthen, President of Council; D. of Norfolk; D. of Bolton; E. of Lindsey, Great Chamberlain; E. of Devon, Steward; Earls of Dorset, Oxford, Shrewsbury, Bedford, Bath, Macclesfield, Nottingham; J. Trevor, kt.; W. Rawlinson & Geo. Hutchins, Commissioners of Great Seal; J. Trenchard, kt. & Littleton Powys, Justices of Chester & of Great Sessions; J. Conway, Bt.; W. Hanmer of Bettisfield; Th. Eyton of Trimley; W. Lloyd of Halghton; W. Minshall, attorney in Flint; Th. Evans of Northope; Th. Whitley of Aston; Ellis Young; Owen Barton: Wales 4/993/5. (27)

Montgomery

1543: 12 March
*Th., Lord Audley, Chancellor; *D. of Norfolk, Treasurer; *D. of Suffolk, President of Council; *J. Russell, kt., Keeper of Privy Seal; *B. of Coventry & Lichfield, President of Council in the Marches of Wales; *B. of St. Asaph; B. of Bangor; Walter, Lord Ferrers; Ed., Lord Powys; *Nich. Hare, Ed. Croft, Rice Mansel, *J. Vernon, kts.; *J. Pakington; *Th. Holte; *David Brooke; *J. ap Rice; *Rich. Hassall; *p J. Salisbury senior; *J. Corbet; *Jas. Leche; *Walter Blount; *Griffith David John; Math. Thomas ap Rice; *W. Herbert; Rich. ap Hywel; Rice ap Maurice ap Owen. *Later additions to list*: *Th. Bromley, serjeant at law; *Adam Mytton; *Rich. Price, clerk; Reginald Williams; Ed. ap Rice; Humph. Lloyd; Lewis Jones: C.193/12/1/ f.45. (27 names plus 7 corrections).

1554: 21 May (Acting)
B. of Winchester, Chancellor; Marquess of Winchester, Treasurer; E. of Arundel; E. of Bedford (J. Russell), Keeper of Privy Seal; B. of Worcester, President of Council in the Marches of Wales; E. of Worcester; Viscount Hereford; B. of St. Asaph; Th. Bromley, Rich. Morgan, Rob. Townshend, Rice Mansel, Ed. Carne, Th. Jones, Th. Stradling, Andrew Corbet, J. Price, Adam Mytton, kts.; J. Pollard; Rich. Hassall; J. Welsh; Griffith Leyson, Ll.D.; Hugh Curwen, Ll.D.; J. Scudamore; W. Symonds; Reg. Corbet; Edm. Plowden; Rich. Germyn; H. Stafford; Ed. Herbert; W. Herbert; Maurice Knyvett, clerk; Math. Price; Humph. Lloyd; Nich. Purcell; Rice ap Maurice ap Owen; J. ap Hugh: Wales 4/124/1. (37)

1555: (Acting)
H. Stafford, kt.; Ed. Herbert; Humph. Lloyd; Th. Williams; Owen ap John ap Hywel Vaughan; W. Herbert; Math. Price; Lewis Jones; Rice ap Maurice ap Owen; J. Bulkeley; Rich. ap Hywel; Nich. Purcell: S.P.11/5/f.59. (12)

1558–59: (Acting)
*Nich. Bacon, kt., Keeper of Great Seal; *Marquess of Winchester, Treasurer; *E. of Arundel, Steward; Bishops of *Bath & Wells, *Chester; *J. Throckmorton, Justice of Chester; *J. Vaughan, *Adam Mytton, *H. Stafford, kts.; *J. Scudamore of Holm; *Chas. Fox; *J. Welsh; *Reg. Corbet; *W. Symonds; *W. Gerard; *Rich. Seaborne; *p Ed. Herbert; *Humph. Lloyd; *Th. Williams; W. Herbert; *Rich. Lloyd; *Rich. Price, clerk; *Nich. Purcell; J. ap Hugh; Rice ap Maurice ap Owen; *Owen ap John ap Hywel Vaughan; *J. Bulkeley: B.M., Lansdowne Ms. 1218/f.39v. (Except for the omission of the *ex officio* members of the commission, the same list also appears in S.P.12/2/17/p.74). (27)

1561: 17 March (Acting)
Bacon; Winchester; Arundel; H. Sidney, kt., President of Council in the Marches of Wales; Bishops of Hereford, Worcester, Bangor, St. Davids, St. Asaph; Throckmorton, Justice of Chester & of Great Sessions; Reg. Corbet, Justice *coram Regina*; Nich. Arnold, Adam Mytton, J. Vaughan, H. Stafford, kts.; Chas. Fox; Rich. Lloyd; J. Scudamore of Holm; W. Gerard; Rich. Seaborne; Geo. Bromley; Ed. Herbert; Humph. Lloyd;

W. Herbert; Hugh Powell; Rich. Lloyd; Owen ap Evan ap Hywel Vaughan; J. Bulkeley; Th. Williams; Rice ap Maurice ap Owen; Griffith Lloyd, clerk; Edm. Lloyd; Rich. Price, clerk; Owen ap Owen; David Price: Wales 4/124/3. (Note that this Gaol File list is considerably larger than the list for 1559 because of its inclusion of all the members of the Council in the Marches of Wales who appeared on the commission). (35)

1561: 23 June (Acting)
Bacon; Winchester; Arundel; Sidney, President of Council in the Marches of Wales; Bishops of Bangor, Hereford, St. Asaph; Throckmorton, Justice of Chester & of Great Sessions; Ed. Herbert; Humph. Lloyd; W. Herbert; Hugh Powell; Rich. Lloyd; Owen ap Evan ap Hywel Vaughan; J. Bulkeley; Th. Williams; Rice ap Maurice ap Owen; Griffith Lloyd, clerk; Edm. Lloyd; Rich. Price, clerk; Owen ap Owen; David Price: Wales 4/124/4. (22)

1562: 13 June
*Bacon; *Winchester; *Arundel; *Sidney; Bishops of *Bangor, *St. Asaph; *Throckmorton, Justice of Chester & of Great Sessions; *p Ed. Herbert; Humph. Lloyd; W. Herbert; Hugh Powell; Rich. Lloyd; Owen ap Evan ap Hywel Vaughan; J. Bulkeley; Rice ap Maurice ap Owen; Griffith Lloyd, clerk; Edm. Lloyd; Rich. Price, clerk; Owen ap Owen: C.66/985/m.41d. (19)

1562: 20 July (Acting)
As on 13 June 1562, except: Th. Williams; David Price, *added*. Humph. Lloyd; J. Bulkeley, *omitted*: Wales 4/124/5. (The apparent addition of Williams and Price may have been the result of using a commission of the peace dated prior to that of 13 June when drawing up the Gaol File list). (19)

1563: 9 August (Acting)
*Bacon; *Winchester; *Arundel; *Sidney, President of Council in the Marches of Wales; Bishops of *Bangor, *St. Asaph; *H., Lord Stafford; *Throckmorton, Justice of Chester & of Great Sessions; *Reg. Corbet, Justice *coram Regina*; *W. Gerard; *Chas. Fox; *Rich. Wye; *Ellis Price, Ll.D.; *Rich. Seaborne; *Rich. Pates; *J. Price; *Rich. Smith; *p Ed. Herbert; W. Herbert; *Rich. Lloyd; *Owen ap Evan ap Hywel Vaughan; Rice ap Maurice ap Owen; *Ralph Hanmer; *J. Price of Newtown; *J. Gwynn; Edm. Lloyd; Hywel ap Owen: Wales 4/125/1. (Details of quorum taken from enrolled commission of 1564: C.66/998/m.10d.) (27)

1563: 6 December (Acting)
As on 9 August 1563: Wales 4/125/2. (27)

1564: 20 March (Acting)
As on 6 December 1563, except: J. Price, clerk, *added*: Wales 4/125/3. (This list is identical to that enrolled under 1564: C.66/998/m.10d.) (28)

1566: 2 September (Acting)
As on 20 March 1564, except: Rich. Price, clerk; Geo. Beynon; J. ap Hugh ap Evan, *added*. H. Sidney; B. of Bangor; Lord Stafford; J. Price, clerk; Owen ap Evan ap Hywel Vaughan; J. Price of Newtown; Hywel ap Owen, *omitted*: Wales 4/125/4. (24)

1567: 23 June (Acting)
As on 2 September 1566, except: H. Sidney; B. of Bangor; Lord Stafford; J. Price of Newtown, *added*. Reg. Corbet, *omitted*: Wales 4/125/5. (Note that some of the changes in the commission which appear in this and other Gaol File lists may be caused by vagaries in drawing up the Gaol File lists and not necessarily by real changes). (27)

1567: 29 September (Acting)
As on 23 June 1567, except: B. of Bangor; Lord Stafford, *omitted*: Wales 4/125/6. (25)

1568: 5 April (Acting)
As on 29 September 1567, except: E. of Pembroke, Steward; B. of Bangor; Th. Tanat; H. Townshend; Ed. Davies; Humph. ap John Wynn, *added*. Ed. Herbert (Sheriff, 1567–8); Geo. Beynon, *omitted*: Wales 4/126/1. (29)

1568: 13 September (Acting)
Bacon; Winchester; E. of Pembroke, Steward; E. of Arundel; Sidney, President of Council in the Marches of Wales; Bishops of St. Asaph, Bangor; Throckmorton, Justice of Chester & of Great Sessions; W. Gerard; Chas. Fox; Rich. Wye; Rich. Seaborne; Ellis Price, Ll.D.; Rich. Pates; J. Price; Rich. Smith; Rich. Price, clerk; W. Herbert; Rich. Lloyd; Rice ap Maurice ap Owen; J. Price; Th. Tanat; J. ap Hugh ap Evan; Ralph Hanmer; H. Townshend; J. Gwynn; Ed. Davies; Edm. Lloyd; Humph. ap John Wynn: Wales 4/126/2. (29)

1570: 1 May (Acting)
As on 13 September 1568, except: Hugh Cholmondeley, kt., Vice-President of Council in the Marches of Wales; Rowland Hayward; Ed. Herbert; Rob. Myddelton; David Lloyd Blayney, *added*. W. Herbert; J. Price (this is the J. Price listed after Rich. Pates); Th. Tanat (Sheriff, 1569–70); Rich. Smith, *omitted*: Wales 4/126/4. (30)

1571: 14 May (Acting)
Bacon; Winchester; Sidney, President of Council in the Marches of Wales; B. of Bangor; Hugh Cholmondeley, kt., Vice-President of Council in the Marches of Wales; Throckmorton, Justice of Chester & of Great Sessions; W. Gerard; Chas. Fox; Ed. Gray; Rowland Hayward; Rich. Seaborne; Ellis Price, Ll.D.; Rich. Pates, Ed. Herbert; Rich. Price, clerk; J. Herbert; J. Price of Newtown; H. Townshend; Th. Tanat; Ed. Davies; Rich. Herbert; Ralph Hanmer; Morgan Gwynn; David Lloyd ap Jenkin; J. Gwynn; J. Wynn senior; Rob. Myddelton; David Lloyd Blayney; Roland ap Hugh; J. Vaughan: Wales 4/127/1. (30)

1571: 22 October (Acting)
As on 14 May 1571, except: B. of St. Asaph; Humph. ap John Wynn, *added*:
Wales 4/127/2. (32)

1572: 22 September (Acting)
*Bacon; *Sidney, President of Council in the Marches of Wales; *B. of
St. Asaph; *B. of Bangor; *Hugh Cholmondeley, kt., Vice-President of
Council in the Marches of Wales; *Throckmorton, Justice of Chester & of
Great Sessions; *Rowland Hayward, kt.; *W. Gerard; *Chas. Fox; *Rich.
Seaborne; *Ellis Price, Ll.D.; *Rich. Pates; *p Ed. Herbert; *Ed. Davies;
*J. Herbert; Rich. Say (not known if was on quorum); *J. Price of New-
town; *J. Vaughan; *Rich. Herbert; Morgan Gwynn; *David Lloyd ap
Jenkin; *Rob. Myddelton; David Lloyd Blayney; Roland ap Hugh;
*Griffith Lloyd; J. Weaver: Wales 4/127/3. (Details of quorum taken from
two lists of about 1573–4 contained in S.P.12/93/part 2/f.34v. & B.M.,
Egerton Ms. 2345/f.44v). (26)

1574: 29 March (Acting)
As on 20 September 1572, except: W., Lord Burghley, Treasurer, *added*.
Rich Say, *omitted*: Wales 4/127/5. (26).

1575: 5 September (Acting)
As on 29 March 1574, except: E. of Leicester; Oliver Lloyd; Th. Tanat;
H. Townshend; Arthur Price, *added*. Hugh Cholmondeley, *omitted*: Wales
4/128/1. (30)

1576: 20 August (Acting)
As on 5 September 1575, except: Rich. Say, *added*: Wales 4/128/2. (31)

1577: 18 March (Acting)
As on 20 August 1576, except: Rich. Say; David Lloyd Blayney (Sheriff,
1576–7), *omitted*: Wales 4/128/4. (29)

1578: 30 June (Acting)
*Bacon; *Burghley, Treasurer; *Sidney, President of Council in the Marches
of Wales; *B. of Worcester, Vice-President of Council in the
Wales; *E. of Leicester, Chamberlain of Chester; Earls of *Worcester,
*Pembroke; Bishops of *Hereford, *Bangor, *St. Davids, *St. Asaph;
*Jas. Croft, kt., Household Controller; *Throckmorton, Justice of Chester
& of Great Sessions; *Andrew Corbet, *J. Perrot, *Nich. Arnold, *Hugh
Cholmondeley, J. Littleton, *J. Huband, kts.; *David Lewis, Ll.D., Judge
of Court of Admiralty; *Geo. Bromley, attorney of Duchy of Lancaster;
*W. Gerard; *W. Aubrey; *Chas. Fox; *W. Glaseor; *Ellis Price, Ll.D.;
*Ed. Leighton; *Rich. Pates; *Ralph Barton; *Jerome Corbet; *J.
Puckering; *Fabian Phillips; *H. Townshend; *W. Leighton; *p Ed.
Herbert of Montgomery; *J. Herbert; *J. Vaughan; *J. Price of Newtown;
*Rich. Herbert; Th. Tanat; Rich. Price, clerk; *David Lloyd ap Jenkin of
Llanidloes; Rob. Myddelton of Middleton Hall; David Lloyd Blayney of
Tregynon; *Griffith Lloyd; Roland ap Hugh; Morgan Gwynn; Rich. Morris:
Wales 4/129/1. (This list matches exactly two other lists of 1578 con-
tained in B.M., Royal Ms. 18.D.III/f.105v & Hatfield House Ms. 223.7 of
which the latter also provides details of the quorum). (48)

1578: 8 September (Acting)
As on 30 June 1578: Wales 4/129/2.   (48)

1579: 16 February (Acting)
As on 8 September 1578, except: Andrew Corbet; J. Herbert: Rich. Price; Rich. Morris (Sheriff, 1578-9), *omitted*: Wales 4/129/3.   (44)

1579: 21 September (Acting)
As on 16 February 1579, except: *Th. Bromley, kt., Chancellor; *J. Price; *J. Herbert; *Arthur Price; *Rich. Morris; Th. Price; Th. Jukes, *added*. Nich. Bacon, kt., *omitted*: Wales 4/129/4. (Details of membership of quorum taken from S.P.12/145/f.54v.)   (50)

1580: 17 October (Acting)
As on 21 September 1579, except: Rich. Price; Rich. ap Hugh of Pencoed, *added*. J. Throckmorton, *omitted*: Wales 4/130/2.   (51)

1581: 24 April (Acting)
As on 17 October 1580, except: Nich. Arnold; J. Herbert; Rich. Price, *omitted*: Wales 4/130/3.   (48)

1582: 10 September (Acting)
As on 24 April 1581, except: J. Herbert; Rich. Price; Oliver Lloyd, *added*. J. Vaughan; Morgan Gwynn (Sheriff, 1581-2), *omitted*: Wales 4/130/5. (Note that the restoration of J. Herbert & Rich. Price is certainly an error, since both were dead by this date. Both were omitted from a list of 16 men active as justices on 20 November 1581 which is contained in Bodleian, Bodley Ms. 904/f.207).   (49)

1583: 7 October (Acting)
*Th Bromley, kt., Chancellor; *Burghley; *Sidney, President of Council in the Marches of Wales; Earls of *Leicester, *Worcester, *Pembroke; Bishops of *Worcester, *Hereford, *Bangor, *St. Asaph; *Croft; *Geo. Bromley, kt. & *H. Townshend, Justices of Chester & of Great Sessions; *David Lewis, Ll.D., Master of Court of Requests; *J. Perrot, *Hugh Cholmondeley, *J. Littleton, *J. Huband, kts.; *J. Puckering, serjeant at law; *W. Aubrey; *Chas. Fox; *W. Glaseor; *Ellis Price, Ll.D.; *Ed. Leighton; *Rich. Pates; *Ralph Barton; *Jerome Corbet; *Fabian Phillips; *W. Leighton; J. Price (not clear if is on quorum); *p Ed. Herbert; *Rich. Herbert of Parke; *Rich. Herbert of Montgomery; *J. Price of Newtown; *Oliver Lloyd; *Arthur Price; *Rich. Morris; *David Lloyd Blayney; *Rice Tanat; *David Lloyd ap Jenkin; Rob. Myddelton; *Griffith Lloyd; Th. Price; Th. Jukes: Wales 4/131/2. (Details of quorum taken from a list of 1584 in E.163/14/8/f.52v).   (44)

1584: 15 June (Acting)
As on 7 October 1583, except: J. Owen Vaughan, *added*. J. Huband, *omitted*: Wales 4/131/3.   (44)

1584: 12 October (Acting)
As on 15 June 1584, except: Rich. Herbert of Parke (Sheriff, 1583–4), *omitted*: Wales 4/131/4. (43)

1585: 7 May (Acting)
As on 12 October 1584, except: Rich. Herbert of Parke, *added*. David Lloyd Blayney, *omitted*: Wales 4/132/1. (43)

1585: 4 October (Acting)
As on 7 May 1585, except: Reginald Williams, *added·*: Wales 4/132/2. (44)

1588: 25 March (Acting)
Christopher Hatton, kt., Chancellor; Burghley; E. of Pembroke, President of Council in the Marches of Wales; E. of Leicester, Steward; B. of St. Asaph; Croft; Bromley & Townshend, Justices of Chester & of Great Sessions; J. Perrot, Hugh Cholmondeley, J. Littleton, kts.; J. Puckering, serjeant at law; W. Aubrey; Chas. Fox; W. Glaseor; Ellis Price, Ll.D.; W. Leighton; Ed. Leighton; Rich. Pates; Ralph Barton; Jerome Corbet; Fabian Phillips; Ed. Herbert; David Powell, D.D.; Rich. Herbert of Parke; Rich. Herbert of Montgomery; Oliver Lloyd; J. Owen Vaughan; J. Price; Reginald Williams; Arthur Price; Rich. Morris; Rice Tanat; Rob. Myddelton; Griffith Lloyd; Th. Price; Th. Jukes; Ed. Price of Llanfyllin: Wales 4/133/3. (38)

1589: 22 September (Acting)
As on 25 March 1588, except: E. of Worcester; Rich. Shuttleworth, kt., Justice of Chester; W. Penrhyn, *added*. E. of Leicester; Geo. Bromley; W. Glaseor; Ralph Barton, *omitted*: Wales 4/133/5. (37)

1590: 18 May (Acting)
As on 22 September 1589, except: Rich. Pates; Oliver Lloyd, *omitted*: Wales 4/134/1. (35)

1590: 26 October (Acting)
As on 15 May 1590, except: W. Williams, *added*. E. of Worcester; Jas. Croft, *omitted*: Wales 4/134/2. (34)

1592: 24 April (Acting)
As on 26 October 1590, except: Ed., Lord Stafford; Jenkin Lloyd; Lewis Blayney; Chas. Lloyd, *added*. J. Littleton; Chas. Fox; J. Owen Vaughan; W. Penrhyn; Th. Price, *omitted*: Wales 4/135/1. (33)

1592: 23 October (Acting)
As on 24 April 1592, except: E. of Essex; Rich. ap Hugh, *added*. Christopher Hatton; J. Perrot; Ed. Leighton (Sheriff, 1591–2); Rob. Myddelton, *omitted*: Wales 4/135/2. (31)

1593: 14 May (Acting)
As on 23 October 1592, except: Ed. Leighton, *added*. Griffith Lloyd, *omitted*: Wales 4/136/1. (31)

1594: 30 May
*J. Puckering, kt., Keeper of Great Seal; *Burghley; *Pembroke, President of Council in the Marches of Wales; *E. of Essex; *B. of St. Asaph; *Ed., Lord Stafford; *Rich. Shuttleworth, kt. & *H. Townshend, Justices of Chester & Great Sessions; *Hugh Cholmondeley, kt.; *W. Aubrey; *Ellis Price, Ll.D.; *W. Leighton; *Jerome Corbet; *Fabian Phillips; *p Rich. Herbert of Montgomery; *J. Hanmer; *Rich. Price; *David Powell, D.D.; W. Williams; *Rich. Herbert of Parke; *J. Price of Newtown; *Reg. Williams; *Arthur Price; Math. Herbert; *Rich. Morris; *Rice Tanat; Jenkin Lloyd; Lewis Blayney; Ed. Price of Llanfyllin; *Griffith Lloyd; *Th. Jukes; Chas. Lloyd; Rich. ap Hugh; W. Penrhyn: C.66/1421/m.15d. (34)

1594: 24 June (Acting)
As on 30 May 1594, except: Reg. Williams (Sheriff, 1593-4), omitted: Wales 4/136/3. (33)

1595: 14 July (Acting)
As on 24 June 1594, except: Reg. Williams, added: Wales 4/137/1. (34)

1595: 15 August
*Puckering; *Burghley; *Pembroke, President of Council in the Marches of Wales; *E. of Essex; *B. of St. Asaph; *Ed., Lord Stafford; *Shuttleworth & *Townshend, Justices of Chester & of Great Sessions; *Hugh Cholmondeley, kt.; *W. Leighton; *Jerome Corbet; *Fabian Phillips; *W. Fowler; *p Rich. Herbert of Montgomery; *Rich. Price; *Rich. Herbert of Parke; *J. Price of Newtown; *Arthur Price; Math. Herbert; *Rich. Morris; Lewis Blayney; *Griffith Lloyd; *Th. Jukes; Chas. Lloyd: C.66/1435/m.20d. General renewal of Welsh commissions on 15 August: Index 4208/f.4v. (24)

1596: 5 February
Commission renewed to add W. Penrhyn: Index 4208/f.10v.

1596: 10 July
Commission renewed to restore Jenkin Lloyd: Index 4208/f.18.

1596: 31 July
As on 15 August 1595, except: *Th. Egerton, kt., Keeper of Great Seal; *W. Herbert; *Jenkin Lloyd; W. Penrhyn, added. J. Puckering, omitted: S.P.13/Case F, no. 11/f.41. Commission renewed to add W. Herbert: Index 4208/f.19. (27)

1596: 9 October
Commission renewed to restore Rice Tanat: Index 4208/f.21.

1596: 21 October
As on 31 July 1596, except: *p Rich. Broughton; *Rice Tanat, added. Rich. Herbert of Montgomery, omitted: C.66/1468/m.16d. Commission renewed to add Rich. Broughton, custos rotulorum: Index 4208/f.21v. (28)

1596: 3 December
Commission renewed to *add* J. Owen of Machynlleth: Index 4208/f.24v.

1597: 3 February
As on 21 October 1596, except: *J. Hanmer; J. Owen of Machynlleth, *added*. Hugh Cholmondeley; Fabian Phillips, *omitted*: C.66/1468/m.31d. Commission renewed to *add* J. Hanmer: Index 4208/f.26v. (28)

1597: 31 October (Acting)
As on 3 February 1597, except: Fabian Phillips, *added*. (This is an error since Phillips was dead). Arthur Price, *omitted*: Wales 4/138/2. (28)

1598: 29 May
Commission renewed to *add* Ed. Price of Vaynor: Index 4208/f.50.

1598: 17 July (Acting)
As on 31 October 1597, except: Ed. Price of Vaynor, *added*. Fabian Phillips; W. Fowler; Rich. Morris, *omitted*: Wales 4/138/1. (26)

1598: 28 July
Commission renewed to *add* Th. Wynn: Index 4208/f.54v.

1598: 4 September
Commission renewed to *add* Owen Vaughan: Index 4208/f.55v.

1598: 7 November
*Th. Egerton, kt., Keeper of Great Seal; *E. of Essex; *E. of Pembroke, President of Council in the Marches of Wales; *B. of St. Asaph; *Ed., Lord Stafford; *Shuttleworth & *Townshend, Justices of Chester & of Great Sessions; *W. Leighton; *p Rich. Broughton; *Jerome Corbet; *W. Herbert; *J. Hanmer; *Rich. Price; *Rich. Herbert of Parke; *J. Price of Newtown; Owen Vaughan; Ed. Price of Vaynor; *Math. Herbert; *Maurice Owen; *Rice Tanat; *Jenkin Lloyd; *Griffith Lloyd; Lewis Blayney; *Th. Jukes; Chas. Lloyd; Th. Wynn; W. Penrhyn; J. Owen of Machynlleth: C.66/1482/m.17d. Commission renewed to *add* Maurice Owen: Index 4208/f.57v. (28)

1599: 22 February
Commission renewed to *add* David Lloyd: Index 4208/f.65.

1599: 2 July (Acting)
As on 7 November 1598, except: David Lloyd, *added*. Jerome Corbet, *omitted*: Wales 4/139/2. (28)

1600: 25 January
Commission renewed to *add* Chas. Herbert; Gilbert Jones; Morgan Glynn: Index 4208/f.81v.

1600: 12 March
As on 2 July 1599, except: *Th., Lord Buckhurst, Treasurer; *Rich.
Lewkenor, kt., Justice of Chester; Chas. Herbert; Gilbert Jones; Morgan
Glynn, *added*. B. of St. Asaph; Rich. Shuttleworth, kt., *omitted*: C.66/1523/
m.30d. Commission renewed to *add* Rich. Lewkenor, kt., Justice of Chester
& of Great Sessions: Index 4208/f.85. (31)

1600: 17 December
As on 12 March 1600, except: *Rich. Leighton, *added*. E. of Essex; E. of
Pembroke, *omitted*: C.66/1549/m.31d. Commission renewed to *add* Rich.
Leighton: Index 4208/f.100. (Both the Earls of Essex and Pembroke may
have been on the commission as originally issued on 17 December. However
they died in February and January 1601 respectively and their names were
probably omitted when the commission finally came to be entered on the
patent roll.) (30)

1602: 12 February
Commission renewed to *omit* Chas. Lloyd: Index 4208/f.129.

1602: 25 February
Commission renewed to *add* B. of St. Asaph: Index 4208/f.130.

1602: 26 March
Commission renewed to appoint W. Herbert as *custos rotulorum*: Index
4208/f.131v.

1602: 17 May
Commission renewed to *restore* Chas. Lloyd: Index 4208/f.134.

1602: 2 July
Commission renewed to *add* Roger Kynaston: Index 4208/f.138.

1602: 25 July
General renewal of Welsh commissions to *add* Ed., Lord Zouch, President
of Council in the Marches of Wales: Index 4208/f.141.

1602: 27 August
Commission renewed to *add* Ed. Price of Newtown: Index 4208/f.142.

1602: 22 December
Commission renewed to *omit* Rich. Herbert of Parke because of outlawry: Index 4208/f.148.

1602: 28 December
*Egerton; *Th., Lord Buckhurst, Treasurer; *Ed., Lord Zouch, President
of Council in the Marches of Wales; *B. of St. Asaph; *Ed., Lord Stafford;
*Rich. Lewkenor, kt. & *H. Townshend, Justices of Chester & of Great
Sessions; *W. Leighton; *Rich. Broughton; *p W. Herbert; *J. Hanmer;
*Rich. Price; *Owen Vaughan; *Rich. Herbert of Parke; *Reg. Williams;
*Ed. Price of Newtown; Roger Kynaston; *Ed. Price of Vaynor; *Math.

Herbert; *Rich. Leighton; *Maurice Owen; *Rice Tanat; *Jenkin Lloyd; *Griffith Lloyd; *Th. Jukes; *Chas. Lloyd; Th. Wynn; W. Penrhyn; J. Owen of Machynlleth; *David Lloyd; *Chas. Herbert; *Gilbert Jones; Morgan Glynn: C.66/1594/m.35d. Commission renewed to *add* Reg. Williams, and to *restore* Rich. Herbert of Parke: Index 4208/f.148.   (33)

1603: (Acting)
As on 28 December 1602, except: *Ed. Herbert, kt., *added*. Rich. Herbert of Parke, *omitted*: C.66/1620/m.14d.   (33)

1604: (Acting)
As in 1603, except: *Th. Hanmer, kt., *added*. Lord Stafford; J. Hanmer; Ed. Price of Newtown; Ed. Price of Vaynor; Th. Wynn; J. Owen of Machynlleth, *omitted*: C.66/1662/m.23d.   (28)

1605: 2 September (Acting)
*Th. Egerton, Lord Ellesmere, Chancellor; *Th., Lord Buckhurst, E. of Dorset, Treasurer; *Zouch, President of Council in the Marches of Wales; *B. of St. Asaph; *Lewkenor & *Townshend, Justices of Chester & of Great Sessions; *p W. Herbert, *Ed. Herbert, *Rich. Price, *Th. Hanmer, kts.; *W. Leighton; *Rich. Broughton; *Owen Vaughan; *Reginald Williams; Roger Kynaston; *Rich. Leighton; *Math. Herbert; *Maurice Owen; *Jenkin Lloyd; *Griffith Lloyd; *Th. Jukes; *Chas. Lloyd; W. Penrhyn; Th. Wynn; *David Lloyd; *Chas. Herbert; *Gilbert Jones; Morgan Glynn: Wales 4/141/1. (Note that Th. Wynn should probably not be included as he was omitted from the patent roll enrolment of 1604 and is also omitted from all Gaol File lists subsequent to the present one. Details of the quorum are taken from C.66/1662/m.23d).   (28)

1606: (Acting)
As on 2 September 1605, except: *Rich. Hussey, kt.; *Rowland Pugh; Cadwalader Owen, B.D.; Rowland Owen; Lewis Gwynn; Ed. Price, *added*. Lord Zouch; Rich. Broughton; Reg. Williams; Griffith Lloyd; Chas. Lloyd; Th. Wynn (see note under previous entry); David Lloyd, *omitted*: C.66/1698/m.31d.   (27)

1607: post 12 September
As in 1606, except: *Ralph, Lord Eure, President of Council in the Marches of Wales (appointed on 12 September 1607); *J. Herbert; *Ed. Price of Newtown; *Ed. Price of Vaynor, *added*. W. Leighton, *omitted*: C.66/1748/m.31d.   (30)

1608–9: (Acting)
As in 1607, except: *E. of Salisbury, Treasurer; *E. of Northampton, Keeper of Privy Seal, *added*. E. of Dorset, *omitted*: C.66/1786/m.31d.   (31)

1609–10: (Acting)
*Ellesmere; *E. of Salisbury, Treasurer; *E. of Northampton, Keeper of Privy Seal; *Ralph, Lord Eure, President of Council in the Marches of Wales; *B. of St. Asaph; *Lewkenor & *Townshend, Justices of Chester & of

Great Sessions; *p W. Herbert, *Ed. Herbert, *Rich. Price, *Th. Hanmer, *Rich. Hussey, *Owen Vaughan, kts.; *Ed. Price of Newtown; *Rob. Leighton; *Ed. Price of Vaynor; *Rich. Leighton; *Rowland Pugh; *Math. Herbert; *Maurice Owen; *Jenkin Lloyd; *Th. Jukes; W. Penrhyn; Cadwalader Owen, B.D.; *Chas. Herbert; *Lewis Gwynn; *Gilbert Jones; Rowland Owen; Rich. Lloyd of Marrington; Morgan Glynn; Ed. Price of Kerry: C.66/1822/m.28d. (Note that Ed. Price of Kerry is not identified as such on the patent roll but can be identified from a Gaol File list of 9 October 1609: Wales 4/142/1). (31)

1610–11: (Acting)

As in 1609–10, except: Roger Kynaston, *added*. Rob. Leighton, *omitted*: C.66/1897/m.20d. (These two apparent changes are probably in error. Kynaston was omitted from the commission in 1609–10, the year that Leighton first appears, occupying the place in the commission formally held by Kynaston. The apparent restoration of Kynaston in 1610–11 in place of Leighton and in his old place on the commission is not borne out by subsequent commissions which again have Leighton's name and omit Kynaston). (31)

1611–12: (Acting)

As in 1610–11, except: *Rob. Leighton, *added*. (See note above). Roger Kynaston (See note above); Ed. Price of Vaynor; Rich. Leighton; Math. Herbert, *omitted*: C.66/1898/m.28d. (The omission of Ed. Price & Rich. Leighton from this enrolled commission may be an error since both reappear in subsequent commissions). (28)

1614: 23 May (Acting)

*Ellesmere; *Northampton; *Eure, President of Council in the Marches of Wales; *B. of St. Asaph; *Rich. Lewkenor & *H. Townshend, kts., Justices of Chester & of Great Sessions; *p W. Herbert, *Ed. Herbert, *Rich. Price, *Th. Hanmer, *Rich. Hussey, kts.; *Rich. Barker; *Owen Vaughan; *Ed. Price of Newtown; Rob. Leighton; Ed. Price of Vaynor; *Rich. Leighton; *Rowland Pugh; *Maurice Owen; *Jenkin Lloyd; *Th. Jukes; W. Penrhyn; Cadwalader Owen, B.D.; J. Vaughan; *Chas. Herbert; *Lewis Gwynn; *Gilbert Jones; Rowland Owen; Rich. Lloyd of Marrington; Morgan Glynn; Rich. Rocke: Wales 4/143/2. (Details of the quorum are taken from an enrolled commission of the same year: C.66/1988/m.28d.) (31)

1614: post 11 July

As on 23 May 1614, except: *E. of Suffolk, Treasurer (Suffolk was appointed on 11 July 1614); Ed. Price of Kerry, *added*. E. of Northampton, *omitted*: C.66/1988/m.28d. (32)

1615: 11 July

Commission renewed to *add* Math. Price: Index 4211/f.7v.

1615: 16 October (Acting)

As in 1614, except: Math. Price, *added*. Rich. Barker; Ed. Price of Newtown (Sheriff, 1614–15); J. Vaughan; Morgan Glynn, *omitted*: Wales 4/143/3. (29)

1615: 23 December
Commission renewed to *restore* Ed. Price: Index 4211/f.12v.

1616: 21 May
Commission renewed to *add* Th. Chamberlain, kt., Justice of Chester & of Great Sessions; David Crewe, kt., serjeant at law: Index 4211/f.19v.

1616: 21 September
Commission renewed to *add* Th. Kerry: Index 4211/f.26v.

1617: 19 March
Commission renewed to *add* Francis Bacon, kt., Keeper of Great Seal; Th., Lord Gerard, President of Council in the Marches of Wales: Index 4211/f.38.

1617: 25 April
Commission renewed to *restore* Ed. Price of Newtown: Index 4211/f.40v.

1617: 7 July
Commission renewed to *add* J. Herbert, kt.: Index 4211/f.44v.

1617: 12 July
Commission renewed to *add* Lewis, B. of Bangor: Index 4211/f.45v.

1617: 30 September
Commission renewed to *add* Rob. Vaughan: Index 4211/f.49v.

1617: 27 November
Commission renewed to *add* Fulk Price, D.D.; Rowland Pugh: Index 4211/f.52v. (Rowland Pugh was probably being restored to the commission at this date since he appears on commissions up to about 1616 when he was apparently omitted. See C.66/2076/m.25d. which is an undated enrolled commission belonging to a date in 1616).

1617: 1 December
*Francis Bacon, kt., Keeper of Great Seal; *E. of Suffolk, Treasurer; *E. of Worcester, Keeper of Privy Seal; *D. of Lennox, Steward; *W., Lord Compton, President of Council in the Marches of Wales; Bishops of *St. Asaph, *Bangor; *Th. Chamberlain & *H. Townshend, kts., Justices of Chester & of Great Sessions; *p W. Herbert, *Ed. Herbert, *Rich. Price, *Th. Hanmer, *Rich. Hussey, *J. Herbert, kts.; Fulk Price, D.D.; Rob. Vaughan; *Ed. Price of Newtown; Rob. Leighton; *Ed. Price of Vaynor; *Rich. Leighton; Rowland Pugh; *Jenkin Lloyd; *Th. Jukes; W. Penrhyn; *Chas. Herbert; *Lewis Gwynn; *Athelstan Owen; Math. Price; Rowland Owen; Th. Kerry; Rich. Lloyd of Marrington; *Ed. Price (of Kerry); Rich. Rocke: C.66/2147/m.24d. Commission renewed to *add* Athelstan Owen: Index 4211/f.53. (This was probably also the date on which the new President of the Council in the Marches of Wales, Lord Compton, who had been appointed on 24 November, was added to the commission). (34)

1618: 11 September
Commission renewed to *add* J. Price, kt.: Index 4211/f.71v. (The Docquet Book entry actually says that Price was restored on this date but there is no trace of his membership of the commission at any earlier time).

1619: 16 February
As on 1 December 1617, except: *J. Price, kt.; Ed. Homes, clerk, *added*. E. of Suffolk; Ed. Price of Vaynor, *omitted*: C.66/2174/m.20d. Commission renewed to *add* Ed. Homes, clerk: Index 4211/f.78v.   (34)

1619: 5 June
Commission renewed to *add* Ed. Fox, kt.: Index 4211/f.84v.

1619: 12 June
Commission renewed to *add* Francis Eure, kt.: Index 4211/f.86v.

1619: 21 June
Commission renewed to *add* J. Blayney: Index 4211/f.88.

1620: 21 July
Commission renewed to *add* Daniel Price, D.D.: Index 4211/f.111.

1620: 4 September (Acting)
As on 16 February 1619, except: Francis Eure, kt.; Ed. Fox, kt.; Daniel Price, D.D.; J. Blayney, *added*. Th. Hanmer; Rich. Leighton, *omitted*. (Two out of the three justices, Rich. Rocke, Rich. Lloyd of Marrington and Ed. Price of Kerry, were also omitted, but damage to the end of the list makes it impossible to say for certain which ones are concerned): Wales 4/145/1. (34)

1620: 4 November
General renewal of Welsh commissions to *add* Jas. Whitlock, kt., serjeant at law, Justice of Chester & of Great Sessions: Index 4211/f.114.

1621: 26 February
*Francis Bacon, kt., Viscount St. Alban, Chancellor; *H., Viscount Mandeville, Treasurer; *Worcester; *Lennox; *E. of Northampton, President of Council in the Marches of Wales; Bishops of *St. Asaph, *Bangor; *Jas. Whitlock, kt., serjeant at law & *H. Townshend, kt., Justices of Chester & of Great Sessions; *p W. Herbert, *Ed. Herbert, *Ed. Fox, *Rich. Price, *Rich. Hussey, *J. Herbert, *J. Price, *Rob. Vaughan, kts.; *Fulk Price, D.D.; *Daniel Price, D.D.; *Ed. Price of Newtown; Rob. Leighton; Rowland Pugh; *Jenkin Lloyd; *Th. Jukes; W. Penrhyn; *Chas. Herbert; *Lewis Gwynn; *Athelstan Owen; J. Blayney; *Math. Price; Rowland Owen; Th. Kerry; Ed. Homes, clerk: C.66/2234/m.43d. General renewal of Welsh commissions to *add* Viscount Mandeville, Treasurer: Index 4211/f.120.   (33)

1621: 20 August
As on 26 February 1621, except: *B. of Lincoln, Keeper of Great Seal; *Rich. Leighton; Arthur Price of Vaynor; Ed. Price of Kerry, *added*. Viscount St. Alban, *omitted*: C.193/13/1/f.121. Commission renewed to *add* Arthur Price of Vaynor; Ed. Price of Kerry: Index 4211/f.128. (The B. of Lincoln, who was appointed Lord Keeper on 16 July, was probably also added on 20 August). (36)

1621: post 29 September
As on 20 August 1621, except: *Lionel Cranfield, Treasurer, *added*. (Cranfield was appointed on 29 September 1621). B. of Bangor; H. Townshend, *omitted*: C.66/2259/m.26d. (35)

1622: 26 January
Commission renewed to *add* Francis Herbert: Index 4211/f.133v.

1622: 29 April
Commission renewed to *add* Marmaduke Lloyd, kt., second Justice of Chester & of Great Sessions: Index 4211/f.138.

1622: 14 October (Acting)
As at the end of 1621, except: B. of Bangor; Marmaduke Lloyd, kt., second Justice of Chester & of Great Sessions; Francis Herbert, *added*. Rich .Price; J. Price (Sheriff, 1621–2); Lewis Gwynn, *omitted*: Wales 4/145/3. (35)

1623: 28 June
As on 14 October 1622, except: *Meredith Morgan, *added*. D. of Lennox; B. of St. Asaph, *omitted*: C.66/2310/m.31d. Commission renewed to *add* Meredith Morgan: Index 4211/f.153v. (Note that the omission of Rowland Pugh and W. Penrhyn is recorded in the Gaol File list of 21 April 1623: Wales 4/145/4.).(34)

1624: 12 April
Commission renewed to *add* J. Davies, D.D., & to *restore* Rowland Pugh: Index 4211/f.164.

1624: 26 August
Commission renewed to *add* Percy Herbert, kt. & Bt.: Index 4211/f.170.

1624: 2 September
Commission renewed to *add* Ed. Vaughan: Index 4211/f.170v.

1625: 1 April
*B. of Lincoln, Keeper of Great Seal; *Jas., Lord Ley, Treasurer; *Viscount Mandeville, President of Council; *Worcester; *Northampton, President of Council in the Marches of Wales; *B. of Bangor; *Th. Chamberlain & *Marmaduke Lloyd, kts., Justices of Chester & of Great Sessions; *Percy Herbert, kt. & Bt.; *p W. Herbert, *Ed. Herbert, *Ed. Fox, *Rich. Hussey, *J. Herbert, kts.; *Daniel Price, D.D.; *Fulk Price, D.D.; *J. Davies, D.D.; *Sampson Eure; *Rob. Brooke; *Ed. Price of Newtown; Rob. Leighton; *Rich. Leighton; *Rowland Pugh; *Jenkin Lloyd; *Th. Jukes; *Ed.

Vaughan; *Chas. Herbert; *Athelstan Owen; J. Blayney; *Math. Price; Rowland Owen; Th. Kerry; Arthur Price of Vaynor; *Francis Herbert; *Meredith Morgan; *Ed. Homes, clerk: C.66/2367/m.29d. General renewal of Welsh commissions: Index 4211/f.180v. (36)

1625: 16 May (Acting)
As on 1 April 1625: Wales 4/146/1. (36)

1625: 1 June
Commission renewed to *add* Andrew Ellis; J. Lloyd: Index 4211/f.189.

1625: 4 July
Commission renewed to *add* Rich. Pugh: Index 4211/f.190.

1625: 22 December
As on 16 May 1625, except: *Th. Coventry, kt., Keeper of Great Seal; Andrew Ellis; J. Lloyd of Dolobran; Rich. Pugh; Lloyd Piers; David Morris, *added*. B. of Lincoln; Th. Chamberlain, *omitted*: B.M., Harleian Ms. 1622/f.99d. General renewal of Welsh commissions to *add* Th. Coventry, Keeper of Great Seal: Index 4211/f.194v. (This commission was probably also the occasion for the addition of Lloyd Piers & David Morris, although there is no Docquet Book entry for them). (40)

1626: 9 March
Commission renewed to *add* J. Bridgeman, kt., Justice of Chester & of Great Sessions: Index 4211/f.198v.

1626: 10 April (Acting)
As on 22 December 1625, except: J. Bridgeman, kt., Justice of Chester, etc., *added*. Ed. Fox; Rich. Hussey; J. Davies; Rob. Leighton; Rich. Leighton; Rowland Pugh (Sheriff, 1625–6); Ed. Vaughan; J. Blayney; Rowland Owen; Th. Kerry; Andrew Ellis; J. Lloyd of Dolobran; David Morris, *omitted*: Wales 4/146/2. (28)

1626: 7 July
Commission renewed to *restore* Lloyd Piers: Index 4211/f.205.

1626: 20 July
*Th. Coventry, kt., Keeper of Great Seal; *E. of Marlborough (Lord Ley), Treasurer; *E. of Manchester (Viscount Mandeville), President of Council; *Worcester; *Northampton, President of Council in the Marches of Wales; *B. of Bangor; *Ed., Lord Herbert; *J. Bridgeman & *Marmaduke Lloyd, kts., Justices of Chester & of Great Sessions; *Percy Herbert, kt. & Bt.; *p W. Herbert, *Ed. Fox, *J. Herbert, kts.; *Daniel Price, D.D.; *Fulk Price, D.D.; *Sampson Eure; *Rob. Brooke; *Ed. Price of Newtown; *Jenkin Lloyd; *Th. Jukes; *Chas. Herbert; *Athelstan Owen; *Math. Price; Arthur Price of Vaynor; *Francis Herbert; *Meredith Morgan; Rich. Pugh; Lloyd Piers; *Ed. Homes, clerk: E.163/18/12/f.100 & C.193/12/2/f.72. Commission renewed to *restore* Ed. Fox, kt.: Index 4211/f.207. (29)

1627: 30 March
Commission renewed to *add* Evan Glynn: Index 4211/f.221d.

1627: 23 April (Acting)
As on 20 July 1626, except: Evan Glynn, *added*. Ed. Price of Newtown; Rich. Pugh (Sheriff, 1626–7), *omitted*: Wales 4/147/1.   (28)

1627: 26 April
Commission renewed to *restore* Evan Glynn: Index 4211/f.223. (There is no indication of how Glynn came to be omitted so soon after his addition on 30 March).

1627: 22 June
Commission renewed to *add* Ed. Price; Rowland Pugh; David Morris: Index 4211/f.228v. (Note that Ed. Price is certainly an error for J. Price of Newtown who can newly be found on commissions from the end of 1627 in place of Ed. Price of Newtown who had disappeared from the commission by 23 April 1627).

1627: 21 October (Acting)
As on 23 April 1627, except: Timothy Turneur; J. Price of Newtown; Rowland Pugh; David Morris, *added*. Rob. Brooke; Athelstan Owen, *omitted*: Wales 4/147/2.   (30)

1627: 20 December
As on 21 October 1627, except: J. Lloyd; Rich. Pugh, *added*. E. of Worcester, *omitted*: C.66/2449/m.31d. Commission renewed to *restore* J. Lloyd: Index 4211/f.237v. (The apparent restoration to the commission of Rich. Pugh may be misleading. He was first added to the commission on 4 July 1625 and appears consistently on commissions enrolled on the patent rolls and included in *libri pacis* until about 1640. However he was regularly omitted from Gaol File lists of justices from 23 April 1627 before reappearing in 1632 and, as in the enrolled commissions, continuing until about 1640).   (31)

1628: 23 February
Commission renewed to *add* Ed. Lloyd: Index 4211/f.240.

1629: 8 July
*Coventry; *Rich., Lord Weston, Treasurer; *Viscount Conway, President of Council; *E. of Manchester, Keeper of Privy Seal; *E. of Pembroke; *Northampton, President of Council in the Marches of Wales; *B. of Bangor; *p W., Lord Powys; *Ed., Lord Herbert; *Bridgeman & *Lloyd, Justices of Chester & of Great Sessions; *Percy Herbert, kt. & Bt.; *Rich. Herbert; *Daniel Price, D.D.; *Fulk Price, D.D.; *Sampson Eure; *Timothy Turneur; *Rowland Pugh; *Ed. Lloyd; *Chas. Herbert; *Math. Price; *Francis Herbert; *Evan Glynn; *Meredith Morgan; J. Lloyd; *David Morris; Rich. Pugh; *Lloyd Piers; *Ed. Homes, clerk: C.66/2495/m.28d & C.66/2527/m.31d. Commission renewed to *add* Rich. Herbert, and to *omit* J. Price (of Newtown), Bt.; J. Herbert, kt.; Arthur Price: Index 4212/p.14. (29)

1630: 22 June
Commission renewed to *add* Athelstan Owen: Index 4212/p.36.

1630: 6 July
As on 8 July 1629, except: *Athelstan Owen, *added*. Viscount Conway;
E. of Pembroke; E. of Northampton; Rowland Pugh, *omitted*: C.66/2536/
m.22d & C.66/2577/m.9d. Commission renewed to *omit* Rowland Pugh:
Index 4212/p.38. (Note that Viscount Conway ought to be included.
However he died in January 1631 and it is possible that his name was omitted
when the commission was finally enrolled).   (26)

1631: 19 November
As on 6 July 1630, except: *Arthur Price, *added*. B. of Bangor; Daniel Price,
D.D., *omitted*: S.P.16/212/f.77. Commission renewed to *restore* Arthur Price:
Index 4212/p.69.   (25)

1632: 22 February
Commission renewed to *restore* Rowland Pugh: Index 4212/p.77.

1632: 9 March
Commission renewed to *restore* J. Blayney: Index 4212/p.78.

1632: 16 May
*Coventry; *E. of Portland (Lord Weston), Treasurer; *Manchester; *E. of
Bridgewater, President of Council in the Marches of Wales; *Ed., Lord
Herbert; *p W., Lord Powys; *Bridgeman & *Lloyd, Justices of Chester &
of Great Sessions; *Percy Herbert, kt. & Bt.; *Rich. Herbert; *Ed. Lloyd,
kt.; *Fulk Price, D.D.; *Sampson Eure; *Timothy Turneur; *Arthur Price;
*Francis Herbert; *Rowland Pugh; *Athelstan Owen; *Chas. Herbert;
J. Blayney; *Math. Price; *Evan Glynn; *Meredith Morgan; J. Lloyd;
*David Morris; Rich. Pugh; *Lloyd Piers; Ed. Lloyd; *Ed. Homes, clerk:
C.66/2598/m.22d & C.66/2623/m.25d. Commission renewed to *add* Ed.
Lloyd: Index 4212/p.82. (Lord Weston was not created E. of Portland until
February 1633, but may have had his new title added when the present
commission was enrolled).   (29)

1632: 29 October (Acting)
As on 16 May 1632, except: Fulk Price; Ed. Homes, *omitted*: Wales 4/149/2.
(27)

1633: 28 October (Acting)
As on 29 October 1632: Wales 4/149/4.   (27)

1634: 5 May (Acting)
As on 28 October 1633: Wales 4/150/1.   (27)

1634: 27 October (Acting)
As on 5 May 1634, except: David Morris, *omitted*: Wales 4/150/2.   (26)

1634: 10 December
Commission renewed to *omit* Percy Herbert, kt. & Bt.: Index 4212/p.150.

1636: post 6 March
*Coventry; *B. of London, Treasurer (appointed on 6 March); *Manchester; *Bridgewater, President of Council in the Marches of Wales; *p W., Lord Powys; *Ed., Lord Herbert; *Bridgeman & *Lloyd, Justices of Chester & of Great Sessions; *Rich. Herbert; *Ed. Lloyd, kt.; *Sampson Eure; *Timothy Turneur; *Arthur Price; *Francis Herbert; *Rowland Pugh; J. Blayney; *Math. Price; *Evan Glynn; *Meredith Morgan; J. Lloyd; Rich. Pugh; *Lloyd Piers; Ed. Lloyd: S.P.16/405/f.81v.   (23)

1638: 3 April
As in 1636, except: *Th. Milward, kt. & *Rich. Prydderch, Justices of Chester & of Great Sessions, *added*. J. Bridgeman; Timothy Turneur, *omitted*: C.66/2725/m.20d. Commission renewed to *add* Th. Milward, kt., serjeant at law, Justice of Chester, etc.: Index 4212/p.287.   (23)

1638: 21 September
*Coventry; *London; *Manchester; *Bridgewater, President of Council in the Marches of Wales; *p W., Lord Powys; *Ed., Lord Herbert; *Th. Milward, kt. & *Rich. Prydderch, Justices of Chester & of Great Sessions; *Marmaduke Lloyd, kt.; *Rich. Herbert; *Ed. Lloyd, kt.; *Sampson Eure; *Arthur Price; *Francis Herbert; *Rowland Pugh; J. Blayney; *Math. Price; *Evan Glynn; Rich. Pugh; Ed. Lloyd: C.66/2761/m.16d. Commission renewed to *omit* Lloyd Piers: Index 4212/p.309.   (20)

1639: 13 May (Acting)
As on 21 September 1638, except: Math. Price, *omitted*: Wales 4/152/3.   (19)

1639: 16 July
Commission renewed to *add* Ed. Corbet: Index 4212/p.349.

1639: Autumn (exact date uncertain)
As on 13 May 1639, except: Ed. Corbet, *added*: Wales 4/152/4.   (20)

1640: 2 May
*J. Finch, kt., Keeper of Great Seal; *London; *Manchester; *Bridgewater, President of Council in the Marches of Wales; *p W., Lord Powys; *Ed., Lord Herbert; *Milward & *Prydderch, Justices of Chester & of Great Sessions; *Marmaduke Lloyd, kt.; *Rich. Herbert; *Ed. Lloyd, kt.; *Sampson Eure; *W. Morgan; Ed. Corbet; *Arthur Price; *Francis Herbert; *Rowland Pugh; J. Blayney; *Math. Price; *Evan Glynn; Rich. Pugh; Ed. Lloyd; Th. Morris: C.66/2858/m.20d. Commission renewed to *add* Th. Morris: Index 4212/p.383. (Note the reappearance of Math. Price who had apparently been omitted before 13 May 1639).   (23)

1640: 12 May
Commission renewed to place Ed. Corbet on quorum: Index 4212/p.384.

1640: 4 December
Commission renewed to *add* J. Price, Bt.; Lloyd Piers; J. Price: Index 4212/p.416.

1640: 12 December
Commission renewed to *add* Rich. Price: Index 4212/p.418.

1641: 3 April
Commission renewed to *add* Walter Waring: Index 4212/p.441.

1641: 17 June
Commission renewed to *add* Arthur Blayney; Th. Jukes: Index 4212/p.453.

1641: 26 August
Commission renewed to *add* Arthur Price, and to *omit* Arthur Blayney; Th. Jukes: Index 4212/p.481.

1641: 26 November
Commission renewed to *add* E. of Pembroke & Montgomery as *custos rotulorum*: Index 4212/p.489.

1643: 27 October
Commission renewed to *add* W., Lord Powys; Herbert Vaughan; Ed. Corbet; Ed. Vaughan, and to appoint the said Herbert Vaughan as *custos rotulorum*: Index 4210/p.46.

1645: 28 November
Commission renewed (no details): Index 4213/p.32.

1647: 22 March
Commission renewed to *add* J. Bradshaw & Peter Warburton, Justices of Chester & of Great Sessions: Index 4213/p.84.

1647: 1 October
Commission renewed (no details): Index 4213/p.98.

1648: 14 January
Commission renewed (no details): Index 4213/p.105.

1648: 13 March (Acting)
E. of Kent; E. of Pembroke & Montgomery; E. of Manchester; W. Lenthall, Speaker of Parliament & Master of Rolls of Chancery; J. Bradshaw & Peter Warburton, Justices of Chester & of Great Sessions; Th. Myddelton, kt.; J. Wittering; Oliver St. John, Solicitor-General; J. Wilde, serjeant at law; Samuel Brown; Edm. Prideaux; Francis Buller; Ed. Vaughan; Th. Hunt; Th. Nichols; J. Corbet; Rowland Hunt; Chas. Lloyd of Garth; Esias Thomas; Samuel Moore; J. Price; Rich. Owen; Th. Owen; Gabriel Wynn; W. Kyffin; Rich. Griffith of Sutton; Evan Lloyd: Wales 4/153/2. (28)

1648: 16 October (Acting)
As on 13 March 1648: Wales 4/153/3. (28)

1649: 30 March
*W. Lenthall, Speaker of House of Commons; *Th., Lord Fairfax; *J. Bradshaw, President of Council; *Bulstrode Whitelock, *Rich. Keble, *J. Lisle, Commissioners of Great Seal; *E. of Pembroke & Montgomery; *E. of Denbigh; *H. Rolle, Chief Justice of Upper Bench; *Oliver St. John, Chief Justice of Court of Common Pleas; *J. Wilde, Chief Baron of Exchequer; *J. Bradshaw & *Peter Warburton, Justices of Chester & of Great Sessions; *Th. Myddelton, *J. Wittering, kts.; *Th. Mytton; *J. Pugh of Mathafarn; *Evan Lloyd; *Jas. Mytton; *Lloyd Piers; *Lewis Owen; *Hugh Price; *Chas. Lloyd of Garth; *Samuel Moore; *Rich. Price; Jas. Kynaston; *J. Price of Parke; Math. Morgan; Rich. Owen; Th. Owen; Gabriel Wynn; *Rich. Vaughan; W. Kyffin; Rich. Griffith of Sutton: C.193/13/3/f.79. Commission renewed on this date (no details): Index 4213/p.147. (34)

1650: 9 March
Commission renewed to appoint E. of Pembroke as *custos rotulorum*: Index 4213/p.179.

1650: 25 July
As on 30 March 1649, except: *Oliver Cromwell, Lord General; *Th. Fell, Justice of Chester & of Great Sessions; *Humph. Mackworth; *Edm. Prideaux; Rob. Griffith of Sutton, *added*. Lord Fairfax; Peter Warburton; Th. Myddelton, kt.; Jas Mytton, *omitted*: Lists published by Th. Walkley (1650), p.69. Commission renewed to *add* Th. Fell, Justice of Chester, etc.; Humph. Mackworth; J. Bradshaw, attorney, and to *omit* Th. Myddelton; Jas. Mytton: Index 4213/p.196. (35)

1651: March (no date given)
*Lenthall; *Oliver Cromwell, Lord General; *Whitelock, *Keble, *Lisle; *p E. of Pembroke & Montgomery; *J. Bradshaw, Chancellor of Duchy of Lancaster; *Rolle; *St. John; *Wilde; *Humph. Mackworth; *Th. Fell, Justice of Chester & of Great Sessions; *Edm. Prideaux; *J. Wittering, kt.; *J. Bradshaw, attorney in Montgomery; *Evan Lloyd; *Lloyd Piers; *Lewis Owen; *Hugh Price; *Rich. Price; J. Kynaston; *J. Price of Parke; Math. Morgan; Rich. Owen; *Rich. Vaughan; Rob. Griffith of Sutton; Lewis Price: Cambridge University Ms. Dd.VIII.1/f.130 & C.193/13/4/ f.123v. Commission renewed to *add* Lewis Price, and to *omit* E. of Denbigh; Th. Mytton; J. Pugh; Chas. Lloyd of Garth; Samuel Moore; Th. Owen; Gabriel Wynn; W. Kyffin: Index 4213/p.212. (27)

1653: 28 July
Commission renewed to *add* Th. Lloyd of Maesmawr; Ed. Price, and to *omit* Lloyd Piers; J. Price; Math. Morgan; Rich. Owen: Index 4213/p.265.

1653: 13 October
Commission renewed to *add* Ed. Vaughan of Tirymynach; Ed. Allen; J. Griffith; Th. Nichols, and to *omit* J. Bradshaw, attorney in Montgomery; Lewis Owen; and others (no details): Index 4213/p.271.

1654: 23 March
Commission renewed according to a general list: Index 4213/p.285.

1654: 30 October (Acting)
Whitelock, Keble, Lisle; J. Bradshaw, Chancellor of Duchy of Lancaster; Humph. Mackworth; Th. Fell, Justice of Chester & of Great Sessions; J. Wittering, kt.; Evan Lloyd; Rich. Price; J. Kynaston; Rich. Vaughan; Rob. Griffith; Th. Lloyd of Maesmawr; Ed. Price; Ed. Vaughan of Tirymynach; Ed. Allen; J. Griffith; Th. Nichols: Wales 4/154/3. (18)

1655: 12 December
*Nathaniel Fiennes & *J. Lisle, Commissioners of Great Seal; *Bulstrode Whitelock, kt., *Th. Widdrington, kt., *Ed. Montagu, & *W. Sydenham, Commissioners of Treasury; *J. Glynn, Chief Justice of Upper Bench; *W. Lenthall, Master of the Rolls; *Oliver St. John, Chief Justice of Common Bench; *J. Bradshaw & *Th. Fell, Justices of Chester & of Great Sessions; *Edm. Prideaux, Attorney-General; *J. Wittering, kt.; *Colonel Jas. Berry; *Evan Lloyd; *Hugh Price; *p Rich. Price; *J. Kynaston; *Rich. Vaughan; *Rob. Griffith; *Lewis Price; *Th. Lloyd of Maesmawr; *Ed. Price; *Ed. Vaughan of Tirymynach; Ed. Allen; J. Griffith; Th. Nichols; Pierce Lloyd; Math. Morgan: C.193/13/6/f.109 & C.193/13/5/f.130. Commission renewed to *add* Colonel Jas. Berry: Index 4213/p.321. (29)

1656: 20 October (Acting)
As on 12 December 1655, except: J. Kynaston, *omitted*: Wales 4/155/2. (28)

1657: 29 March (Acting)
As on 20 October 1656, except: J. Kynaston, *added*: Wales 4/155/3. (29)

1658: 24 September
General renewal of Welsh commissions to *add* Rich. Cromwell, Lord Protector: Index 4213/p.405.

1659: 18 March
Commission renewed to *add* J., Lord Jones; J. Ratcliff; Th. Waller, serjeant at law; Th. Harley; Samuel Price; Chas. Lloyd of Dolobran: Index 4213/p.428.

1659: 8 July
Commission renewed according to a general list: Index 4213/p.438.

1659: 5 October
Commission renewed to *omit* Jas. Berry; Pierce Lloyd: Index 4213/p.443.

1660: 16 March
Commission renewed according to a general list: Index 4213/p.454.

1660: 24 August
Commission renewed to *add* Ed., Lord Herbert of Cherbury, as *custos rotulorum*: Index 4214/p.31.

1660: 12 September
*Ed. Hyde, kt., Chancellor; *E. of Southampton, Treasurer; *D. of Albemarle, General; *Marquess of Ormond, Steward; *E. of Lindsey, Great Chamberlain; *E. of Manchester, Household Chamberlain; *E. of Pembroke & Montgomery; *Percy, Lord Powys; *p Ed., Lord Herbert of Cherbury; *W., Lord Craven; *Timothy Turneur & Rob. Milward, Justices of Chester & of Great Sessions; *W. Herbert; *Math. Price, Bt.; *Rich. Corbet, Bt.; *Th. Myddelton, Bt.; *J. Wittering, kt.; *Ed. Lloyd, kt.; *Th. Myddelton, kt.; *J. Blayney; *J. Purcell; *J. Pugh of Mathafarn; *Roger Palmer; Ed. Lloyd of Berthllwyd; Francis Buller junior; *Andrew Newport; Edm. Waring; *Rich. Herbert; W. Oakley; *Rich. Owen; Roger Mostyn; *J. Price; Math. Morgan; Arthur Weaver; *Th. Morris; *Th. Corbet; *Francis Fitzherbert; J. Blodwel; J. Whittingham; Brockwell Griffiths; Watkin Kyffin; Th. Jukes; Edm. Lloyd of Trefnant: C.220/9/4/ f.110v & B. M., Egerton Ms. 2557/f.109v. Commission renewed to *add* Timothy Turneur & Rob. Milward, Justices of Chester, etc.: Index 4214/ p.39. (The E. of Southampton, appointed Treasurer on 8 September, was probably also added on this occasion).   (43)

1661: 8 April (Acting)
As on 12 September 1660, except: Rob. Griffith of Sutton, *added*. Marquess of Ormond; E. of Manchester; Roger Mostyn (Sheriff, 1660–1), *omitted*: Wales 4/151/3.   (41)

1661: 26 August
Commission renewed to *add* Geoff. Palmer, kt. & Bt., Chief Justice of Chester & of Great Sessions: Index 4214/p.136.

1661: 8 November
General renewal of Welsh commissions to *add* E. of Carbery, President of Council in the Marches of Wales: Index 4214/p.144.

1662: 20 March
Commission renewed to *add* Job Charlton, serjeant at law, Chief Justice of Chester & of Great Sessions; H. Herbert: Index 4214/p.163.

1662: 17 July
As on 8 April 1661, except: *J., Lord Robartes, Keeper of Privy Seal; *D. of Ormond; *E. of Manchester; *E. of Carbery, President of Council in the Marches of Wales; *Job Charlton, Justice of Chester & of Great Sessions; *H. Herbert; *Th. Walcott, King's attorney; Roger Mostyn, *added*. Timothy Turneur, Chief Justice of Chester, *omitted*: C.66/2986/m.33d. Commission renewed to *add* Th. Walcott, King's attorney in Montgomery: Index 4214/p.180.   (48)

1662: 6 October (Acting)
As on 17 July 1662: Wales 4/152/2.   (48)

1663: 27 July
Commission renewed to *add* Th. Tanat: Index 4214/p.211.

1663: 10 August (Acting)
As on 6 October 1662, except: Th. Tanat, *added*. Edm. Lloyd of Trefnant, *omitted*: Wales 4/156/2.   (48)

1663: 13 November
As on 10 August 1663, except: J. Newton of Heightley; *J. Mathews junior, *added*: C.66/3022/m.37d. Commission renewed to *add* J. Mathews junior: Index 4214/p.216. (J. Newton was presumably added on the same date).   (50)

1664: 19 September (Acting)
As on 13 November 1663: Wales 4/156/4.   (50)

1665: 10 April (Acting)
As on 19 September 1664: Wales 4/156/5.   (50)

1665: 28 August (Acting)
As on 10 April 1665, except: J. Purcell, *omitted*: Wales 4/156/6.   (49)

1666: 12 March (Acting)
As on 28 August 1665, except: Th. Myddelton, Bt.; Ed. Lloyd, kt.; Th. Tanat, *omitted*: Wales 4/157/1. (Note that Th. Myddelton should have been omitted well before this, having died in July 1663).   (46)

1666: 27 August (Acting)
As on 12 March 1666: Wales 4/157/2.   (46)

1667: 6 May (Acting)
As on 27 August 1666, except: Percy, Lord Powys; Th. Myddelton, kt.; Arthur Weaver (Sheriff, 1666–7), *omitted*: Wales 4/157/3.   (43)

1667: 1 July
Commission renewed to *omit* Math. Price, Bt.: Index 4214/p.308.

1667: 2 September (Acting)
As on 6 May 1667, except: Th. Myddelton, Bt. (son of Th. M., Bt., who died in 1663); Th. Myddelton, kt.; Th. Tanat; Arthur Weaver, *added*. E. of Southampton; Math. Price, Bt., *omitted*: Wales 4/157/4. (Th. Myddelton, kt. and Th. Tanat should be excluded since both were dead).   (45)

1668: 12 October (Acting)
As on 2 September 1667, except: Percy, Lord Powys, *added*: Wales 4/157/5. (Powys had in fact died in January 1667).   (46)

1669: 5 April
Commission renewed to *add* Math. Price, Bt.; W. Browne; J. Kyffin: Index 4214/p.343.

1669: 6 September (Acting)
Orlando Bridgeman, kt. & Bt., Keeper of Great Seal; Lord Robartes, Keeper of Privy Seal; Dukes of Buckingham, Albemarle, Ormond;

Manchester; E. of Carbery, President of Council in the Marches of Wales; E. of Pembroke & Montgomery; E. of Craven; Ed., Lord Herbert; Job Charlton, kt., serjeant at law & Rob. Milward, Justices of Chester & of Great Sessions; W. Herbert; H. Herbert; Andrew Newport; Math. Price, Bt.; Rich. Corbet, Bt.; Th. Myddelton, Bt.; J. Wittering, kt.; Th. Myddelton, kt. (see note under 2 September 1667); Th. Walcott, King's attorney; J. Pugh of Mathafarn; Roger Palmer; Ed. Lloyd of Berthllwyd; Francis Buller junior; Edm. Waring; Rich. Herbert; W. Oakley; Rich. Owen; Roger Mostyn; J. Newton; J. Price; W. Browne; Math. Morgan; Arthur Weaver; Th. Corbet; Francis Fitzherbert; J. Blodwel; J. Whittingham; Rob. Griffith of Sutton; J. Mathews junior; Watkin Kyffin; Th. Jukes; J. Kyffin: Wales 4/158/2. (45)

1670: 2 May (Acting)
As on 6 September 1669, except: D. of Albemarle; Th. Myddelton, kt., *omitted*: Wales 4/158/3. (43)

1670: 26 September (Acting)
As on 2 May 1670, except: D. of Albemarle, *added*. Watkin Kyffin, *omitted*: Wales 4/158/4. (43)

1670: 15 November
Commission renewed to *add* W. Williams: Index 4214/p.381.

1670: 22 November
Commission renewed to *add* Ed. Vaughan of Llwydiarth; J. Wynn of Dolarddyn: Index 4214/p.381.

1673: 13 January
Commission renewed to *add* E. of Shaftesbury, Chancellor; Lord Clifford, Treasurer; Chas. Lloyd, Bt.; Ed. Lloyd: Index 4214/p.430.

1673: 7 April (Acting)
As on 26 September 1670, except: E. of Shaftesbury, Chancellor; Lord Clifford, Treasurer; Marquess of Worcester, President of Council in the Marches of Wales; E. of St. Albans, Household Chamberlain; Chas. Lloyd, Bt.; Owen Wynn; Ed. Vaughan of Llwydiarth; W. Williams; Math. Price of Parke; Ed. Lloyd; J. Wynn of Dolarddyn, *added*. Orlando Bridgeman; Lord Robartes; D. of Albemarle; E. of Manchester; E. of Pembroke; Th. Myddelton, Bt.; J. Price, *omitted*: Wales 4/159/3. (47)

1673: 6 May
Commission renewed to *add* Rich. Stedman: Index 4214/p.448.

1673: 15 September (Acting)
As on 7 April 1673, except: E. of Shaftesbury, *omitted*: Wales 4/159/4. (46)

1674: 24 March
Commission renewed to *add* Ed. Barret of Bausley; Rice Wynn; David Morris; Humph. Griffith, and to *omit* Th. Corbet; J. Kyffin: Index 4214/

p.475. (This was probably also the occasion of the addition of Geo. Johnson, deputy Justice of Chester & of Great Sessions, who was appointed on 22 January: Index 4214/p.469).

1674: 26 April (Acting)
As on 15 September 1673, except: Heneage, Lord Finch, Keeper of Great Seal; Viscount Latimer, Treasurer; E. of Anglesey, Keeper of Privy Seal; Geo. Johnson, deputy Justice of Chester, etc.; Ed. Barret of Bausley; Rich. Stedman; Rice Wynn; David Morris; Humph. Griffith, *added*. Lord Clifford; Rob. Milward; Th. Corbet; Rob. Griffith; J. Kyffin, *omitted*: Wales 4 /159/5. (50)

1675: 5 July
Commission renewed to *add* W. Pugh; H. Blayney; Edm. Lloyd: Index 4214/p.497.

1675: 20 September (Acting)
Heneage, Lord Finch, Keeper of Great Seal; E. of Danby (Viscount Latimer), Treasurer; E. of Anglesey, Keeper of Privy Seal; Dukes of Buckingham, Monmouth, Ormond; Marquess of Worcester, President of Council in the Marches of Wales; E. of Lindsey, Great Chamberlain; E. of Arlington, Household Chamberlain; Earls of Craven, Carbery; Ed., Lord Herbert; Job Charlton, kt. & Geo. Johnson, Justices of Chester & of Great Sessions; W. Herbert; H. Herbert; Andrew Newport; Math. Price, Bt.; Chas. Lloyd, Bt.; Rich. Corbet, Bt.; J. Wittering, kt.; Owen Wynn; Th. Walcott; Ed. Vaughan of Llwydiarth; W. Pugh of Mathafarn; Roger Palmer; Ed. Lloyd of Berthllwyd; Ed. Barret of Bausley; Francis Buller; Edm. Waring; Rich. Herbert; W. Oakley; Rich. Owen; Roger Mostyn; J. Newton of Heightley; W. Williams; Math. Price of Parke; H. Blayney of Gregynog; W. Browne; Math. Morgan; Arthur Weaver; Rich. Stedman; Rice Wynn; Francis Fitzherbert; J. Blodwel; Humph. Griffith; J. Whittingham; J. Mathews junior; Ed. Lloyd; Edm. Lloyd of Trefnant; Th. Jukes; J. Wynn of Dolarddyn: Wales 4/160/2. (52)

1675: 17 December
Commission renewed to *add* Rob. Leighton: Index 4214/p.505.

1676: 28 February
Commission renewed to *add* David Morris; J. Kyffin: Index 4214/p.508.

1676: 27 March (Acting)
As on 20 September 1675, except: Rob. Leighton; David Morris of Pen-y-bont; J. Kyffin of Bodfach, *added*. Humph. Griffith, *omitted*: Wales 4/160/3. (54)

1676: 25 September (Acting)
As on 27 March 1676, except: Math. Price, Bt.; Roger Palmer; Roger Mostyn; W. Browne; J. Blodwel; J. Whittingham; Th. Jukes, *omitted*: Wales 4/160/4. (47)

1676: 19 December
Commission renewed to *add* Ed. Vaughan of Gwernygoe; Geo. Devereux; Chas. Herbert; Ed. Price of Glanmeheli; Ed. Herbert of Kerry; Rich. Griffith of Sutton; J. Lloyd of Llanhafan; J. Edwards of Rorrington: Index 4214/p.519. (Ed. Herbert of Kerry is probably an error for Rich. Herbert of Kerry who actually appears in subsequent commissions).

1677: 8 February
Commission renewed to *add* Evan Glynn; Rich. Mytton: Index 4214/p.521.

1677: 23 April (Acting)
Finch; Danby; Anglesey; Buckingham; Monmouth; Ormond; Worcester, President of Council in the Marches of Wales; Lindsey; Arlington; Craven; Carbery; E. of Powys; Ed., Lord Herbert; Charlton & Johnson, Justices of Chester & of Great Sessions; H. Herbert; Andrew Newport; Chas. Lloyd, Bt.; Rich. Corbet, Bt.; J. Wittering, kt.; Lewis Meyrick, Attorney-General for Wales; Th. Walcott, King's attorney in Montgomery; Ed. Vaughan of Llwydiarth; Ed. Vaughan of Gwernygoe; W. Pugh of Mathafarn; Math. Morgan; Chas. Herbert; Ed. Lloyd of Berthllwyd; Math. Price of Parke; Francis Buller junior; Edm. Waring; W. Oakley; Rich. Owen; J. Newton of Heightley; W. Williams; Rob. Leighton; H. Blayney; Ed. Price of Glanmeheli; Rich. Herbert; David Morris of Pen-y-bont; J. Mathews; Arthur Weaver; Ed. Barrett of Bausley; J. Kyffin of Bodfach; Rich. Griffith of Sutton; Rich. Stedman; J. Lloyd of Llanhafan; Francis Fitzherbert; J. Wynn of Dolarddyn; Evan Glynn; Rich. Mytton; J. Edwards of Rorrington; Edm. Lloyd of Trefnant: Wales 4/160/5. (53)

1677: 15 May
Commission renewed to *add* Ed. Lloyd of Mathrafal: Index 4214/p.527.

1677: 24 September (Acting)
As on 23 April 1677, except: Geo. Devereux; Ed. Lloyd of Mathrafal, *added*: Wales 4/160/6. (55)

1678: 1 April (Acting)
As on 24 September 1677, except: Chas. Lloyd, Bt., *omitted*: Wales 4/160/7. (54)

1678: 18 April
Commission renewed to *add* Sidney Godolphin: Index 4214/p.542.

1678: 23 July
Commission renewed to *add* Rich. Mostyn: Index 4214/p.547.

1678: 7 October (Acting)
As on 1 April 1678, except: Sidney Godolphin, *added*. Lord Finch, *omitted* (this omission is an error): Wales 4/160/8. (54)

1679: 23 January
Commission renewed to appoint Andrew Newport as *custos rotulorum*: Index 4214/p.555.

1679: 21 April (Acting)
As on 7 October 1678, except: Lord Finch; Rich. Mostyn, *added*. E. of Danby; E. of Powys; Ed., Lord Herbert, *omitted*: Wales 4/161/1.   (53)

1679: 18 December
Commission renewed to *add* H., Lord Herbert, as *custos rotulorum*; Vincent Price; Chas. Wind; Th. Mason; Arthur Weaver: Index 4215/p.18.

1680: 20 April
*Prince Rupert; *Archbishop of Canterbury; *Finch; *E. of Radnor, President of Council; *Anglesey; Dukes of *Albemarle, *Monmouth, *Newcastle, *Lauderdale, *Ormond; *Marquess of Winchester; *Worcester, President of Council in the Marches of Wales; *Lindsey; *Arlington; Earls of *Salisbury, *Bridgewater, *Sunderland, *Essex, *Bath, *Craven, *Halifax, *Carbery; *Viscount Fauconberg; *B. of London; *Laurence Hyde; *H. Coventry; *Francis North, kt., Chief Justice of the Bench; *J. Ernley, kt., Chancellor of Exchequer; *Th. Chichley, kt., Chancellor of Duchy of Lancaster; *W. Temple, Bt.; *Ed. Seymour; *Daniel Finch; *Leoline Jenkins; *Sidney Godolphin; *Geo. Jeffreys, kt. & Bt. and Geo. Johnson, Justices of Chester; *p. Andrew Newport; *Rich. Corbet, Bt.; *J. Wittering, kt.; *Lewis Meyrick, Attorney-General for Wales; *Ed. Vaughan of Llwydiarth; *Ed. Vaughan of Gwernygoe; *W. Pugh of Mathafarn; *Math. Morgan; *Chas. Herbert; *Ed. Lloyd of Berthllwyd; *Ed. Lloyd of Mathrafal; *Ed. Barret of Bausley; *Edm. Lloyd of Trefnant; Edm. Waring; W. Oakley; *Rich. Owen; J. Newton of Heightley; *J. Williams of Ystumcolwyn; *Rob. Leighton; *Daniel Whittingham; *Arthur Devereux; *Ed. Price of Glanmeheli; *Rich. Herbert of Kerry; *David Morris of Pen-y-bont; *J. Mathews; *Arthur Weaver; *Rich. Mostyn; *J. Kyffin of Bodfach; *Rich. Stedman; *J. Lloyd of Llanhafan; *Rich. Wynn; *Evan Glynn; *Rich. Mytton; *J. Edwards of Rorrington; *Vincent Price; *Chas. Wind; *Arthur Weaver; *Th. Mason: C.193/12/4/f.153. Commission renewed to *omit* recusants: Index 4215/p.27. (The *addition* to the Montgomery commission of J. Williams of Ystumcolwyn; Daniel Whittingham; Arthur Devereux; and Rich. Wynn was ordered by a warrant of 5 February 1680 and the *removal* of the Duke of Buckingham; H., Lord Herbert; Francis Buller junior; W. Williams; Rich. Griffith of Sutton by a warrant of 5 February, of Math. Price of Parke by a warrant of 26 April, and of H. Blayney of Gregynog by a warrant of 24 June 1680: *H.M.C., Eleventh Report, Appendix,* Part 2, p.185. All these additions and omissions are reflected in the commission given above, including the removal of Math. Price and H. Blayney who were omitted after 20 April, the date to which the basic commission certainly belongs. This discrepancy is probably to be explained by the delay between the issuing of the commission and its entry in the C.193 entry book, thus giving ample time to make allowance for changes in the commission after 20 April. The omission of Math. Price of Parke from the commission was ordered by the Privy Council on 17 April 1680, nine days before the issue of the warrant to give effect to the order: P.C.2/68/p.482).   (73)

1681: 3 March
Commission renewed to *add* Th. Powys, King's attorney in Montgomery: Index 4215/p.44.

1681: 11 April (Acting)
As on 20 April 1680, except: Geo. Jeffreys, kt., Justice of Chester & of Great Sessions; Job Charlton, kt.; Th. Walcott; Math. Price; H. Blayney, *added*: Wales 4/161/4. (See note under 20 April 1680 re Math. Price and H. Blayney). (78)

1681: 29 August (Acting)
As on 11 April 1681, except: Th. Powys, King's attorney; Sidney Godolphin, *added*. (Note that there are two Sidney Godolphins on the commission). Earls of Salisbury, Sunderland, Essex; Job Charlton; Math. Price; H. Blayney, *omitted*: Wales 4/161/5. (74)

1682: 24 April (Acting)
As on 29 August 1681, except: J. Newton; Arthur Weaver (this is the A. Weaver who appears before Rich. Mostyn), *omitted*: Wales 4/162/1. (72)

1682: 29 July
Commission renewed to *add* J. Price, Bt.: Index 4215/p.69.

1682: 4 September (Acting)
As on 24 April 1682, except: Arthur Weaver, *added*: Wales 4/162/2. (73)

1683: 26 March (Acting)
As on 4 September 1682, except: J. Warren, Justice of Chester & of Great Sessions; J. Newton of Heightley, *added*. Geo. Johnson, *omitted*: Wales 4/162/3. (74)

1684: 18 August (Acting)
As on 26 March 1683, except: Chas., Lord Herbert; Ed. Herbert, kt.; J. Price, Bt., *added*. D. of Monmouth; W. Temple; Geo. Jeffreys; Rich. Mytton, *omitted*: Wales 4/162/5. (Note the long delay between the addition to the commission of J. Price and his appearance on a Gaol File list). (73)

1685: 11 April
Commission renewed to *add* Andrew Newport as *custos rotulorum*: Index 4215/p.126. (This is in fact a reappointment to mark the start of the new reign).

1685: 31 August (Acting)
*Archbishop of Canterbury; *Lord Guilford, Keeper of Great Seal; *E. of Rochester, Treasurer; *Marquess of Halifax, President of Council; *E. of Clarendon, Keeper of Privy Seal; Dukes of *Albemarle, *Newcastle, *Ormond; *D. of Beaufort, President of Council in the Marches of Wales; Marquesses of *Winchester, *Worcester; *Lindsey; *Arlington; Earls of *Bridgewater, *Sunderland, *Bath, *Craven, *Nottingham, *Middleton,

*Carbery; *Viscount Fauconberg; *B. of London; *Sidney, Lord Godol-
phin; *H. Coventry; *J. Ernley, kt.; *Th. Chichley, kt.; *Ed. Seymour;
*Leoline Jenkins, kt.; *Geo. Jeffreys, kt. & Bt.; *Ed. Herbert, kt.; *J.
Warren, Justice of Chester & of Great Sessions; *p Andrew Newport;
*Rich. Corbet, Bt.; *J. Price, Bt.; *J. Wittering, kt.; *Lewis Meyrick,
King's attorney in Wales; *Th. Powys, King's attorney in Montgomery;
*Ed. Vaughan of Llwydiarth; *Ed. Vaughan of Gwernygoe; *W. Pugh of
Mathafarn; *Math. Morgan; *Chas. Herbert; *Ed. Lloyd of Berthllwyd;
*Ed. Lloyd of Mathrafal; *Ed. Barret of Bausley; *Sidney Godolphin;
*Edm. Lloyd of Trefnant; Edm. Waring; W. Oakley; *Rich. Owen; J.
Newton of Heightley; *J. Williams of Colwyn; *Rob. Leighton; *Daniel
Whittingham; *Arthur Devereux; *Ed. Price of Glanmeheli; *Rich.
Herbert of Kerry; *David Morris of Pen-y-bont; *J. Mathews; *Arthur
Weaver; *Rich. Mostyn; *J. Kyffin of Bodfach; *Rich. Stedman; *J. Lloyd
of Llanhafan; *Rice Wynn; *Evan Glynn; *J. Edwards of Rorrington;
*Vincent Price; *Chas. Wind; *Arthur Weaver; *Th. Mason: Wales 4/163/1.
(Details of the quorum are based on a list of 1685 in C.193/12/5/f.179v).   (71)

1686: 8 May (Acting)
As on 31 August 1685: Wales 4/163/2.   (71)

1686: 2 September
Commission renewed to *add* Job Charlton, kt. & Bt., Justice of Chester &
of Great Sessions: Index 4215/p.160. (This was probably also the occasion
of the addition of Ed. Jennings who had been appointed as King's attorney
in Montgomery on 28 April 1686, the day before Charlton was appointed
to his office: Index 4215/p.152).

1686: 17 December
Order by the Privy Council for the *removal* from the Montgomery commission
of J. Wittering, kt.; Math. Morgan; Ed. Vaughan of Gwernygoe; Rich.
Owen; Arthur Devereux; Ed. Price of Glanmeheli; Rich. Stedman; Th.
Mason, and the *addition* of the Earl of Castlemaine; W., Lord Herbert of
Montgomery; Th. Price, kt.; Walter Clopton; Nathaniel Morris; Jas.
Palmer: P.C.2/71/p.378. (These changes are not reflected in the Gaol File
lists until 19 September 1687, the commission having been renewed on 7
June and possibly also on 29 August 1687).

1687: 14 March (Acting)
As on 8 May 1686, except: E. of Mulgrave, Household Chamberlain; Job
Charlton, kt. & Bt., Justice of Chester; Ed. Jennings, King's attorney in
Montgomery; Rob. Price, *added*. Lord Guilford; Marquess of Halifax; E. of
Arlington; E. of Carbery; Leoline Jenkins; Rich. Corbet; Th. Powys; Ed.
Vaughan of Gwernygoe; Ed. Lloyd of Mathrafal; Sidney Godolphin;
J. Newton; J. Williams; Rob. Leighton; J. Lloyd; Arthur Weaver, *omitted*
Wales 4/163/4.   (60)

1687: 7 June
Commission renewed to *add* W., Marquess of Powys, *custos rotulorum*:
Index 4215/p.172.

1687: 29 August
Renewal of all the Welsh commissions, except for Montgomery, for the
addition of the clause of dispensation: Index 4215/p.179. (The clause may
have been added in Montgomery when the commission was renewed on
7 June or the Docquet Book entry of 29 August may simply have omitted
reference to Montgomery in error).

1687: 19 September (Acting)
Archbishop of Canterbury; Lord Jeffreys, Chancellor; E. of Sunderland,
President of Council; Lord Arundell of Wardour, Keeper of Privy Seal;
Dukes of Ormond, Albemarle, Newcastle; D. of Beaufort, President of
Council in the Marches of Wales; Marquesses of Winchester, Powys,
Worcester; E. of Lindsey, Great Chamberlain; E. of Mulgrave, Household
Chamberlain; Earls of Bath, Craven, Castlemaine, Nottingham, Middleton;
Viscounts Montgomery, Fauconberg, Preston; B. of Durham; J., Lord
Belasyse; Sidney, Lord Godolphin; H., Lord Dover; J. Ernley, kt.; Ed.
Herbert, kt.; Job Charlton, kt. & Bt. & J. Warren, Justices of Chester &
of Great Sessions; Rich. Corbet, Bt. J. Price, Bt.; Th. Price, kt.; Ed.
Jennings, King's attorney in Montgomery; Lewis Meyrick, King's attorney
in Wales; Walter Clopton; Nathaniel Morris; Jas. Palmer; Th. Bartlett;
Ed. Vaughan of Llwydiarth; Th. Price; W. Pugh of Mathafarn; H. Newton;
Th. Mostyn; Chas. Herbert; Ed. Lloyd of Berthllwyd; Ed. Barret of
Bausley; Sidney Godolphin; Edm. Waring; W. Oakley; Rob. Price; Rob.
Leighton; Daniel Whittingham; Rich. Herbert of Kerry; David Morris of
Pen-y-bont; J. Mathews; Arthur Weaver; Rich. Mostyn; J. Kyffin of
Bodfach; Rob. Lloyd of Llanhafan; Rice Wynn; Evan Glynn; J. Edwards
of Rorrington; Vincent Price; Chas. Wind; Arthur Weaver: Wales 4/163/5.
(65)

1688: 23 March
Commission renewed to *add* and to *omit* several justices (no details): Index
4215/p.189.

1688: 26 May (Acting)
As on 19 September 1687, except: D. of Albemarle, *omitted*: Wales 4/163/6.
(Note that the Gaol File list has not yet caught up with whatever changes
were made on 23 March). (64)

1688: 24 September (Acting)
Canterbury; Jeffreys; Sunderland; Arundell of Wardour; Dukes of Ormond,
Albemarle, Newcastle; D. of Beaufort, President of Council in the Marches
of Wales; Marquesses of Winchester, Powys, Worcester; E. of Lindsey;
Mulgrave; Earls of Bath, Craven, Castlemaine, Nottingham, Middleton;
Viscounts Montgomery, Preston; B. of Durham; Lords Belasyse, Godol-
phin, Dover; J. Ernley, kt.; Ed. Herbert, kt.; Charlton & Warren, Justices
of Chester & of Great Sessions; W. Williams, kt.; Ed. Jennings, King's
attorney in Montgomery; J. Mathews; W. Williams; Sidney Godolphin;
Rob. Leighton; Th. Lloyd; Th. Price; Bernard Foster; Edm. Lloyd; Th.
Price of Llanfyllin; Rowland Bartlett; Th. Mason; Th. Clopton, clerk;
Chas. Lloyd of Dolobran; Math. Price; Humph. Jones: Wales 4/163/7. (45)

1688: 6 October
General renewal of Welsh commissions: Index 4215/p.200.

1689: 29 August
Commission renewed to *add* J. Trenchard & Littleton Powys, Justices of Chester & of Great Sessions: Index 4215/p.238. (This was probably also the occasion of the addition of the E. of Macclesfield, President of the Council in Wales (appointed on 22 March 1689: Index 4215/p.211), and of Randolph Wynn, King's attorney in Montgomery (appointed on 29 August 1689: Index 4215/p.237).

1690: 5 May (Acting)
Archbishop of Canterbury; Marquess of Carmarthen, President of Council; Marquess of Halifax, Keeper of Privy Seal; D. of Norfolk; D. of Bolton; E. of Lindsey, Great Chamberlain; E. of Devonshire, Steward; Earls of Oxford, Shrewsbury, Bedford, Bath; E. of Macclesfield, President of Council in the Marches of Wales; E. of Nottingham; H., Lord Herbert; J. Maynard, Anthony Keck, W. Rawlinson, kts., Commissioners of the Great Seal; J. Trenchard, serjeant at law & Littleton Powys, Justices of Chester & of Great Sessions; Andrew Newport; J. Price, Bt.; W. Williams, kt. & Bt.; Ed. Vaughan; Price Devereux; W. Pugh; W. Williams; Athelstan Owen; Ed. Lloyd; Math. Morgan; Rich. Stedman; J. Mathews; Rich. Mytton; Rob. Lloyd; Nathaniel Morris; Evan Glynn; Th. Mason; Arthur Vaughan; Th. Lloyd; Chas. Herbert; Math. Price; Arthur Devereux; Rich. Mostyn; J. Edwards; Daniel Whittingham; Meredith Morgan; Rich. Herbert: Wales 4/164/1.   (46)

Carmarthen

1543 : 12 March
*Th., Lord Audley of Walden, Chancellor; *D. of Norfolk, Treasurer; *D. of Suffolk, President of Council; *J. Russell, kt., Keeper of Privy Seal; *B. of Coventry & Lichfield, President of Council in the Marches of Wales; *B. of St. Davids; Walter, Lord Ferrers; *Nich. Hare, Ed. Croft, Rice Mansel, *J. Vernon, kts.; *J. Pakington; *Th. Holte; *David Brooke; *J. ap Rice; *Rich. Hassall; *p. Rich. Devereux; *Th. Jones; J. Phillip; W. Morgan of Kidwelly; Jenkin Lloyd of Kidwelly; Jas. Williams; *Walter Vaughan; *Griffith Dwnn; *J. Lloyd senior; *W. Morgan of Llangathen; *Th. Bryne; Howel ap Rither; Th. Hancock; David Vaughan. *Later additions to list*: *Th. Bromley, serjeant at law; *Adam Mytton; J. Hancock; *J. Goodall: C.193/12/1/f.42v. (30 names plus 4 corrections).

1549 : 4 November (Acting)
Th. Jones, kt.; Griffith Dwnn; Griffith Higgon; W. Morgan; Jas. Williams; J. ap Howel ap John: Wales 4/715/2. (These are the names of the justices of the peace present at the Quarter Sessions held at Carmarthen on the above date).

1555 : (Acting)
B. of St. Davids; Th. Jones, J. Vaughan, Jas. Williams, kts.; Griffith Higgon; David Vaughan of Kidwelly; Griffith Dwnn; H. Jones, kt.; J. Rastell; Th. Phayer; J. ap Howel ap John; J. Lloyd of Llangynnor: S.P.11/5/f.61v. (12)

1558–59 : (Acting)
*Nich. Bacon, kt., Keeper of Great Seal; *Marquess of Winchester, Treasurer; *E. of Arundel, Steward; Bishops of *Bath & Wells, *St. Davids, *Chester; *J. Throckmorton, Justice of Chester; *p Th. Jones, *J. Vaughan, *Adam Mytton, *J. Perrot, H. Jones, Jas. Williams, kts.; *J. Scudamore of Holm; *Chas. Fox; *J. Welsh; *Reg. Corbet; *W. Symonds; *W. Gerard; *Rich. Seaborne; *W. Philipps; J. Rastell; J. ap Howel ap John; *Griffith Dwnn; *Th. Phayer; *J. Vaughan of Carmarthen; Rees William; Th. Gough; Roderick David ap Roderick: B.M., Lansdowne Ms. 1218/f.37. (Except for the omission of the *ex officio* members of the commission, the same list also appears in S.P.12/2/17/p.68). (29)

1561 : (Acting)
*Bacon; *Winchester; *Arundel; *H. Sidney, kt., President of Council in the Marches of Wales; *B. of St. Davids; *Rich. Wye; J. Vaughan, *p H. Jones, kts.; *J. Rastell; J. ap Howel ap John; *J. Vaughan of Carmarthen; Rees William; Th. Gough; David Vaughan; Rees Penry: B.M., Lansdowne Ms. 1218/f.85v. (15)

1562 : 13 June
As in 1561, except: Jas. Williams, kt., *added*: C.66/985/m.41d. (Jas. Williams may have been omitted in error in 1561). (16)

1564: (Acting)
*Bacon; *Winchester; *Arundel; *Sidney, President of Council in the Marches of Wales; *B. of St. Davids; *Rich. Wye; *Reg. Corbet; *J. Throckmorton, Justice of Chester; J. Vaughan, kt.; *p H. Jones, kt.; *W. Gerard; *Chas. Fox; *Rich. Seaborne; *Rich. Pates; *J. Price; *Rich. Smith; *J. Rastell; J. ap Howel ap John; Griffith Rice; *Rees Thomas; David Vaughan; Maurice ap Rees; Rees Penry; *Th. Vaughan of Pembrey: C.66/998/m.10d.   (24)

1573–74: (Acting)
*Bacon; *W., Lord Burghley, Treasurer; *E. of Essex; *Sidney, President of Council in the Marches of Wales; *B. of St. Davids; *Jas. Croft, House-hold Controller; *Hugh Cholmondeley, kt.; *Throckmorton, Justice of Chester; *J. Rastell, Justice of Great Sessions; *p H. Jones, *Jas. Williams, kts.; *W. Gerard; *Chas. Fox; *Rich. Seaborne; *Rich. Pates; *Ed. Davies; *Th. Huet, clerk; *Rich. Vaughan; *Griffith Rice; *J. Vaughan of Carmarthen; Th. Vaughan of Pembrey; *Lewis Gwynn, clerk; J. Thomas ap Henry; *W. Davies; *Philip Williams; *Morgan John Harry; Jenkin David John; Owen Dwnn: S.P.12/93/part 2/f.33 & B.M., Egerton Ms. 2345/f.42.   (28)

1575: 8 August (Acting)
*Bacon; *Burghley; *Essex; *Sidney; *B. of St. Davids; *Croft; *Throck-morton, Justice of Chester; *Geo. Fetiplace, Justice of Great Sessions; *p H. Jones, *Jas. Williams, kts.; *W. Gerard; *Chas. Fox; *Rich. Seaborne; *Rich. Pates; *Ed. Davies; *Th. Huet, clerk; *Rich. Vaughan; *Griffith Rice; *Walter Vaughan; *Th. Vaughan of Pembrey; *Lewis Gwynn, clerk; J. Thomas ap Henry; *W. Penry of Llanedi; *W. Davies; J. Howel ap John; *Philip Williams; *Morgan John Harry; Geo. David Powell; Th. Williams; Jenkin David John; *Griffith Lloyd of the Forest of Glyncothi; Owen Dwnn: Wales 4/716/1. (Details of the quorum taken from a list of 1575 contained in S.P.12/106/part 2/f.4v. which is identical with the one given here except for the addition of J. Perrot, kt., and the omission of J. Howel ap John).   (32)

1577: (Acting)
As on 8 August 1575, except: *J. Perrot, kt.; Th. Lloyd of Llanstephan; Griffith Vaughan of Trimsaran; Rich. Philipps; Rice Thomas Lewis, added. E. of Essex; Ed. Davies; Th. Huet; J. Thomas ap Henry; W. Penry of Llanedi; J. Howel ap John; Jenkin David John; Griffith Lloyd of Glyncothi; Owen Dwnn, omitted: S.P.12/121/f.37v.   (28)

1578: (Acting)
*Bacon; *Burghley; *Sidney, President of Council in the Marches of Wales; *B. of Worcester, Vice-President of Council in the Marches of Wales; Earls of *Worcester, *Pembroke; Bishops of *Hereford, *Bangor, *St. Davids, *St. Asaph; *Croft; *Throckmorton, Justice of Chester; *Andrew Corbet; *J. Perrot, *Nich. Arnold, *Hugh Cholmondeley, *J. Littleton, *J. Huband, *p H. Jones, *Jas. Williams senior, kts.; *J. Puckering, Justice of Great Sessions; *David Lewis, Ll.D.; *Geo. Bromley, attorney of the Duchy of

Lancaster; *W. Gerard; *W. Aubrey; *Chas. Fox; *W. Glaseor; *Ellis Price, Ll.D.; *Ed. Leighton; *Rich. Pates; *Ralph Barton; *Jerome Corbet; *Fabian Phillips; *H. Townshend; *W. Leighton; *Griffith Rice, *Rich. Vaughan; *Th. Vaughan of Pembrey; *Walter Vaughan; *Lewis Gwynn, clerk; *W. Davies; *J. Powell ap John; *Morgan John Harry; Geo. David Powell; Th. Williams; Th. Lloyd of Llanstephan; Griffith Vaughan of Trimsaran; Jenkin David John; Rich. Philipps; *Rice Thomas Lewis. *Later additions to list*: *Th. Bromley, kt., Chancellor; *J. Price; *J. Morgan; *Owen Dwnn; *W. Penry; *Philip Williams; Roderick Gwynn David ap Rees: Hatfield House Ms. 223.7. (50 names plus 7 corrections).

1579: post 26 April
As in 1578, except: *Th. Bromley, kt., Chancellor (appointed on 26 April); *J. Price; *J. Morgan; *Owen Dwnn; *W. Penry; *Philip Williams; Rich. Gwynn ap Rees, *added*. Bacon; Jenkin David John, *omitted*: S.P.12/145/f.50v. (Rich. Gwynn ap Rees is apparently the same person as Roderick Gwynn David ap Rees).   (55)

1581: 20 November (Acting)
B. of St. Davids; H. Jones, kt.; Th. Williams; Geo. Powell; Roderick Gwynn David ap Rees; Griffith Rice; J. Powell; Griffith Lloyd; Lewis Williams; Rich. Philipps; W. Davies; Rice Thomas Lewis; Lewis Gwynn, clerk; Rich. Vaughan; Th. Lloyd; J. Morgan; Walter Vaughan; Th. Vaughan; Griffith Vaughan; Owen Dwnn; W. Penry; Ed. Dunlee; Morgan Jones; Philip Williams: Bodleian, Bodley Ms. 904/f.206v. (B. of St. Davids had in fact died on 7 November 1581).   (24)

1582: (Acting)
Bishops of Hereford, St. Asaph; J. Perrot, H. Jones, Jas. Williams, kts.; W. Aubrey; Griffith Rice; Rich. Vaughan; Th. Vaughan of Pembrey; J. Morgan; Walter Vaughan; Griffith Lloyd; Owen Dwnn; Lewis Gwynn, clerk; W. Penry; W. Davies; J. Powell ap John; Philip Williams; Morgan John Harry; Geo. David Powell; Ed. Dunlee; Th. Lloyd; Griffith Vaughan; Roderick Gwynn David ap Rees; Rich. Philipps; Lewis Williams: B.M., Lansdowne Ms. 35/f.138v. (Note that in the lists between about 1577 and 1583 it is difficult to tell how far the variations between lists represent real changes in the commission of the peace or are caused by inaccuracies on the part of those who copied the commissions at the time).   (26)

1583: (Acting)
As in 1582, except for the omission of the first six names on the 1582 list: B. of Hereford; B. of St. Davids; J. Perrot; H. Jones (Sheriff, 1583–4); Jas. Williams; W. Aubrey: B.M., Royal Ms. 18.D.III/f.99v.   (20)

1584: (Acting)
*Th. Bromley, kt., Chancellor; *Burghley, Treasurer; *H. Sidney, kt., President of Council in the Marches of Wales; Earls of *Worcester, *Pembroke; Bishops of *Hereford, *Bangor, *St. Davids, *St. Asaph; *Croft; *Geo. Bromley, kt., Justice of Chester; *J. Puckering & *Rich. Atkins, Justices of Great Sessions; *J. Perrot, *Hugh Cholmondeley, *J. Littleton,

*p H. Jones, kts.; *W. Aubrey; *Chas. Fox; *Ellis Price, Ll.D.; *Ed. Leighton; *W. Leighton; *H. Townshend; *Rich. Pates; *Ralph Barton; *Jerome Corbet; *Fabian Phillips; *W. Glaseor; *Griffith Rice; *Th. Jones of Emlyn; *Rich. Jones; *Th. Vaughan of Pembrey; *J. Morgan; *Lewis Williams; *Griffith Lloyd; *Owen Dwnn; *Ed. Dunlee; *Roderick Gwynn David ap Rees; *David ap John ap William; *J. Powell ap John; *Philip Williams; *Morgan John Harry; Griffith Vaughan of Trimsaran; Rich. Philipps; Th. Williams. *Later additions to list*: *Christopher Hatton, Chancellor (1587); *Th. Perrot, kt.; *Th. Vaughan; *Walter Vaughan; Walter Rice; Jas. Prydderch; W. Davies of Bettws: E.163/14/8/f.48v. (45 names plus 7 corrections).

1588: 26 February (Acting)
Christopher Hatton, kt., Chancellor; Burghley; E. of Pembroke, President of Council in the Marches of Wales; E. of Worcester; Bishops of St. Davids, St. Asaph; Croft; Bromley, Justice of Chester; Puckering & Atkins, Justices of Great Sessions; J. Perrot, Hugh Cholmondeley, J. Littleton, Th. Perrot, Th. Jones, kts.; W. Aubrey, Ll.D.; Chas. Fox; W. Leighton; H. Townshend; Rich. Pates; Ralph Barton; Jerome Corbet; Fabian Phillips; W. Glaseor; Griffith Rice; Rich. Jones; Walter Rice; J. Morgan; Walter Vaughan; Lewis Williams; Owen Dwnn; Lewis Gwynn; J. Powell; Rich. Philipps; W. Davies of Bettws; David Lloyd; Philip Owen; Th. Williams; Jas. Prydderch: Wales 4/716/2. (39)

1590–91: (Acting)
*Hatton, Chancellor; *Burghley; *Pembroke, President of Council in the Marches of Wales; Bishops of *St. Davids, *St. Asaph; *J. Perrot, kt.; *Rich. Shuttleworth, kt., Justice of Chester; *Puckering & *Atkins, Justices of Great Sessions; *Hugh Cholmondeley, *Th. Perrot, *p. Th. Jones, kts.; *W. Aubrey, Ll.D.; *Ellis Price, Ll.D.; *Ed. Leighton; *W. Leighton; *H. Townshend; *Jerome Corbet; *Fabian Phillips; *Griffith Rice; *Herbert Croft; *Rich. Jones; *J. Morgan; *Lewis Williams; *Walter Vaughan; *Owen Dwnn; Roderick Gwynn David ap Rees; Walter Rice; Th. Williams; *Th. Powell; Morgan John Harry; Philip Williams; Francis Lloyd; Jas. Prydderch; Philip Owen; Jenkin David John; David Lloyd ap Griffith; W. Davies of Bettws: Hatfield House Ms. 278/f.55. (38)

1592–3: (Acting)
As in 1590–91, except: *E. of Essex; *W. Oldisworth, Justice of Great Sessions; *p Ed. Dunlee; *Jas. Lewis; Francis Jones; W. Gwynn, *added*. Hatton; J. Perrot; Th. Jones; Rich. Jones; Lewis Williams; Owen Dwnn; Walter Rice; Jas. Prydderch, *omitted*: Kent Record Office U.350.03. (36)

1594: 20 July
*J. Puckering, kt., Keeper of Privy Seal; *Burghley; *Pembroke, President of Council in the Marches of Wales; *E. of Essex; Bishops of *St. Asaph, *St. Davids; *Shuttleworth, Justice of Chester; *Rich. Atkins & *W. Oldisworth, Justices of Great Sessions; *Hugh Cholmondeley, kt.; *W. Aubrey, Ll.D.; *Ellis Price, Ll.D.; *W. Leighton; *H. Townshend; *Jerome Corbet; *Fabian Phillips; *p Ed. Dunlee; *Herbert Croft; Walter Rice;

*J. Morgan; *Walter Vaughan; Anth. Mansel; Roderick Gwynn David ap Rees; Th. Williams; David Lloyd of Forest; *Th. Powell; Morgan John Harry; *Philip Williams; Francis Lloyd; *Jas. Lewis; Jas. Prydderch; Philip Owen; Jenkin David John; *David Lloyd ap Griffith; W. Davies of Bettws; *W. Gwynn; Francis Jones: C.66/1421/m.15d. (37)

1595: 15 August
As on 20 July 1594, except: *W. Fowler; Rowland Gwynn, *added*. W. Aubrey; Ellis Price; Herbert Croft; Walter Vaughan; Jas. Lewis; Philip Owen; W. Davies of Bettws; Francis Jones, *omitted*: Bodleian, Bodley Ms. 904/f.214. General renewal of Welsh commissions on 15 August: Index 4208/f.4v. (31)

1595: 15 November
As on 15 August 1595, except: *p Th. Jones, kt., *added*: C.66/1435/m.19d. Commission renewed to *add* Th. Jones, kt., as *custos rotulorum*: Index 4208/f.8. (32)

1596: 29 June
As on 15 November 1595, except: *Th. Egerton, kt., Keeper of Great Seal; *Walter Vaughan, *added*. J. Puckering, *omitted*: C.66/1468/m.15d & S.P.13/Case F, no. 11/f.38v. Commission renewed to *add* Walter Vaughan: Index 4208/f.17. (Egerton, who was appointed Lord Keeper on 6 May, was probably also added on this date). (33)

1597: 16 February
Commission renewed to *restore* Francis Jones: Index 4208/f.28.

1597: 12 March
As on 29 June 1596, except: *Francis Jones; David Lloyd Jones, *added*. Hugh Cholmondeley; Fabian Phillips; David Lloyd ap Griffith, *omitted*: C.66/1468/m.30d. Commission renewed to *add* David Lloyd Jones: Index 4208/f.30. (32)

1598: 16 February
Commission renewed to *add* J. Vaughan; Francis Mansel: Index 4208/f.45v.

1598: 18 August
Commission renewed to *restore* W. Davies of Bettws: Index 4208/f.55v.

1598: 30 October
*Th. Egerton, kt., Keeper of Great Seal; *Essex; *Pembroke, President of Council in the Marches of Wales; Bishops of *St. Asaph, *St. Davids; *Shuttleworth, Justice of Chester; *Atkins & *Oldisworth, Justices of Great Sessions; *p Th. Jones, kt.; *W. Leighton; *H. Townshend; *Jerome Corbet; *Walter Rice; *J. Vaughan; *J. Morgan; *Th. Williams; *Anth. Mansel; *Francis Mansel; H. Dunlee; Roderick Gwynn David ap Rees; David Lloyd of Forest; *Th. Powell; Morgan John Harry; Francis Lloyd; *Jas. Prydderch; Rowland Gwynn; David Lloyd ap Griffith; W. Davies of Bettws; *Francis Jones; *W. Gwynn; David Lloyd Jones: C.66/1482/m.16d. Commission renewed to *add* H. Dunlee: Index 4208/f.57. (31)

1599: post 15 May
As on 30 October 1598, except: *Th., Lord Buckhurst, Treasurer, *added*. (Buckhurst was appointed on 15 May); Jerome Corbet; Anth. Mansel, *omitted*: C.66/1493/m.26d.   (30)

1600: 5 June
As in 1599, except: *Rich. Lewkenor, kt., Justice of Chester, *added*. Rich. Shuttleworth, *omitted*: C.66/1523/m.29d. Commission renewed to *add* Rich. Lewkenor, and to place J. Vaughan, Esq., as a knight: Index 4208/f.91. (J. Vaughan does not in fact appear on the commission as it is enrolled).   (30)

1601: (Acting)
As on 5 June 1600, except: E. of Essex; E. of Pembroke; B. of St. Asaph; J. Vaughan; David Lloyd of Forest, *omitted*: C.66/1549/m.30d.   (25)

1602: 18 February
Commission renewed to *add* Th. Parry: Index 4208/f.129v.

1602: 28 June
Commission renewed to *restore* J. Vaughan, kt., and to *add* J. Lloyd: Index 4208/f.137. (This explains why J. Vaughan was not included in the enrolment of the 5 June 1600 commission. He was certainly on the commission as originally issued but had presumably been omitted for some reason, whether accidental or deliberate, when the commission was finally enrolled).

1602: 25 July
General renewal of Welsh commissions to *add* Ed., Lord Zouch, President of Council in the Marches of Wales: Index 4208/f.141.

1602: 13 November
*Egerton; *Lord Buckhurst, Treasurer; *Ed., Lord Zouch, President of Council in the Marches of Wales; *B. of St. Davids; *Rich. Lewkenor, kt., Justice of Chester; *Atkins & *Oldisworth, Justices of Great Sessions; *p Th. Jones, *J. Vaughan, kts.; *W. Leighton; *H. Townshend; *Walter Rice; *J. Morgan; *Th. Williams; *Francis Mansel; H. Dunlee; Roderick Gwynn David ap Rees; *Th. Powell; Jas. Prydderch; David Lloyd ap Griffith; *Th. Parry; W. Davies of Bettws; *Francis Jones; *W. Gwynn; *W. Powell; *Howel Gwynn; David Lloyd Jones; *J. Lloyd: C.66/1594/m.34d. Commission renewed to *add* W. Powell; Howel Gwynn: Index 4208/f.144v.   (28)

1603: post 8 June
As on 13 November 1602, except: *Jas. Ley, Justice of Great Sessions, *added*. (Ley was appointed on 8 June 1603). W. Oldisworth, *omitted*: C.66/1620/m.15d.   (28)

1604: (Acting)
As in 1603, except: *Rich. Daston, Justice of Great Sessions, *added*. Jas. Ley; Roderick Gwynn David ap Rees, *omitted*: C.66/1662/m.21d. (A list contained in B.M., Add. Ms. 38139/f.168v is identical to the one given here except for

the omission of Jas. Prydderch. This omission is not however reflected in other lists of the period immediately after 1604 and is almost certainly an error). (27)

1605: 23 September (Acting)
Lord Ellesmere, Chancellor; E. of Dorset (Lord Buckhurst), Treasurer; Zouch, President of Council in the Marches of Wales; B. of St. Davids; Lewkenor, Justice of Chester; Rich. Atkins & Rich. Daston, Justices of Great Sessions; Walter Rice, H. Jones, H. Townshend, kts.; W. Leighton; J. Morgan; Th. Williams; Francis Mansel; W. Vaughan, Ll.D.; H. Dunlee; Th. Powell; Jas. Prydderch; David Lloyd Griffith; Th. Parry; W. Davies of Bettws; Francis Jones; W. Gwynn; David Lloyd Jones; J. Lloyd: Wales 4/717/1. (25)

1605-6: (Acting)
As on 23 September 1605, except: *J. Vaughan, kt.; *W. Powell; *Howel Gwynn; Jas. Lewis, *added*. Lord Zouch; Th. Powell, *omitted*: C.66/1682/m.4d. (The apparent addition of Vaughan, Powell and Gwynn is misleading since all three had appeared together on the commission since 13 November 1602 until their omission, presumably in error, from the Gaol File list of 23 September 1605). (27)

1606-7: (Acting)
As in 1605-6: C.66/1698/m.28d. (27)

1607: post 12 September
As in 1606-7, except: *Ralph, Lord Eure, President of Council in the Marches of Wales (appointed on 12 September); Rice Rydderch; Maurice Bowen, *added*. Walter Rice, kt.; W. Leighton; Th. Williams; David Lloyd ap Griffith, *omitted*: C.66/1748/m.29d. (26)

1608-9: (Acting)
As at the end of 1607, except: *E. of Salisbury, Treasurer; *E. of Northampton, Keeper of Privy Seal, *added*. E. of Dorset; Francis Jones; Jas. Lewis, *omitted*: C.66/1786/m.29d. (25)

1610-11: (Acting)
As in 1608-9, except: *Geo. Devereux, kt., *added*. Rich. Atkins; J. Morgan, *omitted*: C.66/1822/m.26d. (24)

1611-12: (Acting)
As in 1610-11, except: *Nich. Overbury, Justice of Great Sessions, *added*. Rice Rydderch, *omitted*: C.66/1898/m.26d. (24)

1614: post 11 July
As in 1611-12, except: *E. of Suffolk, Treasurer (appointed on 11 July); Rice Rydderch (probably omitted in error in previous list); Th. Jones, *added*. E. of Salisbury; E. of Northampton; W. Gwynn; W. Powell, *omitted*: C.66/1988/m.26d. (23)

1615: (Acting)
As in 1614: C.66/2047/m.20d. (23)

1616: 5 February
*Ellesmere; *E. of Suffolk, Treasurer; *E. of Worcester, Keeper of Privy Seal; *Ralph, Lord Eure, President of Council in the Marches of Wales; *Lewkenor, Justice of Chester; *Nich. Overbury & *Rich. Daston, Justices of Great Sessions; *J. Vaughan, *p H. Jones, *H. Townshend, kts.; *Francis Mansel; *W. Vaughan, Ll.D.; *J. Lloyd; Maurice Bowen; *W. Davies of Bettws; *Howel Gwynn; Th. Jones; *David Lloyd Jones; Walter Vaughan; J. Prydderch; Morgan Thomas; Rich. Williams: C.66/2076/m.23d. Commission renewed to *add* Walter Vaughan; J. Prydderch; Morgan Thomas; Rich. Williams, and to *omit* H. Dunlee and Rice Rydderch because of their outlawry: Index 4211/f.15v. (22)

1616: 28 June
Commission renewed to *restore* H. Dunlee, his outlawry having been reversed: Index 4211/f.22v.

1616: 9 July
Commission renewed to *add* B. of St. Davids: Index 4211/f.23v.

1616: 12 December
Commission renewed to *add* Griffith Lloyd; Maurice Gwynn, and to *omit* Francis Mansel and J. Prydderch because of outlawry: Index 4211/f.30.

1617: 12 March
Commission renewed to *add* Francis Bacon, kt., Keeper of Great Seal; Th., Lord Gerard, President of Council in the Marches of Wales; Th. William Lloyd, and to *restore* Francis Mansel; J. Prydderch: Index 4211/f.36v.

1617: 16 April
Commission renewed to *add* H. Vaughan: Index 4211/f.40v.

1617: post 24 November
*Francis Bacon, kt., Keeper of Great Seal; *Suffolk; *Worcester; *D. of Lennox, Steward; *W., Lord Compton, President of Council in the Marches of Wales (appointed on 24 November); *B. of St. Davids; *Th. Chamberlain, kt., Justice of Chester; *Overbury & *Daston, Justices of Great Sessions; *J. Vaughan, *p H. Jones, *H. Townshend, kts.; *Francis Mansel; *W. Vaughan, Ll.D.; H. Dunlee; *J. Lloyd; Maurice Bowen; *W. Davies; Th. William Lloyd; *Howel Gwynn; Th. Jones; Walter Vaughan; J. Prydderch; H. Vaughan; Morgan Thomas; Rich. Williams; Maurice Gwynn: C.66/2147/m.22d. (27)

1618: 12 March
Commission renewed to *add* Th. Vaughan, and to *omit* W. Davies: Index 4211/f.60v.

1618–19: (Acting)
As at the end of 1617, except: Th. Vaughan; Griffith Lloyd, *added*. E. of
Suffolk; W. Davies, *omitted*: C.66/2174/m.18d.   (27)

1619: 1 May
Commission renewed to *restore* W. Davies: Index 4211/f.83.

1619: 10 June
Commission renewed to *add* W. Ryves, Justice of Great Sessions, in place
of Rich. Daston: Index 4211/f.85.

1619: 25 June
Commission renewed to *add* Rice Lloyd: Index 4211/f.88v.

1619: 21 December
Commission renewed to *add* Rowland Gwynn: Index 4211/f.96.

1620: 21 July
Commission renewed to *add* J. Stepney, kt.; J. Philipps: Index 4211/f.111.

1620: 4 November
General renewal of Welsh commissions to *add* Jas. Whitlock, kt., Justice of
Chester: Index 4211/f.114.

1620: 2 December
Commission renewed to *add* Rice Rudd: Index 4211/f.115.

1621: 26 February
*Francis Bacon, kt., Viscount St. Alban, Chancellor; *H., Viscount Mande-
ville, Treasurer; *Worcester; *Lennox; *E. of Northampton (Lord
Compton), President of Council in the Marches of Wales; *B. of St. Davids;
*Jas. Whitlock, kt., serjeant at law, Justice of Chester; *Nich. Overbury &
*Ed. Littleton, Justices of Great Sessions; *J. Vaughan, *p H. Jones,
*H. Townshend, *J. Stepney, kts.; *Francis Mansel; *W. Vaughan, Ll.D.;
*J. Philipps; *J. Prydderch; *Walter Vaughan; H. Dunlee; *J. Lloyd;
*H. Vaughan; *Maurice Bowen; *W. Davies; Th. Vaughan; *Th. William
Lloyd; Griffith Lloyd; *Howel Gwynn; Th. Jones; Morgan Thomas;
Rich. Williams; Maurice Gwynn; Rice Lloyd; Rowland Gwynn: C.66/2234/
m.42d. General renewal of Welsh commissions to *add* Viscount Mandeville:
Index 4211/f.120. (Note that Rice Rudd's name is omitted, probably in
error, from the end of the commission).   (33)

1621: 3 July
Commission renewed to *add* J. Hoskins, Justice of Great Sessions: Index
4211/f.126.

1621: 31 August
As on 26 February 1621, except: *B. of Lincoln, Keeper of Great Seal;
*J. Hoskins, Justice of Great Sessions; Rice Rudd (see note above), *added*.
Viscount St. Alban; Ed. Littleton, *omitted*: C.193/13/1/f.111v. (J. Vaughan,

kt., now appears as J., Lord Vaughan). Commission renewed to *add* J., Lord Vaughan: Index 4211/f.128v.   (34)

1621: post 29 September
As on 31 August 1621, except: *Lionel Cranfield, Treasurer, *added*. (Cranfield was appointed on 29 September) B. of St. Davids; H. Townshend; Griffith Lloyd (Sheriff, 1620–1), *omitted*: C.66/2259/m.24d.   (32)

1622: 20 February
Commission renewed to *restore* Griffith Lloyd: Index 4211/f.135.

1622: 28 February
As at the end of 1621, except: *B. of St. Davids; Griffith Lloyd, *added*. Rice Lloyd, *omitted*: C.66/2285/m.32d. Commission renewed to *add* B. of St. Davids: Index 4211/f.136. (The commission describes the Treasurer, Cranfield, as E. of Middlesex, a title which he received on 16 September 1622. However this was probably a correction made to the commission when it was finally enrolled and need not affect the dating of the commission as that of 28 February 1622).   (33)

1623: 5 August
Commission renewed to *add* J. Stedman: Index 4211/f.156v.

1623: 2 December
As on 28 February 1622, except: David Gwynn; J. Stedman, *added*. D. of Lennox, *omitted*: C.66/2310/m.29d. Commission renewed to *add* David Gwynn: Index 4211/f.159.   (34)

1625: 29 January
Commission renewed to *restore* J. Stedman, the late Sheriff: Index 4211/f.175.

1625: 1 April
*B. of Lincoln, Keeper of Great Seal; *Jas., Lord Ley, Treasurer; *Viscount Mandeville; *Worcester; *Northampton, President of Council in the Marches of Wales; *B. of St. Davids; *J., Lord Vaughan; *Th. Chamberlain, kt., Justice of Chester; *Nich. Overbury & *J. Hoskins, Justices of Great Sessions; *J. Philipps, Bt.; *J. Stepney, kt. & Bt.; *Francis Mansel, Bt.; *p H. Jones, kt.; *W. Vaughan, Ll.D.; *Sampson Eure; *Rob. Brooke; *Walter Vaughan; H. Dunlee; *J. Lloyd; *H. Vaughan; David Gwynn; *Maurice Bowen; *W. Davies; *Rice Rudd; Th. Vaughan; *Th. William Lloyd; Griffith Lloyd; *Howel Gwynn; Th. Jones; Morgan Thomas; Rich. Williams; Maurice Gwynn; Rowland Gwynn; J. Stedman: C.66/2367/m.27d. General renewal of Welsh commissions: Index 4211/f.180v. (35)

1625: 22 December
As on 1 April 1625, except: *Th. Coventry, kt., Keeper of Great Seal, *added*. B. of Lincoln; Th. Chamberlain, kt., *omitted*: B.M., Harleian Ms. 1622/f.90v. General renewal of Welsh commissions to *add* Th. Coventry: Index 4211/f.194v.   (34)

1626: 20 March
Commission renewed to *add* J. Bridgeman, kt., Justice of Chester: Index 4211/f.199v.

1626: 20 June
As on 22 December 1625, except: *J. Bridgeman, kt., Justice of Chester; *Rich. Vaughan, kt., *added*. J. Stepney, Bt.; W. Vaughan, Ll.D.; H. Dunlee; Maurice Bowen; W. Davies; Howel Gwynn; Morgan Thomas; Maurice Gwynn, *omitted*: E.163/18/12/f.92 & C.193/12/2/f.67. Commission renewed to *add* Rich. Vaughan, kt.: Index 4211/f.204v.   (28)

1627: 13 July
Commission renewed to *restore* W. Davies: Index 4211/f.231.

1628: 14 March
Commission renewed to *restore* Maurice Bowen: Index 4211/f.242.

1628: 25 April
As on 20 June 1626, except: *Marmaduke Lloyd, kt.; *Timothy Turneur; *Maurice Bowen; *W. Davies, *added*. E. of Worcester; Rob. Brooke, *omitted*: C.66/2449/m.32d. Commission renewed to *add* Marmaduke Lloyd, kt.: Index 4211/f.245.   (30)

1628: 15 August
Commission renewed to *add* Rich. Vaughan: Index 4211/f.254v.

1628: 10 December
Commission renewed to *add* Walter Mansel, Bt.: Index 4211/f.260.

1629: 29 June
*Th., Lord Coventry, Keeper of Great Seal; *Rich., Lord Weston, Treasurer; *Viscount Conway, President of Privy Council; *E. of Manchester (Viscount Mandeville), Keeper of Privy Seal; *E. of Pembroke; *Northampton, President of Council in the Marches of Wales; *Rich., Lord Vaughan; *J. Bridgeman, kt., Justice of Chester; *Overbury & *Hoskins, Justices of Great Sessions; *Walter Mansel, Bt.; *Rice Rudd, Bt.; *p H. Jones, *Marmaduke Lloyd, kts.; *Sampson Eure; *Timothy Turneur; *Walter Vaughan; *J. Lloyd; *H. Vaughan; David Gwynn; *Maurice Bowen; Th. Vaughan; *Th. William Lloyd; *Griffith Lloyd; Th. Jones; Rowland Gwynn; J. Stedman; Rich. Vaughan; J. Gwynn of Gwempa: C.66/2495/ m.26d. Commission renewed to *add* J. Gwynn of Gwempa: Index 4212/ p.10.   (29)

1630: 20 February
Commission renewed to *add* David Williams: Index 4212/p.25.

1630: 25 February
As on 29 June 1629, except: *David Williams; Rich. Philipps of Richmore, *added*: C.66/2527/m.28d. Commission renewed to *add* Rich. Philipps of Richmore: Index 4212/p.26.   (31)

1630: 13 December
As on 25 February 1630, except: Morgan Owen, clerk, *added*. Viscount Conway; E. of Pembroke; E. of Northampton; Maurice Bowen; Th. William Lloyd; J. Gwynn of Gwempa, *omitted*: C.66/2536/m.20d.; C.66/2577/m.11d. & S.P.16/212/f.70v. Commission renewed to *add* Morgan Owen, clerk, and to *omit* J. Lloyd; Maurice Bowen; Th. William Lloyd; J. Gwynn: Index 4212/p.44. (Note that, despite the above Docquet Book entry, J. Lloyd does not in fact appear to have been omitted).   (26)

1632: 27 February
Commission renewed to *add* Francis Lloyd: Index 4211/p.77.

1632: 24 November
*Coventry; *E. of Portland (Lord Weston), Treasurer; *Manchester; *E. of Bridgewater, President of Council in the Marches of Wales; *B. of St. Davids; *Rich., Lord Vaughan; *Bridgeman, Justice of Chester; *Overbury & *Hoskins, Justices of Great Sessions; *Walter Mansel, Bt.; *Rice Rudd, Bt.; *p H. Jones, *Marmaduke Lloyd, kts.; *Sampson Eure; *Timothy Turneur; *Walter Vaughan; *J. Lloyd; *Griffith Lloyd of Ynyswen; *H. Vaughan; David Gwynn; *David Williams; Th. Vaughan; Th. Jones; *Rowland Gwynn; Morgan Owen, clerk; J. Stedman; Rich. Vaughan; Rich. Philipps of Richmore; Francis Lloyd: C.66/2598/m.20d.; C.66/2623/m.23d & C.193/13/2/f.77. Commission renewed to *add* B. of St. Davids: Index 4212/p.94.   (29)

1634: 10 December
As on 24 November 1632, except: Rich., Lord Vaughan, now appears as Rich., E. of Carbery: C.66/2654/m.22d. Commission renewed to *add* Rich., Lord Vaughan, as E. of Carbery: Index 4212/p.151.   (29)

1636: post 6 March
As on 10 December 1634, except: *B. of London, Treasurer, *added* (appointed on 6 March). E. of Portland; B. of St. Davids, *omitted*: S.P.16/405/f.75v.   (28)

1637: 1 July
Commission renewed to *add* Roger, B. of St. Davids; W. Vaughan, kt.; H. Jones; J. Bloom: Index 4212/p.250.

1637: 12 July
Commission renewed to *add* J. Lewis: Index 4212/p.255.

1637: 27 September (Acting)
*Coventry; *B. of London, Treasurer; *Manchester; *Bridgewater, President of Council in the Marches of Wales; *E. of Carbery; *B. of St. Davids; *Bridgeman, Justice of Chester; *Timothy Turneur & *J. Hoskins, Justices of Great Sessions; *Walter Mansel, Bt.; *p H. Jones, kt.; *Marmaduke Lloyd, *W. Vaughan, kts.; *Morgan Owen, D.D.; *Sampson Eure; *H. Jones; *J. Lloyd; *H. Vaughan; David Gwynn; Th. Vaughan; *Rowland Gwynn; J. Stedman; Rich. Vaughan; J. Bloom; Rich. Philipps

of Richmore; Francis Lloyd; J. Lewis: Wales 4/717/4. (Details of quorum based on the commission of 6 March 1638 contained in C.66/2725/m.19d). (27)

1637: 14 December
Commission renewed to appoint H. Jones, Esq., as *custos rotulorum* in place of H. Jones, kt., deceased: Index 4212/p.273.

1638: 6 March
As on 27 September 1637, except: *Rice Rudd, Bt., *added*. (Rudd was probably omitted in error from the list of 27 September 1637). J. Bridgeman, kt.; H. Jones, kt.; J. Lloyd; David Gwynn, *omitted*: C.66/2725/m.19d. Commission renewed to *add* Timothy Turneur, Justice of Great Sessions: Index 4212/p.284. (Note that Turneur had been appointed as Justice on 25 July 1637 (Index 4212/p.257) and therefore appeared in the list of justices of the peace made for the Session of 27 September 1637 in anticipation of the issuing of a new commission of the peace to include him).   (24)

1638: 12 June
*Coventry; *London; *Manchester; *Bridgewater, President of Council in the Marches of Wales; *Carbery; *B. of St. Davids; *Th. Milward, kt., Justice of Chester; *Turneur & *Hoskins, Justices of Great Sessions; *Walter Mansel, Bt.; *Rice Rudd, Bt.; *Marmaduke Lloyd, *W. Vaughan, kts.; *Morgan Owen, D.D.; *Sampson Eure; *p H. Jones; *H. Vaughan; Th. Vaughan; *Rowland Gwynn; J. Stedman; *Rich. Vaughan; J. Bloom; Rich. Philipps of Richmore; Francis Lloyd; J. Lewis: C.66/2761/m.17d. Commission renewed to *add* Daniel Lloyd: Index 4212/p.296.   (25).

1639: 15 March
Commission renewed to *add* J. Platt, Justice of Great Sessions: Index 4212/p.330.

1639: 29 June
Commission renewed to *add* H. Jones (not to be confused with the *custos rotulorum*): Index 4212/p.344.

1640: post 17 January
*J. Finch, kt., Keeper of Great Seal (appointed on 17 January); *London; *Manchester; *Bridgewater, President of Council in the Marches of Wales; *Carbery; *B. of St. Davids; *Milward, Justice of Chester; *Timothy Turneur & *J. Platt, Justices of Great Sessions; *Walter Mansel, Bt.; *Rice Rudd, Bt.; *Marmaduke Lloyd, *W. Vaughan, kts.; *Morgan Owen, D.D.; *Sampson Eure; *W. Morgan; *p H. Jones; *H. Vaughan; Th. Vaughan; *Rowland Gwynn; H. Jones; J. Stedman; *Rich. Vaughan; J. Bloom; Rich. Philipps; Daniel Lloyd; J. Lewis: C.66/2858/m.21d.   (27)

1640: 3 August
Commission renewed to *add* David Lloyd: Index 4212/p.401.

1640: 10 December
Commission renewed to *add* Howel Gwynn: Index 4212/p.416.

1641: 20 August
Commission renewed to *add* Lodowick Lewis; J. Harris, to place J. Bloom on the quorum, and to *omit* Howel Gwynn: Index 4212/p.478.

1642: 24 February
Commission renewed to *add* David Gwynn; J. Vaughan of Llanelly; Nich. Williams; Th. William Lloyd; J. Vaughan of Plasgwyn; H. Middleton; Francis Lloyd of Llanstephan: Index 4212/p.507.

1642: 14 March
Commission renewed to *add* Ed. Vaughan: Index 4212/p.512.

1642: 21 May
Commission renewed to *add* Howel Gwynn: Index 4212/p.523.

1643: 6 April
Commission renewed to *add* Chas. Gwynn; J. Powell, and to place J. Vaughan on the quorum (it is not clear which J. Vaughan is meant): Index 4210/p.12. (David Jenkins who had been appointed as Justice of Great Sessions on 11 March in place of J. Platt, who had been discharged from office at his own request (Index 4210/p.7), was probably also added on this date).

1643: 3 November
Commission renewed to *add* Anth. Rudd; Th. Aubrey: Index 4210/p.49.

1644: 28 May
Commission renewed to appoint E. of Carbery as *custos rotulorum*: Index 4210/p.117.

1647: 20 March
W. Powell & J. Clark appointed as Justices of Great Sessions: Index 4213/p.82. (It is not known when they were formally added to the commission of the peace).

1648: 24 January
Commission renewed (no details): Index 4213/p.105.

1648: 11 August
Commission renewed to *add* Erasmus Philipps, Bt.; H. Rice; Jas. Jones; H. Price; W. Fleming: Index 4213/p.121.

1649: 6 March
*W. Lenthall, Speaker of House of Commons; *Th., Lord Fairfax; *J. Bradshaw, President of the Council; *Bulstrode Whitelock, *Rich. Keble, *J. Lisle, Commissioners of Great Seal; *H. Rolle, Chief Justice of Upper Bench; *W. Powell & *J. Clark, Justices of Great Sessions; *Edm. Prideaux,

Attorney-General; *Erasmus Philipps, Bt.; *Ed. Vaughan, kt.; *Th. Harrison; *Howel Gwynn; *Francis Lloyd of Llangadock; *Rich. Vaughan; *Chas. Gwynn; *Griffith Lloyd; *J. Lloyd of Faerdref; *W. Fleming; *Geo. Jones; J. Powell; Evan Thomas; David Morgan; Th. Morgan; Jas. Jones: C.193/13/3/f.73. Commission renewed (no details): Index 4213/p.143. (The name of Edm. Prideaux, who was not appointed as Attorney-General until 9 April, was probably added to the commission when it was copied into the C.193 entry book). (26)

1649: 12 November
Commission renewed to appoint Th. Harrison as *custos rotulorum*: Index 4213/p.168. (Ed. Freeman, who was appointed attorney in Carmarthen on 27 July 1649 (Index 4213/p.164), was probably also added on this date).

1650: 11 March
Commission renewed to *add* Philip Jones; Rowland Dawkins; J. Russell; Rowland Gwynn; Th. William Lloyd; Stephen Winthrop; J. Franklin; Maurice Morgan, and to *omit* Howel Gwynn; Jas. Jones: Index 4213/p.181.

1650: 25 July
*Lenthall; *Oliver Cromwell, Lord General; *Bradshaw; *Whitelock, *Keble & *Lisle; *Rolle; *Powell & *Clark, Justices of Great Sessions; *Edm. Prideaux, Attorney-General; *p Th. Harrison; *Philip Jones; *Erasmus Philipps, Bt.; *Ed. Vaughan, kt.; *Ed. Freeman, attorney in Carmarthenshire; *J. Lloyd of Faerdref; *Jas. Philipps; *Rowland Dawkins; *David Morgan; *Jenkin Franklin; *Rich. Vaughan; *Maurice Morgan; Chas. Gwynn; *Th. Morgan; *W. Fleming; *J. Russell: *Lists published by Th. Walkley* (1650), p.64. Commission renewed to *add* Jas. Philipps, and to *omit* Francis Lloyd of Llangadock; Griffith Lloyd; Geo. Jones; and others (no further details given in Docquet Book): Index 4213/p.198. (26)

1651: 24 February
As on 25 July 1650, except: *Rowland Gwynn; *Nich. Williams; *Geo. Jones; J. Powell, *added*. Rowland Dawkins; Th. Morgan, *omitted*: C.193/13/4/f.114d & B.M., Stowe Ms. 577/f.61. Commission renewed to *add* Nich. Williams; Geo. Jones; J. Powell, and to *omit* Rowland Dawkins; Th. Morgan: Index 4213/p.209. (Note that Rowland Gwynn had originally been added to the commission on 11 March 1650 but was not included in the commission of 25 July as recorded in Walkley's list, probably in error). (28)

1653: 10 January
*Lenthall; *Cromwell; *Whitelock, *Keble & *Lisle; *Bradshaw; *Rolle; *Powell & *Clark, Justices of Great Sessions; *Edm. Prideaux, Attorney-General; *p Th. Harrison; *Philip Jones; *Erasmus Philipps, Bt.; *Rowland Dawkins; *Ed. Vaughan; *Ed. Freeman, attorney in Carmarthen; *J. Lloyd of Faerdref; *Jas. Philipps; *Geo. Gwynn; *David Morgan; *Jenkin Franklin; *Rich. Vaughan; *Maurice Morgan; *W. Fleming; *Rowland Gwynn; Chas. Gwynn; *J. Russell; *Nich. Williams; *Geo. Jones; J. Powell; David Edwards; J. Vaughan of Plasgwyn; Rich. Lewis; J. Lewis:

Cambridge University Ms. Dd.VIII.1/f.121. Commission renewed to *add* Rowland Dawkins; Geo. Gwynn; David Edwards; J. Vaughan; Rich. Lewis; J. Lewis: Index 4213/p.249.   (34)

1653: 20 August (Acting)
As on 10 January 1653, except: J. Haggatt, Justice of Great Sessions, *added*. W. Powell; J. Clark; Ed. Freeman; Rowland Gwynn, *omitted*: Wales 4/718/1.   (31)

1654: 4 March
Commission renewed according to a general list: Index 4213/p.284.

1654: 14 August (Acting)
As on 20 August 1653, except: Oliver St. John, Chief Justice of Lower Bench; Bennet Hoskins, Justice of Great Sessions; Edm. Jones, Attorney-General of South Wales; Jenkin Lloyd; J. Lloyd of Cilrhiw; Th. Evans, *added*. Oliver Cromwell; Th. Harrison; J. Lloyd of Faerdref; W. Fleming; J. Russell, *omitted*: Wales 4/718/2. (These changes were presumably introduced when the commission was renewed on 4 March 1654).   (32)

1656: 20 March
Commission renewed to *add* Major-General Jas. Berry; Th. Lloyd of Llanllawddog, and to *omit* Rich. Vaughan; Th. Evans; Maurice Morgan; Nich. Williams; J. Lewis: Index 4213/p.329.

1656: 22 July
*Nathaniel Fiennes & *J. Lisle, Commissioners of Great Seal; *Bulstrode Whitelock, kt., *Th. Widdrington, kt., *Ed. Montagu & *W. Sydenham, Commissioners of Treasury; *Philip Jones; *J. Glynn, Chief Justice of Upper Bench; *W. Lenthall, Master of the Rolls; *Oliver St. John, Chief Justice of Common Bench; *J. Haggatt & *Bennet Hoskins, Justices of Great Sessions; *Edm. Prideaux, Attorney-General; *Major-General Jas. Berry; *Erasmus Philipps, Bt.; *p Rowland Dawkins; *Ed. Vaughan; *Edm. Jones, Attorney-General of S. Wales; *W. Russell; *Jas. Philipps; *Geo. Gwynn; *David Morgan; *Jenkin Franklin; *Jenkin Lloyd; *J. Lloyd of Cilrhiw; *Chas. Gwynn; *Geo. Jones; J. Powell; *David Edwards; J. Vaughan; *Rich. Lewis; *Th. Lloyd of Llanllawddog; *J. Vaughan of Derllys; Morgan Jones of Tregib; Owen Brigstock; J. Lewis of Llysnewydd: C.193/13/6/f.101 & C.193/13/5/f.121v. Commission renewed to *add* J. Vaughan of Derllys; Morgan Jones of Tregib; Owen Brigstock; J. Lewis of Llysnewydd: Index 4213/p.344.   (36)

1657: 7 December
Commission renewed to *omit* J. Powell: Index 4213/p.381.

1658: 24 September
General renewal of Welsh commissions to *add* Rich. Cromwell, Lord Protector: Index 4213/p.405.

1659: 28 June
Commission renewed according to a general list: Index 4213/p.434.

1660: 31 March
Commission renewed according to a general list: Index 4213/p.460. (The commission would have included Bennet Hoskins & Th. Manby who were appointed as Justices of Great Sessions on 30 March 1660: Index 4213/p.460).

1660: 6 September
Commission renewed to *add* E. of Carbery, *custos rotulorum;* W. Morton & Simon Degg, Justices of Great Sessions; and others (no details): Index 4214/p.36.

1661: 18 March
*Ed. Hyde, kt., Chancellor; *E. of Southampton, Treasurer; *D. of Albemarle; *Marquess of Ormond, Steward; *E. of Lindsey, Great Chamberlain; *E. of Manchester, Household Chamberlain; *p E. of Carbery; *Francis, Lord Vaughan; *Arthur Annesley; *W. Morton, kt., serjeant at law & *Simon Degg, Justices of Great Sessions; *H. Vaughan, kt.; *Rice Rudd, Bt.; *Ed. Mansel, Bt.; *Ed. Rice, Francis Lloyd, kts.; *J. Vaughan of Golden Grove; *H. Vaughan of Derwydd; *J. Vaughan of Plasgwyn; *H. Middleton; Philip Vaughan; Owen Brigstock; Penry Vaughan; Morgan Jones; J. Vaughan of Cwrt Derllys; Evan Thomas; Lewis Morgan; W. Bevan; *J. Lewis; Th. Lloyd; Rich. Lewis; Th. Vaughan of Abergwili; Th. Lloyd of Berllan; *J. Lloyd; *Jas. Jones; Jonathan Lloyd; W. Gwynn; Nich. Williams; J. Powell junior; Th. Lloyd of Danryallt; Walter Jones: C.220/9/4/f.101 & B.M., Egerton Ms. 2557/f.100. Commission renewed to place Ed. Mansel, Bt., on the quorum: Index 4214/p.91.   (41)

1661: 12 August
Commission renewed to *add* W. Russell, Bt.: Index 4214/p.130.

1661: 8 November
As on 18 March 1661, except: *J., Lord Robartes, Keeper of Privy Seal; *W. Russell, Bt., *added*: C.193/12/3/f.116. General renewal of Welsh commissions to *add* E. of Carbery as President of Council in the Marches of Wales (Carbery was already a member of the Carmarthen commission before his promotion): Index 4214/p.144. (Arthur Annesley now appears as E. of Anglesey).   (43)

1662: 17 July
As on 8 November 1661, except: J. Vaughan of Llanelly, *added*: C.66/2986/ m.30d. Commission renewed to *add* J. Vaughan of Llanelly: Index 4214/ p.178. (J. Lloyd now appears as J. Lloyd, Bt.)   (44)

1662–3: (Acting)
As on 17 July 1662, except: Job Charlton, kt., Justice of Chester, *added*: C.66/3022/m.35d. (Charlton was appointed on 14 March 1662 but was clearly not added to the commission until some time later. Note that this commission was again enrolled for the year 1665–6 (C.66/3074/m.34d) since no fresh commission had apparently been issued in the meantime. The Gaol File list of 3 October 1664 shows however that the real composition of the commission had changed considerably).   (45)

1664: 3 October (Acting)
E. of Clarendon, Chancellor; Southampton; Lord Robartes, Keeper of Privy Seal; Albemarle; Ormond; Lindsey; Manchester; Carbery, President of Council in the Marches of Wales; E. of Anglesey; Francis, Lord Vaughan; Morton & Degg, Justices of Great Sessions; Ed. Mansel, Bt.; W. Russell, Bt.; Francis Lloyd, kt.; J. Vaughan of Golden Grove, kt. of the Bath; H. Vaughan, kt.; J. Vaughan of Llanelly; J. Vaughan of Plasgwyn; H. Middleton; Philip Vaughan; Owen Brigstock; Penry Vaughan; Morgan Jones; J. Vaughan of Cwrt Derllys; Evan Thomas; Lewis Morgan; W. Bevan; Th. Lloyd of Llanllawddog; Rich. Lewis; Th. Lloyd of Berllan; Jas. Jones; W. Gwynn; Nich. Williams; J. Powell junior; Th. Lloyd of Danyrallt: Wales 4/720/4.   (36)

1665: 5 September (Acting)
As on 3 October 1664, except: W. Russell, Bt.; Nich. Williams, *omitted*: Wales 4/720/5. (Both omissions are probably erroneous).   (34)

1666: 18 July
Commission renewed to *add* Fred. Hyde, kt., serjeant at law, Justice of Great Sessions: Index 4214/p.289.

1666: 27 August (Acting)
As on 5 September 1665, except: Job Charlton, kt., Justice of Chester; Fred. Hyde, kt., Justice of Great Sessions; Rice Rudd, Bt.; W. Russell, Bt.; Nich. Williams; W. Jones, *added*. W. Morton, *omitted*: Wales 4/720/6. (Note that Charlton had held office since 1662. His failure to appear on any Gaol File list before the present one was caused by the lack of a new commission of the peace since that of 17 July 1662).   (39)

1667: 24 May
Commission renewed to *add* Rice Rudd, Bt.; Francis Cornwallis, kt.: Index 4214/p.306. (Rice Rudd, Bt., was the successor of his namesake who had died in 1664, but who was erroneously retained in the Gaol File lists until 1666).

1667: 13 June
Commission renewed to *omit* H. Vaughan of Derwydd, kt., and J. Vaughan of Llanelly because of their outlawry: Index 4214/p.307.

1667: 13 June (Acting)
As on 27 August 1666, except: Rice Rudd, Bt.; Francis Cornwallis, kt.; J. Lewis, *added*. E. of Southampton; Rice Rudd, Bt. (died in 1664); J. Vaughan of Plasgwyn; Evan Thomas; W. Bevan; Rich. Lewis, *omitted*: Wales 4/721/1.   (36)

1667: 19 August (Acting)
As on 13 July 1667, except: J. Vaughan of Plasgwyn, *added*. Francis, Lord Vaughan; H. Vaughan; J. Vaughan of Llanelly, *omitted*: Wales 4/721/2.   (34)

1669: 5 April (Acting)
As on 19 August 1667, except: E. of Clarendon; Francis Lloyd; J. Lewis; Nich. Williams; W. Jones, *omitted*: Wales 4/721/5. (Note that the last three names reappear on the list of 23 August 1669). (29)

1669: 22 May
Commission renewed to *add* Altham Vaughan; Walter Vaughan of Llanelly: Index 4214/p.345.

1669: 23 August (Acting)
Orlando Bridgeman, kt. & Bt., Keeper of Great Seal; Robartes; D. of Buckingham; Albemarle; Ormond; Lindsey; Manchester; Carbery, President of Council in the Marches of Wales; E. of Anglesey; J., Lord Vaughan; Job Charlton, kt., Justice of Chester; Fred. Hyde, kt. and Simon Degg, Justices of Great Sessions; Altham Vaughan; Rice Rudd, Bt.; Ed. Mansel, Bt.; W. Russell, Bt.; Francis Cornwallis, kt.; J. Vaughan of Plasgwyn; H. Middleton; Philip Vaughan; Owen Brigstock; Penry Vaughan; Morgan Jones; J. Vaughan of Cwrt Derllys; Walter Vaughan of Llanelly; Lewis Morgan; J. Lewis; Th. Lloyd of Llanllawddog; Th. Lloyd of Berllan; Jas. Jones; W. Gwynn; Nich. Williams; J. Powell junior; Th. Lloyd (of Danyrallt); W. Jones: Wales 4/721/6. (36)

1669: 25 November
Commission renewed to *add* Christopher Middleton: Index 4214/p.356.

1670: 25 July (Acting)
As on 23 August 1669, except: Christopher Middleton, *added*. J. Vaughan of Plasgwyn; H. Middleton, *omitted*: Wales 4/722/1. (35)

1670: 15 December
Commission renewed to *add* Walter Rice; Rich. Bloom: Index 4214/p.383.

1671: 2 March
Commission renewed to *add* Walter Middleton: Index 4214/p.386.

1671: 10 April (Acting)
As on 25 July 1670, except: Walter Rice; Rich. Bloom, *added*: Wales 4/722/2. (Walter Middleton's addition is not yet reflected in the Gaol File lists). (37)

1672: 26 February
Commission renewed to *add* Sackville Crowe, Bt.; Rowland Gwynn: Index 4214/p.408.

1672: 25 March (Acting)
As on 10 April 1671, except: E. of St. Albans, Household Chamberlain; B. of St. Davids; Sackville Crowe, Bt.; J. Lloyd, Bt.; Rowland Gwynn of Glanbran; J. Vaughan of Plasgwyn; Rich. Gwynn; Walter Middleton; Geo. Gwynn; W. Bevan, *added*. Lord Robartes; D. of Albemarle; E. of Manchester; Penry Vaughan; J. Lewis; Th. Lloyd of Llanllawddog, *omitted*: Wales 4/722/3. (41)

1672: 15 July
Commission renewed to *add* Rawleigh Mansel: Index 4214/p.419.

1673: 7 June
Commission renewed to *add* Rich. Vaughan of Torycoed; David Morgan: Index 4214/p.451.

1673: 2 July
Commission renewed to *add* J. Philipps: Index 4214/p.453.

1673: 7 July (Acting)
E. of Shaftesbury, Chancellor; Th., Lord Clifford, Treasurer; Buckingham; Ormond; Marquess of Worcester, President of Council in the Marches of Wales; Earls of Lindsey, Norfolk, St. Albans, Anglesey, Carbery; B. of St. Davids; Job Charlton, kt., Justice of Chester; J., Lord Vaughan; Hyde & Degg, Justices of Great Sessions; Altham Vaughan; Rice Rudd, Bt.; Sackville Crowe, Bt.; Ed. Mansel, Bt.; W. Russell, Bt.; J. Lloyd, Bt.; Francis Cornwallis, kt.; Owen Wynn; Walter Rice; Rawleigh Mansel; W. Gwynn; Rowland Gwynn of Glanbran; J. Vaughan of Plasgwyn; Philip Vaughan; Rich. Vaughan of Torycoed; Owen Brigstock; Morgan Jones; J. Vaughan of Cwrt Derllys; Walter Vaughan of Llanelly; Lewis Morgan; Th. Lloyd of Berllan; Jas. Jones; Rich. Gwynn; Chris. Middleton; Nich. Williams; Walter Middleton; David Morgan; J. Powell junior; Rich. Bloom; W. Bevan: Wales 4/722/4.   (45)

1673: 4 August (Acting)
As on 7 July 1673, except: Th., Viscount Osborne, Treasurer; Th. Lloyd of Danyrallt; J. Philipps; W. Jones, *added*. Lord Clifford, *omitted*: Wales 4/722/5.   (48)

1674: 19 March (Acting)
As on 4 August 1673, except: E. of Norfolk; E. of St. Albans, *omitted*: Wales 4/722/6.   (46)

1674: 24 March
Commission renewed to *add* Roger Mainwaring: Index 4214/p.475.

1675: 15 June
Commission renewed to *add* Ed. Gwynn: Index 4214/p.499.

1675: 2 August (Acting)
As on 19 March 1674, except: Lord Finch, Keeper of Great Seal; E. of St. Albans; Roger Mainwaring, *added*. E. of Shaftesbury; Simon Degg; J. Lloyd; Walter Rice; Rawleigh Mansel; Nich. Williams; Th. Lloyd of Danyrallt; W. Jones; David Morgan, *omitted*: Wales 4/722/7.   (40)

1676: 11 January
Commission renewed to *add* Theophilus Lloyd of Danyrallt: Index 4214 p.506.

1676: 8 May (Acting)
Lord Finch. Chancellor; E. of Danby, Treasurer; Anglesey; Buckingham; D. of Monmouth; Ormond; Marquess of Worcester, President of Council in the Marches of Wales; Lindsey; E. of Arlington; Carbery; B. of St. Davids; J., Lord Vaughan; Charlton, Justice of Chester; Fred. Hyde, kt. & Francis Manley, Justices of Great Sessions; Altham Vaughan; Rice Rudd, Bt.; Sackville Crowe, Bt.; Ed. Mansel, Bt.; W. Russell, Bt.; Owen Wynn; W. Gwynn; J. Vaughan of Plasgwyn; Philip Vaughan; Rich. Vaughan of Torycoed; Owen Brigstock; Morgan Jones; J. Vaughan of Cwrt Derllys; Walter Vaughan of Llanelly; Lewis Morgan; Th. Lloyd of Berllan; Jas. Jones; Rich. Gwynn; Chris. Middleton; Rowland Gwynn; Roger Mainwaring; Walter Middleton; Theophilus Lloyd of Danyrallt; J. Philipps of Dolhaidd; J. Powell junior; Rich. Bloom; W. Bevan: Wales 4/723/1. (42)

1676: 11 May
Commission renewed to *add* Rice Williams: Index 4214/p.512.

1676: 22 May
Commission renewed to *add* Th. Williams of Talley: Index 4214/p.512.

1676: 13 June
Commission renewed to *add* J. Morgan: Index 4214/p.513.

1676: 19 December
Commission renewed to *add* Ed. Vaughan of Penybanc: Index 4214/p.519.

1677: 25 July
Commission renewed to *add* Rich. Jones of Tregib: Index 4214/p.531.

1677: 27 August (Acting)
As on 8 May 1676, except: W. Buckby, Justice of Great Sessions; Rice Williams, kt.; Lewis Meyrick, Attorney-General for Wales; Th. Williams of Talley; J. Morgan; Rich. Brett; Ed. Vaughan of Penybanc; Rich. Jones of Tregib, *added*. Frederick Hyde; Owen Wynn; Philip Vaughan; Morgan Jones, *omitted*: Wales 4/723/2. (46)

1678: 1 March
Commission renewed to *add* Th. Gwynn; W. Brigstock of Llechdwnny; Th. Lloyd of Alltycadno; J. Lloyd of Llanllawddog; J. Scurlock: Index 4214/p.540.

1678: 20 August
Commission renewed to *add* Rich. Vaughan: Index 4214/p.548.

1679: 5 April
Commission renewed to *add* J. Williams of Abercothi: Index 4215/p.4.

1679: 14 April (Acting)
Finch; Danby; Anglesey; Buckingham; Monmouth; Ormond; Worcester,
President of Council in the Marches of Wales; Lindsey; Arlington; Carbery;
B. of St. Davids; J., Lord Vaughan; Charlton, Justice of Chester; Francis
Manley & W. Buckby, Justices of Great Sessions; Altham Vaughan; Rice
Rudd, Bt.; Sackville Crowe, Bt.; Ed. Mansel, Bt.; W. Russell, Bt.; Rice
Williams, kt.; Lewis Meyrick, Attorney-General for Wales; W. Gwynn;
Th. Williams of Talley; J. Vaughan of Plasgwyn; Rich. Vaughan of Tory-
coed; Owen Brigstock; J. Vaughan of Cwrt Derllys; Walter Vaughan of
Llanelly; J. Powell junior; Lewis Morgan; J. Morgan; Th. Lloyd of
Berllandywyll; Jas. Jones; Rich. Gwynn; Rich. Brett; Christopher Middle-
ton; Rowland Gwynn; Th. Gwynn; Roger Mainwaring; W. Brigstock of
Llechdwnny; Walter Middleton; Th. Lloyd of Alltycadno; J. Lloyd of
Llanllawddog; J. Philipps of Dolhaidd; Ed. Vaughan of Penybanc; Rich.
Jones of Tregib; Rich. Bloom; W. Bevan: Wales 4/723/4. (Note that for
some reason, possibly in error, J. Scurlock and Rich. Vaughan, who were
added to the commission on 1 March and 20 August 1678, are not included.
The addition to the commission of J. Williams on 5 April 1679 was too
recent for him to appear in the present list). (49)

1679: 25 August (Acting)
As on 14 April 1679, except: J. Williams of Abercothi, *added*. E. of Danby;
J. Morgan, *omitted*: Wales 4/723/5. (48)

1680: 1 April
*Prince Rupert; *Archbishop of Canterbury; *Finch; *E. of Radnor,
President of Council; Dukes of *Albermarle, *Monmouth, *Newcastle,
*Lauderdale, *Ormond; *Marquess of Winchester; *Marquess of Worcester,
President of Council in the Marches of Wales; Earls of *Lindsey, *Arlington,
*Salisbury, *Bridgewater, *Sunderland, *Essex, *Bath, *Halifax, *p Carbery;
*Viscount Fauconberg; Bishops of *London, *St. Davids; *J., Lord
Vaughan; *Laurence Hyde; *H. Coventry; *Francis North, kt., Chief
Justice of Bench; *J. Ernley, kt., Chancellor of Exchequer; *Th. Chichley,
kt., Chancellor of Duchy of Lancaster; *Ed. Seymour; *W. Temple, Bt.;
*Leoline Jenkins; *Sidney Godolphin; *Francis Manley & *W. Buckby,
Justices of Great Sessions; *Altham Vaughan; *Rice Rudd, Bt.; *Sackville
Crowe, Bt.; *Ed. Mansel, Bt.; *W. Russell, Bt.; *Rice Williams, kt.; *Lewis
Meyrick, Attorney-General for Wales; *W. Gwynn; *Th. Williams of
Talley; *J. Vaughan of Plasgwyn; *Rich. Vaughan of Torycoed; *Owen
Brigstock; *J. Vaughan of Cwrt Derllys; *Walter Vaughan of Llanelly;
*Jas. Protheroe; *J. Powell junior; Lewis Morgan; *J. Morgan; *Th.
Lloyd of Berllandywyll; *Jas. Jones; *J. Williams of Abercothi; *Rich.
Gwynn; *Rich. Brett; *Chris. Middleton; *Rich. Vaughan; *Rowland
Gwynn; *Th. Gwynn; *Roger Mainwaring; *W. Brigstock of Llechdwnny;
*Walter Middleton; *Th. Lloyd of Alltycadno; *J. Lloyd of Llanllawddog;
*Theophilus Lloyd of Danyrallt; *J. Scurlock; *J. Philipps of Dolhaidd;
*Ed. Vaughan of Penybanc; *Rich. Jones of Tregib; Rich. Bloom; W. Jones;
W. Bevan: C.193/12/4/f.139v. Commission renewed to *remove* recusants
and to *add* others (no details): Index 4215/p.26. (The *removal* from the
Carmarthen commission of the Duke of Buckingham and the *addition* of

Jas. Protheroe were ordered by warrants of 5 February 1680: *H.M.C.,*
Eleventh Report, Appendix, Part 2, p.175). (75)

1680: 23 August
Commission renewed to *add* H. Vaughan of Trimsaran; Rawleigh Mansel:
Index 4215/p.35.

1681: 11 April (Acting)
As on 1 April 1680, except: E. of Anglesey, Keeper of Privy Seal; Daniel
Finch; Geo. Jeffreys, Justice of Chester; Rawleigh Mansel, *added*. (Note
that Anglesey & Finch ought probably to have been included on 1 April
1680. Note also that Rawleigh Mansel appears but not H. Vaughan who was
added to the commission on the same date). W. Gwynn; Th. Williams of
Talley; J. Williams of Abercothi; Theophilus Lloyd of Danyrallt, *omitted*:
Wales 4/724/1. (75)

1682: 10 January
Commission renewed to *add* Griffith Lloyd: Index 4215/p.58.

1682: 28 February
Commission renewed to *add* Daniel Lloyd of Llangennech: Index 4215/p.61.

1682: 10 April (Acting)
As on 11 April 1681, except: Chas., Lord Herbert; J. Williams of Abercothi;
Daniel Lloyd of Llangennech; Griffith Lloyd, *added*. D. of Monmouth;
Earls of Salisbury, Sunderland, Essex; W. Temple; Rich. Bloom; Altham
Vaughan; J. Morgan, *omitted*: Wales 4/724/2. (Note that J. Williams had
probably been omitted in error in 1681). (71)

1682: 7 August (Acting)
As on 10 April 1682, except: Rice Rudd; J. Scurlock; W. Jones, *omitted*:
Wales 4/724/3. (68)

1683: 27 February
Commission renewed to *add* Ed. Vaughan of Trimsaran: Index 4215/p.79.

1683: 27 August (Acting)
As on 7 August 1682, except: E. of Sunderland; E. of Conway; Ed. Vaughan
of Trimsaran; J. Williams of Talley; H. Owen of Glasallt; Arthur Gwynn;
W. Jones, *added*. Prince Rupert; E. of Nottingham; E. of Anglesey; D. of
Lauderdale; Walter Vaughan (Sheriff, 1682–3); Jas. Jones; J. Lloyd of
Llanllawddog, *omitted*: Wales 4/724/5. (68)

1684: 28 April (Acting)
As on 27 August 1683, except: Ed. Vaughan of Trimsaran; Th. Lloyd of
Alltycadno (Sheriff, 1683–4), *omitted*: Wales 4/724/6. (66)

1685: 3 March
Commission renewed to reappoint E. of Carbery as *custos rotulorum*: Index
4215/p.121. (Anth. Farrington who was appointed Justice of Great Sessions
in place of Francis Manley on 13 February 1685 (Index 4215/p.117), was
probably also added on this date).

1685: 23 March (Acting)

*Canterbury; *Lord Guilford, Keeper of Great Seal; *E. of Radnor, President of Council; *Marquess of Halifax, Keeper of Privy Seal; *E. of Clarendon; Dukes of *Albemarle, *Newcastle, *Ormond; *D. of Beaufort, President of Council in the Marches of Wales; *Marquess of Winchester; Earls of *Lindsey, *Arlington, *Bridgewater, *Sunderland, *Bath, *Conway, *Nottingham, *Rochester, *p Carbery; *Chas., Lord Herbert; *Viscount Fauconberg; Bishops of *London, *St. Davids; *J., Lord Vaughan; *H. Coventry; *J. Ernley, kt., Chancellor of Exchequer; *Th. Chichley, kt., Chancellor of Duchy of Lancaster; *Ed. Seymour; *Leoline Jenkins, kt.; *Sidney Godolphin; *Geo. Jeffreys, kt. & Bt., Justice of Chester; *W. Buckby & *Anth. Farrington, Justices of Great Sessions; *Sackville Crowe, Bt.; *Ed. Mansel, Bt.; *W. Russell, Bt.; *Rice Williams, kt.; *Lewis Meyrick, Attorney-General for Wales; *J. Vaughan of Plasgwyn; *Rich. Vaughan of Torycoed; *Owen Brigstock; *J. Powell; *Lewis Morgan; *Th. Lloyd of Berllandywyll; *Rawleigh Mansel; *J. Williams of Abercothi; *Rich. Gwynn; *Rich. Brett; *Chris. Middleton; *Rich. Vaughan of Cwrt Derllys; *Rowland Gwynn; *Th. Lloyd of Alltycadno; *Th. Gwynn; *Roger Mainwaring; *W. Brigstock of Llechdwnny; *Walter Middleton; *J. Williams of Talley; *H. Owen of Glasallt; *Arthur Gwynn; *J. Philipps of Dolhaidd; *Daniel Lloyd of Llangennech; *Rich. Jones of Tregib; *Griffith Lloyd; W. Bevan: Wales 4/725/1. (Details of the quorum are based on the list of post 28 September 1685 contained in C.193/12/5/f.164v). (64)

1685: post 28 September

As on 23 March 1685, except: *Marquess of Worcester; *E. of Ailesbury; *J. Vaughan of Cwrt Derllys; *Walter Vaughan of Llanelly; *Jas. Protheroe; *J. Morgan; *Jas. Jones; *Ed. Vaughan of Trimsaran; *Ed. Vaughan of Penybanc; W. Jones, *added*. Lord Guilford; E. of Radnor, E. of Arlington; E. of Conway; Chas., Lord Herbert; Th. Chichley; Leoline Jenkins, *omitted*: C.193/12/5/f.164v. (Geo. Jeffreys, Justice of Chester, was appointed as Chancellor on 28 September 1685. The names of all those apparently added in this list, with the exception of the E. of Ailesbury, had appeared in earlier lists and may have been wrongly omitted from the Gaol File list of 23 March 1685). (67)

1686: 22 March (Acting)

As at the end of 1685, except: Th. Chichley, kt., Chancellor of Duchy of Lancaster, *added*. (He was probably left out in error in 1685) E. of Ailesbury; B. of St. Davids; W. Buckby; J. Vaughan of Llasgwyn; J. Vaughan of Cwrt Derllys; Walter Vaughan of Llanelly; Jas. Protheroe; J. Morgan; Jas. Jones; Ed. Vaughan of Trimsaran, *omitted*: Wales 4/725/2. (This list omits practically all the men who were added in the C.193 list of late 1685 and is so much at variance with the details given there that it is probably based on an outdated commission, possibly that of 3 March 1685. It may therefore be wise to assume that the justices apparently omitted on 22 March 1686 were serving justices of the peace after all, the nature of the records making it very hard to identify the exact period of their service). (58)

1686: 23 June
Commission renewed to appoint J., E. of Carbery (J., Lord Vaughan), as *custos rotulorum* in place of Rich., E. of Carbery: Index 4215/p.156. (J. Mathews, who was appointed as Justice of Great Sessions in place of W. Buckby on 15 June 1686 (Index 4215/p.155), was probably also added on this date).

1686: 23 August (Acting)
As on 22 March 1686, except: E. of Mulgrave; E. of Middleton; B. of St. Davids; Ed. Herbert, kt., Chief Justice of the Bench; J. Matthews, Justice of Great Sessions, *added*. Marquess of Halifax; Rich., E. of Carbery; Daniel Lloyd of Llangennech; W. Jones, *omitted*: Wales 4/725/3. (J., Lord Vaughan now appears as E. of Carbery). (59)

1686: 17 December
Order by the Privy Council to *add* Rob. Price to the Carmarthen commission and to *omit* W. Russell, Bt.: P.C.2/71/p.377.

1687: 7 March (Acting)
Canterbury; Lord Jeffreys, Chancellor; E. of Rochester, Treasurer; E. of Sunderland, President of the Council; Clarendon; Dukes of Albemarle, Newcastle, Ormond; D. of Beaufort, President of Council in the Marches of Wales; Marquesses of Winchester, Worcester; Lindsey; E. of Mulgrave, Household Chamberlain; Earls of Bridgewater, Bath, Nottingham, Middleton, Carbery; Viscount Fauconberg; Bishops of London, St. Davids; Sidney, Lord Godolphin; H. Coventry; J. Ernley, kt., Chancellor of Exchequer; Th. Chichley, kt., Chancellor of Duchy of Lancaster; Ed. Herbert, kt., Chief Justice of the Bench; Ed. Seymour; Anth. Farrington & J. Matthews, Justices of Great Sessions; Sackville Crowe, Bt.; Ed. Mansel, Bt.; W. Russell, Bt.; Rice Williams, kt.; Lewis Meyrick, Attorney-General for Wales; Rich, Vaughan of Torycoed; Owen Brigstock; J. Powell, kt.; Lewis Morgan; Th. Lloyd of Berllandywyll; Rawleigh Mansel; J. Williams of Abercothi; Rich. Gwynn; Rich. Brett; Chris. Middleton; Rich. Vaughan; Rowland Gwynn; Th. Gwynn; Roger Mainwaring; W. Brigstock; Walter Middleton; Th. Lloyd of Alltycadno; Ed. Vaughan of Penybanc; J. Williams of Talley; H. Owen of Glasallt; Arthur Gwynn; Rich. Jones of Tregib; Griffith Lloyd; W. Bevan: Wales 4/725/4. (The Privy Council's orders of 17 December 1686 are not reflected in this list of serving justices). (58)

1687: 29 August
General renewal of Welsh commissions to add the clause of dispensation: Index 4215/p.179. (Edwin Wyatt, deputy Justice of Great Sessions, who was appointed on 16 June 1687 (Index 4215/p.173), was probably added to the commission on this date).

1688: 14 April
Commission renewed (no details): Index 4215/p.191. (J. Tate, kt., who was appointed as Justice of Great Sessions on 25 February. (Index 4215/p.188), was probably added on this date).

1688: 30 August (Acting)

Canterbury; Jeffreys; Sunderland; Lord Arundell of Wardour, Keeper of Privy Seal; Dukes of Albemarle, Newcastle, Ormond; D. of Beaufort, President of Council in the Marches of Wales; Marquesses of Winchester, Powys, Worcester; Earls of Lindsey, Mulgrave, Bath, Nottingham, Middleton, Carbery, Castlemaine; Viscounts Montgomery, Fauconberg, Preston; B. of Durham; B. of St. Davids; Lords Belasyse, Dartmouth, Godolphin, Dover; J. Ernley, kt., Chancellor of Exchequer; Ed. Herbert, kt., Chief Justice of the Bench; Edwin Wyatt, serjeant at law, Justice of Great Sessions; Rice Williams, kt. & Bt.; Th. Owen; Walter Middleton; J. Evans; J. Philipps; Ed. Jones; Chas. Powell; Daniel Lloyd; Th. Lloyd of Llanstephan; Jas. Williams of Dolgwm; Rich. Lloyd: Wales 4/725/5.   (41)

1688: 18 September (Acting)

As on 30 August 1688: Wales 4/725/6.   (41)

1688: 6 October

General renewal of Welsh commissions: Index 4215/p.200.

1688: 27 November

Commission renewed to *add* Rob. Owen, Bt. & others (no details): Index 4215/p.204.

1689: 19 June

Commission renewed to reappoint E. of Carbery as *custos rotulorum*: Index 4215/p.229.

1690: 23 March (Acting)

Archbishop of Canterbury; J. Maynard, Anth. Keck & W. Rawlinson, kts., Commissioners of Great Seal; Marquess of Carmarthen, President of Council; Marquess of Halifax, Keeper of Privy Seal; D. of Norfolk; Earls of Lindsey, Devonshire, Dorset, Bedford, Nottingham, Bath; E. of Macclesfield, President of Council in the Marches of Wales; E. of Carbery, *custos rotulorum*; J. Trenchard, kt., Justice of Chester; W. Wogan, kt. & Marmaduke Gibbs, Justices of Great Sessions; Sackville Crowe, Bt.; Rice Rudd, Bt.; W. Russell, Bt.; Rice Williams, kt.; J. Powell, kt.; Rich. Vaughan; Griffith Rice; Th. Cornwallis; Arthur Shaen; Rowland Gwynn; Chris. Middleton; Th. Lloyd of Berllandywyll; Rich. Gwynn; Griffith Lloyd; Roger Mainwaring; H. Owen; Ed. Vaughan; W. Brigstock; Rawleigh Mansel; Arthur Gwynn; Th. Lloyd of Alltycadno; Rich. Vaughan of Derllys; J. Evans; J. Williams of Abercothi; J. Williams of Talley; Th. Gwynn; H. Lloyd; W. Bevan; Th. Lloyd of Danyrallt: Wales 4/726/3.   (47)

Borough of Carmarthen

1627: 23 July (Acting)
Th. Coventry, kt., Keeper of Great Seal; E. of Marlborough, Treasurer; E. of Manchester, President of Council; E. of Worcester, Keeper of Privy Seal; E. of Northampton, President of Council in the Marches of Wales; B. of St. Davids; J., Lord Vaughan of Golden Grove; J. Bridgeman, kt., Justice of Chester; Nich. Overbury, kt. & J. Hoskins, Justices of Great Sessions; Anthony Johns, Mayor of Carmarthen; Marmaduke Lloyd, kt., Recorder of Carmarthen; Griffith Beynon: Wales 4/717/3. (Unlike the county and borough of Haverfordwest, there is no evidence that a commission of the peace was ever specially issued for the borough of Carmarthen).

1653: 20 August (Acting)
Rich. Thomas, Mayor of Carmarthen; E. of Carbery; Rowland Dawkins; David Edwards; Lodowick Lewis: Wales 4/718/1.

1654: 14 August (Acting)
Ed. Johns, Mayor; Lodowick Lewis, Recorder; E. of Carbery; Rich. Thomas: Wales 4/718/2.

1657: 14 March (Acting)
W. Gower, Mayor; Lodowick Lewis, Recorder; E. of Carbery; Rob. Burtt: Wales 4/719/3.

1658: 30 August (Acting)
Griffith Beynon, Mayor; Edm. Jones, Recorder; E. of Carbery; W. Gower: Wales 4/719/4.

1662: 8 August (Acting)
Geo. Lewis, Mayor; E. of Carbery, President of Council in the Marches of Wales; W. Morton, kt. & Simon Degg. Justices of Great Sessions; Edm. Jones, Recorder; Anth. Jones: Wales 4/720/2.

1663: 20 March (Acting)
Carbery; Morton & Degg; J. Oakley, Mayor; Edm. Jones, Recorder; Geo. Lewis: Wales 4/720/3.

1664: 3 October (Acting)
Carbery; Morton & Degg; Th. Beynon, Mayor; Edm. Jones, Recorder; Rob. Lewis: Wales 4/720/4.

1665: 5 September (Acting)
As on 3 October 1664: Wales 4/720/5.

1666: 27 August (Acting)
Carbery; Fred. Hyde, kt. & Simon Degg, Justices of Great Sessions; J. Scurlock, Mayor; Edm. Jones, Recorder; Th. Beynon: Wales 4/720/6.

1667: 13 June (Acting)
Carbery; Hyde & Degg; Rich. Leigh, Mayor; Edm. Jones, Recorder; J. Scurlock: Wales 4/721/1.

1668: 13 August (Acting)
Carbery; Hyde & Degg; J. Muggull, Mayor; Edm. Jones, Recorder; Rich. Leigh: Wales 4/721/3.

1669: 5 April (Acting)
Carbery; Hyde & Degg; J. Vaughan, Mayor; Edm. Jones, Recorder; J. Muggull: Wales 4/721/5.

1669: 23 August (Acting)
As on 5 April 1669: Wales 4/721/6.

1670: 25 July (Acting)
Carbery; Hyde & Degg; W. Brigstock, Mayor; Edm. Jones, Recorder; J. Scurlock: Wales 4/722/1.

1671: 10 April (Acting)
Carbery; Hyde & Degg; H. Vaughan, Mayor; Edm. Jones, Recorder; W. Brigstock: Wales 4/722/2.

1672: 25 March (Acting)
Carbery; Hyde & Degg; Rob. Lewis, Mayor; Edm. Jones, Recorder; Th. Beynon: Wales 4/722/3.

1673: 7 July (Acting)
Marquess of Worcester, President of Council in the Marches of Wales; E. of Carbery; Hyde & Degg; Altham Vaughan, Mayor; Edm. Jones, Recorder; Rob. Lewis: Wales 4/722/4.

1673: 4 August (Acting)
Altham Vaughan, Mayor; Edm. Jones, Recorder; Rob. Lewis: Wales 4/722/5.

1674: 19 March (Acting)
J. Vaughan, Mayor; Altham Vaughan; Edm. Jones, Recorder: Wales 4/722/6.

1675: 2 August (Acting)
J. Williams, Mayor; E. of Carbery; J. Vaughan; Edm. Jones, Recorder: Wales 4/722/7.

1679: 14 April (Acting)
Th. Newsham, Mayor; Carbery; Edm. Jones, Recorder; J. Oakley: Wales 4/723/4.

1680: 12 April (Acting)
David Jones, Mayor; Carbery; Edm. Jones, Recorder; Th. Newsham: Wales 4/723/6.

1681: 11 April (Acting)
Ed. Gower, Mayor; Carbery; Edm. Jones, Recorder; David Jones: Wales
4/724/1.

1682: 10 April (Acting)
Ed. Jones, Mayor; Carbery; Edm. Jones, Recorder; Ed. Gower: Wales
4/724/2.

1683: 27 August (Acting)
Owen Brigstock, Mayor; Carbery; Rich. Vaughan, Recorder; Ed. Jones:
Wales 4/724/5.

1684: 28 April (Acting)
W. Jones, Mayor; Carbery; Rich. Vaughan, Recorder; Th. Beynon: Wales
4/724/6.

1685: 23 March (Acting)
J. Philipps, Mayor; Carbery; Rich. Vaughan, Recorder; W. Jones: Wales
4/725/1.

1686: 22 March (Acting)
Charles de Lanoy, Mayor; Carbery; Rich. Vaughan, Recorder; J. Philipps:
Wales 4/725/2.

1686: 23 August (Acting)
Charles de Lanoy, Mayor; D. of Beaufort, Recorder; E. of Carbery; Sackville Crowe, Bt., Alderman; Ed. Mansel, Bt., Alderman; Rice Williams,
kt., Alderman; Rich. Vaughan of Cwrt Derllys, Recorder; Edm. Meyrick,
clerk: Wales 4/725/3.

1687: 7 March (Acting)
Sackville Crowe, Bt., Mayor; D. of Beaufort & Rich. Vaughan, Recorders;
Ed. Mansel, Bt., Alderman; Rice Williams, kt., Alderman; Rowland Gwynn,
Alderman; Edm. Meyrick, clerk; Charles de Lanoy: Wales 4/725/4.

1688: 30 August (Acting)
Rowland Gwynn, Mayor; D. of Beaufort & Rich. Vaughan, Recorders;
Sackville Crowe, Bt., Alderman; Ed. Mansel, Bt., Alderman; Rice Williams,
kt., Alderman; Edm. Meyrick, clerk: Wales 4/725/5.

1688: 18 September (Acting)
As on 30 August 1688: Wales 4/725/6.

1690: 31 March (Acting)
J. Ryder, Mayor; E. of Carbery; Rich. Vaughan, Recorder; Martin Beynon:
Wales 4/726/2.

Cardigan

1542: 18 September (Acting)
Th. Audley, kt., Chancellor; D. of Norfolk, Treasurer; D. of Suffolk, President of Council; E. of Southampton, Keeper of Privy Seal; B. of Coventry & Lichfield, President of Council in the Marches of Wales; B. of St. Davids; Walter, Lord Ferrers; Nich. Hare, Ed. Croft, Rice Mansel, J. Vernon, Th. Jones, kts.; J. Pakington; Th. Holte; David Brooke; J. ap Rice; Rich. Hassall; Rich. Devereux; Rich. Herbert; Roland Meyrick, clerk; David Lloyd ap Griffith ap Rice; Morgan ap Rice ap Philip; Philip Williams; Th. Bryne; Lewis David ap Meredith; Jenkin ap Evan Lewis; David ap Evan Lloyd; J. Phillip: Wales 4/883/1. (28)

1543: 12 March
*Th., Lord Audley of Walden, Chancellor; *Norfolk; *Suffolk; *J. Russell, kt., Keeper of Privy Seal; *B. of Coventry & Lichfield, President of Council in the Marches of Wales; Bishops of *St. Asaph, *St. Davids; *p Walter, Lord Ferrers; *Nich. Hare, Ed. Croft, Rice Mansel, *J. Vernon, *W. ap Thomas, kts.; *J. Pakington; *Th. Holte; *David Brooke; *J. ap Rice; *Rich. Hassall; *Rich. Devereux; *Th. Jones; J. Phillip; David ap Evan Lloyd; *Rich. Herbert; *Th. Bryne; *Roland Meyrick, clerk; David Lloyd ap Griffith ap Rice; *Morgan ap Rice ap Philip; Jenkin ap Evan Lewis; Lewis ap David ap Meredith; Philip Williams. *Later additions to list*: *Th. Bromley, serjeant at law; *Adam Mytton; Rich. ap Rice David Lloyd: C.193/12/1/f.43v. (30 names plus 3 corrections).

1547: 19 September (Acting)
D. of Somerset, Protector; W. Paulet, kt., Lord St. John, President of Council; Russell; E. of Worcester; B. of Coventry & Lichfield, President of Council in the Marches of Wales; Bishops of St. Asaph, St. Davids; Walter, Lord Ferrers; Ed., Lord Powys; Rob. Townshend, Th. Bromley, Ed. Willoughby, Ed. Carne, Rice Mansel, Th. Jones, J. Vernon, J. Pakington, J. Price, Adam Mytton, kts.; David Brooke, serjeant at law; Hugh ?, clerk; Rich. Hassall; Geo. Willoughby; Rich. Germyn; Roland Meyrick, clerk; Th. Bryne; David Lloyd ap Griffith ap Rice; David ap Evan Lloyd; Hugh Williams; Lewis ap David ap Meredith; Rees Vaughan ap Rhydderch: Wales 4/883/2. (31)

1555: (Acting)
J. Wogan, kt.; Jas. Williams, kt.; Rich. Herbert; Th. Bryne; J. Powell; J. Price; David ap Evan Lloyd Vaughan; David Lloyd ap Robert; Jas. Morris: S.P.11/5/f.59. (9)

1556: 6 July (Acting)
Archbishop of York, Chancellor; Marquess of Winchester, Treasurer; E. of Arundel, President of Council & Steward; W., Lord Paget, Keeper of Privy Seal; E. of Pembroke, President of Council in the Marches of Wales; E. of Worcester; Viscount Hereford; Bishops of Worcester, St. Davids, St. Asaph, Bangor; J., Lord Chandos; Cuthbert Scott, D.D.; David Brooke, kt.; J. Pollard of Newnham Courtney, kt.; Robert Townshend, Geo. Herbert, Rice Mansel, Ed. Carne, Th. Jones, J. Vaughan, Adam Mytton,

Jas. Williams, kts.; J. Scudamore; Geoff. Clyve, Ll.D.; David Lewis, Ll.D.;
W. Sheldon; W. Symonds; Gilbert Gerard; Reg. Corbet; Geo. Wood;
Edm. Plowden; W. Gerard; Rich. Seaborne; Rich. Herbert; Th. Bryne;
J. Powell; J. Price; Ed. Powell; David ap Evan Lloyd Vaughan; David
Lloyd ap Robert: Wales 4/883/4. (Note that this list gives details of the full
commission, unlike that for 1555 in which only the names of the justices
resident and active in Cardigan are included). (41)

1558–9: (Acting)
*Nich. Bacon, kt., Keeper of Great Seal; *Winchester; *Arundel; Bishops
of *Bath & Wells, *St. Davids, *Chester; *J. Throckmorton, Justice of
Chester; *Th. Jones, *J. Vaughan, *Adam Mytton, *J. Perrot, *Jas.
Williams, kts.; *J. Scudamore of Holm; Chas. Fox; *J. Welsh; *Reg.
Corbet; *W. Symonds; *W. Gerard; *Rich. Seaborne; *Rich. Herbert;
*p J. Price; Lewis David Meredith; Th. Bryne; David ap Llewelyn Lloyd;
*J. Powell; Hugh ap Llewelyn Lloyd; *Ed. Powell; Th. Phayer: B.M.,
Lansdowne Ms. 1218/f.38. (Except for the omission of the *ex officio* members
of the commission, the same list also appears in S.P.12/2/17/f.38). (28)

1561: (Acting)
*Bacon; *Winchester; *Arundel; *H. Sidney, kt., President of Council in
the Marches of Wales; *B. of St. Davids; *Rich. Wye; *J. Vaughan, *H.
Jones, *Jas. Williams, kts.; Rich. Herbert; *J. Powell; *p J. Price; Lewis ap
Meredith; David ap Evan Lloyd; Hugh ap Llewelyn Lloyd: B.M.,
Lansdowne Ms. 1218/f.86. (15)

1562: 13 June
As in 1561, except: Jas. Williams, kt., *omitted*: C.66/985/m.41d. (14)

1564: (Acting)
*Bacon; *Winchester; *Arundel; *Viscount Hereford; *Sidney, President
of Council in the Marches of Wales; Bishops of *Bangor, *St. Davids;
*Rich. Wye; *Reg. Corbet; *Throckmorton, Justice of Chester; *J.
Vaughan, kt.; *W. Gerard; *Chas. Fox; *Rich. Seaborne; *Rich. Pates;
*p J. Price of Eglwysegl; *Rich. Smith; *J. Price; Lewis ap Meredith;
David ap Evan Lloyd; Hugh ap Llewelyn Lloyd; *J. Bradshaw; Hugh
Morgan, Ll.B.; David Lloyd ap Meredith; *Ed. Powell; Jas. Morris:
C.66/998/m.10d. (26)

1573–4: (Acting)
*Bacon; *W., Lord Burghley, Treasurer; *E. of Essex; *Sidney, President
of Council in the Marches of Wales; *B. of St. Davids; *Jas. Croft, House-
hold Controller; *Hugh Cholmondeley, kt.; *Throckmorton, Justice of
Chester; *H. Jones, kt.; *J. Rastell, Justice of Great Sessions; *W. Gerard;
*Chas. Fox; *Rich. Seaborne; *Rich. Pates; *Ed. Davies; *p J. Price;
Lewis Gwynn, Chancellor of St. Davids; *J. Powell; *David ap Evan Lloyd
Vaughan; *Hugh ap Llewelyn Lloyd; *J. Stedman; J. Lloyd of Cilgwyn;
Morgan Lloyd: S.P.12/93/part 2/f.34 & B.M., Egerton Ms. 2345/f.43v. (23)

1575: (Acting)
*Bacon; *Burghley; *Essex; *Sidney, President of Council in the Marches of Wales; *B. of St. Davids; *Croft; *Throckmorton, Justice of Chester; *J. Perrot, *H. Jones, kts.; *Geo. Fetiplace, Justice of Great Sessions; *W. Gerard; *Chas. Fox; *Rich. Seaborne; *Rich. Pates; *Ed. Davies; *p J. Price; *Lewis Gwynn, Chancellor of St. Davids; *J. Powell; *David ap Evan Lloyd Vaughan; *Hugh ap Llewelyn Lloyd; *J. Stedman; Jas. Lewis; J. Lloyd of Cilgwyn; Th. Gwynn ap Morgan Vaughan; *Rich. David Jenkins; Morgan Lloyd; Maurice ap Richard; *Rice Lloyd; *Th. Revell; Th. Griffith: S.P.12/106/part 2/f.6v. (30)

1577: (Acting)
As in 1575, except: E. of Essex; H. Jones; Ed. Davies; Lewis Gwynn; J. Lloyd of Cilgwyn; Th. Gwynn ap Morgan Vaughan; Maurice ap Richard; Rice Lloyd; Th. Revell, *omitted*: S.P.12/121/f.38v. (21)

1578: (Acting)
*Bacon; *Burghley; *Sidney, President of Council in the Marches of Wales; *B. of Worcester; Earls of *Worcester, *Pembroke; Bishops of *Hereford, *Bangor, *St. Davids, *St. Asaph; *Croft; *Throckmorton, Justice of Chester; *Andrew Corbet, *J. Perrot, *Nich. Arnold, *Hugh Cholmondeley, *J. Littleton, *J. Huband, kts.; *J. Puckering, Justice of Great Sessions; *David Lewis, Ll.D.; *Geo. Bromley; *W. Gerard; *W. Aubrey; *Chas. Fox; *W. Glaseor; *Ellis Price, Ll.D.; *Ed. Leighton; *Rich. Pates; *Ralph Barton; *Jerome Corbet; *Fabian Phillips; *H. Townshend; *W. Leighton; *p J. Price of Gogerddan; *David ap Evan Lloyd Vaughan; *Hugh ap Llewelyn Lloyd; *J. Stedman; *Jas. Lewis; Rich. David Jenkins; Morgan Lloyd; J. Powell; Th. Griffith. *Later additions to list*: *Th. Bromley, kt., Chancellor; Th. Gwynn: Hatfield House Ms. 223.7. (42 names plus 2 corrections).

1579: (Acting)
As in 1578, except: *Th. Gwynn, *added*. Hugh ap Llewelyn Lloyd, *omitted*: S.P.12/145/f.52v. (42)

1580: 25 July (Acting)
As in 1579, except: Th. Bromley, kt., Chancellor; Rich. Atkins, Justice of Great Sessions (there are now two such justices); Jenkin Lloyd; Th. Revell, *added*. Nich. Bacon; J. Throckmorton; Andrew Corbet; Nich. Arnold; Th. Gwynn, *omitted*: Wales 4/883/8. (Throckmorton's place as Justice of Chester was taken by Geo. Bromley who had already been a member of the commission before his promotion). (41)

1581: 20 November (Acting)
J. Price; Rich. David Jenkins; Jenkin Lloyd; Th. Griffith; Morgan Lloyd; J. Stedman; Jas. Lewis; J. Powell; Th. Revell: Bodleian, Bodley Ms. 904/f.206v. (This list of justices active in Cardigan on 20 November 1581 excludes all the *ex officio* members listed in earlier commissions). (9)

1582: (Acting)
J. Perrot, kt.; J. Stedman; Jas. Lewis; Jenkin Lloyd; Rich. David Jenkins;
Morgan Lloyd; Th. Revell; J. Powell; Th. Griffith: B.M., Lansdowne Ms.
35/f.139. (9)

1584: (Acting)
*Th. Bromley, kt., Chancellor; *Burghley; *Sidney, President of Council
in the Marches of Wales; Earls of *Worcester, *Pembroke; Bishops of
*Hereford, *Bangor, *St. Davids, *St. Asaph; *Croft; *Geo. Bromley, kt.,
Justice of Chester; *J. Puckering & *Rich. Atkins, Justices of Great
Sessions; *J. Perrot, *Hugh Cholmondeley, *J. Littleton, kts.; *W. Aubrey;
*Chas. Fox; *Ellis Price, Ll.D.; *Ed. Leighton; *W. Leighton; *H.
Townshend; *Rich. Pates; *Ralph Barton; *Jerome Corbet; *Fabian
Phillips; *W. Glaseor; *J. Morgan; *J. Powell; *J. Stedman; *Jas. Lewis;
*Jenkin Lloyd; *Rich. David Jenkins; *Morgan Lloyd; Th. Revell; Th.
Griffith. *Later additions to list*: *Christopher Hatton, Chancellor (1587);
*p Geo. Devereux; *Th. Jones, kt.; *Rich. Price; Jas. Jones; Eynon
Phillips: E.163/14/8/f.51. (36 names plus 6 corrections).

1590–91: (Acting)
*Christopher Hatton, kt., Chancellor; *Burghley; *E. of Pembroke,
President of Council in the Marches of Wales; Bishops of *St. Davids,
*St. Asaph; *J. Perrot, kt.; *Rich. Shuttleworth, kt., Justice of Chester;
*Puckering & *Atkins, Justices of Great Sessions; Geo. Devereux; *Hugh
Cholmondeley, *Th. Jones, kts.; *W. Aubrey; *Ellis Price, Ll.D.; *Ed.
Leighton; *W. Leighton; *H. Townshend; *Jerome Corbet; *Fabian
Phillips; *p Rich. Price; J. Morgan; *J. Powell; *J. Stedman; *Morgan
Lloyd; *Jas. Lewis; *Rich. David Jenkins; *Jenkin Lloyd; *Th. Revell;
Th. Griffith; Th. Parry; Morgan David Lloyd; David Lloyd of Abermad:
Hatfield House Ms. 278/f.57. (32)

1592–3: (Acting)
As in 1590–91, except: *E. of Essex; *W. Oldisworth, Justice of Great
Sessions; *J. Stedman junior; *Maurice Vaughan; Lewis David Gwynn,
added. Hatton; J. Perrot; Th. Jones; Rich. Price; J. Morgan; J. Powell;
Rich. David Jenkins; Morgan David Lloyd, *omitted*: Kent Record Office
U.350.03. (J. Puckering, the former Justice of Great Sessions, is now
Keeper of the Great Seal. Rich. Price's place as *custos rotulorum* is taken by
Fabian Phillips). (29)

1594: 2 August
*J. Puckering, kt., Keeper of Great Seal; *Burghley; *Pembroke, President
of Council in the Marches of Wales; *E. of Essex; *B. of St. Asaph;
*Shuttleworth, Justice of Chester; *Rich. Atkins & *W. Oldisworth,
Justices of Great Sessions; Geo. Devereux; *Hugh Cholmondeley, kt.;
*W. Aubrey; *Ellis Price, Ll.D.; *W. Leighton; *H. Townshend; *Jerome
Corbet; *Fabian Phillips; *p Rich. Price; *Th. Revell; *J. Stedman;
*Morgan Lloyd; *Jas. Lewis; Th. Griffith; *Th. Price; *Rich. Mortimer;
*David Lloyd of Abermad; *J. Stedman junior; Th. Parry; *Maurice
Vaughan; Watkin Thomas; Lewis David Gwynn; David Lloyd Gwynn:
C.66/1421/m.15d. (31)

1595: 15 August
As on 2 August 1594, except: Morgan David Lloyd, *added*. W. Aubrey; Ellis Price; Th. Griffith; Rich. Mortimer; Watkin Thomas; Lewis David Gwynn; David Lloyd Gwynn, *omitted*: C.66/1435/m.20d. General renewal of Welsh commissions on 15 August: Index 4208/f.4v. (This commission is also contained in Bodleian, Bodley Ms. 904/f.214, but with the omission of J. Stedman junior, who was sheriff in 1594-5).   (25)

1596: 21 February
Commission renewed to *restore* J. Stedman junior, late Sheriff: Index 4208/f.12.

1596: 29 June
As on 15 August 1595, except: *Th. Egerton, kt., Keeper of Great Seal; *Rich. Mortimer, *added*. J. Puckering; Th. Revell, *omitted*: C.66/1468/m.16d & S.P.13/Case F, no. 11/f.39v. Commission renewed to *add* Rich. Mortimer: Index 4208/f.17. (Th. Egerton, who was appointed as Lord Keeper on 6 May 1596, was probably also added on this date).   (25)

1597: 16 February
*Th. Egerton, kt., Keeper of Great Seal; *Burghley; *Pembroke, President of Council in the Marches of Wales; *Essex; *B. of St. Asaph; *Shuttleworth, Justice of Chester; *Atkins & *Oldisworth, Justices of Great Sessions; Geo. Devereux, kt.; *W. Leighton; *H. Townshend; *Jerome Corbet; *p Rich. Price; *J. Stedman; *Morgan Lloyd; *Jas. Lewis; *Th. Price; *Rich. Mortimer; Morgan David Lloyd; J. Lloyd; David Lloyd of Abermad; *J. Stedman junior; Th. Parry; Maurice Vaughan: C.66/1468/m.30d. Commission renewed to *add* J. Lloyd: Index 4208/f.27v.   (24)

1598: (Acting)
As on 16 February 1597, except: Lord Burghley, *omitted*: C.66/1482/m.17d. (23)

1599: 28 March
Commission renewed to *add* J. Lewis: Index 4208/f.67.

1599: 28 November
Commission renewed to *add* Geo. Phillips; J. Byrt; David Lloyd ap Hugh, and to *omit* J. Lewis: Index 4208/f.79.

1601: 2 April
Commission renewed to *add* Th. Johnes, kt., and to *omit* Geo. Devereux, kt.: Index 4208/f.107v.

1601: 15 July
*Egerton; *Th., Lord Buckhurst, Treasurer; *Rich. Lewkenor, kt., Justice of Chester; *Atkins & *Oldisworth, Justices of Great Sessions; *Th. Johnes, kt.; *W. Leighton; *H. Townshend; *p Rich. Price; *J. Stedman; *Morgan Lloyd; *Th. Price; J. Lewis of Abernant Bychan; *Rich. Mortimer; J. Lloyd; David Lloyd of Abermad; *J. Stedman junior; Maurice Vaughan; Geo. Phillips; J. Byrt; David Lloyd ap Hugh: C.66/1549/m.31d. Commission renewed to *add* J. Lewis of Abernant Bychan: Index 4208/f.116v.   (21)

1602: 14 January
Commission renewed to *add* J. Lewis senior of Llangrannog: Index 4208
f.127.

1602: 19 February
Commission renewed to *add* David Thomas Parry: Index 4208/f.129v.

1602: 25 July
As on 15 July 1601, except: *Ed., Lord Zouch, President of Council in the
Marches of Wales; David Thomas Parry; J. Lewis senior of Llangrannog,
added: C.66/1594/m.34d. General renewal of Welsh commissions to *add*
Ed., Lord Zouch: Index 4208/f.141.   (24)

1603: post 8 June
As on 25 July 1602, except: *Jas. Ley, Justice of Great Sessions, *added*.
(Ley was appointed on 8 June 1603). W. Oldisworth; H. Townshend,
omitted: C.66/1620/m.14d.   (23)

1604: (Acting)
*Th. Egerton, Lord Ellesmere, Chancellor; *E. of Dorset (Lord Buck-
hurst), Treasurer; *Ed., Lord Zouch, President of Council in the Marches
of Wales; *Lewkenor, Justice of Chester; *Rich. Atkins & *Rich. Daston,
Justices of Great Sessions; *p Rich. Price, *J. Lewis, kts.; *H. Townshend;
*W. Leighton; *J. Stedman; *Th. Price; *Rich. Mortimer; J. Lloyd; David
Lloyd of Abermad; *J. Stedman junior; *Geo. Phillips; David Thomas
Parry; *J. Lewis senior of Llangrannog; *Th. Lloyd; J. Byrt; David
Lloyd ap Hugh; David Gwynn; Ed. Vaughan: C.66/1662/m.21d.   (24)

1605: (Acting)
As in 1604, except: Maurice Vaughan; Evan Gwynn Jenkin, *added*. Ed.,
Lord Zouch; J. Lloyd; David Gwynn, *omitted*: C.66/1682/m.4d.   (23)

1606: (Acting)
As in 1605: C.66/1698/m.28d.   (23)

1607: post 12 September
*Ellesmere; *Dorset; *Ralph, Lord Eure, President of Council in the
Marches of Wales (appointed on 12 September 1607); *Lewkenor, Justice
of Chester; *Atkins & *Daston, Justices of Great Sessions; *p Rich. Price,
*J. Lewis, *H. Townshend, kts.; *J. Stedman; *Th. Price; *Rich. Mortimer;
*David Lloyd of Abermad; *J. Stedman junior; Maurice Vaughan; *Geo.
Phillips; David Thomas Parry; *J. Lewis senior of Llangrannog; *Th.
Lloyd; J. Byrt; David Lloyd ap Hugh; Evan Gwynn Jenkin; Ed. Vaughan:
C.66/1748/m.29d.   (23)

1608–9: (Acting)
As in 1607, except: *E. of Salisbury, Treasurer; *E. of Northampton,
Keeper of Privy Seal; Jas. Price; Geo. Lloyd, *added*. E. of Dorset; J.
Stedman; Th. Price, *omitted*: C.66/1786/m.29d.   (24)

1610–11: (Acting)
As in 1608–9, except: *Nich. Overbury, Justice of Great Sessions; *Th.
Price; Morgan Gwynn, *added*. Rich. Atkins; Rich. Mortimer, *omitted*:
C.66/1822/m.25d.   (25)

1612–13: (Acting)
*Ellesmere; *E. of Salisbury, Treasurer; *E. of Northampton, Keeper of
Privy Seal; *Eure, President of Council in the Marches of Wales; *Lewkenor,
Justice of Chester; *Nich. Overbury & *Rich. Daston, Justices of Great
Sessions; *p Rich. Price, *J. Lewis, *H. Townshend, kts.; *Th. Price;
*David Lloyd of Abermad; *J. Stedman; *Th. Lloyd; Maurice Vaughan;
*Geo. Phillips; David Thomas Parry; Jas. Lewis; *Jas. Price; J. Byrt;
Evan Gwynn Jenkin; *Ed. Vaughan; Geo. Lloyd; Morgan Gwynn:
C.66/1898/m.25d.   (24)

1614: post 11 July
As in 1612–13, except: *E. of Suffolk, Treasurer (appointed on 11 July);
Marmaduke Lloyd, *added*. E. of Salisbury; E. of Northampton; Th. Lloyd;
Morgan Gwynn (Sheriff, 1613–14), *omitted*: C.66/1988/m.26d.   (22)

1615: 12 July
Commission renewed to *add* Th. Jones: Index 4211/f.7v.

1615: 18 September (Acting)
Ellesmere; E. of Suffolk, Treasurer; Eure, President of Council in the
Marches of Wales; Lewkenor, Justice of Chester; Overbury & Daston,
Justices of Great Sessions; Rich. Price, J. Lewis, H. Townshend, kts.; Th.
Price; David Lloyd of Abermad; Jas. Stedman; Maurice Vaughan; Geo.
Phillips; David Thomas Parry; Jas. Lewis; Jas. Price; J. Byrt; Evan Gwynn
Jenkin; Ed. Vaughan; Geo. Lloyd; Morgan Gwynn; Marmaduke Lloyd;
Th. Jones: Wales 4/884/1.   (24)

1616: post 2 January
As on 18 September 1615, except: *E. of Worcester, Keeper of Privy Seal,
added. (Worcester was appointed on 2 January 1616). J. Lewis, kt.; Th.
Price; Maurice Vaughan; Jas. Lewis; Geo. Lloyd, *omitted*: C.66/2076/m.23d.
(20)

1616: 3 July
Commission renewed to *add* J. Lewis, kt.; Th. Price; Maurice Vaughan;
Jas. Lewis: Index 4211/f.24.

1617: 19 March
General renewal of Welsh commissions to *add* Francis Bacon, kt., Keeper
of Great Seal; Th., Lord Gerard, President of Council in the Marches of
Wales: Index 4211/f.38.

1617: post 24 November
As in 1616, except: *Francis Bacon, kt., Keeper of Great Seal; *D. of
Lennox, Steward; *W., Lord Compton, President of Council in the Marches

of Wales; *Th. Chamberlain, kt., Justice of Chester; *J. Lewis, kt.; *Th. Price; Maurice Vaughan; *Jas. Lewis, *added*. Lord Ellesmere; Lord Eure; Rich. Lewkenor; H. Townshend; Jas. Stedman, *omitted*: C.66/2147/m.22d. (Lord Compton was appointed President of Council in the Marches of Wales on 24 November 1617 in place of Lord Gerard whose term of office was too short for him to appear on any of the commissions as finally enrolled on the patent rolls). (23)

1618: 18 February
Commission renewed to *add* J. Stedman: Index 4211/f.58.

1618: 21 November
*Francis Bacon, Lord Verulam, Chancellor; *E. of Worcester, Keeper of Privy Seal; *D. of Lennox, Steward; *E. of Northampton (Lord Compton), President of Council in the Marches of Wales; *Th. Chamberlain, kt., Justice of Chester; *Overbury & *Daston, Justices of Great Sessions; *p Rich. Price, *J. Lewis, *H. Townshend, kts.; *Th. Price; *David Lloyd of Abermad; *J. Price of Strata Florida; Maurice Vaughan; *Geo. Phillips; David Thomas Parry; *Jas. Lewis; *Jas. Price; J. Byrt; Evan Gwynn Jenkin; *Ed. Vaughan; Morgan Gwynn; *Marmaduke Lloyd; Th. Jones; *J. Stedman of Castle Howell: C.66/2174/m.18d. Commission renewed to *add* J. Price of Strata Florida: Index 4211/f.74v. (25)

1619: 10 June
Commission renewed to *add* W. Ryves, Justice of Great Sessions, in place of Rich. Daston: Index 4211/f.85.

1620: 17 February
Commission renewed to *add* Ed. Littleton, Justice of Great Sessions, in place of W. Ryves: Index 4211/f.99v.

1620: 21 July
Commission renewed to *add* Walter Lloyd: Index 4211/f.111.

1620: 4 November
General renewal of Welsh commissions to *add* Jas. Whitlock, kt., Justice of Chester: Index 4211/f.114.

1621: 26 February
*Francis Bacon, Viscount St. Alban, Chancellor; *H., Viscount Mandeville, Treasurer; *Worcester; *Lennox; *Northampton, President of Council in the Marches of Wales; *Jas. Whitlock, kt., serjeant at law, Justice of Chester; *Nich. Overbury & *Ed. Littleton, Justices of Great Sessions; *p Rich. Price, *J. Lewis, *H. Townshend, kts.; *Th. Price; *Walter Lloyd; *David Lloyd of Abermad; *J. Price of Strata Florida; *Geo. Phillips; David Thomas Parry; *Jas. Lewis; *Jas. Price; J. Byrt; *Ed. Vaughan; Morgan Gwynn; *Marmaduke Lloyd; Th. Jones; J. Stedman: C.66/2234/m.41d. General renewal of Welsh commissions to *add* Viscount Mandeville: Index 4211/f.120. (25)

1621: 3 July
Commission renewed to *add* J. Hoskins, Justice of Great Sessions, in place of Ed. Littleton: Index 4211/f.126.

1621: post 29 September
As on 26 February 1621, except: *B. of Lincoln, Keeper of Great Seal; *Lionel Cranfield, Treasurer (appointed on 29 September); *J. Hoskins, Justice of Great Sessions, *added*. Viscount St. Alban; Ed. Littleton; H. Townshend; Jas. Price, *omitted*: C.66/2259/m.24d. (24)

1622: 14 May
Commission renewed to *add* Marmaduke Lloyd, kt.: Index 4211/f.138v. (This is the same man who appears earlier as M. Lloyd, Esq.).

1623: 27 February
As at the end of 1621, except: Rich. Price, kt.; J. Byrt, *omitted*: C.66/2285/m.32d. Commission renewed to appoint J. Lewis, kt., as *custos rotulorum*: Index 4211/f.150. (22)

1623: 18 November
Commission renewed to *add* Th. Price: Index 4211/f.158v. (This is probably in fact a restoration of the Th. Price who appears on earlier lists as late as 27 February 1623. There is no apparent cause for his omission after that date).

1623: 2 December
As on 27 February 1623, except: Evan Gwynn, *added*. D. of Lennox, *omitted*: C.66/2310/m.29d. Commission renewed to *add* Evan Gwynn: Index 4211/f.159. (22)

1625: 1 April
*B. of Lincoln, Keeper of Great Seal; *Jas., Lord Ley, Treasurer; *Viscount Mandeville; *Worcester; *Northampton, President of Council in the Marches of Wales; *Th. Chamberlain, kt., Justice of Chester; *Nich. Overbury, kt. & *J. Hoskins, Justices of Great Sessions; *p J. Lewis, *Marmaduke Lloyd, kts.; *Sampson Eure; *Rob. Brooke; *Th. Price; *Walter Lloyd; *David Lloyd of Abermad; *J. Price of Strata Florida; *Geo. Phillips; David Thomas Parry; *Jas. Lewis; Morgan Gwynn; Th. Jones; *J. Stedman; Evan Gwynn: C.66/2367/m.26d. General renewal of Welsh commissions: Index 4211/f.180v. (23)

1625: 22 December
As on 1 April 1625, except: *Th. Coventry, kt., Keeper of Great Seal; *Ed. Vaughan, *added*. B. of Lincoln; Th. Chamberlain, *omitted*: B.M., Harleian Ms. 1622/f.89d. General renewal of Welsh commissions to *add* Th. Coventry: Index 4211/f.194v. (Note that Ed. Vaughan, who had been a regular member of the commission since 1604, was probably omitted in error from the enrolment of the commission of 1 April 1625). (23)

1626: 20 March
Commission renewed to *add* J. Bridgeman, kt., Justice of Chester, and to appoint E. of Northampton as *custos rotulorum* in place of J. Lewis, kt.: Index 4211/f.199.

1626: 26 June
As on 22 December 1625, except: *J. Bridgeman, kt., Justice of Chester; *Rich. Vaughan, kt., *added.* J. Lewis, kt.; J. Price of Strata Florida; J. Stedman, *omitted*: E.163/18/12/f.91 & C.193/12/2/f.66. Commission renewed to *add* Rich. Vaughan, kt.: Index 4211/f.204.   (22)

1627–8: (Acting)
As on 26 June 1626, except: *Timothy Turneur; *Jas. Lewis, *added.* (There are now two men named Jas. Lewis on the commission). E. of Worcester; Rob. Brooke; Evan Gwynn, *omitted*: C.66/2449/m.33d. (The omission of Evan Gwynn is probably an error since he reappears in later commissions). (21)

1628: 10 December
Commission renewed to *add* Roland Pugh: Index 4211/f.260.

1628: post 14 December
As in 1627–8, except: *Rich., Lord Weston, Treasurer; *Viscount Conway, President of Council; *E. of Pembroke; *Roland Pugh; Evan Gwynn, *added.* E. of Marlborough (Lord Ley); Geo. Phillips; Th. Jones, *omitted*: C.66/2495/m.26d. (Conway was appointed on 14 December 1628).   (23)

1629: (Acting)
As at the end of 1628: C.66/2527/m.27d.   (23)

1630: 8 January
Commission renewed to *add* Hector Phillips: Index 4212/p.21.

1630: 1 July
Commission renewed to appoint Rich., Lord Vaughan, as *custos rotulorum*: Index 4212/p.37.

1630: 13 December
*Th., Lord Coventry, Keeper of Great Seal; *Rich., Lord Weston, Treasurer; *E. of Manchester (Viscount Mandeville), Keeper of Privy Seal; *p Rich., Lord Vaughan; *J. Bridgeman, kt., Justice of Chester; *Overbury & *Hoskins, Justices of Great Sessions; *Marmaduke Lloyd, kt.; *Sampson Eure; *Timothy Turneur; *Jas. Lewis; *Th. Price; *Walter Lloyd; *David Lloyd of Abermad; *Hector Phillips; *Jas. Lewis of Cwmowen; *Ed. Vaughan; Morgan Gwynn; Evan Gwynn; Llewelyn Thomas Parry: C.66/2536/m.20d & C.66/2577/m.11d. Commission renewed to *add* Llewelyn Thomas Parry: Index 4212/p.44. (Note that Viscount Conway who died on 3 January 1631 was probably omitted from this commission when it was enrolled. This commission is also entered in S.P.16/212/f.70).   (20)

1633: 16 February
As on 13 December 1630, except: *Roland Pugh, *added*. David Lloyd of Abermad; Morgan Gwynn, *omitted*: C.66/2598/m.20d. Commission renewed to *restore* Roland Pugh: Index 4212/p.97.   (19)

1634: 25 June
*Coventry; *E. of Portland (Lord Weston), Treasurer; *Manchester; *E. of Bridgewater, President of Council in the Marches of Wales; *p Rich., Lord Vaughan; *Bridgeman, Justice of Chester; *Overbury & *Hoskins, Justices of Great Sessions; *Marmaduke Lloyd, kt.; *Sampson Eure; *Timothy Turneur; *Rich. Price; *Jas. Lewis; *Roland Pugh; *Walter Lloyd; *Th. Price; *Hector Phillips; *Jas. Lewis of Cwmowen; *Ed. Vaughan; *Evan Gwynn; Llewelyn Thomas Parry: C.193/13/2/f.76d. Commission renewed to *add* Rich. Price: Index 4212/p.140.   (21)

1634: 10 December
Commission renewed to *add* E. of Carbery (Rich., Lord Vaughan); J. Pugh: Index 4212/p.150.

1635: 20 August
Commission renewed to *add* David Parry; David Evans: Index 4212/p.179.

1636: 6 February
As on 25 June 1634, except: *David Parry; Morgan Herbert; J. Lloyd of Crynfryn; J. Pugh; David Evans, *added*. Ed. Vaughan; Llewelyn Thomas Parry, *omitted*: C.66/2654/m.22d. Commission renewed to *add* Morgan Herbert; J. Lloyd of Crynfryn: Index 4212/p.191.   (24)

1636: 18 March
As on 6 February 1636, except: *B. of London, Treasurer; H. Vaughan of Cilcenin, *added*. E. of Portland, *omitted*: S.P.16/405/f.74v. Commission renewed to *add* H. Vaughan of Cilcenin: Index 4212/p.198. (The B. of London who was appointed Treasurer on 6 March was presumably added on this date).   (25)

1637: 8 April
Commission renewed to *add* J. Lloyd: Index 4212/p.239.

1637: 12 July
Commission renewed to place J. Lloyd on the quorum: Index 4212/p.254.

1638: 6 March
Commission renewed to *add* Timothy Turneur, Justice of Great Sessions: Index 4212/p.284.

1638: 29 June
*Coventry; *B. of London, Treasurer; *Manchester; *Bridgewater, President of Council in the Marches of Wales; *p E. of Carbery; *Timothy Turneur & *J. Hoskins, Justices of Great Sessions; *Marmaduke Lloyd, kt.; *Sampson Eure; *Jas. Lewis; *Rich. Price; *Roland Pugh; *David

Parry; *Walter Lloyd; *Th. Price; *Hector Phillips; *J. Lloyd; *Jas. Lewis
of Cwmowen; *Evan Gwynn; H. Vaughan of Cilcenin; Morgan Herbert;
David Evans: C.66/2725/m.18d. Commission renewed to *add* Jas. Lewis of
Cwmowen: Index 4212/p.301. (22)

1638: 20 December
As on 29 June 1638, except: *Th. Milward, kt., Justice of Chester; J.
Stedman; J. Pugh, *added*. J. Hoskins; Hector Phillips, *omitted*: C.66/2761/
m.17d. Commission renewed to *add* J. Stedman: Index 4212/p.320. (J. Pugh
may have been omitted in error from the commission of 29 June 1638).   (23)

1639: 15 March
Commission renewed to *add* J. Platt, Justice of Great Sessions: Index
4212/p.330.

1639: 19 July
Commission renewed to *add* Francis Lloyd: Index 4212/p.350.

1640: post 17 January
*J. Finch, kt., Keeper of Great Seal (appointed on 17 January); *London;
*Manchester; *Bridgewater, President of Council in the Marches of Wales;
*p E. of Carbery; *Th. Milward, kt., Justice of Chester; *Timothy Turneur
& *J. Platt, Justices of Great Sessions; *Marmaduke Lloyd, kt.; *Sampson
Eure; *W. Morgan; *Francis Lloyd; *Jas. Lewis; *Rich. Price; *Roland
Pugh; *David Parry; *Walter Lloyd; *Jas. Lewis of Cwmowen; *J.
Stedman; *Th. Price; *J. Lloyd; *Evan Gwynn; *H. Vaughan of Cilcenin;
Morgan Herbert; J. Pugh; David Evans: C.66/2858/m.21d.   (26)

1642: 4 February
Commission renewed to *add* J. Pugh to the quorum: Index 4212/p.504.

1643: 10 February
Commission renewed to *add* Rob. Byrt: Index 4212/p.545 & Index 4210/p.3.

1643: 5 May
Commission renewed to *add* David Jenkins, Justice of Great Sessions:
Index 4210/p.20.

1647: 20 September
Commission renewed (no details): Index 4213/p.98.

1649: 6 March
*W. Lenthall, Speaker of House of Commons; *Lord Fairfax; *J. Bradshaw;
*Bulstrode Whitelock, *Rich. Keble, *J. Lisle, Commissioners of Great
Seal; *H. Rolle, Chief Justice of Upper Bench; *W. Powell & *J. Clark,
Justices of Great Sessions; *Jas. Lewis of Abernant Bychan; *Jas. Phillips
of Tregybi; *J. Lloyd of Faerdref; *Th. Lloyd of Llanbedr; J. Lewis of
Glascrug; J. Lloyd of Ynyshir(?); H. Vaughan of Cilcenin: C.193/13/3/
f.72d. Commission renewed on 6 March (no details): Index 4213/p.143.   (16)

1650: 11 March
Commission renewed to *add* Rich. Lloyd of Llangoedmor, and to *omit* Th.
Lloyd; Th. Vaughan: Index 4213/p.181.

1650: 25 July
Commission renewed to *add* Th. Harrison; H. Vaughan; Th. Parry;
Rawleigh Mansel, and to *omit* J. Lloyd of Ynyshir(?): Index 4213/p.198.

1650: 1 August
*Lenthall; *Oliver Cromwell, Lord General; *Bradshaw; *Whitelock,
*Keble & *Lisle; *Rolle; *W. Powell & *J. Clark, Justices of Great
Sessions; *Edm. Prideaux, Attorney-General; *Th. Harrison; *Ed. Freeman,
Attorney-General in South Wales; *p Jas. Phillips; *H. Vaughan; *Jas.
Lewis; *J. Lloyd of Faerdref; *J. Lewis of Glascrug; *Th. Parry; Rich.
Lloyd of Llangoedmor; Rawleigh Mansel: *Lists published by Th. Walkley*
(1650), p.64. Commission renewed to *add* H. Vaughan, place Th. Parry
on the quorum, and to appoint Jas. Phillips as *custos rotulorum*: Index 4213/
p.198. (20)

1652: 4 March
Commission renewed to *add* Rich. Price, Bt.; Th. Powell: Index 4213/p.233.

1652: 24 March
As on 1 August 1650: Cambridge University Ms. Dd.VIII.1/f.120 &
C.193/13/4/f.113d. Commission renewed to *omit* Rich. Price, Bt.; Th.
Powell: Index 4213/p.235. (20)

1652: 27 April (Acting)
As on 24 March 1652, except: J. Lloyd of Faerdref, *omitted*: Wales 4/884/8.
(19)

1654: 4 March
Commission renewed according to a general list: Index 4213/p.284.

1656: 20 March
*Nathaniel Fiennes & *J. Lisle, Commissioners of Great Seal; *Bulstrode
Whitelock, kt., *Th. Widdrington, kt., *Ed. Montagu, *W. Sydenham,
Commissioners of Treasury; *Philip Jones; *J. Glynn, Chief Justice of
Upper Bench; *W. Lenthall, Master of the Rolls; *Oliver St. John, Chief
Justice of Common Bench; *J. Haggatt & *Bennet Hoskins, Justices of
Great Sessions; *Edm. Prideaux, Attorney-General; *Major-General Jas.
Berry; *Rich. Price, Bt.; *Edm. Jones, Attorney-General in South Wales;
*p Jas. Phillips; *Jas. Lewis; *J. Vaughan; *H. Vaughan; *Rowland
Dawkins; *J. Lewis of Glascrug; *Th. Parry; *Jenkin Lloyd; *Th. Evans;
*Rich. Herbert; *Erasmus Lloyd; Nich. Lewis: C.193/13/6/f.100 &
C.193/13/5/f.120. Commission renewed to *add* Major-General Jas. Berry;
Rowland Dawkins; Nich. Lewis: Index 4213/p.329. (28)

1657: 7 July
Commission renewed to *add* Hector Phillips; Th. Lloyd of Llanfychan; J. Bowen, and to *omit* Th. Evans: Index 4213/p.371.

1657: 7 September (Acting)
As on 20 March 1656, except: Hector Phillips; J. Bowen, *added*. Th. Evans, *omitted*: Wales 4/884/10. (Th. Lloyd of Llanfychan is not listed, although added to the commission on 7 July 1657). (29)

1658: 24 September
General renewal of Welsh commissions to *add* Rich. Cromwell, Lord Protector: Index 4213/p.405.

1659: 28 June
Commission renewed according to a general list: Index 4213/p.435.

1659: 15 August (Acting)
W. Lenthall, Speaker; J. Bradshaw, Th. Tyrrell & J. Fountain, Commissioners of Great Seal; J. Haggatt, Justice of Great Sessions; Jas. Lewis, *custos rotulorum*; J. Jones; Th. Woogan; Rich. Herbert; Th. Evans; Jenkin Lloyd; Th. Price; J. Lewis; David Evans; Th. Knowles; H. Vaughan; Th. Lewis; Abel Griffiths; Rees Gwynn; J. Price: Wales 4/884/12. (20)

1660: post 8 September
*Ed. Hyde, kt., Chancellor; *E. of Southampton, Treasurer (appointed on 8 September); *D. of Albemarle; *Marquess of Ormond, Steward; *E. of Lindsey, Great Chamberlain; *E. of Manchester, Household Chamberlain; *E. of Carbery; *p Francis, Lord Vaughan; *W. Morton, kt. & *Simon Degg, Justices of Great Sessions; *Rich. Price, Bt.; *Walter Lloyd, *Francis Lloyd, kts.; *Jas. Lewis; *J. Vaughan; Jonathan Lloyd; *H. Vaughan; *Lewis Morgan; Th. Jenkins; *Morgan Herbert; Th. Price junior; Th. Parry; J. Lewis; Erasmus Lloyd: C.220/9/4/f.100 & B.M., Egerton Ms. 2557/f.99. (24)

1661: 3 April (Acting)
As at the end of 1660, except: E. of Southampton; E. of Lindsey; Walter Lloyd, kt., *omitted*: Wales 4/885/1. (All three omissions are probably erroneous). (21)

1661: 8 November
As on 3 April 1661, except: *E. of Southampton; *Lord Robartes, Keeper of Privy Seal; *E. of Lindsey; *Walter Lloyd, kt., *added*: C.193/12/3/f.115. General renewal of Welsh commissions to *add* E. of Carbery, President of Council in the Marches of Wales: Index 4214/p.144. (In the case of Cardigan, the E. of Carbery's name was already on the commission before his promotion). (25)

1662: 17 July
*E. of Clarendon, Chancellor; *Southampton; *Lord Robartes, Keeper of Privy Seal; *Albemarle; *Ormond; *Lindsey; *Manchester; *E. of Carbery,

President of Council in the Marches of Wales; *p Francis, Lord Vaughan; *Morton & *Degg, Justices of Great Sessions; *Rich. Price, Bt.; *Walter Lloyd, kt.; *Francis Lloyd, kt.; *Jas. Lewis; *J. Vaughan; *Ed. Freeman; Jonathan Lloyd; *H. Vaughan; *Lewis Morgan; David Lloyd; Ed. Vaughan; Th. Jenkins; Th. Lloyd of Rhiwarthen; *Morgan Herbert; Th. Lloyd of Ynyshir(?); Rich Herbert; J. Lewis; Reginald Jenkins; Erasmus Lloyd; Th. Lloyd of Bronwydd: C.66/2986/m.30d. Commission renewed to *add* Ed. Freeman; David Lloyd of Crynfryn; Ed. Vaughan; Th. Lloyd of Rhiwarthen; Th. Lloyd of Ynyshir(?); Rich. Herbert; Reginald Jenkins; Th. Lloyd of Bronwydd: Index 4214/p.178.   (31)

1663: 27 July
Commission renewed to *add* Jas. Stedman; Th. Lewis: Index 4214/p.211.

1663: 19 August
As on 17 July 1662, except: *Job. Charlton, kt., Justice of Chester; Jas. Stedman; Th. Lewis of Cwmowen; *J. Jones; *Th. Parry; *J. Bowen; Hector Phillips; Nich. Lewis, *added*. Jonathan Lloyd, *omitted*: C.66/3022/m.35d. Commission renewed to *add* J. Jones; Th. Parry; J. Bowen; Hector Phillips; Nich. Lewis: Index 4214/p.213.   (38)

1666: 5 May
*Clarendon; *Southampton; *Robartes; *Albemarle; *Ormond; *Lindsey; *Manchester; *Carbery, President of Council in the Marches of Wales; *p Francis, Lord Vaughan; *Job Charlton, kt., Justice of Chester; *Fred. Hyde, kt. & *Simon Degg, Justices of Great Sessions; *Rich. Price, Bt.; *Walter Lloyd, kt.; *Jas. Lewis; *J. Vaughan; *Ed. Freeman; *H. Vaughan; *Lewis Morgan; *David Lloyd; *Ed. Vaughan; Th. Jenkins; Th. Lloyd of Rhiwarthen; *Morgan Herbert; Th. Lloyd of Ynyshir(?); Rich. Herbert; *Jas. Stedman; Th. Lewis of Cwmowen; J. Lewis; *Reg. Jenkins; *Erasmus Lloyd; Th. Lloyd of Bronwydd; *J. Jones; *Th. Parry; *J. Bowen; Hector Phillips; Nich. Lewis: C.66/3074/m.33d. Commission renewed to *add* Fred. Hyde, kt., serjeant at law, Justice of Great Sessions: Index 4214/p.282.   (37)

1669: 2 March
Commission renewed to *add* Altham Vaughan; H. Sumner, and to appoint E. of Carbery as *custos rotulorum*: Index 4214/p.340.

1669: 17 April (Acting)
Robartes; Albemarle; Ormond; Lindsey; Manchester; Carbery, President of Council in the Marches of Wales; J. Vaughan, kt., serjeant at law, Chief Justice of Common Bench; Charlton, Justice of Chester; Hyde & Degg, Justices of Great Sessions; Rich. Price, Bt.; Ed. Freeman; Lewis Morgan; Hector Phillips; David Lloyd; Ed. Vaughan; Reg. Jenkins; Jas. Lewis; Morgan Herbert; Th. Parry; Jas. Stedman; Nich. Lewis; Erasmus Lloyd; J. Lewis; Th. Lloyd; Th. Lewis; Rich. Herbert; Th. Jenkins; Altham Vaughan: Wales 4/885/6. (Note that for some reason H. Sumner, who was added to the commission on the same date as Altham Vaughan, does not appear in the present list).   (29)

1670: 24 March
Commission renewed to *omit* Morgan Herbert: Index 4214/p.364.

1670: 9 December
Commission renewed to *add* J. Lloyd of Cilgwyn: Index 4214/p.383.

1671: 22 April (Acting)
As on 17 April 1669, except: Orlando Bridgeman, kt. & Bt., Keeper of Great Seal; D. of Buckingham; J. Lloyd of Cilgwyn; H. Sumner, *added*. D. of Albemarle; Reginald Jenkins; Morgan Herbert; Jas. Lewis, *omitted*: Wales 4/885/8. (29)

1672: 1 July
Commission renewed to *add* Th. Price of Llanvrood(?); Th. Powell; Walter Lloyd of Olmarch; J. Lewis of Gurnos; J. Williams of Abernant Bychan: Index 4214/p.417.

1676: 27 January
Commission renewed to *add* Th. Lloyd: Index 4214/p.506.

1678: 30 March (Acting)
Lord Finch, Chancellor; D. of Monmouth; D. of Ormond, Steward; E. of Lindsey, Great Chamberlain; E. of St. Albans, Household Chamberlain; E. of Carbery; Francis North, kt., Chief Justice of Bench; Job Charlton, kt., Justice of Chester; Francis Manley & W. Buckby, Justices of Great Sessions; Altham Vaughan; Owen Wynn; Ed. Vaughan; Ed. Freeman; Lewis Morgan; Th. Price senior of Llanvrood(?); Th. Powell; Erasmus Lloyd; Walter Lloyd of Olmarch; J. Lloyd of Cilgwyn; Hector Phillips; Nich. Lewis; Th. Jenkins; Th. Lloyd of Castle Howell; J. Williams of Abernant Bychan; J. Lewis of Gurnos; Th. Lloyd of Rhiwarthen; H. Sumner; Rich. Herbert; Th. Lewis: Wales 4/885/9. (30)

1679: 26 April (Acting)
As on 30 March 1678, except: Nich. Lewis, *omitted*: Wales 4/885/10. (29)

1679: 30 July
Commission renewed to *add* Th. Lloyd of Bronwydd: Index 4215/p.12.

1680: 1 April
*Prince Rupert; *Archbishop of Canterbury; *Lord Finch, Chancellor; *E. of Radnor, President of Council; *E. of Anglesey, Keeper of Privy Seal; Dukes of *Albemarle, *Newcastle, *Ormond; *Marquess of Winchester; *Marquess of Worcester, President of Council in the Marches of Wales; Earls of *Lindsey, *Arlington, *Salisbury, *Bridgewater, *Sunderland, *Essex, *p Carbery, *Bath, *Halifax; *Viscount Fauconberg; *B. of London; *Laurence Hyde; *H. Coventry; *Francis North, kt., Chief Justice of Bench; *J. Ernley, kt., Chancellor of Exchequer; *Th. Chichley, kt., Chancellor of Duchy of Lancaster; *W. Temple, Bt.; *Ed. Seymour; *Daniel Finch; *Leoline Jenkins; *Sidney Godolphin; *Francis Manley & *W. Buckby, Justices of Great Sessions; *Altham Vaughan; *Th. Price, Bt.; *Lewis

Meyrick, Attorney-General for Wales; *Ed. Vaughan; *Ed. Freeman, King's attorney in Cardigan; *Lewis Morgan; *Th. Price senior of Llanvrood(?); *Th. Powell; *David Lloyd; *Erasmus Lloyd; Walter Lloyd of Olmarch; J. Lewis of Gurnos; *J. Lloyd of Cilgwyn; *Hector Phillips; *Th. Price; *Morgan Herbert; *J. Herbert of Gogerddan; *Th. Jenkins; *Th. Lloyd of Bronwydd; J. Williams of Abernant Bychan; Th. Lloyd of Rhiwarthen; H. Sumner; Rich. Herbert; Th. Lewis of Cwmowen; *Th. Lloyd of Castle Howell: C.193/12/4/f.137v. Commission renewed to *remove* recusants and to *add* others (no details): Index 4215/p.26. (The *removal* from the Cardigan commission of the Duke of Buckingham was ordered by a warrant of 5 February 1680, and the *addition* of Th. Price, Bt.; Th. Price; Morgan Herbert; J. Herbert of Gogerddan by a warrant of the same date: H.M.C., *Eleventh Report, Appendix*, Part 2, p.174). (58)

1681: 28 July
Commission renewed to *omit* J. Williams: Index 4215/p.53.

1682: 4 April (Acting)
As on 1 April 1680, except: D. of Lauderdale; E. of Conway; Chas., Lord Herbert, *added*. Earls of Salisbury, Sunderland, Essex; W. Temple, Bt.; Altham Vaughan; J. Williams, *omitted*: Wales 4/885/13. (55)

1682: 19 August (Acting)
As on 4 April 1682, except: Th. Price, Bt., *omitted*: Wales 4/885/14. (54)

1684: 10 May (Acting)
As on 19 August 1682, except: Prince Rupert; E. of Nottingham (Lord Finch), Chancellor; D. of Lauderdale; Ed. Vaughan; David Lloyd; Erasmus Lloyd; J. Herbert; *omitted*: Wales 4/885/15. (47)

1684: 11 July
Commission renewed to *add* J. Lewis of Coedmore: Index 4215/p.105.

1685: 3 March
Commission renewed to appoint E. of Carbery as *custos rotulorum*: Index 4215/p.121. (This was probably also the occasion of the addition of Anth. Farrington who had been appointed Justice of Great Sessions in place of Francis Manley on 13 February: Index 4215/p.117.)

1685: post 28 September
*Archbishop of Canterbury; *Lord Jeffreys, Chancellor (appointed on 28 September); *E. of Rochester, Treasurer; *Marquess of Halifax, President of Council; *E. of Clarendon, Keeper of Privy Seal; Dukes of *Albemarle, *Newcastle, *Ormond; *D. of Beaufort, President of Council in the Marches of Wales; Marquesses of *Winchester, *Worcester; Earls of *Lindsey, *Ailesbury, *Bridgewater, *Sunderland, *Bath, *Nottingham, *p Carbery; *Viscount Fauconberg; *B. of London; *Sidney, Lord Godolphin; *H. Coventry; *J. Ernley, kt., Chancellor of Exchequer; *Th. Chichley, kt., Chancellor of Duchy of Lancaster; *Ed. Seymour; *W. Buckby & *Anth. Farrington, Justices of Great Sessions; *Altham Vaughan; *Th. Price, Bt.;

*Th. Powell, serjeant at law; *Lewis Meyrick, Attorney-General for Wales; *Ed. Vaughan; *Ed. Freeman, King's attorney in Cardigan; *Lewis Morgan; *Th. Price senior of Llanvrood(?); *David Lloyd; *Erasmus Lloyd; *Walter Lloyd of Olmarch; J. Lewis of Gurnos; *J. Lloyd of Cilgwyn; *Hector Phillips; *Th. Price; *Morgan Herbert; *J. Herbert of Gogerddan; *Th. Jenkins; Th. Lloyd of Rhiwarthen; *David Parry; H. Sumner; *J. Lewis of Coedmore; *Rich. Herbert; *Watkin Lloyd of Wern Newydd; *Morgan Lloyd of Green Grove; *Th. Lewis of Cwmowen; *Rich. Lloyd of Mabws; *Th. Lloyd of Castle Howell: C.193/12/5/f.162.   (55)

1686: 23 June
Commission renewed to add J., E. of Carbery, as custos rotulorum: Index 4215/p.156.

1686: 17 December
Order by the Privy Council for the removal from the Cardigan commission of Hector Phillips and the addition of the Earl of Castlemaine; Rob. Price; Jas. Palmer: P.C.2/71/p.376.

1687: 19 March (Acting)
Canterbury; Jeffreys; Rochester; E. of Sunderland, President of the Council; Clarendon; Dukes of Albemarle, Newcastle, Ormond; D. of Beaufort, President of Council in the Marches of Wales; Marquesses of Winchester, Worcester; E. of Lindsey, Great Chamberlain; E. of Mulgrave, Household Chamberlain; Earls of Middleton, Bridgewater, Bath, Nottingham, Carbery; Viscount Fauconberg; B. of London; Sidney, Lord Godolphin; H. Coventry; J. Ernley, kt., Chancellor of Exchequer; Th. Chichley, kt., Chancellor of Duchy of Lancaster; Ed. Seymour; Ed. Herbert, kt., Chief Justice of the Bench; Anth. Farrington & J. Matthews, Justices of Great Sessions; Th. Powell, serjeant at law; Lewis Meyrick, Attorney-General for Wales; Walter Lloyd of Olmarch; J. Lewis of Pant David; Hector Phillips; Th. Price; Morgan Herbert; J. Herbert of Gogerddan; Th. Lloyd of Bronwydd; Th. Lloyd of Rhiwarthen; David Parry; H. Sumner; J. Lewis of Coedmore; Rich. Herbert; Morgan Lloyd of Green Grove; Th. Lewis of Pant-yr-Odyn; Rich. Lloyd of Mabws; Th. Lloyd of Castle Howell: Wales 4/886/3. (Note that this list reflects the commission as it was before the changes ordered by the Privy Council in December 1686, since there had been no renewal of the commission in the meantime. The 1686 changes would probably have been incorporated for the first time in the renewal of the commission on 29 August 1687). (46)

1687: 29 August
General renewal of Welsh commissions to add the clause of dispensation: Index 4215/p.179. (Edwin Wyatt, Deputy Justice of Great Sessions, who was appointed on 16 June (ibid./p.173), was probably added on this date).

1688: 14 April
Commission renewed (no details): Index 4215/p.191.

1688: 6 October
General renewal of Welsh commissions: Index 4215/p.200.

1688: 27 November
Commission renewed to *add* Morgan Herbert & others (no details): Index
4215/p.204.

1689: 19 June
Commission renewed to reappoint E. of Carbery as *custos rotulorum*: Index
4215/p.229.

1689: 21 September (Acting)
Archbishop of Canterbury; J. Maynard, Anth. Keck & W. Rawlinson, kts.,
Commissioners of Great Seal; Marquess of Carmarthen, President of
Council; Marquess of Halifax, Keeper of Privy Seal; D. of Norfolk; D. of
Bolton; E. of Lindsey, Great Chamberlain; Earls of Devonshire, Dorset,
Bedford, Bath; E. of Macclesfield, President of Council in the Marches of
Wales; E. of Nottingham; E. of Carbery, *custos rotulorum*; J. Trenchard, kt.,
Justice of Chester; W. Wogan, kt. & Marmaduke Gibbs, Justices of Great
Sessions; Carbery Price, kt. & Bt.; J. Vaughan; Hector Phillips; J. Lewis
of Coedmore; J. Herbert; Th. Lloyd of Castle Howell; Walter Lloyd
senior; Walter Lloyd junior; Th. Lewis; Th. Lloyd of Bronwydd; Daniel
Evans; J. Phillips of Dolhaidd; Rich. Lloyd of Mabws; David Lloyd of
Crynfryn; Hugh Lloyd: Wales 4/886/4.   (34)

Pembroke

1543: 12 March
*Th., Lord Audley of Walden, Chancellor; *D. of Norfolk, Treasurer; *D. of Suffolk, President of Council; *J. Russell, kt., Keeper of Privy Seal; *B. of Coventry & Lichfield, President of Council in the Marches of Wales; Bishops of *St. Asaph, *St. Davids; Walter, Lord Ferrers; *Nich. Hare, Ed. Croft, Rice Mansel, *J. Vernon, kts.; *J. Pakington; *Th. Holte; *David Brooke; *J. ap Rice; *Rich. Hassall; *Rich. Devereux; *J. Wogan; *Th. Jones; Th. Lloyd, clerk; *p J. Vaughan; *J. Morgan; Lewis ap Watkin; H. Wirriott; Owen ap Owen; *Th. Bateman; Th. Revell; J. Rastell; J. Sutton. *Later additions to list*: *Th. Jones, kt. (probably the Th. Jones, Esq., who appears above); *Th. Bromley, serjeant at law; *Adam Mytton; J. Barlow, clerk; J. Philipps; Roger Barlow; J. Adams; J. Elliott; the Mayor of Pembroke; the Mayor of Tenby: C.193/12/1/f.43. (30 names plus 10 corrections).

1547: 12 September (Acting)
D. of Somerset, Protector; W. Paulet, kt., Lord St. John, President of Council; J. Russell, kt., Lord Russell, Keeper of Privy Seal; E. of Worcester; B. of Coventry & Lichfield, President of Council in the Marches of Wales; B. of St. Asaph; B. of St. Davids; Walter, Lord Ferrers; Rob. Townshend, Th. Bromley, Ed. Carne, Rice Mansel, Th. Jones, J. Wogan, kts.; ————— (the rest of the list is destroyed): Wales 4/775/1.

1550: 20 February (Acting)
Recognition made on this date before J. Sutton and J. Rastell, Justices of the Peace: Wales 4/775/2.

1554: 24 September (Acting)
B. of Winchester, Chancellor; Marquess of Winchester, Treasurer; E. of Bedford, Keeper of Privy Seal; Earls of Arundel, Pembroke; B. of Worcester, President of Council in the Marches of Wales; Bishops of St. Davids, St. Asaph; Rob. Townshend, Th. Bromley, David Brooke, J. Seyntlowe, Rice Mansel, Th. Jones, Walter Dennys, Ed. Carne, J. Wogan, J. Perrot, Roland Hill, J. Price, Adam Mytton, J. Vaughan, kts.; J. Pollard; Griffith Leyson, Ll.D.; Reg. Corbet; J. Scudamore of Holm Lacy; Rich. Hassall; W. Sheldon; J. Throckmorton; Edm. Plowden; Owen ap Owen; H. Wirriott; J. Rastell; W. Owen; W. ap Rice; Arnold Butler; Morgan Jones; Th. Cathern: Wales 4/775/3. (38)

1555: (Acting)
J. Vaughan, J. Perrot, kts.; H. Wirriott; Th. Cathern; Morgan Jones; W. Rice; Owen ap Owen; J. Rastell; W. Owen; Arnold Butler: S.P.11/5/f.61v. (10)

1558–9: (Acting)
*Nich. Bacon, kt., Keeper of Great Seal; *Marquess of Winchester, Treasurer; *E. of Arundel, Steward; Bishops of *Bath & Wells, *St. Davids, *Chester; *J. Throckmorton, Justice of Chester; *Th. Jones, *J. Vaughan, *Adam Mytton, *J. Perrot, kts.; *J. Scudamore of Holm; *Chas. Fox;

*J. Welsh; *Reg. Corbet; *W. Symonds; *W. Gerard; *Rich. Seaborne; *p Th. Cathern; *W. Philipps; *Morgan Jones; Owen ap Owen; *J. Rastell; *W. Owen; *Th. Phayer; J. Adams; Griffith White; J. ap Owen of Treslowen(?); J. Perrot of Scotsborough; Rees ap Morgan: B.M., Lansdowne Ms. 1218/f.37v. (Except for the omission of the *ex officio* members of the commission, the same list also appears in S.P.12/2/17/p.75). (30)

1561: (Acting)
*Bacon; *Winchester; *Arundel; *H. Sidney, kt., President of Council in the Marches of Wales; *B. of St. Davids; *Rich. Wye; *J. Vaughan, *p J. Perrot, kts.; *Th. Cathern; *W. Philipps; Owen ap Owen; *J. Rastell; Arnold Butler; J. Adams; J. Perrot of Scotsborough; Rees Morgan; J. Bradshaw: B.M., Lansdowne Ms. 1218/f.86. (17)

1562: 13 June
As in 1561: C.66/985/m.14d. (17)

1564: (Acting)
*Bacon; *Winchester; *Arundel; *Viscount Hereford; *Sidney, President of Council in the Marches of Wales; Bishops of *Bangor, *St. Davids; *Rich. Wye; *Reg. Corbet; *J. Throckmorton, Justice of Chester; *J. Vaughan, *p J. Perrot, kts.; *W. Gerard; *Chas. Fox; *Rich. Seaborne; *Rich. Pates; *J. Price; *Rich. Smith; J. Wogan; *Th. Cathern; Owen ap Owen; Griffith White; *J. Rastell; *Arnold Butler; J. Perrot of Scotsborough; *Rees Morgan; J. Bradshaw; *J. Barlow; *W. Jenkins: C.66/998/m.10d. (29)

1567: 31 May (Acting)
Bacon; Winchester; Earls of Pembroke, Arundel; Hereford; Sidney, President of Council in the Marches of Wales; Bishops of St. Davids, Bangor; Rich. Wye, Justice of Great Sessions; Throckmorton, Justice of Chester; J. Perrot, kt.; W. Gerard; Chas. Fox; Rich. Seaborne; Rich. Pates; J. Price; Rich. Smith; J. Wogan of Wiston; Griffith Rice; Griffith White; J. Rastell; Erasmus Saunders; Th. Huet; W. Philipps; J. Wogan of Boulston; J. Perrot of Scotsborough; Rees Morgan; J. Bradshaw; J. Barlow; Rice ap Owen: Wales 4/775/4. (30)

1571: 28 May (Acting)
Bacon; Winchester; Arundel; Hereford; Sidney, President of Council in the Marches of Wales; Bishops of St. Davids, Bangor; J. Rastell, Justice of Great Sessions; Throckmorton, Justice of Chester; J. Perrot, kt.; W. Gerard; Chas. Fox; Rich. Seaborne; Rich. Pates; J. Price; J. Wogan of Wiston; Griffith Rice; Griffith White; Erasmus Saunders; W. Philipps; J. Wogan of Boulston; J. Barlow; Rees Morgan; Th. Huet, clerk: Wales 4/775/6. (24)

1573: 28 September (Acting)
*Bacon; *W., Lord Burghley, Treasurer; *E. of Essex; *Sidney, President of Council in the Marches of Wales; Bishops of *St. Davids, *Bangor; *Jas. Croft, kt., Household Controller; *Hugh Cholmondeley, kt., Vice-

President of Council in the Marches of Wales; *Throckmorton, Justice of Chester; *J. Rastell, Justice of Great Sessions; *p J. Perrot, kt.; *W. Gerard; *Chas. Fox; *Rich. Seaborne; *Rich. Pates; *Ed. Davies; *Th. Huet, clerk; *J. Wogan of Wiston; *J. Barlow; *Griffith White; *Erasmus Saunders; J. Wogan of Boulston; Geo. Wirriott: Wales 4/776/1. (Details of the quorum are taken from two lists of 1573–4 which are identical to the one above except for the addition of the name of Lewis Gwynn, clerk, after J. Wogan of Wiston: S.P.12/93/part 2/f.33v & B.M., Egerton Ms. 2345/ f.43). (23)

1575: 12 September (Acting)
As on 28 September 1573, except: Geo. Fetiplace, Justice of Great Sessions; Lewis Gwynn, clerk; Th. Perrot; Morgan Philipps; Th. Revell; Alban Stepney; Eynon Philipps, added. Hugh Cholmondeley; J. Rastell; J. Barlow (Sheriff, 1574–5); Geo. Wirriott, omitted: Wales 4/776/2. (This list is largely the same as another for 1575 contained in S.P.12/106/part 2/f.5v except that the later list retains the name of J. Barlow, does not include the names of Morgan Philipps and Alban Stepney, and adds the names of H. Adams and Hugh Owen). (26)

1577: (Acting)
*Bacon; *Burghley; *Sidney, President of Council in the Marches of Wales; Bishops of *St. Davids, *Bangor; *Croft; *Throckmorton, Justice of Chester; *Geo. Fetiplace, Justice of Great Sessions; *p J. Perrot, kt.; *W. Gerard; *Chas. Fox; *Rich. Seaborne; *Rich. Pates; *J. Wogan of Wiston; *Th. Perrot; *J. Wogan of Boulston; *Rob. Laugharne, Ll.D.; Griffith White; *J. Barlow; H. Adams; Erasmus Saunders; *Th. Revell; *Hugh Owen; Eynon Philipps; Morgan Philipps; Francis Laugharne: S.P.12/121/f.38. (26)

1578: (Acting)
*Bacon; *Burghley; *Sidney; *B. of Worcester; Earls of *Worcester, *Pembroke; Bishops of *Hereford, *Bangor, *St. Davids, *St. Asaph; *Croft; *Throckmorton, Justice of Chester; *Andrew Corbet; *p J. Perrot, *Nich. Arnold, *Hugh Cholmondeley, *J. Littleton, *J. Huband, kts.; *J. Puckering, Justice of Great Sessions; *David Lewis, Ll.D.; *Geo. Bromley; *W. Gerard; *W. Aubrey; *Chas. Fox; *W. Glaseor; *Ellis Price, Ll.D.; *Ed. Leighton; *Rich. Pates; *Ralph Barton; *Jerome Corbet; *Fabian Phillips; *H. Townshend; *W. Leighton; *J. Wogan of Wiston; *Th. Perrot; *J. Wogan of Boulston; *Rob. Laugharne, Ll.D.; Griffith White; *J. Barlow; H. Adams; Erasmus Saunders; *Th. Revell; *Hugh Owen; Eynon Philips; Morgan Philipps; Francis Laugharne: Hatfield House Ms. 223.7. (46)

1579: (Acting)
As in 1578, except: *Th. Bromley, kt., Chancellor; *J. Price, added. Bacon; Erasmus Saunders; Hugh Owen, omitted: S.P.12/145/f.51v. (45)

1581: 20 November (Acting)
J. Perrot, kt.; Th. Perrot, kt.; Morgan Philipps; J. Wogan of Boulston;
Rob. Laugharne, Ll.D.; Griffith White; J. Barlow; Th. Revell; Francis
Laugharne; H. Adams; Eynon Philipps: Bodleian, Bodley Ms. 904/f.206v.
(This list is confined only to the justices active within the county and omits
the *ex officio* justices included in earlier lists).   (11)

1582: (Acting)
As on 20 November 1581, except: W. Aubrey, *added*: B.M., Lansdowne
Ms.35/f.138v.   (12)

1583: (Acting)
*p J. Perrot, *H. Jones, kts.; *Th. Williams; *Morgan Philipps; *J. Wogan;
*Ed. Dunlee; *Francis Laugharne; *Th. Revell; *Griffith White; *J.
Barlow; *H. Adams; *Rob. Laugharne, Ll.D.; Eynon Philipps; J. Price of
Rickerston; J. Elliott; *Maurice Canon: B.M., Royal Ms. 18.D.III/f.102.
(16)

1584: (Acting)
*Th. Bromley, kt., Chancellor; *Burghley; *Sidney, President of Council
in the Marches of Wales; Earls of *Worcester, *Pembroke; Bishops of
*Hereford, *Bangor, *St. Davids, *St. Asaph; *Croft; *Geo. Bromley, kt.,
Justice of Chester; *J. Puckering & *Rich. Atkins, Justices of Great
Sessions; *p J. Perrot, *Hugh Cholmondeley, *J. Littleton, *Th. Perrot,
kts.; *W. Aubrey; *Chas. Fox; *Ellis Price, Ll.D.; *Ed. Leighton; *W.
Leighton; *H. Townshend; *Rich. Pates; *Ralph Barton; *Jerome Corbet;
*Fabian Phillips; *W. Glaseor; *Morgan Philipps; *J. Morgan; *J.
Wogan of Boulston; *J. Barlow; *Th. Jones of Armeston; H. Adams;
*J. Price of Rickerston; *Th. Revell; *Hugh Owen; *Roland Laugharne;
Geo. Owen; Alban Stepney; *Maurice Canon; J. Elliott: E.163/14/8/f.49v.
(42)

1586: 15 August (Acting)
Bromley; Burghley; Earls of Worcester, Pembroke; Bishops of St. Davids,
St. Asaph; Croft; Bromley, Justice of Chester; Puckering & Atkins, Justices
of Great Sessions; J. Perrot, Hugh Cholmondeley, J. Littleton, Th. Perrot,
kts.; W. Aubrey; Chas. Fox; Ellis Price, Ll.D.; Ed. Leighton; W. Leighton;
H. Townshend; Rich. Pates; Ralph Barton; Fabian Phillips; Jerome
Corbet; W. Glaseor; J. Wogan; J. Barlow; Th. Jones of Armeston; H.
Adams; J. Price of Rickerston; Th. Revell; Hugh Owen; Geo. Owen;
Alban Stepney; J. Bowen; Maurice Canon; J. Elliott; Th. Lloyd: Wales
4/776/4.   (38)

1590-91: (Acting)
*Christopher Hatton, kt., Chancellor; *Burghley; *E. of Pembroke,
President of Council in the Marches of Wales; Bishops of *St. Davids,
*St. Asaph; *p J. Perrot, kt.; *Rich. Shuttleworth, kt., Justice of Chester;
*Puckering & *Atkins, Justices of Great Sessions; *Hugh Cholmondeley,
*Th. Perrot, *J. Wogan, kts.; *W. Aubrey; *Ellis Price, Ll.D.; *Ed.
Leighton; *W. Leighton; *H. Townshend; *Jerome Corbet; *Fabian

Phillips; J. Morgan; J. Philipps; *J. Barlow; *Alban Stepney; *Th. Jones of Armeston; H. Adams; *J. Price of Rickerston; *Th. Revell; *Hugh Owen; Geo. Owen; *Rich. Grafton; Rich. Tothill; J. Owen Philipps; W. Warren of Trewern; Hugh Butler; Th. Lloyd: Hatfield House Ms. 278/f.56. (35).

1592: 21 August (Acting)
J. Puckering, kt., Keeper of Great Seal; Burghley; Pembroke, President of Council in the Marches of Wales; E. of Essex; Bishops of St. Davids, St. Asaph; Shuttleworth, Justice of Chester; Rich. Atkins & W. Oldisworth, Justices of Great Sessions; Hugh Cholmondeley, Th. Perrot, J. Wogan, Ed. Leighton, kts.; W. Aubrey; Ellis Price, Ll.D.; W. Leighton; H. Townshend; Jerome Corbet; Fabian Phillips; J. Barlow; Alban Stepney; Th. Revell; Th. Jones; H. Adams; J. Price; Hugh Owen; Geo. Owen; Edm. Wynstanley; Rich. Grafton; Rich. Tothill; Francis Meyrick: Wales 4/776/5. (31)

1594: 28 June
*Puckering; *Burghley; *Pembroke, President of Council in the Marches of Wales; *p E. of Essex; Bishops of *St. Asaph, *St. Davids; *Shuttleworth, Justice of Chester; *Atkins & *Oldisworth, Justices of Great Sessions; *Geo. Devereux; *Hugh Cholmondeley, *J. Wogan, kts.; *W. Aubrey; *Ellis Price, Ll.D.; *W. Leighton; *H. Townshend; *Jerome Corbet; *Fabian Phillips; J. Philipps; *Alban Stepney; *Th. Revell; *Th. Jones of Armeston; H. Adams; J. Price of Rickerston; Walter Vaughan; *Hugh Owen; *Geo. Owen; Edm. Wynstanley; *Rich. Grafton; *Francis Meyrick; *W. Warren of Trewern: C.66/1421/m.15d. (31)

1594: 16 September (Acting)
As on 28 June 1594, except: B. of St. Davids; Walter Vaughan (Sheriff, 1593–4), omitted: Wales 4/776/6. (29)

1595: 15 August
As on 16 September 1594, except: *B. of St. Davids; *W. Fowler; Rich. Edwards, Chancellor of St. Davids; *Hugh Butler, added. W. Aubrey; Ellis Price; Hugh Owen; W. Warren; J. Philipps (Sheriff, 1594–5), omitted: Bodleian, Bodley Ms. 904/f.213v. (This ms. identifies the present commission as that of 15 August 1595). General renewal on 15 August of all the Welsh commissions: Index 4208/f.4v. (28)

1596: 21 February
As on 15 August 1595, except: J. Philipps, added: C.66/1435/m.20d. Commission renewed to restore J. Philipps, the late Sheriff: Index 4208/f.12. (29)

1596: 29 June
As on 21 February 1596, except: *Th. Egerton, kt., Keeper of Great Seal, added. J. Puckering, omitted: C.66/1468/m.15d & S.P.13/Case F, no. 11/f.39. Commission renewed to add Th. Egerton, Keeper of Great Seal: Index 4208/f.16v. (29)

1596: 30 December
Commission renewed to *add* Hugh Owen: Index 4208/f.25v.

1597: 18 February
Commission renewed to *add* W. Warren: Index 4208/f.28v.

1597: 2 June
Commission renewed to *add* J. Owen Philipps: Index 4208/f.33v.

1597: 8 October
*Th. Egerton, kt., Keeper of Great Seal; *Burghley; *Pembroke, President of Council in the Marches of Wales; *p E. of Essex; Bishops of *St. Asaph, *St. Davids; *Shuttleworth, Justice of Chester; *Atkins & *Oldisworth, Justices of Great Sessions; *Geo. Devereux, *J. Wogan, kts,; *W. Leighton; *H. Townshend; *Jerome Corbet; *W. Fowler; *J. Philipps; *Geo. Owen; *Walter Vaughan; *Alban Stepney; *Hugh Owen; *Th. Revell; *Francis Meyrick; *Th. Jones of Armeston; H. Adams; *J. Price of Rickerston; Edm. Wynstanley; Rich. Edwards, Chancellor of St. Davids; *Rich. Grafton; *Hugh Butler; J. Owen Philipps; W. Warren: C.66/1468/m.30d. Commission renewed to *add* Walter Vaughan: Index 4208/f.40v. (31)

1598: 30 May
Commission renewed to *add* Jas. Perrot: Index 4208/f.50v.

1598: 30 November
As on 8 October 1597, except: *Jas. Perrot; Th. Lloyd, *added*. Lord Burghley; Jerome Corbet; W. Fowler; Walter Vaughan, *omitted*: C.66/1482/m.17d. Commission renewed to *add* Th. Lloyd: Index 4208/f.59v. (29)

1599: post 15 May
As on 30 November 1598, except: *Th., Lord Buckhurst, Treasurer, *added*: C.66/1493/m.27d. (Buckhurst was appointed on 15 May 1599). (30)

1601: 24 March
Commission renewed to appoint Jas. Perrot as *custos rotulorum*, and to *omit* Geo. Devereux, kt.; Francis Meyrick, kt.; and Th. Revell: Index 4208/f.107.

1601: 11 July
*Egerton; *Th., Lord Buckhurst, Treasurer; *B. of St. Davids; *Rich. Lewkenor, kt., Justice of Chester; *Atkins & *Oldisworth, Justices of Great Sessions; *J. Wogan, kt.; *W. Leighton; *H. Townshend; *Geo. Owen; W. Wogan; *J. Philipps; *p Jas. Perrot; *Alban Stepney; Th. Lloyd; *Th. Jones of Armeston; H. Adams; Edm. Wynstanley; *Rich. Grafton; *Hugh Butler; J. Owen Philipps; W. Warren; *Th. Canon: C.66/1549/m.30d. Commission renewed to *add* W. Wogan; Th. Canon, and to *omit* Hugh Owen: Index 4208/f.116. (23)

1602: 15 February
Commission renewed to *add* J. Wogan: Index 4208/f.129.

1602: 2 July
Commission renewed to *add* W. Bradshaw: Index 4208/f.139.

1602: 25 July
General renewal of Welsh commissions to *add* Ed., Lord Zouch, President of Council in the Marches of Wales: Index 4208/f.141.

1602: 20 November
*Egerton; *Buckhurst; *Ed., Lord Zouch, President of Council in the Marches of Wales; *B. of St. Davids; *Lewkenor, Justice of Chester; *Atkins & *Oldisworth, Justices of Great Sessions; *W. Leighton; *H. Townshend; *p Jas. Perrot; *Geo. Owen; *J. Wogan; W. Wogan; *J. Philipps; *Alban Stepney; W. Bradshaw; Th. Lloyd; *Th. Jones of Armeston; H. Adams; Edm. Wynstanley; Hugh Butler; J. Owen Philipps; W. Warren; *Th. Canon; H. White; Devereux Barrett; Nich. Adams: C.66/1594/m.33d. Commission renewed to *add* H. White; Devereux Barrett; Nich. Adams: Index 4208/f.146.   (27)

1603: 19 February
Commission renewed to *add* Th. Price: Index 4208/f.152.

1603: 13 April
*Egerton; *Buckhurst; *Zouch, President of Council in the Marches of Wales; *B. of St. Davids; *Lewkenor, Justice of Chester; *Atkins & *Oldisworth, Justices of Great Sessions; *W. Leighton; *H. Townshend; *Geo. Owen; *p Jas. Perrot, *J. Wogan, W. Wogan, kts.; *J. Philipps; *Alban Stepney; W. Bradshaw; Th. Lloyd; *Th. Jones of Armeston; H. Adams; Edm. Wynstanley; *Hugh Butler; J. Owen Philipps; W. Warren; *Th. Canon; H. White; Devereux Barrett; Nich. Adams; Th. Price: Geo. Owen, *The Description of Pembrokeshire,* Cymmrodorion Record Series, no. 1, ed. H. Owen (London, 1892), vol. 1, pp.159–60.   (28)

1603: 8 August (Acting)
As on 13 April 1603, except: Jas. Ley, Justice of Great Sessions, *added.* W. Oldisworth, *omitted*: Wales 4/777/1.   (28)

1603: 26 September (Acting)
As on 8 August 1603: Wales 4/777/2.   (28)

1604: 17 September (Acting)
As on 26 September 1603, except: Rich. Daston, Justice of Great Sessions, *added.* B. of St. Davids; Jas. Ley; Hugh Butler; H. White (Sheriff, 1603–4), *omitted*: Wales 4/777/4. (The omissions of the B. of St. Davids and H. White are probably erroneous).   (25)

1605: 18 March (Acting)
As on 17 September 1604, except: B. of St. Davids; H. White, *added.* Alban Stepney (Sheriff, 1604–5), *omitted*: Wales 4/777/5.   (26)

1607: 23 March (Acting)
As on 18 March 1605, except: Alban Stepney; Th. Revell; J. Butler; Rice Philipps Scarfe, *added*: Wales 4/778/2.   (30)

1607: 21 September (Acting)
Lord Ellesmere (Th. Egerton), Chancellor; E. of Dorset, Treasurer; Zouch, President of Council in the Marches of Wales; B. of St. Davids; Lewkenor, Justice of Chester; Rich. Atkins & Rich. Daston, Justices of Great Sessions; Jas. Perrot, W. Wogan, J. Wogan, H. Townshend, kts.; W. Leighton; Geo. Owen; J. Philipps; Alban Stepney; Th. Revell; W. Bradshaw; Th. Lloyd; Th. Jones; H. Adams; Edm. Wynstanley; J. Butler; J. Owen Philipps; Rice Philipps Scarfe; W. Warren; Th. Canon; H. White; Devereux Barrett; Nich. Adams; Th. Price: Wales 4/778/3.   (30)

1608: 12 September (Acting)
As on 21 September 1607, except: E. of Salisbury, Treasurer; E. of Northampton, Keeper of Privy Seal; Ralph, Lord Eure, President of Council in Wales; J. Carew, kt., *added*. E. of Dorset; Lord Zouch; W. Leighton; J. Butler (Sheriff, 1607–8); W. Warren; Th. Revell, *omitted*: Wales 4/778/4.   (28)

1609: 11 September (Acting)
*Ellesmere; *E. of Salisbury, Treasurer; *E. of Northampton, Keeper of Privy Seal; *Ralph, Lord Eure, President of Council in the Marches of Wales; *B. of St. Davids; *Lewkenor, Justice of Chester; *Atkins & *Daston, Justices of Great Sessions; *p Jas. Perrot, *W. Wogan, *J. Wogan, *H. Townshend, *J. Carew, kts.; *Geo. Owen; *J. Philipps; *Alban Stepney; *W. Bradshaw; Th. Lloyd; *Th. Jones of Armeston; H. Adams; J. Butler; Edm. Wynstanley; J. Owen Philipps; *Rice Philipps Scarfe; *Th. Canon; H. White; *Devereux Barrett; Nich. Adams; Th. Price: Wales 4/778/5. (Details of the quorum are taken from an enrolled but undated commission of about this time in C.66/1786/m.32d).   (29)

1610: 26 March (Acting)
As on 11 September 1609, except: J. Carew; Th. Price, *omitted*: Wales 4/779/1. (Both omissions appear to be erroneous).   (27)

1611: 15 July (Acting)
As on 26 March 1610, except: Nich. Overbury, Justice of Great Sessions; J. Carew, kt.; Th. Price, *added*. Rich. Atkins; J. Philipps (Sheriff, 1610–11), *omitted*: Wales 4/779/3.   (28)

1611:16 September (Acting)
As on 15 July 1611, except: Alban Stepney, *omitted*: Wales 4/779/4.   (27)

1612: 30 March (Acting)
As on 16 September 1611, except: J. Philipps; J. Stepney, *added*. J. Carew; H. Adams, *omitted*: Wales 4/779/5.   (27)

1613: 2 August (Acting)
As on 30 March 1612, except: Rich. Cuny, *added*. E. of Salisbury; Edm. Wynstanley, *omitted*: Wales 4/779/6. (26)

1613: 13 September (Acting)
As on 2 August 1613, except: Th. Lloyd (Sheriff, 1612–3), *omitted*: Wales 4/780/1. (25)

1615: 7 August (Acting)
*Ellesmere; *E. of Suffolk, Treasurer; *Lord Eure, President of Council in the Marches of Wales; *B. of St. Davids; *Lewkenor, Justice of Chester; *Nich. Overbury & *Rich. Daston, Justices of Great Sessions; *p W. Wogan, *J. Wogan, *H. Townshend, kts.; *J. Philipps; *Th. Canon; *Alban Owen; *J. Stepney; *Th. Price; *W. Bradshaw; *Th. Jones of Armeston; *J. Butler; J. Owen Philipps; *Devereux Barrett; Nich. Adams: Wales 4/780/3. (Details of the quorum are based on the enrolled commission contained in C.66/2047/m.21d. This enrolment also includes the names of Th. Lloyd (omitted from the Gaol File list in 1613), Rice Philipps Scarfe, and Rich. Cuny. However, because of uncertainty as to the exact date of the enrolled commission it is difficult to be sure which list is the more accurate). (21)

1615: 13 September (Acting)
As on 7 August 1615: Wales 4/780/4. (21)

1616: 10 January
Commission renewed to *add* Chas. Bowen; Griffith White; W. Scourfield; H. Lort, and to *omit* W. Bradshaw because of his outlawry and Th. Canon for non-residence: Index 4211/f.13v.

1616: 26 February
*Ellesmere; *Suffolk; *E. of Worcester, Keeper of Privy Seal; *Eure, President of Council in the Marches of Wales; *Rich. Lewkenor, kt., Justice of Chester; *Overbury & *Daston, Justices of Great Sessions; *p W. Wogan, *J. Wogan, *H. Townshend, kts.; *J. Philipps; Alban Owen; *J. Stepney; *Th. Price; *W. Bradshaw; *Th. Jones of Armeston; *J. Butler; J. Owen Philipps; Rich. Cuny; *Devereux Barrett; Nich. Adams; Chas. Bowen; Griffith White; W. Scourfield; H. Lort: C.66/2076/m.25d. Commission renewed to *restore* W. Bradshaw, his outlawry having been reversed: Index 4211/f.17. (25)

1616: 9 July
Commission renewed to *add* Rich., B. of St. Davids: Index 4211/f.23v.

1616: 16 September (Acting)
As on 26 February 1616, except: B. of St. Davids; Th. Chamberlain, kt., Justice of Chester, *added*. Rich Lewkenor: Devereux Barrett (Sheriff, 1615–6), *omitted*: Wales 4/780/5. (Note that Chamberlain, who was appointed on 28 April 1616, was probably added to the commission on the same date as the B. of St. Davids). (25)

1617: 8 March
Commission renewed to *add* Francis Bacon, kt., Keeper of Great Seal; Th., Lord Gerard, President of Council in Wales: Index 4211/f.36. (These two were added in the other Welsh counties on 19 March).

1617: 5 August
Commission renewed to *restore* Th. Canon: Index 4211/f.48.

1617: 15 September (Acting)
As on 16 September 1616, except: Francis Bacon, kt., Keeper of Great Seal; D. of Lennox, Steward; Th., Lord Gerard, President of Wales; Th. Canon; Devereux Barrett, *added*. Lord Ellesmere; Lord Eure; W. Scourfield (Sheriff, 1616–7), *omitted*: Wales 4/780/6.   (27)

1617: post 24 November
As on 15 September 1617, except: *W., Lord Compton, President of Council in the Marches of Wales; W. Scourfield, *added*. Lord Gerard, *omitted*: C.66/2147/m.24d. (Compton was appointed on 24 November 1617).   (28)

1618: 27 July (Acting)
As at the end of 1617, except: J. Owen Philipps, *omitted*: Wales 4/781/1.   (27)

1619: 10 June
Commission renewed to *add* W. Ryves, Justice of Great Sessions, in place of Rich. Daston: Index 4211/f.85.

1620: 17 February
Commission renewed to *add* Ed. Littleton, Justice of Great Sessions, in place of W. Ryves: Index 4211/f.99v.

1620: 3 April (Acting)
As on 27 July 1618, except: Ed. Littleton, Justice of Great Sessions; J. Owen Philipps, *added*. E. of Suffolk; Rich. Daston; Alban Owen (Sheriff, 1619–20), *omitted*: Wales 4/781/3.   (26)

1620: 11 September (Acting)
As on 3 April 1620, except: J. Owen Philipps, *omitted*: Wales 4/781/4.   (25)

1620: 4 November
General renewal of Welsh commissions to *add* Jas. Whitlock, kt., Justice of Chester: Index 4211/f.114.

1621: 19 February
Commission renewed to *add* Jas. Bowen: Index 4211/f.119v.

1621: 26 February
*Francis Bacon, Viscount St. Alban, Chancellor; *H., Viscount Mandeville, Treasurer; *E. of Worcester, Keeper of Privy Seal; *D. of Lennox, Steward; *E. of Northampton (Lord Compton), President of Council in the Marches of Wales; *B. of St. Davids; *Jas. Whitelock, kt., serjeant at law, Justice of

Chester; *Nich. Overbury & *Ed. Littleton, Justices of Great Sessions; *p W. Wogan, *J. Wogan, *H. Townshend, *J. Stepney, kts.; *J. Philipps; *Th. Canon; Alban Owen; *Th. Price; *W. Bradshaw; *Devereux Barrett; *W. Scourfield; *Th. Jones; *J. Butler; Rich. Cuny; Nich. Adams; Chas. Bowen; Griffith White; H. Lort; Jas. Bowen: C.66/2234/m.43d. & B.M., Harleian Ms. 1933/f.26. General renewal of Welsh commissions to *add* Viscount Mandeville: Index 4211/f.120. (Note that Jas. Bowen's name does not appear in the enrolment of this commission on C.66/2234. This is clearly an error).   (28)

1621: 3 July
Commission renewed to *add* J. Hoskins, Justice of Great Sessions, in place of Ed. Littleton: Index 4211/f.126.

1621: post 29 September
As on 26 February 1621, except: *B. of Lincoln, Keeper of Great Seal; *Lionel Cranfield, Treasurer (appointed on 29 September); *J. Hoskins, Justice of Great Sessions, *added*. Viscount St. Alban; B. of St. Davids; Ed. Littleton; H. Townshend, *omitted*: C.66/2259/m.26d.   (27)

1622: 28 February
Commission renewed to *add* W., B. of St. Davids: Index 4211/f.136.

1622: 23 September (Acting)
As at the end of 1621, except: B. of St. Davids, *added*. Devereux Barrett; W. Scourfield, *omitted*: Wales 4/782/1.   (26)

1623: 21 March
*B. of Lincoln, Keeper of Great Seal; *E. of Middlesex (Cranfield) Treasurer; *Viscount Mandeville; *Worcester; *Lennox; *Northampton, President of Council in the Marches of Wales; *Whitlock, Justice of Chester; *Nich. Overbury, kt. & *J. Hoskins, Justices of Great Sessions; *J. Philipps, Bt.; *J. Stepney, kt. & Bt.; *Jas. Perrot, *p W. Wogan, *J. Wogan, kts.; *Th. Canon; Alban Owen; *Th. Price; *W. Bradshaw; *Th. Jones of Armeston; *J. Butler; Rich. Cuny; Nich. Adams; Chas. Bowen; Griffith White; H. Lort; Jas. Bowen: C.66/2285/m.34d. Commission renewed to *restore* Jas. Perrot, kt.: Index 4211/f.150v.   (26)

1623: 17 August
As on 21 March 1623, except: *B. of St. Davids, *added*. D. of Lennox, *omitted*: C.66/2310/m.31d. (Note that Lennox died in February 1624 and was probably included in the 17 August commission as originally issued, being omitted when the commission was later enrolled). Commission renewed to *add* H. Lort: Index 4211/f.156v. (Lort was already a member of the commission, the purpose of this renewal apparently being to promote him in the order of the justices to appear after J. Butler).   (26)

1624: 9 November
Commission renewed to appoint J. Stepney, kt. & Bt., as *custos rotulorum*: Index 4211/f.172.

1625: 26 February
Commission renewed to *add* J. Wogan, Esq.: Index 4211/f.177.

1625: 1 April
*Lincoln; *Jas., Lord Ley, Treasurer; *Mandeville; *Worcester; *North-ampton, President of Council in the Marches of Wales; *B. of St. Davids; *Th. Chamberlain, kt., Justice of Chester; *Overbury & *Hoskins, Justices of Great Sessions; *J. Philipps, Bt.; *p J. Stepney, kt. & Bt.; *Jas. Perrot, *J. Wogan, *Th. Canon, kts.; Sampson Eure; *Rob. Brooke; Alban Owen; *Th. Price; *W. Bradshaw; *J. Wogan; *Th. Jones of Armeston; *J. Butler; *H. Lort; Rich. Cuny; Nich. Adams; Chas. Bowen; Griffith White; Jas. Bowen: C.66/2367/m.30d. General renewal of Welsh commissions: Index 4211/f.180v. (28)

1625: 1 June
Commission renewed to *add* Jenkin Gwynn: Index 4211/f.188v.

1625: 11 August
Commission renewed to appoint E. of Pembroke as *custos rotulorum*: Index 4211/f.192v.

1625: 22 December
As on 1 April 1625, except: *Th. Coventry, kt., Keeper of Great Seal; *p E. of Pembroke; *Jenkin Gwynn, *added*. B. of Lincoln; Th. Chamberlain; J. Stepney; Th. Jones of Armeston, *omitted*: B.M., Harleian Ms. 1622/f.101v. General renewal of Welsh commissions to *add* Th. Coventry: Index 4211/f.194v. (27)

1626: 20 March
As on 22 December 1625, except: *J. Bridgeman, kt., Justice of Chester, *added*. Alban Owen; W. Bradshaw; Jas. Bowen; Jenkin Gwynn, *omitted*: E.163/18/12/f.101v & C.193/12/2/f.73. Commission renewed to *add* J. Bridgeman, kt., Justice of Chester: Index 4211/f.199v. (The commission entered in C.193/12/2/f.73 omits the name of W., B. of St. Davids, and may possibly have been copied after the Bishop's translation to Bath & Wells in September 1626). (24)

1627: 17 September (Acting)
As on 20 March 1626, except: J. Bridgeman; Sampson Eure; Griffith White (Sheriff, 1626–7), *omitted*: Wales 4/783/4. (All these apparent omissions are probably misleading. The omission of Bridgeman may be the result of using an outdated commission. All three names reappear in later lists). (21)

1627: 1 December
As on 17 September 1627, except: *J. Bridgeman, kt., Justice of Chester; *Sampson Eure; *Timothy Turneur; Griffith White; *Jenkin Gwynn, *added*. E. of Worcester; Rob. Brooke, *omitted*: C.66/2449/m.31d. Commission renewed to *restore* Jenkin Gwynn: Index 4211/f.236v. (24)

1629: 20 March
Commission renewed to *add* Rich. Philipps, Bt.; J. Laugharne; Alban Owen; Hugh Bowen: Index 4211/f.266.

1629: 20 June
Commission renewed to *add* Alban Philipps; J. Philipps: Index 4212./p.10.

1629: 3 July
Commission renewed to *add* Hugh Owen; Geo. Bowen; Th. Warren: Index 4212/p.12.

1629: 3 December
*Th. Coventry, kt., Keeper of Great Seal; *Rich., Lord Weston, Treasurer; *Viscount Conway, President of Council; *E. of Manchester (Viscount Mandeville), Keeper of Privy Seal; *E. of Pembroke; *Northampton, President of Council in the Marches of Wales; *J. Bridgeman, kt., Justice of Chester; *Overbury & *Hoskins, Justices of Great Sessions; *Rich. Philipps, Bt.; *Jas. Perrot, *J. Wogan, *Th. Canon, kts.; *Sampson Eure; *Timothy Turneur; *J. Wogan; *Hugh Owen; *Th. Price; *J. Laugharne; *H. Lort; Chas. Bowen; Griffith White; *Jenkin Gwynn; *Alban Owen; Hugh Bowen; *Alban Philipps; Geo. Bowen; J. Philipps; Th. Warren of Trewern: C.66/2495/m.28d. Commission renewed to *restore* Jenkin Gwynn: Index 4212/p.20. (29)

1630: 12 June
As on 3 December 1629: C.66/2527/m.31d. Commission renewed to appoint E. of Pembroke as *custos rotulorum*: Index 4212/p.33. (This is Philip Herbert, brother and heir of W. Herbert, E. of Pembroke, who died in April 1630). (29)

1630: 19 June
Commission renewed to *add* Owen Edwards: Index 4212/p.35.

1631: 23 February
As on 12 June 1630, except: *Owen Edwards, *added*. Viscount Conway; E. of Northampton; Jenkin Gwynn, *omitted*: C.66/2536/m.22d. Commission renewed to *omit* Jenkin Gwynn: Index 4212/p.50. (27)

1631-2: (Acting)
As on 28 February 1631, except: *Marmaduke Lloyd, kt., *added*. Th. Price, *omitted*: C.66/2577/m.9d & S.P.16/212/f.78. (27)

1632: 24 November
As in 1631-2, except: *E. of Bridgewater, President of Council in the Marches of Wales; *B. of St. Davids, *added*: C.66/2623/m.25d. Commission renewed to *add* Theophilus, B. of St. Davids: Index 4212/p.94. (29)

1634: 7 June
As on 24 November 1632, except: *Th. Price, *added*: C.193/13/2/f.85. Commission renewed to *restore* Th. Price: Index 4212/p.137. (30)

1634: 13 November
*Coventry; *E. of Portland (Lord Weston), Treasurer; *Manchester; *p E. of Pembroke; *E. of Bridgewater, President of Council in the Marches

of Wales; *B. of St. Davids; *Bridgeman, Justice of Chester; *Overbury & *Hoskins, Justices of Great Sessions; *Rich. Philipps, Bt.; *J. Stepney, Bt.; *Marmaduke Lloyd, *Jas. Perrot, *J. Wogan, *Th. Canon, kts.; *Sampson Eure; *Timothy Turneur; *J. Wogan; *J. Laugharne; *Hugh Owen; *Th. Price; *H. Lort; Chas. Bowen; Griffith White; *Alban Owen; Hugh Bowen; *Alban Philipps; Geo. Bowen; *J. Philipps; Th. Warren of Trewern; *Owen Edwards: C.66/2654/m.24d. Commission renewed to *add* J. Stepney, Bt.: Index 4212/p.148.   (31)

1636: post 6 March
As on 13 November 1634, except: *B. of London, Treasurer, *added*. E. of Portland; B. of St. Davids, *omitted*: S.P.16/405/f.82d. (The B. of London was appointed on 6 March 1636).   (30)

1637: 21 July
Commission renewed to *add* Arthur Owen: Index 4212/p.256.

1638: 6 March
Commission renewed to *add* Timothy Turneur, Justice of Great Sessions, in place of Nich. Overbury: Index 4212/p.284.

1638: 14 December
*Coventry; *B. of London, Treasurer; *Manchester; *p E. of Pembroke; *Bridgewater, President of Council in the Marches of Wales; *Timothy Turneur & *J. Hoskins, Justices of Great Sessions; *Rich. Philipps, Bt.; *J. Stepney, Bt.; *Marmaduke Lloyd, *Th. Canon, kts.; *Sampson Eure; *J. Wogan; *J. Laugharne; *Hugh Owen; *Th. Price; *H. Lort; Chas. Bowen; Griffith White; *Alban Owen; Hugh Bowen; Arthur Owen; Evan Owen, B.D., Judge of Admiralty in South Wales; Geo. Bowen; *J. Philipps; Th. Warren of Trewern; *Owen Edwards: C.66/2725/m.20d. Commission renewed to *add* Evan Owen, B.D.: Index 4212/p.318. (Another very similar commission of about the same date is contained in C.66/2761/m.16d. This *omits* the name of Evan Owen but *adds* those of Alban Philipps (a regular member of the commission since 1629) and of Th. Milward, kt., Justice of Chester. Milward was appointed on 23 March 1638 and might therefore be expected to appear in the commission of 14 December).   (27)

1639: 15 March
Commission renewed to *add* J. Platt, Justice of Great Sessions, in place of J. Hoskins: Index 4212/p.330.

1640: 17 August (Acting)
London; Manchester; Pembroke; Bridgewater, President of Council in the Marches of Wales; Th. Milward, kt., Justice of Chester; Timothy Turneur & J. Platt, Justices of Great Sessions; Rich. Philipps, Bt.; J. Stepney, Bt.; Marmaduke Lloyd, kt.; Sampson Eure; J. Wogan; Alban Owen; J. Laugharne; Hugh Owen; Th. Price; H. Lort; Griffith White; Hugh Bowen; Arthur Owen; Evan Owen, B.D., Judge of Admiralty in South Wales; Geo. Bowen; J. Philipps; Th. Warren; J. Elliott; Owen Edwards: Wales 4/787/1.   (26)

1640: 30 November
Commission renewed to *add* Roger Lort: Index 4212/p.415.

1641: 4 March
Commission renewed to *add* Lewis Barlow; J. Gunter: Index 4212/p.433.

1641: 22 June
*J., Lord Finch, Keeper of Great Seal; *London; *Manchester, Keeper of
Privy Seal; *p E. of Pembroke; *Bridgewater, President of Council in the
Marches of Wales; *Milward, Justice of Chester; *Turneur & *Platt,
Justices of Great Sessions; *Rich. Philipps, Bt.; *J. Stepney, Bt.; *Marma-
duke Lloyd, kt.; *Sampson Eure; *Rich. Lloyd; *W. Morgan; *J. Wogan;
*Alban Owen; *J. Laugharne; *Hugh Owen; *Th. Price; *Roger Lort;
Griffith White; Hugh Bowen; J. Gunter; Arthur Owen; Lewis Barlow;
*J. Elliott; *Evan Owen, B.D., Judge of Admiralty; Geo. Bowen; *J.
Philipps; Th. Warren of Trewern; J. Edwards: C.66/2858/m.20d. Com-
mission renewed to *add* J. Edwards: Index 4212/p.454. (Note that there is
some doubt as to the exact date of the present commission. The membership
of the commission tallies with the names of those who were added to it in
late 1640 and early 1641, but on the other hand Lord Finch left office as
Keeper of the Great Seal in January 1641 in favour of Sir Edward Littleton
and the Bishop of London left office as Treasurer in May 1641). (31)

1643: 1 April
Commission renewed to *add* E. of Carbery as *custos rotulorum*; Lodowick
Lewis as King's attorney; J. Barlow of Slebech; J. Lloyd of Trerach; Rich.
Bowen; Sampson Lort, and to *omit* Hugh Owen, Bt.; Griffith White;
Arthur Owen; J. Gunter; Geo. Bowen: Index 4212/p.549 & Index 4210/
p.11. (David Jenkins who was appointed as Justice of Great Sessions on
11 March in place of J. Platt, (Index 4210/p.7) was probably also added on
this date).

1647: 10 April
Commission renewed to appoint E. of Pembroke as *custos rotulorum*: Index
4213/p.84. (W. Powell and J. Clark who were appointed as Justices of
Great Sessions on 20 and 22 March, were probably also added on this date:
Index 4213/p.82).

1647: 27 September (Acting)
E. of Pembroke; W. Powell & J. Clark, Justices of Great Sessions; Rich.
Philipps, Bt.; Jas. Lewis; Griffith White; Th. Price; Roger Lort; Arthur
Owen; J. Elliott; Geo. Bowen; Th. Warren; Lewis Barlow; W. Philipps;
Th. Bowen; Herbert Perrot; Sampson Lort: Wales 4/787/4. (17)

1649: 6 March
*W. Lenthall, Speaker of House of Commons; *Lord Fairfax; *J. Bradshaw;
*Bulstrode Whitelock, *Rich. Keble, *J. Lisle, Commissioners of Great
Seal; *E. of Pembroke; *H. Rolle, Chief Justice of Upper Bench; *W.
Powell & *J. Clark, Justices of Great Sessions; *Erasmus Philipps, Bt.;
*Jas. Lewis; *Th. Price; *Roger Lort; *J. Elliott; *Herbert Perrot; Sampson

Lort; H. White; Rich. Lehunt; *Th. Wogan; Walter Cuny: C.193/13/3/f.80.
Commission renewed on 6 March (no details): Index 4213/p.143.   (21)

1649: 23 March (Acting)
As on 6 March 1649, except: J. Bradshaw, *omitted* (probably in error):
Wales 4/788/1.   (20)

1650: 9 March
Commission renewed to *appoint* E. of Pembroke as *custos rotulorum,* and to
add Th. Harrison; Jas. Philipps; W. Barbar; J. Mathias; Maurice Morgan:
Index 4213/p.179.

1650: 25 July
*Lenthall; *Oliver Cromwell, Lord General; *Bradshaw; *Whitelock,
*Keble & *Lisle; *p E. of Pembroke; *Rolle; *Powell & *Clark, Justices
of Great Sessions; *Th. Harrison; *Ed. Freeman, attorney-general in South
Wales; *Erasmus Philipps, Bt.; *Roger Lort; *Jas. Philipps; *Sampson
Lort; *H. White; *Herbert Perrot; *Jas, Lewis; *Th. Parry; *J. Mathias;
*Th. Jones; Maurice Morgan: *Lists published by Th. Walkley* (1650), p.70
& B.M., Stowe Ms. 577/f.68. Commission renewed to *add* Jas. Philipps;
Th. Parry; Th. Jones, and to *omit* J. Elliott; Rich. Lehunt; Th. Wogan;
Walter Cuny; W. Barbar: Index 4213/p.196. (Note that it is not clear why
Jas. Philipps was added on this date since his inclusion in the commission
had already been ordered on 9 March).   (23)

1650: 19 August (Acting)
As on 25 July 1650, except: Sampson Lort (Sheriff, 1649–50), *omitted*:
Wales 4/788/2.   (22)

1650: 16 September (Acting)
As on 19 August 1650: Wales 4/788/3.   (22)

1652: 22 July
*Lenthall; *Cromwell; *Whitelock, *Keble & *Lisle; *p E. of Pembroke;
*Bradshaw; *Rolle; *Powell & *Clark, Justices of Great Sessions; *Th.
Harrison; *Erasmus Philipps, Bt.; *Hugh Owen, Bt.; *Roger Lort; *Ed.
Freeman, attorney-general in South Wales; *Jas. Philipps; *Sampson Lort;
*H. White; *Herbert Perrot; *Jas. Lewis; *W. Philipps; Lewis Barlow;
J. Elliott; *Maurice Canon; *Th. Parry; Jas. Price; J. Horsey; *J. Mathias;
*Th. Jones; Maurice Morgan; Th. Owen; J. Lloyd: Cambridge University
Ms. Dd.VIII.1/f.131 & C.193/13/4/f.125. Commission renewed to *add*
W. Philipps; Lewis Barlow; J. Elliott; Maurice Canon; Jas. Price; J.
Horsey: Index 4213/p.242. (Note that, although there is no specific reference
in the Docquet Book, it is likely that Th. Owen and J. Lloyd were also
added on this date).   (32)

1652: 6 September (Acting)
As on 22 July 1652, except: Hugh Owen, Bt.; Roger Lort (Sheriff, 1651–2);
Th. Owen; J. Lloyd, *omitted*: Wales 4/788/5. (Some of these omissions may
be in error, but there is no certain way of deciding this).   (28)

1653: 20 August (Acting)
As on 6 September 1652, except: J. Haggatt, Justice of Great Sessions; Edm. Jones, attorney-general in South Wales; Roger Lort, *added*. W. Powell; J. Clark; J. Horsey, *omitted*: Wales 4/788/6. (J. Haggatt was appointed as Justice of Great Sessions on 12 July 1653: Index 4213/p.260). (28)

1654: 4 March
Commission renewed according to a general list: Index 4213/p.284.

1654: 15 March (Acting)
Whitelock, Keble & Lisle; Rolle; W. Lenthall, Master of Rolls; Oliver St. John, Chief Justice of Common Bench; J. Haggatt, Justice of Great Sessions; Edm. Prideaux, Attorney-General; Erasmus Philipps, Bt.; Roger Lort; Edm. Jones, attorney-general in South Wales; Jas. Philipps; Sampson Lort; Herbert Perrot; Jas. Lewis; J. Ireton, Alderman of the City of London; J. Humphreys; J. Elliott; Maurice Canon; Th. Parry; Th. Jones; J. Lloyd; J. Mathias; Th. Knowles; Geo. Hayward; Rich Castell; Maurice Morgan; Th. Owen; Geo. William Griffith: Wales 4/789/1. (This presumably represents the commission as renewed on 4 March even though the Great Session for which the present Gaol File list was drawn up followed very closely). (29)

1654: 21 August (Acting)
As on 15 March 1654, except: Bennet Hoskins, Justice of Great Sessions, *added*. Rich. Keble; Th. Jones, *omitted*: Wales 4/789/2. (28)

1655: 2 April (Acting)
As on 21 August 1654, except: Rich. Keble; Hugh Owen, Bt., *added*. Maurice Canon; Geo. William Griffith, *omitted*: Wales 4/789/3. (Note that in the list of justices for Haverfordwest, which is of the same date and contained in the same file, Keble's place is taken by Th. Widdrington, kt.). (28)

1655: 20 August (Acting)
As on 2 April 1655, except: Th. Widdrington, kt., Commissioner of the Great Seal, *added*. Rich. Keble; J. Ireton, *omitted*: Wales 4/789/4. (Ireton's omission is probably an error). (27)

1656: 20 March
Commission renewed to *add* Major-General Jas. Berry; Rowland Dawkins; Arthur Owen; Th. Wogan of Llanstinan, and to *omit* Maurice Canon; Th. Owen; Th. Jones; J. Mathias; Maurice Morgan; Geo. William Griffith: Index 4213/p.330. (Note that Canon and Geo. William Griffith had been prematurely omitted in the Gaol File list of 2 April 1655).

1656: 22 July
*Nathaniel Fiennes & *J. Lisle, Commissioners of Great Seal; *Bulstrode Whitelock, kt., *Th. Widdrington, kt., *Ed. Montagu & *W. Sydenham, Commissioners of Treasury; *Philip Jones; *J. Glynn, Chief Justice of Upper Bench; *W. Lenthall, Master of the Rolls; *Oliver St. John, Chief

Justice of Common Bench; *J. Haggatt & *Bennet Hoskins, Justices of Great Sessions; *Edm. Prideaux, Attorney-General; *Major-General Jas. Berry; *Erasmus Philipps, Bt.; *Hugh Owen, Bt.; *Roger Lort; *Edm. Jones, attorney-general in South Wales; *Rowland Dawkins; *p Jas. Philipps; *Arthur Owen; *Sampson Lort; *Herbert Perrot; *Jas. Lewis; *J. Ireton, Alderman of London; *J. Humphreys; *Th. Parry; *J. Lloyd; *Th. Wogan of Llanstinan; *Jas. ap Rice; *H. White; J. Elliott; Th. Knowles; Geo. Hayward; Rich. Castell; Rich. Brown; Rees Williams: C.193/13/6/f.110v & C.193/13/5/f.131v. Commission renewed to *add* Jas. ap Rice; H. White; Rich. Brown; Rees Williams: Index 4213/p.345. (37)

1657: 20 March (Acting)
As on 22 July 1656: Wales 4/790/1. (37)

1657: 31 August (Acting)
As on 20 March 1657, except: H. White (Sheriff in 1657), *omitted*: Wales 4/790'2. (36)

1658: 2 August
Commission renewed to *add* W. Scourfield; Isaac Lloyd; Jas. Lloyd; J. Protherough; Th. Cozen: Index 4213/p.402.

1658: 6 September (Acting)
As on 31 August 1657, except: W. Scourfield; Isaac Lloyd; Jas. Lloyd; J. Protherough; Th. Cozen, *added*. Jas. ap Rice; H. White, Rich. Castell, *omitted*: Wales 4/790/4. (38)

1658: 24 September
General renewal of Welsh commissions to *add* Rich. Cromwell, Lord Protector: Index 4213/p.405.

1659: 28 June
Commission renewed according to a general list: Index 4213/p.435.

1659: 8 August (Acting)
W. Lenthall, Speaker; J. Bradshaw, Th. Tyrrell & J. Fountain, Commissioners of Great Seal; J. Haggatt, Justice of Great Sessions; Erasmus Philipps, Bt.; Th. Wogan; Jas. Lewis; Roger Lort; J. Elliott senior; H. White; Herbert Perrot; Sampson Lort; Rich. Castell; Th. Knowles; J. Lort; J. Elliott junior; Griffith Davies; Rowland Wogan; W. Scourfield; Th. Lloyd; Rich. Brown: Wales 4/790/5. (22)

1660: 27 March
Commission renewed according to a general list: Index 4213/p.459.

1660: post 8 September
*Ed. Hyde, kt., Chancellor; *E. of Southampton, Treasurer (appointed on 8 September); *D. of Albemarle; *Marquess of Ormond, Steward; *E. of Lindsey, Great Chamberlain; *E. of Manchester, Household Chamberlain; *p E. of Pembroke; *E. of Carbery; *W. Morton, kt. & *Simon Degg,

Justices of Great Sessions; *Erasmus Philipps, Bt.; *J. Stepney, Bt.; *Hugh Owen, kt. & Bt.; *Essex Meyrick; *Rowland Laugharne; *Roger Lort; *Arthur Owen; H. White; Hugh Butler; *Lewis Barlow; *W. Scourfield; *Herbert Perrot; Hugh Bowen; *W. Philipps; *Th. Parry; *Lewis Morgan; Jas. Bowen; Th. Owen; Geo. Hayward; *Isaac Lloyd; Th. Warren; Th. Wogan of Llanstinan; Jas. Lloyd; *J. Mathias: C.220/9/4/f.112 & B.M., Egerton Ms. 2557/f.111.   (34)

1661: 8 November
As at the end of 1660, except: *Lord Robartes, Keeper of Privy Seal, *added:* C.193/12/3/f.127. General renewal of Welsh commissions to *add* E. of Carbery, President of Council in the Marches of Wales: Index 4214/p.144. (In the case of Pembroke, the E. of Carbery was already a member of the commission before his promotion).   (35)

1662: 17 July
*E. of Clarendon (Ed. Hyde), Chancellor; *Southampton; *Lord Robartes, Keeper of Privy Seal; *Albemarle; *Ormond; *Lindsey; *Manchester; *E. of Carbery, President of Council in the Marches of Wales; *p E. of Pembroke; *Morton & *Degg, Justices of Great Sessions; *Erasmus Philipps, Bt.; *J. Stepney, Bt.; *Hugh Owen, kt. & Bt.; *Roger Lort; *Herbert Perrot, kt.; *Essex Meyrick; *Rowland Laugharne; *Arthur Owen; *Hugh Butler; *Lewis Barlow; *W. Scourfield; Hugh Bowen; *W. Philipps; *Th. Parry; *Lewis Morgan; Jas. Bowen; Geo. Hayward; *Ed. Freeman; *Rich. Walter; W. Mordant; Th. Wogan of Llanstinan; J. Laugharne; Jas. Lloyd; Th. Powell; Th. Corbet: C.66/2986/m.33d. Commission renewed to *add* Ed. Freeman; Rich. Walter; W. Mordant; J. Laugharne of Llanerthen; Th. Powell of Greenhill; Th. Corbet: Index 4214/p.178.   (36)

1663: 6 April (Acting)
As on 17 July 1662, except: H. White, *added.* Roger Lort; W. Scourfield (Sheriff, 1662–3), *omitted*: Wales 4/792/1. (Note that H. White was included in the commission at the end of 1660. Since there is no record evidence that he was deliberately omitted from the commission after that time it is likely that his omission from the enrolment of the 17 July 1662 commission was an error).   (35)

1663: 27 July
As on 6 April 1663, except: *Job Charlton, kt., Justice of Chester; *J. Lort, kt. & Bt.; *W. Scourfield, *added.* Th. Powell, *omitted*: C.66/3022/m.37d. Commission renewed to *add* J. Lort, kt. & Bt.: Index 4214/p.211.   (37)

1664: 29 July (Acting)
Clarendon; Southampton; Robartes; Albemarle; Ormond; Lindsey; Manchester; Carbery, President of Council in the Marches of Wales; Pembroke; Morton & Degg, Justices of Great Sessions; Erasmus Philips, Bt.; J. Stepney, Bt.; J. Lort, kt. & Bt.; Herbert Perrot, kt.; Essex Meyrick; Rowland Laugharne; Arthur Owen; H. White; Hugh Butler; Lewis Barlow; W. Scourfield; Hugh Bowen; W. Philipps; Th. Parry; Lewis Morgan; Jas. Bowen; Geo.

Hayward; Ed. Freeman; Rich. Walter; W. Mordant; Th. Wogan of Llanstinan; J. Laugharne; Jas. Lloyd; Th. Corbet: Wales 4/792/3. (Note that Job Charlton, kt., Justice of Chester, is not included). (35)

1664: 26 September (Acting)
As on 29 July 1664, except: Hugh Butler, *omitted*: Wales 4/792/4. (34)

1665: 22 February
Commission renewed to *omit* Essex Meyrick; H. White; Index 4214/p.253.

1665: 12 May
Commission renewed to *add* Hugh Owen: Index 4214/p.259.

1665: 12 August (Acting)
As on 26 September 1664, except: Job Charlton, kt., Justice of Chester; Hugh Owen, kt. & Bt.; Hugh Owen; Walter Vaughan of Slebech; Th. Lloyd of Morvil, *added*. Essex Meyrick; H. White; Geo. Hayward, *omitted*: Wales 4/792/5. (36)

1665: 30 August (Acting)
Clarendon; Southampton; Robartes; Albemarle; Ormond; Lindsey; Manchester; Carbery, President of Council in the Marches of Wales; Pembroke; Job Charlton, kt., serjeant at law, Justice of Chester; Morton & Degg, Justices of Great Sessions; Erasmus Philipps, Bt.; J. Stepney, Bt.; Hugh Owen, kt. & Bt.; J. Lort, kt. & Bt.; Herbert Perrot, kt.; Hugh Owen; Rowland Laugharne; Arthur Owen; Walter Vaughan of Slebech; Lewis Barlow; W. Scourfield; Hugh Bowen; W. Philipps; Th. Parry; Lewis Morgan; Jas. Bowen; Ed. Freeman; Rich. Walter; W. Mordant; Th. Lloyd of Morvil; Th. Wogan of Llanstinan; J. Laugharne; Jas. Lloyd; Th. Corbet: Wales 4/787/2. (Note that this file is wrongly indexed as belonging to 17 Charles I). (36)

1666: 18 July
Commission renewed to *add* Fred. Hyde, kt., serjeant at law, as Justice of Great Sessions in place of W. Morton: Index 4214/p.289.

1666: 20 August (Acting)
As on 30 August 1665, except: Fred. Hyde, kt., Justice of Great Sessions; Hugh Butler; Geo. Hayward, *added*. W. Morton; Herbert Perrot (Sheriff, 1665-6), *omitted*: Wales 4/793/1. (Note that Butler and Hayward had probably been left out in error from the Gaol File list of 30 August 1665 and that Perrot was probably wrongly omitted from the present list). (37)

1667: 19 July (Acting)
As on 20 August 1666: Wales 4/793/2. (37)

1667: 26 August (Acting)
As on 19 July 1667, except: Herbert Perrot, kt., *added*. Wales 4/793/3. (38)

1668: 7 August (Acting)
Southampton; Robartes; Albemarle; Ormond; Lindsey; Manchester; Carbery, President of Council in the Marches of Wales; Pembroke; Charlton, Justice of Chester; Fred. Hyde, kt. & Simon Degg, Justices of Great Sessions; Erasmus Philipps, Bt.; J. Stepney, Bt.; Hugh Owen, kt. & Bt.; J. Lort, kt. & Bt.; Herbert Perrot, kt.; Hugh Owen; Rowland Laugharne; Arthur Owen; Hugh Butler; Walter Vaughan; W. Scourfield; Hugh Bowen; W. Philipps; Th. Parry; Lewis Morgan; Jas. Bowen; Geo. Hayward; Ed. Freeman; Rich. Walter; W. Mordant; Th. Lloyd of Morvil; Th. Wogan; Jas. Lloyd; J. Laugharne; Th. Corbet: Wales 4/793/4.   (36)

1668: 25 August (Acting)
As on 7 August 1668, except: Lewis Barlow, *added*: Wales 4/793/5.   (37)

1669: 12 April (Acting)
As on 25 August 1668, except: Hugh Butler; Walter Vaughan; Geo. Hayward; Th. Wogan; Lewis Barlow, *omitted*: Wales 4/793/6. (The first four men are probably correctly omitted at this point since marginal comments on the Gaol File lists of 1668 give them as dead. Lewis Barlow is probably omitted in error).   (32)

1669: 30 August (Acting)
As on 12 April 1668, except: Hugh Butler; Walter Vaughan; Geo. Hayward; Th. Wogan, *added*. (See note above). Th. Lloyd of Morvil, *omitted*: Wales 4/793/7.   (35).

1670: 11 March
Commission renewed to *add* E. of Pembroke as *custos rotulorum*: Index 4214/p.363. (This is W. Herbert, E. of Pembroke, who succeeded his father, Philip, in December 1669. Note that the absence of any renewal of the Pembrokeshire commission of the peace between 18 July 1666 and 11 March 1670 makes it very difficult to be sure of the true state of the commission in these years).

1670: 11 April (Acting)
As on 30 August 1669, except: Lewis Barlow; Th. Lloyd of Morvil, *added*. D. of Albemarle; Hugh Butler; Walter Vaughan; Geo. Hayward; Th. Wogan, *omitted*: Wales 4/794/1.   (32)

1670: 1 August (Acting)
As on 11 April 1670, except: D. of Albemarle, *added*. E. of Southampton, *omitted*: Wales 4/794/2. (Note that Albemarle died in January 1670 and that his restoration to the Gaol File list is an error. It is unlikely that his son was added in his place since the latter did not hold the office of General which had ensured his father's position on the commission. Southampton had in fact died in 1667 and should have been left out well before this).   (32)

1671: 17 April (Acting)
As on 1 August 1760, except: E. of Southampton, *added*. (See note above); D. of Albemarle; Hugh Owen; J. Laugharne; Jas. Bowen (Sheriff, 1670–1), *omitted*: Wales 4/794/3. (Note that the omission of Laugharne is probably incorrect since he reappears in the next Gaol File list).   (29)

1671: 25 July
Commission renewed to *add* Lewis Wogan; J. Lort; Rich. Philipps; Maurice Wogan; Griffith Dawes: Index 4214/p.398.

1671: 9 September (Acting)
Orlando Bridgeman, kt. & Bt., Keeper of Great Seal; D. of Buckingham; Ormond; Lindsey; E. of St. Albans, Household Chamberlain; Carbery, President of Council in the Marches of Wales; Pembroke; B. of St. Davids; Charlton, Justice of Chester; Hyde & Degg, Justices of Great Sessions; Erasmus Philipps, Bt.; J. Stepney, Bt.; Hugh Owen, Bt.; J. Lort, kt. & Bt.; Herbert Perrot, kt.; Essex Meyrick; Rowland Laugharne; Arthur Owen; Hugh Butler; Isaac Lloyd; Lewis Wogan of Boulston; W. Scourfield; Hugh Bowen; W. Philipps; Th. Parry; Lewis Morgan; Jas. Bowen; Ed. Freeman; Walter Middleton; Rich. Walter; J. Lort; W. Mordant; Rich. Philipps; Th. Lloyd of Morvil; Griffith Dawes; Th. Wogan of Llanstinan; Maurice Wogan; J. Laugharne; Th. Jones; Jas. Lloyd; Th. Corbet: Wales 4/794/4.   (42)

1672: 19 January
Commission renewed to *add* Rowland Laugharne of St. Brides; David Morgan of Coed Lloyd; W. Owen of Henllys; Arthur Laugharne of Llanrheithan: Index 4214/p.406.

1672: 1 April (Acting)
As on 9 September 1671, except: Rowland Laugharne; David Morgan; W. Owen; Arthur Laugharne, *added*. Lewis Wogan (Sheriff, 1671–2); Rich. Walter; J. Laugharne, *omitted*: Wales 4/794/5.   (43)

1672: 2 September (Acting)
As on 1 April 1672: Wales 4/794/6.   (43)

1673: 14 July (Acting)
As on 2 September 1672, except: Lewis Wogan of Boulston, *added*. J. Lort, Bt.; Hugh Butler; Th. Wogan of Llanstinan; J. Lort, Esq., *omitted*: Wales 4/794/7.   (40)

1673: 3 December
Commission renewed to *add* J. Thomas; W. Meare: Index 4214/p.467.

1674: 25 May (Acting)
As on 14 July 1673, except: Heneage Finch, kt. & Bt., Keeper of Great Seal; Viscount Latimer, Treasurer; E. of Anglesey, Keeper of Privy Seal; Marquess of Worcester, President of Wales; J. Thomas of Haverfordwest; W. Meare, *added*. Orlando Bridgeman; Maurice Wogan; Th. Parry, *omitted*: Wales 4/794/9. (All the additions were presumably made at the renewal of the commission on 3 December 1673).   (43)

1674: 29 July
Commission renewed to *add* E. of Pembroke as *custos rotulorum*: Index 4214/p.481. (W. Herbert, E. of Pembroke, died on 8 July 1674 and was succeeded by his half-brother, Philip Herbert).

1674: 12 September (Acting)
Heneage Finch, kt. & Bt., Keeper of Great Seal; Lord Latimer, Treasurer; E. of Anglesey, Keeper of Privy Seal; Buckingham; Ormond; Marquess of Worcester, President of Council in the Marches of Wales; Lindsey; St. Albans; Pembroke; Carbery; B. of St. Davids; Charlton, Justice of Chester; Fred. Hyde, kt. & Francis Manley, Justices of Great Sessions; Simon Degg, kt.; Erasmus Philipps, Bt.; J. Stepney, Bt.; Hugh Owen, Bt.; Herbert Perrot, kt.; Essex Meyrick; Rowland Laugharne; Arthur Owen; Rowland Laugharne of St. Brides; Isaac Lloyd; David Morgan of Coed Lloyd; J. Thomas of Haverfordwest; Lewis Wogan of Boulston; W. Scourfield; Arthur Laugharne; Hugh Bowen; W. Philipps; W. Owen; Ed. Freeman; Lewis Morgan; Jas. Bowen; Walter Middleton; Th. Corbet; W. Mordant; Rich. Philipps; Th. Lloyd; Jas. Lloyd; Th. Jones; Griffith Dawes; W. Meare of Eastington: Wales 4/795/1. (44)

1675: 28 June
Commission renewed to *add* David Williams of Hean Castle: Index 4214/p.497.

1676: 15 May (Acting)
As on 12 September 1674, except: D. of Monmouth; E. of Arlington, Household Chamberlain; David Williams, *added*. E. of St. Albans; Simon Degg; Rowland Laugharne (the first of that name on the 1674 list); Isaac Lloyd, *omitted*: Wales 4/795/4. (Laugharne and Lloyd were probably left out in error since both reappear later). (43)

1676: 28 August (Acting)
As on 15 May 1676, except: J. Stepney, Bt.; Th. Jones, *omitted*: Wales 4/795/5. (Th. Jones may be wrongly omitted since he reappears later. Stepney is probably correctly left out since he died at about this time, the exact date being unknown: see *Dictionary of Welsh Biography*, p.924). (41)

1677: 7 August
Commission renewed to *add* Geo. Owen, D.D.: Index 4214/p.532.

1677: 3 September (Acting)
Finch; E. of Danby, Treasurer; Anglesey; Buckingham; Albemarle; Ormond; Marquess of Worcester, President of Council in the Marches of Wales; Lindsey; E. of Arlington, Household Chamberlain; Pembroke; Carbery; B. of St. Davids; Charlton, Justice of Chester; Francis Manley & W. Buckby, Justices of Great Sessions; Erasmus Philipps, Bt.; J. Stepney, Bt.; Hugh Owen, Bt.; Herbert Perrot, kt.; Lewis Meyrick, Attorney-General in Wales; Essex Meyrick; Rowland Laugharne; Arthur Owen; Rowland Laugharne of St. Brides; David Morgan of Coed Lloyd; Isaac Lloyd; J. Thomas of Haverfordwest; Lewis Wogan of Boulston; W. Scourfield;

Arthur Laugharne; Hugh Bowen; W. Philipps; W. Owen; Lewis Morgan; Jas. Bowen; Ed. Freeman; Walter Middleton; Th. Corbet; W. Mordant; Rich. Philipps; Geo. Owen, D.D.; Th. Lloyd of Morvil; Griffith Dawes; W. Meare of Eastington; David Williams of Hean Castle; Maurice Wogan; Jas. Lloyd; Th. Jones: Wales 4/795/7. (Note that J. Stepney, Bt., was probably dead by the time this list was drawn up). (48)

1677: 28 November
Commission renewed to *add* J. Barlow, Bt.; Th. Canon; Th. Hayward; Griffith Hawkwell: Index 4214/p.535.

1678: 25 March (Acting)
As on 3 September 1677, except: J. Barlow, Bt.; Th. Hayward; Griffith Hawkwell, *added*. B. of St. Davids; Job Charlton; Rowland Laugharne of St. Brides; Isaac Lloyd; Jas. Bowen; Maurice Wogan; Th. Jones, *omitted*: Wales 4/795/8. (44)

1678: 23 July
Commission renewed to *add* J. Owen of Trecwn: Index 4214/p.547.

1678: 2 September (Acting)
As on 25 March 1678, except: J. Stepney, Bt., *omitted* (see earlier note): Wales 4/795/9. (The new commission containing J. Owen had probably not arrived in time to form the basis of the present Gaol File list). (43)

1679: 21 April (Acting)
As on 2 September 1678, except: B. of St. Davids; Job Charlton, Justice of Chester, *added*. E. of Danby; Arthur Owen; W. Owen, *omitted*: Wales 4/796/1. (Charlton was wrongly omitted from the list of 25 March 1678). (42)

1680: 20 April
*Prince Rupert; *Archbishop of Canterbury; *Lord Finch, Chancellor; *E. of Radnor, President of Council; *E. of Anglesey, Keeper of Privy Seal; Dukes of *Albemarle, *Monmouth, *Newcastle, *Lauderdale, *Ormond; *Marquess of Winchester; *Marquess of Worcester, President of Council in the Marches of Wales; Earls of *Lindsey, *Arlington, *Salisbury, *Bridgewater, *Essex, *Sunderland, *p Pembroke, *Bath, *Halifax, *Carbery; *Viscount Fauconberg; Bishops of *London, *St. Davids; *Laurence Hyde; *H. Coventry; *Francis North, kt., Chief Justice of the Bench; *J. Ernley, kt., Chancellor of Exchequer; *Th. Chichley, kt., Chancellor of Duchy of Lancaster; *W. Temple, Bt.; *Daniel Finch; *Ed. Seymour; *Leoline Jenkins; *Sidney Godolphin; *Francis Manley & *W. Buckby, Justices of Great Sessions; *Erasmus Philipps, Bt.; *J. Stepney, Bt.; *Hugh Owen, Bt.; *J. Barlow, Bt.; *Herbert Perrot, kt.; *Lewis Meyrick, King's attorney in Wales; *Essex Meyrick; *Arthur Owen; *Rowland Laugharne of St. Brides; *Isaac Lloyd; *J. Canon; *David Morgan of Coed Lloyd; *J. Thomas of Haverfordwest; *Lewis Wogan of Boulston; *W. Scourfield; Arthur Laugharne; Hugh Bowen; *W. Philipps; W. Owen; Lewis Morgan; Jas. Bowen; *Ed. Freeman; *Walter Middleton;

*Th. Corbet; W. Mordant; Th. Hayward; *Griffith Hawkwell; *Rich. Philipps; *Geo. Owen, D.D.; *Th. Lloyd of Morvil; *J. Owen of Trecwn; *Griffith Dawes; *W. Meare of Eastington; *Lewis Barlow; *Hector Phillips; *David Williams of Hean Castle; Th. Jones; *Jas. Lloyd: C.193/12/4/f.155v. Commission renewed to *omit* recusants (no details): Index 4215/p.27. (The *removal* from the Pembroke commission of the Duke of Buckingham; Rowland Laugharne; Maurice Wogan was ordered by a warrant of 5 February 1680 and the *addition* of Lewis Barlow; Hector Phillips by a warrant of the same date: *H.M.C., Eleventh Report, Appendix,* Part 2, p.188. Rowland Laugharne should not be confused with his name-sake, Rowland Laugharne of St. Brides, who remained on the commission in 1680. On the evidence of Gaol File lists Maurice Wogan appears already to have left the commission by 1678 but in view of the measures to remove him in 1680 this must be an error).   (75)

1680: 23 August (Acting)
As on 20 April 1680, except: Job Charlton, kt., Justice of Chester, *added*. J. Thomas of Haverfordwest; Isaac Lloyd; W. Owen; Jas. Bowen; Lewis Barlow, *omitted*: Wales 4/796/3. (Note that Charlton should not be included at this date since he was removed from office in April 1680).   (71)

1680: 13 September (Acting)
As on 23 August 1680, except: Lewis Barlow, *added*: Wales 4/796/4. (Barlow should probably have been included in the 23 August list).   (72)

1681: 26 December
Commission renewed to *add* Jas. ap Rice: Index 4215/p.58.

1682: 17 April (Acting)
As on 13 September 1680, except: Chas., Lord Herbert; W. Owen; Jas. ap Rice, *added*. D. of Monmouth; Earls of Salisbury, Sunderland, Essex; W. Temple; Job Charlton; Rich. Philipps; Lewis Barlow, *omitted*: Wales 4/797/1.   (67)

1682: 14 August (Acting)
As on 17 April 1682, except: Th. Chichley; Ed. Seymour; Leoline Jenkins; J. Stepney; W. Owen; Th. Hayward, *omitted*: Wales 4/797/2. (The first three names are omitted in error).   (61)

1683: 2 April (Acting)
As on 14 August 1682, except: Th. Chichley; Ed. Seymour; Leoline Jenkins, *added*. Prince Rupert; E. of Nottingham (Lord Finch); D. of Lauderdale; David Williams (Sheriff, 1682–3), *omitted*: Wales 4/797/3.   (60)

1683: 3 September (Acting)
As on 2 April 1683, except: J. Barlow; Herbert Perrot, *omitted*: Wales 4/797/4. (Barlow's name is probably left out in error).   (58)

1683: 5 October
Commission renewed to *add* E. of Pembroke as *custos rotulorum*: Index 4215/p.91. (Philip Herbert, E. of Pembroke, died in August 1683 and was succeeded by his brother Thomas).

1684: 5 May (Acting)
As on 3 September 1683, except: D. of Lauderdale; J. Barlow, Bt.; David Williams, *added*. Ed. Seymour; Leoline Jenkins; Th. Chichley; Th. Corbet; W. Mordant; J. Owen (Sheriff, 1683-4), *omitted*: Wales 4/797/5. (Note that Lauderdale had been dead since 1682. There is no reason to suppose that all of the names here omitted were correctly left out).   (55)

1685: 9 March
Commission renewed to reappoint E. of Pembroke as *custos rotulorum*: Index 4215/p.122. (Anth. Farrington who was appointed as Justice of Great Sessions in place of Francis Manley on 13 February (ibid./p.117), was probably also added on this date. Note that, as in the years 1666 to 1670, there are very few renewals of the commission of the peace between 1680 and 1685 and it is therefore very hard to discover the true state of the commission. In the absence of other sources it is impossible to be certain which changes in the commission are genuine and which are merely errors on the part of the clerk who drew up the *nomina ministrorum* for insertion in the Gaol File at each Great Session).

1685: 30 March (Acting)
Archbishop of Canterbury; Lord Guilford, Keeper of Great Seal; E. of Rochester, Treasurer; Marquess of Halifax, President of Council; E. of Clarendon, Keeper of Privy Seal; Dukes of Albemarle, Newcastle, Ormond; D. of Beaufort, President of Council in the Marches of Wales; Marquesses of Winchester, Worcester; E. of Lindsey, Great Chamberlain; E. of Arlington, Household Chamberlain; Earls of Bridgewater, Sunderland, Pembroke, Bath, Nottingham, Carbery; Viscount Fauconberg; Bishops of London, St. Davids; Sidney, Lord Godolphin; H. Coventry; J. Ernley, kt., Chancellor of Exchequer; Th. Chichley, kt., Chancellor of Duchy of Lancaster; Ed. Seymour; Leoline Jenkins; Geo. Jeffreys, kt. & Bt., Chief Justice; W. Buckby & Anth. Farrington, Justices of Great Sessions; Erasmus Philipps, Bt.; Hugh Owen, Bt.; J. Barlow, Bt.; Lewis Meyrick, Attorney-General in Wales; Essex Meyrick; Arthur Owen; Rowland Laugharne of St. Brides; J. Canon; Lewis Wogan of Boulston; W. Scourfield; Arthur Laugharne; Hugh Bowen; W. Philipps; Lewis Morgan; Walter Middleton; Th. Corbet; W. Mordant; Griffith Hawkwell; Geo. Owen, D.D.; Th. Lloyd of Morvil; J. Owen of Trecwn; Griffith Dawes; W. Meare of Eastington; Hector Phillips; David Williams of Hean Castle; Jas. ap Rice; Jas. Lloyd: Wales 4/798/1.   (58).

1685: 31 August (Acting)
As on 30 March 1685, except: Leoline Jenkins, *omitted*: Wales 4/798/2.   (57)

1685: post 28 September
As on 31 August 1685, except: E. of Mulgrave, Household Chamberlain, *added*. Lord Guilford; Marquess of Halifax; E. of Arlington, *omitted*: C.193/12/5/f.182v. (Geo. Jeffreys, the former Chief Justice, was appointed Lord Chancellor on 28 September).   (55)

1686: 12 January
Commission renewed to *add* J. Philipps: Index 4215/p.142. (Th. Geers, who was appointed as Justice of Great Sessions in place of W. Buckby on 18 December 1685 (Index 4215/p.141), was probably also added on this date).

1686: 30 August (Acting)
As at the end of 1685, except: Ed. Herbert, kt., Chief Justice of King's Bench; Th. Geers, Justice of Great Sessions; J. Philipps, *added*. E. of Carbery; B. of St. Davids; W. Buckby; W. Meare of Eastington; Jas. ap Rice, *omitted*: Wales 4/798/4. (53)

1686: 17 December
By order of the Privy Council, Rob. Price and W. Barlow were to be *added* and Hugh Owen, Bt., and Hector Phillips, *omitted* from the Pembrokeshire commission: P.C.2/71/p.378.

1687: 14 March (Acting)
Canterbury; Lord Jeffreys, Chancellor; Rochester; Clarendon; Dukes of Albemarle, Newcastle, Ormond; D. of Beaufort, President of Council in the Marches of Wales; Marquesses of Winchester, Worcester; Lindsey; E. of Mulgrave, Household Chamberlain; Earls of Bridgewater, Sunderland, Pembroke, Bath, Nottingham; Viscount Fauconberg; Bishops of London, St. Davids; Lord Godolphin; H. Coventry; J. Ernley, kt., Chancellor of Exchequer; Th. Chichley, kt., Chancellor of Duchy of Lancaster; Ed. Herbert, kt., Chief Justice of Pleas *coram Rege*; Ed. Seymour; Anth. Farrington, Justice of Great Sessions; Erasmus Philipps, Bt.; Hugh Owen, Bt.; J. Barlow, Bt.; Lewis Meyrick, Attorney-General in Wales; Essex Meyrick; Arthur Owen; Rowland Laugharne of St. Brides; J. Canon; Lewis Wogan of Boulston; W. Scourfield; Arthur Laugharne; Hugh Bowen; W. Philipps; Walter Middleton; Th. Corbet; W. Mordant; Griffith Hawkwell; Geo. Owen, D.D.; Th. Lloyd of Morvil; J. Owen of Trecwn; Griffith Dawes; Hector Phillips; J. Philipps; J. Williams of Hean Castle; Jas. Lloyd: Wales 4/778/1. (Note that this file is wrongly indexed as belonging to the reign of James I. Note also that the changes in the commission ordered by the Privy Council in December 1686 have not yet been performed). (52)

1687: 29 August (Acting)
As on 14 March 1687, except: Marquess of Worcester, *omitted*: Wales 4/798/5. (51)

1687: 29 August
General renewal of Welsh commissions to add the clause of dispensation: Index 4215/p.179. (Edwin Wyatt, Justice of Great Sessions, who was appointed on 16 June (Index 4215/p.173), was probably added on this date. This renewal of the commission was of course too late to affect the composition of the Gaol File list of justices of the same date).

1688: 14 April
Commission renewed (no details): Index 4215/p.191.

1688: 27 August (Acting)

Canterbury; Jeffreys; E. of Sunderland, President of Council; Lord Arundell of Wardour, Keeper of Privy Seal; Dukes of Albemarle, Newcastle, Ormond; D. of Beaufort, President of Council in the Marches of Wales; Marquesses of Winchester, Powys, Worcester; Lindsey; Mulgrave; Earls of Bath, Nottingham, Middleton, Pembroke, Castlemaine; Viscounts Montgomery, Fauconberg, Preston; Bishops of Durham, St. Davids; Lords Belasyse, Dartmouth, Godolphin, Dover; J. Ernley, kt., Chancellor of Exchequer; Ed. Herbert, kt., Chief Justice; Edwin Wyatt, serjeant at law, Justice of Great Sessions; W. Barlow senior; Walter Middleton; Geo. Lort; Ed. Philipps; Th. Owen; W. Barlow junior; W. Skyrme; Jenkin Jones; J. Lewis; W. Warren; Geo. Meare: Wales 4/798/6. (41)

1688: 17 September (Acting)

As on 27 August 1688, except: J. Tate, Justice of Great Sessions, *added*. Wales 4/798/7. (42)

1688: 6 October

General renewal of Welsh commissions: Index 4215/p.200.

1689 11 June

Commission renewed (no details): Index 4215/p.228.

1689: 16 September (Acting)

Archbishop of Canterbury; J. Maynard, Anth. Keck & W. Rawlinson, kts., Commissioners of Great Seal; Marquess of Carmarthen, President of Council; Marquess of Halifax, Keeper of Privy Seal; D. of Norfolk; D. of Bolton; E. of Lindsey, Great Chamberlain; E. of Devonshire, Steward; E. of Dorset, Household Chamberlain; Earls of Oxford, Shrewsbury, Bedford, Bath, Pembroke; E. of Macclesfield, President of Council in the Marches of Wales; E. of Nottingham; J. Trenchard, kt., Justice of Chester; Erasmus Philipps, Bt.; Hugh Owen, Bt.; J. Barlow, Bt.; W. Wogan, Justice of Great Sessions; Ed. Philipps; Hector Phillips; Lewis Wogan of Wiston; Lewis Wogan of Boulston; Essex Meyrick; Arthur Owen; Rowland Laugharne; W. Scourfield; J. Owen of Trecwn; Griffith Dawes; Hugh Bowen; Geo. Lort; W. Skyrme; Hugh Wogan; David Williams; J. Williams; Th. Lloyd of Grove; J. Barlow; Griffith Hawkwell; Geo. Bowen; Jas. Lloyd; W. Warren; Chas. Philipps; J. Philipps; J. Lewis; Walter Middleton; W. Mordant; Th. Corbet; Arthur Laugharne: Wales 4/799/1. (52)

County & Borough of Haverfordwest

1555: (Acting)
Mayor of Haverfordwest; Arnold Butler; Rich. Taylor; J. Rastell; Rich. Howell; W. Owen: S.P.11/5/f.60.

1558-59 (Acting)
*Nich. Bacon, kt., Keeper of Great Seal; *Marquess of Winchester, Treasurer; *E. of Arundel, Steward; Bishops of *Bath & Wells, *Chester; *J. Throckmorton, Justice of Chester; *J. Vaughan, *Adam Mytton, kts.; *J. Scudamore of Holm; Chas. Fox; *J. Welsh; *Reg. Corbet; *W. Symonds; *W. Gerard; *Rich. Seaborne; *Mayor of Haverfordwest; *Arnold Butler; Rich. Taylor; *J. Rastell; *Rich. Howell; W. Owen; Rees ap Morgan; Th. Cathern: B.M., Lansdowne Ms. 1218/f.42v. (Except for the omission of the *ex officio* members of the commission, the same list also appears in S.P.12/2/17/p.76).

1561: (Acting)
*Bacon; *Winchester; *Arundel; *H. Sidney, kt., President of Council in the Marches of Wales; *J. Perrot, kt.; *Rich. Wye; *Mayor of Haverfordwest; *Th. Cathern; *Arnold Butler; Rich. Taylor; *J. Rastell, Hugh Harris; *Rees ap Morgan; W. Davies; *W. Morris Gwynn; Th. Brown: B.M., Lansdowne Ms. 1218/f.89.

1562: 13 June
As in 1561: C.66/985/m.41d.

1564: (Acting)
As on 13 June 1562: C.66/998/m.11d. (J. Perrot is marked as *custos rotulorum*).

1567: 31 May (Acting)
Bacon; Winchester; Arundel; Sidney, President of Council in the Marches of Wales; Rich. Wye, Justice of Great Sessions; Geo. Pynde, Mayor of Haverfordwest; J. Perrot, kt.; J. Rastell; Rees Morgan; Rich. Taylor; W. Morris Gwynn; Th. Brown: Wales 4/775/4.

1571: 28 May (Acting)
Bacon; Winchester; Arundel; Viscount Hereford; Sidney, President of Council in the Marches of Wales; J. Throckmorton, kt., Justice of Chester; J. Rastell, Justice of Great Sessions; J. Perrot, kt.; J. Voyle, Mayor of Haverfordwest; W. Morris Gwynn; Rich. Taylor; Rees Morgan; Geo. Pynde; J. David; Samuel Taylor: Wales 4/775/6.

1573: 28 September (Acting)
Bacon; Arundel; E. of Essex; Sidney, President of Council in the Marches of Wales; Throckmorton, Justice of Chester; Rastell, Justice of Great Sessions; J. Perrot, kt.; Rich. Taylor; Geo. Pynde; J. David; W. Gwynn, Mayor of Haverfordwest: Wales 4/776/1.

HAVERFORDWEST COUNTY AND BOROUGH, 1555 TO 1689

1573-4: (Acting)
*Bacon; *W., Lord Burghley, Treasurer; *Essex; *Sidney, President of Council in the Marches of Wales; *Hugh Cholmondeley, kt., Vice-President of Wales; *Throckmorton, Justice of Chester; *Mayor of Haverfordwest; *J. Perrot, kt.; *Rastell, Justice of Great Sessions; *Rich. Taylor; *W. ap Rice; *Rees Morgan; *W. Morris Gwynn; J. Davies; Geo. Pynde; Otwell Taylor: S.P.12/93/part/f.36v & B.M., Egerton Ms. 2345/f.47d.

1575: 12 September (Acting)
Bacon; E. of Arundel; E. of Essex; Sidney, President of Council in the Marches of Wales; Geo. Fetiplace, Justice of Great Sessions; Throckmorton, Justice of Chester; J. Perrot, kt., Mayor of Haverfordwest; W. Gwynn; Geo. Pynde: Wales 4/776/2.

1578: (Acting)
*Bacon; *Burghley; *Sidney; *Throckmorton, Justice of Chester; *Mayor of Haverfordwest; *J. Perrot, kt.; *Th. Simion, Ll.D.; *W. Morris Gwynn; J. Davies; Geo. Pynde; Maurice Canon; J. Garmon: Hatfield House Ms. 223.7.

1586: 15 August (Acting)
Th. Bromley, kt., Chancellor; J. Puckering & Rich. Atkins, Justices of Great Sessions; J. Perrot, kt.; Th. Perrot, Mayor of Haverfordwest; Jenkin Davies; Maurice Canon; J. Garmon: Wales 4/776/4.

1592: 21 August (Acting)
J. Puckering, kt., Keeper of Great Seal; Burghley, Treasurer; E. of Pembroke, President of Council in the Marches of Wales; Th. Perrot, kt.; W. Walter, Mayor of Haverfordwest; Jenkin Davies; Maurice Walter; Morgan Voyle; Rich. Bateman: Wales 4/776/5.

1594: 16 September (Acting)
Puckering; Burghley; Pembroke; Rich. Atkins & W. Oldisworth, Justices of Great Sessions; H. Morton, Mayor of Haverfordwest; Jenkin Davies; Maurice Walter; Morgan Voyle; W. Walter; Rich. Bateman: Wales 4/776/6.

1595: 15 August
General renewal of Welsh commissions (this would presumably include that for Haverfordwest): Index 4208/f.4v.

1601: 17 October
*Th. Egerton, kt., Keeper of Great Seal; *Th., Lord Buckhurst, Treasurer; *Atkins & *Oldisworth, Justices of Great Sessions; *p Mayor of Haverfordwest; *Jas. Perrot; *Alban Stepney; *Th. Revell; *Jenkin Davies; *W. Davies; Morgan Voyle; Maurice Walter; W. Walter; Rich. Bateman: C.181/1/f.4v. Commission renewed to *add* Jas. Perrot: Index 4208/f.123v. (The C.181 series of Entry Books contains commissions of the peace issued for boroughs and other kinds of commissions. Unlike the county commissions of the peace contained in the C.193 Entry Books or enrolled on the Patent Rolls, these commissions are dated and so provide a confirmation of the dates provided by the Docquet Books).

1602: 25 July
General renewal of Welsh commissions to *add* Ed., Lord Zouch, President of Council in the Marches of Wales (Haverfordwest is not mentioned but would probably be included): Index 4208/f.141.

1603: 25 February
*Egerton; *Buckhurst; *Atkins & *Oldisworth, Justices of Great Sessions; *p Mayor of Haverfordwest; *Jas. Perrot; *Alban Stepney; *Th. Revell; *Jenkin Davies; *Th. Canon; *W. Davies; Morgan Voyle; W. Walter; Rich. Bateman: C.181/1/f.39. Commission renewed to *add* Th. Canon: Index 4208/f.152v.

1603: 9 May
As on 25 February 1603: C.181/1/f.44. (There is no Docquet Book entry to correspond with this commission because of the loss of the Book for the first half of the reign of James I. The commission was probably formally renewed to mark the start of the new reign).

1603: 8 August (Acting)
Egerton; Buckhurst; Rich. Atkins & Jas. Ley, Justices of Great Sessions; J. Hill, Mayor of Haverfordwest; Jas. Perrot, kt.; Alban Stepney; Th. Revell; Jenkin Davies; Th. Canon; W. Davies; Morgan Voyle; W. Walter; Rich. Bateman: Wales 4/777/1.

1603: 10 September
As on 8 August 1603: C.181/1/f.66. (This commission was probably issued formally to add Jas. Ley, the new Justice of Great Sessions).

1603: 26 September (Acting)
As on 10 September 1603: Wales 4/777/2.

1604: 1 March
*Lord Ellesmere (Th. Egerton), Chancellor; *Buckhurst; *Lord Zouch, President of Council in the Marches of Wales; *Rich. Atkins & *Rich. Daston, Justices of Great Sessions; *p Mayor of Haverfordwest; *Jas. Perrot, kt.; *Alban Stepney; *Th. Revell; *Jenkin Davies; *Th. Canon; *W. Davies; Morgan Voyle; W. Walter; Rich. Bateman: C.181/1/f.83.

1604: 13 August (Acting)
Ellesmere; Buckhurst; Zouch; Atkins & Daston, Justices of Great Sessions; Geo. Carne, Mayor of Haverfordwest; Jas. Perrot, kt.; Alban Stepney; Th. Revell; Jenkin Davies; Th. Canon; Morgan Voyle; W. Walter; Rich. Bateman: Wales 4/777/3.

1604: 17 September (Acting)
As on 13 August 1604: Wales 4/777/4.

1605: 18 March (Acting)
Ellesmere; E. of Dorset (Lord Buckhurst), Treasurer; Atkins & Daston, Justices of Great Sessions; Jas. Perrot, kt., Mayor of Haverfordwest; Alban Stepney; Th. Revell; Jenkin Davies; Th. Canon; Morgan Voyle; W. Davies; W. Walter; Rich. Bateman: Wales 4/777/5.

1607: 23 March (Acting)
Ellesmere; Dorset; Zouch, President of Council in the Marches of Wales; B. of St. Davids; Rich. Lewkenor, kt., Justice of Chester; Atkins & Daston, Justices of Great Sessions; Arnold Tanke, Mayor of Haverfordwest; Jas. Perrot, kt.; Alban Stepney; Th. Canon; Jenkin Davies; W. Walter; Morgan Voyle; Rich. Bateman; W. Davies: Wales 4/778/2.

1607: 21 September (Acting)
As on 23 March 1607, except: Lord Zouch, *omitted*: Wales 4/778/3.

1608: 12 September (Acting)
Ellesmere; E. of Salisbury, Treasurer; B. of St. Davids; Lewkenor, Justice of Chester; Atkins & Daston, Justices of Great Sessions; Rich. Knethell, Mayor of Haverfordwest; Jas. Perrot, kt.; Alban Stepney; Jenkin Davies; Th. Canon; Morgan Voyle; Rich. Bateman; W. Davies: Wales 4/778/4.

1609: 11 September (Acting)
Ellesmere; Salisbury; E. of Northampton, Keeper of Privy Seal; B. of St. Davids; Lewkenor, Justice of Chester; Atkins & Daston, Justices of Great Sessions; Rice James, Mayor of Haverfordwest; Jas. Perrot, kt.; Alban Stepney; Jenkin Davies; Morgan Voyle; W. Walter; Th. Canon; Rich. Bateman; W. Davies: Wales 4/778/5.

1610: 26 March (Acting)
Ellesmere; Salisbury; Northampton; Ralph, Lord Eure, President of Council in the Marches of Wales; B. of St. Davids; Lewkenor, Justice of Chester; Atkins & Daston, Justices of Great Sessions; J. Howell, Mayor of Haverfordwest; Jas. Perrot, kt.; Alban Stepney; Jenkin Davies; Morgan Voyle; W. Walter; Th. Canon; Rich. Bateman; W. Davies: Wales 4/779/1.

1610: 24 September (Acting)
Ellesmere; Salisbury; Atkins & Daston, Justices of Great Sessions; J. Howell, Mayor of Haverfordwest; Jas. Perrot, kt.; Alban Stepney; Jenkin Davies; Th. Canon; Morgan Voyle; W. Walter; Rich. Bateman: W. Davies: Wales 4/779/2.

1611: 15 July (Acting)
Ellesmere; Salisbury; Lord Eure, President of Council in the Marches of Wales; Nich. Overbury & Rich. Daston, Justices of Great Sessions; W. Thomas, Mayor of Haverfordwest; Jas. Perrot, kt.; J. Wogan, kt.; Alban Stepney; Th. Canon; Morgan Voyle; Rich. Bateman; W. Davies: Wales 4/779/2. (This list comes from the same file as the preceding one).

1611: 16 September (Acting)
As on 15 July 1611: Wales 4/779/4.

1612: 30 March (Acting)
Ellesmere; Salisbury; Eure; Overbury & Daston, Justices of Great Sessions; Th. Canon, Mayor of Haverfordwest; Jas. Perrot, kt.; J. Wogan, kt.; J. Stepney; W. Davies; Morgan Voyle; Rich. Bateman; W. Thomas: Wales 4/779/5.

1613: 13 September (Acting)
Ellesmere; Eure; Overbury & Daston, Justices of Great Sessions; W.
Davies, Mayor of Haverfordwest; Jas. Perrot, kt.; J. Wogan, kt.; Th.
Canon; J. Stepney; Morgan Voyle; Rich. Bateman: Wales 4/780/1.

1614: 3 August
*Ellesmere; *E. of Suffolk, Treasurer; *Eure; *Overbury & *Daston,
Justices of Great Sessions; *p Mayor of Haverfordwest; *Jas. Perrot, kt.;
J. Wogan, kt.; J. Stepney; *Th. Canon; *W. Davies; Morgan Voyle;
W. Walter; Rich. Bateman; J. Bateman: C.181/2/f.213v.

1614: 12 September (Acting)
Ellesmere; Suffolk; Eure; Overbury & Daston, Justices of Great Sessions;
J. Kynner, Mayor of Haverfordwest; Jas. Perrot, kt.; J. Wogan, kt.; J.
Stepney; Th. Canon; W. Davies; Morgan Voyle; J. Bateman: Wales
4/780/2.

1615: 14 August (Acting)
Ellesmere; Suffolk; Eure; Overbury & Daston, Justices of Great Sessions;
Math. Synnett, Mayor of Haverfordwest; Jas. Perrot, kt.; J. Wogan, kt.;
Th. Canon; J. Stepney; Morgan Voyle; J. Kynner; W. Davies; J. Bateman:
Wales 4/780/3.

1615: 5 September
Commission renewed to *add* J. Kynner: Index 4211/f.9v.

1615: 18 September (Acting)
As on 14 August 1615: Wales 4/780/4. (This list is too close to 5 September
1615 for the new commission to have arrived).

1616: 16 September (Acting)
Ellesmere; Suffolk; Eure; Overbury & Daston, Justices of Great Sessions;
J. Bateman, Mayor of Haverfordwest; Jas. Perrot, kt.; J. Wogan, kt.;
Th. Canon; J. Stepney; W. Davies; Morgan Voyle: Wales 4/780/5. (John
Kynner, who was added to the commission on 5 September 1615, is not
listed).

1617: 8 March
Renewal of Pembrokeshire commission to *add* Francis Bacon, kt., Keeper of
Great Seal; Th., Lord Gerard, President of Council in the Marches of
Wales: Index 4211/f.36. (The Haverfordwest commission is not mentioned
but was probably renewed at the same time).

1617: 5 September
*Francis Bacon, kt., Keeper of Great Seal; *E. of Suffolk, Treasurer; *E. of
Worcester, Keeper of Privy Seal; *Th., Lord Gerard, President of Council
in the Marches of Wales; *Overbury & *Daston, Justices of Great Sessions;
*p Mayor of Haverfordwest; *Jas. Perrot, kt.; J. Wogan, kt.; J. Stepney;
*Th. Canon; J. Kynner; *W. Davies; Morgan Voyle; J. Bateman; J. White:
C.181/2/f.296. Commission renewed to *add* J. White: Index 4211/f.49.

1617: 15 September (Acting)

Bacon; Suffolk; Gerard, President of Council in the Marches of Wales; Overbury & Daston, Justices of Great Sessions; Roger Walter, Mayor of Haverfordwest; Jas. Perrot, kt.; J. Wogan, kt.; J. Stepney; Th. Canon; W. Davies; Morgan Voyle; J. Bateman: Wales 4/780/6. (The new commission of 5 September had probably not arrived at the time of this session).

1618: 27 July (Acting)

Bacon; Suffolk; E. of Worcester, Keeper of Privy Seal; W., Lord Compton President of Council in the Marches of Wales; Overbury & Daston, Justices of Great Sessions; W. Bateman, Mayor of Haverfordwest; Jas. Perrot, J. Wogan, J. Stepney, kts.; Th. Canon; W. Davies; Morgan Voyle; J. Bateman; Roger Walter; J. White: Wales 4/781/1.

1619: 13 September (Acting)

Bacon; Suffolk; Worcester; E. of Northampton (Lord Compton), President of Council in the Marches of Wales; Nich. Overbury & W. Ryves, Justices of Great Sessions; Roger Walter, Mayor of Haverfordwest; Jas. Perrot, J. Wogan, J. Stepney, kts.; Th. Canon; W. Davies; Morgan Voyle; J. Bateman; W. Bateman; J. White: Wales 4/781/2.

1620: 3 April (Acting)

Bacon; Suffolk; Worcester; Northampton; Nich. Overbury & Ed. Littleton, Justices of Great Sessions; J. Stepney, kt., Mayor of Haverfordwest; Jas. Perrot, J. Wogan, kts.; Th. Canon; W. Davies; Morgan Voyle; J. Bateman; Roger Walter; J. White: Wales 4/781/3.

1620: 11 September (Acting)

As on 3 April 1620: Wales 4/781/4.

1622: 23 September (Acting)

B. of Lincoln, Keeper of Great Seal; Lord Cranfield, Treasurer; Viscount Mandeville, President of Council; Worcester; Northampton; Nich. Overbury & J. Hoskins, Justices of Great Sessions; Jenkin Howell, Mayor of Haverfordwest; J. Stepney, kt. & Bt.; Jas. Perrot, J. Wogan, kts.; Th. Canon; Morgan Voyle; W. Davies; J. Bateman; J. Warren; J. White: Wales 4/782/1.

1623: 8 September (Acting)

B. of Lincoln; E. of Middlesex (Lord Cranfield); Worcester; Northampton; Overbury & Hoskins, Justices of Great Sessions; Th. Adams, Mayor of Haverfordwest; J. Stepney, kt. & Bt.; Jas. Perrot, J. Wogan, Th. Canon, kts.; W. Davies; Morgan Voyle; J. Bateman; Jenkin Howell; J. White: Wales 4/782/2.

1624: 26 July (Acting)

Lincoln; Worcester; Northampton; Overbury & Hoskins, Justices of Great Sessions; Jas. Perrot, kt., Mayor of Haverfordwest; J. Stepney, kt. & Bt.; J. Wogan, Th. Canon, kts.; W. Davies; Morgan Voyle; Th. Adams; J. White: Wales 4/782/3.

1625: 1 April
General renewal of Welsh commissions: Index 4211/f.180v. (Haverfordwest was probably included in this renewal although there is no specific mention of this).

1625: 24 June
*Lincoln; *Jas., Lord Ley, Treasurer; *Northampton, President of Council in the Marches of Wales; *Overbury & *Hoskins, Justices of Great Sessions; *p Mayor of Haverfordwest; J. Stepney, kt. & Bt.; *Jas. Perrot, J. Wogan, *Th. Canon, kts.; *W. Davies; Morgan Voyle; J. White; *Roger Walter: C.181/3/f.181v. Commission renewed to *add* Roger Walter: Index 4211/f.189v.

1625: 19 September (Acting)
Lincoln; Ley; Viscount Mandeville; E. of Worcester, Keeper of Privy Seal; Northampton; Overbury & Hoskins, Justices of Great Sessions; W. Meyler, Mayor of Haverfordwest; Jas. Perrot, J. Wogan, Th. Canon, kts.; Morgan Voyle; Roger Walter; J. White: Wales 4/783/1.

1625: 22 December
General renewal of Welsh commissions to *add* Th. Coventry, kt., Keeper of Great Seal: Index 4211/f.194d. (Haverfordwest is not mentioned specifically but was probably included in this renewal).

1626: 3 April (Acting)
Th. Coventry, kt., Keeper of Great Seal; Ley; Mandeville; Worcester; Northampton; Overbury & Hoskins, Justices of Great Sessions; J. White, Mayor of Haverfordwest; Jas. Perrot, J. Wogan, Th. Canon, kts.; Morgan Voyle; W. Meyler: Wales 4/783/2.

1626: 18 September (Acting)
As on 3 April 1626: Wales 4/783/3.

1628: 7 April (Acting)
Coventry; E. of Marlborough (Lord Ley); Worcester; Mandeville; Northampton; Overbury & Hoskins, Justices of Great Sessions; J. Barlow, Mayor of Haverfordwest; Jas. Perrot, J. Wogan, Th. Canon, kts.; Morgan Voyle; J. White; W. Bowen: Wales 4/783/5.

1629: 20 March
*Coventry; *Rich., Lord Weston, Treasurer; *Northampton; *Overbury & *Hoskins, Justices of Great Sessions; *p Mayor of Haverfordwest; *Jas. Perrot, *J. Wogan, *Th. Canon, kts.; Morgan Voyle; Maurice Canon; W. Bateman; J. Warren; J. White; W. Meyler; W. Bowen: C.181/3/f.263. Commission renewed to *add* Maurice Canon; W. Bateman; J. Warren; W. Meyler; W. Bowen: Index 4211/f.266.

1629: 5 June
Commission renewed to *omit* J. Warren: Index 4211/f.268.

1630: 13 September (Acting)
Coventry; Weston; Overbury & Hoskins, Justices of Great Sessions; Roger Beavans, Mayor of Haverfordwest; Jas. Perrot, J. Wogan, Th. Canon, kts.; Morgan Voyle; Maurice Canon; W. Bateman; J. White; W. Meyler; W. Bowen; Etheldred Wogan: Wales 4/784/1.

1631: 28 March (Acting)
Coventry; Weston; Overbury & Hoskins, Justices of Great Sessions; W. Bateman, Mayor of Haverfordwest; Jas. Perrot, J. Wogan, Th. Canon, kts.; Morgan Voyle; W. Meyler; J. White; W. Bowen; Maurice Canon; Roger Beavans: Wales 4/784/2.

1631: 19 September (Acting)
As on 28 March 1631: Wales 4/784/3.

1632: 26 March (Acting)
Coventry; Weston; Overbury & Hoskins, Justices of Great Sessions; Th. Canon, kt., Mayor of Haverfordwest; Jas. Perrot, J. Wogan, kts.; Morgan Voyle; Maurice Canon; W. Bateman; J. White; W. Meyler; W. Bowen: Wales 4/785/1.

1632: 17 September (Acting)
As on 26 March 1632, except: Morgan Voyle, *omitted*: Wales 4/785/2.

1633: 23 September (Acting)
Coventry; Weston; E. of Bridgewater, President of Council in the Marches of Wales; Overbury & Hoskins, Justices of Great Sessions; W. Williams, Mayor of Haverfordwest; Jas. Perrot, J. Wogan, Th. Canon, kts.; Maurice Canon; W. Bateman; J. White; W. Bowen; W. Meyler: Wales 4/785/3.

1634: 15 September (Acting)
Coventry; E. of Portland (Lord Weston); Overbury & Hoskins, Justices of Great Sessions; Jas. Perrot, kt., Mayor of Haverfordwest; J. Wogan, Th. Canon, kts.; Maurice Canon; W. Bateman; W. Meyler; J. White; W. Bowen; W. Williams: Wales 4/786/1.

1634: 13 November
*Coventry; *Portland; *Overbury & *Hoskins, Justices of Great Sessions; *p Mayor of Haverfordwest; *J. Stepney, Bt.; *Jas. Perrot, *J. Wogan, *Th. Canon, kts.; Morgan Voyle; Maurice Canon; W. Bateman; J. Warren; J. White; W. Meyler; W. Bowen: C.181/4/f.187v. Commission renewed to *add* J. Stepney, Bt.: Index 4212/p.148.

1635: 26 June
*Coventry; *Portland; *Overbury & *Hoskins, Justices of Great Sessions; *p Mayor of Haverfordwest; *J. Stepney, Bt.; *Jas. Perrot, *J. Wogan, *Th. Canon, kts.; Morgan Voyle; Maurice Canon; W. Bateman; J. White; W. Meyler; W. Bowen: C.181/5/f.21. Commission renewed to *omit* J. Warren who was inserted in the commission by mistake at the previous renewal: Index 4212/p.172. (This remark about J. Warren should probably not be taken at face value).

1636: 25 July (Acting)
Coventry; Overbury & Hoskins, Justices of Great Sessions; J. Warren, Mayor of Haverfordwest; J. Stepney, Bt.; Jas. Perrot, J. Wogan, Th. Canon, kts.; Maurice Canon; W. Bateman; J. White; W. Meyler; W. Bowen: Wales 4/786/2.

1636: 12 September (Acting)
As on 25 July 1636, except: J. White, *omitted*: Wales 4/786/3.

1638: 6 March
*Coventry; *B. of London, Treasurer; *Timothy Turneur & *J. Hoskins, Justices of Great Sessions; *p Mayor of Haverfordwest; *J. Stepney, Bt.; *Th. Canon, kt.; Maurice Canon; W. Bateman; W. Meyler; W. Bowen: C.181/5/f.99v. Commission renewed to *add* Timothy Turneur, Justice of Great Sessions: Index 4212/p.284.

1638: 26 March (Acting)
Coventry; London; Turneur & Hoskins, Justices of Great Sessions; J. Barlow, Mayor of Haverfordwest; J. Stepney, Bt.; Th. Canon, kt.; Maurice Canon; W. Bateman; W. Meyler; W. Bowen: Wales 4/786/4.

1639: 15 March
*Coventry; *London; *Timothy Turneur & *J. Platt, Justices of Great Sessions; *p Mayor of Haverfordwest; *J. Stepney, Bt.; Maurice Canon; W. Bateman; W. Meyler; W. Bowen: C.181/5/f.133. Commission renewed to *add* J. Platt, Justice of Great Sessions: Index 4212/p.330.

1640: 17 August (Acting)
London; Turneur & Platt, Justices of Great Sessions; Roger Beavans, Mayor of Haverfordwest; J. Stepney, Bt.; Maurice Canon; W. Bateman; W. Meyler; W. Bowen; Etheldred Wogan: Wales 4/787/1.

1641: 11 February
*Ed. Littleton, kt., Keeper of Great Seal; *London; *Turneur & *Platt, Justices of Great Sessions; *p Mayor of Haverfordwest; *J. Stepney, Bt.; Maurice Canon; W. Bateman; W. Meyler; *W. Bowen; *J. Davies: C.181/5/f.188. Commission renewed to *add* J. Davies, gentleman: Index 4212/p.428.

1647: 23 August (Acting)
W. Powell & J. Clark, Justices of Great Sessions; Etheldred Wogan, Mayor of Haverfordwest; J. Stepney, Bt.; Maurice Canon; W. Bateman; W. Meyler; W. Bowen; Roger Beavans; J. Davies: Wales 4/787/4.

1649: 23 March (Acting)
W. Lenthall, Speaker of House of Commons; Lord Fairfax; Bulstrode Whitelock, Rich. Keble, J. Lisle, Commissioners of Great Seal; W. Powell & J. Clark, Justices of Great Sessions; W. Williams, Mayor of Haverford-west; J. Stepney, Bt.; Maurice Canon; W. Meyler; W. Bowen; J. Davies; J. Prinn: Wales 4/788/1.

1650: 16 September (Acting)
Lenthall; Oliver Cromwell; Whitelock, Keble & Lisle; H. Rolle, Chief Justice of Upper Bench; Powell & Clark, Justices of Great Sessions; W. Bowen, Mayor of Haverfordwest; J. Stepney, Bt.; Maurice Canon; W. Meyler; W. Williams; J. Davies: Wales 4/788/3.

1651: 15 September (Acting)
Lenthall; Cromwell; Whitelock, Keble & Lisle; J. Bradshaw, President of Council; E. of Pembroke; Rolle; Powell & Clark, Justices of Great Sessions; Th. Williams, Mayor of Haverfordwest; J. Stepney, Bt.; Maurice Canon; W. Meyler; W. Bowen; J. Davies: Wales 4/788/4.

1653: 20 August (Acting)
Lenthall; Cromwell; Whitelock, Keble & Lisle; Bradshaw; Pembroke; Rolle; J. Haggatt, Justice of Great Sessions; W. Walter, Mayor of Haverfordwest; J. Stepney, Bt.; W. Meyler; W. Bowen: Wales 4/788/6.

1653: 17 September (Acting)
As on 20 August 1653: Wales 4/788/7.

1654: 15 March (Acting)
Lenthall; Whitelock, Keble & Lisle; Bradshaw; Pembroke; Rolle; Haggatt, Justice of Great Sessions; H. Bowen, Mayor of Haverfordwest; J. Stepney, Bt.; W. Meyler; W. Bowen; W. Walter: Wales 4/789/1.

1654: 21 August (Acting)
Whitelock & Lisle; Rolle; Lenthall; Oliver St. John, Chief Justice of Common Bench; J. Haggatt & Bennet Hoskins, Justices of Great Sessions; H. Bowen, Mayor of Haverfordwest; J. Stepney, Bt.; W. Meyler; W. Bowen; W. Walter: Wales 4/789/2.

1655: 15 March
Whitelock, Widdrington & Lisle; Rolle; W. Lenthall, Master of the Rolls; St. John; Haggatt & Hoskins, Justices of Great Sessions; Edm. Jones, attorney-general of South Wales; Mayor of Haverfordwest; Jas. Philipps; W. Meyler; W. Bowen; W. Williams; W. Walter; Arnold Thomas; H. Bowen; Th. Davies: C.181/6/p.96. Commission renewed according to a general list: Index 4213/p.306.

1655: 2 April (Acting)
As on 15 March 1655: Wales 4/789/3. (The name of the Mayor of Haverfordwest in 1655 is inserted as W. Davies).

1655: 20 August (Acting)
As on 2 April 1655: Wales 4/789/4.

1656: 24 March (Acting)
Nathaniel Fiennes & J. Lisle, Commissioners of Great Seal; Bulstrode Whitelock, kt. & Th. Widdrington, kt., Commissioners of Treasury; J. Glynn, Chief Justice of Upper Bench; W. Lenthall, Master of the Rolls;

Oliver St. John, Chief Justice of Common Bench; Haggatt & Hoskins, Justices of Great Sessions; Edm. Jones, attorney-general of South Wales; Rich. Bateman, Mayor of Haverfordwest; Jas. Philipps; W. Meyler; W. Bowen; W. Williams; W. Walter; Arnold Thomas; H. Bowen; Th. Davies: Wales 4/789/5.

1656: 22 July
Fiennes & Lisle; Whitelock & Widdrington; Philip Jones, one of the Council; Glynn; Lenthall; St. John; Haggatt & Hoskins, Justices of Great Sessions; Hugh Owen, Bt.; Edm. Jones, attorney-general of South Wales; p Mayor of Haverfordwest; Jas. Philipps; W. Meyler; W. Bowen; W. Williams; W. Walter; Arnold Thomas; H. Bowen; Th. Davies; Rich. Castell; Rich. Brown; Rowland Gethin: C.181/6/p.183. Commission renewed to *add* Hugh Owen, Bt.; Rich. Castell; Rich. Brown; Rowland Gethin: Index 4213/p.345. (Gethin's first name appears as Richard in the original Docquet Book entry but other sources make it clear that it should be Rowland).

1656: 11 August (Acting)
As on 24 March 1656, except: Rich. Bateman, *omitted* and replaced as Mayor by Jas. Philipps: Wales 4/789/6. (The new commission of 22 July had clearly not reached Haverfordwest by this date).

1657: 20 March (Acting)
Fiennes & Lisle; Whitelock & Widdrington; Philip Jones; Glynn; Lenthall; St. John; Haggatt & Hoskins, Justices of Great Sessions; Hugh Owen, Bt., Mayor of Haverfordwest; Jas. Philipps; W. Meyler; W. Williams; W. Walter; Arnold Thomas; Th. Davies; H. Bowen; Rich. Castell; Rich. Brown; Rowland Gethin: Wales 4/790/1.

1657: 31 August (Acting)
As on 20 March 1657, except: Edm. Jones, attorney-general of South Wales, *added*: Wales 4/790/2.

1658: 29 March (Acting)
Fiennes & Lisle; Whitelock & Widdrington; Jones; Glynn; Lenthall; St. John; Haggatt & Hoskins, Justices of Great Sessions; Edm. Jones, attorney-general of South Wales; Arnold Thomas, Mayor of Haverfordwest; Hugh Owen, Bt.; Jas. Philipps; W. Meyler; W. Williams; W. Walter; Th. Davies; H. Bowen; Rich. Castell; Rich. Brown; Rowland Gethin: Wales 4/790/3.

1658: 6 September (Acting)
As on 29 March 1658: Wales 4/790/4.

1658: 24 September
General renewal of Welsh commissions to *add* Rich. Cromwell, Lord Protector: Index 4213/p.405. (Haverfordwest is not mentioned in this renewal but may have been included).

1659: 8 August (Acting)

Fiennes; Lisle; Whitelock; Jones; Glynn; Lenthall; St. John; Widdrington; J. Haggatt, Justice of Great Sessions; Edm. Jones, attorney-general of South Wales; Lewis Barron, Mayor of Haverfordwest; Hugh Owen, Bt.; Jas. Philipps; W. Meyler; W. Williams; Arnold Thomas; Th. Davies; W. Walter; H. Bowen; Rich. Castell; Rowland Gethin: Wales 4/790/5. (The corresponding Gaol File list for the county of Pembroke on the same date differs considerably from that for Haverfordwest in the details of the *ex officio* members of the commission. This is almost certainly because a new commission had been issued for Pembroke on 28 June 1659 while that for Haverfordwest was probably as old as 22 July 1656. However Haverfordwest was to receive a new commission on 19 October 1659 which brought it back into line with Pembroke).

1659: 29 August (Acting)

J. Haggatt, Justice of Great Sessions; Lewis Barron, Mayor of Haverfordwest; Arnold Thomas: Wales 4/790/6. (The truncated state of this list is probably the result of uncertainty in Haverfordwest as to the real condition of the commission of the peace caused by the situation described above. J. Haggatt and Lewis Barron could still safely be listed as justices of the peace since both would be *ex officio* members of any new commission, but it is not clear why Arnold Thomas should still be named).

1659: 19 October

*W. Lenthall, Speaker & Master of the Rolls; *J. Bradshaw, *Th. Tyrrell & *J. Fountain, Commissioners of Great Seal; *p Mayor of Haverfordwest; *Sampson Lort; *Th. Wogan; *H. Bowen; *Herbert Perrot; *W. Meyler; *Rich. Castell; Anthony Stokes; Arnold Thomas: C.181/6/p.402. Commission renewed according to a general list: Index 4213/p.444.

1660: 11 September

*Ed. Hyde, kt., Chancellor; *E. of Southampton, Treasurer; *D. of Albemarle, General; *Marquess of Ormond, Steward; *E. of Lindsey, Great Chamberlain; *E. of Manchester, Household Chamberlain; *W. Morton, kt. & *Simon Degg, Justices of Great Sessions; *p H. Jones, Mayor of Haverfordwest; *J. Stepney, Bt.; *Hugh Owen, Bt.; *Herbert Perrot, kt.; *W. Philipps; *Isaac Lloyd; Geo. Hayward; Rich. Bateman; *W. Williams; *H. Bowen; *W. Meyler; *Th. Davies; Lewis Barron; W. Walter; Math. Prinn; J. Williams: C.181/7/p.50. Commission renewed (no details): Index 4214/p.39.

1660: 2 October (Acting)

Hyde; Southampton; Albemarle; Ormond; Lindsey; Manchester; Morton & Degg, Justices of Great Sessions; Philip Wall, Mayor of Haverfordwest; J. Stepney, Bt.; Hugh Owen, Bt.; Herbert Perrot, kt.; W. Philipps; Isaac Lloyd; Geo. Hayward; H. Jones; Rich. Bateman; W. Williams; H. Bowen; W. Meyler; Th. Davies; Lewis Barron; W. Walter; Math. Prinn; J. Williams: Wales 4/791/1.

1661: 28 March (Acting)

As on 2 October 1660, except: H. Jones, *omitted*: Wales 4/791/2.

1661: 16 September (Acting)
As on 28 March 1661: Wales 4/791/3.

1662: 17 July
*Morton & *Degg, Justices of Great Sessions; *p Mayor of Haverfordwest;
*J. Stepney, Bt.; *Hugh Owen, Bt.; *Herbert Perrot, kt.; *W. Philipps;
*Rowland Laugharne; *Rich. Walter; *Th. Cozen; *Geo. Hayward; *H.
Jones; *W. Williams; *W. Meyler; *Th. Davies; Lewis Barron; Math.
Prinn; J. Williams: C.181/7/p.163. Commission renewed to *add* Rowland
Laugharne; Rich. Walter; Th. Cozen, and to *omit* Isaac Lloyd; Rich. Bate-
man; H. Bowen: Index 4214/p.179.

1662: 16 August (Acting)
E. of Clarendon (Ed. Hyde), Chancellor; E. of Southampton, Treasurer;
Lord Robartes, Keeper of Privy Seal; D. of Albemarle, General; D. of
Ormond, Steward; E. of Lindsey, Great Chamberlain; E. of Manchester,
Household Chamberlain; E. of Carbery, President of Council in the Marches
of Wales; Morton & Degg, Justices of Great Sessions; J. Stepney, Bt.,
Mayor of Haverfordwest; Hugh Owen, Bt.; Herbert Perrot, kt.; W. Philipps;
Rowland Laugharne; Rich. Walter; Th. Cozen; Geo. Hayward; W. Williams;
W. Meyler; Lewis Barron; Math. Prinn: Wales 4/791/4.

1663: 6 April (Acting)
As on 16 August 1662, except: Th. Cozen, *omitted*. Lewis Barron is now
Mayor: Wales 4/792/1.

1663: 3 September (Acting)
As on 6 April 1663, except: Th. Cozen, *added*: Wales 4/792/2.

1664: 29 July (Acting)
As on 3 September 1663, except: J. Williams is now Mayor: Wales 4/792/3.

1664: 26 September (Acting)
As on 29 July 1664: Wales 4/792/4.

1665: 12 August (Acting)
Clarendon; Southampton; Robartes; Albemarle; Ormond; Lindsey;
Manchester; Carbery; Morton & Degg, Justices of Great Sessions; W.
Brown, Mayor of Haverfordwest; J. Stepney, Bt.; Hugh Owen, Bt.;
Herbert Perrot, kt.; Rowland Laugharne; W. Philipps; Rich. Walter;
Th. Cozen; W. Williams; Lewis Barron; J. Williams; Math. Prinn: Wales
4/792/5.

1665: 30 August (Acting)
As on 12 August 1665: Wales 4/787/2. (This file is wrongly indexed as
belonging to 17 Charles I).

1666: 18 July
*Clarendon; *Southampton; *Robartes; *Albemarle; *Ormond; *Lindsey;
*Manchester; *Frederick Hyde, kt. & *Simon Degg, Justices of Great

Sessions; *p Mayor of Haverfordwest; *J. Stepney, Bt.; *Hugh Owen, Bt.;
*Herbert Perrot, kt.; *W. Philipps; *Rowland Laugharne; *Rich. Walter;
*Th. Cozen; *Geo. Hayward; *H. Jones; *W. Williams; *W. Meyler;
*Th. Davies; Lewis Barron; Math. Prinn; J. Williams: C.181/7/p.367.
Commission renewed to *add* Fred. Hyde, kt., Justice of Great Sessions:
Index 4214/p.289.

1666: 6 August (Acting)
As on 18 July 1666, except: Th. Cozen appears as Mayor of Haverfordwest:
Wales 4/787/3. (This file is wrongly indexed as belonging to 18 Charles I).

1666: 20 August (Acting)
As on 6 August 1666, except: E. of Carbery, President of Wales, *added*:
Wales 4/793/1.

1666: 11 December
*Clarendon; *Southampton; *Robartes; *Albemarle; *Ormond; *Lindsey;
*Manchester; *Carbery; *Hyde & *Degg, Justices of Great Sessions;
*p Mayor of Haverfordwest; *Erasmus Philipps, Bt.; *J. Stepney, Bt.;
*Hugh Owen, Bt.; *Herbert Perrot, kt.; *Walter Vaughan; *Isaac Lloyd;
*J. Thomas; *W. Philipps; *Rowland Laugharne; *Rich. Walter; Th.
Cozen; Geo. Hayward; H. Jones; W. Williams; W. Meyler; Th. Davies;
W. Brown; J. Williams; Th. Bowen: C.181/7/p.372. Commission renewed
to *add* Erasmus Philipps, Bt.; Walter Vaughan; Isaac Lloyd; J. Thomas;
W. Brown; Th. Bowen: Index 4214/p.296.

1667: 19 July (Acting)
As on 11 December 1666, except: Rich. Walter is now Mayor: Wales
4/793/2.

1667: 26 August (Acting)
As on 19 July 1667: Wales 4/793/3.

1668: 7 August (Acting)
Southampton; Robartes; Albemarle; Ormond; Lindsey; Manchester;
Carbery; Hyde & Degg, Justices of Great Sessions; Rich. Walter, Mayor of
Haverfordwest; Erasmus Philipps, Bt.; J. Stepney, Bt.; Hugh Owen, Bt.;
Herbert Perrot, kt.; Walter Vaughan; Isaac Lloyd; W. Philipps; J. Thomas;
Rowland Laugharne; Th. Cozen; W. Brown; J. Williams; Th. Bowen:
Wales 4/793/4.

1668: 25 August (Acting)
As on 7 August 1668, except: Walter Vaughan, *omitted*: Wales 4/793/5.

1669: 12 April (Acting)
Southampton; Robartes; Albemarle; Ormond; Lindsey; Manchester;
Carbery; Hyde & Degg, Justices of Great Sessions; Th. Bowen, Mayor of
Haverfordwest; Erasmus Philipps, Bt.; J. Stepney, Bt.; Hugh Owen, Bt.;
Herbert Perrot, kt.; Walter Vaughan; Isaac Lloyd; J. Thomas; W. Philipps;
Rowland Laugharne; Rich. Walter; Th. Cozen; Geo. Hayward; H. Jones;
W. Williams; W. Meyler; Th. Davies; W. Brown; J. Williams: Wales
4/793/6.

1669: 30 August (Acting)
As on 12 April 1669, except: Walter Vaughan; Geo. Hayward; H. Jones; W. Williams; W. Meyler; Th. Davies, *omitted*: Wales 4/793/7. (All of the men left out on this date had been marked as dead and omitted from the commission in the course of 1668 and then wrongly restored in April 1669).

1670: 11 April (Acting)
Southampton; Robartes; Ormond; Lindsey; Manchester; Carbery; Hyde & Degg, Justices of Great Sessions; J. Thomas, Mayor of Haverfordwest; Erasmus Philipps, Bt.; J. Stepney, Bt.; Hugh Owen, Bt.; Herbert Perrot, kt.; Isaac Lloyd; W. Philipps; Rowland Laugharne; Rich. Walter; Th. Cozen; W. Brown; J. Williams; Th. Bowen: Wales 4/794/1.

1670: 1 August (Acting)
As on 11 April 1670, except: E. of Southampton, *omitted*: Wales 4/794/2.

1671: 17 April (Acting)
Robartes; Ormond; Lindsey; Manchester; Carbery; Hyde & Degg, Justices of Great Sessions; Rich. Fowler, Mayor of Haverfordwest; Erasmus Philipps, Bt.; J. Stepney, Bt.; Herbert Perrot, kt.; Isaac Lloyd; J. Thomas; W. Philipps; Rowland Laugharne; Rich. Walter; Th. Cozen; W. Brown; J. Williams; Th. Bowen: Wales 4/794/3.

1671: 9 September (Acting)
As on 17 April 1671: Wales 4/794/4.

1672: 1 April (Acting)
Robartes; Ormond; Manchester; Carbery; Hyde & Degg, Justices of Great Sessions; Balthazar Wolford, Mayor of Haverfordwest; Erasmus Philipps, Bt.; J. Stepney, Bt.; Herbert Perrot, kt.; Isaac Lloyd; J. Thomas; W. Philipps; Rowland Laugharne; Th. Cozen; W. Brown; J. Williams; Th. Bowen; Rich. Fowler: Wales 4/794/5.

1672: 2 September (Acting)
As on 1 April 1672: Wales 4/794/6.

1673: 14 July (Acting)
Robartes; Ormond; Manchester; Carbery; Hyde & Degg, Justices of Great Sessions; Rob. Prust, Mayor of Haverfordwest; Erasmus Philipps, Bt.; J. Stepney, Bt.; Herbert Perrot, kt.; Isaac Lloyd; J. Thomas; W. Philipps; Rowland Laugharne; Th. Cozen; W. Brown; J. Williams; Th. Bowen; Balthazar Woolford: Wales 4/794/7.

1673: 11 August (Acting)
As on 14 July 1673: Wales 4/794/8.

1674: 25 May (Acting)
Robartes; Ormond; Manchester; Carbery; Hyde & Degg, Justices of Great Sessions; J. Lloyd, Mayor of Haverfordwest; Erasmus Philipps, Bt.; J. Stepney, Bt.; Herbert Perrot, kt.; Isaac Lloyd; J. Thomas; W. Philipps; Rowland Laugharne; Th. Cozen; W. Brown; J. Williams; Th. Bowen: Wales 4/794/9.

1674: 12 September (Acting)

As on 25 May 1674, except: Rob. Prust, *added*: Wales 4/795/1. (In the original Gaol File list the name of Francis Manley, who was appointed as a Justice of Great Sessions in place of Simon Degg in August 1674, appears as an insertion made after the list was drawn up. Manley does not however appear in later lists until 1677 because no new commission to incorporate his name was issued for Haverfordwest. Comparison with the commission for Pembroke also shows that in the years between about 1670 and 1677 the *ex officio* portion of the Haverfordwest commission, i.e. the names of the major officers of state, bore less and less relation to the true situation. This was caused by the lack of any new commission for Haverfordwest between 11 December 1666 and 10 July 1677. The names of the active portion of the commission, i.e. beginning with the name of the Mayor of Haverfordwest, may however be taken as accurate).

1675: 8 April (Acting)

Robartes; Ormond; Manchester; Carbery; Hyde & Degg, Justices of Great Sessions; J. Bateman, Mayor of Haverfordwest; Erasmus Philipps, Bt.; J. Stepney, Bt.; Herbert Perrot, kt.; Isaac Lloyd; J. Thomas; W. Philipps; Rowland Laugharne; Th. Cozen; J. Williams; W. Brown; Th. Bowen; J. Lloyd: Wales 4/795/2.

1675: 9 August (Acting)

As on 8 April 1675, except: Isaac Lloyd, *omitted*: Wales 4/795/3.

1676: 15 May (Acting)

Robartes; Ormond; Manchester; Carbery; Hyde & Degg, Justices of Great Sessions; Roger Davies, Mayor of Haverfordwest; Erasmus Philipps, Bt.; J. Stepney, Bt.; Herbert Perrot, kt.; J. Thomas; W. Philipps; Th. Cozen; W. Brown; J. Williams; Th. Bowen; J. Bateman: Wales 4/795/4.

1676: 28 August (Acting)

As on 15 May 1676, except: J. Stepney, *omitted*: Wales 4/795/5.

1677: 16 April (Acting)

Robartes; Ormond; Manchester; Carbery; Hyde & Degg, Justices of Great Sessions; Herbert Perrot, kt., Mayor of Haverfordwest; Erasmus Philipps, Bt.; J. Thomas; W. Philipps; Th. Cozen; J. Williams; W. Brown; Th. Bowen; Roger Davies: Wales 4/795/6.

1677: 10 July

Commission renewed to *add* Hugh Owen, Bt.; Lewis Wogan of Boulston; Th. Hayward; Rob. Prust; J. Bateman; J. Fowler; Benjamin Twyning: Index 4214/p.529.

1677: 3 September (Acting)

Lord Finch, Chancellor; E. of Danby, Treasurer; E. of Anglesey, Keeper of Privy Seal; D. of Monmouth; D. of Ormond, Steward; E. of Lindsey, Great Chamberlain; E. of Arlington, Household Chamberlain; E. of Carbery; Francis Manley & W. Buckby, Justices of Great Sessions; Th. Cozen,

Mayor of Haverfordwest; Erasmus Philipps, Bt.; Hugh Owen, Bt.; Herbert Perrot, kt.; Lewis Wogan of Boulston; Th. Hayward; J. Thomas; W. Philipps; Th. Bowen; Roger Davies; Rob. Prust; J. Bateman; J. Fowler; Benjamin Twyning: Wales 4/795/7.

1677: 14 September
Commission renewed to add Geo. Owen, D.D.; Arthur Owen junior; Chas. Stepney; Rich. Jones; J. Williams; Lewis Barron; Roger Davies; J. Lloyd: Index 4214/p.533.

1678: 25 March (Acting)
Finch; Danby; Anglesey; Monmouth; Ormond; Lindsey; Arlington; Carbery; Manley & Buckby, Justices of Great Sessions; Jas. Wolford, Mayor of Haverfordwest; Erasmus Philipps, Bt.; Hugh Owen, Bt.; Herbert Perrot, kt.; Geo. Owen, D.D.; Lewis Wogan of Boulston; Th. Hayward; J. Thomas; W. Philipps; Arthur Owen junior; Th. Cozen; Chas. Stepney; Rich. Jones; Th. Bowen; Rob. Prust; W. Brown; J. Bateman; Lewis Barron; Roger Davies; J. Lloyd; J. Fowler; Benjamin Twyning: Wales 4/795/8.

1678: 7 September (Acting)
As on 25 March 1678, except: J. Williams, *added*. Arthur Owen; Th. Cozen, *omitted*: Wales 4/795/9.

1679: 21 April (Acting)
Finch; Danby; Anglesey; Monmouth; Ormond; Lindsey; Arlington; Carbery; Manley & Buckby, Justices of Great Sessions; J. Williams, Mayor of Haverfordwest; Erasmus Philipps, Bt.; Herbert Perrot, kt.; Lewis Wogan; Th. Hayward; J. Thomas; W. Philipps; Geo. Owen, D.D.; Th. Cozen; Th. Bowen; Rob. Prust; J. Bateman; J. Lloyd; Roger Davies; J. Fowler; Rich. Jones; Benjamin Twyning: Wales 4/796/1.

1679: 1 September (Acting)
As on 21 April 1679, except: Hugh Owen, Bt., *added*: Wales 4/796/2.

1680: 23 August (Acting)
Finch; Danby; Anglesey; Monmouth; Ormond; Lindsey; Arlington; Carbery; Manley & Buckby, Justices of Great Sessions; W. Davies, Mayor of Haverfordwest; Erasmus Philipps, Bt.; Hugh Owen, Bt.; Herbert Perrot, kt.; Lewis Wogan; Th. Hayward; W. Philipps; Geo. Owen, D.D.; J. Williams; Th. Bowen; Rob. Prust; J. Bateman; J. Lloyd; Roger Davies; Rich. Jones; J. Fowler; Benjamin Twyning: Wales 4/796/3. (The Haverfordwest commission does not appear to have been purged in 1680 as in other counties. As a result of this the *ex officio* portion of the commission remained out of date until the commission was renewed on 29 July 1682).

1681: 4 April (Acting)
Finch; Danby; Anglesey; Monmouth; Ormond; Carbery; Manley & Buckby, Justices of Great Sessions; Lewis Wogan, Mayor of Haverfordwest; Erasmus Philipps, Bt.; Hugh Owen, Bt.; Herbert Perrot, kt.; Th. Hayward;

W. Philipps; Geo. Owen, D.D.; J. Williams; Th. Bowen; Rob. Prust;
J. Bateman; Roger Davies; W. Davies; Rich. Jones; J. Fowler (his name
was erased after the list was made); Benjamin Twyning: Wales 4/796/5.

1681: 5 September (Acting)
Finch; Danby; Anglesey; Monmouth; Ormond; Lindsey; Arlington;
Carbery; Manley & Buckby, Justices of Great Sessions; Lewis Wogan,
Mayor of Haverfordwest; Erasmus Philipps, Bt.; Hugh Owen, Bt.; Herbert
Perrot, kt.; Geo. Owen, D.D.; Th. Hayward; W. Philipps; Arthur Owen
junior; Chas. Stepney; Rich. Jones; Th. Bowen; Rob. Prust; J. Bateman;
J. Williams; Roger Davies: Wales 4/796/6.

1682: 17 April (Acting)
Finch; Danby; Anglesey; Monmouth; Lindsey; Arlington; Carbery;
Manley & Buckby, Justices of Great Sessions; Th. Bowen, Mayor of
Haverfordwest; Erasmus Philipps, Bt.; Hugh Owen, Bt.; Herbert Perrot,
kt.; Geo. Owen, D.D.; Lewis Wogan; Th. Hayward; W. Philipps; Arthur
Owen junior; Rob. Prust; J. Bateman; J. Williams; Roger Davies; J. Fowler:
Wales 4/797/1.

1682: 29 July
Commission renewed to *add* Jas. Woolford & J. Woolford, Aldermen:
Index 4215/p.69.

1682: 14 August (Acting)
As on 17 April 1682, except: D. of Ormond; Rich. Jones, *added*. Th.
Hayward; J. Williams, *omitted*: Wales 4/797/2. (The new commission of
29 July had evidently not arrived by this date).

1683: 2 April (Acting)
E. of Radnor, President of Council; Anglesey; Ormond; Lindsey; Arlington;
Carbery; Manley & Buckby, Justices of Great Sessions; Rob. Prust, Mayor
of Haverfordwest; Erasmus Philipps, Bt.; Hugh Owen, Bt.; Herbert Perrot,
kt.; Geo. Owen, D.D.; Lewis Wogan of Boulston; W. Philipps; Arthur
Owen; Rich. Jones; Th. Bowen; J. Bateman; Roger Davies; Jas. Woolford;
J. Woolford; J. Fowler: Wales 4/797/3.

1683: 3 September (Acting)
As on 2 April 1683, except: E. of Nottingham, Chancellor, *added*. Geo.
Owen, *omitted*: Wales 4/797/4. (In fact the Earl of Nottingham who had
been Chancellor since 1675, was replaced on his death in December 1682 by
Sir Francis North, but as on other occasions the Haverfordwest commission
had not been renewed to show the change).

1684: 5 May (Acting)
Radnor; Anglesey; Ormond; Lindsey; Arlington; Carbery; Manley &
Buckby, Justices of Great Sessions; Roger Davies, Mayor of Haverfordwest;
Erasmus Philipps, Bt.; Hugh Owen, Bt.; Geo. Owen, D.D.; Lewis Wogan;
W. Philipps; Arthur Owen; Th. Bowen; J. Bateman; Rob. Prust; Jas.
Woolford; Rich. Jones; J. Woolford; J. Fowler: Wales 4/797/5.

1684: 15 September (Acting)
As on 5 May 1684, except: Rich. Jones, *omitted*: Wales 4/797/6.

1685: 30 March (Acting)
J. Fowler, Mayor of Haverfordwest; Erasmus Philipps, Bt.; Hugh Owen, Bt.; Geo. Owen, D.D.; Lewis Wogan; W. Philipps; Arthur Owen; Th. Bowen; Rob. Prust; J. Bateman; Jas. Woolford; Rich. Jones; J. Woolford: Wales 4/798/1. (The *ex officio* members of the commission were probably omitted in the expectation that a new commission would soon be issued to mark the start of the reign of James II).

1685: 31 August (Acting)
J. Fowler, Mayor of Haverfordwest; Roger Davies, Alderman: Wales 4/798/2. (No other justices of the peace are named).

1686: 29 March (Acting)
W. Brown, Mayor of Haverfordwest; J. Fowler, Alderman: Wales 4/798/3.

1686: 6 July
Commission renewed to *add* J. Mathews, Justice of Great Sessions: Index 4215/p.158.

1686: 30 August (Acting)
Lord Jeffreys, Chancellor; E. of Rochester, Treasurer; E. of Sunderland, President of Council; E. of Clarendon, Keeper of Privy Seal; D. of Ormond, Steward; D. of Beaufort, President of Council in the Marches of Wales; E. of Lindsey, Great Chamberlain; E. of Mulgrave, Household Chamberlain; Anth. Farrington & J. Mathews, Justices of Great Sessions; W. Brown, Mayor of Haverfordwest; Erasmus Philipps, Bt.; Hugh Owen, Bt.; Geo. Owen, D.D.; Lewis Wogan of Boulston; W. Wogan; W. Philipps; Arthur Owen; Hugh Wogan; Roger Davies; Rob. Prust; J. Bateman; J. Fowler: Wales 4/798/4.

1687: 14 March (Acting)
Jeffreys; Rochester; Sunderland; Clarendon; Ormond; Beaufort; Lindsey; Mulgrave; Farrington & Mathews, Justices of Great Sessions; W. Bowen, Mayor of Haverfordwest; Erasmus Philipps, Bt.; Hugh Owen, Bt.; Geo. Owen, D.D.; Lewis Wogan; W. Philipps; Arthur Owen; Hugh Wogan; Roger Davies; Rob. Prust; J. Bateman; J. Fowler; W. Brown: Wales 4/778/1. (This file is wrongly indexed under the reign of James I).

1687: 29 August (Acting)
As on 14 March 1687, except: W. Wogan, *added*. J. Mathews, *omitted*: Wales 4/798/5.

1687: 29 August
General renewal of Welsh commissions to add the clause of dispensation: Index 4215/p.179. (The Haverfordwest commission was probably included in this renewal. Note that Haverfordwest does not appear to have shared in the purge of the commissions which was ordered by the Privy Council on 17 December 1686: P.C.2/71/p.363, et seq.).

1688: 27 August (Acting)
Jeffreys; Rochester; Sunderland; Clarendon; Beaufort; Lindsey; Mulgrave; Edwin Wyatt & J. Tate, Justices of Great Sessions; Th. Poyer, Mayor of Haverfordwest; Erasmus Philipps, Bt.; Hugh Owen, Bt.; Geo. Owen, D.D.; Lewis Wogan; W. Wogan; W. Philipps; Arthur Owen; Hugh Wogan; Roger Davies; Rob. Prust; J. Bateman; J. Fowler; W. Brown; W. Bowen: Wales 4/798/6.

1688: 17 September (Acting)
As on 27 August 1688, except: W. Philipps, *omitted*: Wales 4/798/7.

1689: 16 September (Acting)
W. Wogan & Marmaduke Gibbs, Justices of Great Sessions; Rob. Prust, Mayor of Haverfordwest; Hugh Wogan; Rob. Prust; J. Bateman; J. Fowler; W. Brown; Th. Poyer: Wales 4/799/1.

Brecon

1543: 12 March
*Lord Audley of Walden, Chancellor; *D. of Norfolk, Treasurer; *D. of Suffolk, President of Council; *J. Russell, kt., Keeper of Privy Seal; E. of Worcester; *B. of Coventry & Lichfield, President of Council in the Marches of Wales; Bishops of *St. Asaph, *St. Davids; Walter, Lord Ferrers; *Nich. Hare, Ed. Croft, Rice Mansel, *J. Vernon, *p W. Vaughan, kts.; *J. Pakington; *Th. Holte; *David Brooke; *J. ap Rice; *Rich. Hassall; J. Morgan; *Th. Havard; Ed. Games; Lewis ap Watkin; Christopher Vaughan; Th. Whitney; Ed. ap Gwilym; Roger Vaughan; W. Aubrey; W. Games. *Later additions to list*: *Th. Bromley, serjeant at law; *Adam Mytton; *W. Herbert of Brecon; Rich. Herbert: C.193/12/1/f.40. (29 names plus 4 corrections).

1555: (Acting)
Roger Vaughan, kt.; Watkin Herbert; Th. Havard; J. Games; W. Games; Ed. Games; Andrew Winter: S.P.11/5/f.61.   (7)

1559: 17 July (Acting)
Bishops of *Bath & Wells, *Chester; *J. Throckmorton, Justice of Chester; *Adam Mytton, *J. Vaughan, *p Roger Vaughan, kts.; *J. Scudamore of Holm; *Chas. Fox; *David Lewis, Ll.D.; *J. Welsh; *Reg. Corbet; *W. Symonds; *W. Gerard; *Rich. Seaborne; *Watkin Herbert; *Th. Havard; J. Games; Th. Solers senior; *Ed. Games; J. Lloyd: Wales 4/320/1. (Details of the quorum are taken from the list of 1559 contained in S.P.12/2/17/p.66. Note that unlike the 1555 list the present one includes the names of members of the Council in the Marches of Wales as well as those of the justices from within Breconshire. Another copy of the commission appears in B.M., Lansdowne Ms. 1218/f.35).   (20)

1560: 14 October (Acting)
Nich. Bacon, kt., Keeper of Great Seal; Marquess of Winchester, Treasurer; E. of Arundel, Steward; H. Sidney, kt., President of Council in the Marches of Wales; Bishops of Hereford, Worcester, St. Davids, St. Asaph; J. Throckmorton, Justice of Chester; Reg. Corbet; W. Gerard; Nich. Arnold, Adam Mytton, J. Vaughan, Roger Vaughan, kts.; David Lewis, Ll.D.; Chas. Fox; J. Scudamore of Holm; Rich. Wye; Rich. Seaborne; Rich. Pates; Alexander Whitehead; Th. Huet, clerk; Watkin Herbert; Th. Havard; Rowland Vaughan; J. Games; J. Lloyd; Th. Solers junior; Andrew Winter; Philip Jones: Wales 4/320/2.   (31)

1561: 28 July (Acting)
Bacon; Winchester; Arundel; Sidney; B. of St. Davids; W. Gerard; Roger Vaughan, kt.; David Lewis, Ll.D.; Rowland Vaughan; Th. Huet, clerk; Watkin Herbert; J. Lloyd; Th. Solers; Andrew Winter; Philip Jones: Wales 4/320/3. (B.M., Lansdowne Ms. 1218/f.84v. contains a list for 1561 which is identical to the present one, except for the inclusion of J. Games. This second list also shows Roger Vaughan as *custos rotulorum*).   (15)

1561: 1 September (Acting)
As on 28 July 1561: Wales 4/320/4.   (15)

1562: 12 February (?)
As on 1 September 1561, except: J. Games, *added*: C.66/985/m.40d. (Note that there is some doubt about the date of this commission. Its enrolment on the patent roll is not specifically dated, being immediately preceded by a commission for Durham of 12 February 1562). (16)

1562: 6 July (Acting)
As on 12 February 1562, except: E. of Pembroke; J. Throckmorton, Justice of Chester; Ed. Herbert, *added*. J. Games, *omitted*: Wales 4/320/5. (18)

1562: 14 September (Acting)
As on 6 July 1562, except: E. of Pembroke; J. Throckmorton, *omitted*: Wales 4/320/6. (16)

1563: 19 July (Acting)
As on 14 September 1562: Wales 4/321/1. (16)

1563: 11 October (Acting)
Bacon; Winchester; Arundel; Sidney, President of Council in the Marches of Wales; B. of St. Davids; W. Gerard; Reg. Corbet; Throckmorton, Justice of Chester; Roger Vaughan, kt.; Chas. Pye; Rich. Wye; Rich. Seaborne; Rich. Pates; J. Price; Rich. Smith; Ed. Games; Th. Huet, clerk; Walter Herbert; J. Lloyd; Andrew Winter; Christopher Vaughan; Philip Jones; Ed. Herbert: Wales 4/321/2. (23)

1564: 10 July (Acting)
As on 11 October 1563: Wales 4/321/3. (23)

1564: 25 September (Acting)
As on 10 July 1564: Wales 4/321/4. (The commission which is enrolled on the 1564 patent roll (C.66/998/m.10d) is identical to the present Gaol File list). (23)

1565: 28 May (Acting)
As on 25 September 1564, except: W. Games, *added*. Ed. Games, *omitted*: Wales 4/321/5. (23)

1565: 15 October (Acting)
As on 28 May 1565, except: J. Walbeof, *added*. Walter Herbert, *omitted*: Wales 4/321/6. (23)

1566: 15 July (Acting)
*Bacon; *Winchester; *Arundel; *Sidney, President of Council in the Marches of Wales; *B. of St. Davids; *W. Gerard, Justice of Great Sessions; *Reg. Corbet; *Throckmorton, Justice of Chester; *p Roger Vaughan, kt.; *Chas. Fox; *Rich. Wye; *Rich. Seaborne; *Rich. Pates; *J. Price; *Rich. Smith; *Th. Huet, clerk; *W. Games; *J. Lloyd; Ed. Herbert; Philip Jones; *Christopher Vaughan; *Andrew Winter; J. Walbeof: Wales 4/322/1. (Details of the quorum are taken from the 1564 commission

contained in C.66/998/m.10d., with the exception of justices added to the commission since 1564 for whom reference was made to a commission of 1573 contained in S.P.12/93/part 2/p.32). (23)

1566: 14 October (Acting)
As on 15 July 1566: Wales 4/322/2. (23)

1567: 23 June (Acting)
As on 14 October 1566, except: David Lewis, Ll.D., Judge of Admiralty; Th. Lewis; Rich. Price; Owen ap Evan Bedo, *added*. Reg. Corbet; J. Lloyd, *omitted*: Wales 4/322/3. (25)

1567: 13 October (Acting)
As on 23 June 1567: Wales 4/322/4. (25)

1568: 24 May (Acting)
As on 13 October 1567, except: Jas. Gamond; H. Vaughan, *added*. Ed. Herbert (Sheriff, 1567-8), *omitted*: Wales 4/322/5. (26)

1568: 18 October (Acting)
As on 24 May 1568, except: E. of Pembroke, Steward, *added*. David Lewis; Th. Lewis, *omitted*: Wales 4/322/6. (David Lewis was probably wrongly omitted). (25)

1569: 11 July (Acting)
As on 18 October 1568, except: David Lewis, Ll.D., *added*: Wales 4/323/1. (26)

1569: 19 September (Acting)
As on 11 July 1569: Wales 4/323/2. (26)

1570: 18 September (Acting)
*Bacon; *Winchester; *Viscount Hereford; *Sidney, President of Council in the Marches of Wales; *B. of St. Davids; *Throckmorton, Justice of Chester; *Gerard, Justice of Great Sessions; *Hugh Cholmondeley, *p Roger Vaughan, kts.; *David Lewis, Ll.D., Judge of Admiralty; *Chas. Fox; *J. Rastell; *Rich. Seaborne; *Rich. Pates; *Rich. Smith; *Th. Huet, clerk; *W. Games; *Ed. Herbert; *Rich. Price; Philip Jones; W. Worthing; J. Walbeof; *H. Vaughan; *Chas. Aubrey; Jas. Gamond; Owen ap Evan Bedo: Wales 4/323/3. (Details of the quorum are based on the commission of 1573 contained in S.P.12/93/part 2/p.32). (26)

1571: 9 July (Acting)
As on 18 September 1570, except: Jas. Croft, kt., Household Controller; J. Games; W. Watkins, *added*. Rich. Smith; W. Games (Sheriff, 1570-1); W. Worthing, *omitted*: Wales 4/323/4. (26)

1572: 7 July (Acting)
As on 9 July 1571, except: W. Games, *added*. Marquess of Winchester; Roger Vaughan; J. Games; Rich. Price, *omitted*: Wales 4/323/5. (The omission of J. Games is probably an error since he again appears in the next list). (23)

1572: 22 September (Acting)
As on 7 July 1572, except: Th. Vaughan; J. Games, *added*: Wales 4/323/6. (25)

1573: 22 June (Acting)
As on 22 September 1572, except: W., Lord Burghley, Treasurer; W., Lord Howard of Effingham, Keeper of Privy Seal; Rich. Price, *added*: Wales 4/324/1. (Note that Lord Howard had already left office as Keeper of the Privy Seal by the time this Gaol File list was drawn up (Howard held office from July 1572 till before May 1573). The delay in his appearing in a Gaol File list may have been caused by delay in issuing a new commission of the peace). (28)

1573: 21 September (Acting)
As on 22 June 1573: Wales 4/324/2. (28)

1573-4: (Acting)
*Bacon; *Lord Burghley, Treasurer; *E. of Essex (former Viscount Hereford); *Sidney, President of Council in the Marches of Wales; *B. of St. Davids; *Jas. Croft, kt., Household Controller; *Hugh Cholmondeley, kt.; *Throckmorton, Justice of Chester; *Gerard, Justice of Great Sessions; *David Lewis, Ll.D., Judge of Admiralty; *Chas. Fox; *J. Rastell; *Rich. Seaborne; *Rich. Pates; *Th. Huet, clerk; *W. Games; *p Rich. Price; *Ed. Herbert; W. Watkins; Philip Jones; J. Games; J. Walbeof; *H. Vaughan; *Chas. Aubrey; Th. Vaughan; Jas. Gamond; Owen ap Evan Bedo: S.P.12/93/part 2/f.32 & B.M., Egerton Ms. 2345/f.40. (27)

1574: 19 July (Acting)
As in 1573-4, except: Chas. Walcott, *added*: Wales 4/324/3. (28)

1574: 4 October (Acting)
As on 19 July 1574: Wales 4/324/4. (28)

1575: 4 July (Acting)
As on 4 October 1574, except: W. Vaughan; J. Aubrey, *added*. B. of St. Davids; Hugh Cholmondeley; J. Rastell; Chas. Aubrey (Sheriff, 1574-5); Philip Jones, *omitted*: Wales 4/324/5. (25)

1575: 17 October (Acting)
Bacon; Burghley; Sidney, President of Council in the Marches of Wales; Essex; B. of St. Davids; Croft; Throckmorton, Justice of Chester; Gerard, Justice of Great Sessions; David Lewis, Ll.D., Judge of Admiralty; Chas. Fox; Rich. Seaborne; Rich. Pates; Th. Huet, clerk; W. Games; Rich. Price; Th. Vaughan; Ed. Herbert; J. Games; W. Vaughan; H. Vaughan; W. Watkins; J. Aubrey; Jas. Gamond; J. Walbeof; Owen ap Evan Bedo: Wales 4/324/6. (25)

1576: 30 July (Acting)
As on 17 October 1575, except: Chas. Walcott, *added*. J. Games (Sheriff, 1575-6), *omitted*: Wales 4/325/1. (Walcott may have been wrongly omitted on 17 October 1575). (25)

1576: 8 October (Acting)
As on 30 July 1576, except: E. of Essex, *omitted*: Wales 4/325/2.   (24)

1577: 22 April (Acting)
As on 8 October 1576, except: Hugh Cholmondeley, kt.; J. Games, *added*.
Jas. Gamond, *omitted*: Wales 4/325/3.   (25)

1577: 7 October (Acting)
As on 22 April 1577, except: E. of Essex; David Williams, *added*. W.
Vaughan; H. Vaughan; Owen ap Evan Bedo, *omitted*: Wales 4/325/4. (Note
that the E. of Essex died in September 1576 and was therefore correctly
omitted from the Gaol File list of 8 October 1576. His restoration in the
present list is a clear error).   (24)

1578: 30 June (Acting)
*Bacon; *Burghley; *Sidney, President of Council in the Marches of Wales;
*B. of Worcester, Vice-President of Council in the Marches of Wales; Earls
of *Worcester, *Pembroke; Bishops of *Hereford, *Bangor, *St. Davids,
*St. Asaph; *Croft; *Throckmorton, Justice of Chester; *Andrew Corbet,
*J. Perrot, *Nich. Arnold, *Hugh Cholmondeley, *J. Littleton, *J. Huband,
kts.; *W. Gerard, Justice of Great Sessions; *David Lewis, Ll.D., Judge
of Admiralty; *Geo. Bromley, Attorney of Duchy of Lancaster; *W. Aubrey,
Ll.D.; *Chas. Fox; *W. Glaseor; *Ellis Price, Ll.D.; *Ed. Leighton; *Rich.
Pates; *Ralph Barton; *Jerome Corbet; *J. Puckering; *Fabian Phillips;
*H. Townshend; *W. Leighton; *Th. Huet, clerk; *W. Games; *p Rich.
Price; Th. Vaughan; *Ed. Herbert; *J. Games; *J. Aubrey; W. Watkins;
J. Walbeof; Chas. Walcott; *David Williams: Wales 4/325/5. (Details of
the quorum are taken from an almost identical list of the Brecon justices in
1578 contained in Hatfield House Ms. 223.7).   (44)

1578: 29 September (Acting)
As on 30 June 1578, except: W. Games (Sheriff, 1577–8), *omitted*: Wales
4/325/6.   (43)

1579: 27 July (Acting)
As on 29 September 1578, except: Th. Bromley, kt., Chancellor; J. Price;
Th. Games; H. Vaughan, *added*. Nich. Bacon, *omitted*: Wales 4/326/1.   (46)

1579: 15 October (Acting)
As on 27 July 1579, except: David Lewis, *omitted* (probably in error):
Wales 4/326/2.   (45)

1580: 11 July (Acting)
As on 15 October 1579, except: Edm. Walter, Deputy Justice of Great
Sessions; David Lewis, Ll.D., *added*. Th. Games (Sheriff, 1579–80), *omitted*:
Wales 4/326/3.   (46)

1580: 19 September (Acting)
As on 11 July 1580, except: Ed. Aubrey; Th. Powell; Rich. Herbert, *added*.
Andrew Corbet; Nich. Arnold, *omitted*: Wales 4/326/4.   (47)

1581 : 17 July (Acting)
As on 19 September 1580, except: Th. Estcourt, Justice of Great Sessions;
Th. Games, *added*. J. Throckmorton; W. Gerard; Chas. Walcott (Sheriff,
1580–1), *omitted*: Wales 4/326/5.   (46)

1581 : 21 September (Acting)
As on 17 July 1581: Wales 4/326/6.   (46)

1582 : 16 July (Acting)
*Th. Bromley, kt., Chancellor; *Burghley; *Sidney, President of Council
in the Marches of Wales; *B. of Worcester, Vice-President of Council in the
Marches of Wales; Earls of *Worcester, *Pembroke; Bishops of *Hereford,
*Bangor, *St. Davids, *St. Asaph; *Croft; *Geo. Bromley, kt., Justice of
Chester; *Edm. Walter & *Th. Estcourt, Justices of Great Sessions; *J.
Perrot, *Hugh Cholmondeley, *J. Littleton, *J. Huband, kts.; *J. Puckering,
serjeant at law; *David Lewis, Ll.D., Master in Chancery; *Chas. Fox;
*W. Aubrey, Ll.D.; *W. Glaseor; *Ellis Price, Ll.D.; *Ed. Leighton;
*Rich. Pates; *Ralph Barton; *Jerome Corbet; *Fabian Phillips; *H.
Townshend; *W. Leighton; *J. Price; *p Rich. Price; *Th. Games; *Th.
Huet, clerk; *Ed. Herbert; *Th. Vaughan; *J. Games; *Ed. Aubrey;
*W. Watkins; *J. Aubrey; David Williams; Chas. Walcott; Lewis Gunter;
H. Vaughan; *Th. Powell; Rich. Herbert; J. Walbeof; Wales 4/327/1.
(Details of the quorum are based on the list of 1584 contained in E.163/
14/8/f.44v).   (48)

1582 : 24 September (Acting)
As on 16 July 1582: Wales 4/327/2.   (48)

1583 : 8 July (Acting)
As on 24 September 1582, except: Walter Prosser, *added*: Wales 4/327/3.   (49)

1583 : 23 September (Acting)
As on 8 July 1583, except: B. of St. Davids; Th. Huet; H. Vaughan; J.
Walbeof, *omitted*: Wales 4/327/4.   (45)

1584 : 20 July (Acting)
As on 23 September 1583, except: B. of St. Davids; J. Walbeof, *added*.
(Walbeof may have been wrongly left out in 1583). B. of Worcester; J.
Huband; David Lewis, *omitted*: Wales 4/327/5.   (44)

1584 : 21 September (Acting)
As on 20 July 1584, except: J. Price, *omitted*: Wales 4/327/6.   (43)

1585 : 12 July (Acting)
As on 21 September 1584, except: Rob. Knollys; Hugh Powell; W. Herbert;
W. Vaughan; Rice Lloyd, *added*. B. of Bangor; Ed. Herbert; Ed. Aubrey
(Sheriff, 1584–5); Th. Powell, *omitted*: Wales 4/328/1.   (44)

1585 : 20 September (Acting)
As on 12 July 1585, except: B. of Hereford, *omitted*: Wales 4/328/2.   (43)

1586: 28 March (Acting)
As on 20 September 1585, except: B. of Hereford, *added*: Wales 4/328/3.   (44)

1586: 5 September (Acting)
As on 28 March 1586, except: H. Sidney, *omitted*: Wales 4/328/4.   (43)

1587: 24 July (Acting)
As on 5 September 1586, except: Christopher Hatton, kt., Chancellor; Ed. Aubrey, *added*. Th. Bromley; B. of Hereford; W. Glaseor; Ralph Barton; Rich. Price (Sheriff, 1586–7); Lewis Gunter, *omitted*: Wales 4/328/5.   (39)

1587: 2 October (Acting)
As on 24 July 1587: Wales 4/328/6.   (39)

1588: 25 March (Acting)
*Burghley; *E. of Pembroke, President of Council in the Marches of Wales; *E. of Worcester; Bishops of *St. Davids, *St. Asaph; *Croft; *Bromley, Justice of Chester; *Walter & *Estcourt, Justices of Great Sessions; *J. Perrot, *Hugh Cholmondeley, *J. Littleton, kts.; *J. Puckering, serjeant at law; *W. Aubrey; *Chas. Fox; *Ellis Price, Ll.D.; *Ed. Leighton; *W. Leighton; *H. Townshend; *Rich. Pates; *Jerome Corbet; *Fabian Phillips; *p Rob. Knollys; *Th. Games; *David Williams; *Ed. Aubrey; *Th. Vaughan; *J. Games; W. Herbert; *W. Watkins; Chas. Walcott; W. Vaughan; Rich. Herbert; Rice Lloyd; J. Walbeof; Walter Prosser: Wales 4/329/1. (Details of the quorum are based on the list of 1590–1 contained in Hatfield House Ms. 278/f.52).   (36)

1589: 17 March (Acting)
As on 25 March 1588, except: Hatton, Chancellor; Gregory Price; J. Aubrey; Lewis Gunter, *added*. E. of Worcester; Rich. Pates; J. Games (Sheriff, 1588–9), *omitted*: Wales 4/329/3.   (37)

1589: 8 September (Acting)
As on 17 March 1589: Wales 4/329/4.   (37)

1590: 25 May (Acting)
As on 8 September 1589, except: J. Games; Hugh Powell, *added*: Wales 4/329/5.   (39)

1591: 5 July (Acting)
As on 25 May 1590, except: J. Price; Roger Vaughan; Roger Williams, *added*. Jas. Croft; Geo. Bromley; Chas. Fox; Rob. Knollys; Th. Vaughan; Hugh Powell; W. Watkins, *omitted*: Wales 4/330/1.   (35)

1591: 20 or 27 September (Acting). (The exact date is uncertain because of damage to the records).
As on 5 July 1591, except: Rich. Shuttleworth, kt., Justice of Chester; Rob. Knollys; W. Watkins, *added*. (Knollys & Watkins had probably been wrongly omitted on 5 July). J. Littleton; Ed. Aubrey, *omitted*: Wales 4/330/2.   (36)

1592: 6 June (Acting)
As in September 1591, except: Christopher Hatton; J. Perrot; J. Puckering; Th. Games; W. Vaughan (Sheriff, 1591–2); Lewis Gunter, *omitted*: Wales 4/330/3. (30)

1592: 25 September (Acting)
As on 6 June 1592, except: Watkin Vaughan; Ed. Aubrey; H. Vaughan; W. Powell, *added*: Wales 4/330/4. (34)

1593: 16 July (Acting)
As on 28 September 1592, except: J. Puckering, kt., Keeper of Great Seal; E. of Essex, *added*: Wales 4/330/5. (36)

1593: 24 September (Acting)
As on 16 July 1593: Wales 4/330/6. (36)

1594: 28 June
*J. Puckering, kt., Keeper of Great Seal; *Burghley; *Pembroke, President of Council in the Marches of Wales; *E. of Essex; Bishops of *St. Asaph, *St. Davids; *Rich. Shuttleworth, kt., Justice of Chester; *Geo. Kingsmill & *Th. Estcourt, Justices of Great Sessions; *W. Aubrey; *Hugh Cholmondeley, kt.; *David Williams, serjeant at law; *Ellis Price, Ll.D.; *W. Leighton; *H. Townshend; *Jerome Corbet; *Fabian Phillips; *p Rob. Knollys; *Gregory Price; *Watkin Vaughan; *Ed. Aubrey; *J. Aubrey; *J. Games; W. Herbert; *W. Watkins; *J. Price; Chas. Walcott; *W. Vaughan; Rich. Herbert; *J. Walbeof; *Roger Vaughan; Roger Williams; Rice Lloyd; H. Vaughan; W. Powell; Walter Prosser; Th. Gunter: C.66/1421/m.15d. (37)

1594: 29 July (Acting)
As on 28 June 1594, except: Walter Prosser (Sheriff, 1593–4), *omitted*: Wales 4/331/1. (36)

1595: 14 April (Acting)
As on 29 July 1594, except: Walter Prosser; J. Herbert, *added*. Ellis Price; Gregory Price (Sheriff, 1594–5), *omitted*: Wales 4/331/2. (36)

1595: 15 August
*Puckering; *Burghley; *Pembroke, President of Council in the Marches of Wales; *Essex; Bishops of *St. Asaph, *St. Davids; *Shuttleworth, Justice of Chester; *Kingsmill & *Estcourt, Justices of Great Sessions; *Hugh Cholmondeley, kt.; *David Williams, serjeant at law; *W. Leighton; *H. Townshend; *Jerome Corbet; *Fabian Phillips; *p Rob. Knollys; *Watkin Vaughan; *Ed. Aubrey; *J. Aubrey; *J. Games; *J. Price; Rich. Herbert; *J. Walbeof; *Roger Vaughan; Roger Williams; *Walter Prosser; *J. Herbert: Bodleian, Bodley Ms. 904/f.214v. (This commission is identified as that of 15 August 1595 in the ms. which is a register of the Council in the Marches of Wales). General renewal of Welsh commissions on 15 August 1595: Index 4208/f.4v. (27)

1596: 29 January
Commission renewed to *restore* Gregory Price, late Sheriff; H. Vaughan: Index 4208/f.10.

1596: 8 July
As on 15 August 1595, except: *Th. Egerton, kt., Keeper of Great Seal; *Gregory Price; *H. Vaughan; *W. Watkins; J. Games junior, *added*. J. Puckering; Watkin Vaughan; J. Aubrey, *omitted*: C.66/1468/m.15d & S.P.13/Case F, no. 11/f.36v. Commission renewed to *restore* W. Watkins and to *add* J. Games junior: Index 4208/f.18. (29)

1596: 1 December
Commission renewed to *add* J. Games of Buckland: Index 4208/f.24.

1597: 14 March (Acting)
As on 8 July 1596, except: W. Vaughan; J. Games of Buckland; Th. Gunter, *added*. Hugh Cholmondeley, *omitted*: Wales 4/332/1. (31)

1597: 14 July
*Th. Egerton, kt., Keeper of Great Seal; *Burghley; *Pembroke, President of Council in the Marches of Wales; *Essex; Bishops of *St. Asaph, *St. Davids; *Shuttleworth, Justice of Chester; *Kingsmill & *Estcourt, Justices of Great Sessions; *David Williams, serjeant at law; *W. Leighton; *H. Townshend; *Jerome Corbet; *p Rob. Knollys; *Gregory Price; *H. Vaughan; *Ed. Aubrey; *J. Games of Newton; *W. Watkins; *J. Price; Rich. Herbert; *J. Walbeof; *Roger Vaughan; Roger Williams; *Walter Prosser; *J. Games of Aberbran; J. Games of Buckland; J. Herbert: C.66/1468/m.30d. Commission renewed to *omit* W. Vaughan; Th. Gunter: Index 4208/f.37. (Note that the service of W. Vaughan & Th. Gunter on the commission presents some problems. Both are given in the commission of 28 June 1594 (C.66/1421/m.15d) but are omitted from that of 15 August 1595 (Bodleian, Bodley Ms. 904/f.214v.) They then reappear in the Gaol File list of 14 March 1597 (Wales 4/332/1). After their formal omission from the commission on 14 July 1597 (Index 4208/f.37) their names, as is to be expected, are left out of future patent roll enrolments of the commission. They do not however disappear from the Gaol File lists until that of 18 September 1598 (Wales 4/332/4). It is possible that both men were continuously members of the commission between 28 June 1594 and 14 July 1597 but there is no easy way of confirming whether or not this was the case). (28)

1598: 22 February
Commission renewed to *add* Chas. Walcott: Index 4208/f.46v.

1598: 15 March
As on 14 July 1597, except: W. Aubrey, Ll.D.; Chas. Walcott, *added*. Burghley; Walter Prosser, *omitted*: C.66/1482/m.16d. Commission renewed to *add* W. Aubrey, Ll.D.: Index 4208/f.47. (Prosser's name is omitted from the list of justices in the patent roll enrolment of the commission but appears among the members of the quorum. However his name is omitted

from the Gaol File list of 12 September 1597 (Wales 4/332/2) so it is probably correct to treat him as no longer being a member of the commission).   (28)

1599: 2 March
Commission renewed to *add* W. Vaughan of Tretower: Index 4208/f.65v.

1599: 30 June
As on 15 March 1598, except: *Th., Lord Buckhurst, Treasurer; *J. Croke, Recorder of London and Justice of Great Sessions; *W. Vaughan of Tretower, *added*. Geo. Kingsmill; Jerome Corbet; J. Price, *omitted*: C.66/1493/m.26d. Commission renewed to *add* J. Croke, Recorder of London & Justice of Great Sessions: Index 4208/f.72. (Lord Buckhurst, who was appointed Treasurer on 15 May 1599, was probably added on the same date).   (28)

1599: 24 November
Commission renewed to *add* W. Walbeof: Index 4208/f.79v.

1600: 5 July
*Egerton; *Lord Buckhurst, Treasurer; *Essex; *Pembroke, President of Council in the Marches of Wales; Bishops of *St. Asaph, *St. Davids; *Rich. Lewkenor, kt., Justice of Chester; *J. Croke, Recorder of London & *Geo. Calfield, Justices of Great Sessions; *David Williams, serjeant at law; *W. Leighton; *H. Townshend; *p Rob. Knollys; *H. Vaughan; W. Aubrey, Ll.D.; *Ed. Aubrey; *J. Games of Newton; *W. Watkins; *W. Vaughan of Tretower; Chas. Walcott; Rich. Herbert; W. Walbeof; *Roger Vaughan; Roger Williams; J. Games of Aberbran; J. Games of Buckland; *J. Herbert: C.66/1523/m.28d. Commission renewed to *add* Geo. Calfield, Justice of Great Sessions: Index 4208/f.93.   (27)

1602: 25 July
As on 5 July 1600, except: *Ed., Lord Zouch, President of Council in the Marches of Wales, *added*. E. of Essex; E. of Pembroke; B. of St. Asaph, *omitted*: C.66/1594/m.32d. General renewal of Welsh commissions to *add* Lord Zouch, President of Council in the Marches of Wales: Index 4208/f.141. (25)

1603: 8 August (Acting)
*Th. Egerton, Lord Ellesmere, Chancellor; *Buckhurst; *Ed., Lord Zouch, President of Council in the Marches of Wales; *B. of St. Davids; *Lewkenor, Justice of Chester; *Croke & *Calfield, Justices of Great Sessions; *David Williams, *J. Games, *H. Williams, kts.; *W. Leighton; *H. Townshend; *p Rob. Knollys; *H. Vaughan; *W. Aubrey, Ll.D.; *Ed. Aubrey; *W. Watkins; *W. Vaughan of Tretower; *Chas. Walcott; Rich. Herbert; *Roger Vaughan; Roger Williams; J. Games of Aberbran; J. Games of Buckland: Wales 4/334/1. (Details of the quorum are based on the commission for 1603-4 enrolled on C.66/1620/m.15d. This enrolment also includes the names of W. Walbeof and J. Herbert who are both omitted from the present and all later Gaol File lists but who remain on patent roll entries until 1604 (C.66/1662/m.20d) and 1608-9 respectively (C.66/1786/m.28d).   (24)

1604: 30 July (Acting)
As on 8 August 1603, except: Francis Tate, Justice of Great Sessions, *added*.
Geo. Calfield; Roger Williams (Sheriff, 1603–4), *omitted*: Wales 4/334/2.   (23)

1604: 17 September (Acting)
As on 30 July 1604: Wales 4/334/3.   (23)

1605: 25 March (Acting)
As on 17 September 1604, except: Roger Williams, *added*: Wales 4/334/4.
(24)

1605: 5 August (Acting)
As on 25 March 1605, except: W. Aubrey, kt., *added*. Ed. Aubrey, kt.,
omitted: Wales 4/334/5.   (24)

1606: 28 July (Acting)
Ellesmere; E. of Dorset (Lord Buckhurst), Treasurer; Zouch, President of
Council in the Marches of Wales; B. of St. Davids; David Williams, kt.,
Justice *coram Rege*; *Lewkenor, Justice of Chester; J. Croke, kt. & Francis
Tate, Justices of Great Sessions; Rob. Knollys, J. Games, H. Williams,
W. Aubrey, H. Townshend, kts.; W. Leighton; H. Vaughan; W. Aubrey,
Ll.D.; W. Watkins; W. Vaughan of Tretower; Chas. Walcott; Rich.
Herbert; Roger Williams; Howel Gwynn; J. Games of Aberbran; J. Games
of Buckland; Rice Williams; Lewis Lewis: Wales 4/335/1.   (26)

1606: 15 September (Acting)
As on 28 July 1606, except: J. Games of Buckland (Sheriff, 1606), *omitted*:
Wales 4/335/2.   (25)

1608: 8 August (Acting)
Ellesmere; E. of Salisbury, Treasurer; E. of Northampton, Keeper of Privy
Seal; Ralph, Lord Eure, President of Council in the Marches of Wales;
B. of St. Davids; David Williams, kt., Justice *coram Rege*; Geo. Snigg, kt.,
Baron of Exchequer & Justice of Great Sessions; Lewkenor, Justice of
Chester; Francis Tate, Justice of Great Sessions; Rob. Knollys, J. Games,
H. Williams, W. Aubrey, H. Townshend, kts.; H. Vaughan; W. Aubrey,
Ll.D.; W. Watkins; J. Games of Aberbran; Chas. Walcott; Rich. Herbert;
Roger Williams; Howel Gwynn; J. Games of Buckland; Rice Williams:
Wales 4/335/3.   (24)

1609: 27 March (Acting)
As on 8 August 1608, except: Lewis Lewis, *added*. W. Aubrey, kt. (Sheriff,
1608–9), *omitted*: Wales 4/335/4.   (24)

1609: 11 September (Acting)
As on 27 March 1609: Wales 4/335/5.   (24)

1610: 13 August (Acting)
*Ellesmere; *Salisbury; *Northampton; *Eure, President of Council in
the Marches of Wales; *B. of St. Davids; *David Williams, kt.; *Geo.

Snigg, kt., Baron of Exchequer & Justice of Great Sessions; *Lewkenor, Justice of Chester; *Francis Tate, Justice of Great Sessions; *p Rob. Knollys, *J. Games, *H. Williams, *W. Aubrey, *H. Townshend, kts.; *H. Vaughan; W. Aubrey, Ll.D.; *W. Watkins; *J. Games of Aberbran; Th. Price; *Chas. Walcott; Rich. Herbert; Roger Williams; *Howel Gwynn; J. Games of Buckland; Rice Williams; Lewis Lewis: Wales 4/336/1. (Details of the quorum are taken from the enrolled commission for 1610 contained in C.66/1897/m.18d.) (26)

1611: 26 August (Acting)
As on 13 August 1610, except: Roderick Gwynn, *added*. W. Watkins, *omitted* (perhaps in error): Wales 4/336/2. (26)

1612: 23 March (Acting)
As on 26 August 1611, except: Chas. Vaughan, *added*. W. Aubrey, kt.; Chas. Walcott, *omitted*: Wales 4/336/3. (25)

1612: 24 August (Acting)
As on 23 March 1612, except: W. Watkins, *added*: Wales 4/336/4. (26)

1613: 22 March (Acting)
As on 24 August 1612, except: E. of Salisbury; David Williams; W. Watkins; Rice Williams (Sheriff, 1612–3), *omitted*: Wales 4/337/1. (22)

1613: 30 August (Acting)
As on 22 March 1613, except: Chas. Vaughan, kt.; Ed. Games; Rice Williams, *added*. J. Games of Buckland, *omitted*: Wales 4/337/2. (24)

1614: post 11 July
*Ellesmere; *E. of Suffolk, Treasurer (appointed on 11 July); *Eure, President of Council in the Marches of Wales; *B. of St. Davids; *Geo. Snigg, kt., Baron of Exchequer & Justice of Great Sessions; *Lewkenor, Justice of Chester; *Francis Tate, Justice of Great Sessions; *Rob. Knollys, *H. Williams, *p Chas. Vaughan, *H. Townshend, kts.; *H. Vaughan; W. Aubrey, Ll.D.; Ed. Games; *Chas. Walcott; *J. Games of Aberbran; Chas. Vaughan; *Th. Price; Rich. Herbert; *Howel Gwynn; *Rice Williams; J. Williams: C.66/1988/m.26d. (22)

1615: 20 March (Acting)
As in 1614: Wales 4/337/4. (22)

1615: 12 July
Commission renewed to *add* Llewelyn Gwilym: Index 4211/f.6.

1615: 21 August (Acting)
As on 20 March 1615, except: B. of St. Davids, *omitted*: Wales 4/337/5. (The new commission including Gwilym had evidently not arrived by this date). (21)

1616: 10 July
Commission renewed to *add* B. of St. Davids: Index 4211/f.23v.

1616: 9 September (Acting)
*Ellesmere; *Suffolk; *Eure, President of Council in the Marches of Wales; *Geo. Snigg, kt., Baron of Exchequer & Justice of Great Sessions; *Lewkenor, Justice of Chester; *Francis Tate, Justice of Great Sessions; *Rob. Knollys, *H. Williams, *p Chas. Vaughan, *H. Townshend, kts.; *H. Vaughan; W. Aubrey, Ll.D.; Ed. Games; *Chas. Walcott; *J. Games of Aberbran; Chas. Vaughan; *Th. Price; Rich. Herbert; *Howel Gwynn; J. Williams; Llewelyn Gwilym: Wales 4/338/2. (Details of the quorum are based on the commission for 1616 enrolled in C.66/2076/m.23d. The 10 July commission had apparently not yet arrived).   (21)

1617: 1 February
Commission renewed to *restore* Chas. Walcott, and to *add* W. Rumsey: Index 4211/f.32v.

1617: 19 March
Commission renewed to *add* Francis Bacon, kt., Keeper of Great Seal; Th., Lord Gerard, President of Council in the Marches of Wales: Index 4211/f.38. (Walter Pye, who was appointed as Justice of Great Sessions in place of Geo. Snigg on 8 February (Index 4211/f.33), was probably also added on this date).

1617: 22 August
Commission renewed to appoint H. Williams, kt., as *custos rotulorum* in place of Chas. Vaughan, kt.: Index 4211/f.48.

1617: 8 September (Acting)
As on 9 September 1616, except: Bacon, Keeper of Great Seal; E. of Worcester, Keeper of Privy Seal; D. of Lennox, Steward; Lord Gerard, President of Council in the Marches of Wales; Th. Chamberlain, kt., Justice of Chester; Walter Pye & Andrew Powell, Justices of Great Sessions; B. of St. Davids, *added*. Lord Ellesmere; Lord Eure; Geo. Snigg; Rich. Lewkenor; Francis Tate; Rich. Herbert; Howel Gwynn (Sheriff, 1616–7), *omitted*: Wales 4/338/4.   (22)

1618: 23 March (Acting)
As on 8 September 1617, except: W., Lord Compton, President of Council in the Marches of Wales; Howel Gwynn, *added*. Lord Gerard, *omitted*: Wales 4/338/3.   (23)

1618: 14 September (Acting)
*Francis Bacon, kt., Keeper of Great Seal; *Suffolk; *E. of Worcester, Keeper of Privy Seal; *D. of Lennox, Steward; *Lord Compton, President of Council in the Marches of Wales; *B. of St. Davids; *Th. Chamberlain, kt., Justice of Chester; *Walter Pye & *Andrew Powell, Justices of Great Sessions; *Rob. Knollys, *p H. Williams, *Chas. Vaughan, *H. Townshend, kts.; *H. Vaughan; *Th. Price; W. Aubrey, Ll.D.; Ed. Games; *Chas. Walcott; *J. Games of Aberbran; Chas. Vaughan; *Howel Gwynn; J. Williams; Llewelyn Gwilym: Wales 4/339/2. (Details of the quorum are taken from the commission of 1618 enrolled in C.66/2147/m.18d).   (23)

1619: 22 March (Acting)
As on 14 September 1618, except: E. of Suffolk; Rob. Knollys, *omitted*:
Wales 4/339/1. (21)

1620: 29 May
Commission renewed to *add* Ed. Williams: Index 4211/f.105v.

1620: 4 November
General renewal of Welsh commissions to *add* Jas. Whitlock, kt., Justice of
Chester: Index 4211/f.114.

1621: 26 February
*Francis Bacon, Viscount St. Alban, Chancellor; *Viscount Mandeville,
Treasurer; *Worcester; *Lennox; *E. of Northampton (Lord Compton),
President of Council in the Marches of Wales; *B. of St. Davids; *Jas.
Whitlock, kt., Justice of Chester; *Pye & *Powell, Justices of Great
Sessions; *p H. Williams, *Chas. Vaughan, *H. Townshend, kts.; J. Games
of Aberbran; Ed. Games; *H. Vaughan; *Th. Price; W. Aubrey, Ll.D.;
*Chas. Walcott; Chas. Vaughan; *Howel Gwynn; J. Williams; Llewelyn
Gwilym; Ed. Williams: C.66/2234/m.41d & B.M., Harleian Ms. 1933/f.24.
Commission renewed to *add* Viscount Mandeville, Treasurer: Index 4211/
f.120. (23)

1621: post 29 September
As on 26 February 1621, except: *B. of Lincoln, Keeper of Great Seal;
*Lionel Cranfield, Treasurer, *added*. Viscount St. Alban; B. of St. Davids;
H. Townshend, *omitted*: C.66/2259/m.24d. (Cranfield was appointed
Treasurer on 29 September 1621). (22)

1622: 28 February
Commission renewed to *add* W., B. of St. Davids: Index 4211/f.136.

1622: 9 September (Acting)
As at the end of 1621, except: W., B. of St. Davids; Blanch Parry, *added*.
J. Williams (Sheriff, 1621–2), *omitted*: Wales 4/340/4. (23)

1623: 6 February
*B. of Lincoln, Keeper of Great Seal; *E. of Middlesex (Lionel Cranfield),
Treasurer; *Viscount Mandeville, President of Council; *Worcester; *Lennox;
*Northampton, President of Council in the Marches of Wales; *B. of St.
Davids; *Whitlock, Justice of Chester; *Pye & *Powell, Justices of Great
Sessions; *p H. Williams, *Chas. Vaughan, kts.; Ed. Games; *J. Games of
Aberbran; *H. Vaughan; *Th. Price; W. Aubrey, Ll.D.; *Chas. Walcott;
Chas. Vaughan; *Howel Gwynn; J. Williams; Llewelyn Gwilym; Ed.
Williams; Blanch Parry: C.66/2285/m.31d. Commission renewed to *restore*
J. Williams, late Sheriff: Index 4211/f.148v. (24)

1623: 26 May
As on 6 February 1623, except: *W. Aubrey, kt., *added*. D. of Lennox,
omitted: C.66/2310/m.29d. Commission renewed to *add* W. Aubrey, kt.:
Index 4211/f.152. (24)

1624: 1 May
Commission renewed to *restore* Chas. Vaughan, late Sheriff: Index 4211/f.164.

1624: 11 May
Commission renewed to *add* J. Price: Index 4211/f.164v.

1624: 19 June
Commission renewed to *add* H. Rumsey: Index 4211/f.168d.

1625: 1 April
*Lincoln; *Jas., Lord Ley, Treasurer; *Mandeville; *Worcester; *Northampton, President of Council in the Marches of Wales; *B. of St. Davids; *Th. Chamberlain, kt., Justice of Chester; *Pye & *Powell, Justices of Great Sessions; *p H. Williams, *Chas. Vaughan, *W. Aubrey, kts.; *Sampson Eure; *Rob. Brooke; Ed. Games; *J. Games of Aberbran; *H. Vaughan; *Th. Price; *W. Aubrey, Ll.D.; *Chas. Walcott; *Chas. Vaughan; *Howel Gwynn; J. Williams; *J. Price; *H. Rumsey; Llewelyn Gwilym; Ed. Williams; Blanch Parry: C.66/2367/m.27d. General renewal of Welsh commissions: Index 4211/f.180v. (28)

1625: 22 December
As on 1 April 1625, except: *Th. Coventry, kt., Keeper of Great Seal, *added*. B. of Lincoln; Th. Chamberlain, *omitted*: B.M., Harleian Ms. 1622/ f.88v. General renewal of Welsh commissions to *add* Th. Coventry: Index 4211/f.194v. (27)

1626: 20 March
*Th. Coventry, kt., Keeper of Great Seal; *Jas. Ley, E. of Marlborough, Treasurer; *E. of Manchester (Viscount Mandeville), President of Council; *Worcester; *Northampton, President of Council in the Marches of Wales; *B. of St. Davids; *J. Bridgeman, kt., Justice of Chester; *Pye & *Powell, Justices of Great Sessions; *p H. Williams, kt.; *Chas. Vaughan, kt.; *Sampson Eure; *Rob. Brooke; *Ed. Games; *Th. Price; *J. Games of Aberbran; Th. Gwynn; *Chas. Walcott; *Chas. Vaughan; *J. Price; Ed. Williams; Blanch Parry: E.163/18/12/f.90. Commission renewed to *add* J. Bridgeman, kt., Justice of Chester; Th. Gwynn: Index 4211/ff.199, 200. (Another copy of the 20 March 1626 commission is entered in C.193/12/2/ f.65v. but omits the Bishop of St. Davids and was probably therefore made after the Bishop's translation to Bath & Wells in September 1626). (22)

1626: 31 July (Acting)
As on 20 March 1626, except: Chas. Vaughan, kt., *omitted*: Wales 4/342/3. (Vaughan's omission may be an error since he reappears in Gaol File lists and enrolled commissions from 1628). (21)

1626: 18 September (Acting)
As on 31 July 1626: Wales 4/342/4. (21)

1627: 10 September (Acting)
As on 18 September 1626: Wales 4/342/6. (21)

1627: 1 December
Commission renewed to *restore* J. Williams: Index 4211/f.236.

1628: 31 March (Acting)
As on 10 September 1627, except: Chas. Vaughan, kt.; Timothy Turneur; J. Williams, *added*. Rob. Brooke, *omitted*: Wales 4/343/1.   (23)

1628: 25 April
Commission renewed to *add* Marmaduke Lloyd, kt.; Index 4211/f.245.

1628: 1 August
As on 31 March 1628, except: *Marmaduke Lloyd, kt.; Rich. Games, *added*. E. of Worcester, *omitted*: C.66/2449/m.33d. Renewed to *add* Rich. Games: Index 4211/f.253.   (24)

1628: 8 September (Acting)
As on 1 August 1628, except: Rich., Lord Weston, Treasurer; E. of Pembroke, Steward, *added*. B. of St. Davids, *omitted*: Wales 4/343/2.   (25)

1629: 23 March (Acting)
As on 8 September 1628: Wales 4/343/3.   (25)

1630: 24 March
Commission renewed to *add* Th. Games of Aberbran: Index 4212/p.27.

1630: 24 April
*Coventry; *Lord Weston, Treasurer; *Viscount Conway, President of Privy Council; *Manchester; *E. of Pembroke, Steward; *Northampton, President of Council in the Marches of Wales; *Bridgeman, Justice of Chester; *Pye & *Powell, Justices of Great Sessions; *p H. Williams, *Chas. Vaughan, *Marmaduke Lloyd, kts.; *Sampson Eure; *Timothy Turneur; *H. Williams; *Ed. Games; *Th. Price; *Th. Games of Aberbran; Th. Gwynn; *Chas. Walcott; *Chas. Vaughan; *J. Williams; *J. Price; *Ed. Williams; Blanch Parry; Rich. Games: C.66/2527/m.27d. Commission renewed to *add* H. Williams: Index 4212/p.30.   (26)

1630: 26 July (Acting)
As on 24 April 1630, except: E. of Pembroke, *omitted*: Wales 4/343/5.   (25)

1630: 13 September (Acting)
As on 26 July 1630, except: E. of Northampton, *omitted*: Wales 4/343/6.   (24)

1631: 1 August (Acting)
As on 13 September 1630, except: Chas. Vaughan, kt.; Th. Gwynn (Sheriff, 1630–1), *omitted*: Wales 4/344/1. (Chas. Vaughan is omitted from Gaol File lists up to 25 July 1636 but his omission is not borne out by any enrolled commission in this period and may be regarded as uncertain).   (22)

1632: 23 July (Acting)
As on 1 August 1631, except: E. of Bridgewater, President of Council in

the Marches of Wales; Walter Rumsey, Justice of Great Sessions; Th. Gwynn, *added*. Viscount Conway; Andrew Powell; Th. Price, *omitted*: Wales 4/344/2. (22)

1632: 17 August
Commission renewed to *add* Th. Price, and to *omit* Th. Games of Aberbran; Chas. Walcott: Index 4212/p.90.

1632: 24 November
Commission renewed to *add* Theophilus, B. of St. Davids: Index 4212/p.94.

1632: 14 December
Commission renewed to *add* J. Walbeof: Index 4212/p.95.

1633: 16 March
*Coventry; *E. of Portland (Lord Weston), Treasurer; *Manchester; *E. of Bridgewater, President of Council in the Marches of Wales; *B. of St. Davids; *Bridgeman, Justice of Chester; *Walter Pye, kt. & *Walter Rumsey, Justices of Great Sessions; *p H. Williams, *Chas. Vaughan, *Marmaduke Lloyd, kts.; *Sampson Eure; *Timothy Turneur; *H. Williams; *Ed. Games; *Th. Price; Th. Gwynn; *Chas. Vaughan; *J. Williams; *J. Price; (Roger Williams); J. Walbeof; Ed. Williams; Blanch Parry; Rich. Games; J. Stedman: C.66/2598/m.20d. Commission renewed to *add* Roger Williams & J. Stedman: Index 4212/p.103. (Note that through an error Roger Williams does not appear in the enrolment of this commission upon the patent roll. His place in the commission can however be found by examination of later Brecon commissions). (26)

1634: 8 February
As on 16 March 1633, except: Geoff. Jeffreys, *added*: C.66/2623/m.22d & C.193/13/2/f.75v. Commission renewed to *add* Geoff. Jeffreys: Index 4212/p.122. (27)

1634: 1 September (Acting)
As on 8 February 1634, except: Chas. Vaughan, kt. (see note under 1 August 1631); Ed. Games, *omitted*: Wales 4/345/2. (25)

1635: 16 March (Acting)
As on 1 September 1634: Wales 4/345/3. (25)

1635: 13 June
Commission renewed to *add* Howel Gwynn: Index 4212/p.168.

1635: 31 August (Acting)
As on 16 March 1635, except: Howel Gwynn, *added*. E. of Portland, *omitted*: Wales 4/345/4. (25)

1636: 31 October
Commission renewed to appoint H. Williams, Esq., as *custos rotulorum* in place of his father, H. Williams, kt., deceased: Index 4212/p.221.

1636: 16 December
Commission renewed to *add* Th. Games: Index 4212/p.222.

1636: 22 December
*Coventry; *B. of London, Treasurer; *Manchester; *Bridgewater, President of Council in the Marches of Wales; *Bridgeman, Justice of Chester; *Walter Rumsey, Justice of Great Sessions; *Chas. Vaughan, *Marmaduke Lloyd, kts.; *Sampson Eure; *Timothy Turneur; *p H. Williams; *W. Morgan, King's attorney; *Th. Games; *Th. Price; Th. Gwynn; *Chas. Vaughan; *J. Price; *Rich. Games; *Howel Gwynn; *J. Williams; Roger Williams; J. Walbeof; Ed. Williams; Blanch Parry; J. Stedman; Geoff. Jeffreys: S.P.16/405/f.73v. Commission renewed to *add* W. Morgan: Index 4212/p.223. (26)

1637: 11 August
Commission renewed to *add* Meredith Lewis: Index 4212/p.259.

1637: 4 September (Acting)
As on 22 December 1636, except: Meredith Lewis, *added*. Chas. Vaughan, kt.; Chas. Vaughan, Esq. (Sheriff, 1636–7); Roger Williams; Blanch Parry, *omitted*: Wales 4/346/4. (This time Chas. Vaughan, kt., seems to be correctly omitted since he also disappears from the enrolled commission of about this period). (23)

1638: 26 March (Acting)
*Coventry; *London; *Manchester; *Bridgewater, President of Council in the Marches of Wales; *Marmaduke Lloyd, kt. & *Walter Rumsey, Justices of Great Sessions; *Sampson Eure; *Timothy Turneur; *p H. Williams; *W. Morgan, King's attorney in Brecon; *Th. Games; *Th. Price; *Th. Gwynn; *J. Price; *Rich. Games; *Howel Gwynn; *J. Williams; J. Stedman; J. Walbeof; Ed. Williams; Geoff. Jeffreys; Meredith Lewis: Wales 4/347/1. (Details of the quorum are based on the enrolled commission for 1637–8 contained in C.66/2761/m.18d.) (22)

1638: 24 September (Acting)
As on 26 March 1638, except: Th. Milward, kt., Justice of Chester, *added*. Wales 4/347/2. (23)

1639: 1 April (Acting)
As on 24 September 1638, except: Th. Milward; Meredith Lewis (Sheriff, 1638–9), *omitted*: Wales 4/347/3. (21)

1639: 19 August (Acting)
As on 1 April 1639: Wales 4/347/4. (21)

1640: 23 March (Acting)
As on 19 August 1639, except: Meredith Lewis, *added*. Lord Coventry; J. Stedman, *omitted*: Wales 4/348/1. (20)

1640: 17 July
Commission renewed to *add* Ed. Rumsey: Index 4212/p.398.

1640: 17 August (Acting)
As on 23 March 1640, except: H. Williams (Sheriff, 1639–40); Ed. Williams, *omitted*: Wales 4/348/2. (18)

1640: 11 September
Commission renewed to *add* Roger Vaughan: Index 4212/p.406.

1641: 30 March
Commission renewed to *add* Herbert Price; J. Herbert; Morgan Aubrey: Index 4212/p.440.

1641: 5 April (Acting)
Lord Littleton, Keeper of Great Seal; London; Manchester; Bridgewater, President of Council in the Marches of Wales; Th. Milward, kt., Justice of Chester; Lloyd & Rumsey, Justices of Great Sessions; Sampson Eure, serjeant at law; Rich. Lloyd; W. Morgan; H. Williams; Th. Price; J. Price; Herbert Price; Th. Games; Th. Gwynn; J. Williams; Rich. Games; Howel Gwynn; Geoff. Jeffreys; W. Morgan, King's attorney in Brecon; J. Walbeof; J. Herbert; Morgan Aubrey; Ed. Rumsey; Roger Vaughan; Meredith Lewis: Wales 4/348/3. (27)

1641: 31 August
Commission renewed to *add* Chas. Walbeof, and to *omit* Howel Gwynn: Index 4212/p.483.

1641: 4 October (Acting)
As on 5 April 1641, except: Chas. Walbeof, *added*. Howel Gwynn; J. Walbeof, *omitted*: Wales 4/348/4. (Note that this list was first of all made up on the basis of the commission of 30 March 1641 since it was corrected after its completion to add Chas. Walbeof and omit Howel Gwynn). (26)

1642: 21 May
Commission renewed to appoint Howel Gwynn as *custos rotulorum*: Index 4212/p.523.

1642: 29 August (Acting)
As on 4 October 1641, except: Howel Gwynn, *added*. B. of London, *omitted*: Wales 4/349/2. (26)

1643: 4 February
Commission renewed to *restore* W. Morgan as King's attorney in Brecon: Index 4210/p.1.

1643: 16 or 18 March
Commission renewed to *add* J. Jeffreys: Index 4212/p.547 & Index 4210/p.9. (Both the above dates appear in the records).

1643: 24 April (Acting)
Littleton; D. of Richmond & Lennox, Steward; E. of Arundel; Bridgewater, President of Council in the Marches of Wales; Viscount Saville, Household

Treasurer; Viscount Falkland, Chief Secretary; Peter Wyche, kt., House-hold Controller; Ed. Nicholas, kt., Chief Secretary; Milward, Justice of Chester; Lloyd & Rumsey, Justices of Great Sessions; Sampson Eure, kt., serjeant at law; Rich. Lloyd, kt.; W. Morgan, King's attorney in Brecon; W. Morgan; H. Williams; Th. Price; J. Price; Herbert Price; Th. Games; Th. Gwynn; Howel Gwynn; J. Williams; Rich. Games; J. Jeffreys; J. Herbert; Morgan Aubrey; Roger Vaughan; Meredith Lewis; Chas. Walbeof; Ed. Williams: Wales 4/349/1. (31)

1643: 26 June
Commission renewed to *add* Walter Pye, kt.; W. Watkins of Tregoyd; Lewis Lloyd; Rees Gwynn: Index 4210/p.24.

1643: 18 September (Acting)
As on 24 April 1643: Wales 4/349/3. (31)

1644: 6 May (Acting)
As on 18 September 1643, except: Viscount Falkland; Th. Games, *omitted*: Wales 4/349/4. (Note that the commission containing the four men added on 26 June 1643 does not appear to have reached its destination). (29)

1647: 22 March
Commission renewed to *add* W. Lewis, Bt.: Index 4213/p.85. (J. Eltonhead & J. Parker who were appointed as Justices of Great Sessions on 20 March (Index 4213/p.82) were probably also added on this date).

1647: 30 August (Acting)
E. of Manchester; W. Lenthall, Speaker of Parliament & Master of the Rolls; J. Eltonhead & J. Parker, Justices of Great Sessions; W. Lewis, Bt.; Hoo Games; Chas. Walbeof; Ed. Williams; Geo. Parry; Ed. Rumsey; Ed. Games; Roger Vaughan; Meredith Lewis; Th. Lewis: Wales 4/349/5. (14)

1647: 27 September (Acting)
As on 30 August 1647: Wales 4/349/5. (Both 1647 Gaol File lists are contained in the same file). (14)

1647: 10 November
Commission renewed to *add* Philip, Lord Herbert, as *custos rotulorum*: Index 4213/p.100.

1648: 20 March (Acting)
As on 27 September 1647, except: Geo. Parry; Ed. Games, *omitted*: Wales 4/349/6. (12)

1649: 6 March
Commission renewed (no details): Index 4213/p.143.

1649: 16 March
Commission renewed to *add* J. Norbury, Justice of Great Sessions: Index 4213/p.144.

1649: 30 July (Acting)
W. Lenthall, Speaker of Parliament; Lord Fairfax, General; Bulstrode Whitelock, Rich. Keble, J. Lisle, Commissioners of Great Seal; H. Rolle, Chief Justice of Upper Bench; J. Eltonhead & J. Norbury, Justices of Great Sessions; Th. Horton; Howel Gwynn; Ed. Rumsey; Ed. Games; H. Williams; Ed. Vaughan; Jas. Parry; Th. Williams; W. Watkins; Lewis Jones: Wales 4/350/1. (18)

1649: 12 November
*Lenthall; *Fairfax; *J. Bradshaw, President of the Council; *Whitelock, *Keble & *Lisle; *Rolle; *Eltonhead & *Norbury, Justices of Great Sessions; *Edm. Prideaux, Attorney-General; *Th. Harrison; *Ed. Rumsey; *Ed. Games; *Roger Havard of Llanddew; *Th. Gunter of Llanfihangel-Talyllyn; W. Watkins; Lewis Jones; *Chas. Walbeof; *Th. Lewis; *Meredith Lewis; *Roger Games; Th. Bowen; J. Williams: C.193/13/3/ f.71v. Commission renewed to *add* Th. Harrison: Index 4213/p.168. (The name of Ed. Walbeof appears as a correction to the basic list). (23)

1650: 9 March
Commission renewed to appoint Th. Harrison as *custos rotulorum* and to *add* Philip Jones; Th. Watkins; Ed. Williams; Chas. Walbeof: Index 4213/p.180. (Chas. Walbeof may be a clerical error for Ed. Walbeof).

1650: 25 March (Acting)
As on 12 November 1649, except: Ed. Freeman, Attorney-General of South Wales; Philip Jones; H. Williams; Ed. Williams; Th. Williams; Th. Watkins, *added*. Roger Havard of Llanddew; Th. Gunter; W. Watkins (Sheriff, 1649–50); Ed. Walbeof; Th. Lewis; Meredith Lewis; Roger Games; Th. Bowen; J. Williams, *omitted*: Wales 4/350/2. (21)

1650: 29 July (Acting)
As on 25 March 1650, except: W. Watkins, *added*: Wales 4/350/3. (22)

1650: 11 October
*Lenthall; *Oliver Cromwell, Lord General; *Bradshaw; *Whitelock, *Keble & *Lisle; *Rolle; *Eltonhead & *Norbury, Justices of Great Sessions; *Prideaux, Attorney-General; *Ed. Freeman, Attorney-General of South Wales; *p Th. Harrison; *Philip Jones; *Chas. Walbeof; *Ed. Rumsey; *Ed. Games; *Roger Havard of Acton; *H. Williams; Ed. Williams; Th. Williams; W. Watkins; Lewis Jones; Th. Watkins: *Lists published by Th. Walkley* (1650), p.63. Commission renewed to *add* Roger Havard: Index 4213/p.201. (23)

1651: 10 July
Commission renewed to *add* David Gwynn of Hay; Th. Lloyd of Llangamarch: Index 4213/p.222.

1651: 18 December
Commission renewed to *add* W. Jones, to *omit* David Gwynn; Roger Havard; Th. Lloyd, and to place Lewis Jones; W. Watkins on the quorum: Index 4213/p.227.

1652: 4 March
*Lenthall; *Cromwell; *Whitelock, *Keble & *Lisle; *Bradshaw; *Rolle; *Eltonhead & *Norbury, Justices of Great Sessions; *Prideaux; *p Th. Harrison; *Ed. Freeman, Attorney-General of South Wales; *Philip Jones; *Ed. Rumsey; *Ed. Games; *H. Williams; Ed. Williams; *Meredith Lewis; *J. Williams; Th. Williams; *W. Watkins; *Lewis Jones; Th. Watkins; W. Jones: C.193/13/4/f.112 & B.M., Stowe Ms. 577/f.60. (The copy of the commission contained in B.M., Stowe Ms. 577 is identical to the C.193 version except for the omission of J. Bradshaw). Commission renewed to *add* Meredith Lewis; J. Williams, and to *omit* Chas. Walbeof: Index 4213/p.233. (24)

1653: 10 January
Commission renewed to *add* Geo. Gwynn, and to *omit* Th. Williams: Index 4213/p.249.

1653: 18 March
As on 4 March 1652, except: *H., Lord Herbert of Raglan; *Geo. Gwynn, *added*. Th. Williams, *omitted*: Cambridge University Ms. Dd.VIII.1/f.118v. Commission renewed to *add* Lord Herbert of Raglan: Index 4213/p.255. (25)

1654: 18 March
Commission renewed according to a general list: Index 4213/p.285.

1655: 16 April (Acting)
Whitelock, Keble & Lisle; H., Lord Herbert of Raglan; Philip Jones, one of the Council; H. Rolle, Chief Justice of Upper Bench; Oliver St. John, Chief Justice of Common Bench; J. Corbet, Justice of Great Sessions; Edm. Prideaux, Attorney-General; Edm. Jones, Attorney-General of South Wales; Geo. Gwynn; Ed. Games; H. Williams; Ed. Williams; Meredith Lewis; J. Williams; W. Watkins; Th. Watkins; W. Jones; David Morgan of Llanwenarth: Wales 4/351/3. (20)

1655: 30 August
Commission renewed to *add* W. Foxwist, Justice of Great Sessions: Index 4213/p.317.

1656: 20 March
Commission renewed to *add* Major-General Jas. Berry; Rowland Dawkins; Evan Lewis; W. Jones of Buckland: Index 4213/p.330.

1656: 7 April (Acting)
*Nathaniel Fiennes & *J. Lisle, Commissioners of Great Seal; *Bulstrode Whitelock, kt., *Th. Widdrington, kt., *Ed. Montagu & *W. Sydenham,

Commissioners of Treasury; *p Philip Jones; *Lord Herbert of Raglan;
*J. Glynn, Chief Justice of Upper Bench; *W. Lenthall, Master of the Rolls;
*Oliver St. John, Chief Justice of Common Bench; *J. Corbet & *W.
Foxwist, Justices of Great Sessions; *Edm. Prideaux, Attorney-General;
*Major-General Jas. Berry; *Rowland Dawkins; *Edm. Jones, Attorney-
General of South Wales; *Geo. Gwynn; *H. Williams; *Ed. Williams;
*Meredith Lewis; *J. Williams; *W. Watkins; *Th. Watkins; David
Morgan of Llanwenarth; Evan Lewis; W. Jones; W. Jones of Buckland:
Wales 4/351/4. (Details of the quorum are taken from the commission of
18 July entered in C.193/13/6/f.99).   (28)

1656: 18 July
As on 7 April 1656, except: J. Games of Aberbran, added: C.193/13/6/f.99.
Commission renewed to add J. Games: Index 4213/p.344.   (29)

1656: 18 August (Acting)
As on 18 July 1656: Wales 4/351/5.   (29)

1656: 18 December
As on 18 August 1656, except: *W. Morgan, added: C.193/13/5/f.119.
Commission renewed to add W. Morgan: Index 4213/p.354.   (30)

1657: 30 March (Acting)
As on 18 December 1656, except: Lord Herbert, omitted: Wales 4/352/1.
(29)

1657: 10 August (Acting)
As on 30 March 1657, except: Lord Herbert, added (he was apparently left
out in error in March): Wales 4/352/2.   (30)

1658: 12 April (Acting)
As on 10 August 1657, except: Ed. Williams (Sheriff in 1658), omitted:
Wales 4/352/3.   (29)

1658: 23 August (Acting)
As on 12 April 1657: Wales 4/352/4.   (29)

1658: 24 September
General renewal of Welsh commissions to add Rich. Cromwell, Lord
Protector: Index 4213/p.405.

1659: 28 June
Commission renewed according to a general list (no details): Index 4213/
p.435.

1660: 27 February
Commission renewed according to a general list (no details): Index 4213/
p.452.

1660: 8 August
Commission renewed to *add* W. Lewis, Bt., *custos rotulorum*, and others (no details): Index 4212/p.24.

1660: 10 September (Acting)
*Ed. Hyde, kt., Chancellor; *D. of Albemarle, General; *Marquess of Ormond, Steward; *E. of Manchester, Household Chamberlain; *E. of Carbery; *H., Lord Herbert of Raglan; *Rich. Lloyd, kt., Justice of Great Sessions; *p W. Lewis Bt.; *H. Williams, Bt.; *Herbert Price; *Walter Vaughan of Porthaml; Th. Price; Milborne Williams; *Geo. Gwynn; *J. Jeffreys; *Th. Lewis; *J. Williams of Park; *Th. Williams, Recorder of Brecon; *H. Williams of Caebalfa; *Meredith Lewis; *J. Herbert; Lewis Morgan; Walter Vaughan of Trebarried; Morgan Aubrey; Marmaduke Lloyd; *J. Stedman; Th. Williams; Ed. Williams; Hugh Powell; Jas. Watkins; Th. Bowen; Roland Lloyd: Wales 4/353/1. (Details of the quorum are taken from the commission of late 1660 as entered in C.220/9/4/f.99 & B.M., Egerton Ms. 2557/f.98. These two copies of the Brecon commission are almost identical to the present Gaol File list, the main differences being in the order of the names). (32)

1660: post 8 September
As on 10 September 1660, except: *E. of Southampton, Treasurer (appointed on 8 September); *E. of Lindsey, Great Chamberlain, *added*. Rich. Lloyd, Justice of Great Sessions, *omitted*: C.220/9/4/f.99 & B.M., Egerton Ms. 2557/f.98. (33)

1661: 17 August
Commission renewed to *add* Rich. Lloyd, kt. & Arthur Trevor, Justices of Great Sessions; Edm. Jones; W. Morgan of Newton; Ed. Powell: Index 4214/p.134.

1661: 26 August
Commission renewed to *add* H. Williams of Llangattock; J. Morgan of Wenallt; W. Lloyd of Llangamarch: Index 4214/p.136.

1661: 14 October
Commission renewed to *omit* Milborne Williams: Index 4214/p.142.

1661: 8 November
*E. of Clarendon, Chancellor; *E. of Southampton, Treasurer; *Lord Robartes, Keeper of Privy Seal; *Albemarle; *Ormond; *E. of Lindsey, Great Chamberlain; *Manchester; *E. of Carbery, President of Council in the Marches of Wales; *H., Lord Herbert of Raglan; *Rich. Lloyd, kt. & *Arthur Trevor, Justices of Great Sessions; *p W. Lewis, Bt.; *Herbert Price, Bt.; *H. Williams, Bt.; *Lewis Morgan, King's attorney in Brecon; *Marmaduke Lloyd; *Walter Vaughan of Porthaml; Th. Price; *Geo. Gwynn; *J. Jeffreys; *Edm. Jones; *Th. Lewis; *J. Stedman; *J. Herbert; W. Morgan of Newton; Walter Vaughan of Trebarried; Hugh Powell; *Th. Williams, Recorder of Brecon; Th. Williams; *H. Williams; *Meredith Lewis; Ed. Powell; Jas. Watkins; Th. Bowen; Roland Lloyd: C.66/2986/

m.29d & C.193/12/3/f.113v. General renewal of Welsh commissions to *add* E. of Carbery, President of Council in the Marches of Wales: Index 4214/p.144. (35)

1662: 7 April (Acting)
As on 8 November 1661, except: Walter Vaughan of Porthaml; J. Herbert (Sheriff, 1661–2); Roland Lloyd, *omitted*: Wales 4/353/4. (32)

1662: 1 September (Acting)
As on 7 April 1662: Wales 4/353/5. (32)

1663: 31 August (Acting)
As on 1 September 1662, except: J. Herbert, kt., *added*: Wales 4/353/6. (33)

1664: 28 March (Acting)
Clarendon; Southampton; Robartes; Albemarle; Ormond; Lindsey; Manchester; Carbery, President of Council in the Marches of Wales; H., Lord Herbert of Raglan; Lloyd & Trevor, Justices of Great Sessions; W. Lewis, Bt.; H. Williams, Bt.; Herbert Price, Bt.; J. Herbert, kt.; H. Williams; Lewis Morgan, King's attorney in Brecon; Geo. Gwynn; Th. Lewis; Walter Vaughan; J. Jeffreys; Meredith Lewis; Marmaduke Lloyd; Th. Price; Th. Williams; Edm. Jones; Jas. Watkins; Hugh Powell; J. Stedman; W. Morgan of Newton; Th. Williams; Ed. Powell; Th. Bowen: Wales 4/354/1. (33)

1665: 27 March (Acting)
As on 28 March 1664: Wales 4/354/4. (33)

1666: 9 April (Acting)
As on 27 March 1665, except: H. Williams, Bt.; Hugh Powell (Sheriff, 1665–6), *omitted*: Wales 4/355/1. (31)

1666: 18 April
Commission renewed to *add* David Gwynn of Park: Index 4214/p.281.

1666: 12 May
Commission renewed to *add* W. Le Hunt: Index 4214/p.282.

1666: 10 September (Acting)
As on 9 April 1666, except: Job Charlton, kt., Justice of Chester; David Gwynn of Park; W. Le Hunt, *added*. J. Herbert, kt., *omitted*: Wales 4/354/5. (Note that Charlton had held office since 1662 but does not appear in any Gaol File list before the present one because the commission of the peace for Brecon was not renewed between 8 November 1661 and 18 April 1666). (33)

1666: 4 December
Commission renewed to *omit* David Gwynn of Park: Index 4214/p.296.

1667: 12 February
Commission renewed to *add* J. Williams of Cwmdu: Index 4214/p.300.

1667: 1 March
Commission renewed to *add* Th. Street as Justice of Great Sessions in place of Arthur Trevor: Index 4214/p.302.

1667: 20 June
Commission renewed to *add* Roland Gwynn of Tymawr: Index 4214/p.308.

1667: 9 September (Acting)
Clarendon; Robartes; Albemarle; Ormond; Marquess of Worcester; Lindsey; Manchester; Carbery, President of Council in the Marches of Wales; Job Charlton, kt., Justice of Chester; Rich. Lloyd, kt. & Th. Street, Justices of Great Sessions; W. Lewis, Bt.; Herbert Price, Bt.; Lewis Morgan, King's attorney in Brecon; Marmaduke Lloyd; Th. Price; Geo. Gwynn; Roland Gwynn; J. Jeffreys; Edm. Jones; W. Le Hunt; Th. Lewis; W. Morgan of Newton; Walter Vaughan; Hugh Powell; Th. Williams; H. Williams; Th. Williams of Abercamlais; J. Williams; Meredith Lewis; Ed. Powell; Jas. Watkins; Th. Bowen: Wales 4/355/2. (33)

1669: 19 April (Acting)
As on 9 September 1667, except: J. Stedman, *added*. E. of Clarendon; W. Morgan of Newton; Jas. Watkins (Sheriff, 1668–9), *omitted*: Wales 4/356/1. (31)

1669: 11 June
Commission renewed to *add* Th. Hodgkins: Index 4214/p.345.

1669: 6 December
Commission renewed to *add* Daniel Williams: Index 4214/p.357.

1670: 11 January
Commission renewed to *add* Ed. Games: Index 4214/p.359.

1670: 5 December
Commission renewed to *add* J. Gwynn of Glyntowy; J. Morgan of Wenallt, and to *omit* Th. Williams: Index 4214/p.382.

1670: 15 December
Commission renewed to *add* Th. Lane; Marmaduke Gwynn: Index 4214/p.383.

1671: 2 March
Commission renewed to *add* Christopher Middleton: Index 4214/p.386.

1671: 11 September (Acting)
Orlando Bridgeman, kt. & Bt., Keeper of Great Seal; D. of Buckingham, Master of the Horse; Ormond; Worcester; Lindsey; Manchester; Carbery, President of Council in the Marches of Wales; B. of Llandaff; Charlton, Justice of Chester; Lloyd & Street, Justices of Great Sessions; W. Lewis, Bt.; Herbert Price, Bt.; Lewis Morgan, King's attorney in Brecon; Marmaduke Lloyd; Th. Price; Th. Lane; Geo. Gwynn; Roland Gwynn; J. Jeffreys;

Edm. Jones; W. Le Hunt; Th. Lewis; Marmaduke Gwynn; J. Stedman; Th. Hodgkins; W. Morgan of Newton; Walter Vaughan; Ed. Games; Hugh Powell; J. Gwynn; H. Williams; Ed. Powell; Jas. Watkins; Th. Bowen; J. Williams of Cwmdu; Daniel Williams; J. Morgan of Wenallt; Christopher Middleton: Wales 4/356/3. (39)

1672: 21 March
Commission renewed to *add* Ed. Lewis of the Van: Index 4214/p.411.

1672: 22 April (Acting)
As on 11 September 1671, except: E. of St. Albans, Household Chamberlain; Owen Wynn; Ed. Lewis of the Van, *added*. E. of Manchester, *omitted*: Wales 4/356/4. (41)

1672: 22 June
Commission renewed to *add* J. Stedman: Index 4214/p.416. (This may be the same J. Stedman who appears on the commission before 1672).

1672: 5 July
Commission renewed to *add* Ed. Herbert: Index 4214/p.418.

1672: 27 September
Commission renewed to *add* H. Rumsey: Index 4214/p.423.

1673: 16 January
Commission renewed to *add* E. of Shaftesbury, Chancellor; Th., Lord Clifford, Treasurer; Jasper Miller: Index 4214/p.431.

1673: 6 May
Commission renewed to *omit* Marmaduke Gwynn: Index 4214/p.448.

1673: 16 May
Commission renewed to *add* Th. Williams of Abercamlais: Index 4214/p.449.

1673: 19 May (Acting)
As on 22 April 1672, except: E. of Shaftesbury, Chancellor; Lord Clifford, Treasurer; H. Rumsey; Jasper Miller; Ed. Herbert, *added*. Orlando Bridgeman, *omitted*: Wales 4/357/1. (45)

1673: 27 June
Commission renewed to *add* Ed. Williams; J. Gunter: Index 4214/p.452.

1673: 8 July
Commission renewed to *restore* Marmaduke Gwynn: Index 4214/p.455.

1673: 8 September (Acting)
E. of Shaftesbury, Chancellor; Viscount Osborne, Treasurer; E. of Anglesey, Keeper of Privy Seal; Buckingham; Ormond; Marquess of Worcester, President of Council in the Marches of Wales; Lindsey; E. of St. Albans, Household Chamberlain; E. of Carbery; B. of Llandaff; Charlton, Justice of

Chester; Lloyd & Street, Justices of Great Sessions; W. Lewis, Bt.; Herbert Price, Bt.; Owen Wynn; Lewis Morgan, King's attorney in Brecon; Ed. Lewis of the Van; Th. Price; Th. Lane; Geo. Gwynn; Roland Gwynn; J. Jeffreys; Edm. Jones; Marmaduke Lloyd; W. Le Hunt; Th. Lewis; Marmaduke Gwynn; J. Stedman; Th. Hodgkins; W. Morgan; Walter Vaughan of Trebarried; Ed. Games; Hugh Powell; J. Gwynn of Glyntawe; Th. Williams; H. Williams; Ed. Powell; Jas. Watkins; J. Gunter; Th. Bowen; J. Williams of Cwmdu; Daniel Williams; Jasper Miller; J. Morgan; Ed. Herbert; Christopher Middleton; H. Rumsey; Ed. Williams: Wales 4/357/2. (49)

1674: 27 April
Commission renewed to *add* Th. Williams, M.D., and to *omit* H. Rumsey; J. Williams: Index 4214/p.476.

1674: 8 December
Commission renewed to *add* J. Williams; H. Proger: Index 4214/p.486.

1675: 1 March
Commission renewed to *add* Th. Walker: Index 4214/p.491.

1675: 12 April (Acting)
As on 8 September 1673, except: Lord Finch, Keeper of Great Seal; E. of Danby, Treasurer; D. of Monmouth; E. of Arlington, Household Chamberlain; Th. Williams, M.D.; Th. Walker; H. Proger, *added*. E. of Shaftesbury; Lord Clifford; E. of St. Albans; Geo. Gwynn; H. Rumsey, *omitted*: Wales 4/357/4. (Note that the brief omission of J. Williams between 27 April and 8 December 1674 does not figure in these changes). (51)

1675: 19 June
Commission renewed to *add* Th. Mansel of Briton Ferry: Index 4214/p.496.

1675: 23 August (Acting)
As on 12 April 1675, except: B. of Llandaff; Ed. Lewis, *omitted*: Wales 4/357/5. (49)

1675: 11 October
Commission renewed to *add* Barzillay Jones: Index 4214/p.501.

1676: 17 February
Commission renewed to *add* H. Rumsey: Index 4214/p.507.

1676: 28 February
Commission renewed to *add* Rich. Williams: Index 4214/p.509.

1676: 3 April (Acting)
Lord Finch, Chancellor; E. of Danby, Treasurer; Anglesey; Dukes of Buckingham, Monmouth, Ormond; Worcester, President of Council in the Marches of Wales; Lindsey; E. of Arlington, Household Chamberlain; Carbery; Charlton, Justice of Chester; Lloyd & Street, Justices of Great

Sessions; W. Lewis, Bt.; Herbert Price, Bt.; Th. Williams, kt. & Bt.; Owen Wynn; Lewis Morgan, King's attorney in Brecon; Th. Price; Th. Lane; J. Jeffreys; Edm. Jones; Marmaduke Lloyd; W. Le Hunt; Th. Lewis; Marmaduke Gwynn; J. Stedman; H. Rumsey; W. Morgan of Newton; Walter Vaughan; Ed. Games; Hugh Powell; J. Gwynn; Th. Williams; Th. Walker; Ed. Powell; Jas. Watkins; J. Gunter; Th. Bowen; H. Proger; J. Williams of Cwmdu; Daniel Williams; Jasper Miller; J. Morgan; Ed. Herbert; Christopher Middleton; Barzillay Jones; Ed. Williams; Th. Mansel of Briton Ferry; Rich. Williams of Caebalfa: Wales 4/357/6.   (50)

1676: 8 June
Commission renewed to *omit* Th. Hodgkins; Marmaduke Gwynn; J. Gunter; Ed. Herbert; Jasper Miller; Barzillay Jones; J. Gwynn: Index 4214/p.513. (Note that Th. Hodgkins does not appear in the Gaol File list of 3 April 1676. His omission on that occasion may however have been an error).

1676: 14 December
Commission renewed to *add* Jasper Miller: Index 4214/p.519.

1677: 7 May (Acting)
As on 3 April 1676, except: Lewis Meyrick, *added*. Rich. Lloyd; Marmaduke Gwynn; J. Gwynn; J. Gunter; Ed. Herbert; Barzillay Jones, *omitted*: Wales 4/358/1.   (45)

1677: 6 November
Commission renewed to appoint Th. Williams, kt. & Bt., as *custos rotulorum*: Index 4214/p.534.

1678: 7 July
Commission renewed to *add* Marmaduke Gwynn; Lewis Lewis: Index 4214/p.547.

1679: 28 April (Acting)
As on 7 May 1677, except: Marmaduke Gwynn; Lewis Lewis, *added*. W. Lewis, Bt.; Herbert Price, Bt.; Ed. Powell; Th. Bowen, *omitted*: Wales 4/358/3.   (43)

1679: 29 April
Commission renewed to *add* Philip Parry: Index 4215/p.6.

1679: 13 November
Commission renewed to *add* Rich. Jeffreys: Index 4215/p.15.

1679: 9 December
Commission renewed to appoint Marquess of Worcester as *custos rotulorum*: Index 4215/p.17.

1680: 1 April
*Prince Rupert; *Archbishop of Canterbury; *Lord Finch, Chancellor; *E. of Radnor, President of Council; *E. of Anglesey, Keeper of Privy

Seal; Dukes of *Albemarle, *Monmouth, *Newcastle, *Lauderdale, *Ormond; *Marquess of Winchester; *p Marquess of Worcester, President of Council in the Marches of Wales; Earls of *Lindsey, *Arlington, *Salisbury, *Bridgewater, *Sunderland, *Essex, *Bath, *Halifax, *Carbery; *Viscount Fauconberg; *B. of London; *B. of St. Davids; *Laurence Hyde; *H. Coventry; *Francis North, kt., Chief Justice of Bench; *J. Ernley, kt., Chancellor of Exchequer; *Th. Chichley, kt., Chancellor of Duchy of Lancaster; *W. Temple, Bt.; *Ed. Seymour; *Daniel Finch; *Leoline Jenkins; *Sidney Godolphin; *Th. Street & *Owen Wynn, Justices of Great Sessions; *J. Ashburnham; *Lewis Meyrick, King's attorney in Wales; *Lewis Morgan, King's attorney in Brecon; Th. Price; *Th. Lane; *J. Jeffreys; *Edm. Jones; *Marmaduke Lloyd; *W. Le Hunt; *Th. Walker; *Th. Lewis; *J. Stedman; W. Morgan of Newton; *Walter Vaughan of Trebarried; *Ed. Games; Hugh Powell; Th. Williams; Jas. Watkins; *H. Proger; *J. Williams of Cwmdu; *Lewis Lewis; *Daniel Williams; *Philip Parry; *Jasper Miller; *Rich. Jeffreys; Christopher Middleton; *Ed. Williams; *W. Powell, clerk: C.193/12/4/f.135v. Commission renewed to remove recusants and add others (no details): Index 4215/p.26. (The *omission* from the Brecon commission of the Duke of Buckingham; Th. Williams, kt. & Bt.; Marmaduke Gwynn; J. Morgan of Wenallt was ordered by a warrant of 5 February 1680 and that of Rich. Williams by a warrant of 26 April. The *addition* of J. Ashburnham was ordered by a warrant of 5 February and of W. Powell, clerk, by one of 12 February 1680: *H.M.C., Eleventh Report, Appendix,* Part 2, p.174. The details of the revised commission published in 1680 by N.S., Esq. (p.24) also record the omission at some stage during the year of H. Rumsey and Th. Mansel of Briton Ferry. The order for the omission of Rich. Williams was given by the Privy Council on 17 April 1680 (P.C.2/68/p.483) and was given effect by the warrant of 26 April, this correction to the commission issued on 1 April probably being made when the commission was inserted in the C.193 entry book).   (64)

1681: 28 March (Acting)
As on 1 April 1680, except: E. of Ossory, *added*. Th. Lewis; J. Williams of Cwmdu, *omitted*: Wales 4/358/6.   (63)

1682: 18 February
Commission renewed to *omit* Marmaduke Lloyd; Walter Vaughan; Th. Mansel; Hugh Powell; Ed. Williams: Index 4215/p.60. (Note that Mansel had already been omitted in 1680).

1682: 3 April (Acting)
As on 28 March 1681, except: Chas., Lord Herbert; Geo. Jeffreys, kt., Justice of Chester; Rob. Wright, kt., Justice of Great Sessions, *added*. D. of Monmouth; Earls of Salisbury, Sunderland, Ossory, Essex; W. Temple; Th. Street; Marmaduke Lloyd; Walter Vaughan; Hugh Powell; Jas. Watkins; Ed. Williams, *omitted*: Wales 4/359/1. (The additions were probably made in the commission of 18 February).   (54)

1682: 14 August
Commission renewed to *add* J. Williams; Ed. Williams, and to *omit* Th. Williams; Daniel Williams: Index 4215/p.69.

1682: 23 September (Acting)
As on 4 April 1682, except: J. Williams; Ed. Williams, *added*. E. of Anglesey; Th. Williams; Daniel Williams, *omitted*: Wales 4/359/2. (53)

1683: 8 March
Commission renewed to *add* Marmaduke Gwynn: Index 4215/p.80.

1683: 2 April (Acting)
Canterbury; Francis North, kt., Keeper of Great Seal; E. of Radnor, President of Council; Marquess of Halifax, Keeper of Privy Seal; Dukes of Albemarle, Newcastle, Ormond; D. of Beaufort (Marquess of Worcester), President of Council in the Marches of Wales; Marquess of Winchester; Lindsey; Arlington; Earls of Bridgewater, Sunderland, Bath, Conway, Nottingham, Rochester, Carbery; Chas., Lord Herbert; Viscount Fauconberg; Bishops of London, St. Davids; H. Coventry; J. Ernley, kt., Chancellor of Exchequer; Th. Chichley, kt., Chancellor of Duchy of Lancaster; Ed. Seymour; Leoline Jenkins, kt.; Sidney Godolphin; Geo. Jeffreys, kt. & Bt., Justice of Chester; Rob. Wright, kt. & Owen Wynn, Justices of Great Sessions; J. Ashburnham; Lewis Meyrick, King's attorney in Wales; Lewis Morgan, King's attorney in Brecon; Th. Price; Th. Lane; J. Jeffreys; Edm. Jones; W. Le Hunt; Th. Walker; Marmaduke Gwynn; J. Stedman; W. Morgan of Newton; Ed. Games; H. Proger; Lewis Lewis; J. Williams; Ed. Williams; Philip Parry; Jasper Miller; Rich. Jeffreys; Christopher Middleton; W. Powell, clerk: Wales 4/359/3. (53)

1683: 24 September (Acting)
As on 2 April 1683, except: Edm. Jones, *omitted*: Wales 4/359/4. (52)

1684: 25 March
Commission renewed to *add* Ed. Jones: Index 4215/p.100.

1684: 29 March (Acting)
As on 24 September 1683, except: Ed. Jones, *added*. E. of Conway; Geo. Jeffreys, *omitted*: Wales 4/359/5. (51)

1684: 11 August (Acting)
As on 29 March 1684, except: B. of St. Davids, *omitted*: Wales 4/359/6. (50)

1685: 3 March
Commission renewed to *add* D. of Beaufort as *custos rotulorum*; W. Bowen: Index 4215/p.121. (J. Powell who was appointed as Justice of Great Sessions on 13 February (Index 4215/p.117) was probably also added on this date).

1685: 13 April (Acting)
As on 11 August 1684, except: E. of Clarendon, Keeper of Privy Seal; Geo. Jeffreys, kt. & Bt., Justice of Chester; J. Powell, Justice of Great Sessions; W. Bowen of Talyllyn, *added*. E. of Radnor; Rob. Wright; Jasper Miller, *omitted*: Wales 4/360/1. (51)

1685: 21 September (Acting)
As on 13 April 1685, except: Francis North, Lord Guilford; E. of Arlington; Leoline Jenkins, *omitted*: Wales 4/360/2. (48)

1685: post 28 September
*Canterbury; *Geo., Lord Jeffreys, Chancellor (appointed on 28 September); *E. of Rochester, Treasurer; *Halifax; *E. of Clarendon, Keeper of Privy Seal; Dukes of *Albemarle, *Newcastle, *Ormond; *p D. of Beaufort, President of Council in the Marches of Wales; Marquesses of *Winchester, *Worcester; Earls of *Lindsey, *Ailesbury, *Bridgewater, *Sunderland, *Bath, *Nottingham, *Carbery; *Viscount Fauconberg; Bishops of *London, *St. Davids; *Sidney, Lord Godolphin; *H. Coventry; *J. Ernley, kt., Chancellor of Exchequer; *Th. Chichley, kt., Chancellor of Duchy of Lancaster; *Ed. Seymour; *Owen Wynn, serjeant at law & *J. Powell, Justices of Great Sessions; *J. Ashburnham, Bt.; *Lewis Meyrick, King's attorney in Wales; *Lewis Morgan, King's attorney in Brecon; Th. Price; *Th. Lane; *J. Jeffreys; *Ed. Jones; *W. Le Hunt; *Th. Walker; *Marmaduke Gwynn; *J. Stedman; *W. Morgan of Newton; *Ed. Games; *H. Proger; *Lewis Lewis; *J. Williams; *Ed. Williams; *Philip Parry; *W. Bowen of Talyllyn; *Rich. Jeffreys; Christopher Middleton; *W. Powell, clerk: C.193/12/5/f.159v. (50)

1686: 15 June
Th. Geers appointed as Justice of Great Sessions in place of J. Powell: Index 4215/p.155. (There is no indication of the date on which he was added to the commission).

1686: 17 December
Order by Privy Council that Francis Gwynn; Rob. Price; W. Winter; W. Lee should be *added* to the Brecon commission, and J. Ashburnham, *omitted*: P.C.2/71/p.376. (A memorandum of the same date ordered that the members of the Privy Council should be added to the commissions of the peace: Ibid./p.379).

1687: 26 June
D. of Beaufort recommends appointment of Sir Edward Williams as a J.P.: N.L.W. Ms. 11020.E.

1687: 29 August
General renewal of Welsh commissions to add the clause of dispensation: Index 4215/p.179.

1688: 2 April
Commission renewed to *add* certain justices and to *omit* others (no details): Index 4215/p.190.

1688: 24 September (Acting)
Canterbury; Jeffreys; E. of Sunderland, President of Council; Lord Arundell of Wardour, Keeper of Privy Seal; Dukes of Ormond, Albemarle, Newcastle; D. of Beaufort, President of Council in the Marches of Wales;

Marquesses of Winchester, Powys, Worcester; Lindsey; E. of Mulgrave, Household Chamberlain; Earls of Bath, Castlemaine; Viscounts Fauconberg, Preston, Montgomery; Bishops of Durham, St. Davids; Lords Belasyse, Dartmouth, Godolphin, Dover; J. Ernley, kt., Chancellor of Exchequer; Ed. Herbert, kt., Chief Justice of the Bench; Owen Wynn & Th. Geers, Justices of Great Sessions; Th. Williams, kt. & Bt.; Ed. Williams, kt.; Rob. Price; W. Winter; W. Lee; Th. Price; J. Jeffreys; Chas. Lloyd; W. Le Hunt; W. Watkins; Philip Parry; Lewis Jones of Talyllyn; Samuel Pritchard; Th. Bradford; Owen Wynn; J. Walters of Brecon; Th. Gwynn of Penygwryd; Walter Vaughan of Trebarried; Ed. Williams; J. Williams; Jas. Parry of Trostre; Rich. Price; Lewis Hubbard: Wales 4/361/5.   (51)

1688: 6 October
General renewal of Welsh commissions: Index 4215/p.200.

1689: 19 April (Acting)
Archbishop of Canterbury; J. Maynard, Anthony Keck & W. Rawlinson, kts., Commissioners of Great Seal; Marquess of Carmarthen, President of Council; Marquess of Halifax, Keeper of Privy Seal; D. of Norfolk; D. of Bolton; Marquess of Worcester; E. of Lindsey, Great Chamberlain; E. of Devonshire, Steward; E. of Dorset, Household Chamberlain; Earls of Oxford, Shrewsbury, Bedford, Bath; E. of Macclesfield, President of Council in the Marches of Wales; E. of Nottingham; J. Trenchard, kt., Justice of Chester; Ed. Williams, Bt.; Roland Gwynn, kt.; H. Morgan of Tredegar; J. Ashburnham; J. Powys of Coedmore; Rich. Williams of Caebalfa; Ed. Jones; Bussey Mansel; Geoff. Jeffreys; J. Jeffreys; Chas. Morgan; Walter Vaughan; Daniel Williams; Marmaduke Lloyd; J. Morgan; Walter Williams; Rich. Jeffreys; Jasper Miller; Geo. Gwynn; Gwynn Vaughan; J. Walbeof; Samuel Williams; J. Lewis of Llangorse; W. Powell; Francis Lloyd; Rich. Price; Rob. Rumsey; Jas. Donne: Wales 4/362/2.   (47)

1689: 28 May
Commission renewed to *add* Th. Geers & H. Chauncy, kt., Justices of Great Sessions, and to appoint Roland Gwynn, kt., as *custos rotulorum*: Index 4215/p.225.

1689: 26 September
Commission renewed to *add* J. Stedman; Marmaduke Gwynn and others: Index 4215/p.239.

Glamorgan

1536: 24 February
*E. of Worcester; Leyshon, Abbot of Neath; Lewis, Abbot of Margam; Th. Gamage, kt.; Rice Mansel, kt.; *Walter Herbert; Geo. Herbert; Geo. Mathew; Th. Stradling; Arnall Butler; Milo Mathew; *Ed. Lewis; Howel Carne; Edm. Turner; Rob. ap William Mathew; *J. Broune; *Th. Atkins; *Lewis Blethin; *J. Bassett: C.66/667/m.26d. (Note that this is *not* a commission of the peace and of oyer and terminer as it is described in *Letters & Papers of Reign of Henry VIII*, 10, no. 392 (48) but is a commission appointing the E. of Worcester, etc., as justices in eyre. This commission is included for the sake of comparison with later commissions of the peace with which it has similarities in membership. For a discussion of the background to the commission see W. R. B. Robinson, 'Early Tudor Policy towards Wales', part 3, *Bulletin of Board of Celtic Studies*, 21, 1965–66, p.343, n.4).   (19)

1541: 2 October (Acting)
Prisoner brought before Th. Stradling, Justice of the Peace in Glamorgan: Wales 4/591/1/item 5. (This is the earliest reference found for a Justice of the Peace acting in any Welsh county, the next in date being 6 October 1541 in Caernarvon: see Caernarvonshire list).

1541: 25 November (Acting)
Prisoner brought before Geo. Mathew, Justice of the Peace: Wales 4/591/1/item 4.

1541: 24 December (Acting)
Prisoner brought before Ed. Lewis and Milo Mathew, Justices of the Peace: Wales 4/591/1/item 8.

1542: pre 27 March (Acting)
Indictment of prisoner before Th. Stradling; Ed. Lewis; Rich. Carne; Geo. Mathew; Milo Mathew, Justices of the Peace: Wales 4/591/1/item 3. (This item is undated. 27 March was the date of the Great Session for which the present Gaol File was produced).

1542: 27 March (Acting)
Th. Audley, kt., Chancellor; D. of Norfolk, Treasurer; D. of Suffolk, President of Council; E. of Southampton, Keeper of Privy Seal; E. of Worcester; B. of Coventry & Lichfield, President of Council in Wales & the Marches; B. of St. Davids; Walter, Lord Ferrers; Nich. Hare, Ed. Croft, J. Vernon, Ed. Carne, Th. Gamage, kts.; J. Pakington; Th. Holte; David Brooke; J. ap Rice; Rich. Hassall; W. Herbert; Geo. Herbert; Th. Stradling; J. Bassett; Ed. Lewis; Rich. Carne; Geo. Mathew; Milo Mathew: Wales 4/591/1. (26 names).

1543: 12 March
*Audley; *Norfolk; *Suffolk; *J. Russell, kt., Keeper of Privy Seal; E. of Worcester; *B. of Coventry & Lichfield, President of Council in the Marches of Wales; Bishops of *St. Asaph, *St. Davids; Walter, Lord Ferrers; *Nich. Hare, Ed. Croft, Rice Mansel, *J. Vernon, *Ed. Carne, Th. Gamage, kts.;

*J. Pakington; *Th. Holte; *David Brooke; *J. ap Rice; *Rich. Hassall; *Walter Herbert; *p W. Herbert; *Geo. Herbert; *Th. Stradling; *J. Bassett; *Ed. Lewis; Roger Carne; *Geo. Mathew; Milo Mathew. *Later additions to list*: *Th. Bromley, serjeant at law; *Adam Mytton; H. Morgan, clerk; Th. Bowen; J. Mathew; Christopher Turberville; Mayor of Cardiff: C.193/12/1/f.41. (29 names plus 7 corrections).

1548: 28 May (Acting)
D. of Somerset, Protector; the Earl Marshal; W. Paulet, kt., Lord St. John, President of Council; J. Russell, kt., Lord Russell, Keeper of Privy Seal; E. of Worcester; B. of Coventry & Lichfield, President of Council in the Marches of Wales; Bishops of St. Asaph, Llandaff; Walter Devereux, kt., Lord Ferrers; W. Herbert, Rob. Townshend, J. Pakington, kts.; David Brooke, serjeant at law; J. ap Rice, Rice Mansel, Geo. Herbert, Ed. Carne, Adam Mytton, kts.; Rich. Germyn; H. Morgan, clerk; Geo. Mathew; Ed. Lewis; W. Bassett; Jas. Thomas; Roger Carne; Th. Bowen: Wales 4/591/3. (26)

1549: 1 July (Acting)
Somerset; Rich., Lord Rich., Chancellor; St. John; Russell; E. of Warwick, Great Chamberlain & President of Council in the Marches of Wales; E. of Worcester; Bishops of Worcester, Llandaff; Walter, Lord Ferrers; Ed., Lord Powys; W., Lord Herbert; Rob. Townshend, Th. Bromley, Ed. Carne, Rice Mansel, J. Pakington, Geo. Herbert, Th. Holcrofte, J. Talbot, Roland Hill, W. Bruerton, Th. Jones, W. Herbert, Hugh Cholmondeley, J. Salisbury, J. Puleston, J. ap Rice, Th. Stradling, Adam Mytton, kts.; Griffith Leyson, Ll.D.; Rich. Hassall; Geo. Willoughby; H. Morgan Thomas; J. Bassett; Math. Herbert; Geo. Mathew; Roger Carne; Th. Bowen; W. Bassett; Jas. Thomas; Rob. Gamage: Wales 4/591/4. (41)

1554: 7 May (Acting)
B. of Winchester, Chancellor; Marquess of Winchester, (Lord St. John), Treasurer; E. of Arundel, Steward; E. of Bedford (Lord Russell), Keeper of Privy Seal; E. of Pembroke; B. of Worcester, President of Council in the Marches of Wales; E. of Worcester; Walter, Viscount Hereford (Lord Ferrers); Bishops of St. Asaph, Llandaff; Th. Bromley, Rich. Morgan, David Brooke, Rob. Townshend, Ed. Carne, Geo. Herbert, Th. Jones, Th. Stradling, Andrew Corbet, J. Wogan, J. ap Rice, Adam Mytton, kts.; J. Pollard; Rich. Hassall; J. Welsh; Griffith Leyson, Ll.D.; J. Scudamore; W. Symonds; Reg. Corbet; Edm. Plowden; W. Herbert; Rob. Gamage; Geo. Mathew; W. Bassett; Ed. Stradling; Jas. Thomas; Ed. Lewis: Wales 4/591/5. (Note that the name Rich. Morgan is probably an error for Rice Mansel.) (37)

1555: (Acting)
B. of Llandaff; Geo. Herbert, Rice Mansel, Ed. Carne, Th. Stradling, kts.; W. Herbert; Rob. Gamage; Geo. Mathew; W. Bassett; Ed. Stradling; Jas. Thomas; Ed. Lewis; Jas. Button; W. Carne: S.P.11/5/f.61. (Note that this list includes only the justices from within the county of Glamorgan and omits all the *ex officio* members of the commission). (14)

1555: 7 October (Acting)
B. of Winchester, Chancellor; Marquess of Winchester, Treasurer; Arundel; Bedford; Archbishop of York, President of Council in the Marches of Wales; Earls of Worcester, Pembroke; Viscount Hereford; Bishops of Hereford, St. Davids, Llandaff; J. Bridges, kt., Lord Chandos; David Brooke, Rob. Townshend, Geo. Herbert, Rice Mansel, Andrew Corbet, Ed. Carne, Th. Jones, Th. Stradling, J. Vaughan, J. Wogan, J. ap Rice, Adam Mytton, Geo. Mathew, kts.; J. Pollard; Rich. Hassall; J. Welsh; W. Gerard; Griffith Leyson, Ll.D.; Hugh Curwen, Ll.D.; J. Scudamore; J. Oteley; W. Symonds; Reg. Corbet; Geo. Wood; Edm. Plowden; Rich. Seaborne; W. Herbert; Ed. Mansel; Rob. Gamage; W. Bassett; Ed. Stradling; Jas. Thomas; Ed. Lewis; Jas. Button; W. Carne: Wales 4/591/6. (47)

1557: 18 October (Acting)
Archbishop of York, Chancellor; Marquess of Winchester, Treasurer; Arundel; W., Lord Paget, Keeper of Privy Seal; E. of Pembroke, President of Council in the Marches of Wales; E. of Worcester; Viscount Hereford; Bishops of Worcester, Gloucester, St. Davids, Bangor, Llandaff, Chester, St. Asaph; H., Lord Stafford; David Brooke, Geo. Herbert, Rice Mansel, Ed. Carne, Th. Jones, Roger Vaughan, Adam Mytton, Geo. Mathew, kts.; J. Scudamore; J. Williams, Ll.D.; Geoff. Gwilym, Ll.D.; David Lewis, Ll.D.; J. Smyth, Ll.D.; W. Sheldon; W. Symonds; J. Welsh; Reg. Corbet; Gilbert Gerard; Edm. Plowden; W. Wightman; W. Gerard; Rich. Seaborne; W. Herbert; Ed. Mansel; Rob. Gamage; W. Bassett; Jas. Thomas; Ed. Lewis; Rob. Stradling; David Evans: Wales 4/591/7. (45)

1558–9: (Acting)
*Nich. Bacon, kt., Keeper of Great Seal; *Winchester; *Arundel; *p E. of Pembroke; Bishops of *Bath & Wells, *Llandaff, *Chester; *J. Throckmorton, Justice of Chester; *Rice Mansel, *Ed. Carne, *J. Vaughan, *Adam Mytton, *Th. Stradling, Geo. Mathew, kts.; *J. Scudamore of Holm; Chas. Fox; *J. Smyth, Ll.D.; *J. Welsh; *Reg. Corbet; *W. Symonds; *W. Gerard; *Rich. Seaborne; Ed. Lewis; *W. Herbert; *Ed. Mansel; Rob. Gamage; Jas. Thomas; Rob. Stradling; *David Evans: B.M., Lansdowne Ms. 1218/f.35v. (Except for the omission of the *ex officio* members of the commission, the same list also appears in S.P.12/2/17/ p.72). (29)

1561: (Acting)
*Bacon; *Winchester; *Arundel; *p E. of Pembroke; *H. Sidney, kt., President of Council in the Marches of Wales; Bishops of *Llandaff, *St. Davids; *Geo. Herbert, kt.; David Lewis, Ll.D.; *W. Herbert of Swansea; *W. Herbert of Cogan Pill; Ed. Mansel; *Ed. Lewis; Rob. Gamage; *David Evans; *W. Bassett; *Leyshon Price; W. Evans, Ll.B.; Milo Button; David Kemeys: B.M., Lansdowne Ms. 1218/f.84v. (20)

1562: 13 June
As in 1561: C.66/985/m.41d. (20)

1564: (Acting)
*Bacon; *Winchester; *Arundel; *p E. of Pembroke; *Sidney, President of Council in the Marches of Wales; *B. of St. Davids; *W. Gerard; *Reg. Corbet, Justice of Great Sessions; *J. Throckmorton, Justice of Chester; *Geo. Herbert, kt.; *David Lewis, Ll.D.; *Chas. Fox; *Rich. Wye; *Rich. Seaborne; *Rich. Pates; *J. Price; *Rich. Smith; *W. Herbert of Cogan Pill; Ed. Mansel; *Ed. Lewis; Rob. Gamage; *David Evans; *W. Bassett; Christopher Turberville; *Leyshon Price; Th. Lewis; W. Evans, Ll.B.; W. Jenkins; Milo Button; *David Kemeys: C.66/998/m.10d.   (30)

1573–4: (Acting)
*Bacon; *W., Lord Burghley, Treasurer; *p E. of Pembroke; *Sidney, President of Council in the Marches of Wales; Bishops of *St. Davids, *Llandaff; *Jas. Croft, kt., Household Controller; *Hugh Cholmondeley, kt.; *Throckmorton, Justice of Chester; *W. Gerard, Justice of Great Sessions; *David Lewis, Ll.D.; *Ed. Mansel, kt.; *Chas. Fox; *Rich. Seaborne; *Rich. Pates; *W. Herbert of Swansea; *W. Herbert of Cardiff; Ed. Lewis; *W. Evans, Ll.B.; *W. Mathew; *W. Bassett; *Ed. Stradling; Th. Carne; *Th. Lewis; *Th. Morgan; Nich. Herbert; *Leyshon Price; *Ed. Kemeys; Anth. Mansel; Milo Button: S.P.12/93/part 2/f.32v & B.M., Egerton Ms. 2345/f.41.   (30)

1575: (Acting)
As in 1573–4, except: *W., B. of Llandaff; *J. Gibbon, Ll.D.; J. Thomas, *added*. Hugh, B. of Llandaff; Hugh Cholmondeley; Ed. Lewis, *omitted*: S.P.12/106/part 2/f.2v.   (30)

1577: 15 April (Acting)
Bacon; Burghley; Pembroke; Sidney, President of Council in the Marches of Wales; Bishops of St. Davids, Llandaff; Croft; Throckmorton, Justice of Chester; Gerard, Justice of Great Sessions; David Lewis, Ll.D., Judge of Admiralty Court; W. Herbert of Swansea, kt.; Ed. Mansel, kt.; Ed. Stradling, kt.; J. Gibbon, Ll.D., Master in Chancery; Chas. Fox; Rich. Seaborne; Rich. Pates; W. Evans, Ll.B.; W. Mathew; W. Bassett; Th. Carne; Th. Lewis; Th. Morgan; Leyshon Price; Ed. Kemeys; Anth. Mansel; Milo Button; J. Thomas: Wales 4/592/1.   (28)

1578: (Acting)
*Bacon; *Burghley; *Sidney; *B. of Worcester; *E. of Worcester; *p E. of Pembroke; Bishops of *Hereford, *Bangor, *St. Davids, *St. Asaph, *Llandaff; *Croft; *Throckmorton, Justice of Chester; *Andrew Corbet, *W. Herbert, *J. Perrot, *Nich. Arnold, *Hugh Cholmondeley, *J. Littleton, *J. Huband, *Ed. Mansel, *Ed. Stradling, kts. *Gerard, Justice of Great Sessions; *David Lewis, Ll.D., Judge of Admiralty; *Geo. Bromley; *W. Aubrey; *Chas. Fox; *W. Glaseor; *Ellis Price, Ll.D.; *Ed. Leighton; *Rich. Pates; *Ralph Barton; *Jerome Corbet; *J. Puckering; *Fabian Phillips; *H. Townshend; *W. Leighton; *W. Mathew; *W. Evans, Ll.B.; *Th. Morgan, Queen's attorney in South Wales; *W. Bassett; Th. Lewis; W. Herbert of Cardiff; Nich. Herbert; *Leyshon Price; Anth. Mansel; Milo Button; Ed. Kemeys: Hatfield House Ms. 223.7.   (48)

1579: (Acting)
As in 1578, except: *Th. Bromley, kt., Chancellor; *Edm. Walter, Justice of Great Sessions; *J. Gibbon; *J. Price, *added*. Bacon, *omitted*: S.P.12/145/ f.48d. (51)

1581: 20 November (Acting)
Ed. Mansel, Ed. Stradling, W. Herbert, kts.; W. Evans; W. Mathew; Th. Lewis; Nich. Herbert; Ed. Kemeys; Anth. Mansel; Milo Button; W. Bassett; W. Carne; Leyshon Price; Jenkin Franklin: Bodleian, Bodley Ms. 904/f.206v. (Note that this list of the justices acting in Glamorgan on the above date excludes the *ex officio* members of the commission). (14)

1582: (Acting)
W. Herbert, J. Perrot, Ed. Mansel, Ed. Stradling, kts.; J. Puckering, serjeant at law; J. Price; W. Mathew; W. Evans; W. Bassett; Th. Lewis; W. Herbert of Cardiff; Nich. Herbert; Leyshon Price; Anth. Mansel; Milo Button; Ed. Kemeys; W. Carne; Jenkin Franklin: B.M., Lansdowne Ms. 35/f.108v. (18)

1585: 5 July (Acting)
*Th. Bromley, kt., Chancellor; *Burghley; *H. Sidney, kt., President of Council in the Marches of Wales; *Worcester; *p E. of Pembroke; Bishops of *Hereford, *Bangor, *St. Davids, *St. Asaph; *Croft; *Geo. Bromley, kt., Justice of Chester; *Edm. Walter & *Th. Estcourt, Justices of Great Sessions; *W. Herbert, *J. Perrot, *Hugh Cholmondeley, *J. Littleton, *Ed. Mansel, *Ed. Stradling, kts.; *J. Puckering, serjeant at law; *Rob. Sidney; *W. Aubrey; *Chas. Fox; *Ellis Price, Ll.D.; *Ed. Leighton; *W. Leighton; *H. Townshend; *Rich. Pates; *Ralph Barton; *Jerome Corbet; *Fabian Phillips; *W. Glaseor; *W. Mathew; *W. Evans, Ll.B.; *W. Bassett; *Th. Lewis; *Nich. Herbert; *Leyshon Price; Anth. Mansel; Th. Mansel; Milo Button; Rich. Gwynn; J. Carne; Jenkin Franklin: Wales 4/592/2. (Details of the quorum are taken from the list of 1584 contained in E.163/14/8/f.45v). (44)

1590–1: (Acting)
*Christopher Hatton, kt., Chancellor; *Burghley; *p E. of Pembroke, President of Council in the Marches of Wales; Bishops of *St. Davids, *St. Asaph; *J. Perrot, kt.; *Rich. Shuttleworth, kt., Justice of Chester; *Walter & *Estcourt, Justices of Great Sessions; *W. Herbert, *Hugh Cholmondeley, *Ed. Stradling, *Rob. Sidney, kts.; *J. Puckering, serjeant at law; *W. Aubrey; *Ellis Price, Ll.D.; *Ed. Leighton; *W. Leighton; *H. Townshend; *Jerome Corbet; *Fabian Phillips; Th. Mansel; *Th. Lewis; *Th. Carne; *Nich. Herbert; *Anth. Mansel; *H. Mathew; Ed. Lewis; Milo Button; *Ed. Kemeys; Rich. Bassett; J. Carne; Rob. Thomas; Leyshon Evans; Roger Seys; Geo. Williams; Jenkin Franklin: Hatfield House Ms. 278/f.53. (37)

1592–3: (Acting)
As in 1590–1, except: *E. of Essex; *B. of Llandaff; *J. Herbert, Master of Requests; *H. Mathew of Llandaff; Edm. Mathew; *Ed. Pritchard, *added*.

Christopher Hatton; J. Perrot; W. Leighton, *omitted*: Kent Record Office Ms. U.350.03. (40)

1594: 28 June
*J. Puckering, kt., Keeper of Great Seal; *Burghley; *p E. of Pembroke, President of Council in the Marches of Wales; *E. of Essex; Bishops of *St. Asaph, *Llandaff; *Rich. Shuttleworth, kt., Justice of Chester; *Geo. Kingsmill & *Th. Estcourt, Justices of Great Sessions; *J. Herbert, Master of Requests; *W. Herbert, *Hugh Cholmondeley, *Ed. Stradling, *Rob. Sidney, *Th. Mansel, kts.; *W. Aubrey; *Ellis Price, Ll.D.; *W. Leighton; *H. Townshend; *Jerome Corbet; *Fabian Phillips; *Th. Lewis; *Anth. Mansel; *Nich. Herbert; *H. Mathew; Ed. Lewis; *Milo Button; *Ed. Kemeys; *Rich. Bassett; J. Carne; *H. Mathew of Llandaff; Rob. Thomas; Leyshon Evans; Edm. Mathew; *Ed. Pritchard; Roger Seys; Geo. Williams; Jenkin Franklin: C.66/1421/m.15d.   (38)

1594: 22 July (Acting)
As on 28 June 1594, except: B. of St. Davids; Ed. Leighton, kt.; Th. Carne; J. Gwynn; Th. Aubrey, *added*. Th. Mansel, kt., *omitted*: Wales 4/592/5. (Note that it is possible that the commission of 28 June may not have reached Glamorgan by 22 July and that the present list is therefore based on a commission of earlier than 28 June. Th. Mansel was Sheriff in 1593-4 and should therefore have been omitted from the 28 June commissiom. It is likely that the commission was entered on the patent roll after the end of Mansel's term as Sheriff so that his name was then restored).   (42)

1595: 15 August
*Puckering; *Burghley; *p E. of Pembroke, President of Council in the Marches of Wales; *Essex; *B. of St. Asaph; *Shuttleworth, Justice of Chester; *Kingsmill & *Estcourt, Justices of Great Sessions; *J. Herbert, Master of Requests; *W. Herbert, *Hugh Cholmondeley, *Ed. Stradling, *Rob. Sidney, *Th. Mansel, kts.; *W. Leighton; *H. Townshend; *Jerome Corbet; *Fabian Phillips; *Anth. Mansel; *Nich. Herbert; *H. Mathew; Ed. Lewis; *Rich. Bassett; *H. Mathew of Llandaff; J. Gwynn; Leyshon Evans; Edm. Mathew; *Th. Aubrey; *Ed. Pritchard; Roger Seys: Bodleian, Bodley Ms. 904/f.214v. General renewal of Welsh commissions on 15 August 1595: Index 4208/f.4v. (The version of the present commission entered on the patent roll (C.66/1435/m.19d) is identical to the one given here except for its inclusion of Ed. Kemeys. Kemeys was Sheriff of Glamorgan in 1594-5 and hence correctly left out of the commission on 15 August 1595, but by the time the commission was enrolled on the patent roll his term of office would have ended and he was therefore put back on the commission).   (30)

1595: 1 December
Commission renewed to *add* Th. Bawdripp: Index 4208/f.8v.

1596: 14 February
Commission renewed to *restore* Ed. Kemeys, late Sheriff of Glamorgan: Index 4208/f.11.

1596: 16 July
As on 15 August 1595, except: *Th. Egerton, kt., Keeper of Great Seal; *Ed. Kemeys; Th. Bawdripp, *added*. J. Puckering, *omitted*: S.P.13/Case F, no. 11/f.37v. Commission renewed to *add* Th. Egerton, kt., Keeper of Great Seal: Index 4208/f.18v.   (32)

1596: 3 September
Commission renewed to *add* Th. Carne: Index 4208/f.20.

1596: 6 November
As on 16 July 1596, except: *Th. Carne; Roland Morgan, *added*. Th. Bawdripp, *omitted*: C.66/1468/m.15d. Commission renewed to *add* Roland Morgan: Index 4208/f.22.   (33)

1597: 16 February
As on 6 November 1596, except: J. Carne, *added*. Hugh Cholmondeley; Fabian Phillips, *omitted*: C.66/1468/m.29d. Commission renewed to *restore* J. Carne: Index 4208/f.28.   (32)

1598: 11 May
*Th. Egerton, kt., Keeper of Great Seal; *Essex; *p E. of Pembroke, President of Council in the Marches of Wales; *B. of St. Asaph; *Shuttleworth, Justice of Chester; *Kingsmill & *Estcourt, Justices of Great Sessions; *J. Herbert, Master of Requests; *W. Herbert, *Ed. Stradling, *Rob. Sidney, *Th. Mansel, kts.; *W. Leighton; *H. Townshend; *Jerome Corbet; *Anth. Mansel; Nich. Herbert; H. Mathew; Ed. Lewis; *Ed. Kemeys; *Rich. Bassett; *Th. Carne; J. Carne; H. Mathew of Llandaff; *Roland Morgan; Edm. Mathew; Ed. Carne; *Th. Aubrey; *Ed. Pritchard; Roger Seys: C.66/1482/m.16d. Commission renewed to *add* Ed. Carne, and to *omit* Leyshon Evans: Index 4208/f.49.   (30)

1599: 30 June
As on 11 May 1598, except: *Th., Lord Buckhurst, Treasurer; *J. Croke, Recorder of London, Justice of Great Sessions, *added*. Geo. Kingsmill; Jerome Corbet; Roger Seys, *omitted*: C.66/1493/m.26d. Commission renewed to *add* J. Croke, Justice of Great Sessions: Index 4208/f.72. (Lord Buckhurst, who was appointed as Treasurer on 15 May 1599, was added to the commission on this date).   (29)

1600: 5 July
As on 30 June 1599, except: *Rich. Lewkenor, kt., Justice of Chester; *Geo. Calfield, Justice of Great Sessions; Th. Lewis, *added*. Rich. Shuttleworth; Th. Estcourt; H. Mathew; Ed. Kemeys, *omitted*: C.66/1523/m.28d. Commission renewed to *add* Geo. Calfield, Justice of Great Sessions: Index 4208/f.93. (Rich. Lewkenor and Th. Lewis were presumably added on the same date).   (28)

1601: 5 February
Commission renewed to *add* W. Mathew of Llandaff; W. Price of Briton Ferry: Index 4208/f.102.

1601: 26 February
As on 5 July 1600, except: W. Mathew of Llandaff; W. Price of Briton Ferry, *added*. E. of Essex; E. of Pembroke; B. of St. Asaph; H. Mathew of Llandaff, *omitted*. J. Herbert now appears as *custos rotulorum*: C.66/1549/m.30d. Commission renewed to appoint J. Herbert, Queen's Secretary, as *custos rotulorum*: Index 4208/f.104. (26)

1601: 4 December
Commission renewed to *add* Morgan Meyrick, and to *omit* J. Carne; W. Mathew: Index 4208/f.126.

1602: 20 January
Commission renewed to *add* Geo. Lewis: Index 4208/f.127.

1602: 18 February
Commission renewed to *add* Rich. Seys: Index 4208/f.129v.

1602: 21 May
Commission renewed to *restore* J. Carne; W. Mathew: Index 4208/f.134v.

1602: 25 July
General renewal of Welsh commissions to *add* Ed., Lord Zouch, President of Council in the Marches of Wales: Index 4208/f.141.

1602: 6 August
Commission renewed to *add* W. Wood, Ll.D.: Index 4208/f.141v.

1602: 13 August
*Egerton; *Lord Buckhurst, Treasurer; *Ed., Lord Zouch, President of Council in the Marches of Wales; *p J. Herbert, kt., Queen's Second Secretary; *Rich. Lewkenor, kt., Justice of Chester ;*J. Croke, Recorder of London & *Geo. Calfield, Justices of Great Sessions; *Rob. Sidney, *W. Herbert, *Ed. Stradling, *Th. Mansel, kts.; *W. Leighton; *H. Townshend; *W. Wood, Ll.D., Master in Chancery; *Anth. Mansel; *Ed. Lewis; *Ed. Kemeys; *Rich. Bassett; *Th. Carne; *J. Carne; *Th. Aubrey; W. Mathew of Llandaff; Roland Morgan; Leyshon Evans; Ed. Carne; W. Price of Briton Ferry; *Ed. Pritchard; Rich. Seys; Geo. Lewis; Morgan Meyrick; Th. Lewis: C.66/1594/m.33d. Commission renewed to *restore* Ed. Kemeys; Leyshon Evans: Index 4208/f.141v. (31)

1603: (Acting)
*Egerton; *Buckhurst; *Zouch, President of Council in the Marches of Wales; *p W., E. of Pembroke; *Rob., Lord Sidney of Penshurst; *J. Herbert, kt., King's Second Secretary; *Lewkenor, Justice of Chester; *J. Croke, kt., serjeant at law, Justice of Great Sessions; *W. Herbert, *Ed. Stradling, *Th. Mansel, *Roland Morgan, kts.; *W. Leighton; *H. Townshend; *W. Wood, Ll.D., Master in Chancery; *Anth. Mansel; *Edm. Mathew; *Ed. Lewis; *Ed. Kemeys; *Rich. Bassett; *Th. Carne; *J. Carne; *Th. Aubrey; W. Mathew of Llandaff; Leyshon Evans; Ed. Carne; W. Price of Briton Ferry; *Ed. Pritchard; Rich. Seys; Morgan Meyrick; Th. Lewis: C. 66/1620/m.15d. (31)

1604-5: (Acting)
As in 1603, except: *Francis Tate, Justice of Great Sessions; Ed. Button, *added*: C.66/1662/m.22d & B.M., Add. Ms. 38139/f.172.   (33)

1605: 1 April (Acting)
*Th. Egerton, Lord Ellesmere, Chancellor; *E. of Dorset (Lord Buckhurst), Treasurer; *Zouch, President of Council in the Marches of Wales; *p E. of Pembroke; *Lord Sidney of Penshurst; *Herbert; *Lewkenor, Justice of Chester; *J. Croke, kt. & *Francis Tate, Justices of Great Sessions; *W. Herbert, *Ed. Stradling, *Th. Mansel, *Ed. Lewis, *Roland Morgan, *H. Townshend, kts.; *W. Leighton; *W. Wood, Ll.D.; *Anth. Mansel; *Edm. Mathew; *Ed. Kemeys; *Rich. Bassett; *Th. Carne; *J. Carne; *Th. Aubrey; W. Mathew of Llandaff; Leyshon Evans; Ed. Carne; *W. Price of Briton Ferry; *Ed. Pritchard; Rich. Seys; Morgan Meyrick; Th. Lewis; Ed. Button: Wales 4/594/3. (Details of the quorum are taken from the patent roll entry of 1604-5: C.66/1662/m.22d).   (33)

1605-6: (Acting)
As on 1 April 1605, except: *Maurice Griffith, *added*. Lord Zouch, *omitted*: C.66/1682/m.2d.   (33)

1606-7: (Acting)
As in 1605-6, except: Edm. Mathew, *omitted*: C.66/1698/m.30d.   (32)

1607: post 12 September
*Ellesmere; *Dorset; *Ralph, Lord Eure, President of Council in the Marches of Wales (appointed on 12 September); *p E. of Pembroke; *Rob. Sidney, Viscount Lisle; *B. of Llandaff; *Herbert; *Lewkenor, Justice of Chester; *Croke & *Tate, Justices of Great Sessions; *W. Herbert, *Ed. Stradling, *Th. Mansel, *Ed. Lewis, Lewis Mansel, *Roland Morgan, *J. Carne, *H. Townshend, kts.; *Ed. Kemeys; *Rich. Bassett; *Th. Aubrey; *W. Mathew of Llandaff; Leyshon Evans; Ed. Carne; *W. Price of Briton Ferry; *Ed. Pritchard; *J. Stradling; *Maurice Griffith; *Rich. Seys, attorney; Morgan Meyrick; Th. Lewis; *Ed. Button; Math. Price: S.P.14/33/f.74. (The commission enrolled on the patent roll for 1607-8 (C.66/1748/m.30d) is identical to the present one except for the replacement of J. Croke by Geo. Snigg, kt., who was appointed as a Justice of Great Sessions on 14 May 1608).   (33)

1608-9: (Acting)
As at the end of 1607, except: *E. of Salisbury, Treasurer; *E. of Northampton, Keeper of Privy Seal; Th. Mathew; Hugh Jones, *added*. E. of Dorset, *omitted*: C.66/1786/m.30d.   (36)

1610: 6 August (Acting)
*Ellesmere; *E. of Salisbury, Treasurer; *E. of Northampton, Keeper of Privy Seal; *Eure, President of Council in the Marches of Wales; *p E. of Pembroke; *Viscount Lisle; *B. of Llandaff; *Herbert; *Geo. Snigg, kt., Baron of Exchequer & Justice of Great Sessions; *Lewkenor, Justice of Chester; *Francis Tate, Justice of Great Sessions; *Th. Mansel, *Ed. Lewis

Lewis Mansel, *Roland Morgan, *J. Carne, *H. Townshend, *J. Stradling, *Th. Aubrey, kts.; *Rich. Bassett; *W. Mathew of Llandaff; Leyshon Evans; Ed. Carne; *W. Price of Briton Ferry; *Ed. Pritchard; *Maurice Griffith; *Rich. Seys, King's attorney in Glamorgan; *Ed. Button; Th. Lewis; Math. Price; Th. Mathew; Hugh Jones; W. Herbert: Wales 4/594/5. (Details of the quorum are based on the commission for 1609–10 contained in C.66/1822/m.27d.)   (33)

1610–11: (Acting)
As on 6 August 1610, except: Morgan Meyrick, added: C.66/1897/m.19d. (34)

1611–12: (Acting)
As in 1610–11, except: Maurice Griffith, omitted: C.66/1898/m.27d.   (33)

1613: 23 August (Acting)
Ellesmere; Northampton; Eure, President of Council in the Marches of Wales; Pembroke; Lisle; B. of Llandaff; Herbert; Snigg, Baron of Exchequer & Justice of Great Sessions; Lewkenor, Justice of Chester; Tate, Justice of Great Sessions; Th. Mansel, kt. & Bt.; J. Stradling, kt. & Bt.; Roland Morgan, J. Carne, H. Townshend, Th. Aubrey, kts.; Rich. Bassett; W. Mathew; Rob. Robotham, Archdeacon of Llandaff; Ed. Carne; W. Price of Briton Ferry; Rich. Seys, King's attorney in Glamorgan; Ed. Button; David Kemeys; W. Thomas; W. Lewis; David Pritchard; Th. Lewis; Morgan Meyrick; Math. Price; W. Bawdripp; Th. Mathew; Hugh Jones; W. Herbert: Wales 4/595/1.   (34)

1614: post 11 July
As on 23 August 1613, except: *E. of Suffolk, Treasurer (appointed on 11 July 1614); *Ed. Lewis, kt., added. E. of Northampton; Th. Mathew, omitted: C.66/1988/m.28d.   (34)

1614–5: (Acting)
As in 1614: C.66/2047/m.21d.   (34)

1616: post 2 January
As in 1614–5, except: *E. of Worcester, Keeper of Privy Seal (appointed on 2 January); *Th. Mathew, added. Rich. Bassett; W. Lewis, omitted: C.66/2076/m.24d.   (34)

1617: 19 March
Commission renewed to add Francis Bacon, kt., Keeper of Great Seal; Th., Lord Gerard, President of Council in the Marches of Wales: Index 4211/f.38. (It is likely that Walter Pye and Andrew Powell who were appointed as Justices of Great Sessions in February 1617, were also added to the commission on this date).

1617: post 24 November
*Francis Bacon, kt., Keeper of Great Seal; *E. of Suffolk, Treasurer; *E. of Worcester, Keeper of Privy Seal; *D. of Lennox, Steward; *W., Lord

Compton, President of Council in the Marches of Wales (appointed on 24 November 1617); *p E. of Pembroke, Household Chamberlain; *Lisle; *B. of Llandaff; *Th. Chamberlain, kt., Justice of Chester; *Walter Pye & *Andrew Powell, Justices of Great Sessions; *Th. Mansel, kt. & Bt.; *J. Stradling, kt. & Bt.; *Ed. Lewis, *Roland Morgan, *H. Townshend, *Th. Aubrey, kts.; *W. Mathew of Llandaff; Rob. Robotham, Archdeacon of Llandaff; *Ed. Carne; *W. Price of Briton Ferry; *Rich. Seys, King's attorney in Glamorgan; *Ed. Button; *W. Thomas; *W. Lewis; David Pritchard; Morgan Meyrick; *Math. Price; W. Bawdripp; *Th. Mathew; Hugh Jones; W. Herbert: C.66/2147/m.23d.   (32)

1618: 9 February
Commission renewed to *add* J. Carne: Index 4211/f.56v.

1618: 16 March (Acting)
As in 1617, except: J. Carne, *added*: Wales 4/596/2.   (33)

1618: 9 June
*Lord Verulam (Francis Bacon), Chancellor; *Worcester; *Lennox; *E. of Northampton (Lord Compton), President of Council in the Marches of Wales; *p E. of Pembroke; *Lisle; *Chamberlain, Justice of Chester; *Pye & *Powell, Justices of Great Sessions; *Th. Mansel, kt. & Bt.; *J. Stradling, kt. & Bt.; *Ed. Lewis, *Lewis Mansel, *Roland Morgan, *H. Townshend, *Th. Aubrey, kts.; *J. Carne; *W. Mathew of Llandaff; Rob. Robotham, Archdeacon of Llandaff; *Ed. Carne; *W. Price of Briton Ferry; *Th. Mathew; *Rich. Seys, King's attorney in Glamorgan; *Ed. Button; *W. Thomas; *W. Lewis; David Pritchard; Morgan Meyrick; *Math. Price; W. Bawdripp; Hugh Jones; W. Herbert: C.66/2174/m.19d. Commission renewed to *restore* Lewis Mansel, kt.: Index 4211/f.64. (Note that Lord Compton was created E. of Northampton on 2 August 1618, after the issue of the present commission. His new title was probably put into the commission when it was entered on the patent roll).   (32)

1619: 12 July
Commission renewed to *add* David Evans: Index 4211/f.90.

1619: 3 November
Commission renewed to *add* Theophilus, B. of Llandaff: Index 4211/f.92v.

1620: 4 November
General renewal of Welsh commissions to *add* Jas. Whitlock, kt., Justice of Chester: Index 4211/f.114.

1621: 26 February
*Viscount St. Alban (Nich. Bacon), Chancellor; *Viscount Mandeville, Treasurer; *Worcester; *Lennox; *Northampton, President of Council in the Marches of Wales; *p E. of Pembroke; *E. of Leicester (Viscount Lisle); *B. of Llandaff; *Jas Whitlock, kt., Justice of Chester; *Pye & *Powell, Justices of Great Sessions; *Th. Mansel, kt. &Bt.; *J. Stradling, kt. & Bt.; *Ed. Lewis, *Lewis Mansel, *Roland Morgan, *H. Townshend, *Th.

Aubrey, *W. Lewis, kts.; *J. Carne; *W. Mathew of Llandaff; *Rob. Robotham, Archdeacon of Llandaff; *Ed. Carne; *W. Price; *Th. Mathew; *Rich. Seys, King's attorney in Glamorgan; *Ed. Button; *W. Thomas; David Pritchard; Morgan Meyrick; *Math. Price; W. Bawdripp; Hugh Jones; W. Herbert; David Evans: C.66/2234/m.43d & B.M., Harleian Ms. 1933/f.28. Commission renewed to *add* Viscount Mandeville: Index 4211/f.120. (35)

1622: 28 February
Commission renewed to *add* W. Mathew: Index 4211/f.136.

1622: 5 June
Commission renewed to *add* Ed. Stradling, kt.: Index 4211/f.139v.

1622: 7 August
Commission renewed to *add* Rich. Bassett, clerk: Index 4211/f.143v.

1622: 17 October
Commission renewed to *add* Morgan Jones, clerk: Index 4211/f.145.

1622: 2 December
Commission renewed to *add* H. Mansel: Index 4211/f.146v.

1623: 10 February
*B. of Lincoln, Keeper of Great Seal; *E. of Middlesex, Treasurer; *Viscount Mandeville, President of Council ;*Worcester; *Lennox; *p E. of Pembroke; *Northampton, President of Council in the Marches of Wales; *Leicester; *B. of Llandaff; *Whitlock, Justice of Chester; *Pye & *Powell, Justices of Great Sessions; *Th. Mansel, kt. & Bt.; *J. Stradling, kt. & Bt.; *Ed. Lewis, *Lewis Mansel, *Roland Morgan, *Th. Aubrey, *W. Lewis, *Ed. Stradling, Raleigh Bussey, kts.; *J. Carne; *W. Mathew of Llandaff; Rob. Robotham, Archdeacon of Llandaff; *Ed. Carne; *W. Price of Briton Ferry; *Th. Mathew; *Rich. Seys, King's attorney in Glamorgan; *Ed. Button; *W. Thomas; David Pritchard; Morgan Meyrick; Math. Price; H. Mansel; W. Bawdripp; W. Herbert; David Evans; Rich. Bassett; Morgan Jones: C.66/2285/m.33d. Commission renewed to *add* Raleigh Bussey, kt.: Index 4211/f.148v. (Note that the W. Mathew who was added to the commission on 28 February 1622 does not appear in the present list, possibly because of an error in enrolling the commission on the patent roll). (39)

1623: 26 July
Commission renewed to *add* W. Powell: Index 4211/f.156.

1623: 12 September
Commission renewed to *add* W. Herbert, and to *omit* Rich. Seys: Index 4211/f.157.

1624: 18 February
As on 10 February 1623, except: W. Mathew; *W. Powell; W. Herbert, *added.* D. of Lennox; Raleigh Bussey; Rich. Seys; Ed. Button; W. Thomas,

omitted: C.66/2310/m.30d. Commission renewed to *restore* Th. Mansel, kt. & Bt., late Sheriff: Index 4211/f.161. (Note that there are two W. Herberts on the commission). (37)

1624: 13 May
Commission renewed to *add* Edm. Thomas; W. Bassett: Index 4211/f.165.

1624: 16 June
Commission renewed to *add* Rich. Seys: Index 4211/f.167.

1624: 2 October
Commission renewed to *add* Th. Morgan, kt.: Index 4211/f.171.

1625: 28 March (Acting)
Lincoln; Mandeville; Worcester; Pembroke; Northampton, President of Council in the Marches of Wales; Leicester; B. of Llandaff; Whitlock, Justice of Chester; Pye & Powell, Justices of Great Sessions; Th. Mansel, kt. & Bt.; J. Stradling, kt. & Bt.; Ed. Lewis, Lewis Mansel, Th. Aubrey, W. Lewis, Ed. Stradling, Th. Morgan, kts.; J. Carne; W. Mathew of Llandaff; Rob. Robotham, Archdeacon of Llandaff; Ed. Carne; W. Price of Briton Ferry; Edm. Thomas; W. Bassett; Th. Mathew; Rich. Seys, King's attorney in Glamorgan; David Pritchard; W. Herbert of Swansea; Math. Price; H. Mansel; W. Mathew of Aberaman; W. Bawdripp; W. Herbert of Cogan; W. Powell; David Evans; Rich. Bassett, clerk: Wales 4/597/1. (37)

1625: 1 April
*Lincoln; *Jas., Lord Ley, Treasurer; *Mandeville; *Worcester; (*p E. of Pembroke); *Northampton, President of Council in the Marches of Wales; *Leicester; *B. of Llandaff; *Th. Chamberlain, kt., Justice of Chester; *Pye & *Powell, Justices of Great Sessions; *Th. Mansel, kt. & Bt.; *J. Stradling, kt. & Bt.; *Ed. Lewis, *Lewis Mansel, *Th. Aubrey, *W. Lewis, *Ed. Stradling, *Th. Morgan, kts.; *Sampson Eure; *Rob. Brooke; *J. Carne; *W. Mathew of Llandaff; Rob. Robotham, Archdeacon of Llandaff; *Ed. Carne; *W. Price of Briton Ferry; *Edm. Thomas; *W. Bassett; *Th. Mathew; *Rich. Seys, King's attorney in Glamorgan; David Pritchard; *W. Herbert of Swansea; *Math. Price; H. Mansel; W. Mathew of Aberaman; W. Bawdripp; W. Herbert of Cogan; *W. Powell; *David Evans; Rich. Bassett, clerk: C.66/2367/m.29d. General renewal of Welsh commissions: Index 4211/f.180v. (Note that in the form the commission is enrolled on the patent roll the Earl of Pembroke, the *custos rotulorum* for Glamorgan, is omitted. However there is no reason to suppose that he was left out at this point since he appears in earlier and subsequent commissions). (40)

1625: 22 December
As on 1 April 1625, except: *Th. Coventry, kt., Keeper of Great Seal, *added*. B. of Lincoln; Th. Chamberlain, *omitted*: B.M., Harleian Ms. 1622/f.97. General renewal of Welsh commissions to *add* Th. Coventry: Index 4211/f.194v. (39)

1626: 20 March
Commission renewed to *add* J. Bridgeman, kt., Justice of Chester: Index 4211/f.199v.

1626: 15 May
As on 22 December 1625, except: *J. Bridgeman, kt., Justice of Chester, *added.* E. of Leicester; W. Mathew of Llandaff; Rob. Robotham; Math. Price; Rich. Bassett, *omitted*: E.163/18/12/f.97v. Commission renewed to *restore* W. Herbert of Cogan; W. Bassett: Index 4211/f.203. (There is no indication of when these two men had been omitted from the commission or for what reason). (35)

1626: 4 October
Commission renewed to *restore* Math. Price: Index 4211/f.209v.

1626: 19 October
As on 15 May 1626, except: Anth. Gwynn; Math. Price, *added*: C.193/12/2/f.70v. (37)

1627: 29 June
*Th. Coventry, kt., Keeper of Great Seal; *E. of Marlborough (Lord Ley), Treasurer; *E. of Manchester (Viscount Mandeville), President of Council; *p E. of Pembroke; *Northampton, President of Council in the Marches of Wales; *J. Bridgeman, kt., Justice of Chester; *Pye & *Powell, Justices of Great Sessions; *Th. Mansel, kt. & Bt.; *J. Stradling, kt. & Bt.; *Lewis Mansel, *Th. Aubrey, *W. Lewis, *Ed. Stradling, *Th. Morgan, kts.; *Sampson Eure; *Timothy Turneur; *J. Carne; *Ed. Carne; *Th. Mathew; *Edm. Thomas; *W. Bassett; *Rich. Seys, King's attorney in Glamorgan; *Anth. Gwynn; David Pritchard; *W. Herbert of Swansea; *W. Herbert of Cogan; *Math. Price; H. Mansel; W. Mathew; *W. Powell; *David Evans; *W. Carne: C.66/2449/m.31d. Commission renewed to *add* W. Carne: Index 4211/f.230. (33)

1629: 6 March
Commission renewed to *add* Th. Lewis: Index 4211/f.265v.

1629: 29 June
As on 29 June 1627, except: *Rich., Lord Weston, Treasurer; *Viscount Conway, President of Council; *B. of Llandaff; *Th. Lewis; *Jenkin Morgan, *added*. E. of Marlborough, *omitted*: C.66/2495/m.27d. Commission renewed to *add* W., B. of Llandaff; Jenkin Morgan: Index 4212/p.10. (Note that Theophilus Field, the predecessor of William Murray as Bishop of Llandaff, was translated to St. Davids on 12 July 1627 and may therefore have been included in the commission of 29 June 1627 as it was originally issued and before its enrolment on the patent roll). (37)

1629: 23 November
As on 29 June 1629, except: *Anth. Mansel, kt., *added*: C.66/2527/m.30d. Commission renewed to *add* Anth. Mansel, kt.: Index 4212/p.18. (38)

1630: 28 January
Commission renewed to *add* Th. Lewis, kt.: Index 4212/p.21.

1630: 12 June
Commission renewed to appoint Philip, E. of Pembroke & Montgomery, as *custos rotulorum*: Index 4212/p.33. (The Earl's elder brother, William, Earl of Pembroke, died in April 1630).

1630: 26 June
*Coventry; *Lord Weston, Treasurer; *Manchester; *p E. of Pembroke; Bishops of *St. Davids, *Llandaff; *Bridgeman, Justice of Chester; *Pye & *Powell, Justices of Great Sessions; *Th. Mansel, kt. & Bt.; *J. Stradling, kt. & Bt.; *Lewis Mansel, *Th. Aubrey, *W. Lewis, *Ed. Stradling, *Th. Morgan, *Th. Lewis, *Anth. Mansel, kts.; *Sampson Eure; *Timothy Turneur; *J. Carne; *Ed. Carne; *Th. Mathew; *Edm. Thomas; *W. Bassett; *Rich. Seys, King's attorney in Glamorgan; *Anth. Gwynn; *W. Herbert of Swansea; *W. Herbert of Cogan; H. Mansel; W. Mathew; *W. Powell; *David Evans; *W. Carne; *Th. Lewis; *Jenkin Morgan; Th. Mansel: C.66/2536/m.21d. Commission renewed to *add* Th. Mansel: Index 4212/p.36. (Note that Viscount Conway, who died in January 1631, was probably included in this commission at the time of its issue but was omitted at the time of its entry on the patent roll. The present basic commission is also enrolled on two later patent rolls (C.66/2577/m.10d & C.66/2654/m.23d), except for the addition of Marmaduke Lloyd, kt., and the omission of Andrew Powell who died in 1631).   (37)

1631: 30 November
As on 26 June 1630, except: *Walter Rumsey, Justice of Great Sessions; *Marmaduke Lloyd, kt.; *Lewis Morgan, kt., *added*. Andrew Powell, *omitted*: S.P.16/212/f.75. Commission renewed to *add* Lewis Morgan, kt.: Index 4212/p.70. (Note that the inclusion of Walter Rumsey in this list taken from a *Liber Pacis* of February 1632 is misleading. He was not in fact formally added to the Glamorgan commission until 12 July, 1632 several months after the addition of J. Aubrey who was placed in the commission in February 1632. It is likely that Rumsey, who was appointed as a Justice of Great Sessions in place of Andrew Powell in September 1631, was unofficially added to the commission when it was being copied for purposes of reference into the present *Liber Pacis*).   (39)

1632: 11 February
Commission renewed to *add* J. Aubrey: Index 4212/p.74.

1632: 12 July
As on 30 November 1631, except: *E. of Bridgewater, President of Council in the Marches of Wales; *J. Aubrey, *added*: C.66/2598/m.22d. Commission renewed to *add* Walter Rumsey, Justice of Great Sessions: Index 4212/p.88. (See note under 30 November 1631 on Rumsey's appointment as Justice. The present commission is also entered in C.66/2623/m.24d & C.193/13/2/f.81v. but with the omission of Lewis Morgan, kt., who had probably died when the entries were made).   (41)

1635: 17 March
Commission renewed to *add* Ed. Thomas: Index 4212/p.159.

1635: 20 August
Commission renewed to *add* E. of Leicester: Index 4212/p.178.

1636: 9 July
*Coventry; *B. of London, Treasurer; *Manchester; *p E. of Pembroke;
*E. of Bridgewater, President of Council in the Marches of Wales; *E. of
Leicester; *B. of Llandaff; *Bridgeman, Justice of Chester; *Marmaduke
Lloyd, kt. & Walter Rumsey, Justices of Great Sessions; *Lewis Mansel,
kt. & Bt.; *J. Stradling, kt. & Bt.; *Th. Aubrey, *W. Lewis, *Ed. Stradling,
*Th. Morgan, *Th. Lewis, *Anth. Mansel, kts.; *Sampson Eure; *Timothy
Turneur; *J. Carne; *J. Aubrey; *Nich. Kemeys; *Th. Mathew; *Edm.
Thomas; *Rich. Seys, King's attorney in Glamorgan; *Anth. Gwynn;
*W. Herbert of Swansea; *W. Herbert of Cogan; H. Mansel; W. Mathew;
*W. Powell; *David Evans; Ed. Thomas; *W. Carne; *Th. Lewis; *Jenkin
Morgan; Th. Mansel: S.P.16/405/f.79v. Commission renewed to *add* Nich.
Kemeys: Index 4212/p.213. (Walter Rumsey is not included in the com-
mission as entered in S.P.16/405 but this is clearly an oversight).   (38)

1637: 5 June
Commission renewed to *add* Marmaduke Mathew: Index 4212/p.246.

1640: 3 March
Commission renewed to *add* Philip Morgan; Rich. Bassett: Index 4212/p.372.

1640: 11 June
Commission renewed to *add* Morgan, B. of Llandaff; Rich. Bassett, Ll.B.:
Index 4212/p.388.

1640: 17 July
*J. Finch, kt., Keeper of Great Seal; *London; *Manchester; *p E. of
Pembroke; *Bridgewater, President of Council in the Marches of Wales;
*Leicester; *B. of Llandaff; *Th. Milward, kt., Justice of Chester; *Lloyd &
*Rumsey, Justices of Great Sessions; *Ed. Stradling, kt. & Bt.; *Th.
Aubrey, *W. Lewis, *Th. Morgan, *Th. Lewis, *Anth. Mansel, kts.; *Rich.
Lloyd; *Sampson Eure; *Philip Morgan; *J. Carne; *J. Aubrey; *Nich.
Kemeys; *Th. Mathew; *W. Carne; Rich. Bassett; *Anth. Gwynn; *W.
Herbert of Swansea; *W. Herbert of Cogan; H. Mansel; *W. Powell;
*David Evans; *Ed. Thomas; Th. Carne; *Th. Lewis; *Jenkin Morgan;
Th. Mansel; Marmaduke Mathew; Rich. Bassett, Ll.B.: C.66/2858/m.20d.
Commission renewed to *add* Th. Carne: Index 4212/p.397.   (38)

1640: 4 August
Commission renewed to *add* Ed. Pritchard: Index 4212/p.401.

1640: 10 December
Commission renewed to *add* Ed. Stradling: Index 4212/p.416.

1641: 9 September
Commission renewed to *add* Ed. Evans: Index 4212/p.484.

1642: 14 March
Commission renewed to *add* Rob. Button: Index 4212/p.512.

1642: 15 August
Commission renewed to *add* Chas. Kemeys; Humph. Mathews; W. Thomas: Index 4212/p.541.

1643: 5 December
Commission renewed to *add* Th. Gwynn, Ll.D.; W. Gibbs; J. Gibbs: Index 4210/p.54.

1644: 10 January
Commission renewed to *omit* Philip, Lord Herbert, and to appoint J. Aubrey, kt. & Bt., as *custos rotulorum*: Index 4210/p.138.

1645: 3 February
Commission renewed to *add* Th. Evans of Neath: Index 4210/p.144.

1646: 11 August
Commission renewed (no details): Index 4213/p.54.

1647: 16 January
Commission renewed to *add* Philip, Lord Herbert; Algernon Sidney; W. Herbert of Cogan; W. Powell; Philip Gamage; Watkin Lougher; Geo. Boughen; H. Bowen; Ed. Lewis: Index 4213/p.74.

1647: 22 March
Commission renewed to *add* J. Eltonhead & J. Parker, Justices of Great Sessions: Index 4213/p.84.

1649: 6 March
Commission renewed (no details): Index 4213/p.143.

1649: 16 March
Commission renewed to *add* J. Norbury, Justice of Great Sessions: Index 4213/p.144.

1649: 10 October
*W. Lenthall, Speaker of Parliament; *Lord Fairfax, General; *J. Bradshaw, President of Council; *Bulstrode Whitelock, *Rich. Keble & *J. Lisle, Commissioners of Great Seal; *E. of Pembroke; *Philip, Lord Herbert; *Oliver Cromwell; *Algernon Sidney; *H. Rolle, Chief Justice of Upper Bench; *J. Eltonhead & *J. Norbury, Justices of Great Sessions; *Th. Lewis, kt.; *W. Powell, serjeant at law; *Rich. Cromwell; *Walter Strickland; *W. Lewis; *Bussey Mansel; *Michael Oldsworth; *Th. Parry; *Edm. Pritchard; *Evan Seys; *Humph. Wyndham; *W. Herbert of Cottam; *Ed. Stradling; Rich. Jones; *Philip Jones; H. Bowen; J. Herbert;

*J. Price; Th. Evans; *Rowland Dawkins; J. Gibbs; W. Deere; Ed. Gamage: C.193/13/3/f.77. Commission renewed to *add* Philip, Lord Herbert; Th. Parry; W. Deere: Index 4213/p.166. (36)

1650: 9 March
*Lenthall; *p Oliver Cromwell; *Bradshaw; *Whitelock, *Keble & *Lisle; *Pembroke; *Algernon Sidney; *Rolle; *Eltonhead & *Norbury, Justices of Great Sessions; *Th. Harrison; *Ed. Freeman, Attorney-General of South Wales; *Th. Lewis, kt.; *W. Powell, serjeant at law; *Rich. Cromwell; *Walter Strickland; *W. Lewis; *Bussey Mansel; *Michael Oldsworth; *Th. Parry; *Edm. Pritchard; *Evan Seys; *Humph. Wyndham; *W. Herbert of Cottam; *Ed. Stradling; Rich. Jones; *Philip Jones; H. Bowen; J. Herbert; J. Price; Th. Evans; *Rowland Dawkins; J. Gibbs; W. Deere; Ed. Gamage; Th. Butler: *Lists published by Th. Walkley* (1650), p.68. Commission renewed to appoint Oliver Cromwell, Lieut-General & Governor of Ireland as *custos rotulorum*, and to *add* Th. Harrison; Th. Butler; Ed. Freeman, Attorney-General of South Wales: Index 4213/p.179. (37)

1651: 24 February
*Lenthall; *p Oliver Cromwell; *Whitelock, *Keble & *Lisle; *Pembroke; *J. Bradshaw, Chancellor of Duchy of Lancaster; *Sidney; *Rolle; *Rich. Cromwell; *Eltonhead & *Norbury, Justices of Great Sessions; *Th. Harrison; *Walter Strickland; *Philip Jones; *Michael Oldsworth; *Ed. Freeman, Attorney-General of South Wales; *Th. Lewis, kt.; *W. Powell, serjeant at law; *W. Lewis; *Bussey Mansel; *Edm. Pritchard; *Evan Seys; *Humph. Wyndham; *W. Herbert of Cottam; *Ed. Stradling; *J. Price; *H. Bowen; *J. Herbert; *Rowland Dawkins; *J. Gibbs; *Rich. Jones; W. Deere; Edm. Gamage; *W. Butler; Rice Powell: C.193/13/4/f.120v.; Cambridge University Ms. Dd.VIII.1/f.127 & B.M., Stowe Ms. 577/f.64. Commission renewed to *add* W. Butler, and to *omit* Th. Butler; Th. Evans; Th. Parry: Index 4213/p.207. (36)

1653: 28 July
Commission renewed to *add* Edm. Thomas of Wenvoe: Index 4213/p.265. (J. Corbet who was appointed as Justice of Great Sessions on 12 July 1653 (Index 4213/p.260), was probably also added on this date).

1653: 30 September
Commission renewed to *add* H. Morgan; Th. Evans of Eglwysilan; Th. Lougher; Evan Lewis; J. Bowen; Rob. Thomas, and to *omit* others (no details): Index 4213/p.268. (In the original Docquet Book J. Bowen's name could also possibly be J. Brown).

1654: 18 March
Commission renewed according to a general list: Index 4213/p.285.

1655: 30 August
Commission renewed to *add* W. Foxwist, Justice of Great Sessions: Index 4213/p.317.

1656: 20 March
*Rich. Cromwell; *Nathaniel Fiennes & *J. Lisle, Commissioners of Great
Seal; *Bulstrode Whitelock, kt., *Th. Widdrington, kt., *Ed. Montagu &
*W. Sydenham, Commissioners of Treasury; *E. of Pembroke; *Philip,
Viscount Lisle; *Walter Strickland; *p Philip Jones; *J. Glynn, Chief
Justice of Upper Bench; *W. Lenthall, Master of the Rolls; *Oliver St.
John, Chief Justice of Common Bench; *J. Corbet & *W. Foxwist, Justices of
Great Sessions; *Edm. Prideaux, Attorney-General; *Major-General Jas.
Berry; *W. Lewis; *Edm. Jones, Attorney-General of South Wales;
*Bussey Mansel; *Michael Oldsworth; *Edm. Thomas of Wenvoe; *Row-
land Dawkins; *W. Herbert of Swansea; *Evan Seys, attorney in Glam-
organ; *Humph. Wyndham; *Herbert Evans; *Ed. Stradling; *J. Price;
*J. Herbert; *J. Gibbs; *Rich. Jones; *Edm. Gamage; *Rice Powell; H.
Morgan; Evan Lewis; J. Bowen; J. Gawler; Rob. Thomas; Th. Evans;
Morgan Morgan: C.193/13/6/f.106v & C.193/13/5/f.127v. Commission
renewed to *add* Major-General Jas. Berry; Morgan Morgan; J. Gawler, and
to *omit* Ed. Pritchard; Th. Lougher: Index 4213/p.330.   (42)

1658: 25 March
Commission renewed to *add* David Evans: Index 4213/p.390.

1658: 24 September
General renewal of Welsh commissions to *add* Rich. Cromwell, Lord
Protector: Index 4213/p.405.

1659: 28 June
Commission renewed according to a general list: Index 4213/p.435.

1659: 19 October
Commission renewed to *add* Mark Grimes: Index 4213/p.444.

1660: 19 April
Commission renewed according to a general list: Index 4213/p.462. (J.
Corbet & J. Ratcliffe, who were appointed as Justices of Great Sessions on
30 March 1660 (Index 4213/p.460), were probably added on this date).

1660: 30 July
Commission renewed to appoint E. of Pembroke as *custos rotulorum*: Index
4214/p.21.

1660: 4 September
Commission renewed to *add* Th. Thomas; W. Bassett, Ll.D.; and the Justices
of Great Sessions: Index 4214/p.35. (There was in fact only one Justice of
Great Sessions to add, Rich. Lloyd, kt., who was appointed in July 1660 in
place of Corbet and Ratcliffe).

1660: post 8 September
*Ed. Hyde, kt., Chancellor; *E. of Southampton, Treasurer (appointed on
8 September); *D. of Albemarle, General; *Marquess of Ormond, Steward;
*E. of Lindsey, Great Chamberlain; *E. of Manchester, Household Chamber-

lain; *Marquess of Worcester; *p E. of Pembroke; *E. of Leicester; *E. of
Carbery; *H., Lord Herbert; *W., Lord Herbert; *Rich. Lloyd, kt., Justice
of Great Sessions; *Ed. Mansel, Bt.; *Ed. Thomas, Bt.; *J. Aubrey, kt. &
Bt.; *W. Lewis, Bt.; *Rich. Bassett, *W. Lewis, *Th. Lewis, kts.; *Evan
Seys, serjeant at law; *W. Bassett, Ll.D.; *Rob. Thomas; Milo Button;
*Th. Lewis; W. Bassett of Beaupre; *Bussey Mansel; *W. Herbert; *Edm.
Thomas; *W. Thomas; *Herbert Evans; *Humph. Wyndham; Th. Carne;
*Ed. Freeman; David Jenkins; *Rich. Lewis; David Mathew; Th. Stradling
junior; *Rob. Button; *J. Wyndham; Th. Mathew; *Th. Stradling senior;
J. Van; *Th. Thomas; Ed. Mathew; Rich. Lougher; Gabriel Lewis;
*Lambrock Stradling; *J. Carne; Walter Thomas of Dan-y-graig; Edm.
Gamage; Ed. Turberville; *H. Bassett; Chas. Bowen; Rich. Seys: C.220/9/4/
f.107. (55)

1660: 15 November
As in September 1660, except: Rob. Button, *omitted*: B.M., Egerton Ms.
2557/f.106. Commission renewed to *omit* Rob. Button at his own request:
Index 4214/p.53. (54)

1661: 26 August
Commission renewed to *add* Rich. Lloyd, kt. & Arthur Trevor, Justices of
Great Sessions: Index 4214/p.136.

1661: 8 November
As on 15 November 1660, except: *J., Lord Robartes, Keeper of Privy
Seal; *Arthur Trevor, Justice of Great Sessions, *added*. Marquess of
Worcester, *omitted*: C.193/12/3/f.122. General renewal of Welsh commissions
to *add* E. of Carbery, President of Council in the Marches of Wales: Index
4214/p.144. (Carbery was already a member of the Glamorgan commission
in his private capacity before this date). (55)

1662: 17 July
*E. of Clarendon (Ed. Hyde), Chancellor; *Southampton; Lord Robartes,
Keeper of Privy Seal; *Albemarle; *Ormond; *Worcester; *Lindsey;
*Manchester; *E. of Carbery, President of Council in the Marches of Wales;
*p E. of Pembroke; *E. of Leicester; *H., Lord Herbert; *W., Lord Herbert;
*Rich. Lloyd, kt. & *Arthur Trevor, Justices of Great Sessions; *Ed.
Mansel, Bt.; *Ed. Thomas, Bt.; *J. Aubrey, kt. & Bt.; *W. Lewis, Bt.;
*Rich. Bassett, *W. Lewis, *Th. Lewis, kts.; *Evan Seys, serjeant at law;
*W. Bassett, Ll.D.; *Rob. Thomas; Milo Button; *Th. Lewis; W. Lewis
of Beaupre; *Bussey Mansel; *W. Herbert; *Edm. Thomas; *W Thomas;
*Herbert Evans; *Humph. Wyndham; Th. Carne; *J. Gibbs; *Th. Evans;
*Ed. Freeman; David Jenkins; *Rich. Lewis; David Mathew; Th. Stradling
junior; *J. Wyndham; Th. Mathew; *Th. Stradling senior; J. Van; *Th.
Thomas; Ed. Mathew; Rich. Lougher; Gabriel Lewis; Ed. Herbert of
Cogan; *Lambrock Stradling; *J. Carne; Walter Thomas of Dan-y-graig;
W. Herbert of Cilybebyll; Edm. Gamage; Ed. Turberville; *H. Bassett;
Chas. Bowen; Rich. Seys: C.66/2986/m.32d. Commission renewed to *add*
J. Gibbs; Th. Evans; Ed. Herbert; W. Herbert: Index 4214/p.179. (60)

1664: 13 December
Commission renewed to *add* Miles Mathews: Index 4214/p.246.

1667: 1 March
Commission renewed to *add* Th. Street as Justice of Great Sessions in place of Arthur Trevor: Index 4214/p.302.

1668: 8 May
Commission renewed to *add* Philip Hoby of Neath Abbey: Index 4214/p.326.

1669: 23 April
Commission renewed to *add* Christopher Middleton: Index 4214/p.343.

1670: 11 March
Commission renewed to *add* W., E. of Pembroke, as *custos rotulorum*: Index 4214/p.363.

1670: 15 December
Commission renewed to *add* Edm. Lewis: Index 4214/p.383.

1672: 21 March
Commission renewed to *add* Ed. Lewis of the Van: Index 4214/p.411.

1672: 10 August
Commission renewed to *add* Philip Jones of Fonmon; David Evans of Neath: Index 4214/p.421.

1673: 13 January
Commission renewed to *add* E. of Shaftesbury, Chancellor; Th., Lord Clifford, Treasurer; Martin Button: Index 4214/p.430.

1674: 25 June
Commission renewed to *add* J. Jones; Rich. Morgan: Index 4214/p.478.

1674: 29 July
Commission renewed to *add* Philip, E. of Pembroke, as *custos rotulorum*: Index 4214/p.481.

1675: 19 June
Commission renewed to *add* Th. Mansel of Briton Ferry: Index 4214/p.496.

1675: 18 November
Commission renewed to *add* W., B. of Llandaff: Index 4214/p.503.

1677: 1 February
Commission renewed to *add* Marmaduke Gibbs: Index 4214/p.521.

1677: 24 April
Commission renewed to *add* H. Milbourne: Index 4214/p.527.

1677: 12 May
Commission renewed to *omit* Rich. Seys: Index 4214/p.527.

1677: 14 May (Acting)
Lord Finch, Chancellor; E. of Danby, Treasurer; E. of Anglesey, Keeper of
Privy Seal; Dukes of Buckingham, Monmouth, Ormond; Marquess of
Worcester, President of Council in the Marches of Wales; E. of Lindsey,
Great Chamberlain; E. of Arlington, Household Chamberlain; Earls of
Pembroke, Leicester, Carbery; B. of Llandaff; Job Charlton, kt., serjeant
at law, Justice of Chester; Th. Street & Owen Wynn, Justices of Great
Sessions; Ed. Mansel, Bt.; J. Aubrey, kt. & Bt.; W. Lewis, Bt.; Herbert
Evans, Bt.; Evan Seys, serjeant at law; Lewis Meyrick, Attorney-General
for Wales; Rob. Thomas, Bt.; Milo Button; Th. Lewis; Bussey Mansel;
W. Herbert; Ed. Thomas; H. Milbourne; Philip Hoby; W. Thomas;
Humph. Wyndham; Th. Carne; David Jenkins; Rich. Bassett; Rich. Lewis;
David Mathew; Th. Stradling junior; J. Wyndham; J. Jones; Ed. Freeman;
Th. Stradling senior; J. Carne; Ed. Mathew; J. Van; Rich. Lougher;
Christopher Middleton; David Evans; W. Herbert of Cilybebyll; Marma-
duke Gibbs; Edm. Gamage; Rich. Seys; Th. Mansel of Briton Ferry:
Wales 4/599/3. (Note that this list is based on the commission of 24 April
not that of 12 May). (53)

1677: 11 June
Commission renewed to *add* W. Thomas of Dan-y-graig; Geo. Bowen of
Kittle Hill: Index 4214/p.528.

1677: 28 July
Commission renewed to *add* Rich. Seys: Index 4214/p.532.

1677: 7 August
Commission renewed to *omit* Rich. Seys; Marmaduke Gibbs: Index 4214
p.532.

1677: 22 November
Commission renewed to *add* Ed. Stradling, Bt.: Index 4214/p.535.

1678: 11 May
Commission renewed to *omit* H. Milbourne: Index 4214/p.543.

1679: 5 May (Acting)
Finch; Danby; Anglesey; Dukes of Buckingham, Monmouth, Ormond;
Marquess of Worcester, President of Council in the Marches of Wales;
Lindsey; Arlington; Pembroke; Carbery; B. of Llandaff; Charlton, Justice
of Chester; Street & Wynn, Justices of Great Sessions; Ed. Mansel, Bt.;
J. Aubrey, kt. & Bt.; Ed. Stradling, Bt.; Evan Seys, serjeant at law; Lewis
Meyrick, Attorney-General for Wales; Rob. Thomas, Bt.; Th. Lewis;
Bussey Mansel; W. Herbert; Humph. Wyndham; Th. Carne; David Jenkins;
Rich. Bassett; Rich. Lewis; David Mathew; Th. Stradling junior; J.
Wyndham; Ed. Freeman; Th. Stradling senior; J. Van; Rich. Lougher;
J. Carne; Christopher Middleton; David Evans; W. Herbert of Cilybebyll;
Edm. Gamage; Th. Mansel; W. Thomas; Geo. Bowen: Wales 4/599/5. (44)

1679: 18 November
Commission renewed to *add* Oliver Jones: Index 4215/p.15.

1679: 4 December
Commission renewed to *add* J. Aubrey, Bt.: Index 4215/p.16.

1680: 20 April
*Prince Rupert; *Archbishop of Canterbury; *Finch; *E. of Radnor, President of Council; Anglesey; Dukes of *Albemarle, *Monmouth, *Newcastle, *Lauderdale, *Ormond; *Marquess of Winchester; *Marquess of Worcester, President of Council in the Marches of Wales; Earls of *Lindsey, *Arlington, *Salisbury, *Bridgewater, *Sunderland, *Essex, *p Pembroke, *Bath, *Halifax, *Carbery; *Viscount Fauconberg; Bishops of *London, *Llandaff; *Laurence Hyde; *H. Coventry; *Francis North, kt., Chief Justice of Bench; *J. Ernley, kt., Chancellor of Exchequer; *Th. Chichley, kt., Chancellor of Duchy of Lancaster; *W. Temple, Bt.; *Ed. Seymour; *Daniel Finch; *Leoline Jenkins; *Sidney Godolphin; *Th. Street & *Owen Wynn, Justices of Great Sessions; *J. Aubrey, Bt.; *Ed. Stradling, Bt.; *Lewis Meyrick, King's attorney in Wales; *Th. Lewis; *Bussey Mansel; *W. Herbert; *Oliver Jones; *W. Thomas; Th. Carne; *David Jenkins; *Rich. Bassett; *Rich. Lewis; David Mathew; Th. Stradling junior; *J. Wyndham; *Ed. Freeman; *Th. Stradling senior; J. Van; Rich. Lougher; *J. Carne; *Christopher Middleton; *David Evans of Neath; W. Herbert of Cilybebyll; Edm. Gamage; Geo. Bowen of Kittle Hill: C.193/12/4/f.149. Commission renewed to *omit* recusants: Index 4215/p.27. (The *removal* from the Glamorgan commission of the Duke of Buckingham; Rob. Thomas, Bt.; Evan Seys, serjeant at law; Humph. Wyndham and Th. Mansel of Briton Ferry was ordered by a warrant of 5 February 1680 and that of Ed. Mansel, Bt., by one of 18 February: *H.M.C., Eleventh Report, Appendix*, Part 2, p.179. According to the details of the changes in the Glamorgan commission published in 1680 by N.S., Esq., (p.26), Rich. Seys was also omitted at some stage during the year. The *addition* to the commission of Francis Gwynn was ordered by the Privy Council on 17 April: P.C.2/68/p.482). (62)

1681: 4 April (Acting)
As on 20 April 1680, except: Job Charlton, kt., Justice of Chester, *added*: Wales 4/599/7. (63)

1682: 4 March
Commission renewed to *add* Th. Morgan of Llanrhymny, and to *omit* Bussey Mansel; W. Thomas of Llanbradach: Index 4215/p.62.

1683: 9 April (Acting)
As on 4 April 1681, except: Chas., Lord Herbert; Rob. Wright, Justice of Great Sessions; Th. Morgan of Llanrhymny, *added*. Prince Rupert; Lord Finch; D. of Monmouth; Marquess of Winchester; Earls of Salisbury, Sunderland, Essex; W. Temple; Job Charlton; Th. Street; Bussey Mansel; Oliver Jones (Sheriff, 1682–3); W. Thomas; David Mathew; Th. Stradling senior; Edm. Gamage, *omitted*: Wales 4/599/8. (50)

1683: 5 October
Commission renewed to *add* Th., E. of Pembroke, as *custos rotulorum*: Index 4215/p.91.

1684: 27 May
Commission renewed to *add* Ed. Mansel, Bt.: Index 4215/p.102.

1684: 10 July
Commission renewed to *add* Rowland Dawkins: Index 4215/p.105.

1684: 18 December
Commission renewed to *add* J. Rumsey: Index 4215/p.111.

1685: 21 February
Commission renewed to *add* Th., E. of Pembroke, *custos rotulorum*: Index 4215/p.118. (Owen Wynn & J. Powell who were appointed as Justices of Great Sessions on 13 February (Index 4215/p.117), were probably also added on this date).

1685: 20 April (Acting)
As on 9 April 1683, except: Marquess of Winchester; E. of Sunderland; Geo. Jeffreys, kt. & Bt., Justice of Chester; J. Powell, Justice of Great Sessions; Ed. Mansel, Bt.; Oliver Jones; J. Rumsey; Th. Lewis of Llanishen; Rowland Dawkins, *added*. E. of Radnor; E. of Anglesey; D. of Lauderdale; Rob. Wright, *omitted*: Wales 4/599/9. (55)

1685: post 28 September
*Archbishop of Canterbury; *Geo., Lord Jeffreys, Chancellor (appointed on 28 September); *E. of Rochester, Treasurer; *Marquess of Halifax, President of Council; *E. of Clarendon, Keeper of Privy Seal; Dukes of *Albemarle, *Newcastle, *Ormond; *D. of Beaufort, President of Council in the Marches of Wales; Marquesses of *Winchester, *Worcester; Earls of *Lindsey, *Mulgrave, *Bridgewater, *Sunderland, *p Pembroke, *Bath, *Nottingham, *Carbery; *Viscount Fauconberg; Bishops of *London, *Llandaff; *Sidney, Lord Godolphin; *H. Coventry; *J. Ernley, kt., Chancellor of Exchequer; *Th. Chichley, kt., Chancellor of Duchy of Lancaster; *Ed. Seymour; *Owen Wynn & *J. Powell, Justices of Great Sessions; *J. Aubrey, Bt.; *Ed. Mansel, Bt.; *Ed. Stradling, Bt.; *Rich. Bassett, kt.; *Lewis Meyrick, King's attorney in Wales; *Th. Lewis; *W. Herbert; *Oliver Jones; *Th. Morgan of Llanrhymny; Th. Carne; *David Jenkins; *Rich. Lewis; *J. Rumsey; Th. Stradling junior; *J. Wyndham; *Ed. Freeman; *Th. Lewis of Llanishen; J. Van; Rich. Lougher; *J. Carne; *Christopher Middleton; *David Evans of Neath; W. Herbert of Cilybebyll; Rowland Dawkins; *Geo. Bowen of Kittle Hill: C.193/12/5/f.175. (54)

1686: 17 December
Order by Privy Council that Francis Gwynn; Rich. Carne; W. Thomas; Christopher Turberville of Penllyn; Christopher Turberville; Rob. Price, should be *added* to the Glamorgan commission and that Geo. Bowen should be *omitted*: P.C.2/71/p.377. (A memorandum of the same date ordered the members of the Privy Council to be added to the commission of the peace: P.C.2/71/p.379).

1687: 29 August
General renewal of Welsh commissions to add the clause of dispensation:
Index 4215/p.179.

1688: 2 April
Commission renewed to *add* certain justices and to *omit* others (no details):
Index 4215/p.190.

1688: 12 September
Commission renewed to *add* Rich. Bassett, kt., and others: Index 4215/p.198.

1688: 6 October
General renewal of Welsh commissions: Index 4215/p.200.

1689: 11 June
Commission renewed to *add* Th. Geers & H. Chauncy, kt., Justices of Great
Sessions: Index 4215/p.228.

1689: 9 September (Acting)
Archbishop of Canterbury; J. Maynard, Anthony Keck, W. Rawlinson, kts.,
Commissioners of Great Seal; Marquess of Carmarthen, President of Council;
Marquess of Halifax, Keeper of Privy Seal; D. of Norfolk; D. of Bolton;
Marquess of Worcester; E. of Lindsey, Great Chamberlain; E. of Devonshire,
Steward; E. of Dorset, Household Chamberlain; Earls of Oxford, Shrews-
bury, Bedford, Pembroke, Bath; E. of Macclesfield, President of Council
in the Marches of Wales; E. of Nottingham; J. Trenchard, kt., Justice of
Chester; Ed. Mansel, Bt.; Chas. Kemeys, Bt.; J. Aubrey, Bt.; Roland Gwynn,
kt.; Rich. Bassett, kt.; Humph. Mackworth, kt.; Humph. Edwyn, kt.;
J. Wyndham, serjeant at law; Th. Mansel; Th. Morgan; Rich. Lewis; Th.
Lewis; Bussey Mansel; David Jenkins; W. Herbert; Francis Gwynn;
Rich. Seys; Ed. Mathew; W. Wyndham; Chas. Mathew; Th. Lewis of
Llanishen; W. Thomas; Ed. Mathew; Th. Button; Rich. Lougher; Oliver
St. John; Ed. Mansel; Marmaduke Gibbs; W. Herbert of Cilybebyll; David
Evans; Rowland Dawkins; Geo. Bowen: Wales 4/600/1.   (52)

APPENDIX

RICE MERRICK, ESQ., *A Booke of Glamorganshire Antiques,* 1578, ed. J. A. Corbett (London, 1887), pp.115–116: List of Justices of Great Sessions and of the Peace.

Comparison of the names on this list with those obtained from other sources shows that practically all the men listed served as justices of the peace in Glamorgan at various times between 1541 and 1577, which compares well with the date at which Rice Merrick was writing. The only exceptions are William Carne of Sully† and John Carne of Nash, who cannot be traced until 1581 and 1585 respectively, and Matthew Herbert†, Christopher Fleming, Roger Williams and David Jones, who do not appear at all in other extant sources. These are not serious inconsistencies since there are many gaps in the evidence on the state of the Glamorgan commission before 1578. Rice Merrick's list, as quoted here, has been annotated to indicate the year in which each justice first appears, but for the reasons already explained these dates are only a general guide. The spelling of names has also been modernised.

JUSTICES OF ASSIZE (i.e. of Great Sessions)
John Pakington, kt. (1542).
John Pollard, kt. (1554).
Symon Esquyor.
William Gerard. (1573–4).

Custos Rotulorum
George Herbert, kt. (1548).
William, Earl of Pembroke (1554), with George Herbert as his deputy.
Henry, Earl of Pembroke (1570), with Edward Lewis as his deputy and, after the latter's death, his son Thomas Lewis.

CLERKS OF THE PEACE
(These names do not form part of the commission of the peace).
Roger Carne.
David John Yghan, appointed by Sir George Herbert, deputy *custos rotulorum.*
William Herbert, appointed by Sir George Herbert, deputy *custos rotulorum.*
Rice Merrick, appointed by William, Earl of Pembroke, and afterwards by Henry, Earl of Pembroke.

A catalogue of Justices of the Peace, inhabiting or having possessions in Glamorgan, which have been in the Commission of the Peace.
Anthony Kitchen, Bishop of Llandaff (consecrated in 1545 and presumably added to the commission soon afterwards).
George Herbert, kt. (1542).
Rice Mansel, kt. (1543).
Thomas Stradling, kt. (1541).
Edward Carne, kt. (1542).
George Mathew, kt. (1541).
Matthew Herbert (date unknown). †
William Bassett (1548).

†: See Index

Edward Lewis (1541).
John Thomas Bassett (1542).
Christopher Fleming (date unknown).
Richard Carne (1542).
John Mathew (after 1543).
A note against these last three names says that they were 'long in the commission being dead'.
Miles Mathew of Llandaff (1541).
Christopher Turberville (after 1543).
Robert Stradling (1557).
Roger Carne (1543).
John Smyth, Ll.D. (1557).
Henry Morgan, clerk (after 1543).
Hugh Jones, Bishop of Llandaff (consecrated in 1567 and presumably added to the commission soon afterwards).
William James, Ll.B. (possibly an error for William Evans, Ll.B. who first appears in 1561).
Edward Mansel, kt. (1561).
William Herbert (1542).
Edward Stradling of Llantwit (1554).
James Thomas (1548).
James Button (1555).
William Herbert, kt. (1548).
Leyshon Price (1561).
David Kemeys (1561).
Thomas Lewis (1564).
Thomas Carne (1573–4).
William Mathew (1573–4).
William Jenkins (1564).
Roger Williams (date unknown).
David Jones (date unknown).
William Carne of Sully (1581).†
Edward Stradling, kt. (1577).
John Carne of Nash (1585).
Nicholas Herbert (1573–4).
Miles Button (1561).
Edward Kemeys (1573–4).
Thomas Morgan of Machen (1573–4).
John Gibbon, Ll.D. (1577).
William Blethin, Bishop of Llandaff (consecrated in 1575 and presumably added to the commission soon afterwards).
Anthony Mansel (1573–4).
John Thomas (1577).

† : See Index

Radnor

1542: 13 March (Acting)

Lord Audley of Walden, Chancellor; D. of Norfolk, Treasurer; D. of Suffolk, President of Council; E. of Southampton, Keeper of Privy Seal; E. of Worcester; B. of Coventry & Lichfield, President of Council in the Marches of Wales; B. of St. Davids; Walter, Lord Ferrers; Nich. Hare, Ed. Croft, Rice Mansel, J. Vernon, kts.; J. Pakington; Th. Holte; David Brooke; J. ap Rice; Rich. Hassall; J. Baker; J. Bradshaw; Hugh David Lewis; J. Knill; Rich. Blike; J. ap Rice; Lewis John; Th. Lloyd: Wales 4/461/1. (25)

1543: 12 March

*Audley; *Norfolk; *Suffolk; *J. Russell, kt., Keeper of Privy Seal; Worcester; *B. of Coventry & Lichfield, President of Council in the Marches of Wales; Bishops of *St. Asaph, *St. Davids; Lord Ferrers; *Nich. Hare, Ed. Croft, Rice Mansel, *J. Vernon, kts.; *J. Pakington; *Th. Holte; *David Brooke; *J. ap Rice; *Rich. Hassall; *p J. Baker; J. Bradshaw; *J. Knill; Rich. Blike; J. ap Rice; Lewis John; *Rice ap Gwilym; Th. Lloyd; Peter Lloyd. *Later additions to list*: *Th. Bromley, serjeant at law; *Adam Mytton: C.193/12/1/f.41v. (27 names plus 2 corrections).

1552: 21 March (Acting)

B. of Ely, Chancellor; Marquess of Winchester, Treasurer; D. of Northumberland, Earl Marshal & Steward; E. of Bedford (J. Russell), Keeper of Privy Seal; Marquess of Northampton; E. of Shrewsbury; E. of Pembroke, President of Council in the Marches of Wales; E. of Worcester; Walter, Viscount Hereford; B. of St. Asaph; J. Pollard; Rob. Townshend, Th. Bromley, J. Savage, Rich. Cotton, Anthony Kingston, J. Seyntlowe, Geo. Herbert, Rice Mansel, Th. Jones, kts.; Walter Dennys, Ed. Carne, Roland Hill, Jas. Croft, Rob. Acton, Nich. Arnold, J. Price, Adam Mytton, Th. Morgan, Roger Vaughan, W. Brereton, J. Salisbury, Chas. Herbert, kts.; Griffith Leyson, Ll.D.; J. Herbert; Reginald Corbet; J. Scudamore; Rich. Hassall; W. Sheldon; J. Throckmorton; Edm. Plowden; Rice Gwilym; J. Bradshaw senior; J. Knill; Stephen Price; Peter Lloyd; Stephen Price; Rich. Blike; Rich. Morris: Wales 4/461/2. (49)

1554: 23 April (Acting)

B. of Winchester, Chancellor; Marquess of Winchester, Treasurer; E. of Arundel, Steward; Bedford; B. of Worcester, President of Council in the Marches of Wales; Earls of Worcester, Pembroke; Viscount Hereford; B. of St. Asaph; Th. Bromley, Rich. Morgan, David Brooke, Rob. Townshend, kts.; J. Pollard; Rice Mansel, Ed. Carne, Geo. Herbert, Th. Jones, Th. Stradling, Andrew Corbet, J. Wogan, Adam Mytton, J. Price, kts.; W. Symonds; Rich. Hassall; J. Welsh; Griffith Leyson, Ll.D.; Hugh Curwen, Ll.D.; J. Scudamore; Reg. Corbet; Edm. Plowden; Rich. Germyn; Chas. Vaughan; J. Knill; J. Bradshaw senior; Rich. Morris; Peter Lloyd; Jas. Price; Rich. Blike; Stephen Price; Evan Lewis: Wales 4/461/3. (41)

1554: 23 July (Acting)
As on 23 April 1554, except: B. of St. Asaph; Rich. Germyn; J. Bradshaw (Sheriff, 1553–4), *omitted*: Wales 4/461/4. (38)

1555: 21 October (Acting)
As on 23 July 1554, except: B. of Hereford; B. of St. Davids; J. Bridges, kt., Lord Chandos; J. Vaughan, kt.; W. Gerard; J. Oteley; Geo. Wood; Rich. Seaborne, *added*. E. of Bedford; Th. Bromley; Rich. Morgan; J. Wogan; J. Price; Griffith Leyson; Rich. Morris; Peter Lloyd (Sheriff, 1554–5); Chas. Vaughan, *omitted*: Wales 4/461/6. (37)

1556: 18 May (Acting)
Archbishop of York, Chancellor; Winchester, Treasurer; Arundel; E. of Pembroke, President of Council in the Marches of Wales; E. of Worcester; Viscount Hereford; Bishops of Hereford, St. Davids; H., Lord Stafford; J. Bridges, kt., Lord Chandos; J. Pollard, David Brooke, Rob. Townshend, Geo. Herbert, Rice Mansel, Ed. Carne, Th. Jones, Th. Stradling, J. Vaughan, J. Wogan, Adam Mytton, kts.; J. Williams; J. Welsh; W. Gerard; J. Scudamore; W. Symonds; Reg. Corbet; Geo. Wood; Edm. Plowden; Rich. Seaborne; J. Knill; Jas. Price; Rich. Blike; Evan Lewis: Wales 4/461/7. (34)

1556: 14 September (Acting)
As on 18 May 1556, except: J. Oteley; Chas. Vaughan; Peter Lloyd, *added*. Lord Stafford; J. Williams, *omitted*: Wales 4/462/1. (35)

1557: 21 June (Acting)
York; Winchester; Arundel; E. of Pembroke, President of Council in the Marches of Wales; Worcester; Viscount Hereford; Bishops of Hereford, St. Davids; Lord Chandos; David Brooke, J. Pollard, Geo. Herbert, Rice Mansel, Ed. Carne, Th. Jones, Th. Stradling, J. Vaughan, J. Wogan, Adam Mytton, kts.; W. Symonds; J. Welsh; W. Gerard; J. Scudamore; J. Oteley; Reg. Corbet; Geo. Wood; Edm. Plowden; Rich. Seaborne; J. Knill; Chas. Vaughan; Jas. Price; Rich. Blike; Peter Lloyd; Stephen Price; J. Bradshaw senior; Ed. Price; J. Bedo: Wales 4/462/2. (After this list the following names, probably representing changes made to the commission after the holding of the session of 21 June, were added in the same hand in a separate column: W., Lord Paget, Keeper of Privy Seal; Bishops of Worcester, Gloucester, Bangor, Chester, St. Asaph; H., Lord Stafford; W. Pye, clerk, Dean of Chichester; Roger Vaughan, kt.; J. Salisbury, kt.; Geoff. Glynn, Ll.D.; David Lewis, Ll.D.; W. Sheldon; Gilbert Gerard; W. Wightman). (37)

1557: 30 August (Acting)
York; Winchester; Arundel; W., Lord Paget, Keeper of Privy Seal; Pembroke, President of Council in the Marches of Wales; Worcester; Viscount Hereford; Bishops of Worcester, Gloucester, St. Davids, Bangor, Chester, St. Asaph; H., Lord Stafford; David Brooke, kt.; W. Pye, clerk, Dean of Chichester; Geo. Herbert, Rice Mansel, Ed. Carne, Th. Jones, Roger Vaughan, J. Salisbury, J. Vaughan, Adam Mytton, kts.; W. Symonds;

J. Scudamore; Geoff. Glynn, Ll.D.; David Lewis, Ll.D.; W. Sheldon; J. Welsh; Reg. Corbet; Geo. Wood; Gilbert Gerard; W. Wightman; Edm. Plowden; W. Gerard; Rich. Seaborne; J. Knill; Chas. Vaughan; Th. Lewis; J. Bradshaw senior; Jas. Price; Peter Lloyd; Stephen Price; Ed. Price; J. Bedo of Presteigne: Wales 4/462/3. (46)

1558: 23 May (Acting)
As on 30 August 1557, except: J. Williams, Ll.D.; Evan Lewis; Rob. Vaughan, *added*. E. of Arundel; W. Pye; Geoff. Glynn; J. Knill (Sheriff, 1557–8), *omitted*: Wales 4/462/4. (45)

1558: 26 September (Acting)
As on 23 May 1558: Wales 4/462/5. (45)

1559: 10 July (Acting)
*Nich. Bacon, kt., Keeper of Great Seal; *Winchester; *Arundel; Bishops of *Bath & Wells, *Chester; *J. Throckmorton, Justice of Chester; *J. Vaughan, *Adam Mytton, kts.; *W. Symonds; *J. Scudamore of Holm; *Chas. Fox; *J. Welsh; *Reg. Corbet; *W. Gerard; *Rich. Seaborne; Chas. Vaughan; *p Ed. Price; *Jas. Price; *Th. Lewis; *Evan Lewis; J. Bradshaw senior; Peter Lloyd; Stephen Price; Rob. Vaughan; *J. Bedo of Presteigne; Morgan Meredith: Wales 4/463/1. (Details of the quorum are taken from the commissions of 1559 and 1561 contained in S.P.12/2/17/ p.77 & B.M., Lansdowne Ms. 1218/f.85). (26)

1560: 22 April (Acting)
As on 10 July 1559, except: B. of Bath & Wells; B. of Chester; W. Symonds; Morgan Meredith (Sheriff, 1559–60), *omitted*: Wales 4/463/2. (22)

1560: 21 October (Acting)
As on 22 April 1560, except: H. Sidney, kt., President of Council in the Marches of Wales; Bishops of Hereford, Worcester, St. Davids, St. Asaph; Nich. Arnold, kt.; Rich. Wye; Rich. Pates; Th. Huet, clerk, *added*: Wales 4/463/3. (31)

1561: 21 July (Acting)
*Bacon; *Winchester; *Arundel; *H. Sidney, kt., President of Council in the Marches of Wales; *B. of Hereford; *W. Gerard; *p Ed. Price; *Th. Huet, clerk; Chas. Vaughan; *Th. Lewis; *Evan Lewis; Stephen Price; Peter Lloyd; J. Bradshaw senior; *J. Bedo of Presteigne; Morgan Meredith; Maurice ap Rees: Wales 4/463/4. (Details of the quorum are taken from the commission of 1561 contained in B.M., Lansdowne Ms. 1218/f.85). (17)

1561: 8 September (Acting)
As on 21 July 1561: Wales 4/463/5. (17)

1562: 13 June
*Bacon; *Winchester; *Arundel; *Sidney; Bishops of *Hereford, *St. Davids; *W. Gerard; *Th. Huet, clerk; Chas. Vaughan; *Th. Lewis;

*p Ed. Price; *Evan Lewis; *Stephen Price; Peter Lloyd; *J. Bedo of Presteigne; Morgan Meredith; J. Bradshaw senior; Maurice ap Rees: C.66/985/m.41d. (18)

1562: 13 July (Acting)
As on 13 June 1562, except: J. Throckmorton, Justice of Chester; Jas. Price; Rich. Powell; Rob. Vaughan; J. Madock, *added*. Evan Lewis (Sheriff, 1561–2); Stephen Price, *omitted*: Wales 4/463/6. (21)

1563: 26 July (Acting)
As on 13 July 1562, except: Evan Lewis; W. Fowler; H. Stanley, *added*. J. Throckmorton; J. Madock, *omitted*: Wales 4/464/1. (22)

1563: 18 October (Acting)
*Bacon; *Winchester; *Arundel; *Sidney, President of Council in the Marches of Wales; Bishops of *Hereford, *St. Davids; *W. Gerard; *Reg. Corbet, Justice of Pleas *coram Regina*; *J. Throckmorton, Justice of Chester; *Chas. Fox; *Rich. Wye; *Rich. Seaborne; *Rich. Pates; *J. Price; *Rich. Smith; *p Th. Lewis; *Jas. Price; Chas. Vaughan; Evan Lewis; Ed. Price; *W. Fowler; *Th. Huet, clerk; Peter Lloyd; J. Bradshaw senior; J. Bedo of Presteigne; Morgan Meredith; Rich. Powell; Rob. Vaughan; H. Stanley; Maurice ap Rees: Wales 4/464/2. (Details of the quorum are taken from the undated commission of 1564 contained in C.66/998/m.10d. This commission is identical in content to the present list but slightly different in the order in which the justices are named). (30)

1564: 2 October (Acting)
As on 18 October 1563: Wales 4/464/4. (30)

1565: 8 October (Acting)
As on 2 October 1564: Wales 4/464/6. (30)

1566: 22 July (Acting)
As on 8 October 1565, except: Ed. Herbert; Griffith Jones, *added*. Ed. Price (Sheriff, 1565–6); Peter Lloyd, *omitted*: Wales 4/465/1. (30)

1566: 21 October (Acting)
As on 22 July 1566: Wales 4/465/2. (30)

1567: 30 June (Acting)
As on 21 October 1566, except: Ed. Price, *added*. Reg. Corbet, *omitted*: Wales 4/465/3. (30)

1567: 27 October (Acting)
As on 30 June 1567, except: J. Bradshaw, *omitted*: Wales 4/465/4. (29)

1568: 31 May (Acting)
As on 27 October 1567, except: E. of Pembroke, Steward; J. Bradshaw; Lewis Lloyd, *added*. Rich. Powell; Rob. Vaughan (Sheriff, 1567–8), *omitted*: Wales 4/465/5. (30)

1568: 25 October (Acting)
As on 31 May 1568, except: Owen Phillips, *added*. J. Bradshaw, *omitted*:
Wales 4/465/6. (30)

1569: 18 July (Acting)
As on 25 October 1568, except: J. Bradshaw; Rob. Vaughan, *added*: Wales
4/466/2. (32)

1569: 26 September (Acting)
As on 18 July 1569: Wales 4/466/1. (32)

1570: 3 July (Acting)
Bacon; Winchester; Arundel; Sidney, President of Council in the Marches
of Wales; Bishops of Hereford, St. Davids; Hugh Cholmondeley, kt.,
Vice-President of Wales; W. Gerard, Justice of Great Sessions; Throck-
morton, Justice of Chester; Chas. Fox; Rich. Seaborne; Rich. Pates;
Th. Huet, clerk; W. Fowler; Ed. Herbert; Chas. Vaughan; Th. Lewis;
Jas. Price; Ed. Price; Evan Lewis; Morgan Meredith; J. Bedo of Presteigne;
J. Bradshaw; Griffith Jones; H. Stanley; Lewis Lloyd; Rob. Vaughan;
Maurice ap Rees; Owen Phillips; David Lloyd Meredith: Wales 4/466/3.
(30)

1570: 25 September (Acting)
As on 3 July 1570: Wales 4/466/4. (30)

1571: 16 July (Acting)
As on 25 September 1570, except: Jas. Croft, kt., Household Controller,
added. E. of Arundel; Jas. Price (Sheriff, 1570–1), *omitted*: Wales 4/466/5. (29)

1571: 24 September (Acting)
As on 16 July 1571: Wales 4/466/6. (29)

1572: 14 July (Acting)
*Bacon; *Sidney, President of Council in the Marches of Wales; Bishops of
*Hereford, *St. Davids; *Jas. Croft, kt., Household Controller; *Hugh
Cholmondeley, kt., Vice-President of Council in the Marches of Wales;
*Throckmorton, Justice of Chester; *Gerard, Justice of Great Sessions;
*Chas. Fox; *Rich. Seaborne; *Rich. Pates; *Ed. Davies; *Th. Huet,
clerk; *p W. Fowler; *Jas. Price; *Th. Lewis; *Evan Lewis; *Morgan
Meredith; J. Bedo of Presteigne; *J. Bradshaw; Th. Whitney; H. Stanley;
David Lloyd Meredith: Wales 4/467/1. (Details of the quorum are taken
from the commission of 1573–4 contained in S.P.12/93/part 2/p.33 & B.M.,
Egerton Ms. 2345/f.41v.) (23)

1572: 29 September (Acting)
As on 14 July 1572, except: David Lloyd Meredith, *omitted* (possibly in
error): Wales 4/467/2. (22)

1573: 29 June (Acting)
As on 29 September 1572, except: W., Lord Burghley, Treasurer; Ed. Price;
David Lloyd Meredith, *added*: Wales 4/467/3. (25)

1573: 28 September (Acting)
As on 29 June 1573, except: Owen Phillips; Maurice ap Rees; Lewis Lloyd of Norton, *added*. Th. Whitney, *omitted* (perhaps in error): Wales 4/467/4. (27)

1574: 26 July (Acting)
As on 28 September 1573, except: J. Price of Whitton; Rob. Vaughan; Th. Whitney, *added*. David Lloyd Meredith, *omitted*: Wales 4/467/5. (29)

1574: 11 October (Acting)
As on 26 July 1574, except: David Lloyd Meredith, *added*: Wales 4/467/6. (30)

1575: 11 July (Acting)
As on 11 October 1574, except: Hugh Cholmondeley; Jas. Price; Evan Lewis (Sheriff, 1574–5), *omitted*: Wales 4/468/1. (27)

1575: 24 October (Acting)
As on 11 July 1575, except: Edm. Walter, *added*: Wales 4/468/2. (28)

1576: 6 August (Acting)
As on 24 October 1575, except: Evan Lewis, *added*: Wales 4/468/3. (29)

1576: 15 October (Acting)
*Bacon; *Lord Burghley, Treasurer; *Sidney, President of Council in the Marches of Wales; Bishops of *Hereford, *St. Davids; *Croft; *Throckmorton, Justice of Chester; *Gerard, Justice of Great Sessions; *Chas. Fox; *Rich. Seaborne; *Rich. Pates; *Ed. Davies; *Edm. Walter; *p W. Fowler; *Th. Huet, clerk; *J. Price; *Th. Lewis; *J. Bradshaw; *Ed. Price; *Evan Lewis; *Morgan Meredith; Lewis Lloyd of Norton; Owen Phillips; Rob. Vaughan; *David Lloyd Meredith; H. Stanley; Th. Whitney; Maurice ap Rees: Wales 4/468/4. (Details of the quorum are taken from the list of 1575 contained in S.P.12/106/part 2/f.3v). (28)

1577: 20 April (Acting)
As on 15 October 1576, except: Hugh Lloyd, *added*: Wales 4/468/5. (29)

1577: 14 October (Acting)
As on 20 April 1577: Wales 4/468/6. (29)

1578: 7 July (Acting)
*Bacon; *Burghley; *Sidney, President of Council in the Marches of Wales; *B. of Worcester, Vice-President of Council in the Marches of Wales; Earls of *Worcester, *Pembroke; Bishops of *Hereford, *Bangor, *St. Davids, *St. Asaph; *Jas. Croft, kt., Household Controller; *Throckmorton, Justice of Chester; *Andrew Corbet, *J. Perrot, *Nich. Arnold, *Hugh Cholmondeley, *J. Littleton, *J. Huband, kts.; *Gerard, Justice of Great Sessions; *David Lewis, Ll.D., Judge of Admiralty; *Geo. Bromley, Attorney of Duchy of Lancaster; *W. Aubrey; *Chas. Fox; *W. Glaseor; *Ellis Price, Ll.D.; *Ed. Leighton; *Rich. Pates; *Ralph Barton; *Jerome

Corbet; *J. Puckering; *Fabian Phillips; *H. Townshend; *W. Leighton; *p W. Fowler; *J. Price of Mynachty; *Th. Lewis; *Ed. Price; *J. Bradshaw; Th. Wigmore; *David Lloyd Meredith; *Evan Lewis; Morgan Meredith; Owen Phillips; Hugh Lloyd; Roger Vaughan of Clyro: Wales 4/469/1. (Details of the quorum are taken from the list for 1578 contained in Hatfield House Ms. 223.7). (45)

1578: 6 October (Acting)
As on 7 July 1578: Wales 4/469/2. (45)

1579: 3 August (Acting)
As on 6 October 1578, except: Th. Bromley, kt., Chancellor; Edm. Walter, Justice of Great Sessions; Clement Price; J. Price of Pilleth; Lewis Lloyd, *added*. Bacon; Andrew Corbet, *omitted*: Wales 4/469/3. (48)

1579: 12 October (Acting)
As on 3 August 1579: Wales 4/469/4. (48)

1580: 18 July (Acting)
As on 12 October 1579, except: Andrew Corbet, kt.; Jas. Whitney, kt.; H. Stanley; J. Baskerville, *added*. Nich. Arnold; J. Throckmorton; Th. Wigmore (Sheriff, 1579–80), *omitted*: Wales 4/469/5. (49)

1580: 26 September (Acting)
As on 18 July 1580: Wales 4/469/6. (49)

1581: 24 July (Acting)
As on 26 September 1580, except: Th. Estcourt, Justice of Great Sessions; Th. Wigmore, *added*. W. Gerard; Andrew Corbet; Evan Lewis (Sheriff, 1580–1), *omitted*: Wales 4/470/1. (48)

1581: 2 October (Acting)
As on 24 July 1581, except: J. Croft, *added*. Roger Vaughan, *omitted*: Wales 4/470/2. (48)

1581: 20 November (Acting)
Jas. Whitney, kt.; W. Fowler; Clement Price; Th. Lewis; Ed. Price; J. Bradshaw; Th. Wigmore; David Lloyd Meredith; Hugh Lloyd; J. Price; Morgan Meredith; Owen Phillips; Lewis Lloyd; H. Stanley; Roger Vaughan; J. Baskerville: Bodleian, Bodley Ms. 904/f.206v. (Note that the form of the present list differs from that of the Gaol File lists in including only the names of the Radnorshire men on the commission and omitting all the *ex officio* members). (16)

1582: 23 July (Acting)
As on 2 October 1581, except: B. of St. Davids; Morgan Meredith (Sheriff, 1581–2), *omitted*: Wales 4/470/3. (46)

1582: 1 October (Acting)
*Th. Bromley, kt., Chancellor; *Burghley; *Sidney, President of Council in the Marches of Wales; *B. of Worcester, Vice-President of Council in the Marches of Wales; Earls of *Worcester, *Pembroke; Bishops of *Hereford, *Bangor, *St. Asaph; *Croft; *Geo. Bromley, kt., Justice of Chester; *Edm. Walter & *Th. Estcourt, Justices of Great Sessions; *J. Perrot, *Hugh Cholmondeley, *J. Littleton, *J. Huband, *Jas. Whitney, kts.; *J. Puckering; *David Lewis, Ll.D., Master in Chancery; *Chas. Fox; *W. Aubrey; *W. Glaseor; *Ellis Price, Ll.D.; *Ed. Leighton; *Rich. Pates; *Ralph Barton; *Jerome Corbet; *Fabian Phillips; *H. Townshend; *W. Leighton; *J. Price; *p W. Fowler; *Ed. Price; *J. Bradshaw; *Evan Lewis; *Th. Lewis; *Lewis Lloyd; *Th. Wigmore; J. Croft; David Lloyd Meredith; *H. Stanley: Wales 4/470/4. (Details of the quorum are based on the list of 1584 contained in E.163/14/8/f.47). (42)

1583: 15 July (Acting)
As on 1 October 1582, except: Hugh Lloyd; J. Price of Pilleth; J. Weaver, *added*. Evan Lewis; Lewis Lloyd, *omitted*: Wales 4/470/5. (43)

1583: 30 September (Acting)
As on 15 July 1583, except: Evan Lewis, Morgan Meredith; Owen Phillips; Lewis Lloyd, *added*. B. of Worcester; J. Croft; David Lloyd Meredith, *omitted*: Wales 4/470/6. (44)

1584: 27 July (Acting)
As on 30 September 1583, except: Lewis Lloyd (Sheriff, 1583–4), *omitted*: Wales 4/471/1. (43)

1584: 28 September (Acting)
As on 27 July 1584, except: B. of St. Davids; J. Croft; Brian Crowther, *added*. (These additions appear to have been made after the production of the basic list). David Lewis; J. Huband; J. Price, *omitted*: Wales 4/471/2. (43)

1585: 19 July (Acting)
As on 28 September 1584, except: Clement Price; Lewis Lloyd; David Lloyd Meredith, *added*. B. of Hereford; Owen Phillips; J. Weaver (Sheriff, 1584–5), *omitted*: Wales 4/471/3. (43)

1585: 27 September (Acting)
As on 19 July 1585, except: J. Garmon, *added*: Wales 4/471/4. (44)

1586: 12 September (Acting)
As on 27 September 1585, except: Roger Vaughan; J. Weaver, *added*. B. of Bangor; J. Bradshaw (Sheriff, 1585–6), *omitted*: Wales 4/471/6. (44)

1587: 31 July (Acting)
*Christopher Hatton, kt., Chancellor; *Burghley; *E. of Worcester; *E. of Pembroke, President of Council in the Marches of Wales; Bishops of *St. Davids, *St. Asaph; *Croft; *Bromley, Justice of Chester; *Walter &

*Estcourt, Justices of Great Sessions; *J. Perrot, *Hugh Cholmondeley, *J. Littleton, kts.; *J. Puckering, serjeant at law; *Chas. Fox; *W. Aubrey; *Ellis Price, Ll.D.; *Ed. Leighton; *W. Leighton; *H. Townshend; *Rich. Pates; *Ralph Barton; *Jerome Corbet; *Fabian Phillips; *W. Glaseor; *p W. Fowler; *Th. Lewis; *J. Bradshaw; Clement Price; *Th. Wigmore; *Roger Vaughan; *Evan Lewis; *Morgan Meredith; *Lewis Lloyd; David Lloyd Meredith; *Hugh Lloyd; *J. Price of Pilleth; *H. Stanley; J. Croft; *J. Weaver; Brian Crowther; J. Garmon: Wales 4/472/1. (Details of the quorum are based on the commission of 1584 contained in E.163/14/8/ f.47). (42)

1587: 10 October (Acting)
As on 31 July 1587, except: Clement Price (Sheriff, 1587), *omitted*: Wales 4/472/2. (41)

1588: 1 April (Acting)
As on 10 October 1587, except: Clement Price, *added*. Hugh Lloyd (Sheriff, 1587–8), *omitted*: Wales 4/472/3. (41)

1588: 16 September (Acting)
As on 1 April 1588, except: J. Bradshaw, *omitted*: Wales 4/472/4. (40)

1589: 24 March (Acting)
As on 16 September 1588, except: Gelly Meyrick; Hugh Lloyd; Th. Price, *added*. E. of Worcester; B. of St. Asaph; Rich. Pates; Ralph Barton; W. Glaseor; Evan Lewis (Sheriff, 1588–9), *omitted*: Wales 4/472/5. (37)

1589: 15 September (Acting)
As on 24 March 1589, except: B. of St. Asaph, *added*. Geo. Bromley, *omitted*: Wales 4/472/6. (37)

1590: 18 May (Acting)
As on 15 September 1589, except: Evan Lewis, *added*: Wales 4/473/1. (38)

1590: 5 October (Acting)
As on 18 May 1590, except: Th. Vaughan, *added*: Wales 4/473/2. (39)

1591: 28 June (Acting)
As on 5 October 1590, except: Rich. Shuttleworth, kt., Justice of Chester, *added*. J. Littleton; Chas. Fox; J. Croft; Th. Vaughan, *omitted*: Wales 4/473/3. (36)

1591: 27 September (Acting)
*Hatton; *Burghley; *Pembroke, President of Council in the Marches of Wales; Bishops of *St. Davids, *St. Asaph; *J. Perrot, kt.; *Rich. Shuttleworth, kt., Justice of Chester; *Walter & *Estcourt, Justices of Great Sessions; *Hugh Cholmondeley, kt.; *J. Puckering, serjeant at law; *W. Aubrey, Ll.D.; *Ellis Price, Ll.D.; *Ed. Leighton; *W. Leighton; *H. Townshend; *Jerome Corbet; *Fabian Phillips; *p W. Fowler; *Th. Wigmore; *Roger Vaughan; *Th. Lewis; Clement Price; *Evan Lewis;

*Gelly Meyrick; *Morgan Meredith; *Lewis Lloyd; J. Croft; David Lloyd Meredith; *Hugh Lloyd; *J. Price of Pilleth; *H. Stanley; Th. Vaughan; *J. Weaver; Brian Crowther; J. Garmon: Wales 4/473/4. (Details of the quorum are taken from the list of 1590–91 contained in Hatfield House Ms. 278/f.54). (36)

1592: 3 July (Acting)
As on 27 September 1591, except: Th. Price, *added*. Christopher Hatton; J. Puckering, *omitted*: Wales 4/473/5. (35)

1592: 18 September (Acting)
As on 3 July 1592, except: J. Puckering, *added*. J. Perrot; H. Stanley, *omitted*: Wales 4/473/6. (Note that although Puckering was appointed as Keeper of the Great Seal in May 1592 he is not described as such in the Gaol File lists for Radnor until 9 July 1593). (34)

1593: 9 July (Acting)
As on 18 September 1592, except: E. of Essex; David Williams; Jas. Price; Th. Peniston, *added*. J. Croft; J. Garmon; Th. Price, *omitted*: Wales 4/474/1. (35).

1593: 1 October (Acting)
As on 9 July 1593: Wales 4/474/2. (35)

1594: 28 June
*J. Puckering, kt., Keeper of Great Seal; *Burghley; *Pembroke, President of Council in the Marches of Wales; *E. of Essex; *B. of St. Asaph; *Shuttleworth, Justice of Chester; *Geo. Kingsmill & *Th. Estcourt, Justices of Great Sessions; *Hugh Cholmondeley, kt.; *W. Aubrey; *Ellis Price, Ll.D.; *W. Leighton; *H. Townshend; *Jerome Corbet; *Fabian Phillips; *David Williams, serjeant at law; *p W. Fowler; *Th. Wigmore; *Roger Vaughan; *Jas. Price; *Gelly Meyrick; *Th. Peniston; *Th. Lewis; *Edm. Wynstanley; *Rich. Fowler; *Evan Lewis; *Morgan Meredith; Clement Price; *Lewis Lloyd; David Lloyd Meredith; *Hugh Lloyd; *J. Price of Pilleth; *H. Stanley; Th. Vaughan; *J. Weaver; Brian Crowther: C.66/1421/m.15d. (36)

1595: 15 August
As on 28 June 1594, except: W. Bradshaw, *added*. W. Aubrey; Ellis Price; Th. Wigmore (Sheriff, 1594–5); Evan Lewis; Morgan Meredith; David Lloyd Meredith; Hugh Lloyd; H. Stanley, *omitted*: C.66/1435/m.19d & Bodleian, Bodley Ms. 904/f.214v. General renewal of Welsh commissions on 15 August: Index 4208/f.4v. (29)

1596: 29 March (Acting)
As on 15 August 1595, except: Jas. Price (Sheriff, 1595–6); J. Weaver *omitted*: Wales 4/475/1. (27)

1596: 16 July
As on 29 March 1596, except: *Th. Egerton, kt., Keeper of Great Seal; *Jas. Price, *added*. J. Puckering; Th. Vaughan, *omitted*: S.P.13/Case F, no. 11/f.38. Commission renewed to *add* Th. Egerton, kt., Keeper of Great Seal: Index 4208/f.18v. (27).

1596: 11 November
As on 16 July 1596, except: Hugh Lloyd, *added*: C.66/1468/m.15d. Commission renewed to *restore* Hugh Lloyd: Index 4208/f.22v. (28)

1597: 3 February
Commission renewed to *add* Humphrey Cornwall: Index 4208/f.26v.

1597: 17 February
Commission renewed to *add* David Lloyd Meredith: Index 4208/f.28v.

1597: 21 March (Acting)
As on 11 November 1596, except: David Lloyd Meredith; Humph. Cornwall, *added*. Hugh Cholmondeley; Fabian Phillips; Rich. Fowler (Sheriff, 1596–7), *omitted*: Wales 4/475/3. (27)

1597: 6 May
*Th. Egerton, kt., Keeper of Great Seal; *Burghley; *Pembroke, President of Council in the Marches of Wales; *Essex; *B. of St. Asaph; *Shuttleworth, Justice of Chester; *Kingsmill & *Estcourt, Justices of Great Sessions; *Gelly Meyrick, kt.; *David Williams, serjeant at law; *W. Leighton; *H. Townshend; *Jerome Corbet; *p W. Fowler; *Roger Vaughan; *Jas. Price; *Th. Peniston; *Th. Lewis; *Edm. Wynstanley; W. Bradshaw; *Rich. Fowler; *David Lloyd Meredith; Clement Price; Humph. Cornwall; *Lewis Lloyd; *Hugh Lloyd; *J. Price of Pilleth; *Th. Vaughan of Llowes; *Brian Crowther: C.66/1468/m.30d. Commission renewed to *restore* Th. Vaughan: Index 4208/f.32v. (29)

1597: 19 September (Acting)
As on 6 May 1597, except: Rich. Fowler, *omitted*: Wales 4/475/4. (Note that Rich. Fowler was Sheriff of Radnor in 1596-7 and was therefore correctly omitted from the details of the commission as recorded in the Gaol Files of this period. The commission of 6 May may have been entered on the patent roll after the end of Fowler's term as Sheriff and his consequent restoration to the commission, and would not therefore record his temporary omission). (28)

1598: 9 March
Commission renewed to appoint Gelly Meyrick as *custos rotulorum*: Index 4208/f.46v.

1598: 27 March (Acting)
As on 19 September 1597, except: Rich. Fowler, *added*. W. Fowler; J. Price of Pilleth (Sheriff, 1597–8), *omitted*: Wales 4/476/1. (27)

1598: 4 December
As on 27 March 1598, except: *J. Price of Pilleth; Evan Vaughan, *added*.
Lord Burghley; Jerome Corbet, *omitted*: C.66/1482/m.16d. Commission
renewed to *add* Evan Vaughan: Index 4208/f.60. (27)

1599: 30 June
Commission renewed to *add* J. Croke, Recorder of London & Justice of
Great Sessions: Index 4208/f.72.

1599: 7 July
As on 4 December 1598, except: *Th., Lord Buckhurst, Treasurer; *J.
Croke, Justice of Great Sessions; J. Bradshaw; Ed. Price, *added*. Geo.
Kingsmill, *omitted*: C.66/1493/m.26d. Commission renewed to *add* J.
Bradshaw; Ed. Price: Index 4208/f.73. (30)

1600: 14 March
Commission renewed to *omit* Roger Vaughan: Index 4208/f.85v.

1600: 5 July
Commission renewed to *add* Geo. Calfield, Justice of Great Sessions; Roger
Vaughan: Index 4208/f.93.

1600: 1 August
*Egerton; *Th., Lord Buckhurst, Treasurer; *Essex; *Pembroke, President
of Council in the Marches of Wales; *B. of St. Asaph; *Rich. Lewkenor,
kt., Justice of Chester; *J. Croke, Recorder of London & *Geo. Calfield,
Justices of Great Sessions; *David Williams, serjeant at law; *W. Leighton;
*H. Townshend; *Roger Vaughan; *Jas. Price; *Th. Peniston; *Th.
Lewis; *Edm. Wynstanley; W. Bradshaw; *p Rich. Fowler; *David Lloyd
Meredith; Clement Price; Humph. Cornwall; J. Bradshaw; Ed. Price;
*Lewis Lloyd; *Hugh Lloyd; *J. Price of Pilleth; *Th. Vaughan of Llowes;
*Brian Crowther; Evan Vaughan: C.66/1523/m.28d. Commission renewed
to *omit* Gelly Meyrick, and to appoint Rich. Fowler as *custos rotulorum*:
Index 4208/f.94v. (29)

1600: 10 December
Commission renewed to *omit* Clement Price: Index 4208/f.99.

1601: 16 March (Acting)
As on 1 August 1600, except: E. of Essex; E. of Pembroke; Clement Price;
Lewis Lloyd, *omitted*: Wales 4/477/1. (25)

1601: 17 August (Acting)
As on 16 March 1601, except: J. Bradshaw (Sheriff, 1600–1), *omitted*:
Wales 4/477/2. (24)

1602: 22 March (Acting)
As on 17 August 1601, except: J. Bradshaw, *added*. J. Price of Pilleth (Sheriff,
1601–2), *omitted*: Wales 4/477/3. (24)

1602: 8 May
Commission renewed to *omit* David Lloyd Meredith: Index 4208/f.133v.

1602: 21 May
Commission renewed to *restore* J. Price: Index 4208/f.135. (Price was the former Sheriff of Radnor. He wrongly appears as Jas. Price in the Docquet Book).

1602: 6 July
Commission renewed to *add* J. Townshend: Index 4208/f.139v.

1602: 25 July
General renewal of Welsh commissions to *add* Ed., Lord Zouch, President of Council in the Marches of Wales: Index 4208/f.141.

1602: 9 December
*Egerton; *Buckhurst; *Ed., Lord Zouch, President of Council in the Marches of Wales; *Lewkenor, Justice of Chester; *Croke & *Calfield, Justices of Great Sessions; *David Williams, serjeant at law; *W. Leighton; *H. Townshend; *Roger Vaughan; *Jas. Price; *J. Townshend; *Th. Peniston; *Th. Lewis; *Edm. Wynstanley; W. Bradshaw; *p Rich. Fowler; Humph. Cornwall; J. Bradshaw; Ed. Price; *Lewis Lloyd; *Hugh Lloyd; *J. Price of Pilleth; *Th. Vaughan of Llowes; *Brian Crowther; Evan Vaughan; J. Lloyd of Gweneryn(?): C.66/1594/m.33d. Commission renewed to *add* J. Lloyd: Index 4208/f.147v. (27)

1603: 1 August (Acting)
Egerton; Buckhurst; Zouch, President of Council in the Marches of Wales; Lewkenor, Justice of Chester; Croke & Calfield, Justices of Great Sessions; David Williams, serjeant at law; W. Leighton; H. Townshend; Jas. Price; J. Townshend; Th. Peniston; Th. Lewis; Edm. Wynstanley; W. Bradshaw; Rich. Fowler; J. Bradshaw; Hugh Lloyd; J. Price; Th. Vaughan; Brian Crowther; Evan Vaughan: Wales 4/478/1. (The absence of J. Lloyd from this list may indicate that the list is based on the commission of 25 July 1602 rather than that of 9 December 1602). (22)

1604: 24 September (Acting)
As on 1 August 1603, except: Francis Tate, Justice of Great Sessions; David Lloyd Meredith; Humph. Cornwall; J. Lloyd, *added*. Geo Calfield; Th. Peniston; Evan Vaughan (Sheriff, 1603–4), *omitted*: Wales 4/478/3. (23)

1605: 18 March (Acting)
As on 24 September 1604, except: Evan Vaughan, *added*. J. Townshend (Sheriff, 1604–5), *omitted*: Wales 4/478/4. (23)

1605: 29 July (Acting)
As on 18 March 1605, except: J. Townshend, kt.; W. Vaughan; Hugh Lewis, *added*. Th. Vaughan, *omitted*: Wales 4/478/5. (25)

1606: 21 July (Acting)
As on 29 July 1605, except: Roger Bradshaw, D.D., *added*. David Lloyd Meredith; Hugh Lloyd, *omitted*: Wales 4/479/1. (24)

1606: 8 September (Acting)
As on 21 July 1606, except: Th. Lewis, *omitted*: Wales 4/479/2. (23)

1607: 17 August (Acting)
As on 8 September 1606, except: Jas. Price of Pilleth; Th. Powell, *added*. Lord Zouch; Jas. Price; Humph. Cornwall; J. Bradshaw, *omitted*: Wales 4/479/3. (21)

1607: 28 September (Acting)
*Th. Egerton, Lord Ellesmere, Chancellor; *E. of Dorset (Lord Buckhurst), Treasurer; *Ralph, Lord Eure, President of Council in the Marches of Wales; *David Williams, kt., Justice *coram Rege*; *J. Croke, Justice *coram Rege* & of Great Sessions; *Lewkenor, Justice of Chester; *Francis Tate, Justice of Great Sessions; *J. Townshend, kt.; *H. Townshend, kt.; *W. Leighton; Roger Bradshaw, D.D.; *Edm. Wynstanley; *W. Bradshaw; *p Rich. Fowler; *W. Vaughan; *J. Price of Pilleth; *Jas. Price of Pilleth; *Brian Crowther; Evan Vaughan; J. Lloyd; Hugh Lewis; Th. Powell: Wales 4/479/4. (Details of the quorum are based on the commissions for 1606–7 and 1607–8 enrolled on C.66/1698/m.31d & C.66/1748/m.32d). (22)

1608: 4 April (Acting)
As on 28 September 1607, except: Jas. Price of Mynachty; J. Bradshaw, *added*. W. Leighton *omitted*: Wales 4/479/5. (23)

1608: 15 August (Acting)
As on 4 April 1608, except: E. of Salisbury, Treasurer; E. of Northampton, Keeper of Privy Seal; Geo. Snigg, kt., Baron of Exchequer & Justice of Great Sessions, *added*. E. of Dorset; J. Croke, *omitted*: Wales 4/479/6. (24)

1609: 3 April (Acting)
As on 15 August 1608: Wales 4/480/1. (24)

1610: 23 March (Acting)
As on 3 April 1609, except: Chas. Walcott, *added*. Th. Powell, *omitted*: Wales 4/480/3. (24)

1610: 20 August (Acting)
As on 23 March 1610, except: Rowland Meyrick, *added*: Wales 4/480/4. (25)

1611: 4 March (Acting)
As on 20 August 1610, except: Th. Powell, *added*. Jas. Price of Pilleth (Sheriff, 1610–11), *omitted*: Wales 4/480/5. (25)

1611: 2 September (Acting)
As on 4 March 1611, except: H. Williams, kt., *added*: Wales 4/480/6. (26)

1612: 30 March (Acting)
As on 2 September 1611, except: Jas. Price of Pilleth, *added*. Edm. Wynstanley; J. Lloyd, *omitted*: Wales 4/481/1. (25)

1612: 17 August (Acting)
*Ellesmere; *E. of Northampton, Keeper of Privy Seal; *Eure, President of Council in the Marches of Wales; Williams, Justice *coram Rege*; *Geo. Snigg, kt., Baron of Exchequer & Justice of Great Sessions; *Rich. Lewkenor, Justice of Chester; *Francis Tate, Justice of Great Sessions; H. Williams, *J. Townshend, *H. Townshend, kts.; *Jas. Price of Mynachty; *W. Bradshaw; *p Rich. Fowler; Chas. Walcott; *J. Bradshaw; *W. Vaughan; *J. Price of Pilleth; Rowland Meyrick; *Jas. Price of Pilleth; *Brian Crowther; Evan Vaughan; Hugh Lewis; Th. Powell: Wales 4/481/2. (Details of the quorum are taken from the commission for 1611–2 enrolled in C.66/1898/m.29d). (23)

1614: 28 March (Acting)
As on 17 August 1612, except: W. Leighton; J. Lloyd, *added*. David Williams; Th. Powell, *omitted*: Wales 4/481/4. (23)

1614: post 11 July
*Ellesmere; *E. of Suffolk, Treasurer (appointed on 11 July); *Eure, President of Council in the Marches of Wales; *Snigg, Baron of Exchequer & Justice of Great Sessions; *Lewkenor, Justice of Chester; *Tate, Justice of Great Sessions; H. Williams, *J. Townshend, *H. Townshend, kts.; *Roger Bradshaw, D.D.; *Jas. Price of Mynachty; *W. Bradshaw; *p Rich. Fowler; Chas. Walcott; *J. Bradshaw; *W. Vaughan; *J. Price of Pilleth; Rowland Meyrick; W. Leighton; J. Lloyd; *Jas. Price of Pilleth; *Brian Crowther; Evan Vaughan; Hugh Lewis; Th. Powell: C.66/1988/m.29d. (Note that Roger Bradshaw ceases to appear in Gaol File lists after 30 March 1612 and Th. Powell in lists after 28 March 1614. Both men may therefore be included in the present patent roll enrolment in error). (25)

1615: 23 December
Commission renewed to *add* Rich. Jones: Index 4211/f.12v.

1616: 7 March
*Ellesmere; *Suffolk; *E. of Worcester, Keeper of Privy Seal; *Eure, President of Council in the Marches of Wales; *Snigg, Baron of Exchequer & Justice of Great Sessions; *Lewkenor, Justice of Chester; *Tate, Justice of Great Sessions; H. Williams, *J. Townshend, *H. Townshend, kts.; *W. Bradshaw; *p Rich. Fowler; *J. Price of Pilleth; Chas. Walcott; *W. Vaughan; Rowland Meyrick; *Jas. Price of Pilleth; J. Lloyd; *Brian Crowther; Evan Vaughan; Rich. Jones: C.66/2076/m.25d. Commission renewed to *omit* Jas. Price: Index 4211/f.17v. (Note that the dating of this commission raises difficulties. The Docquet Book entry actually states that the renewal of the commission was made to *restore* Jas. Price. This however seems unlikely since there is no evidence of the omission prior to 7 March 1616 of either of the Prices included in earlier commissions, Jas. Price of Mynachty and Jas. Price of Pilleth. However the Gaol File list of 2 September

1616 indicates that Jas. Price of Mynachty had been omitted from the commission during that year (Wales 4/481/3). There is also a renewal of the commission on 29 August 1616 to *restore* Jas. Price (Index 4211/f.26). The evidence therefore points to Jas. Price of Mynachty and to his *omission* on 7 March 1616 and *restoration* on 29 August 1616). (21)

1616: 29 August
Commission renewed to *restore* Jas. Price: Index 4211/f.26.

1617: 19 March
Commission renewed to *add* Francis Bacon, kt., Keeper of Great Seal; Th., Lord Gerard, President of Council in the Marches of Wales: Index 4211/f.38.

1617: 14 April (Acting)
Francis Bacon, kt., Keeper of Great Seal; Suffolk; Worcester; D. of Lennox, Steward; Th., Lord Gerard, President of Council in the Marches of Wales; Th. Chamberlain, kt., Justice of Chester; Walter Pye & Andrew Powell, Justices of Great Sessions; H. Williams, H. Townshend, kts.; Jas. Price of Mynachty; Rich. Fowler; W. Bradshaw; J. Price of Pilleth; J. Lloyd; Chas. Walcott; W. Vaughan; Rowland Meyrick; Jas. Price of Pilleth; Brian Crowther; Evan Vaughan; Rich. Jones: Wales 4/482/4. (22)

1617: 18 July
Commission renewed to *add* J. Townshend, kt.; Ezekiel Weston: Index 4211/f.47v.

1617: 4 November
Commission renewed to *add* Chas. Williams: Index 4211/f.50v.

1617: 1 December
As on 14 April 1617, except: *W., Lord Compton, President of Council in the Marches of Wales; *J. Townshend, kt.; *Ezekiel Weston; Samuel Parker; Chas. Williams, *added*. Lord Gerard, *omitted*: C.66/2147/m.24d. Commission renewed to *add* Samuel Parker: Index 4211/f.52v. (Compton was appointed as President of Council in the Marches of Wales on 24 November 1617 and was presumably therefore added on 1 December). (26)

1618: 7 July
Commission renewed to *add* Humphrey Walcott: Index 4211/f.68.

1618: 28 November
*Lord Verulam (Nich. Bacon), Chancellor; *Worcester; Lennox; *E. of Northampton (Lord Compton), President of Council in the Marches of Wales; *Chamberlain, Justice of Chester; *Pye & *Powell, Justices of Great Sessions; *J. Townshend, H. Williams, *H. Townshend, kts.; *p Rich. Fowler; *Jas. Price of Mynachty; *W. Bradshaw; *J. Price of Pilleth; *J. Lloyd; Chas. Walcott; *W. Vaughan; Rowland Meyrick; *Jas. Price of Pilleth; *Brian Crowther; Evan Vaughan; Humph. Walcott; Rich. Jones; *Ezekiel Weston; Chas. Williams; *Epiphan Haworth: C.66/2174/m.20d. Commission renewed to *add* Epiphan Haworth: Index 4211/f.74v. (26)

1619: 12 July
Commission renewed to *add* Evan Vaughan, D.D.: Index 4211/f.90v.

1619: 13 September (Acting)
As on 28 November 1618, except: Evan Vaughan, D.D., *added*. H. Townshend, *omitted*: Wales 4/483/3. (26)

1620: 10 April (Acting)
As on 13 September 1619, except: H. Townshend, kt., *added*. Chas. Williams, *omitted*: Wales 4/483/4. (26)

1620: 6 May
Commission renewed to *restore* Chas. Williams: Index 4211/f.104v.

1620: 4 November
General renewal of Welsh commissions to *add* Jas. Whitlock, kt., Justice of Chester: Index 4211/f.114.

1620: 23 November
Commission renewed to *add* J. Reade: Index 4211/f.115.

1621: 26 February
*Viscount St. Alban (Nich. Bacon), Chancellor; *Viscount Mandeville, Treasurer; *Worcester; *Lennox; *Northampton, President of Council in the Marches of Wales; *B. of St. Davids; *Jas. Whitlock, kt., Justice of Chester; *Pye & *Powell, Justices of Great Sessions; *J. Townshend, H. Williams, *H. Townshend, kts.; Evan Vaughan, D.D.; *p Rich. Fowler; *Jas. Price of Mynachty; *W. Bradshaw; *J. Price of Pilleth; *J. Lloyd; Chas. Walcott; *W. Vaughan; Rowland Meyrick; *Jas. Price of Pilleth; *Brian Crowther; Evan Vaughan; Humph. Walcott; Rich. Jones; *Ezekiel Weston; *Chas. Williams; Epiphan Haworth; J. Reade: B.M., Harleian Ms. 1933/f.25. Commission renewed to *add* Viscount Mandeville: Index 4211/ f.120. (Details of the quorum are based on the patent roll enrolment of the present commission in C.66/2234/m.44d. The patent roll entry is identical to the Harleian version of the commission except for the omission of the Bishop of St. Davids and J. Price of Pilleth. These differences are explained by the Bishop's translation to Carlisle in June 1621 and the disappearance from the commission of J. Price by 2 April 1621 (Wales 4/484/1). The commission was clearly entered on the patent roll after these two justices had left the commission). (30)

1621: post 29 September
As on 26 February 1621, except: *B. of Lincoln, Keeper of Great Seal; *Lionel Cranfield, Treasurer, *added*. (Cranfield was appointed on 29 September). Viscount St. Alban; B. of St. Davids; H. Townshend; J. Price of Pilleth, *omitted*: C.66/2259/m.27d. (28)

1622: 8 February
Commission renewed to appoint W. Vaughan as *custos rotulorum*: Index 4211/f.134v.

1622: 15 April (Acting)
As at the end of 1621, except: Rich. Fowler; Ezekiel Weston; J. Reade (Sheriff, 1621–2), *omitted*: Wales 4/484/3. (25)

1622: 8 July
Commission renewed to *add* Griffith Jones: Index 4211/f.140v.

1622: 2 September
Commission renewed to *omit* J. Townshend, kt.; Jas. Price of Mynachty; J. Lloyd; Chas. Walcott; Rowland Meyrick; Humph. Walcott: Index 4211/f.144.

1623: 2 December
Commission renewed to *restore* J. Reade, late Sheriff: Index 4211/f.159.

1624: 9 March
*B. of Lincoln, Keeper of Great Seal; *E. of Middlesex (Lionel Cranfield), Treasurer; *Viscount Mandeville, President of Council; *Worcester; *Northampton, President of Council in the Marches of Wales; *Whitlock, Justice of Chester; *Pye & *Powell, Justices of Great Sessions; *H. Williams, kt.; *Evan Vaughan, D.D.; *p W. Vaughan; *Jas. Price of Pilleth; *W. Bradshaw; *Brian Crowther; Evan Vaughan; *Rich. Jones; *Chas. Williams; *Epiphan Haworth; J. Reade; *Griffith Jones; Hugh Lloyd of Caerfagu: C.66/2310/m.31d. Commission renewed to *add* Hugh Lloyd: Index 4211/f.163. (21)

1624: 10 May
Commission renewed to *add* Rich. Fowler: Index 4211/f.164v. (This name is written as Flower in the original Docquet Book and patent roll entries).

1625: 22 February
Commission renewed to *add* Jas. Phillips; Nich. Taylor: Index 4211/f.176v.

1625: 4 March
Commission renewed to *add* W. Fowler: Index 4211/f.177.

1625: 1 April
*Lincoln; *Jas., Lord Ley, Treasurer; *Mandeville; *Worcester; *Northampton, President of Council in the Marches of Wales; *Th. Chamberlain, kt., Justice of Chester; *Pye & *Powell, Justices of Great Sessions; *H. Williams, kt.; *Evan Vaughan, D.D.; *Sampson Eure; *Rob. Brooke; *p W. Vaughan; W. Fowler; *Jas. Price of Pilleth; *W. Bradshaw; *Brian Crowther; Evan Vaughan; Humph. Walcott; *Rich. Jones; *Chas. Williams; *Epiphan Haworth; *Griffith Jones; Hugh Lloyd; *Rich. Fowler; Jas. Phillips; Nich. Taylor: C.66/2367/m.30d. General renewal of Welsh commissions: Index 4211/f.180v. (27)

1625: 22 December
As on 1 April 1625, except: *Th. Coventry, kt., Keeper of Great Seal, *added*. B. of Lincoln; Th. Chamberlain, *omitted*: B.M., Harleian Ms. 1622/f.103. General renewal of Welsh commissions to *add* Th. Coventry: Index 4211/f.194v. (26)

1626: 20 March
As on 22 December 1625, except: *J. Bridgeman, kt., Justice of Chester, *added*. W. Bradshaw; Chas. Williams; Epiphan Haworth; Hugh Lloyd; Jas. Phillips, *omitted*: E.163/18/12/f.102v. Commission renewed to *add* J. Bridgeman: Index 4211/f.199. (22)

1626: 7 September
As on 20 March 1626, except: Evan Vaughan, D.D., *omitted*: C.193/12/2/ f.73v. Commission renewed to *omit* Evan Vaughan: Index 4211/f.209. (21)

1627: 5 January
Commission renewed to *restore* Hugh Lloyd: Index 4211/f.214v.

1627: 15 March
*Th. Coventry, kt., Keeper of Great Seal; *E. of Marlborough (Lord Ley), Treasurer; *E. of Manchester (Viscount Mandeville), President of Council; *Northampton, President of Council in the Marches of Wales; *J. Bridgeman, kt., Justice of Chester; *Pye & *Powell, Justices of Great Sessions; *H. Williams, kt.; *Sampson Eure; *Timothy Turneur; *p W. Vaughan; W. Fowler; *Jas. Price of Pilleth; *Brian Crowther; Evan Vaughan; Humph. Walcott; *Rich. Jones; *Hugh Lloyd of Caerfagu; *Griffith Jones; Nich. Taylor; Roderick Gwynn of Llavell: C.66/2449/m.30d. Commission renewed to *add* Roderick Gwynn: Index 4211/f.220v. (21)

1629: 20 February
Commission renewed to *add* Th. Jenner: Index 4211/f.264v.

1629: 6 March
*Coventry; *Rich., Lord Weston, Treasurer; *Viscount Conway, President of Council; *E. of Manchester, Keeper of Privy Seal; *E. of Pembroke, Steward; *Northampton, President of Council in the Marches of Wales; *Bridgeman, Justice of Chester; *Pye & *Powell, Justices of Great Sessions; *H. Williams, kt.; *Sampson Eure; *Timothy Turneur; *p W. Vaughan; W. Fowler; *Jas. Price of Pilleth; *Brian Crowther; Evan Vaughan; Humph. Walcott; *Rich. Jones; *Hugh Lloyd; *Jas. Phillips; Nich. Taylor; Roderick Gwynn of Llavell; *Rob. Williams; Th. Jenner: C.66/ 2495/m.29d & C.66/2527/m.31d. Commission renewed to *add* Jas. Phillips; Rob. Williams: Index 4211/f.265v. (25).

1629: 14 September (Acting)
As on 6 March 1629, except: Hugh Lloyd, *omitted*: Wales 4/487/4. (The apparent omission of Hugh Lloyd between March and 14 September may be misleading since he may be omitted in error from the present list. Note that the list also includes the name of Griffith Jones who had disappeared from the commission of 6 March 1629 either at the time of its issue or when it was later enrolled. Jones was however omitted from the Gaol File list by the time of the next such surviving list of 20 September 1630). (25)

1630: 23 January
Commission renewed to *restore* Chas. Williams: Index 4212/p.21. (Williams had been omitted on or before 20 March 1626: E.163/18/12/f.102v).

1630: 20 September (Acting)
As on 14 September 1629, except: Chas. Williams; Hugh Lloyd, *added*. E. of Pembroke; E. of Northampton; Griffith Jones, *omitted*: Wales 4/487/5. (24)

1631: 8 August (Acting)
As on 20 September 1630, except: E. of Bridgewater, President of Wales, *added*. Viscount Conway; Andrew Powell; Jas. Phillips (Sheriff, 1630–1), *omitted*: Wales 4/488/1. (22)

1632: 30 July (Acting)
As on 8 August 1631, except: Walter Rumsey, Justice of Great Sessions; Marmaduke Lloyd, kt.; Jas. Phillips, *added*. Roderick Gwynn (Sheriff, 1631–2), *omitted*: Wales 4/488/3. (24)

1633: 15 April (Acting)
As on 30 July 1632, except: Roderick Gwynn of Llavell, *added*. Hugh Lloyd, *omitted*: Wales 4/488/5. (24)

1633: 9 September (Acting)
As on 15 April 1633, except: Jas. Phillips, *omitted*: Wales 4/488/6. (23)

1633: 20 December
*Coventry; *E. of Portland (Lord Weston), Treasurer; *Manchester; *E. of Bridgewater, President of Council in the Marches of Wales; *Bridgeman, Justice of Chester; *Walter Pye, kt. & *Walter Rumsey, Justices of Great Sessions; *H. Williams, *Marmaduke Lloyd, kts.; *Sampson Eure; *Timothy Turneur; *p W. Vaughan; W. Fowler; *Jas. Price of Pilleth; *Brian Crowther; Evan Vaughan; Humph. Walcott; *Rich. Jones; J. Price; *Chas. Williams; *Nich. Taylor; Roderick Gwynn of Llavell; *Rob. Williams; Th. Jenner: C.193/13/2/f.86. Commission renewed to *add* J. Price: Index 4212/p.120. (Note that the version of this commission enrolled on C.66/2623/m.25d. still includes the name of Jas. Phillips whom the Gaol File lists show had disappeared from the commission by 9 September 1633). (24)

1634: 8 September (Acting)
As on 20 December 1633: Wales 4/489/2. (24)

1634: 19 December
Commission renewed to *add* Nich. Meredith: Index 4212/p.151.

1635: 23 March (Acting)
As on 8 September 1634, except: Nich. Meredith, *added*. Brian Crowther, *omitted*: Wales 4/489/3. (24)

1635: 30 April
Commission renewed to *add* Hugh Lewis: Index 4212/p.163.

1636: 1 July
Commission renewed to *add* Morgan Vaughan; Herbert Weston: Index
4212/p.211.

1637: 2 January
*Coventry; *B. of London, Treasurer; *Manchester; *Bridgewater, President
of Council in the Marches of Wales; *Bridgeman, Justice of Chester;
*Marmaduke Lloyd, kt. & *Walter Rumsey, Justices of Great Sessions;
*H. Williams, kt.; *Sampson Eure; *Timothy Turneur; *p W. Vaughan;
W. Fowler; *Jas. Price of Pilleth; *Rob. Williams; Evan Vaughan; Humph.
Walcott; *J. Powell of Stanage; *Rich. Jones; J. Price; Nich. Meredith;
*Chas. Williams; *Hugh Lewis; *Nich. Taylor; Roderick Gwynn of
Llavell; *Th. Jenner; Morgan Vaughan; Herbert Weston: S.P.16/405/f.83v.
Commission renewed to *add* J. Powell of Stanage: Index 4212/p.225.   (27)

1637: 27 March (Acting)
As on 2 January 1637, except: H. Williams, kt.; J. Price (Sheriff in 1637),
omitted: Wales 4/489/5.   (25)

1638: 16 February
As on 27 March 1637, except: *H. Williams, kt.; Maurice Lewis, *added*.
J. Bridgeman; Timothy Turneur; Evan Vaughan, *omitted*: C.66/2725/m.20d.
Commission renewed to *add* Maurice Lewis: Index 4212/p.279.   (24)

1639: 25 March (Acting)
As on 16 February 1638, except: H. Williams, kt.; Chas. Williams, *omitted*:
Wales 4/490/2.   (22)

1639: 26 August (Acting)
As on 25 March 1639, except: Hugh Lewis, *omitted*: Wales 4/490/3.   (21)

1640: 16 March (Acting)
As on 26 August 1639, except: J. Finch, kt., Keeper of Great Seal; *added*.
Lord Coventry; J. Powell (Sheriff, 1639–40), *omitted*: Wales 4/490/4.   (20)

1640: 1 June
*J. Finch, kt., Keeper of Great Seal; *London; *Manchester; *Bridgewater,
President of Council in the Marches of Wales; *Th. Milward, kt., Justice of
Chester; *Lloyd & *Rumsey, Justices of Great Sessions; *Sampson Eure;
*W. Morgan; *p W. Vaughan; W. Fowler; *Jas. Price of Pilleth; *Rob.
Williams; Humph. Walcott; *J. Powell of Stanage; *Rich. Jones; Nich.
Meredith; Hugh Lloyd of Caerfagu; Roderick Gwynn of Llavell; Th.
Jenner; Morgan Vaughan; Herbert Weston; Maurice Lewis; W. Beaumont:
C.66/2858/m.19d. Commission renewed to *add* Hugh Lloyd of Caerfagu;
W. Beaumont: Index 4212/p.387. (Note that J. Powell was Sheriff of Radnor
in 1639–40 and was therefore correctly omitted from the Gaol File list of
16 March 1640. His term of office had presumably ended and he had been
restored by the time the commission was enrolled).   (24)

1640: 24 August (Acting)
As on 1 June 1640, except: J. Powell, *omitted* (see note above): Wales 4/490/5. (23)

1641: 21 January
Commission renewed to *add* Chas. Price as *custos rotulorum*: Index 4212/p.423.

1641: 19 March
Commission renewed to *add* Brian Crowther: Index 4212/p.435.

1641: 24 March
Commission renewed to *add* Rob. Williams: Index 4212/p.438.

1641: 29 March (Acting)
Ed. Littleton, kt., Keeper of Great Seal; London; Manchester; Bridgewater, President of Council in the Marches of Wales; Milward, Justice of Chester; Lloyd & Rumsey, Justices of Great Sessions; Sampson Eure, serjeant at law; Rich. Lloyd; W. Morgan; Chas. Price; W. Fowler; Rob. Williams; Humph. Walcott; J. Powell of Stanage; Rich. Jones; Nich. Meredith; Hugh Lloyd; Roderick Gwynn; Th. Jenner; Morgan Vaughan; Herbert Weston; Maurice Lewis; W. Beaumont: Wales 4/491/1. (Note that this list is based on the commission as renewed on 21 January 1641. The commissions in which Brian Crowther and Rob. Williams were added had not yet reached the county. Note also that the addition of Rob. Williams to the commission on 24 March meant that there were two men of that name acting as justices of the peace). (24)

1641: 27 September (Acting)
As on 29 March 1641, except: Rob. Williams; Brian Crowther, *added*. Walter Rumsey, *omitted* (in error): Wales 4/491/2. (25)

1641: 26 November
Commission renewed to *add* Evan Davies: Index 4212/p.489.

1643: 26 June
Commission renewed to *add* Walter Pye, Bt.: Index 4210/p.24.

1643: 14 August (Acting)
As on 27 September 1641, except: Walter Rumsey; Evan Davies, *added*. B. of London; Rob. Williams; Th. Jenner, *omitted*: Wales 4/491/5. (The commission issued to add Walter Pye had evidently not yet arrived in the county). (24)

1644: 13 May (Acting)
As on 14 August 1643, except: E. of Bridgewater, *omitted*: Wales 4/492/1. (23)

1645: 3 February
Commission renewed to appoint Rich. Jones as *custos rotulorum*: Index 4210/p.143.

1648: 1 September
Commission renewed (no details): Index 4213/p.121.

1649: 9 March
Commission renewed (no details): Index 4213/p.144.

1649: 16 March
*W. Lenthall, Speaker of Parliament; *Lord Fairfax, General; *J. Bradshaw, President of Council; *Bulstrode Whitelock, *Rich. Keble, *J. Lisle, Commissioners of Great Seal; *E. of Pembroke; *H. Rolle, Chief Justice of Upper Bench; *J. Eltonhead & *J. Norbury, Justices of Great Sessions; *J. Thynne; *J. Venn; *Silvanus Taylor; *H. Williams of Caebalfa; *Rich. Fowler of Abbey Cwmhir; *W. Beaumont of Bryngwyn; *Th. Baskerville; *J. Williams of Brongynllwyd(?); *J. Williams of Scynlais; Hugh Lewis of Hendwall(?); David Lloyd of Diserth; Peter Taylor of Eveniog(?): C.193/13/3/f.80v. Commission renewed to *add* J. Norbury, Justice of Great Sessions: Index 4213/p.144.   (22)

1649: 2 April (Acting)
As on 16 March 1649, except: J. Bradshaw, *omitted*: Wales 4/493/1.   (21)

1649: 23 July (Acting)
As on 2 April 1649: Wales 4/493/2.   (21)

1650: 9 March
*Lenthall; *p Oliver Cromwell; *Bradshaw; *Whitelock, *Keble & *Lisle; *Rolle; *Eltonhead & *Norbury; *Th. Harrison; *Ed. Freeman, Attorney-General of S. Wales; *J. Thynne; *J. Venn; *Silvanus Taylor; *H. Williams of Caebalfa; *Rich. Fowler of Abbey Cwmhir; *W. Beaumont of Bryngwyn; *Th. Baskerville; *J. Williams of Brongynllwyd(?); *J. Williams of Scynlais; Hugh Lewis; David Lloyd; Peter Taylor; Rich. King; J. Dauntsey; Nich. Taylor: *Lists published by Th. Walkley* (1650), p.71. Commission renewed to *add* Oliver Cromwell, Lieutenant-General & Governor of Ireland, as *custos rotulorum*, and to *add* Th. Harrison; Rich. King; J. Dauntsey; Nich. Taylor: Index 4213/p.179.   (26)

1651: 27 February
Commission renewed to place Hugh Lewis of Hendwall(?) on the quorum: Index 4213/p.207.

1651: 14 May
Commission renewed to *add* Rich. Cromwell; Peter Price of Glasgwm; Rich. King of Llanbister; J. Yardley of Llangunllo; Hugh Price of Mynachty; J. Walsham of Knill, and to *omit* J. Thynne; J. Venn; Silvanus Taylor; Hugh Lewis of Hendwall (?); Rich. Fowler of Abbey Cwmhir; W. Beaumont of Bryngwyn; Th. Baskerville; J. Williams of Scynlais; David Lloyd of Diserth: Index 4213/p.215.

1651: 26 June
*Lenthall; *p Oliver Cromwell; *Whitelock, *Keble & *Lisle; *Bradshaw; *Rolle; *Eltonhead & *Norbury, Justices of Great Sessions; *Th. Harrison; *Ed. Freeman, Attorney-General of S. Wales; *Rich. Cromwell; *Silvanus Taylor; *H. Williams of Caebalfa; *Nich. Taylor of Presteigne; *Peter Taylor of Eveniog(?); *J. Dauntsey of Glasgwm; *J. Williams of Brongynllwyd(?); *Peter Price of Glasgwm; *Rich. King of Llanbister; J. Yardley of Llangunllo; Hugh Price of Mynachty; J. Walsham of Knill: C.193/13/4/f.126 & Cambridge University Ms. Dd.VIII.1/f.132v. Commission renewed to *add* Silvanus Taylor: Index 4213/p.216.   (23)

1652: 16 August (Acting)
As on 26 June 1651, except: J. Dauntsey (Sheriff, 1651–2), *omitted*: Wales 4/493/7.   (22)

1653: 29 August (Acting)
Silvanus Taylor; H. Williams; Nich. Taylor; J. Dauntsey; Peter Price; Rich. King; Peter Taylor; J. Yardley; J. Walsham: Wales 4/494/1. (Note that for some unspecified reason all the *ex officio* members of the commission are omitted from the present list).   (9)

1654: 23 March
Commission renewed according to a general list: Index 4213/p.286.

1654: 17 April (Acting)
Whitelock, Keble & Lisle; Rolle; W. Lenthall, Master of the Rolls; Oliver St. John, Chief Justice of Common Bench; J. Corbet, Justice of Great Sessions; Edm. Prideaux, Attorney-General; Edm. Jones, Attorney-General of S. Wales; Geo. Gwynn; Silvanus Taylor; H. Williams; Nich. Taylor; Peter Taylor; J. Dauntsey; J. Williams, *custos rotulorum*; Peter Price; Rich. King; J. Yardley; Hugh Price of Mynachty: Wales 4/494/2.   (20)

1654: 14 August (Acting)
As on 17 April 1654: Wales 4/494/3.   (20)

1655: 30 August
Commission renewed to *add* W. Foxwist, Justice of Great Sessions: Index 4213/p.317.

1655: 17 September (Acting)
As on 14 August 1654, except: Nathaniel Fiennes, Commissioner of Great Seal; J. Glynn, Chief Justice of Upper Bench; W. Foxwist, Justice of Great Sessions; J. Walsham, *added*. Bulstrode Whitlock; Rich. Keble; H. Rolle, *omitted*: Wales 4/494/4.   (21)

1656: 20 March
*Nathaniel Fiennes & *J. Lisle, Commissioners of Great Seal; *Bulstrode Whitelock, kt., *Th. Widdrington, kt., *Ed. Montagu & *W. Sydenham, Commissioners of Treasury; *p Philip Jones; *J. Glynn, Chief Justice of Upper Bench; *W. Lenthall, Master of the Rolls; *Oliver St. John, Chief

Justice of Common Bench; *J. Corbet & *W. Foxwist, Justices of Great Sessions; *Edm. Prideaux, Attorney-General; *Major-General Jas. Berry; *Rowland Dawkins; *Edm. Jones, Attorney-General of S. Wales; *Geo. Gwynn; *H. Williams of Caebalfa; *Samuel Powell of Stanage; *Nich. Taylor; *Rich. Fowler; *J. Dauntsey of Glasgwm; J. Walsham; *J. Williams of Brongynllwyd(?); *Peter Price of Glasgwm; *Rich. King; J. Yardley; Hugh Price of Mynachty; J. Probert of Llowes; Peter Taylor: C.193/13/6/f.112. Commission renewed to *add* Major-General Jas. Berry; Rowland Dawkins; Samuel Powell of Stanage; Rich. Fowler; J. Probert of Llowes, to *omit* Silvanus Taylor, and to appoint Philip Jones as *custos rotulorum*: Index 4213/p.330. (30)

1656: 18 December
As on 20 March 1656, except: Griffith Jones, *added*. Peter Price, *omitted*: C.193/13/5/f.133. Commission renewed to *add* Griffith Jones, and to *omit* Peter Price: Index 4213/p.354. (30)

1657: 6 April (Acting)
As on 18 December 1656: Wales 4/495/1. (30)

1657: 17 August (Acting)
As on 6 April 1657: Wales 4/495/2. (30)

1658: April (Acting)
As on 17 August 1657: Wales 4/495/3. (30)

1658: 24 September
General renewal of Welsh commissions to *add* Rich. Cromwell, Lord Protector: Index 4213/p.405.

1659: 4 July
Commission renewed according to a general list: Index 4213/p.437.

1659: 21 July
Commission renewed to *add* Nich. Taylor; Samuel Powell: Index 4213/p.440.

1659: 15 August (Acting)
W. Lenthall, Speaker & Master of the Rolls; J. Bradshaw, Th. Tyrrell & J. Fountain, Commissioners of Great Seal; J. Corbet, Justice of Great Sessions; Silvanus Taylor; J. James; Geo. Gwynn; Rob. Weaver; J. Walsham; J. Dauntsey; J. Williams; Nich. Taylor; Samuel Powell; J. Bull; Gabriel Taylor; Peter Taylor; J. Dauntsey junior: Wales 4/495/5. (18)

1660: 27 March
Commission renewed according to a general list: Index 4213/p.459.

1660: 24 August
Commission renewed to *add* Ed. Harley as *custos rotulorum*: Index 4214/p.30.

1660: post 8 September
*Ed. Hyde, kt., Chancellor; *E. of Southampton, Treasurer (appointed on 8 September); *D. of Albemarle, General; *Marquess of Ormond, Steward; *E. of Lindsey, Great Chamberlain; *E. of Manchester, Household Chamberlain; *E. of Carbery; *Arthur Annesley; *Rich. Lloyd, kt., Justice of Great Sessions; *p Ed. Harley; *Rob. Harley; *Geo. Gwynn; *Rich. Fowler; *Jas. Price; *H. Williams; *Lewis Morgan; Th. Lewis; Th. Corbet; Rob. Martin; *Samuel Powell; *Evan Davies; *Nich. Taylor; *Andrew Phillips; Chas. Lewis; H. Probert; Herbert Weston; Griffith Jones; Hugh Powell; Nich. Meredith; Th. Eccleston: C.220/9/4/f.113 & B.M., Egerton Ms. 2557/f.112.   (30)

1661: 25 June
Commission renewed to *add* Rob. Curtler: Index 4214/p.116.

1661: 26 August
Commission renewed to *add* Rich. Lloyd, kt. & Arthur Trevor, Justices of Great Sessions: Index 4214/p.136.

1661: 8 November
As at the end of 1660, except: *J., Lord Robartes, Keeper of Privy Seal; *Arthur Trevor, Justice of Great Sessions; Rob. Curtler, *added*: C.193/12/3/ f.128. General renewal of Welsh commissions to *add* E. of Carbery, President of Council in the Marches of Wales: Index 4214/p.144. (Carbery was already on the Radnor commission in his private capacity before this date).   (33)

1662: 31 July
*E. of Clarendon (Ed. Hyde), Chancellor; *Southampton; *Lord Robartes, Keeper of Privy Seal; *Albemarle; *Ormond; *Lindsey; *Manchester; *E. of Carbery, President of Council in the Marches of Wales; *E. of Anglesey (Arthur Annesley); *Rich. Lloyd, kt. & *Arthur Trevor, Justices of Great Sessions; *p Ed. Harley, kt.; *Rob. Harley; *Geo. Gwynn; *Rich. Fowler; *Jas. Price; *H. Williams; *Lewis Morgan; Th. Lewis; Th. Corbet; Rob. Martin; *Samuel Powell; *Evan Davies; *Nich. Taylor; *Andrew Phillips; *Th. Lewis of Mynachty; Chas. Lewis; H. Probert; Herbert Weston; Griffith Jones; Hugh Powell; Nich. Meredith; Th. Eccleston; Rob. Curtler: C.66/2986/m.34d. Commission renewed to *add* Th. Lewis of Mynachty: Index 4214/p.183.   (34)

1662: 25 August (Acting)
As on 31 July 1662: Wales 4/496/5.   (34)

1664: 21 March (Acting)
As on 25 August 1662, except: H. Williams (Sheriff, 1663-4); Th. Lewis of Mynachty, *omitted*: Wales 4/497/1.   (32)

1664: 25 July (Acting)
As on 21 March 1664: Wales 4/497/2.   (32)

1665: 20 March (Acting)
As on 25 July 1664, except: H. Williams; Th. Lewis of Mynachty, *added*.
Rob. Martin; Hugh Powell; Th. Eccleston (Sheriff, 1664–5), *omitted*:
Wales 4/497/3. (31)

1666: 17 September (Acting)
Clarendon; Southampton; Robartes; Albemarle; Ormond; Lindsey;
Manchester; Carbery, President of Council in the Marches of Wales;
Anglesey; Lloyd & Trevor, Justices of Great Sessions; Ed. Harley, kt. of
the Bath; Rob. Harley, kt.; Geo. Gwynn; Rich. Fowler; Jas. Price; H.
Williams; Lewis Morgan; Th. Lewis; Th. Corbet; Rob. Martin; Samuel
Powell; Evan Davies; Nich. Taylor; Andrew Phillips; Th. Lewis of
Mynachty; Chas. Lewis; H. Probert; Herbert Weston; Griffith Jones;
Hugh Powell; Nich. Meredith; Th. Eccleston; Rob. Curtler: Wales 4/491/4.
(This file is wrongly listed as that of 18 Charles I). (34)

1666: 11 December
Commission renewed to *omit* Nich. Meredith: Index 4214/p.296.

1667: 1 March
Commission renewed to *add* Th. Street as Justice of Great Sessions in place
of Arthur Trevor: Index 4214/p.302.

1667: 16 September (Acting)
As on 17 September 1666, except: Job Charlton, kt., serjeant at law, Justice
of Chester; Th. Street, Justice of Great Sessions, *added*. E. of Southampton;
Arthur Trevor; Chas. Lewis; Nich. Meredith, *omitted*: Wales 4/491/6. (Note
that Charlton had held office since 1662 but is not included in any Gaol File
list before the present one because the Radnor commission of the peace was
not renewed between 31 July 1662 and 11 December 1666. This file is
wrongly listed as that of 19 Charles I). (32)

1670: 25 April (Acting)
As on 16 September 1667, except: Chas. Lewis, *added*. E. of Clarendon;
Lord Robartes; D. of Albemarle; D. of Ormond, *omitted*: Wales 4/498/3.
(29)

1671: 2 March
Commission renewed to *add* Th. Vaughan of Bugeildy; Ezekiel Weston;
Ed. Price: Index 4214/p.386.

1671: 8 May (Acting)
As on 25 April 1670, except: Orlando Bridgeman, kt., Chancellor; D. of
Buckingham; D. of Ormond; B. of Hereford; B. of Llandaff; Th. Vaughan
of Bugeildy; Ezekiel Weston; Ed. Price, *added*. Andrew Phillips; Chas.
Lewis; Th. Eccleston, *omitted*: Wales 4/498/4. (34)

1671: 4 September (Acting)
As on 8 May 1671: Wales 4/498/5. (34)

1672: 5 July
Commission renewed to *add* Ed. Davies; David Williams; Nich. Meredith: Index 4214/p.418.

1673: 12 May
Commission renewed to *add* Th. Brown: Index 4214/p.449.

1674: 24 March
Commission renewed to *add* Ed. Freeman: Index 4214/p.475.

1674: Autumn (Acting)
Lord Finch, Keeper of Great Seal; Viscount Latimer, Treasurer; E. of Anglesey, Keeper of Privy Seal; Dukes of Buckingham, Ormond; Marquess of Worcester, President of Council in the Marches of Wales; E. of Lindsey; E. of St. Albans, Household Chamberlain; E. of Carbery; Bishops of Hereford, Llandaff; Job Charlton, kt., Justice of Chester; Rich. Lloyd, kt. & Th. Street, Justices of Great Sessions; Ed. Harley, kt. of the Bath; Ed. Freeman, King's attorney in Radnor; Owen Wynn; Rich. Fowler; Jas. Price; H. Williams; Lewis Morgan; Th. Lewis of Harpton; Th. Corbet; Rob. Martin; Samuel Powell; Ed. Davies; Nich. Meredith; Th. Lewis of Mynachty; H. Probert; Herbert Weston; Th. Vaughan of Bugeildy; Griffith Jones; Ed. Price; Rob. Curtler; Th. Brown: Wales 4/499/3. (35)

1674: 17 November
Commission renewed to *add* Jas. Lloyd: Index 4214/p.485.

1674: 14 December
Commission renewed to *add* H. Osborne, kt.; Rich. Crowther; J. Davies: Index 4214/p.486.

1675: 5 April (Acting)
As in the autumn of 1674, except: D. of Monmouth; E. of Arlington, Household Chamberlain; H. Osborne, kt.; Rich. Crowther; J. Davies; Jas. Lloyd, *added*. E. of St. Albans, *omitted*: Wales 4/499/4. (40)

1675: 19 April
Commission renewed to *add* W. Probert: Index 4214/p.493.

1676: 28 February
Commission renewed to *add* Rich. Williams: Index 4214/p.509.

1677: 17 September (Acting)
As on 5 April 1675, except: Rob. Harley, kt.; Rich. Williams; W. Probert, *added*. B. of Llandaff; Rich. Lloyd, *omitted*: Wales 4/500/2. (41)

1678: 19 November
Commission renewed to *add* J. Morgan; J. Walsham: Index 4214/p.551.

1678: 19 December
Commission renewed to *add* Ed. Davies: Index 4214/p.554.

1679: 7 June
Commission renewed to *add* W. Probert: Index 4215/p.8.

1679: 28 November
Commission renewed to *add* Nich. Taylor: Index 4215/p.16.

1680: 20 April
*Prince Rupert; *Archbishop of Canterbury; *Lord Finch, Chancellor; *E. of Radnor, President of Council; *E. of Anglesey, Keeper of Privy Seal; Dukes of *Albemarle, *Monmouth, *Newcastle, *Lauderdale, *Ormond; *Marquess of Winchester; *Marquess of Worcester, President of Council in the Marches of Wales; Earls of *Lindsey, *Arlington, *Salisbury, *Bridgewater, *Sunderland, *Essex, *Bath, *Halifax, *Carbery; *Viscount Fauconberg; *B. of London; *B. of Hereford; *Laurence Hyde; *H. Coventry; *Francis North, kt., Chief Justice of Bench; *J. Ernley, kt., Chancellor of Exchequer; *Th. Chichley, kt., Chancellor of Duchy of Lancaster; *W. Temple, Bt.; *Ed. Seymour; *Daniel Finch; *Leoline Jenkins; *Sidney Godolphin; *Th. Street & *Owen Wynn, Justices of Great Sessions; *J. Morgan, Bt.; *Ed. Harley, kt. of the Bath; *Rich. Derham, kt.; *Lewis Meyrick, Attorney-General for Wales; *Ed. Freeman, King's attorney in Radnor; *Rich. Williams; *Rich. Fowler; *Lewis Morgan; Th. Lewis of Harpton; *Samuel Powell; *Ed. Davies; *Th. Lewis of Mynachty; *Ed. Price; H. Probert; Th. Vaughan of Bugeildy; *Nich. Taylor; *J. Davies; *J. Walsham; Griffith Jones; *W. Probert; *Nich. Meredith; *Jas. Lloyd: C.193/12/4/f.158. Commission renewed to remove recusants: Index 4215/p.27. (The *omission* from the Radnor commission of the Duke of Buckingham was ordered by a warrant of 5 February 1680 and the *addition* of Rich. Derham, kt., by a warrant of 26 April: *H.M.C., Eleventh Report, Appendix,* Part 2, p.188. On 17 April 1680 the Privy Council ordered the *addition* to the commission of Rich. Derham, kt., and the *omission* of Rich. Williams and Rich. Derham, Esq.: P.C.2/68/pp.482–3). (58)

1680: 13 September (Acting)
As on 20 April 1680, except: Job Charlton, kt., Justice of Chester; Rich. Derham, Esq., *added*. Rich. Derham, kt.; *omitted*: Wales 4/500/7. (The reappearance of Rich. Derham, Esq., and the omission of Rich. Derham, kt., combined with the retention of Rich. Williams, seem to suggest that the changes in the commission ordered in April 1680 were not carried out. It is possible however that the present list was based on an outdated commission issued in 1679 and not on the most recent one issued in April 1680. The apparent addition to the commission of Job Charlton is misleading since he was superseded as Justice of Chester by Geo. Jeffreys who was appointed on 27 April 1680). (59)

1681: 19 September (Acting)
As on 13 September 1680, except: D. of Monmouth; Th. Street; Th. Lewis of Harpton; Th. Lewis of Mynachty; Griffith Jones, *omitted*: Wales 4/501/1. (54)

1682: 11 March
Commission renewed to *add* Chas., Lord Herbert, as *custos rotulorum*: Index 4215/p.63.

1682: 2 October (Acting)
As on 19 September 1681, except: E. of Conway; Chas., Lord Herbert; Rob. Wright, kt., Justice of Great Sessions, *added*. Earls of Salisbury, Sunderland, Essex; W. Temple; Job Charlton; Ed. Harley; Th. Vaughan, *omitted*: Wales 4/501/2. (50)

1683: 26 March (Acting)
As on 2 October 1682, except: Griffith Jones, *added*. Prince Rupert; Lord Finch; E. of Anglesey; D. of Lauderdale, *omitted*: Wales 4/501/3. (47)

1683: 7 July
Commission renewed to *omit* H. Probert; Nich. Meredith: Index 4215/p.85.

1683: 2 August
Commission renewed to *add* Ed. Lewis: Index 4215/p.88.

1684: Spring (Acting)
As on 26 March 1683, except: E. of Sunderland; Ed. Lewis of Mynachty, *added*. Ed. Price; H. Probert; J. Davies (Sheriff, 1683–4); Griffith Jones; Nich. Meredith, *omitted*: Wales 4/501/5. (44)

1685: 3 March
Commission renewed to appoint Marquess of Worcester (Chas., Lord Herbert) as *custos rotulorum*: Index 4215/p.121. (J. Powell who was appointed as Justice of Great Sessions in place of Rob. Wright on 13 February (Index 4215/p.117), was probably also added on this date).

1685: post 28 September
*Archbishop of Canterbury; *Geo., Lord Jeffreys, Chancellor (appointed on 28 September); *E. of Rochester, Treasurer; *E. of Clarendon, Keeper of Privy Seal; Dukes of *Albemarle, *Newcastle, *Ormond; *D. of Beaufort, President of Council in the Marches of Wales; *Marquess of Winchester; *p Marquess of Worcester; Earls of *Lindsey, *Mulgrave, *Bridgewater, *Sunderland, *Bath, *Nottingham, *Carbery; *Viscount Fauconberg; Bishops of *London, *Hereford; *Sidney, Lord Godolphin; *H. Coventry; *J. Ernley, kt., Chancellor of Exchequer; *Th. Chichley, kt., Chancellor of Duchy of Lancaster; *Ed. Seymour; *Owen Wynn, serjeant at law & *J. Powell, Justices of Great Sessions; *Rich. Derham, kt. & Bt.; *J. Morgan, Bt.; *Lewis Meyrick, King's attorney in Wales; *Ed. Freeman, King's attorney in Radnor; *Rich. Williams; *Rich. Fowler; *Lewis Morgan; *Samuel Powell; *Ed. Davies; *Jas. Lloyd; *Nich. Taylor; *Ed. Lewis of Mynachty; *J. Walsham; *W. Probert: C.193/12/5/f.185. (41)

1686: 15 June
Th. Geers appointed as Justice of Great Sessions in place of J. Powell: Index 4215/p.155. (It is not known when he was added to the commission).

1686: 17 December
Order by Privy Council that Francis Gwynn; Jas. Baskerville; Rob. Price; Anthony Lochard should be *added* to the Radnor commission and that Rich. Derham, kt., should be *omitted*: P.C.2/71/p.378.

1687: 21 March (Acting)
As at the end of 1685, except: Marquess of Halifax, President of Council; Th. Geers, Justice of Great Sessions, *added*. E. of Mulgrave; E. of Bridgewater; E. of Carbery; J. Powell; Ed. Freeman; Rich. Fowler; Samuel Powell, *omitted*: Wales 4/503/1. (This list is based on an outdated commission since it includes the Marquess of Halifax as President of the Council despite his replacement by the Earl of Sunderland in December 1685. This also explains why there is no sign of the changes in the commission ordered in December 1686. These may not have taken effect until the renewal of the commission on 29 August 1687. The replacement of J. Powell as Justice of Great Sessions by Th. Geers must have been noted on the initiative of the clerk who drew up the list of justices for the session of March 1687). (36)

1687: 29 August
General renewal of Welsh commissions to add the clause of dispensation: Index 4215/p.179.

1687: 12 September (Acting)
Canterbury; Jeffreys; E. of Sunderland, President of Council; Lord Arundell of Wardour, Keeper of Privy Seal, Dukes of Ormond, Albemarle, Newcastle; D. of Beaufort, President of Council in the Marches of Wales; Marquesses of Winchester, Powys, Worcester; E. of Lindsey, Great Chamberlain; E. of Mulgrave, Household Chamberlain; Earls of Bath, Nottingham, Middleton; Viscounts Fauconberg, Preston; B. of Durham; B. of Hereford; Lords Belasyse, Dartmouth, Godolphin, Dover; J. Ernley, kt., Chancellor of Exchequer; Ed. Herbert, kt., Chief Justice of King's Bench; Owen Wynn & Th. Geers, Justices of Great Sessions; J. Morgan, Bt.; Lewis Meyrick, King's attorney in Wales; Francis Gwynn; Jas. Baskerville; Rich. Williams; Rob. Price; Anth. Lochard; Rich. Fowler; Lewis Morgan; Ed. Davies; Jas. Lloyd; Nich. Taylor; Ed. Lewis of Mynachty; J. Walsham; W. Probert: Wales 4/503/2. (43)

1688: 2 April (Acting)
As on 12 September 1687: Wales 4/503/4. (43)

1688: 2 April
Commission renewed to *add* certain justices and to *omit* others (no details): Index 4215/p.190.

1688: 6 October
General renewal of Welsh commissions: Index 4215/p.200.

1689: 28 May
Commission renewed to appoint Roland Gwynn, kt., as *custos rotulorum*: Index 4215/p.225. (Th. Geers and H. Chauncy, kt., who were appointed as Justices of Great Sessions on 15 November 1688 (Index 4215/p.203), were probably also added on this date).

1689: 23 September (Acting)
Archbishop of Canterbury; J. Maynard, Anthony Keck & W. Rawlinson, kts., Commissioners of Great Seal; Marquess of Carmarthen, President of Council; Marquess of Halifax, Keeper of Privy Seal; D. of Norfolk; D. of Bolton; E. of Lindsey, Great Chamberlain; E. of Devonshire, Steward; E. of Dorset, Household Chamberlain; Earls of Oxford, Shrewsbury, Bedford, Bath; E. of Macclesfield, President of Council in the Marches of Wales; E. of Nottingham; J. Trenchard, kt., Justice of Chester; Standish Hartstongue, Bt.; J. Morgan, Bt.; Ed. Harley, kt. of the Bath; Roland Gwynn, kt.; Lacon Child, kt.; Rich. Williams; Ed. Lewis; Th. Vaughan; Herbert Weston; Ed. Price; Nich. Taylor; Th. Lewis of Harpton; H. Probert; Evan Bowen; Jeremiah Powell; J. Walsham; Peter Ricketts; Ed. Davies; Ed. Hollorth; J. Tranter; W. Morgan: Wales 4/504/2. (39)

Monmouth

1542: 10 January to 2 June (Acting)

The following justices of the peace were acting in Monmouthshire at various places in the county between these two dates: Walter Herbert; Rich. Morgan; H. Lewis; Anth. Walsh; Math. Herbert; Lewis Blethin; Chas. Herbert; Jas. Whitney; W. John Thomas; Roland Morgan; Th. Herbert; Hugh Huntley, Justices' clerk: E.372/387/m.27. (These details come from the account of Walter Herbert, Sheriff of Monmouth, as enrolled upon the Pipe Roll).

1543: 9 February

*Th. Audley, kt., Chancellor; *D. of Norfolk, Treasurer; *D. of Suffolk, President of Council; *J. Russell, kt., Keeper of Privy Seal; E. of Worcester; *B. of Coventry & Lichfield, President of Council in the Marches of Wales; Walter, Lord Ferrers; *Nich. Hare, *Edm. Mervyn, kts.; *W. Portman, serjeant at law; Ed. Croft, Rice Mansel, *J. Vernon, kts.; *J. Pakington; *Th. Holte; *David Brooke; *J. ap Rice; *Rich. Hassall; *Walter Herbert; *Chas. Herbert; *Anthony Walsh; Th. Morgan; *H. Lewis; *Rich. Morgan; *Th. Etkyns; W. Morgan; Th. Herbert; Jas. Whitney; W. John Thomas; *Nich. Arnold; Reg. ap Howel; *Roland Morgan; Math. Herbert; *Rich. Goldsmith; David Morgan Kemeys; J. Kemeys: C.66/720/m.4d. (Printed in *Letters & Papers of Reign of Henry VIII*, 18, p.124).   (36 names)

1543: 12 March

*Audley; *Norfolk; *Suffolk; *Russell; Worcester; *B. of Coventry & Lichfield, President of Council in the Marches of Wales; *B. of St. Asaph; Lord Ferrers; *Nich. Hare, *Edm. Mervyn, kts.; *W. Portman, serjeant at law; Ed. Croft, Rice Mansel, *J. Vernon, W. Morgan, kts.; *J. Pakington; *Th. Holte; *David Brooke; *J. ap Rice; *Rich. Hassall; *Walter Herbert; *Chas. Herbert; *Anth. Walsh; Th. Morgan; *H. Lewis; *p Rich. Morgan; *Th. Etkyns; *Lewis Blethin; W. Morgan; Th. Herbert; Jas. Whitney; W. John Thomas; *Nich. Arnold; Walter ap Robert; Reg. ap Howel; *Roland Morgan; Math. Herbert; *Rich. Goldsmith; David Morgan Kemeys; J. Kemeys. *Later additions to list*: *Th. Bromley, serjeant at law; *Adam Mytton; *W. Jones of Caerleon; Th. Gunter; J. Gunter: C.193/12/1/f.39v. (W. Morgan, kt., may be the same man as W. Morgan, Esq., lower down the commission and would therefore have been reinstated higher up the list after receiving his knighthood). (40 names plus 5 corrections).

1544: 27 February

*Audley; *Norfolk; *Suffolk; *Russell; Worcester; *B. of Coventry & Lichfield, President of Council in the Marches of Wales; Lord Ferrers; *Nich. Hare, *Edm. Mervyn, kts.; *W. Portman, serjeant at law; Ed. Croft, Rice Mansel, *J. Vernon, kts.; *Th. Bromley, serjeant at law; *J. Pakington; *Th. Holte; *David Brooke; *J. ap Rice; *Rich. Hassall; *Adam Mytton; *Walter Herbert; *Chas. Herbert; *Anth. Walsh; Th. Morgan; *H. Lewis; *p Rich. Morgan; *Th. Etkyns; W. Morgan; Th. Herbert; Jas. Whitney; W. John Thomas; *Nich. Arnold; Reg. ap Howel; *Roland Morgan; Math. Herbert; *W. Jones of Caerleon; *Rich. Goldsmith; David Morgan Kemeys; J. Kemeys; J. Gunter: C.67/74/m.21.

(This commission is printed in *Letters & Papers of Reign of Henry VIII*, 20, part 1, p.319). (40)

1547: 26 May
D. of Somerset, Protector; *W. Paulet, kt., Lord St. John, President of Council; Russell; Worcester; *B. of Coventry & Lichfield, President of Council in the Marches of Wales; Bishops of *St. Asaph, *Llandaff; Walter, Lord Ferrers; Ed., Lord Powys; *Rob. Townshend, *Edm. Mervyn, kts.; *Th. Bromley, serjeant at law; *W. Portman, kt., serjeant at law; Rich. Devereux; *Ed. Carne, Rice Mansel, kts.; Th. Morgan; *J. Pakington, *J. ap Rice, *Adam Mytton, kts.; *David Brooke, serjeant at law; *p Rich. Morgan, serjeant at law; Hugh Curwen, clerk (this name is given as Coren in the original roll); *Rich. Hassall; *Walter Herbert; *Geo. Willoughby; *Rich. Germyn; *Chas. Herbert; *Th. Etkyns; *H. Lewis; W. John Thomas; *Roland Morgan; Math. Herbert; W. Herbert of Colbrooke; W. Jones of Caerleon; Walter ap Robert; Reg. ap Howel: C.66/801/m.24d. (This commission is printed in *Calendar of Patent Rolls, 1547–8*, p.86). (37)

1555: (Acting)
Chas. Herbert, kt.; Th. ap Morgan, kt.; David Lewis, Ll.D.; W. Herbert of Colbrooke; H. Lewis; Walter ap Robert; W. John ap Roger; Th. Herbert of Wonastow; Roland Morgan; Reg. ap Howel; W. Morgan of Llantarnam; J. Philip Morgan of Skenfrith: S.P.11/5/f.61. (The present list omits all the *ex officio* justices who appear in earlier commissions). (12)

1558–9: (Acting)
*Nich. Bacon, kt., Keeper of Great Seal; *Marquess of Winchester, Treasurer; *E. of Arundel, Steward; E. of Worcester; Bishops of *Bath & Wells, *Llandaff, *Chester; *Ed. Saunders, kt.; *J. Whiddon, kt.; *J. Throckmorton, Justice of Chester; *p Th. Somerset; *J. Vaughan, *Adam Mytton, kts.; Chas. Fox; *David Lewis, Ll.D.; *J. Smyth, Ll.D.; *J. Scudamore of Holm; *J. Welsh; *Reg. Corbet; *W. Symonds; *W. Gerard; *Rich. Seaborne; *W. Herbert; *W. Morgan of Llantarnam; W. Morgan of Tredegar; W. Herbert of Colbrooke; *Walter ap Robert; *Roland Morgan; *Geo. James of Troy; *Roger Williams; *Anth. Welsh; W. John ap Roger; *W. John Thomas; Th. Herbert of Wonastow; Reg. ap Howel: B.M., Lansdowne Ms. 1218/f.34v. (The same list is also contained in S.P.12/2/17/p.49, except for the omission of the first ten names which are those of the *ex officio* members of the commission). (35)

1561: (Acting)
*Bacon; *Winchester; *Arundel; *Worcester; *H. Sidney, kt., President of Council in the Marches of Wales; *B. of Hereford; *Ed. Saunders, kt., Chief Baron of the Exchequer; *Th. Carus, serjeant at law; *p Th. Somerset; Chas. Somerset; Th. Morgan, kt.; *David Lewis, Ll.D.; W. Herbert of St. Julian's; *W. Morgan of Llantarnam; *Reg. ap Howel; *W. Morgan of Tredegar; W. Herbert of Colbrooke; *Roland Morgan; W. John ap Roger; *Roger Williams; *W. John Thomas of Treowen: B.M., Lansdowne Ms. 1218/f.83v. (21)

1562: (Acting)
As in 1561, except: *B. of Llandaff; Th. Herbert; *W. Evans, Ll.B., *added*.
W. Herbert of St. Julian's; Roger Williams, *omitted*: C.66/985/m.40d. (22)

1564: (Acting)
*Bacon; *Winchester; *Arundel; Earls of *Worcester, *Pembroke; *Sidney,
President of Council in the Marches of Wales; *B. of Hereford; *Ed.
Saunders, kt.; *Th. Carus; *Reg. Corbet, Justice *ad placita*; *J. Throck-
morton, Justice of Chester; *Chas. Somerset; *Th. Morgan, kt.; *W.
Gerard; *Chas. Fox; *Rich. Wye; *Rich. Seaborne; *Rich. Pates; *J.
Price; *Rich. Smith; *David Lewis, Ll.D.; W. Herbert; *W. Morgan of
Llantarnam; Th. Herbert; *p Roland Morgan; W. Herbert of Colbrooke;
*Roger Williams; W. John ap Roger; W. Evans, Ll.B.: C.66/998/m.10d.
(29)

1573-4: (Acting)
*Bacon; *W., Lord Burghley, Treasurer; *Worcester; *Pembroke; *Sidney,
President of Council in the Marches of Wales; Bishops of *Hereford,
*Llandaff; *Jas. Croft, kt., Household Controller; *Ed. Saunders, kt.,
Chief Baron of Exchequer; *W. Lovelace, serjeant at law; *Hugh Cholmon-
deley, kt.; *Throckmorton, Justice of Chester; *Chas. Somerset, kt.;
*David Lewis, Ll.D., Judge of Court of Admiralty; *W. Gerard; *Chas.
Fox; *Rich. Seaborne; *Rich. Pates; *p Roland Morgan; *W. Morgan of
Llantarnam; *W. Herbert of Colbrooke; W. Morgan of Pencoed; *Chris.
Welsh; Th. Herbert of Wonastow; *W. Evans, Ll.B.; *Th. Morgan of
Machen; Geo. James of Troy; H. Herbert; Rees Morgan; W. Lewis of
St. Pierre; Edm. Morgan; W. John ap Roger: S.P.12/93/part 2/f.32v &
B.M., Egerton Ms. 2345/f.38v. (32)

1577: (Acting)
*Bacon; *Burghley; *Worcester; *Pembroke; *H. Sidney, kt., President
of Council in the Marches of Wales; Bishops of *Hereford, *Llandaff;
*Ed., Lord Herbert; *Croft; *Throckmorton, Justice of Chester; *Chas.
Somerset, *Th. Herbert, *W. Morgan, kts.; *David Lewis, Ll.D.; *W.
Gerard; *Chas. Fox; *Rich. Seaborne; *Rich. Pates; *p Roland Morgan;
*W. Morgan of Llantarnam; *W. Herbert of Colbrooke; *Chris. Welsh;
*W. Evans, Ll.B.; *Th. Morgan of Machen; *W. Cecill; H. Herbert; *W.
Powell of Lampith; Rees Morgan; W. Lewis of St. Pierre; Edm. Morgan;
W. John ap Roger; Math. Herbert of Christchurch; Th. Watkins; Geo. ap
Robert; Walter Jones: S.P.12/121/f.34v. (35)

1578: (Acting)
*Bacon; *Burghley; *Sidney, President of Council in the Marches of Wales;
*B. of Worcester, Vice-President of Council in the Marches of Wales;
*Worcester; *Pembroke; Bishops of *Hereford, *Bangor, *St. Davids,
*St. Asaph, *Llandaff; *Ed., Lord Herbert; *Croft; *Roger Manwood,
Justice of Common Pleas; *Francis Wyndham, serjeant at law; *Throck-
morton, Justice of Chester; *Andrew Corbet, *J. Perrot, *Nich. Arnold,
*Hugh Cholmondeley, *J. Littleton, *J. Huband, *Chas. Somerset, *Th.
Herbert, *W. Morgan, kts.; *David Lewis, Ll.D.; *Geo. Bromley, attorney

of Duchy of Lancaster; *W. Gerard; *W. Aubrey; *Chas. Fox; *W. Glaseor; *Ellis Price, Ll.D.; *Ed. Leighton; *Rich. Pates; *Jerome Corbet; *Ralph Barton; *J. Puckering; *Fabian Phillips; *H. Townshend; *W. Leighton; *Roland Morgan of Tredegar; *W. Herbert of St. Julian's; *W. Morgan of Llantarnam; *W. Herbert of Colbrooke; *Chris. Welsh of Llanwarne; *W. Evans, Ll.B.; *Th. Morgan of Machen, son of Roland Morgan; *W. Cecill; H. Herbert, son of Th. Herbert; *W. Powell of Lampith; Rees Morgan; W. Lewis of St. Pierre; Edm. Morgan, brother of Roland Morgan; W. John ap Roger; Math. Herbert of Christchurch or of Colbrooke; Th. Watkins of Caerwent; *Walter Jones of Dingestow: B.M., Royal Ms. 18.D.III/f.92v. (Details of the quorum are taken from another list of 1578 contained in Hatfield House Ms. 223.7. This latter list is almost identical in its basic form to the one given above but is heavily corrected). (57)

1579: (Acting)
As in 1578, except: *Th. Bromley, kt., Chancellor; *W. Ayloff, Justice of Queen's Bench; *J. Price; *Milo Herbert; *H. Morgan; *Geo. James; J. Jones, *added*. Nich. Bacon, kt.; Roger Manwood; W. Powell, *omitted*: S.P.12/145/f.45v. (W. Herbert of St. Julian's now appears as a knight and *custos rotulorum* for the county). (61)

1582: (Acting)
B. of Llandaff; Ed., Lord Herbert; Chas. Somerset, Th. Herbert, W. Morgan, W. Herbert, kts.; Roland Morgan; Roger Williams; Math. Herbert of Colbrooke; Th. Morgan; Geo. James; W. Evans, Ll.B.; W. Cecill; Edm. Morgan; Rees Morgan; J. Jones; W. Lewis; Th. Williams; W. John ap Roger; W. Lewis of Abergavenny; Walter Jones: B.M., Lansdowne Ms. 35/f.138. (The *ex officio* members of the commission are excluded from this list). (21)

1584: (Acting)
*Th. Bromley, kt., Chancellor; *Burghley; *Sidney, President of Council in the Marches of Wales; *Worcester; *Pembroke; Bishops of *Hereford, *Bangor, *St. Asaph, *Llandaff; *Ed., Lord Herbert; *Croft; *Roger Manwood, kt., Chief Baron of Exchequer; *Francis Wyndham; *Geo. Bromley, kt., Justice of Chester; *J. Perrot, *Hugh Cholmondeley, *J. Littleton, *Chas. Somerset, *Th. Herbert, *W. Morgan, *p W. Herbert of St. Julian's, kts.; *J. Puckering, serjeant at law; *W. Aubrey; *Chas. Fox; *Ellis Price, Ll.D.; *Ed. Leighton; *W. Leighton; *H. Townshend; *Rich. Pates; *Ralph Barton; *Jerome Corbet; *Fabian Phillips; *W. Glaseor; *Roland Morgan; *Roger Williams; *Math. Herbert of Colbrooke; *Th. Morgan of Machen; *Geo. James; *W. Evans, Ll.B.; *W. Cecill; *Ed. Morgan; Rees Morgan; J. Jones; *W. Lewis of St. Pierre; *Edm. Morgan; Th. Williams; *W. John ap Roger; W. Lewis of Abergavenny. *Later additions to basic list*: *Christopher Hatton, kt., Chancellor; *Th. Morgan of Tredegar; *Ed. Morgan; Chas. Herbert; Th. Morgan: E.163/14/8/f.43v. (48 names plus 5 corrections).

1590–1 : (Acting)
*Christopher Hatton, kt., Chancellor; *Burghley; *p E. of Pembroke, President of Council in the Marches of Wales; *Worcester; *B. of St. Asaph; *B. of Llandaff; *J. Perrot, kt.; *Roger Manwood, kt., Chief Baron of Exchequer; *Francis Wyndham, Justice of the Bench; *Rich. Shuttleworth, kt., Justice of Chester; *J. Herbert, *Hugh Cholmondeley, *Chas. Somerset, *W. Herbert of St. Julian's, kts.; *J. Puckering, serjeant at law; *W. Aubrey; *Ellis Price, Ll.D.; *Ed. Leighton; *W. Leighton; *H. Townshend; *Jerome Corbet; *Fabian Phillips; *Th. Morgan of Tredegar; Ed. Morgan; *H. Jones; *Math. Herbert of Colbrooke; W. Cecill; Chas. Herbert; J. Jones; H. Herbert; Th. Morgan; *H. Morgan; *Roland Morgan; *W. John ap Roger; Ed. Kemeys of Kemeys; W. Baker of Abergavenny: Hatfield House Ms. 278/f.51. (36)

1592–3 : (Acting)
As in 1590–1, except: *E. of Essex; *W. Periam, kt., Chief Baron of Exchequer; *J. Clench, Justice *ad placita*; *Rice Kemeys; *W. Morgan, *added*. Christopher Hatton; J. Perrot; Roger Manwood; Francis Wyndham; Ed. Morgan; H. Jones, *omitted*: Kent Record Office Ms. U.350.03. (35)

1594 : 18 February
*J. Puckering, kt., Keeper of Great Seal; *Burghley; *Pembroke, President of Council in the Marches of Wales; *Worcester; *E. of Essex; Bishops of *St. Asaph, *Llandaff; *W. Periam, kt., Chief Baron of Exchequer; *J. Clench, Justice *ad placita*; *Shuttleworth, Justice of Chester; *W. Aubrey, Master of Requests; *J. Herbert, Master of Requests; *Hugh Cholmondeley, *Chas. Somerset, kts.; *Ellis Price, Ll.D.; *W. Leighton; *H. Townshend; *Jerome Corbet; *Fabian Phillips; *Th. Morgan of Tredegar; *Math. Herbert of Colbrooke; *Nich. Herbert; W. Cecill; Chas. Herbert; J. Jones; *H. Herbert; Th. Morgan; *H. Morgan; *Roland Morgan; Ed. Kemeys of Kemeys; ᵗRice Kemeys; *W. Morgan; W. Baker of Abergavenny; Walter Jones; H. Williams: C.66/1421/m.14d. (35)

1596 : 17 February
*Puckering; *Burghley; *p E. of Pembroke, President of Council in the Marches of Wales; *Worcester; *Essex; *W., Lord Herbert; *B. of St. Asaph; *Periam, Chief Baron of Exchequer; *Math. Owens, Baron of Exchequer; *Shuttleworth, Justice of Chester; *J. Herbert, Master of Requests; *Hugh Cholmondeley, *Chas. Somerset, kts.; *W. Leighton; *H. Townshend; *Jerome Corbet; *Fabian Phillips; *Th. Morgan of Tredegar; *Math. Herbert of Colbrooke; *Nich. Herbert; W. Cecill; *H. Herbert; Th. Morgan; *H. Morgan; W. Baker of Abergavenny; H. Billingsley: C.66/1435/m.19d. Commission renewed to *add* W., Lord Herbert: Index 4208/f.11v. (26)

1596 : post 11 May
As on 17 February 1596, except: *Th. Egerton, kt., Keeper of Great Seal (appointed on 11 May 1596); *B. of Llandaff; J. Gainsford, *added*. J. Puckering, *omitted*: C.66/1468/m.14d & S.P.13/Case F, no. 11/f.36. (28)

1597: 12 February
Commission renewed to *add* Rice Kemeys: Index 4208/f.27v.

1597: 22 February
Commission renewed to *add* J. Arnold; W. Morgan: Index 4208/f.29v.

1597: 8 July
As in 1596, except: Rice Kemeys; J. Arnold; W. Morgan; H. Williams, *added*. Hugh Cholmondeley; Fabian Phillips, *omitted*: C.66/1468/m.29d. Commission renewed to *add* H. Williams: Index 4208/f.37. (30)

1598: 29 May
Commission renewed to *add* W. Rawlins: Index 4208/f.50.

1598: 5 July
Commission renewed to *add* H., Lord Herbert; Rob. Hopton: Index 4208/f.52.

1598: 22 July
As on 8 July 1597, except: *H., Lord Herbert; *J. Clench, Justice *ad placita*; H. Morgan of Penllwynsarth; W. Rawlins; Rob. Hopton, *added*. Lord Burghley; W., Lord Herbert; Math. Owens; W. Cecill; H. Herbert, *omitted*: C.66/1482/m.15d. Commission renewed to *add* H. Morgan of Penllwynsarth: Index 4208/f.54v. (30)

1599: 30 June
*Th. Egerton, kt., Keeper of Great Seal; *Th., Lord Buckhurst, Treasurer; *Essex; *p E. of Pembroke, President of Council in the Marches of Wales; *Worcester; *B. of St. Asaph; *B. of Llandaff; *H., Lord Herbert; *Periam, Chief Baron of Exchequer; *J. Clench, Justice *ad placita*; *Shuttleworth, Justice of Chester; *Herbert, Master of Requests; *W. Leighton; *H. Townshend; *Th. Morgan of Tredegar; Rob. Hopton; W. Morgan of Machen; *Nich. Herbert; *Roland Morgan; *J. Gainsford; *Rice Kemeys; J. Arnold; H. Morgan of Penllwynsarth; Th. Morgan; *H. Billingsley; W. Baker of Abergavenny; W. Morgan of Newport; H. Williams of Mathern; W. Rawlins; Ed. Kemeys: C.66/1493/m.25d. Commission renewed to *add* W. Morgan of Machen; Ed. Kemeys: Index 4208/f.71v. (Lord Buckhurst who was appointed as Treasurer on 15 May 1599, was probably also added to the commission on this date). (30)

1600: 16 May
Commission renewed to *omit* J. Arnold: Index 4208/f.88.

1600: 10 June
As on 30 June 1599, except: *Rich. Lewkenor, kt., Justice of Chester, *added*. Rich. Shuttleworth; J. Arnold, *omitted*: C.66/1523/m.28d. Commission renewed to place W. Baker and Ed. Kemeys on the quorum at the request of the Chief Baron of the Exchequer: Index 4208/f.91. (29)

1600: 10 December
Commission renewed to *add* Math. Herbert of Colbrooke: Index 4208/f.99.

1601: 26 February
Commission renewed to appoint E. of Worcester as *custos rotulorum*: Index 4208/f.104v.

1601: 29 May
Commission renewed to *add* Valentine Pritchard: Index 4208/f.111.

1601: 20 June
Commission renewed to *add* Th. Somerset: Index 4208/f.114.

1601: 6 July
Commission renewed to *add* Roland Williams: Index 4208/f.116.

1601: 7 August
*Egerton; *Buckhurst; *p E. of Worcester; *B. of Llandaff; *H., Lord Herbert; *J. Herbert, Queen's Second Secretary; *Th. Walmesley & *Peter Warburton, Justices of Assize; *Rich. Lewkenor, kt., Justice of Chester; *Th. Somerset; *W. Leighton; *H. Townshend; *Th. Morgan of Tredegar; *Math. Herbert of Colbrooke; Rob. Hopton; W. Morgan of Machen; *Nich. Herbert; *Roland Morgan; *J. Gainsford; *Rice Kemeys; H. Morgan of Penllwynsarth; Th. Morgan; *H. Billingsley; *W. Baker of Abergavenny; W. Morgan of Newport; W. Rawlins; *Ed. Kemeys; Valentine Pritchard; Roland Williams; W. Price: C.66/1549/m.28d. Commission renewed to *add* W. Price: Index 4208/f.120d. (30)

1601: 19 December
Commission renewed to *omit* W. Rawlins: Index 4208/f.126v.

1602: 15 May
Commission renewed to *add* Francis, B. of Llandaff: Index 4208/f.134v.

1602: 26 June
Commission renewed to *add* Christopher Yelverton, Justice of Assize: Index 4208/f.137.

1602: 20 July
*Egerton; *Buckhurst; *Ed., Lord Zouch, President of Council in the Marches of Wales; *p E. of Worcester; *B. of Llandaff; *H., Lord Herbert; *Herbert, Queen's Second Secretary; *Peter Warburton & *Christopher Yelverton, Justices of Assize; *Lewkenor, Justice of Chester; Th. Somerset; *W. Leighton; *H. Townshend; *Th. Morgan of Tredegar; *Math. Herbert of Colbrooke; Rob. Hopton; W. Morgan of Machen; *Roland Morgan; *J. Gainsford; *Rice Kemeys; H. Morgan of Penllwynsarth; Th. Morgan; *H. Billingsley; *W. Baker of Abergavenny; W. Morgan of Newport; W. Rawlins; *Ed. Kemeys; Valentine Pritchard; Roland Williams: C.66/1594/m.32d. Commission renewed to *add* Ed., Lord Zouch, and to *restore* W. Rawlins: Index 4208/f.140. (29)

1603: 19 February
Commission renewed to *omit* Rob. Hopton: Index 4208/f.151v.

1603: (Acting)
As on 20 July 1602, except: *Ed. Phillips, kt., Justice of Assize, *added*. Peter Warburton; Rob. Hopton; Th. Morgan, *omitted*: C.66/1620/m.16d.   (27)

1604-5: (Acting)
*Th. Egerton, Lord Ellesmere, Chancellor; *E. of Dorset (Lord Buckhurst), Treasurer; *Zouch, President of Council in the Marches of Wales; *p E. of Worcester; *B. of Llandaff; *H., Lord Herbert; *Ed., Lord Abergavenny; *J. Herbert, kt., King's Second Secretary; *Christopher Yelverton & David Williams, kts., Justices of Assize; *Lewkenor, Justice of Chester; *Th. Somerset, *Edm. Morgan, *Walter Montague, *H. Billingsley, *Roland Morgan, kts.; *H. Townshend; *W. Leighton; *Th. Morgan of Tredegar; *Chas. Somerset; *W. Herbert; *J. Gainsford; *Rice Kemeys; *H. Morgan of Penllwynsarth; *W. Baker of Abergavenny; W. Morgan of Newport; W. Rawlins; *Ed. Kemeys; Valentine Pritchard; Roland Williams; W. Price; Andrew Powell; *Chas. Jones; Hugh Jones: C.66/1662/m.23d.   (34)

1605-6: (Acting)
As in 1604-5, except: *Rob. Hopton; *Maurice Griffith, Ll.B., *added*. Lord Zouch; Th. Morgan of Tredegar, *omitted*: C.66/1682/m.16d.   (34)

1606-7: (Acting)
As in 1605-6, except: W. Baker, *omitted*: C.66/1698/m.16d.   (33)

1607: post 12 September
*Ellesmere; *Dorset; *Ralph, Lord Eure, President of Council in the Marches of Wales (appointed on 12 September 1607); *p E. of Worcester; *B. of Llandaff; *H., Lord Herbert; *Ed., Lord Abergavenny; *Herbert, King's Second Secretary; *Yelverton & *Williams, Justices of Assize; *Lewkenor, Justice of Chester; *Th. Somerset, *Edm. Morgan, *Walter Montague, *H. Billingsley, *Roland Morgan, *H. Townshend, kts.; *Chas. Somerset; *W. Powell of Llansoy; *W. Herbert; *Rob. Hopton; *J. Gainsford; *Rice Kemeys; *H. Morgan of Penllwynsarth; W. Morgan of Newport; *W. Rawlins; *Ed. Kemeys; *Valentine Pritchard; Roland Williams; *Maurice Griffith; *W. Price; Roger Bathern; Andrew Powell; *Chas. Jones; Hugh Jones: C.66/1748/m.17d & S.P.14/33/f.43v.   (35)

1608-9: (Acting)
As at the end of 1607, except: *E. of Salisbury, Treasurer; *E. of Northampton, Keeper of Privy Seal, *added*. W. Herbert; Rice Kemeys; W. Morgan of Newport, *omitted*: C.66/1786/m.17d.   (34)

1609-10: (Acting)
As in 1608-9, except: *J. Croke, kt., Justice of Assize; Rob. Robotham, Archdeacon of Llandaff; Giles Morgan, *added*. H. Townshend, *omitted*: C.66/1822/m.14d.   (36)

1610–11: (Acting)
As in 1609–10, except: *H. Townshend, kt., *added.* J. Croke; Andrew
Powell; Ed. Kemeys, *omitted*: C.66/1897/m.10d. (34)

1611–2: (Acting)
As in 1610–1, except: *Andrew Powell; Th. Morgan; *Ed. Kemeys; Nich.
Nott, *added.* Maurice Griffith, *omitted*: C.66/1898/m.15d. (37)

1614: post 11 July
*Ellesmere; *E. of Suffolk, Treasurer (appointed on 11 July 1614); *Eure,
President of Council in the Marches of Wales; *p E. of Worcester; *B. of
Llandaff; *H., Lord Herbert; *Ed., Lord Abergavenny; *Herbert, King's
Second Secretary; *J. Croke & *J. Doderidge, kts., Justices of Assize;
*Lewkenor, Justice of Chester; *Th. Somerset, *Edm. Morgan, *Walter
Montague, *H. Billingsley, *Roland Morgan, *H. Townshend, *Chas.
Jones, kts.; *Chas. Somerset; *Andrew Powell; *Rob. Hopton; Th. Morgan
of Llanrhymny; *J. Gainsford; *H. Morgan of Penllwynsarth; Rob.
Robotham, Archdeacon of Llandaff; *W. Rawlins; *Ed. Kemeys; *Valentine
Pritchard; *W. Price; W. Jones; Roger Bathern; H. Morgan; W. Jones of
Abergavenny; Hugh Jones; Nich. Nott: C.66/1988/m.15d. (35)

1614–5: (Acting)
As in the previous commission: C.66/2047/m.12d. (35)

1615: 11 July
*Ellesmere; *Suffolk; *p E. of Worcester; *Eure, President of Council in
the Marches of Wales; *B. of Llandaff; *H., Lord Herbert; *Ed., Lord
Abergavenny; *Herbert, King's Second Secretary; *Peter Warburton &
*J. Croke, kts., Justices of Assize; *Lewkenor, Justice of Chester; *Th.
Somerset, *Edm. Morgan, *Walter Montague, *Roland Morgan, *H.
Townshend, *Chas. Jones, kts.; *Th. Chamberlain, serjeant at law; *Chas.
Somerset; *Andrew Powell; *Rob. Hopton; Th. Morgan of Llanrhymny;
*J. Gainsford; *H. Morgan of Penllwynsarth; Rob. Robotham, Archdeacon
of Llandaff; *Ed. Kemeys; *Valentine Pritchard; *W. Price; W. Jones;
Giles Morgan; Roger Bathern; H. Morgan of Le Friers; Nich. Nott:
C.66/2076/m.15d. Commission renewed to *add* Peter Warburton, Justice of
Assize: Index 4211/f.7v. (33)

1616: 12 December
Commission renewed to *omit* Giles Morgan because of outlawry: Index
4211/f.30.

1616: 23 December
Commission renewed to *restore* Giles Morgan: Index 4211/f.31.

1617: 24 February
Commission renewed to *restore* W. Jones: Index 4211/f.34v.

1617: 19 March
Commission renewed together with the twelve commissions for Wales to *add* Francis Bacon, kt., Keeper of Great Seal; Th., Lord Gerard, President of Council in the Marches of Wales: Index 4211/f.38.

1617: 1 December
As on 11 July 1615, except: *Francis Bacon, kt., Chancellor; *D. of Lennox, Steward; *E. of Pembroke, Household Chamberlain; *W., Lord Compton, President of Wales; W. Jones of Abergavenny; Hugh Jones, *added*. Lord Ellesmere; Lord Eure; J. Herbert; Rich. Lewkenor; Walter Montague, *omitted*: C.66/2147/m.14d. Commission renewed to *restore* Hugh Jones: Index 4211/f.52v. (Lord Compton was appointed as President of the Council in the Marches of Wales in place of Lord Gerard on 24 November 1617. Th. Chamberlain appears as Justice of Chester in place of Rich. Lewkenor. Note that the commission now contains two men named W. Jones).   (34)

1618: 4 December
Commission renewed to *add* Nich. More: Index 4211/f.76.

1619: 19 February
*Lord Verulam (Nich. Bacon), Chancellor; *p E. of Worcester, Keeper of Privy Seal; *D. of Lennox, Steward; *E. of Pembroke, Household Chamberlain; *E. of Northampton (Lord Compton), President of Council in the Marches of Wales; *B. of Hereford; *H., Lord Herbert; *Ed., Lord Abergavenny; *Warburton & *Croke, Justices of Assize; *Th. Chamberlain, kt., Justice of Chester; *Th. Somerset, *Edm. Morgan, *Roland Morgan, *H. Townshend, *Chas. Jones, kts.; *Chas. Somerset; *Andrew Powell; *Rob. Hopton; Th. Morgan of Llanrhymny; *J. Gainsford; *H. Morgan of Penllwynsarth; *Geo. Milbourne; Rob. Robotham, Archdeacon of Llandaff; *Ed. Kemeys; *Valentine Pritchard; *W. Price; W. Jones; Giles Morgan; Roger Bathern; H. Morgan of Le Friers; W. Jones of Abergavenny; Hugh Jones; Nich. Nott; Nich. More: C.66/2174/m.11d. Commission renewed to *add* Geo. Milbourne: Index 4211/f.79v.   (35)

1619: 3 November
Commission renewed to *add* Theophilus, B. of Llandaff: Index 4211/f.92v.

1620: 16 February
Commission renewed to *add* Humph. Winch, kt., Justice of Assize: Index 4211/f.98v.

1620: 26 June
Commission renewed to *add* Chas. Williams: Index 4211/f.108

1620: 8 July
Commission renewed to *add* J. Hoskins: Index 4211/f.109v.

1620: 21 August
Commission renewed to *add* W. Blethin; Nich. Kemeys: Index 4211/f.112.

1620: 4 November
Commission renewed together with the twelve commissions for Wales to *add* Jas. Whitlock, kt., Justice of Chester: Index 4211/f.114.

1621: 26 February
*Viscount St. Alban (Nich. Bacon), Chancellor; *Viscount Mandeville, Treasurer; *p E. of Worcester; *Lennox; *E. of Pembroke; *Northampton, President of Council in the Marches of Wales; Bishops of *Hereford, *Llandaff; *H., Lord Herbert; *Ed., Lord Abergavenny; *Peter Warburton & *Humph. Winch, kts., Justices of Assize; *Jas. Whitlock, kt., Justice of Chester; *Th. Somerset, *Edm. Morgan, *Roland Morgan, *H. Townshend, *Chas. Jones, kts.; *Chas. Somerset; *Andrew Powell; *Rob. Hopton; *J. Hoskins; *Th. Morgan of Llanrhymny; *Chas. Williams; *J. Gainsford; *H. Morgan of Penllwynsarth; *Geo. Milbourne; Rob. Robotham, Archdeacon of Llandaff; *Ed. Kemeys; *W. Price; W. Jones; Giles Morgan; Nich. Kemeys; H. Morgan of Le Friers; W. Jones of Abergavenny; Hugh Jones; *Nich. More; W. Blethin: C.66/2234/m.34d. Commission renewed to *add* Viscount Mandeville, Treasurer: Index 4211/f.120. (Another copy of the present commission is contained in B.M., Harleian Ms. 1933/f.27. This second version is identical to the one given here except that it omits the Earl of Pembroke and includes Valentine Pritchard. The omission of Pembroke is probably an error since the Earl appears in later commissions. It is likely that Pritchard was in the commission as it was originally issued but that he died between the time of issue and that of enrolment). (38)

1621: 21 December
As on 26 February 1621, except: *B. of Lincoln, Keeper of Great Seal; *Lionel, Lord Cranfield, Treasurer; *W. Morgan, kt., *added*. Viscount St. Alban; Peter Warburton; H. Townshend, *omitted*: C.66/2259/m.14d. Commission renewed to *add* W. Morgan, kt.: Index 4211/f.132v. (38)

1622: 20 February
Commission renewed to *add* Ed. Morgan: Index 4211/f.135.

1622: 8 July
Commission renewed to *add* J. ap William Parry, and to *omit* Giles Morgan: Index 4211/f.141.

1622: 2 September
Commission renewed to *add* Herbert Jones, clerk: Index 4211/f.144.

1623: 27 February
*B. of Lincoln, Keeper of Great Seal; *E. of Middlesex (Lord Cranfield), Treasurer; *Viscount Mandeville, President of Privy Council; *p E. of Worcester; *Lennox; *Pembroke; *E. of Northampton, President of Council in the Marches of Wales; Bishops of *Hereford, *Llandaff; *H., Lord Herbert; *Humph. Winch & *W. Jones, kts., Justices of Assize; *Whitlock, Justice of Chester; *Th. Somerset, *Walter Pye, *W. Morgan, *Edm. Morgan, *Roland Morgan, *Chas. Jones, *Chas. Williams, kts.; *Chas. Somerset; *Andrew Powell; *J. Hoskins; Th. Morgan of Llan-

rhymny; *J. Gainsford; *H. Morgan of Penllwynsarth; *Geo. Milbourne; Rob. Robotham, Archdeacon of Llandaff; *Ed. Morgan; *W. Price; W. Jones; *Giles Morgan; Nich. More; Nich. Kemeys; H. Morgan of Le Friers; W. Jones of Abergavenny; Hugh Jones; W. Blethin; J. ap William Parry; Herbert Jones, clerk: C.66/2285/m.22d. Commission renewed to *restore* Giles Morgan: Index 4211/f.149v. (40)

1623: 2 July
Commission renewed to *omit* Th. Morgan of Llanrhymny: Index 4211/f.154.

1623: 17 July
Commission renewed to *add* Th. Morgan of Cefn Mably: Index 4211/f.155v.

1624: 5 January
Commission renewed to *add* H. Morgan of Bedwellty: Index 4211/f.160.

1625: 22 February
Commission renewed to *add* Jas. Whitlock, kt., as a Justice of Assize and to *add* W. Baker: Index 4211/f.176v.

1625: 4 March
Commission renewed to *add* W. Kemeys: Index 4211/f.177.

1625: 1 April
General renewal of commissions: Index 4211/f.180v.

1625: 19 May
Commission renewed to *add* David Lewis; Lewis Van: Index 4211/f.187v.

1625: 12 July
Commission renewed to *add* Th. Morgan, kt.: Index 4211/f.191.

1625: 22 December
*Th. Coventry, kt., Keeper of Great Seal; *Jas., Lord Ley, Treasurer; *Mandeville; *p E. of Worcester; *Pembroke; *Northampton, President of Council in the Marches of Wales; Bishops of *Hereford, *Llandaff; *W. Jones & *Jas. Whitlock, kts., Justices of Assize; *Walter Pye, kt., Attorney of Court of Wards; *Edm. Morgan, *W. Morgan, *Chas. Jones, *Chas. Williams, *Th. Morgan, kts.; *J. Hoskins, serjeant at law; *Rob. Robotham, D.D.; *Chas. Somerset; *Andrew Powell; *Th. Morgan of Cefn Mably; *H. Morgan of Bedwellty; *J. Gainsford; *H. Morgan of Penllwynsarth; *Geo. Milbourne; *Ed. Morgan; W. Jones; *Herbert Jones, B.D.; *Nich. More; *Nich. Kemeys; *W. Blethin; *David Lewis; *W. Kemeys; *J. ap William Parry: B.M., Harleian Ms. 1622/f.51v. Commission renewed to *add* Th. Coventry, Keeper of Great Seal: Index 4211/f.194v. (Note that there is no sign in this or any later copy of the commission of Lewis Van who was added to the commission on 19 May 1625). (34)

1626: 3 March
Commission renewed to *add* J. Doderidge, kt., Justice of Assize; W. Baker: Index 4211/f.197. (The new Justice of Chester, Sir John Bridgeman, who was appointed on 4 January 1626, was probably also added on this date).

1626: 26 June
As on 22 December 1625, except: *J. Doderidge, kt., Justice of Assize; *J. Bridgeman, kt., Justice of Chester; *Giles Morgan; *W. Price; *W. Baker, *added*. Jas. Whitlock, *omitted*: E.163/18/12/f.53v. Commission renewed to *restore* Giles Morgan: Index 4211/f.204. (Another copy of this commission contained in C.193/12/2/f.36 also includes the name of H., Lord Herbert, but this is not confirmed in any later commission). (38)

1627: 25 January
Commission renewed to *add* W. Morgan: Index 4211/f.215v.

1627: 11 May
As on 26 June 1626, except: *W. Herbert of Colbrooke; *W. Morgan, *added*. E. of Worcester, *omitted*: C.66/2449/m.40d. Commission renewed to *add* W. Herbert of Colbrooke: Index 4211/f.223v. (39)

1628: 1 April
Commission renewed to *add* E. of Pembroke as *custos rotulorum*: Index 4211/f.243v.

1629: 8 July
*Coventry; *Rich., Lord Weston, Treasurer; *Viscount Conway, President of Privy Council; *E. of Manchester (Viscount Mandeville), Keeper of Privy Seal; *p E. of Pembroke; *Northampton, President of Council in the Marches of Wales; *B. of Hereford; *W., B. of Llandaff; *Jones & *Whitlock, Justices of Assize; *J. Bridgeman, kt., Justice of Chester; *Walter Pye, kt., Attorney of Court of Wards; *Edm. Morgan, *W. Morgan, *Chas. Jones, *Chas. Williams, *Th. Morgan, kts.; *J. Hoskins, serjeant at law; *Chas. Somerset; *Ed. Morgan; *Andrew Powell; *Th. Morgan of Cefn Mably; *H. Morgan of Bedwellty; *W. Herbert of Colbrooke; *J. Gainsford; *H. Morgan of Penllwynsarth; W. Jones; *Geo. Milbourne; *Giles Morgan; *W. Morgan; *W. Kemeys; *Nich. More; *W. Price; *J. ap William Parry; *Herbert Jones, B.D.; *Nich. Kemeys; *David Lewis; *W. Baker: C.66/2495/m.16d. Commission renewed to *add* W., B. of Llandaff: Index 4212/p.14. (38)

1629: 8 December
As on 8 July 1629, except: *Walter Rumsey, *added*: C.66/2527/m.15d. Commission renewed to *add* Walter Rumsey: Index 4212/p.20. (39)

1630: 26 February
Commission renewed to *add* J. Dunlee, D.D.: Index 4212/p.26. (Dunlee does not in fact appear in any recorded commission of this period).

1630: 12 June
Commission renewed to *add* Philip, E. of Pembroke & Montgomery, as *custos rotulorum*: Index 4212/p.33. (The Earl's elder brother, William, Earl of Pembroke, died in April 1630).

1631: 25 May
As on 8 December 1629, except: Philip, E. of Pembroke; *B. of St. Davids; Edm. Morgan; H. Probert, *added*. Viscount Conway; E. of Northampton; W., E. of Pembroke; W. Morgan, Esq., *omitted*: C.66/2577/m.18d & C.66/2654/m.12d. Commission renewed to *add* Edm. Morgan; H. Probert: Index 4212/p.57. (Another copy of this commission is contained in S.P.16/ 212/f.42 but with the omission of Andrew Powell and H. Morgan of Penllwynsarth who had probably died by the time the list was copied). (39)

1632: 29 June
*Coventry; *E. of Portland (Lord Weston), Treasurer; *Manchester; *p E. of Pembroke; Bishops of *Hereford, *St. Davids, *Llandaff; *W. Jones, kt., Justice of Assize; *Th. Trevor, kt., Baron of Exchequer & Justice of Assize; *Bridgeman, Justice of Chester; *Walter Pye, kt., Attorney of Court of Wards; *Edm. Morgan, *W. Morgan, *Chas. Jones, *Chas. Williams, *Th. Morgan, kts.; *J. Hoskins, serjeant at law; *Chas. Somerset; *Ed. Morgan; *Th. Morgan of Cefn Mably; *H. Morgan of Bedwellty; *W. Herbert of Colbrooke; *J. Gainsford; W. Jones; *Geo. Milbourne; *Giles Morgan; *W. Kemeys; *Walter Rumsey; Edm. Morgan; H. Probert; *Nich. More; *W. Price; *J. ap William Parry; *Herbert Jones, B.D.; *Nich. Kemeys; *David Lewis; *W. Baker: C.66/2598/m.11d. Commission renewed to *add* Th. Trevor, kt., Baron of Exchequer & Justice of Assize: Index 4212/p.85. (37)

1636: post 6 March
As on 29 June 1632, except: *B. of London, Treasurer (appointed on 6 March); *E. of Bridgewater, President of Council in the Marches of Wales; *Humph. Davenport, kt., Chief Baron of Exchequer, *added*. E. of Portland; B. of Hereford; B. of St. Davids; Th. Trevor; Walter Pye; J. Gainsford; J. ap William Parry; Nich. Kemeys, *omitted*: S.P.16/405/f.45v. (Note that there is no recorded renewal of the Monmouth commission between 29 June 1632 and 23 May 1637 to show the true rate at which the commission was changing). (32)

1637: 23 May
Commission renewed to *add* Rich. Herbert: Index 4212/p.244.

1637: 21 July
Commission renewed to *add* J. Parry, and to *omit* Chas. Williams, kt.; Th. Morgan, kt.; Chas. Somerset; H. Morgan of Bedwellty; Giles Morgan, for not attending the judge to be sworn: Index 4212/p.257.

1637: 11 August
Commission renewed to *restore* Nich. Kemeys: Index 4212/p.259.

1637: 23 November

*Coventry; *B. of London, Treasurer; *Manchester; *p E. of Pembroke; *E. of Bridgewater, President of Council in the Marches of Wales; *B. of Llandaff; *Humph. Davenport, kt., Chief Baron of Exchequer; *W. Jones, kt., Justice of Assize; *Rich. Herbert; *Edm. Morgan, *W. Morgan, *Chas. Williams, kts.; *J. Hoskins, serjeant at law; *Th. Morgan of Machen; *Nich. Kemeys; *W. Herbert of Colbrooke; *Ed. Morgan; W. Jones; *Geo. Milbourne; *W. Kemeys; *Walter Rumsey; Edm. Morgan; *Nich. More; *Herbert Jones, B.D.; *David Lewis, *W. Baker; J. Parry: C.66/2725/m.11d. Commission renewed to *restore* Chas. Williams, kt.: Index 4212/p.270. (27)

1638: 13 July

As on 23 November 1637, except: *Th. Milward, kt., Justice of Chester; *Th. Morgan, kt.; J. Walter, *added*: C.66/2761/m.24d. Commission renewed to *add* J. Walter: Index 4212/p.304. (Th. Milward who was appointed as Justice of Chester on 23 March 1638, was probably added to the commission on this date. It is also likely that this is the date of the restoration to the commission of Th. Morgan, kt., who had been omitted on 21 July 1637). (30)

1638: 20 November

Commission renewed to *restore* H. Morgan of Bedwellty: Index 4212/p.315.

1638: 27 November

Commission renewed to place W. Jones on the quorum: Index 4212/p.316.

1639: 23 February

Commission renewed to *restore* H. Probert: Index 4212/p.327.

1639: 16 July

Commission renewed to *add* Th. Trevor, kt., Baron of Exchequer & Justice of Assize: Index 4212/p.349.

1640: post 17 January

*J. Finch, kt., Keeper of Great Seal (appointed on 17 January); *London; *Manchester; *p E. of Pembroke; *Bridgewater, President of Council in the Marches of Wales; *B. of Llandaff; *Davenport, Chief Baron of Exchequer; *Jones, Justice of Assize; *Th. Milward, kt., Justice of Chester; *Rich. Herbert; *Edm. Morgan, *W. Morgan, *Chas. Williams, *Th. Morgan, *Nich. Kemeys, kts.; *Walter Rumsey; *Th. Morgan of Machen; *H. Morgan of Bedwellty; *Ed. Morgan; *W. Herbert of Colbrooke; *W. Morgan; *W. Kemeys; *H. Probert; Edm. Morgan; *Nich. More; *David Lewis; *W. Baker; J. Parry: C.66/2858/m.30d. (28)

1640: 3 March

Commission renewed to *add* Philip Morgan: Index 4212/p.374.

1640: 11 June

Commission renewed to *add* Morgan, B. of Llandaff: Index 4212/p.388.

1641: 4 March
Commission renewed to *add* W. Morgan: Index 4212/p.433.

1641: 10 August
Commission renewed to *add* Ed. Henden, Baron of Exchequer & Justice of Assize: Index 4212/p.476.

1643: 17 June
Commission renewed to *add* Ed. Morgan of Pencoed; W. Herbert of Colbrooke; Edm. Morgan of Penllwynsarth; W. Morgan of Pencrug (Pencraig?); Th. Price; Roger Williams; Th. Hughes: Index 4210/p.23.

1643: 3 December
Commission renewed to *add* Th. Gwynn, Ll.D.: Index 4210/p.54.

1645: 10 January
Commission renewed to *omit* Philip, Lord Herbert, and to appoint Ed. Kemeys, kt. & Bt., as *custos rotulorum*: Index 4210/p.138.

1645: 8 March
Commission renewed to *add* Th. Morgan of Llanrhymny as a justice of the peace and a member of the quorum: Index 4210/p.148.

1646: 13 July
Commission renewed (no details): Index 4213/p.52.

1646: 18 November
Commission renewed to *add* Trevor Williams, Bt.: Index 4213/p.68.

1647: 22 March
Commission renewed to *add* H. Baker; W. Blethin; Roger Williams; Chris. Catchmay: Index 4213/p.83.

1648: 27 February
Commission renewed to *add* Serjeant Turner as Justice of Assize (his full name is not given): Index 4213/p.109.

1649: 27 February
Commission renewed (no details): Index 4213/p.142.

1649: 3 July
*W. Lenthall, Speaker of House of Commons; *Th., Lord Fairfax; *J. Bradshaw, President of Council; *Bulstrode Whitelock, *Rich. Keble, *J. Lisle, Commissioners of Great Seal; *E. of Pembroke; *H. Rolle, Chief Justice of Upper Bench; *J. Wilde, Chief Baron of Exchequer; *Philip Jermyn & *Rob. Nicholas, Justices of Assize; *Oliver Cromwell; *Edm. Prideaux, Attorney-General; *Th. Morgan; *Rich. Cromwell; *W. Herbert; *H. Herbert; *Edm. Morgan; *Th. Herbert; *Th. Hughes; *W. Jones; *J. Parry; *J. Walter; *Roger Williams; *Ed. Herbert; H. Baker; W. Blethin; Th. Williams; Chris. Catchmay; Jas. Pritchard; W. Parker; Rob. Jones; Roger Oates; Rice Williams: C.193/13/3/f.44. Commission renewed to *add* Rob. Nicholas, Justice of Assize: Index 4213/p.157.   (34)

1650: 5 March
Commission renewed to appoint Oliver Cromwell, as *custos rotulorum*, to *add* Th. Harrison; J. Nicholas, and to *omit* Th. Morgan: Index 4213/p.177.

1650: 11 May
Commission renewed to *add* Walter Morgan: Index 4213/p.186.

1650: 23 July
*Lenthall; *p Oliver Cromwell; *Bradshaw; *Whitelock, *Keble & *Lisle; *Rolle; *Wilde; *Rich. Aske, Justice of Assize; *Philip Jermyn; *Rob. Nicholas; *Edm. Prideaux, Attorney-General; *Th. Harrison; *Rich. Cromwell; *W. Herbert; *H. Herbert; *Edm. Morgan; *Th. Herbert; *Th. Hughes; *W. Jones; *J. Parry; *J. Walter; *Roger Williams; *Ed. Herbert; *J. Nicholas; H. Baker; W. Blethin; Th. Williams; Chris. Catchmay; Jas. Pritchard; W. Parker; Rob. Jones; Roger Oates; Rice Williams; Walter Morgan: *Lists published by Th. Walkley* (1650), p.37. Commission renewed to *add* Rich. Aske, Justice of Assize: Index 4213/p.195. (It is not clear whether Philip Jermyn or Rob. Nicholas was supplanted as a result of Aske's appointment). (35)

1651: 21 February
Commission renewed to *omit* Walter Morgan: Index 4213/p.209.

1651: 10 July
Commission renewed 'for writing the same in English': Index 4213/p.221.

1652: 26 February
Commission renewed to *add* Peter Warburton, Justice of Assize: Index 4213/p.232.

1652: 22 July
Commission renewed to *add* Rob. Nicholas & J. Greene, Justices of Assize: Index 4213/p.253.

1652: 18 December
As on 23 July 1650, except: *H., Lord Herbert of Raglan; *Peter Warburton, Justice of Assize; *J. Greene, serjeant at law, Justice of Assize; *Rob. Hatton, serjeant at law, *added*. Philip Jermyn; W. Herbert; Walter Morgan, *omitted*: C.193/13/4/f.65. Commission renewed to *add* H., Lord Herbert of Raglan: Index 4213/p.248. (36)

1653: 5 March
*Lenthall, Speaker; *p Oliver Cromwell; *Whitelock, *Keble and *Lisle; *J. Bradshaw, Chancellor of Duchy of Lancaster; *H., Lord Herbert of Raglan; *Rolle; *Wilde; *Philip Jermyn & *Peter Warburton, Justices of Assize; *Edm. Prideaux, Attorney-General; *Th. Harrison; *Rich. Cromwell; *H. Herbert; *Edm. Morgan; *Th. Herbert; *Th. Hughes; *W. Jones; *J. Parry; *J. Walter; *Roger Williams; *Ed. Herbert; *J. Nicholas; H. Baker; W. Blethin; Th. Williams; Chris. Catchmay; Jas. Pritchard;

W. Parker; Rob. Jones; Roger Oates; Rice Williams: Cambridge University
Ms. Dd.VIII.1/f.69. Commission renewed to *add* Philip Jermyn, Justice of
Assize: Index 4213/p.253. (33)

1653: 18 July

Commission renewed to *add* J. Lambert; Philip Jones; Francis Blethin;
Rich. Jones of Llanmartin; J. Ward of Newport; David Morgan of Llanwenarth; Th. Evans of Trelleck; Walter Jenkins of Skenfrith Hundred;
J. Morgan junior of Llangwm, and to *omit* H., Lord Herbert; Edm. Morgan
and others (no details): Index 4213/p.264.

1654: 25 February

Commission renewed according to a general list: Index 4213/p.282.

1654: 18 July

Commission renewed to *add* Mr. Justice Glynn, Justice of Assize: Index
4213/p.293.

1655: 24 February

Commission renewed to *add* Mr. Baron Thorpe (Baron of Exchequer),
Justice of Assize: Index 4213/p.304.

1655: 10 March

Commission renewed to *omit* Edm. Morgan; Th. Herbert; Th. Evans:
Index 4213/p.305.

1655: 2 August

Commission renewed to *add* Rob. Nicholas, Baron of Exchequer & Peter
Warburton, Justices of Assize: Index 4213/p.315.

1656: 3 March

Commission renewed to *add* W. Steele, Chief Baron of Exchequer & Rob.
Nicholas, Baron of Exchequer as Justice of Assize: Index 4213/p.327.

1656: 8 July

*p Rich. Cromwell; *Nathaniel Fiennes & *J. Lisle, Commissioners of
Great Seal; *Bulstrode Whitelock, kt., *Th. Widdrington, kt., *Ed.
Montagu, *W. Sydenham, Commissioners of Treasury; *Major-General
J. Lambert; *H., Lord Herbert; *Philip Jones; *J. Glynn, Chief Justice of
Upper Bench; *W. Lenthall, Master of the Rolls; *Oliver St. John, Chief
Justice of Common Bench; *W. Steele, Chief Baron of Exchequer & *Rob.
Nicholas, Baron of Exchequer, Justices of Assize; *Hugh Wyndham,
Justice of Common Bench; *J. Bradshaw, Chief Justice of Chester; *Edm.
Prideaux, Attorney-General; *Major-General Jas. Berry; *J. Nicholas;
*W. Blethin; *Rice Williams; *W. Jones; *J. Walter; *Roger Williams;
*Ed. Herbert; *H. Baker; *Chris. Catchmay; Edm. Thomas; Walter
Morgan; W. Parker; *Rob. Jones; Francis Blethin; Rich. Jones of Llan-
martin; David Morgan of Llanwenarth; J. Morgan junior of Llangwm:
C.193/13/6/f.59v. Commission renewed to *add* Major-General Jas. Berry;
Edm. Thomas, to *omit* Th. Hughes; J. Ward; Walter Jenkins, and to appoint
Lord Rich. Cromwell, as *custos rotulorum*: Index 4213/p.340. (36)

1657: 4 March
Commission renewed to *add* Rob. Nicholas & J. Fountain, Justices of
Assize: Index 4213/p.361.

1657: 4 July
Commission renewed to *add* Erasmus Earle, Justice of Assize: Index
4213/p.371.

1658: 11 March
Commission renewed to *add* Rob. Nicholas & Rich. Newdigate, Justices of
Assize: Index 4213/p.387.

1658: 20 July
Commission renewed to *add* Ed. Green: Index 4213/p.400.

1658: 18 September
Commission renewed to *add* Rich. Cromwell, Lord Protector: Index
4213/p.404.

1659: 28 June
Commission renewed according to a general list: Index 4213/p.435.

1660: 23 March
Commission renewed according to a general list: Index 4213/p.458.

1660: 20 July
Commission renewed to appoint Lord Herbert of Raglan, as *custos rotulorum*:
Index 4214/p.17.

1660: post 8 September
*Ed. Hyde, kt., Chancellor; *E. of Southampton, Treasurer (appointed on
8 September); *D. of Albemarle, General; *Marquess of Ormond, Steward;
*E. of Lindsey, Great Chamberlain; *E. of Manchester, Household Chamber-
lain; *E. of Pembroke; *p H., Lord Herbert of Raglan; *W., Lord Herbert
of Cardiff; *Ed., Lord Herbert of Cherbury; *Th. Malet, kt. & *Chris.
Turner, kt., Justices of Assize; *Trevor Williams, Bt.; *Ed. Morgan, Bt.;
*Ed. Williams, Bt.; *Geo. Probert, kt.; *Th. Morgan of Machen; *W.
Morgan; *H. Probert; Th. Lewis of St. Pierre; *Chas. Van; *Chas. Proger
Herbert; Th. Hughes; *W. Morgan of Penrick; Ed. Kemeys of Kemeys;
H. Morgan; Th. Morgan of Lansore; W. Herbert; *Lewis Morgan; *Edm.
Jones; Walter Rumsey junior; W. Jones; Chas. Hughes; *Philip Cecill;
Th. Williams; Rich. Baker; Roger Oates: C.220/9/4/f.57 & B.M., Egerton
Ms. 2557/f.57. (37)

1661: 16 February
Commission renewed to *add* Baynham Throckmorton junior, kt.: Index
4214/p.81.

1661: 1 August
Commission renewed to *add* H. Baker; Wadham Wyndham, kt., Justice of
Assize: Index 4214/p.127.

1661: 8 November
As in September 1660, except: *J., Lord Robartes, Keeper of Privy Seal; *E. of Carbery, President of Council in the Marches of Wales; *Rob. Hyde, kt. & *Th. Tyrrell, kt., Justices of Assize; *Wadham Wyndham, kt.; *Baynham Throckmorton junior, kt.; *Edm. Morgan; *H. Baker; Roger Williams, *added*. Th. Malet; Chris. Turner; Ed. Williams, Bt.; Rich. Baker; Roger Oates, *omitted*: C.193/12/3/f.69 & C.66/2986/m.18d. General renewal of commissions for Wales and Monmouth to *add* E. of Carbery, President of Council in the Marches of Wales: Index 4214/p.144. (41)

1662: 17 July
Commission renewed to *add* W. Jones: Index 4214/p.178.

1663: 9 April
Commission renewed to *add* J. Walter: Index 4214/p.202.

1663: 27 July
As on 8 November 1661, except: *Th. Waller, serjeant at law; *Job Charlton, kt., Justice of Chester; *W. Morton, kt., serjeant at law; *W. Jones of Treowen; *Arthur Trevor; Walter Pritchard; J. Walter, *added*. Rob. Hyde; Th. Tyrrell; Ed. Kemeys; W. Jones, *omitted*: C.66/3022/m.20d. Commission renewed to *add* Walter Pritchard: Index 4214/p.211. (Examination of the corrections made to copies of the commissions of about this period suggests that the W. Jones who was omitted was in fact W. Jones of Treowen and that the reason for his removal was to promote him in the order of justices). (44)

1664: 3 August
Commission renewed to *add* Rich. Rainsford, kt., Baron of Exchequer & Justice of Assize: Index 4214/p.238.

1664: 19 December
Commission renewed to *add* Chas. Price: Index 4214/p.246.

1665: 1 August (Acting)
*E. of Clarendon, Chancellor; *Southampton; *Lord Robartes, Keeper of Privy Seal; *Albemarle; *Ormond; *Lindsey; *Manchester; *E. of Carbery, President of Council in the Marches of Wales; *E. of Pembroke; *p H., Lord Herbert of Raglan; *W., Lord Herbert of Cardiff; *Ed., Lord Herbert of Cherbury; *Th. Tyrrell, kt. & *Wadham Wyndham, kt., Justices of Assize; *Job Charlton, kt., Justice of Chester; *W. Morton, kt., serjeant at law; *Baynham Throckmorton, kt. & Bt.; *Trevor Williams, Bt.; *Ed. Morgan Bt.; *Geo. Probert, kt.; *W. Morgan; *W. Jones of Treowen; *Arthur Trevor; *H. Probert; *Edm. Morgan; Th. Lewis of St. Pierre; *Chas. Van; *Chas. Proger Herbert; Th. Hughes; *W. Morgan of Penrick; H. Morgan; Th. Morgan of Lansore; *H. Baker; W. Herbert; *Lewis Morgan; *Edm. Jones; Walter Rumsey; Chas. Price; Chas. Hughes; Walter Pritchard; Roger Williams; J. Walter; *Philip Cecill; Th. Williams: Assize 5/2. (Details of the quorum are based on the commission of 14 July 1666 contained in C.66/3074/m.20d.) (44)

1666: 14 July

As on 1 August 1665, except: D. of Buckingham; Th. Twisden, kt. & Bt., Justice *ad placita*; Samuel Browne, Justice of the Bench, *added*. Th. Tyrrell; Wadham Wyndham, *omitted*: C.66/3074/m.20d. Commission renewed to *add* Th. Twisden, and to *omit* Th. Tyrrell: Index 4214/p.288. (45)

1667: 12 July

Commission renewed to *add* H. Milbourne: Index 4214/p.310.

1667: 5 August

Commission renewed to *add* Jas. Herbert; Herbert Evans; H. Guise, and to *omit* Trevor Williams, Bt.; H. Morgan; Chas. Van: Index 4214/p.311.

1667: 23 September

Commission renewed to *add* J. Arnold; Th. Herbert of Usk: Index 4214 p.312.

1668: 25 June

Commission renewed to *add* Mr. Justice Wyse: Index 4214/p.330.

1669: 16 July

Commission renewed to *add* Th. Morgan of Llanrhymny; W. Jones of Llantrissent: Index 4214/p.348.

1671: 24 February

Commission renewed to *add* Ed. Turner, Baron of Exchequer, as Justice of Assize: Index 4214/p.385.

1671: 21 July

Commission renewed to *add* Ed. Turner, Chief Baron of Exchequer & J. Archer, Justices of Assize; Trevor Williams, Bt.: Index 4214/p.398.

1672: 21 March

Commission renewed to *add* Ed. Lewis of the Van: Index 4214/p.411.

1674: 24 March

Commission renewed to *add* H. Probert; Trevor Morgan: Index 4214/p.475.

1674: 25 June

Commission renewed to *add* Rowland Pritchard: Index 4214/p.478.

1675: 18 November

Commission renewed to *add* W., B. of Llandaff: Index 4214/p.503.

1675: 17 December

Commission renewed to *add* W. Kemeys: Index 4214/p.505.

1677: 24 November

Commission renewed to *omit* J. Arnold; H. Probert: Index 4214/p.535.

1679: 18 March
Commission renewed to *add* Rob. Gunter; Walter Evans; Ed. Perkins: Index 4215/p.2.

1679: 16 April
Commission renewed to *add* Ed. Morgan; H. Probert; J. Arnold; Edm. Morgan; Chas. Van; Roger Oates: Index 4215/p.5.

1679: 20 November
Commission renewed to *omit* Th. Herbert of Usk: Index 4215/p.15.

1680: 8 March
*Prince Rupert; *Archbishop of Canterbury; *Lord Finch, Chancellor; *E. of Radnor, President of Council; *E. of Anglesey, Keeper of Privy Seal; Dukes of *Albemarle, *Monmouth, *Newcastle, *Lauderdale, *Ormond; *Marquess of Winchester; *Marquess of Worcester, President of Council in the Marches of Wales; Earls of *Lindsey, *Arlington, *Salisbury, *Bridgewater, *Sunderland, *Essex, *Bath, *Halifax, *Carbery; *Viscount Fauconberg; *B. of London; *B. of Llandaff; *Laurence Hyde; *H. Coventry; *Francis North, kt., Chief Justice of Bench; *J. Ernley, kt., Chancellor of Exchequer; *Th. Chichley, kt., Chancellor of Duchy of Lancaster; *W. Temple, Bt.; *Ed. Seymour; *Daniel Finch; *Leoline Jenkins; *Sidney Godolphin; *Ed. Atkyns, kt., Baron of Exchequer; *W. Ellys, kt., Justice of Bench; *Th. Raymond, kt., Justice *ad placita*; *Creswell Levinz, kt., Attorney-General; *Heneage Finch, Solicitor-General; *Job Charlton, kt., Justice of Bench; *Baynham Throckmorton, kt. & Bt.; *Ed. Morgan, Bt.; *W. Morgan; *Jas. Herbert of Colbrooke, kt.; *Th. Lewis of St. Pierre; *Th. Morgan of Lansore; *Edm. Jones; *J. Arnold; *W. Herbert; *W. Jones of Llantrissent; *H. Baker; *Rob. Gunter; *Lewis Morgan; *Walter Evans; *Chas. Price; *Chas. Van; Th. Morgan of Llanrhymny; J. Walter; *Rowland Pritchard; *W. Kemeys; *Trevor Morgan; *W. Wolseley; *J. Gabb; *J. Gwynn; *Ed. Nicholas: C.193/12/4/f.77d. Commission renewed to *omit* recusants (no details): Index 4215/p.23. (The *removal* from the Monmouth commission of the Duke of Buckingham; Trevor Williams, Bt.; Ed. Perkins; Roger Williams and Roger Oates was ordered by a warrant of 21 February 1680 and the *addition* of W. Wolseley; J. Gabb; J. Gwynn and Ed. Nicholas by a warrant of the same date: *H.M.C., Eleventh Report, Appendix,* Part 2, p.185. According to the details of the changes in the Monmouth commission published in 1680 by N.S., Esq., (p.13), H. Probert, Edm. Morgan and Th. Herbert were also omitted from the commission at some time during the year. These three omissions in fact appear in the commission given above as that of 8 March but it is likely that they were made after this date and noted when the commission was being copied into the C.193 entry book). (65)

1680: 11 June
Commission renewed to *add* J. Ernle, kt.: Index 4215/p.30. (The addition of J. Ernle, kt., was ordered by a warrant of 2 June: *H.M.C., Eleventh Report, Appendix,* Part 2, p.185).

1681: 26 July
Commission renewed to *omit* Ed. Morgan, Bt.; Trevor Morgan; Chas. Price: Index 4215/p.53.

1681: 4 August (Acting)
Rupert; Canterbury; E. of Nottingham (Lord Finch), Chancellor; Radnor; Anglesey; Dukes of Albemarle, Newcastle, Lauderdale, Ormond; Marquess of Winchester; Marquess of Worcester, President of Council in the Marches of Wales; Earls of Lindsey, Arlington, Bridgewater, Bath, Halifax, Conway, Carbery; Viscounts Fauconberg, Hyde; Bishops of London, Llandaff; Chas., Lord Herbert; Daniel, Lord Finch; H. Coventry; Francis North, kt., Chief Justice of Bench; J. Ernley, kt., Chancellor of Exchequer; Th. Chichley, kt., Chancellor of Duchy of Lancaster; Ed. Seymour; Leoline Jenkins, kt.; Sidney Godolphin; Th. Raymond, kt., Justice *ad placita*; Creswell Levinz, kt., Justice of Bench; Rob. Sawyer, kt., Attorney-General; Heneage Finch, Solicitor-General; Baynham Throckmorton, kt. & Bt.; J. Ernle, kt.; Jas. Herbert of Colbrooke, kt.; Th. Lewis of St. Pierre; Th. Morgan of Lansore; Edm. Jones; J. Arnold; W. Herbert; W. Jones of Llantrissent; Rob. Gunter; Lewis Morgan; Walter Evans; Chas. Van; Th. Morgan of Llanrhymny; J. Walter; Rowland Pritchard; W. Kemeys; W. Wolseley; J. Gabb; J. Gwynn; Ed. Nicholas: Assize 5/5. (56)

1682: 9 March
Commission renewed to *omit* Chas. Van: Index 4215/p.63.

1682: 11 July
Commission renewed to *add* Chas. Kemeys, Bt.; H. Morgan: Index 4215/p.66.

1683: 2 August
Commission renewed to *add* Th. Walcott, serjeant at law, Justice of Assize: Index 4215/p.88.

1683: 8 December
Commission renewed to *add* Th. Herbert: Index 4215/p.93.

1684: 27 May
Commission renewed to *add* Ed. Mansel, Bt.: Index 4215/p.102.

1684: 10 July
Commission renewed to *add* H. Milbourne: Index 4215/p.105.

1684: 18 December
Commission renewed to *add* J. Rumsey: Index 4215/p.111.

1685: 3 March
Commission renewed to *add* Duke of Beaufort as *custos rotulorum*: Index 4215/p.121.

1685: post 28 September

*Archbishop of Canterbury; *Geo., Lord Jeffreys, Chancellor (appointed on 28 September); *E. of Rochester, Treasurer; *Marquess of Halifax, President of Council; *E. of Clarendon, Keeper of Privy Seal; Dukes of *Norfolk, *Albemarle, *Newcastle, *Ormond; *p D. of Beaufort, President of Council in the Marches of Wales; Marquesses of *Winchester, *Worcester; Earls of *Lindsey, *Ailesbury, *Bridgewater, *Sunderland, *Bath, *Nottingham, *Carbery; *Viscount Fauconberg; Bishops of *London, *Llandaff; *Sidney, Lord Godolphin; *H. Coventry; *J. Ernley, kt., Chancellor of Exchequer; *Th. Chichley, kt., Chancellor of Duchy of Lancaster; *Ed Seymour; *Th. Street, kt., Justice of Bench; *Rich. Holloway, kt., Justice *ad placita*; *Rob. Sawyer, kt., Attorney-General; *Heneage Finch, Solicitor-General; *Chas. Kemeys, Bt.; *Ed. Mansel, Bt.; *J. Ernle, kt.; *Jas. Herbert of Colbrooke, kt.; *H. Milbourne; *Th. Lewis of St. Pierre; *Th. Morgan of Lansore; *Edm. Jones; *W. Herbert; *W. Jones of Llantrissent; *Th. Herbert; *Rob. Gunter; *Lewis Morgan; *Walter Evans; *Rich. Lyster; *David Evans; *Ed. Jones; Th. Morgan of Llanrhymny; J. Walter; *J. Rumsey; *Edm. Morgan; *W. Wolseley; *H. Morgan; *J. Gabb; *J. Gwynn: C.193/12/5/f.94. (56)

1686: 17 December

Order by Privy Council that Lord Abergavenny; Rich. Vaughan; Geo. Scudamore; Philip Jones of Llanarth; Anth. Powell; Rich. Croft; Th. Morgan of Tredegar and Roderick Gwynn should be *added* to the Monmouth commission, and that Th. Lewis of St. Pierre and Th. Morgan of Llanrhymny should be *omitted*: P.C.2/71/p.370.

1687: 19 February

Commission renewed (no details): Index 4215/p.167.

1687: 4 March (Acting)

Canterbury; Jeffreys; E. of Sunderland, President of Council; Clarendon; Dukes of Norfolk, Ormond, Albemarle, Newcastle; D. of Beaufort, President of Council in the Marches of Wales; D. of Queensberry; Marquesses of Winchester, Worcester; Earls of Lindsey, Mulgrave, Oxford, Huntingdon, Peterborough, Chesterfield, Bath, Craven, Powys, Berkeley, Nottingham, Rochester, Plymouth, Perth, Moray, Middleton, Melfort, Tyrconnell; Viscounts Fauconberg, Preston; Bishops of Durham, Llandaff; Geo., Lord Abergavenny; H., Lord Arundell of Wardour; J., Lord Belasyse; Geo., Lord Dartmouth; Sidney, Lord Godolphin; H., Lord Dover; J. Ernley, kt., Chancellor of Exchequer; Th. Chichley, kt., Chancellor of Duchy of Lancaster; Ed. Herbert, kt., Chief Justice *ad placita*; Rich. Holloway, kt., Justice *ad placita*; Ed. Lutwich, kt., Justice of Bench; Rob. Sawyer, kt., Attorney-General; Th. Powis, kt., Solicitor-General; Chas. Kemeys, Bt.; Ed. Mansel, Bt.; Jas. Herbert of Colbrooke, kt.; Rich. Vaughan; Geo. Scudamore; Philip Jones of Llanarth; Anth. Powell; Rich. Croft; Th. Morgan of Tredegar; Roderick Gwynn; H. Milbourne; Th. Morgan of Lansore; W. Herbert; W. Jones of Llantrissent; Th. Herbert; Rob. Gunter; Lewis Morgan; Walter Evans; Rich. Lyster; David Evans; Ed. Jones; J. Walter; J. Rumsey; Edm. Morgan; W. Wolseley; H. Morgan; J. Gabb; J. Gwynn: Assize 5/6. (75)

1687: 18 May
D. of Beaufort recommends appointment of Th. Morgan of Llanrhymny as J.P.: N.L.W. Ms. 11020.E.

1687: 11 August
Commission renewed to *add* the clause of dispensation: Index 4215/p.178.

1687: 12 November
Commission renewed to *add* Th. Morgan of Llanrhymny: Index 4215/p.181.

1688: 2 April
Commission renewed (no details): Index 4215/p.190.

1688: 6 October
General renewal of commissions of Wales and Monmouth: Index 4215/p.200.

1689: 21 May
Commission renewed (no details): Index 4215/p.224. (The E. of Macclesfield who was appointed as President of Council in the Marches of Wales on 22 March 1689 (ibid./p.211), was probably added to the commission on this date).

1689: 18 July
Commission renewed to *add* Hopton Williams; Roderick Gwynn: Index 4215/p.234.

APPENDIX

SUBSIDY ASSESSMENTS OF THE JUSTICES OF THE PEACE IN MONMOUTHSHIRE IN 1609.

This list, which omits the *ex officio* portion of the commission, compares very closely with the information obtained elsewhere on the state of the Monmouthshire commission at about this date. As presented here, the details of the subsidy assessment are left out since the names of the justices are of more relevance. The list is however printed in full in J. H. Gleason, *The Justices of the Peace in England, 1558 to 1640* (Oxford, 1969), p.255.

Th. Somerset, Edm. Morgan, Walter Montagu, H. Billingsley, Roland Morgan, H. Townshend, W. Powell, kts.; Chas. Somerset; W. Herbert; Rob. Hopton; J. Gainsford; Rice Kemeys; H. Morgan; W. Morgan of Newport; W. Rawlins; Ed. Kemeys; Valentine Pritchard; Roland Williams; W. Jones; Maurice Griffith; W. Price; Roger Bathern; Andrew Powell; Chas. Jones; Hugh Jones: Huntington Library, Ellesmere Ms. 2513/f.16v. (This ms. does not unfortunately include details for any other Welsh county).

Notes on Layout and Use of Index

1. Each county is indexed separately and in the same order in which it appears in the volume. This involves the repetition of the names of *ex officio* justices but has the advantage that justices belonging to the most prominent county families are grouped together. It is also possible to discover easily which of these families were active in neighbouring counties.

2. Justices of the same name are indexed in the chronological order of their first appearance.

3. When an official post is given after a name in the index, the post is that held at the time of the justice's first appearance in the lists. Any subsequent changes in office can be found by consulting the lists.

4. When there is doubt as to the continuity of a justice's service on the commission or as to the identity of a justice, a new entry is made in the index. Thus a John Jones who appears in 1640 may or may not be the same person as a John Jones who is listed in 1650 and is treated as two individuals. Conversely, there may be some occasions where the nature of the evidence has produced a single index entry covering the careers of two men of the same name.

5. The date given in brackets after each name in the index is that of the *entry* in which the justice first appears. It is not necessarily the date on which the justice was first appointed to the commission, unless the entry specifically states this.

6. Calculating the Length of Service of a Justice of the Peace

The length of a justice's membership of the commission of the peace can be found by consulting the pages referred to in the index. In some instances the evidence cited in the text will give an exact date both for the beginning and for the end of a justice's period of service. But in many more cases the evidence will be less clear.

Defects and gaps in the records, especially in those for the sixteenth century, often make it impossible to give more than an approximate date for the appointment of justices to the commission. It should also be noted that the Crown Office Docquet Books (P.R.O., C.231: formerly described as P.R.O. Indexes), which record the dates of issue of new commissions of the peace as well as the names of newly appointed justices, sometimes fail to mention all the men who were appointed on a particular date. There are also grounds for suspecting that the clerks responsible for the Docquet Books sometimes forgot to enter any details of commissions which are otherwise known to have been issued.

Calculation of the date at which a justice ceased to belong to the commission is far more difficult. On this point the lists in this volume should be used circumspectly and with due reference to any notes included in the text or to independent sources of information. If a justice was removed from the commission by administrative action, this is clearly stated. However, the majority of justices probably died in office and were not formally excluded from the commission until a new one was issued, sometimes a considerable time later. In the information which the clerk of the peace provided twice a year for the justices of Great Sessions, dead justices were usually omitted from the commission. But the clerk frequently failed to do this systematically so that dead justices sometimes reappeared on later copies of the commission and were provided with a posthumous career which lasted until a new commission was issued. Unless the date on which a justice died can easily be discovered from other means of reference, it is often difficult to be sure whether or not this has happened in any given case. This problem is commented on further in the Introduction, p.xxii.

In order to economise on space, the available information on the commissions of the peace has been abbreviated to provide full details for about one year in every three. The entries for the intervening years record in summary form the names of justices who had been added to or omitted from the commission. This means that the end of a justice's career may be given in one of two ways. Either the summary entry of the commission will state that the justice had been omitted since the date of the previous commission, or, in the case of a full copy of the commission, the justice will simply fail to appear. Unless these conditions are satisfied, or there is a specific statement that the justice had been removed from the commission by official order, it can generally be assumed that the justice concerned was still a member of the commission.

Two examples will serve to illustrate the problems. In the lists of justices of the peace for the county of Caernarvon, Sir Hugh Cholmondeley is first recorded in a list of justices acting in the year 1573–74. It is possible that his career actually began in that year, but there is unfortunately no evidence on the state of the commission between the preceding entry, for 1564, and that of 1573–4. Without further information, it can safely be inferred only that Cholmondeley first joined the commission at some point between 1564 and 1573–4. Cholmondeley's departure from the commission is recorded in the entry for the commission of 9 June 1597. He had still been a member of the commission on 8 July 1596 and had presumably been left out at some point between those two dates. Another example is that of Sir Roger Mostyn, whose first known appearance in the commission for Caernarvon is on 26 February 1621 and who last appears in 1640. He is no longer listed on 6 July 1649 when the full details of the commission next survive. Since the commission of 6 July 1649 was at least the tenth to have been issued for the county since 1640, Mostyn's career could have ended at any time between those two dates. In the case of a prominent member of society like Mostyn, it would be relatively easy to discover whether he ceased to be a justice of the peace because of death or political reasons and when this took place. For lesser figures, the problems are obviously much less tractable and correspondingly greater care is needed in interpreting the evidence provided by the lists in this volume.

Pates, Rich. (1564) 19–20
Peick, Hugh (1542) 17 (see also Peke, Hugh (1543))
Peke, Hugh (1543) 17 (see also Peick, Hugh (1542))
Pembroke, E. of (1578–9) 19–22
Pembroke, E. of (1628) 28
Pembroke, E. of (1649) 30
Perrot, J., kt. (1578–9) 19–21
Phillips, Fabian (1578–9) 19–22
Powell, Th. (1558–9) 18–19
Powell, Th., Justice of Great Sessions (1685) 35
Price, Ellis, Ll.D. (1561) 18–21
Price, Hugh (1656) 32
Price, J. (1564) 19–20
Price, Th. (1686) 36
Prideaux, Edm., Attorney-General (1649) 31–2
Prowde, Lewis, Justice of Great Sessions (1609–10) 24–5
Prydderch, Rich., Second Justice of Chester (1638) 29–30
Puckering, J. (1578–9) 19–21
Pugh, Th. (1643) 30
Pugh, W., of Penrhyn (1686) 36
Puleston, Hugh (1564) 19
Puleston, J. (1543) 17
Puleston, Roland (1573–4) 19–23

Radnor, E. of, President of Privy Council (1680) 34–5
ap Rice, J. (1543) 17
ap Richard, J. ap Hugh (1579) 20
ap Richard, Rob. (1592–3) 21
ap Richard, Rob. (1603) 23–4
Robartes, J., Lord, Keeper of Privy Seal (1661) 33
ap Robert, Roland (1575) 19–21
ap Robert, Th. ap William (1543) 17
Roberts, W., clerk (1551) 17
Rolle, H., Chief Justice of Upper Bench (1649) 31
Rowland, H., Dean of Bangor (1595) 21
Rowlands, J. (1686) 36
Rupert, Prince (1680) 34
Russell, J., kt., Keeper of Privy Seal (1543) 17
Russell, W., kt. (1590–1) 20–1

St. Asaph, B. of (1543) 17–27
St. Davids, B. of (1578–9) 19
St. John, Oliver, Chief Justice of Common Pleas (1649) 31–2
Salisbury, E. of, Treasurer (1608–9) 24
Salisbury, E. of (1680) 34
Scudamore, J., of Holm (1558–9) 18
Seaborne, Rich. (1558–9) 18–19
Seymour, Ed. (1680) 34–5
Seys, Evan, Justice of Great Sessions (1656) 32
Shepherd, W., Justice of Great Sessions (1659) 32

Shuttleworth, Rich., kt. Justice of Chester (1590–1) 20–2
Sidney, H., kt., President of Council in Marches of Wales (1561) 18–20
Smith, Rich. (1564) 19
Southampton, E. of, Treasurer (1660) 33
Stoddart, W. (1649) 31–2
Suffolk, D. of, President of Council (1543) 17
Suffolk, E. of, Treasurer (1614) 24–5
Sunderland, E. of (1680) 34–5
Sydenham, W., Commissioner of Treasury (1656) 32
Symonds, W. (1558–9) 18

Temple, W., Bt. (1680) 34
Thomas, Griffith (1635) 29–30
Thomas, Rees (1561) 18–20 (see also Thomas, Rice (1552))
Thomas, Rice (1552) 18 (see also Thomas, Rees (1561))
Thomas, Roland, D.C.L. (1564) 19–20
Thomas, W. (1575) 19–20
Thomas, W. (1596) 21–9
Thomas, W. (1625) 27
Thomas, W. (1630) 28–9
Thomas, W. (1670) 34
ap Thomas, David Lloyd (1558) 18–19
Throckmorton, J., Justice of Chester (1558–9) 18–19
Townshend, H. (1578–9) 19–26
Turneur, Timothy (1627) 28–9
Twistleton, Geo. (1650) 31–2
Twistleton, Geo. (1686) 36

Vaughan, Griffith (1543) 17 (see also Fychan, Gruffydd ap Robert (1550))
Vaughan, Griffith (1584) 20–1
Vaughan, Griffith (1614) 24–5
Vaughan, H. Roland (1594) 21
Vaughan, J., kt. (1558–9) 18
Vaughan, Rich. (1573–4) 19–20
Vaughan, Rich. (1602) 23
Vaughan, Rich. (1627) 28–9
Vaughan, Rich., Justice of Great Sessions (1659) 32
Vaughan, Th. (1590–1) 21–6
Vaughan, Th. (1660) 33
Vaughan, Th. (1680) 34–6
Vaughan, W. (1605) 23–4
Vaughan, W. (1616) 25–9
Vaughan, W. (1660) 33
Vernon, J., kt. (1543) 17

Walcott, Th., Justice of Great Sessions (1680) 34–5
Welsh, J. (1558–9) 18
Weston, Rich., Lord (later E. of Portland), Treasurer (1628) 28–9
Weston, Rich., Justice of Great Sessions (1632) 29
Whitelock, Bulstrode, Commissioner of Great Seal (1649) 30–2

Merioneth

Denbigh

Myddelton, Th., kt. (1660) 78–80
Myddelton, Th., Bt. (1660) 78–80
Myddelton, Th., kt. (1673) 83
Myddelton, Th., Bt. (1674) 84–8
Myddelton, Timothy (1667) 81–3
Myddelton, W. (1599) 61–72
Mytton, Adam (1543) 54
Mytton, Th. (1649) 76

Needham, Th. (1614) 64–70
Newcastle, E. of (1680) 86–90
Nicholas, Ed., kt. (1644) 75
Nicholas, J. (1656) 77
Norfolk, D. of, Treasurer (1543) 54
Norfolk, D. of (1689) 91
North, Francis, kt., Chief Justice of Bench
  (1680) 86–8
Northampton, E. of, Keeper of Privy Seal
  (1608) 64

Ormond, Marquess of, Steward (1660)
  78–90
Osborne, Viscount (later E. of Danby),
  Treasurer (1673) 83–5
Owen, J. (1553) 54
Owen, Leighton (1649) 76
Owen, Peter (1568) 56–9
Owen, Rob., kt. (1689) 91
Owen, W., of Llunddun (1660) 79–87
Oxford, E. of (1689) 91

Pakington, J. (1543) 54
Palmer, Geoff., kt. & Bt., Attorney-
  General (1661) 79–80
Panton, J. (1617) 65–6
Parry, Gabriel, B.D. (1638) 73–4
Parry, J., of Llanbedr (1633) 72
Parry, J., of Tywysog (1686) 90
Parry, J., of Coedmarchan (1687) 90
Parry, J. (1689) 91
Parry, Rich., Dean of Bangor (1599) 62–3
Parry, Rich. (1674) 83–6, 88–90
Parry, Simon (1614) 64–70
Parry, W., of Hendre (1660) 78–87
Pates, Rich. (1559) 55–9
Peck, J. (1649) 76–80
Pembroke, E. of, President of Council in
  Marches of Wales (1553) 54, 56–62
Pembroke, E. of (1629) 70–1
Pembroke & Montgomery, E. of (1649)
  76
Penrhyn, W. (1596) 61–8
Perrot, J., kt. (1579) 57–60
Phillips, Fabian (1579) 58–61
Plowden, Edm. (1553) 54
Pollard, J. (1553) 54
Powell, David, D.D. (1588) 59–62
Powell, Rob., Chancellor of St. Asaph
  (1672) 83–7
Powell, Th. (1579) 58–62
Powell, Th., Bt. (1636) 72–5
Powell, Th., Bt. (1660) 78–91
Powys, Marquess of (1687) 90

Powys, Th., King's attorney in Denbigh
  (1680) 86–9
Preston, Viscount (1687) 90
Price, Ed. (1602) 63
Price, Ellis, clerk (1543) 54
Price, Ellis (1555) 54–60
Price, J., kt. (1553) 54
Price, J. (1553) 54
Price, J., of Derwen (1558–9) 54–8
Price, J., of Eglwysegl (1558–9) 54–60
Price, Rob., of Geeler (1643) 74
Price, Rob., of Geeler (1660) 78–82
Price, Rob. (1686) 90
Price, Th. (1592) 60–4
Price, W. (1642) 74–5
Price, W. (1660) 79–86, 88–90
Prideaux, Edm., Attorney-General (1650)
  76
Pritchard, Hugh (1653) 77–8
Pritchard, Rob., clerk (1619) 67–9
Prydderch, Rich., Justice of Chester
  (1638) 73–5
Puckering, J. (1579) 58–60
Pugh, W. (1686) 90
Puleston,—(1659) 78
Puleston, Ed., kt. (1555) 54–5
Puleston, Geo. (1621) 67–72
Puleston, Hugh (1569) 56
Puleston, J., senior (1543) 54
Puleston, J., junior (1543) 54
Puleston, J. (1648) 76–84
Puleston, J., kt. (1684) 89
Puleston, Rob. (1553) 54–9
Puleston, Roger, kt. (1543) 54
Puleston, Roger (1581) 58–65
Puleston, Roger, kt. (1684) 89–90

Radnor, E. of, President of Council (1680)
  86–9
Ravenscroft, Th. (1643) 74–6
Ravenscroft, Th., of Pickhill (1655) 77
Ravenscroft, Th. (1656) 77
Rawlinson, W., Commissioner of Great
  Seal (1689) 90
ap Rice, David ap Robert (1543) 54
ap Rice, J. (1543) 54
ap Rice, J., junior (1543) 54
ap Richard, Th. Wynn (1591) 60–2
Richmond & Lennox, D. of, Steward
  (1644) 75
Robartes, J., Lord, Keeper of Privy Seal
  (1661) 79–81
ap Robert, Tudor (1543) 54–5
Roberts, Hugh (1667) 81
Roberts, J. (1624) 68
Robinson, J. (1643) 74–5
Robinson, J. (1656) 77–87
Robinson, W. (1618) 66–72
Rogers, J. (1569) 56
Rolle, H., Chief Justice of Upper Bench
  (1649) 76
Rossindale, Th. (1677) 84–5
Royden, J. (1643) 72–5

Flint

Borough of Carmarthen

Cardigan

Pembroke

Glamorgan

Radnor

Sidney, H., kt., President of Council in Marches of Wales (1561) 345–7
Smith, Rich. (1564) 346
Smyth, J., Ll.D. (1558–9) 345
Somerset, D. of, Protector (1547) 345
Somerset, Chas. (1546) 346
Somerset, Chas. (1604–5) 351, 369
Somerset, Th. (1558–9) 345
Somerset, Th. (1601) 350–4, 369
Southampton, E. of, Treasurer (1660) 362–3
Steele, W., Chief Baron of Exchequer (1656) 361
Street, Th., kt., Justice of Bench (1685) 367
Suffolk, D. of, President of Council (1543) 344
Suffolk, E. of, Treasurer (1614) 352
Sunderland, E. of (1680) 365, 367
Sydenham, W., Commissioner of Treasury (1656) 361
Symonds, W. (1558–9) 345

Temple, W., Bt. (1680) 365
Thomas, Edm. (1656) 361
Thomas, W. John (1542) 344–5
Thomas, W. John, of Treowen (1561) 345
Thorpe, Mr. Baron (1655) 361
Throckmorton, Baynham, junior, kt. (1660) 362–3
Throckmorton, Baynham, kt. & Bt. (1680) 365–6
Throckmorton, J., Justice of Chester (1558–9) 345–6
Townshend, H. (1578) 347–54, 369
Townshend, Rob., kt. (1547) 345
Trevor, Arthur (1663) 363
Trevor, Th., kt., Justice of Assize (1632) 357–8
Turner, Chris., kt., Justice of Assize (1660) 362–3
Turner, Ed., Justice of Assize (1671) 364
Turner, Serjeant, Justice of Assize (1648) 359
Twisden, Th., kt. & Bt. (1666) 364
Tyrconnell, E. of (1687) 367
Tyrrell, Th., kt., Justice of Assize (1661) 363–4

Van, Chas. (1660) 362–6
Van, Lewis (1625) 355
Vaughan, J., kt. (1558–9) 345
Vaughan, Rich. (1686) 367
Vernon, J., kt. (1543) 344

Walcott, Th., kt., Justice of Assize (1683) 366
Waller, Th., serjeant at law (1663) 363
Walsh, Anth. (1542) 344 (this is probably the same as Anth. Welsh (1558–9))
Walter, J. (1638) 358
Walter, J. (1649) 359–61, 363, 365–7
Warburton, Peter, Justice of Assize (1602) 350–4

Warburton, Peter, Justice of Assize (1652) 360–1
Ward, J., of Newport (1653) 361
Watkins, Th., of Caerwent (1577) 346–7
Welsh, Anth. (1558–9) 345 (see also Anth. Walsh (1542))
Welsh, Chris., of Llanwarne (1573–4) 346–7
Welsh, J. (1558–9) 345
Weston, Rich., Lord (later E. of Portland), Treasurer (1629) 356–7
Whiddon, J., kt. (1558–9) 345
Whitelock, Bulstrode, Commissioner of Great Seal (1649) 359–61
Whitlock, Jas., kt., Justice of Chester (1620) 354–7
Whitney, Jas. (1542) 344
Widdrington, Th., kt., Commissioner of Treasury (1656) 361
Wilde, J., Chief Baron of Exchequer (1649) 359–60
Williams, Chas. (1620) 353–8
Williams, David, Justice of Assize (1604–5) 351
Williams, Ed. Bt .(1660) 362–3
Williams, H. (1594) 348
Williams, H., of Mathern (1597) 349
Williams, Hopton (1689) 368
Williams, Rice (1649) 359–61
Williams, Roger (1558–9) 345–6
Williams, Roger (1582) 347
Williams, Roger (1643) 359–61
Williams, Roger (1661) 363, 365
Williams, Roland (1601) 350–1, 369
Williams, Th. (1582) 347
Williams, Th. (1649) 359–60
Williams, Th. (1660) 362–3
Williams, Trevor, Bt. (1646) 359
Williams, Trevor, Bt. (1660) 362–5
Willoughby, Geo. (1547) 345
Winch, Humph., kt., Justice of Assize (1624) 353–4
Winchester, Marquess of (1680) 365–7
Wolseley, W. (1680) 365–7
Worcester, B. of, Vice-President of Council in Marches of Wales (1578) 346
Worcester, E. of (1543) 344–8, 350–6
Worcester, Marquess of, President of Council in Marches of Wales (1680) 365–6 (see also Beaufort, D. of (1685))
Wye, Rich. (1564) 346
Wyndham, Francis, serjeant at law (1578) 346–8
Wyndham, Hugh, Justice of Common Bench (1656) 361
Wyndham, Wadham, kt. (1660) 362–4
Wyse, Mr. Justice (1668) 364

Yelverton, Christopher, Justice of Assize (1602) 350–1

Zouch, Ed., Lord, President of Council in Marches of Wales (1602) 350–1